InTASC Standard		Content in Chapters
		Chapter 11: What Are Standards and Benchmarks? Chapter 11: Standards for Content Chapter 13: What Makes Teaching Strategies Work? Chapter 14: What Role Does Technology Play in the Lives of Teachers and Learners? Chapter 14: Why Integrate Technology in Teaching? Chapter 14: How Do Teachers Use Technology to Manage the Classroom?
8	**Instructional Strategies**	Chapter 2: Teaching Students From Diverse Racial and Ethnic Groups Chapter 2: Providing Equity in Schools Chapter 2: Teaching English-Language Learners Chapter 2: Delivering an Equitable Education for Girls and Boys Chapter 2: Addressing Religion in Public Schools Chapter 3: How Are Students With Disabilities Integrating Schools? Chapter 13: What Are Teaching Strategies? Chapter 13: What Makes Teaching Strategies Work? Chapter 13: How Are Different Strategies Used for Differing Purposes? Chapter 14: What Role Does Technology Play in the Lives of Teachers and Learners? Chapter 14: Why Integrate Technology in Teaching? Chapter 14: How Can Teachers Manage the Use of Technology and Use Technology to Manage the Classroom?
9	**Professional Learning and Ethical Practice**	Chapter 1: Being a Professional Chapter 1: Code of Ethics Chapter 1: How Do You Keep Track of Your Growth as a Teacher? Chapter 2: Teaching Students From Diverse Racial and Ethnic Groups Chapter 2: Providing Equity in Schools Chapter 2: Teaching English-Language Learners Chapter 2: Delivering an Equitable Education for Girls and Boys Chapter 2: Supporting LGBTQ Students Chapter 2: Addressing Religion in Public Schools Chapter 3: How Do Class and Culture Affect Teaching and Learning? Chapter 6: How Has Teaching Evolved? Chapter 10: Contemporary Legal Issues and Their Deliberations Chapter 10: Continuing Legal Dilemmas Related to Education Chapter 10: Students' Rights and Protections Chapter 10: Teachers' Responsibilities, Rights, and Liabilities Chapter 14: How Can Teachers Manage the Use of Technology and Use Technology to Manage the Classroom? Chapter 16: What Are Keys to Succeeding in Your Teacher Education Program? Chapter 16: What Are the Keys to Being Hired as a Beginning Teacher? Chapter 16: How Does a Master Teacher Think About the Joy of Teaching?
10	**Leadership and Collaboration**	Chapter 4: How Does Social Context Challenge Educators? Chapter 4: How Does Social Context Influence What Is Taught? Chapter 5: How Does Culture Influence Families and Their Children? Chapter 5: What Happens When Students' Cultures Come to School? Chapter 5: How Should Teachers Work With Parents and Communities? Chapter 6: How Did Public Schools Come to Be? Chapter 6: How Did Schools Become Designed Based On the Age of Students? Chapter 6: What Has Influenced the School Curriculum? Chapter 6: How Has the Educational System Contributed to Equality? Chapter 6: How Has Teaching Evolved? Chapter 8: How Are Schools Staffed and Organized? Chapter 8: What Is the Relationship of Schools to the School District and the State? Chapter 8: What Are Today's Issues In the Workplace Called School? Chapter 9: How Is Governance Different From the Structures of Government? Chapter 9: What Is the Role of the Federal Government in Education? Chapter 9: How Are Schools Paid For and How Is the Money Spent? Chapter 9: How Do Schools Spend the Money? Chapter 9: What Are Some of the School Finance Issues and Challenges? Chapter 16: In What Ways Can Candidates and Teachers Be Leaders?

Making a Difference in Teaching

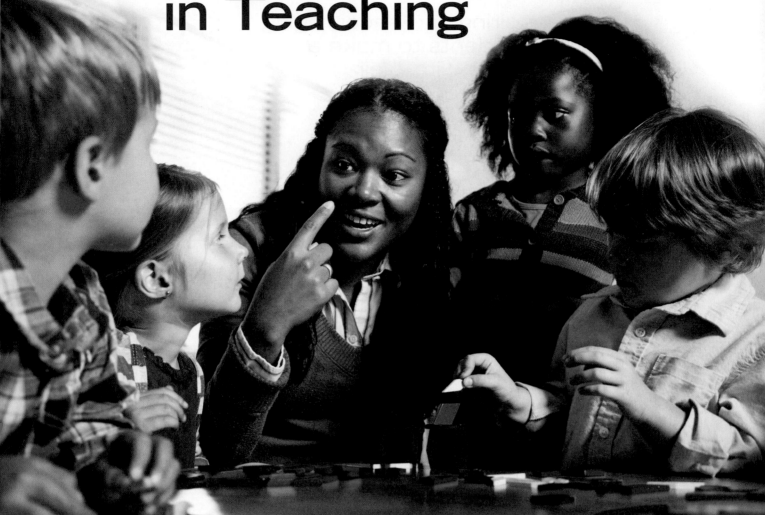

- First-hand stories
- Evidence-based practices
- Engaging interviews
- Student-centered approach to learning
- True-to-life challenges

INSTRUCTOR:
Pamela Sanders
INDIANA UNIVERSITY NORTHWEST

"This book is an asset to any future educator. It is great for future reference when the class ends"

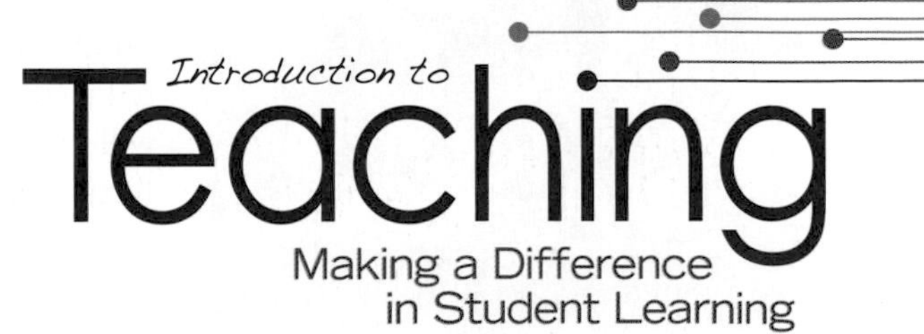

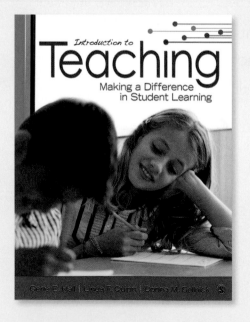

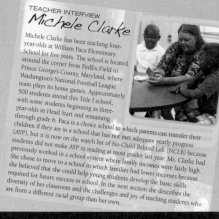

SAGE Is Making a Difference

with comprehensive and free online resources designed to support and enhance both instructors' and students' experiences.

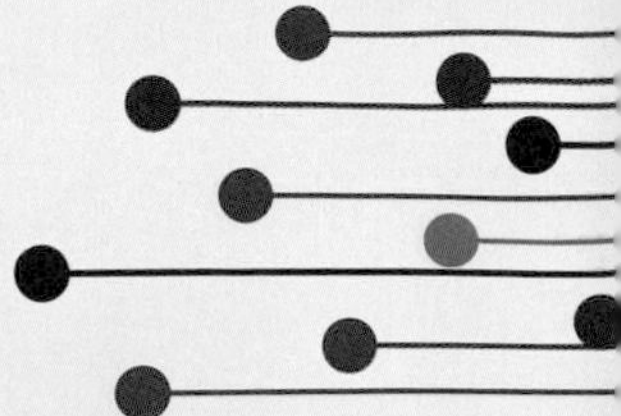

Instructors benefit from access to the password-protected **Instructor Teaching Site**, which contains a test bank in Word and Diploma software, as well as PowerPoint slides, and original classroom videos, featuring interviews with elementary and secondary teachers.

The site also includes course syllabi, discussion questions, classroom activities, portfolio activities, suggested answers to class discussion questions, and SAGE handbook and encyclopedia articles, as well as SAGE journal articles.

Students maximize their understanding through the free, open-access **Student Study Site**, which presents valuable resources such as eFlashcards, web quizzes, web resources, SAGE reference and journal articles, unique and original SAGE video, external video links, audio links, and web exercises.

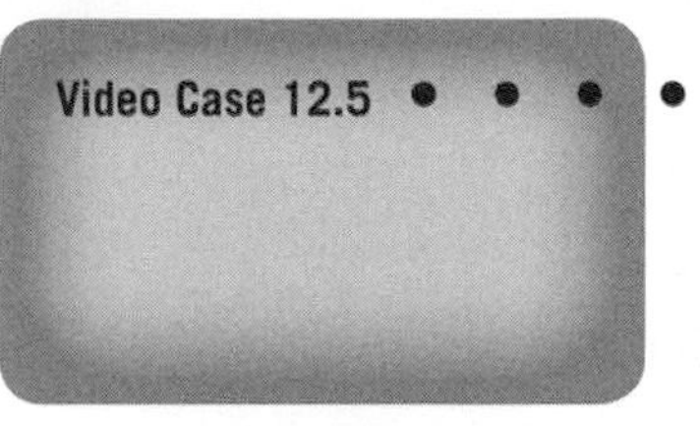

Video Case Links: Original videos showcase elementary and secondary teachers and their classrooms, and are accompanied by author-created reflection questions.

Audio Links: Links to podcasts and audio resources cover important topics and are designed to supplement key points within the text.

Video Links: Carefully selected, web-based video resources feature relevant interviews, lectures, personal stories, inquiries, and other content for use in independent or classroom-based explorations of key topics.

Deeper Look Links: These include links to recent, relevant full-text articles from SAGE's leading research journals, as well as links to articles from SAGE handbooks and encyclopedias.

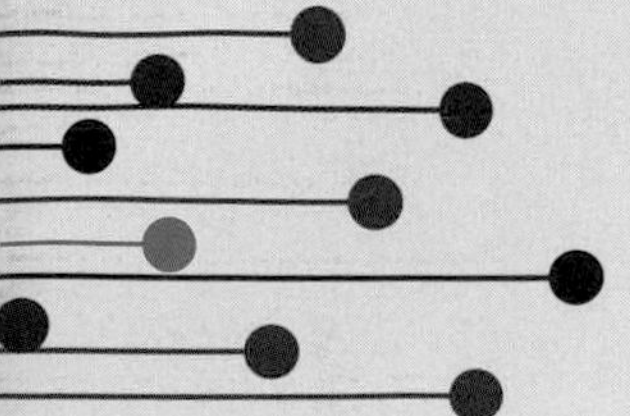

Features That Make a Difference

Contributed by real teachers like you, these features are as inspirational as they are informative.

Teachers' Lounge features

provide students with inspirational, joyful, or humorous stories, related to the chapter content, as reported by a teacher.

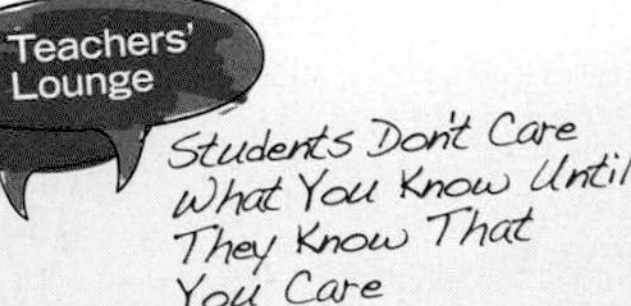

Students Don't Care What You Know Until They Know That You Care

It has been my experience while teaching middle and high school that students from diverse groups do not care what you have to say until they know that you care. Teaching is getting students to do what you want them
while having them think it is their idea, because
ly loves their own ideas. Which takes me into
ce I had with two of my middle school
nderson, North Carolina. Teaching math
it is not their favorite subject can be
d one student in particular who was
d I tutored him after school. We
dent–mentor relationship that was
ce because the student lacked any
ily welcomed my relationship with
I was granted permission to take
the student and his brother for an afternoon out on the town. We went to the movies and had dinner in a nice restaurant and spent time enjoying each other's company at my expense. At the time this did not seem to be a big deal to me; however, it was a huge deal to the students. The students became ambassadors for me at the school and model students. The students realized that I really cared about them and that I wanted the best for them. The new challenge was that every student wanted to go to dinner and a movie with me now. You never know what you may be to a student and what need you fill. When you let them know you care, they will allow you to lead them where they need to go.

Peter M. Eley, PhD,
Fayetteville State University

Chapter-opening teacher interviews

include questions and responses from teachers from across the country and relate directly to the chapter content.

TEACHER INTERVIEW

Lena Mann

Lena Mann is a high school math teacher at Pinon High School, a public school located on the Navajo Reservation in North Eastern Arizona. More than 425 students are enrolled in the high school. Ms. Mann says that after 42 years in the classroom she still enjoys coming to work every day. *I walk into the classroom and all of the problems that I had outside of the classroom disappear.*

Challenging Assumptions boxes

use scholarly research to help debunk many of the myths about teaching.

Challenging Assumptions

What matters most in classroom management?

The Assumption

Many beginning teachers worry most about their ability to manage the movement and behavior of their students. They have heard horror stories and observed unfortunate examples of teachers who have little or no effect on getting students ready for learning. Having no control over a classroom is a frequent concern of teacher education candidates. Cooperating teachers who work with practicum or student teachers may advise them to begin the year with a stern and strict attitude, and to reserve smiles for later in the year. Experienced teachers often advise new teachers not to become a friend too soon. So what really works in classroom management, and how is a new teacher to approach this aspect of teaching?

The Research

There are probably as many approaches to managing a classroom as there are teachers who implement one course of action or another. What approach works for each teacher really does depend on individual attitudes and capabilities. Certainly having a high level of self-efficacy is important. Teachers who view themselves as capable of managing a classroom are more likely to be successful doing so then a teacher who is unsure. One way researchers have approached the study of effective classroom management is to observe teacher behaviors and document those behaviors that result in positive student actions and attitudes.

The study cited here looked at two teachers who represented contrasting styles of classroom management. One teacher used an authoritarian style of classroom management and the other used a style that encouraged students to take responsibility for their own behavior. Three variables— student interactions (behaviors), teacher questioning, and quality of teaching—were used to analyze the effectiveness of the teacher's management styles. Both teachers used lower-level questioning skills and it was determined in the study that the overall quality of instruction was poor. The study found that neither of these two teachers' classroom management styles effected "consistent positive student interactions." The study concluded that the "quality of instruction is central to the interplay between student's interactions and teacher's classroom management practices."

Implications

While this study is of a very small scope, and perhaps the teachers who participated in the study did not employ the most effective instructional strategies, it does provide a small piece of evidence regarding the connection between management style and instructional practices. When students are engaged in learning they are more likely to exhibit positive behaviors. The success of the approach a teacher uses for classroom management may be highly influenced by the instructional practices that are in place. Teachers who teach well usually have little problems with classroom management.

Source: Jeanpierre, B. J (2005). Two urban elementary science classrooms: The interplay between student interactions and classroom management practices. *Education, 124*(4), 664–676.

Features That Make a Difference

Contributed by real teachers like you, these features are as inspirational as they are informative.

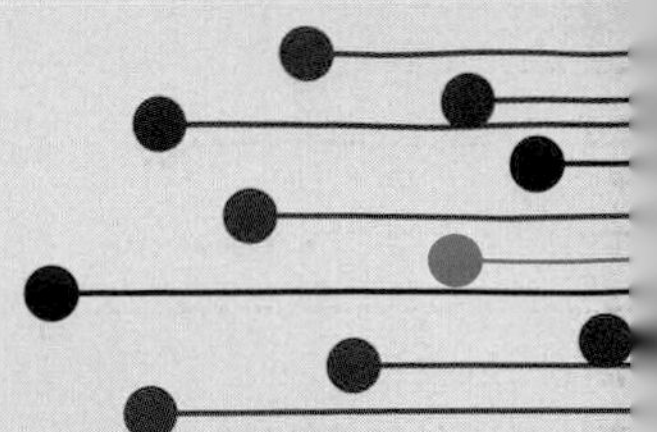

Focus questions

help direct students to the main concepts of the chapter.

The InTASC Correlation Chart

provided in the inside front cover of this text prepares students to meet InTASC standards.

***Understanding and Using Evidence* boxes**

help readers examine a set of data, develop an interpretation, and offer a recommendation.

End-of-chapter pedagogical features

include chapter summaries, discussion questions, self-assessments, a field guide for learning, and more.

UNDERSTANDING AND USING EVIDENCE

Licensure Test Scores

Each state sets the qualifying or cut score that test takers must achieve before they can receive a license to teach in the state. These scores differ across states as shown below.

Test	AR	CT	LA	MS	NV	OH	PA	VA
Biology: Content Knowledge	–	152	150	135	154	148	147	155
Elementary Education: Curriculum, Instruction, & Assessment	–	163	–	135	158	–	168	–
Elementary Education: Content Knowledge	–	–	150	–	–	–	–	143
English Language, Literature, & Composition: Content Knowledge	159	172	160	157	150	167	160	172
Mathematics: Content Knowledge	116	137	125	123	144	139	136	147
Social Studies: Content Knowledge	155	162	149	143	152	157	157	161

Your Task: Respond to the following questions:

1. What does this table tell you about becoming qualified in these eight states?
2. Why are scores not indicated for some states?
3. Why do some states require higher scores than others?

Source: Website of the Educational Testing Service (ETS) at http://www.ets.org/praxis/prxstate.html

WHAT IS YOUR CURRENT LEVEL OF UNDERSTANDING TODAY'S STUDENTS?

One of the indicators of understanding is to examine how complex your thinking is when asked questions that require you to use the concepts and facts introduced in this chapter.

Answer the following questions as fully as you can. Then use the Complexity of Thinking rubric to self-assess the degree to which you understand and can use the ideas presented in this chapter.

1. How can you bring the cultures of your students into the classroom?
2. What impact does the socioeconomic status of students' families have on teachers' expectations for the academic performance of students?
3. What is the teacher's responsibility for teaching students who are not authorized to be in the country?
4. How can boys and girls be damaged with education that focuses on the stereotypical roles of females and males?
5. What can teachers do to help eliminate the bullying of LGBTQ students?
6. What are some ways in which the religious diversity of a community can impact a school?

Complexity of Thinking Rubric

Indicators	Parts & Pieces	Unidimensional	Organized	Integrated	Extensions
	Elements/concepts are talked about as isolated and independent entities.	One or a few concepts are addressed, while others are under-developed.	Deliberate and structured consideration of all key concepts/elements.	All key concepts/elements are included in a view that addresses interconnections.	Integration of all elements and dimensions with extrapolation to new situations.
Relationships between the diversity of students and teaching and learning	Identifies the types of student diversity that exists without being able to explain the relationships to teaching and learning	Describes a few of the impacts that diversity has on teaching and learning	Provides examples of how student diversity can influence teaching and learning across cultural groups	Analyzes the role of the teacher in using student diversity effectively to help students learn	Explains how teachers can adjust their teaching to use student diversity positively to improve learning across cultural groups and develops a plan for increasing his/her knowledge about cultural groups with which they have limited knowledge

STUDENT:
Holly Jones
INDIANA UNIVERSITY NORTHWEST

"I really like the focus questions, self-assessment, and discussion questions. They help with discussions in the classroom—asking students questions about what they have learned or read—and can help you better understand the book yourself."

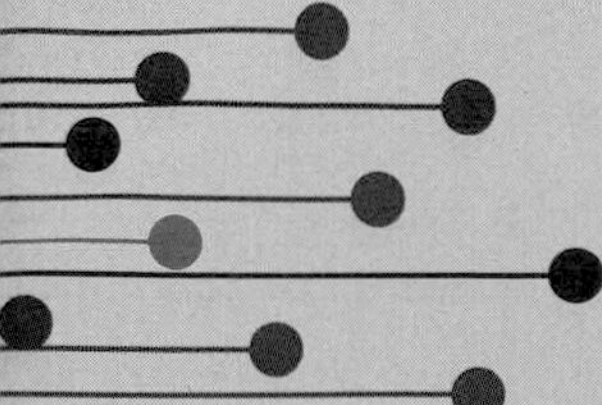

Technology Makes a Difference

Your students can Engage-Reflect-Learn with the FREE Interactive eBook.

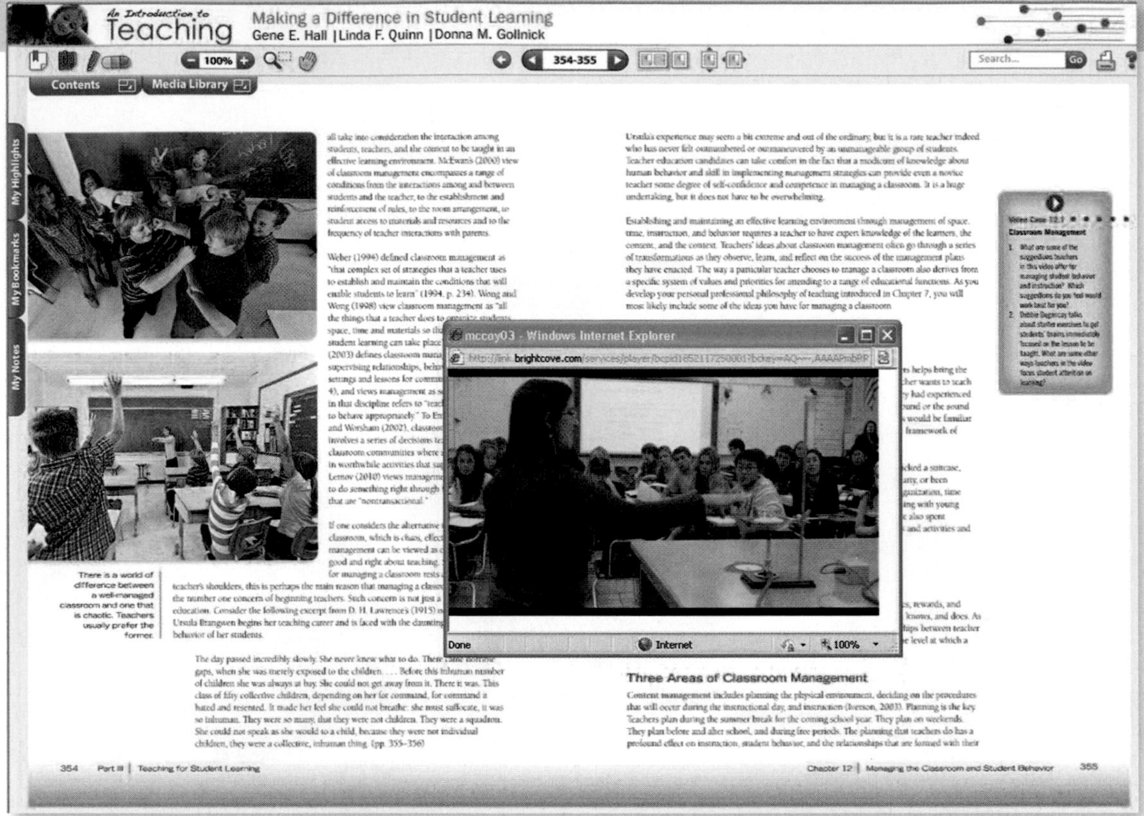

Introduction to Teaching is available as an Interactive eBook, which can be packaged free with the book or purchased separately.

The interactive eBook offers integrated video clips of real classroom scenarios, as well as links to additional web, audio, and video resources.

This dynamic eBook enriches the text for visual learners and fully integrates chapter specific video, and audio material to engage all students. Students can link directly from the "page" to video, audio, additional enrichment readings, glossary terms, and other relevant resources, bringing the text to life in a way that a traditional print text can't.

Students will have access to study tools such as highlighting, bookmarking, note-taking, and an organized media library that allows accessing all media assets in each chapter.

Video Links • Audio Links • Video Cases • Deeper Look Links

Explore and ENGAGE with an eBook demo today!
Try a demo at this link **www.sagepub.com/hall/demo**

YOU Are Making a Difference

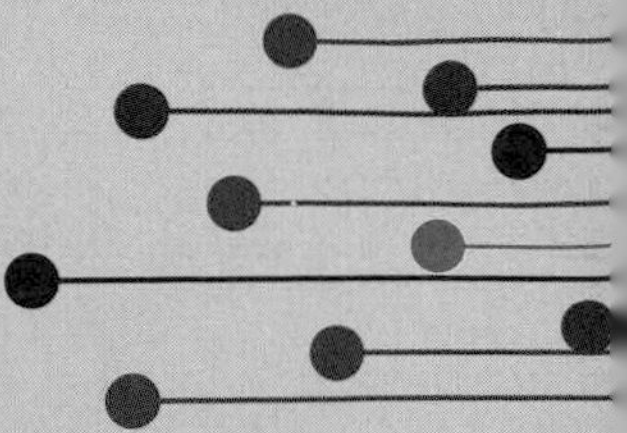

by sharing your feedback every step of the way. We would like to say thank you to our reviewers for your valuable contributions to this project.

Pamela W. Aerni—Longwood University
Catron Allred—Albuquerque Technical Vocational Institute
Elaine Bacharach Coughlin—Pacific University
Angie Bales—Bossier Parish Community College
Tanisha Billingslea—Cameron University
Sherrie Bosse—University of South Dakota
Amy Brodeur—St. Francis University
Jesse Chenven—Central New Mexico Community College
Pamela Chibucos—Owens Community College
Garnet Chrisman—University of the Cumberlands
H. Jurgen Combs—Shenandoah University
Diane G. Corrigan—Cleveland State University
Elaine Coughlin—Pacific University
Charles Edward Craig, Jr.—Tennessee Technical University
Darryl M. De Marzio—University of Scranton
Thomas S. Dickinson—DePauw University
Peter Eley—Fayetteville State University
Rebecca Fredrickson—Texas Woman's University
Jill E. Gelormino—St. Joseph's Collge
Carol Gilles—University of Missouri
Cyndi Giorgis—University of Nevada - Las Vegas
Talisha Givan—Henderson State University
Amanda Lee Glaze—Jacksonville State University
Claudia Green—Corban University
Pam Green—Southwestern College
Steven R. Greenberg—Bridgewater State University
Janice A. Grskovic—Indiana University Northwest
Sam Guerriero—Butler University
Nina Gunther Phillips—Bryn Athyn College
Harry Gutelius—Eastern University
Felecia A. B. Hanesworth—Medaille College
Glenda Hathaway—Cleveland State University
Dana Hilbert—Cameron University
Bethany Hill-Anderson—McKendree University
Jennifer Holloway—Cameron University at RSU
Johnnie Humphrey—John Tyler Community College
MeHee Hyun—Antioch University Los Angeles
Angie Jones Bales—Bossier Parish Community College
Rebekah D. Kelleher—Wingate University
Eileen Kendrick—Northwestern State University - Natchitoches
Sophie Ladd—University of Nevada - Las Vegas
Leonard Larsen—DMACC
Dana Lewis Haraway—James Madison University
Emily Lin—University of Nevada - Las Vegas
Nina Mazloff—Becker College
Reney McAtee—Tennessee State University
Kathy J. McKee—Multnomah University
Deena McKinney—East Georgia College
Sarah K. McMahan—Texas Woman's University
Belete Mebratu—Medaille College
Linda A. Mitchell—Jacksonville State University
Robert Allen Moody—Fort Hayes State University
Madonna Murphy—University of St. Francis
George Noblit—University of North Carolina at Chapel Hill
Mary Ann Pangle—Tennessee State University - Nashville
Denise Patmon—University of Massachusetts, Boston
Lauri Pepe Bousquet—Le Moyne College
Rebecca Pitkin—Dickinson State University
Thomas A. Raunig—University of Great Falls
Donna Redman—University of La Verne
Suzanne Roberts—Florida College
Philip Russell—University Of Arkansas - Fort Smith
Marjorie Schiller—Central Arizona College
Brian Schultz—Northeastern Illinois University
Eric-Gene J. Shrewsbury—Patrick Henry Community College
Richard K. Simmons—College of DuPage
Darlene Smith—Walters State Community College
Janet Stramel—Fort Hays State University
Douglas Sturgeon—Shawnee State University
Lucia Torchia-Thompson—Reading Area Community College
Curtis Visca—Saddleback College
David Vocke—Towson University
Karen A. Vuurens—South Texas College Mid-Valley Campus
Harold Waters—Southern Wesleyan University
Gail Watson—County College of Morris
Camy Weber Davis—Oakland City University
Colleen M. Wilson—Jacksonville University
Theri Wyckoff—College of Southern Nevada
William Yerger—Eastern University

Schools where SAGE proprietary classroom video was filmed:

Newbury Park High School (Newbury Park, CA)
La Mariposa Elementary School (Camarillo, CA)
Sleepy Hollow High School (Sleepy Hollow, NY)

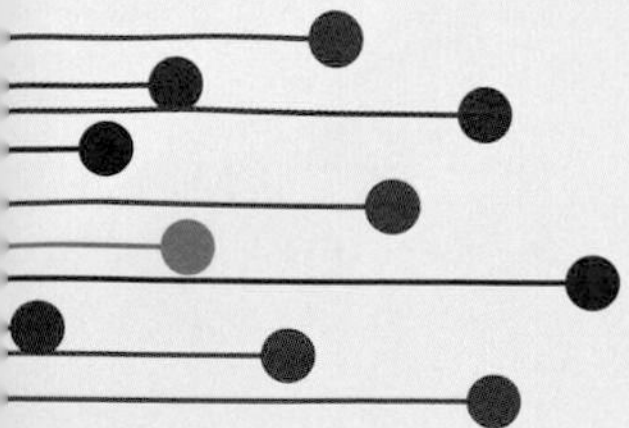

Price Makes a Difference

SAGE Offers Real Content at a Real Value

STUDENT:
Shirley Erby
INDIANA UNIVERSITY NORTHWEST

"The lower price is highly important in today's escalating economy. I would gladly purchase the textbook because of its value pricing."

Costs students
$40–$70 LESS than competing Introduction to Teaching texts

Introduction to Teaching

DEDICATION

The authors dedicate this book to all the great teachers we have known—from early childhood teachers to research university professors. We are blessed with having had more of them than we can name here. We have great memories of their deep knowledge and skillful teaching, their helpfulness, and their cheerful willingness to offer guidance. They taught us to learn and laugh at the same time. They found joy in their teaching and brought true joy to our learning. We thank each and every one of them and the thousands of other exceptional teachers who have made a difference in learning for their students, and who have found joy in teaching.

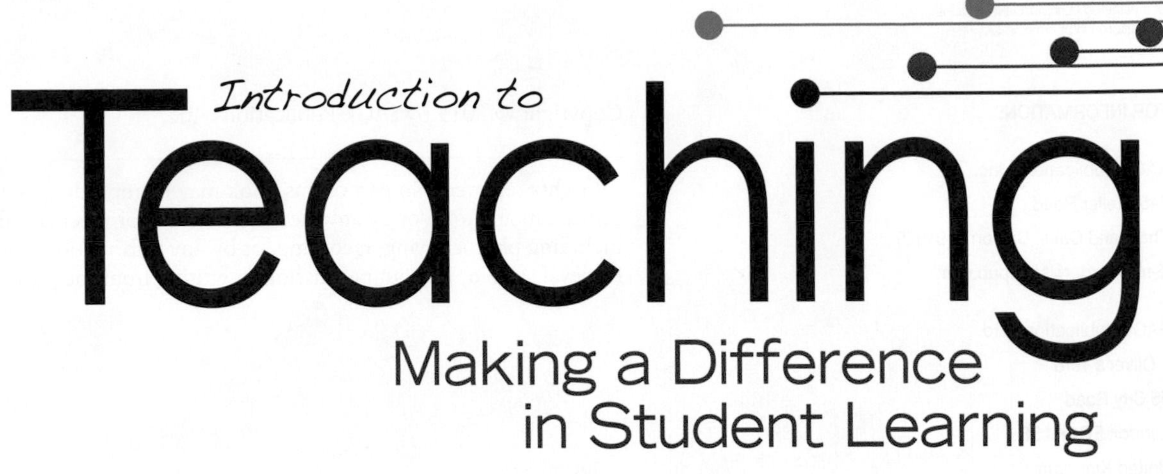

Introduction to Teaching

Making a Difference in Student Learning

Gene E. Hall | Linda F. Quinn | Donna M. Gollnick

University of Nevada, Las Vegas

University of Nevada, Las Vegas

National Council for Accreditation of Teacher Education

Los Angeles | London | New Delhi
Singapore | Washington DC

Los Angeles | London | New Delhi
Singapore | Washington DC

FOR INFORMATION:

SAGE Publications, Inc.
2455 Teller Road
Thousand Oaks, California 91320
E-mail: order@sagepub.com

SAGE Publications Ltd.
1 Oliver's Yard
55 City Road
London EC1Y 1SP
United Kingdom

SAGE Publications India Pvt. Ltd.
B 1/I 1 Mohan Cooperative Industrial Area
Mathura Road, New Delhi 110 044
India

SAGE Publications Asia-Pacific Pte. Ltd.
3 Church Street
#10-04 Samsung Hub
Singapore 049483

Acquisitions Editor: Diane McDaniel
Associate Editors: Megan Krattli/Theresa Accomazzo
Assistant Editor: Rachael LeBlond
Editorial Assistant: Megan Koraly
Production Editors: Astrid Virding/Libby Larson
Copy Editor: Terri Lee Paulsen
Typesetter: C&M Digitals (P) Ltd.
Proofreader: Scott Oney
Indexer: Michael Ferreira
Cover Designer: Rose Storey
Marketing Manager: Terra Schultz
Permissions Editor: Adele Hutchinson

Printed in Canada

A catalog record of this book is available from the Library of Congress.

978-1-4522-0291-4

This book is printed on acid-free paper.

12 13 14 15 16 10 9 8 7 6 5 4 3 2 1

Brief Contents

Preface xxx
Acknowledgments xxxv

Part I. Today's Teachers, Students, and Schools 1

1. Becoming a Teacher 3
2. Today's Students 37
3. Addressing Learners' Individual Needs 67
4. Social Context of Schools 99
5. Families and Communities 129

Part II. The Foundations of Education 157

6. History of Schools in the United States 159
7. Developing a Philosophy of Teaching and Learning 191
8. Organizing Schools for Learning 223
9. Governance and School Finance 251
10. The Law as It Relates to Teaching and Learning 283

Part III. Teaching for Student Learning 317

11. Standards, Curriculum, and Accountability 319
12. Managing the Classroom and Student Behavior 351
13. Teaching Strategies 383
14. Using Technology to Improve Student Learning 415
15. Assessing Student Learning and Results 445

Part IV. Becoming Tomorrow's Highly Effective Teacher 479

16. Succeeding in Your Teacher Education Program, and Beyond 481

Glossary 513
References 520
Photo Credits 529
Index 531
About the Authors 546

Detailed Contents

Preface xxx
Acknowledgments xxxv

Part I. Today's Teachers, Students, and Schools 1

1. Becoming a Teacher 3

Teacher Interview: Katie Johnston 2
Questions to Consider 3
Learning Outcomes 4
Introduction 4
Why Teach? 5
The Joy of Teaching 5
Intrinsic and Extrinsic Rewards 6
The Laughs 6
Making a Difference 7
The Teaching Profession 8
Being a Professional 9
Setting and Upholding Standards 9
Specialized Knowledge 10
Code of Ethics 11
Obligation to Practice in Acceptable Ways 11
What Do Teachers Need to Know? 11
Teacher Education Programs 11
Ways Programs Are Organized and Why 12
Different Pathways to Licensure 12
Where the Jobs Are 14
What Do Teacher Education Candidates Need to Do? 17
How to Get Off to a Good Start in Your Teacher Education Program 17
Test of Basic Skills 18
Learn About Assessment Practices 18
Pass Licensure Tests 18
Spend Time in Schools 22
Professional Development Schools 22
Teachers' Lounge 23
School District/University Partnership Schools 23
Challenging Assumptions 24
Become a Member of a Teaching and Learning Team 25
Understanding and Using Evidence 26
Understand the Role of Your Mentor or Cooperating Teacher 27
How Do You Keep Track of Your Growth as a Teacher? 28
Know the Standards 28
Student Standards 28
Teacher Standards 28
Begin a Portfolio 29
Reflect on Your Observations and Practice in Schools 30
Begin Collaborating With Peers and Professors 30
Connecting to the Classroom 31
Field Guide for Learning More About Becoming a Teacher 33

2. Today's Students 37

Teacher Interview: Michele Clarke 36

Questions to Consider 37
Introduction 37
Learning Outcomes 38
How Racially and Ethnically Diverse Are Our Schools? 39
Race and Ethnicity of the Population 39
The Impact of Immigration 40
Race and Ethnicity in Schools 41
Teaching Students From Diverse Racial and Ethnic Groups 42
The Achievement Gap 42
Race in the Classroom 44
Ethnic Studies 44
Ethnocentric Curriculum 45
How Do Economics Affect Students and Schools? 45
Economic Diversity of Students 45
Students in Low-Income Families 45
Homeless Students 47
Middle-Class Families 47
Providing Equity in Schools 48
Teacher Expectations 48
Tracking 49
What If Students' Native Languages Are Not English? 49
Teaching English-Language Learners 50

Understanding and Using Evidence 51

Bilingual Education 52
English as a Second Language (ESL) 52
What Is the Relationship of Gender and Education? 53
Differences Between Females and Males 53
Delivering an Equitable Education for Girls and Boys 54

Challenging Assumptions 55

Teachers' Lounge 56

How Is Sexual Orientation Addressed in Schools? 56
Sexual Identity 57
Supporting LGBTQ Students 58
What Do the Religious Beliefs of Students Have to Do With Schools? 58
Religious Diversity 59
Addressing Religion in Public Schools 59

Connecting to the Classroom 60

Field Guide for Learning More About Today's Students 63

3. Addressing Learners' Individual Needs 67

Teacher Interview: Brandy Donald 66

Questions to Consider 67
Learning Outcomes 68
Introduction 68
What Are Key Characteristics of Students With Disabilities? 69
Established Disability Categories 70
Learning Disabilities 70
Speech Impairment 70
Mental Retardation 71
Emotionally Disturbed 71
Other Disabilities 71
Autism, a Spectrum 71
School Experiences for Students With Disabilities 72
Inclusion 72
Parental Involvement 72
Disproportionate Placement 73

What Are Some Ways of Distinguishing Students in Terms of Academic Ability? 73
Intelligence as a Basic Ability 73
Intelligence as One Ability 74
Multiple Intelligences 74
Implications of Academic Abilities for Teaching and Learning 75
Understanding and Using Evidence 76
Do All Students Develop in the Same Way? 76
Stages of Cognitive Development 77
Maturation 78
Activity 78
Sensorimotor Stage (0–2 years) 78
Preoperational Stage (2–7 years) 78
Concrete Operational Stage (7–11 years) 78
Formal Operational Stage (11 years to adult) 78
Human Brain Development 79
Different Neural Circuits Develop at Different Ages 79
Impoverishment Effects Can Be Long Lasting 80
The Brain Has Plasticity 80
Implications of Developmental Models for Teaching and Learning 81
How Do Class and Culture Affect Teaching and Learning? 81
Socioeconomic Status as a Way to See Each Student as Exceptional 82
Relationships Between Family Status and the Quantity of Words Heard 82
Relationships Between Family Status and the Quality of Words Heard 83
The Vocabulary Gap Continues to Widen 83
Implications of Vocabulary Development for Teaching and Learning 83
Culture as a Source of Student Exceptionality 84
Elements of Culture: A Quick Review 84
The Meaning in the Symbols 85
Culture in the Classroom 86
Safe and Caring Classroom Environment 86
Bullying Can Come in Two Ways 87
Implications of Class and Culture for Teaching and Learning 87
Characteristics of Students as Learners 89
What Are Some of the Most Common Ways of Categorizing Students? 89
Gifted and Talented Education (GATE) 89
Struggling Students 90
Students at Risk 90
Challenging Assumptions 91
Teachers' Lounge 92
Early Warning Indicators of Students Dropping Out 92
Implications for Teaching and Learning From Placing Students in Categories 93
Connecting to the Classroom 93
Field Guide for Learning More About Addressing Learners' Individual Needs 96

4. The Social Context of Schools 99
Teacher Interview: Ava Evbuoma 98
Questions to Consider 99
Introduction 99
Learning Outcomes 100
How Does Social Context Challenge Educators? 100
Academic Performance 100
The Federal Mandate 101
The Importance of a Teacher 101
The Sociopolitical Context 101
Understanding and Using Evidence 102
Deficit Ideology 103
Stereotyping 104
Students Leaving School Early 104
Why Students Drop Out of School 105
The Cost of Dropping Out 106
School-to-Prison Pipeline 107

Challenging Assumptions 108
How Does Social Context Influence What Is Taught? 108
Social Construction of Knowledge 109
Whose Knowledge 110
Multiple Perspectives 111
Multicultural Education 111
Culturally Responsive Teaching 112
Social Justice Education 113
How Are Students Affected by Social Context? 114
Health and Fitness 115
Nutrition 115
Physical Activity 116
Sexuality 117
Sexual Behavior 117
Teen Pregnancy 117
Sex Education 118
Violence 118
Child Abuse 118
Bullying 119
Teachers' Lounge 120
Gangs 121
Suicide 121
Substance Abuse 121
Connecting to the Classroom 123
Field Guide for Learning More About the Social Context of Schools 125

5. Families and Communities **129**
Teacher Interview: Arlene M. Costello 128
Questions to Consider 129
Learning Outcomes 130
Introduction 130
How Do the Public and Educators View Education? 130
Teacher Quality 131
Problems With Schools 132
Standards and Academic Success 132
In What Types of Families Do Students Live? 133
Diversity of Families 133
Size of Families 134
How Does Culture Influence Families and Their Children? 135
Characteristics of Culture 136
Cultural Relativism 136
Biculturalism and Multiculturalism 137
School Culture 137
Traditions 137
Hidden Curriculum 138
What Happens When Students' Cultures Come to School? 138
Religious Beliefs 139
Prayer in School 139
Books to Read 139
Religious Beliefs in Schools 140
Use of Native Languages 140
Learning English 141
Maintaining the Native Language 142
How Should Teachers Work With Parents and Communities? 143
Challenging Assumptions 143
Working With Families as Partners for Student Learning 144
Understanding and Using Evidence 146
Communications 147
Teachers' Lounge 148
Working With Diverse Families 149
Family and Teacher Organizations 150

Relationship of Schools to the Community 151
Partnerships 151
Bringing the Community Into the School 152
Connecting to the Classroom 152
Field Guide for Learning More About Families and Communities 155

Part II. The Foundations of Education 157

6. History of Schools in the United States 159
Teacher Interview: Marvin Kuhn 158
Questions to Consider 159
Introduction 159
Learning Outcomes 160
How Did Public Schools Come to Be? 160
Schools in the Colonies 160
Creating a System of Public Education 161
How Did Schools Become Designed Based on the Age of Students? 163
Understanding and Using Evidence 164
Elementary Schools 164
High Schools 165
Middle Level Education 167
Early Childhood Education 168
What Has Influenced the School Curriculum? 170
The Industrial Revolution 171
Progressivism: Curriculum for Reform 171
Sputnik I 172
How Has the Educational System Contributed to Equality? 173
First Americans 173
Resistance to Conversion 173
Boarding Schools 175
American Indian Control 176
African Americans 176
Participation in Schools After the Revolutionary War 176
Education in the South 177
Education at the Beginning of the 20th Century 177
School Desegregation 178
Latinos 179
The Battle for the Use of Spanish 179
Equity for Puerto Ricans 180
Asian Americans 181
How Has Teaching Evolved? 181
Teachers' Lounge 182
Teacher Preparation 183
Teacher Behavior 183
Challenging Assumptions 184
Connecting to the Classroom 185
Field Guide for Learning More About the History of Schools in the United States 187

7. Developing a Philosophy of Teaching and Learning 191
Teacher Interview: Heather Cyra 190
Questions to Consider 191
Learning Outcomes 192
Introduction 192
How Do Teachers Develop Personal Philosophies Toward Teaching and Learning? 192
Developing a Personal Philosophy of Teaching 193
The Influence of Stories in Building a Personal Philosophy of Teaching 194
Defining Events in Building a Personal Philosophy of Teaching 195
Taking Stock of Your Beliefs 196
Taking Stock of Your Students 196

How Do Students Learn? 197
Ideas About How Students Learn 198
John Dewey (1859–1952) 198
Hilda Taba (1902–1967) 199
Ralph W. Tyler (1902–1994) 200
Paulo Freire (1921–1997) 200
Eleanor Duckworth (1935–) 201
Howard Earl Gardner (1943–) 201
Grant Wiggins (1952–) 202
Diane McCarty (1954–) 202
Conflicting Perspectives in Teaching and Learning 202
The Necessity of Evaluating Ideas 204
Having a Research-Based Perspective 204
How Does Educational Psychology Help Teachers Understand Student Learning? 205
Research on Teaching and Learning 205
Translating Educational Psychological Perspectives Into Teaching Practice 206
Johann Pestalozzi (1746–1827), Jean Piaget (1896–1980), and Abraham Maslow (1908–1970) 206
Ivan Pavlov (1849–1936), Edward Thorndike (1874–1949), and Burrhus Frederick Skinner (1904–1990) 206
Lev Vygotsky (1896–1934) 207
How Do Philosophical Perspectives Help Teachers Understand Student Learning? 207
Metaphysics, Epistemology, and Axiology 208
The Metaphysical Questions of Content or Child 208
Ways of Knowing, Learning, and Teaching 209
The Role of Values and Ethics in the Classroom 209
Teachers' Lounge 210
Philosophical Perspectives' Influence on Teaching and Learning 210
Confucianism 210
Idealism and Realism 211
Perennialism and Essentialism 211
Pragmatism and Progressivism 212
Existentialism 212
The Presence of Educational Philosophies in Classrooms 213
Teacher-Focused Classrooms 213
Understanding and Using Evidence 215
Challenging Assumptions 216
Student-Focused Classrooms 217
The Changing Focus 217
Using Philosophy to Problem Solve 217
Connecting to the Classroom 218
Field Guide for Learning More About Developing a Philosophy of Teaching and Learning 220

8. Organizing Schools for Learning 223
Teacher Interview: Dr. Kim Friel 222
Questions to Consider 223
Learning Outcomes 224
Introduction 224
How Are Schools Staffed and Organized? 225
Roles of the Adult Workers in Schools 225
Principal 225
Assistant or Vice Principals and Deans 226
Teachers 226
Department Chairs and Teacher Leaders 226
Other School-Based Staff 227
Organization Charts 227
Communication Is Important 228
Organizing for Horizontal Communication 229
Variations in the Teachers' Role 229
Variations in Teaching Responsibilities 229
Professional Learning Communities 231

Organizing Students for Learning 232
Self-Contained Classroom 232
Organizing Students for Work 233
What Is the Relationship of Schools to School Districts and the State? 233
Challenging Assumptions 234
Organization of School Districts 235
School District Organization 235
School District Superintendent 236
District Office–Based School Support Personnel 237
School Boards 237
Teachers' Lounge 238
School Boards as Policy Bodies 238
School Board Responsibilities 239
Organization of Education at the State Level 239
Executive: State Governors 240
Legislative: State Legislatures 240
Judicial: State Courts 241
State Board of Education 241
Chief State School Officer 241
The Role of the Federal Government 242
What Are Today's Issues in the Workplace Called Schools? 242
Questions About the Organization of Schools 242
Class Size: What's Best? 242
Understanding and Using Evidence 243
Why Are Schools Organized the Way They Are? 244
What Should Be the Role of School Boards? 244
What About School Safety? 245
Connecting to the Classroom 246
Field Guide for Learning More About Organizing Schools for Learning 248

9. Governance and School Finance 251
Teacher Interview: Dr. Italia Negroni 250
Questions to Consider 251
Learning Outcomes 252
Introduction 252
How Is Governance Different From the Structures of Government? 252
Governance Can Be Good or Bad 253
Characteristics of Good Governance 253
Characteristics of Bad Governance 254
There Are Politics 255
What Is the Role of the Federal Government in Education? 256
The U.S. Constitution and the States' Responsibility for Education 256
The Tenth Amendment—Grants Responsibility to the States 257
The First Amendment—Freedom of Speech and Religion 257
The Fourteenth Amendment—Due Process 257
Three Parts of the Federal Government: Three Sources of Education Policy 258
Executive: President of the United States 258
Legislative: U.S. Congress 259
Judicial: U.S. Supreme Court 259
U.S. Department of Education 259
ESEA Past and Future 260
Elements of No Child Left Behind (NCLB) 260
Teachers' Lounge 262
As the Realities and Consequences of NCLB Came to Fruition There Were Waivers 263
Growth Scores: A Different Way 263
Reauthorization of ESEA, 2012 and Beyond 264
Rewarding School Success 264
Graduating Every Student 264
Placing Effective Teachers and Leaders 264

Improving STEM Education 264
Teacher Incentive Pay 264
How Are Schools Paid for, and How Is the Money Spent? 265
Finding the Money to Pay for Schools 266
Income Tax 266
Property Tax 267
Sales Tax 267
Federal Government Sources of Funds 267
Citizens Fight Back 268
Seeking Additional Sources of Funding for Schools 268
Lotteries and Gambling 269
Creative Sources of Funds for Schools 269
School Carnivals, Field Events, and Parent–Teacher Organizations 270
School–Business Partnerships 270
Each of These Fundraising Activities Has a Price 270
A Possible Source of Revenue That Was Never Considered Before 270
Challenging Assumptions 271
How Do Schools Spend the Money? 272
Distribution of Revenue: By Different Levels of Government 272
Per-Pupil Expenditure 273
Balancing the Budget in Tight Times 273
What Are Some of the School Finance Issues and Challenges? 274
School Finance: Equal and Enough 274
Two Fundamental Finance Questions 274
Different Levels of Government: Roles and Consequences 275
Centralization Versus Local Control 276
Widespread Variations or a National Curriculum? 276
Understanding and Using Evidence 277
Connecting to the Classroom 278
Field Guide for Learning More About Governance and School Finance 280

10. The Law as It Relates to Teaching and Learning 283
Teacher Interview: Michael Simpson 282
Questions to Consider 283
Introduction 285
Learning Outcomes 284
Contemporary Legal Issues and Their Deliberations 285
Social Media: Uses, Misuses, and Issues 286
Teachers' Use of MySpace 286
Cyberbullying 286
Sexting 287
Copying Documents and Other Material From the Internet 288
Accessing Material on the Web That Has a Copyright 288
Copyright Guidelines for Teachers and Students 289
Finding Out If Something Has a Copyright 290
Continuing Legal Dilemmas Related to Education 290
Separation of Church and State 291
Using Public Funds to Pay for Transportation to Catholic Schools 291
Two Continuing Questions 291
The Place of Religious Activities in Public Schools 293
Prayer at School Events 293
Celebration of Religious Holidays in Schools 293
Funding of Public Schools: Equity and Equality 294
What the U.S. Constitution Says About Funding 294
View of the States About the Funding of Schools 294
Segregation, Desegregation, and the Risks of Resegregation 294
Separate but Equal Was Constitutional 294
Separate but Equal Becomes Unconstitutional 295
Release From Court Order 295

Risk of Resegregation 295
In Summary: Solving Dilemmas Takes Time 295
Understanding and Using Evidence 296
Students' Rights and Protections 296
Statutes Related to Students With Disabilities 298
The Least Restrictive Environment 298
Inclusion 298
Paying for Special Education 299
Student and Teacher Qualifications Under IDEA 299
Student Rights 299
Family Privacy Rights 299
State Interests Versus Individual Rights 300
Public High Schools 300
Sports for Girls 300
Undocumented Students 301
Students' Freedom of Expression 301
Teachers' Lounge 302
Student Body Search 302
Locker Search 302
Teachers' Responsibilities, Rights, and Liabilities 303
Teacher Responsibilities as a School District Employee 303
Determining the Content of the Curriculum 303
When Parents Disagree With Teachers 304
Corporal Punishment 304
Reporting Child Abuse 305
The Basis for Student Grouping 305
Teacher and School Accountability 306
Beginning Teacher Nonrenewal and Dismissal 306
Due Process 306
Individual Teacher Rights and Responsibilities 307
Teacher Freedom of Public Expression 307
Teacher Dress 307
Drug Testing of Teachers 307
Challenging Assumptions 308
Teacher Liability 309
Law and Ethics Are Not the Same 309
The Perspective of the Law: Is It Legal? 310
The Ethical Perspective: What Is Right? 310
Resolving Dilemmas: Legal and Ethical Processes 310
Making the Final Decision 311
A Final Thought 312
Connecting to the Classroom 312
Field Guide for Learning More About the Law as It Relates to Teaching and Learning 314

Part III. Teaching for Student Learning 317

11. Standards, Curriculum, and Accountability 319

Teacher Interview: Lorraine (Reina) Floyd 318
Questions to Consider 319
Learning Outcomes 320
Introduction 320
What Are Standards and Benchmarks? 321
Characteristics of Standards 322
Common Core Standards 323
Standards for Content 324
Developing the Content Standards 325
Organizing the Standards 325
Using the Standards 328
Using Benchmarks 328
Keeping Track of Benchmarks and Standards in Lesson Planning 329

Knowing the Standards 330
Standards for Students 330
Standards for Teachers 331
Standards for Professional Education Areas 332
Standards for Undergraduates 333
Standards for Colleges of Education and Universities 334
Standards for Professional Practice 334
Standards for Teacher Professional Growth 334
Knowing When Students Have Met the Standards 335
Understanding and Using Evidence 336
What Is Curriculum? 337
Characteristics of Curriculum 338
Challenging Assumptions 339
Teachers' Lounge 343
Teachers Making Curriculum Come Alive 343
Accountability Measures Through Standards, Benchmarks, and Curriculum 344
Value-Added Assessment of Teacher Effectiveness 344
School Accountability 344
Connecting to the Classroom 345
Field Guide for Learning More About Standards, Curriculum, and Accountability 347

12. Managing the Classroom and Student Behavior 351
Teacher Interview: Lena Mann 350
Questions to Consider 351
Learning Outcomes 352
Introduction 352
What Is Classroom Management? 353
Using What You Already Know About Classroom Management 355
Frameworks for Learning About Classroom Management 355
Three Areas of Classroom Management 355
The Personal and Parental Affect in Classroom Management 356
The Paradoxes of Classroom Management 357
How Do You Build a Personal Philosophy of Classroom Management? 358
Theorists, Theories, and Models 358
Behavior Modification 358
Assertive Discipline 359
Social-Emotional and Group Dynamics Management Approaches 359
Teachers' Lounge 361
Instruction and Communication Approaches to Classroom Management 361
Understanding and Using Evidence 362
Challenging Assumptions 364
What Constitutes a Well-Managed Classroom? 365
Room Arrangement 365
Helping Students Be Comfortable in the Room You Have Arranged 366
Managing Paperwork 366
Students Managing Classroom Paperwork 367
A Multidimensional Look at Classroom Management 367
Multidimensionality 367
Simultaneity 367
Immediacy 368
Unpredictable and Public 368
History 368
Management of Movement on School Grounds and in Hallways 368
Routines, Rules, and Schedules 369
The Characteristics of a Well-Managed Classroom 370
What Is the Connection Between Discipline and Management? 371
Four Stages of Classroom Life That Influence Behavior 371

Forming 372
Storming 372
Norming 372
Performing 372
The Importance of Communication in Behavior Management 372
Basic Rules of Engagement 373
How Do Teachers Manage the Stress of Managing a Classroom? 374
Three Dimensions of Psychological Support for Teachers 375
Emotional-Physical Support 375
Psychosocial Support 375
Personal-Intellectual Support 375
Laughter in the Classroom 375
Connecting to the Classroom 376
Field Guide for Learning More About Managing the Classroom and Student Behavior 378

13. Teaching Strategies 383
Teacher Interview: Jason Choi 382
Questions to Consider 383
Learning Outcomes 385
Introduction 385
What Are Teaching Strategies? 386
Generic Teaching Strategies 387
Lecture 388
Questioning and Discussions 390
Grouping 393
Understanding and Using Evidence 394
Role Play, Simulation, and Drama 397
Reflective Learning/Inquiry 398
Viewing Teaching Strategies as Direct or Indirect Instruction 399
Teachers' Lounge 400
A Constructivist Approach to Teaching 400
Activity Learning 401
Never Just One 401
What Makes Teaching Strategies Work? 401
The Importance of Planning 402
Challenging Assumptions 403
Instructional Theory Into Practice 404
The Planning Cycle 404
Getting Students Ready to Learn 405
Bracketing or: Let's See, Where Was I? 406
Sponges 406
Evaluating Learning 406
Teacher Work Sample or Analysis of Student Work 407
Understanding the Connection Between Teaching Strategies and Curriculum 407
How Are Different Strategies Used for Different Purposes? 407
Culturally Relevant Teaching Strategies 408
Multiple Intelligences 408
Inclusion Strategies: Least Restrictive Environment (LRE) 409
Strategies for English Language Learners (ELL) 409
Homework as a Teaching Strategy 409
Connecting to the Classroom 410
Field Guide for Learning More About Teaching Strategies 412

14. Using Technology to Improve Student Learning 415
Teacher Interview: Nira Dale 414
Questions to Consider 415
Learning Outcomes 416
Introduction 416
What Role Does Technology Play in the Lives of Teachers and Learners? 417
The Evolving Face of Technology 419
The Cloud 419

Technology for Communication 419
Social Networking 420
Technology Changing the Teacher–Learner Relationship 421
Why Integrate Technology in Teaching? 423
Technology for Teaching 424
Smart Boards, MP3 Players, and Tablets 425
Digital Cameras 426
Video Recording 426
Teachers' Lounge 427
Learning Games 428
Audio Recordings 428
Teachers Using Technology Effectively 428
Using Technology With Diverse Learners 429
Software to Enhance Teaching and Learning 429
Challenging Assumptions 430
Difficulties in Teaching With Technology 431
Students Using Technology for Learning 431
Presentations and Research 431
Student Work Samples 432
Learning My Way on My Time 432
How Can Teachers Manage the Use of Technology and Use Technology to Manage the Classroom? 433
Managing the Use of Technology 433
Technology for Managing the Classroom 434
Creating a Technology-Rich Learning Environment 435
How Can Teachers Integrate Technology Into Their Own Professional Development? 435
Educational Technology Standards for Teachers 435
Using the Internet for Professional Development 437
Understanding and Using Evidence 438
Using Technology for Self-Improvement 439
Connecting to the Classroom 440
Field Guide for Learning More About Using Technology to Improve Student Learning 442

15. Assessing Student Learning and Results 445
Teacher Interview: Dr. Elliott Asp 444
Questions to Consider 445
Learning Outcomes 446
Introduction 446
Why Is Assessing So Important? 447
The Whys and Hows for Assessing 447
Formative Versus Summative Assessments 448
Purposes for Assessing 448
Considering the Quality of Assessments 449
Two Very Different Kinds of Tests 451
Norm-Referenced Tests (NRTs) 451
Criterion-Referenced Tests (CRTs) 451
Comparing NRT and CRT Test Scores 452
Characteristics of Effective Assessments 452
Level of Difficulty 452
Validity 453
Reliability 453
Performance Tasks 453
Authentic 454
Assessing for Different Types of Learning 454
Accommodating Different Types of Learners 454
Accommodating Special Needs Students 455
Accommodating ELL Students 457
What Are Some Ways to Test Student Learning? 457
Checking for Understanding Within Lessons 458
Teacher Observation 458
Teacher Questioning 459

Challenging Assumptions 460
Student Self-Reflection 461
Objective Tests 461
Watch Out for Bias in Test Items 461
Subjective Tests 463
Short-Answer Items 463
Essay Test Items 463
Teachers' Lounge 464
Open-Ended Formats 465
Which Format Is Best? 465
Rubrics Are an Important and Informative Assessment Tool 467
How Do Teachers Use Formative Assessments to Adjust Instruction and Improve Student Learning? 467
Four Levels of Formative Assessment 468
Teachers' Instructional Adjustments 468
Understanding and Using Evidence 469
Students' Learning Tactic Adjustments 470
Classroom Climate Shift From Traditional to Formative Assessment 470
Schoolwide Implementation of a Formative Assessment–Centered Culture 470
Response to Intervention (RTI) 471
Student Improvement Team (SIT) and RTI 472
Don't Forget the Achievement Gap 473
Connecting to the Classroom 473
Field Guide for Learning More About Assessing Student Learning and Results 475

Part IV. Becoming Tomorrow's Highly Effective Teacher 479

16. Succeeding in Your Teacher Education Program, and Beyond 481
Teacher Interview: Amber Velasquez 480
Questions to Consider 481
Learning Outcomes 482
Introduction 482
What Are Keys to Succeeding in Your Teacher Education Program? 483
Understanding Your Concerns 484
What Are Your Concerns Right Now? 484
Describing Teacher Concerns 485
There Is a Developmental Pattern to Teacher Concerns 486
Assessing Your Concerns 486
Implications of the Concerns Model for Teacher Education Candidates 487
Monitoring Your Concerns About Teaching 487
Implications for You 487
Understanding and Using Evidence 488
What About Ms. Velasquez's Concerns? 488
Strive for Quality in Your Teaching 489
Elliott's General Model of Effective Instruction 490
The Importance of Each and Every Field Experience 490
Challenging Assumptions 492
What Are the Keys to Being Hired as a Beginning Teacher? 492
Requirements for Obtaining a Teacher License 493
Getting Your First Teaching Position 493
Where to Look for Teaching Positions 494
Ideas for Your Professional Resume 494
Teacher Dispositions Are Very Important 496
In What Ways Can Candidates and Teachers Be Leaders? 496
Different Ways Teachers Can Lead 497
Formal Teacher Leadership 497
Working With Parents 497
Informal Teacher Leadership 498
Leading Adults Is a Big Challenge for Beginning Teachers 499
Career Path Options for Teachers 499

Teachers' Lounge 500

Becoming a School Administrator 500
Graduate Studies 501

How Does a Master Teacher Think About the Joy of Teaching? 501
Joy and Satisfaction in Teaching Can Be Career Long 502
"First of All, I Love Kids" 503
"I Saw That I Was Making a Difference" 503
"I Loved Sharing With Others" 504
"I Was Always Bringing Human Interest Stories to Share With the Kids" 504
You Need to Have a Notion of What You Want Your Classroom to Be Like Before You Get There 505
Serendipity Occurs as We Are Concluding the Interview With Mrs. Schneider 505
An Epilogue 506

Connecting to the Classroom 506

Field Guide for Learning More About Succeeding in Your Teacher Education Program, and Beyond 509

Glossary 513
References 520
Photo Credits 529
Index 531
About the Authors 546

Preface

Welcome to *Introduction to Teaching: Making a Difference in Student Learning,* which has been developed by an expert team of authors who have wide-ranging experiences and deep knowledge about today's schools and teacher education. Our combined experiences as teachers, teacher educators, and scholars add up to more than 100 years! We are fully engaged in today's schools, always experimenting with new approaches to teacher education, and frequently collaborating with colleagues across the United States and in other countries.

The members of our author team have a strong commitment to improving teacher education, and we have each worked on that goal in a variety of ways.

Over the last few years, as we would meet and see what is happening in schools, we came to the conclusion that most of the textbooks for introduction to teacher education courses do not accurately represent how schools and instruction are changing. Similarly, in many teacher education programs the increased emphasis on state-mandated testing, standards, and assessing are not receiving as much attention as is needed. We strongly believe that future teachers need an introduction to teaching textbook that is heavily grounded in the new paradigm for schools, which is focused on student learning.

We decided to write an introduction to teaching textbook that is grounded in today's schools, places a heavy emphasis on understanding student learning, and acknowledges the challenges of teaching while also emphasizing the joy to be found in this profession.

A quick look through most introduction to teaching textbooks can leave the impression that they all are the same. However, a closer look reveals there can be significant differences between these texts. The differences go beyond how the books are organized and their design. The overall philosophy of textbooks for the introduction to teaching course can vary dramatically. In this book we have worked to ensure that the view of teaching we reflect is grounded in what today's schools are really like and where they are headed in the future. The examples, discussion questions, and field activities throughout promote deep understanding of what it takes to become a teacher who improves student learning.

Our goal in writing this introduction to teaching textbook is to help future teachers prepare for one of the most important, challenging, and worthwhile professions there is. We all know from our own experience when we were students what it means to have an exceptional teacher. We also know what it means to have a teacher who is not. By combining our more than 100 years of experience, we have written a textbook that will help students become one of those exceptional teachers.

Themes

We have identified several key themes that are carried across each of the chapters in this text. Each theme is foundational to what we see exceptional teachers doing.

Focus on Learning.The most important theme of this book, as is reflected in the subtitle, is *making a difference in student learning.* In the past, including when each of us went through our teacher education program, the major focus was on describing what *teachers* do. Today, the focus has shifted to *student learning.* The most important purpose of teaching and schools is to have all students learning. High-quality teachers are always thinking about how what they are doing is affecting student learning.

Understanding and Using Data. Most of today's schools have more data available than can be used effectively. The importance of data should not be underestimated. However, learning how to use data and making decisions based on data are new skills for most teachers.

Real Educators, Real Schools, and Real Students. Given that each of us has been a teacher and teacher educator for a long time, we knew that it would be important to include the words of teachers and other education professionals. Therefore, every chapter begins with an interview of a real educator who is working in schools and school districts at this time. Several of the chapters begin with an interview of a first- or second-year teacher. Because schools cannot succeed without good leaders, other chapters begin with an interview of a school or district administrator, and the opening interview for one of the chapters is an attorney for the National Education Association. There is no escaping the importance of legal aspects of education, so we thought it would be important for you to read firsthand about the legal perspective and how it affects the ability of all students to learn.

Using Technology for Learning. We all see how the many types of technology are being used by students. Integrating technology into instruction can be powerful, and so uses of technology are referenced throughout this book. In addition, this text provides users with access to several useful and innovative technology-based resources, one of which is a set of videos of real classrooms. These videos were produced specifically for this book. We asked expert teachers with interesting classrooms to share what they are doing.

Facing Challenges. Now is not only a very important time to become a teacher; it is also a time during which schools are facing many very difficult problems. Today's students are more diverse than ever before. For the first time in the history of the United States there are governors and legislators who are questioning the importance of public schools and reducing their support of teachers. The downturn in the economy has become another challenge. In a textbook designed to introduce aspiring teachers to real schools, we must address these serious challenges and explore ways to deal with them.

Joy in Teaching. We would be remiss if we did not also address the important theme of *joy* in teaching. There is much joy in teaching, but it is easy to overlook it when confronted with all the work and challenges. So, throughout this text we have made reference to joy in teaching. There are cartoons throughout, as well as a special feature called Teachers' Lounge. For this feature we asked teachers and colleagues to share humorous, touching, and insightful stories from their experiences.

Features

As you read this text, you will find interesting and useful features.

Teacher Interviews open each chapter and offer an authentic look at what it means to be a teacher today. Each chapter-opening interview is paired with Questions to Consider that are designed to stimulate students' critical thinking about the chapter topic and prepare them to engage more deeply with the material that follows.

Learning Outcomes at the beginning of each chapter guide students to think about what they should take away from their reading.

Marginal Icons throughout the chapters direct students to relevant video and audio resources as well as journal articles and reference resources that will allow them to take a "deeper look" at areas of particular interest to them.

Summaries close each chapter and are designed to help students focus on key chapter content.

Discussion Questions challenge students to think critically and apply what they have read.

Self-Assessments allow students to examine their own level of understanding of the chapter content by using a Complexity of Thinking rubric to identify areas of weakness that may require additional study or attention.

The **Field Guide for Learning** concludes each chapter and provides students opportunities to extend their learning beyond the pages of this book. Each field guide represents a critical resource to help students develop the knowledge and skills that we find in expert educators by providing suggestions for classroom observation activities, reflection questions to promote journaling, portfolio builders, and suggested books and websites for further study.

Stories and Examples are important ways to learn about teaching (and improving student learning), and so, each chapter includes plenty of these to illustrate the basic ideas.

We also have a number of engaging boxed features:

Understanding and Using Evidence boxes present a set of research findings or data and ask students to form an understanding of the information and to attempt their own analysis. Follow-up information and sample answers are provided on the ancillary website.

Challenging Assumptions boxes engage students in confronting "common sense" conclusions they may hold about education practices that are, in fact, not supported by research. We have provided examples of surprising research information that we hope will encourage students to question the obvious, and be rigorous when investigating and implementing teaching strategies.

Teachers' Lounge boxes feature inspirational, humorous, and unexpected classroom moments shared by educators from across the country. These offer students a behind-the-scenes glimpse at the stories teachers share with one another in the teachers' lounge that define the day-to-day experience of what it means to be a teacher.

Video Case boxes feature video clips that bring the reality of the modern classroom into focus. Each box features two or three questions that prime students to think critically about the accompanying video.

Connecting to the Classroom boxes offer a convenient summary of suggestions for teaching best practices presented in the chapter.

Ancillaries

Our book offers a robust ancillary package with numerous resources to support instructors and students.

Instructor Teaching Site

A password-protected site, available at **www.sagepub.com/hall**, features resources that have been designed to help instructors plan and teach their courses. These resources include an extensive test bank, chapter-specific PowerPoint presentations, lecture notes, sample syllabi for semester and quarter courses, discussion questions, class activities, portfolio activities, suggested answers to the end-of-chapter questions, and links to the video, audio, and Deeper Look SAGE journal articles and reference resources featured in the margins of the text.

Student Study Site

An open-access student study site is available at **www.sagepub.com/hall**. This site provides access to the videos, audio clips, and Deeper Look SAGE journal articles and reference resources featured in the margins of the text, as well as several study tools including eFlashcards, web quizzes, web resources, and web exercises.

Interactive eBook

Introduction to Teaching: Making a Difference in Student Learning is also available as an **Interactive eBook**, which can be packaged free with the book or purchased separately. The interactive eBook offers links to video cases, Deeper Look materials including SAGE journal articles and reference articles, as well as additional audio, video and web resources.

A Final Important Note

Teaching is hard work; in fact, becoming an exceptional teacher is very hard work. Although we have years of experience in schools and thinking about teaching and learning, we still have times when we wonder about our own effectiveness and what we could be doing differently that would help our students learn more. All the thinking, doing, and reflecting that is necessary to be an exceptional teacher can be exhausting. It is important that teacher candidates and teachers have a life outside of teaching. To paraphrase an old saying, if you only teach you will indeed become a dull teacher. You will see in several of the Teacher Interviews that our interviewees have made reference to what they do outside of teaching. For example, Brandy Donald runs half marathons and Amber Velasquez is very active in her community. Joyce Schneider, the retired teacher in the last chapter, is serving on a board of directors that is developing a new children's science museum.

To be an exceptional teacher requires having a balance. Teachers can't be "on" 24 hours a day, seven days a week. Teachers need time to power down and regenerate. This is one of the reasons the photos we have inserted below are of ourselves in nonprofessional educator settings. Teaching is hard work and you rarely stop thinking about it, so it is important to have life outside of school.

As competitive as we are, it still is important to be able to say to others, and to yourself: **Have fun!**

Gene E. Hall, professor, husband, father, grandfather, and road racer

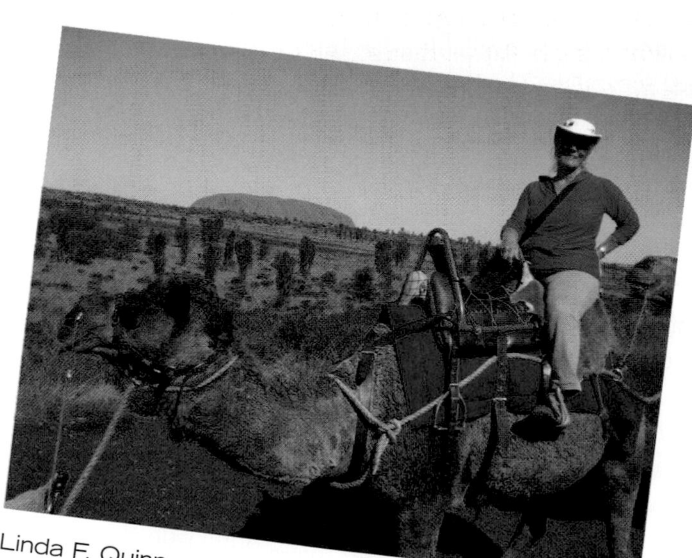

Linda F. Quinn, professor, wife, mother, grandmother, and traveler

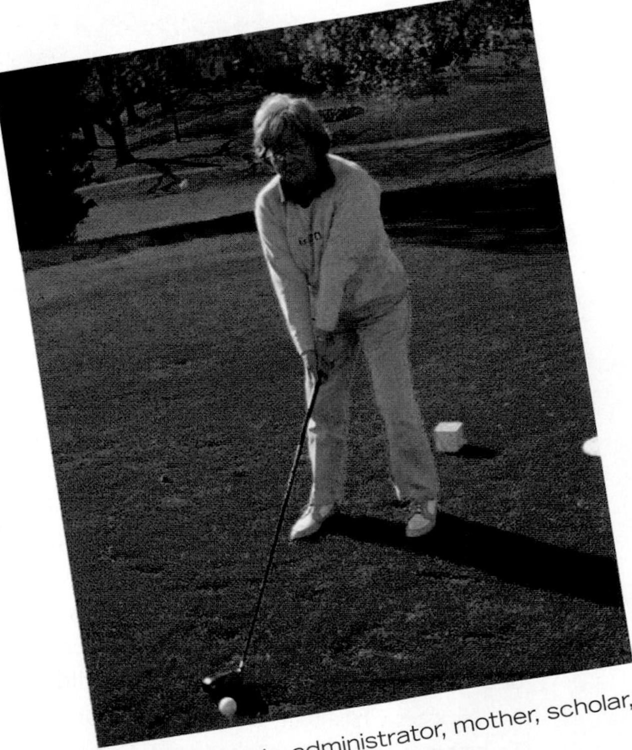

Donna Gollnick, administrator, mother, scholar, and golfer

Acknowledgments

The authors want to express their appreciation for the many talented colleagues and professionals who have contributed to the creation of this book. The thoughtful and insightful contributions of our real educators, the constructive feedback from reviewers, and the Teachers' Lounge authors who shared their experiences all have made this book better, more informative, and grounded in the best of teaching and schooling.

Based on all our experiences in producing this book, we see ourselves as being fortunate to now be members of the SAGE author family. It has been a positive, professional, and successful experience. Without the insight and leadership of Diane McDaniel, executive editor, we would not have had this opportunity. The editorial and production team have been highly professional and good at what they do. Megan Krattli, associate editor, has been our day-to-day pace setter. Without her patient, yet persistent, probing and communicating we would not now have such a good textbook. Many others at SAGE have contributed their expertise including TerriLee Paulsen, copy editor; Terra Schultz, marketing manager; Rachael Leblond, assistant editor; Megan Ann Koraly, editorial assistant; and Astrid Virding and Libby Larson, production editors. This has truly been a team effort where each of us has shared and learned. To all, we say thank you.

Another important set of contributors were the teacher educators who took of their time to review early drafts of our manuscripts. The reviews were substantive and constructive. Also, the reviews arrived in time so that we authors were able to refer to them in clarifying (what we thought were perfect) explanations, making changes (by emphasizing and adding important points), and being reminded of why this book is based not only in what schools are like today, but in how important it is to keep pointing out the joy in teaching and learning.

Pamela W. Aerni, Longwood University

Angie Jones Bales, Bossier Parish Community College

Tanisha Billingslea, Cameron University

Lauri Pepe Bousquet, Le Moyne College

Jesse Chenven, Central New Mexico Community College

Pamela Chibucos, Owens Community College

Garnet Chrisman, University of the Cumberlands

H. Jurgen Combs, Shenandoah University

Diane G. Corrigan, Cleveland State University

Elaine Bacharach Coughlin, Pacific University

Charles Edward Craig, Jr., Tennessee Technical University

Camy Weber Davis, Oakland City University

Darryl M. De Marzio, University of Scranton

Thomas S. Dickinson, DePauw University

Rebecca Fredrickson, Texas Woman's University

Jill E. Gelormino, St. Joseph's College

Carol Gilles, University of Missouri

Amanda Lee Glaze, Jacksonville State University

Claudia Green, Corban University

Pam Green, Southwestern College

Steven R. Greenberg, Bridgewater State University

Janice A. Grskovic, Indiana University Northwest

Sam Guerriero, Butler University

Felecia A. B. Hanesworth, Medaille College

Dana Lewis Haraway, James Madison University

Dana Hilbert, Cameron University

Bethany Hill-Anderson, McKendree University

Jennifer Holloway, Cameron University at RSU

Johnnie Humphrey, John Tyler Community College

MeHee Hyun, Antioch University Los Angeles

Rebekah D. Kelleher, Wingate University

Leonard Larsen, DMACC

Nina Mazloff, Becker College

Reney McAtee, Tennessee State University

Kathy J. McKee, Multnomah University

Deena McKinney, East Georgia College

Sarah K. McMahan, Texas Woman's University

Linda A. Mitchell, Jacksonville State University

Madonna Murphy, University of St. Francis

George Noblit, University of North Carolina at Chapel Hill

Denise Patmon, University of Massachusetts, Boston

Nina Gunther Phillips, Bryn Athyn College

Rebecca Pitkin, Dickinson State University

Thomas A. Raunig, University of Great Falls

Donna Redman, University of La Verne

Suzanne Roberts, Florida College

Phillip Russell, University of Arkansas, Fort Smith

Brian Schultz, Northeastern Illinois University

Marjorie Schiller, Central Arizona College

Eric-Gene J. Shrewsbury, Patrick Henry Community College

Richard K. Simmons, College of DuPage

Darlene Smith, Walters State Community College

Janet Stramel, Fort Hayes State University

Douglas Sturgeon, Shawnee State University

Lucia Torchia-Thompson, Reading Area Community College

Curtis Visca, Saddleback College

David Vocke, Towson University

Harold Waters, Southern Wesleyan University

Gail Watson, County College of Morris

Colleen M. Wilson, Jacksonville University

Today's Teachers, Students, and Schools

Chapter 1 Becoming a Teacher

Chapter 2 Today's Students

Chapter 3 Addressing Learners' Individual Needs

Chapter 4 The Social Context of Schools

Chapter 5 Families and Communities

TEACHER INTERVIEW

Katie Johnston

Meet Katie Johnston, first-grade teacher of 22 first-graders at Shell Rock Elementary School in the Waverly–Shell Rock Community School District in Northeastern Iowa. Shell Rock Elementary is one of four elementary centers in the district and services 160 PreK–4 students. There are 10 full-time teachers and specialists at Shell Rock Elementary. The rural and somewhat bucolic setting of Shell Rock Elementary provides a close-knit community of teachers and learners. Ms. Johnston earned her degree in teacher education at Wartburg College in Waverly, Iowa.

Becoming a Teacher

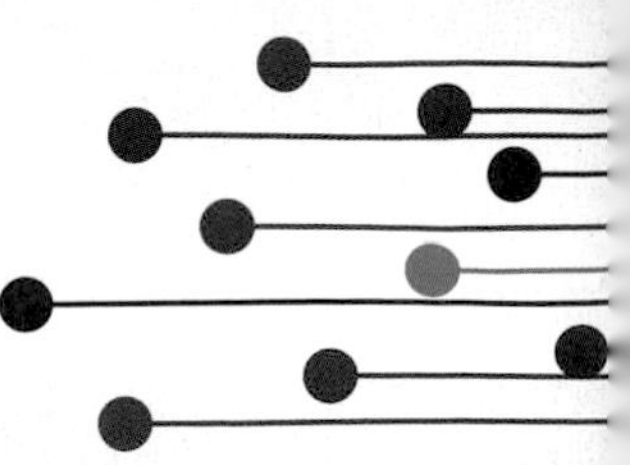

Why did you choose teaching as a career?

I wasn't really one of those people who knew that I wanted to be a teacher. I was interested in getting a degree in music. However, the summer after my senior year in high school, I worked with kids with special needs and so when I showed up on campus for my first year as a university freshman I changed all of my courses from music to education.

How did you get started in your teacher education program?

At Wartburg, I was very fortunate to have placements early in the program and in a variety of settings throughout the program. My placement in sixth grade for student teaching helped me so much. All the teachers on the sixth-grade team were so supportive of me that I really wanted a sixth-grade position for my first job. Now, I love teaching first grade and I am determined to grow professionally.

How did you prepare for your first placement as a teacher?

Fortunately, I knew I had a job in April so I was able to meet with the current teacher who was changing grade levels. She helped me with ideas and resources. I had a mentor during my two-year probationary period, and she gave me excellent advice regarding writing lesson plans and understanding why it was important to script them.

Where do you find joy in teaching?

There are so many different ways to find joy in teaching. I love listening to students' stories. I also really enjoy being able to build strong relationships with families. It is a great joy when I see my students begin to enjoy reading and be excited about learning. I had to make a huge mental shift from thinking I might become a sixth-grade teacher to the reality that I was going to be teaching first grade. Sometimes I am surprised at the level of understanding first-graders have about things adults take for granted. For example, during my second year of teaching I got married and I told my students that I was going to be gone for a while and that my name would change. When I came back to be their teacher, they were expecting someone else. I guess since they thought I would have a new name I wouldn't be the same person. Things like that can keep a smile in your heart for a long time.

How would you describe excellence in teaching?

To me excellence is really about being responsive and flexible in meeting the needs of your students. Instruction must really be based on academic strengths of the students. It is absolutely necessary for teachers to see each student as a whole being in order to be excellent. Excellent teachers learn to use resources in the community and help from parents because teaching is a big job and you can't expect to be able to do it all yourself.

Questions to Consider

1. Ms. Johnston's experience working with special needs students led her to teaching. What other experiences in people's lives might lead them toward choosing teaching as a career?
2. What are some of the joyful images that come to mind when you think about being a teacher?
3. Would teaching in a rural setting such as Shell Rock Elementary School be much different from teaching in a large urban area? Why? Why not?
4. Are beginning teachers usually hired in the grade level of their choice? Why? Why not?

In what ways, as a teacher, do you focus on student learning?

I really try to always hold student learning as the measure for what I plan for my lessons; to make sure I am on track with my strategies and learning goals. Focusing on student learning allows me to focus my instructional practices. First-graders have one assessment so both the student and I are not burdened with testing. I also base my lessons off of the common core standards. First-grade teachers in the district meet once a week to discuss learning strategies. The content and standards we must teach to are clear, but teachers are given some leeway in how those standards should be met so we can match instruction to individual student needs.

How would you describe the relationship between teaching and assessment?

It is a love–hate relationship. I think the word *assessment* has gotten a bad rap because we associate assessment with standardized tests that teachers are forced to do. Formative assessments are at the core of our instructional practices.

Learning Outcomes

After reading this chapter, you should be able to

1. Recognize the range of variables that influence teachers and teaching.
2. Know the steps one can take to earn a teaching license.
3. Understand the reasons educators consider teaching a profession similar to law and medicine.
4. Understand the ways to find the job that you desire.
5. Understand how to develop patterns of behavior that will contribute to a successful career as a teacher.
6. Be aware of the importance of keeping track of personal and professional growth as a teacher.

INTRODUCTION

Teaching is a noble profession. It is a joyful profession. It can be fun to help others learn. Teaching is also hard work. Teaching is a demanding profession that requires making hundreds of decisions during a school day, managing 20 to 40 students hour after hour, analyzing data about learning, and interacting with parents and colleagues. Teaching has never been easy even in earlier times when the classroom was a one-room schoolhouse. In addition to making sure all of their students were learning, teachers in former times had to build the fires to keep the school warm and sweep up after the students went home. Teaching requires high levels of sustained energy, effort, and motivation. Since you are reading this text, you are no doubt thinking about teaching as a career.

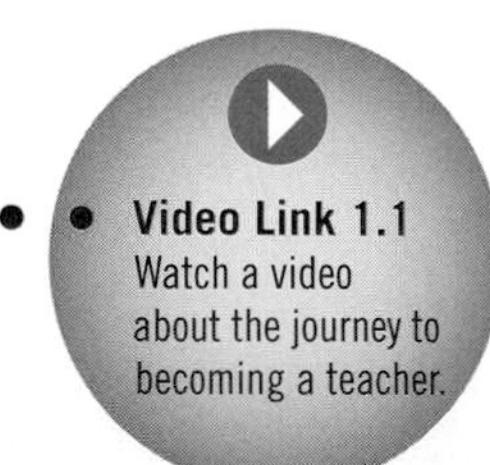

Video Link 1.1
Watch a video about the journey to becoming a teacher.

Is teaching the right choice for you? Some candidates in teaching have started along this career path because they enjoyed going to school. Some follow in the footsteps of parents, aunts, or uncles. Others want to be part of kids' lives, to advocate for children, and to give children exciting, meaningful experiences to help them become educated adults. Many remember a favorite teacher and want to have the same influence on others that that teacher had on them. Teaching seems familiar because we have all spent so much of our lives in classrooms. It is possible to think that teaching can't be too difficult because many of our teachers made it seem easy. We saw teaching through the eyes of the students, not the teachers. Teachers have a very different view of classrooms.

This text will help you explore whether teaching is the right profession for you and what it means to view classrooms from a teacher's perspective. This text will help you understand the diversity of students, communities, and schools in the United States. It will introduce you to the theoretical foundations supporting the teaching profession and explain some of the basic skills needed to manage a classroom and help students learn. This text will shed light on the realities of teaching that teachers face today as well as the joys they experience as part of the teaching profession.

WHY TEACH?

Katie Johnston's original plan for her future didn't include becoming a teacher. She had other goals, other desires than to spend her days in classrooms with children and young adults. But when she had the opportunity to actually teach special needs children, her fate was sealed. Her interactions with the boys and girls in the summer program brought her an immense sense of accomplishment and joy. And so, she became a teacher.

Teachers get to work with people of all sizes, and every day brings something to be happy about.

What brought you to consider a career in teaching? Most teachers say they want to teach because they care about children and youth and believe they can make a difference in the lives of their students. In a survey of teachers by the National Education Association (NEA; 2003), over half of the teachers also indicated that they originally chose teaching because of the value of education to society. Many secondary teachers report they chose teaching because they love the subject they are teaching. Some chose teaching because they love to learn. Many people have wanted to teach for as long as they can remember. Over half of the new teachers in surveys by the Public Agenda indicate they would be satisfied with a job that involves the work they love to do, allows enough time to be with family, contributes to society, provides the support they need, has job security, and gives the sense of being respected and appreciated (Farkas, Johnson, & Foleno, 2000). Teaching does all of these.

The Joy of Teaching

If it isn't fun, why do it? Teachers have to be able to laugh, to get their students to laugh, and to laugh with their students. Learning should be fun. Smiles and laughter can brighten up any situation, relieve stress, and possibly make whatever difficult task is at hand less daunting. The joy that bubbles up when a group of students are pleasantly surprised or excited should never be squelched. New teachers are well familiar with the adage "Don't smile until Christmas." Nothing could be further from the truth. A bit of silliness now and then does not exclude the serious aspects of teaching. A favorite science methods professor of mine made every class a delight. He would laugh, joke, and tease us into learning complex concepts. He often reminded us that he was serious, not somber about science education, and then he would smile. It is the playfulness and spirit of teachers that endears them to students. And it is what students remember of their teachers.

The joy and rewards of teaching vary from teacher to teacher. The best teachers truly enjoy working with children and youth. They find a challenge in ensuring that underserved students learn at high levels and take joy in the academic success of all students. Former teacher and author Jonathan Kozol shares ideas about how to put the fun back into learning in his latest book, *Letters to a Young Teacher.* Francesca, the first-grade teacher Kozol shares teaching stories with, finds joy amidst her struggles to reach the most recalcitrant of students. Kozol tells Francesca, *"I think teaching is a beautiful profession and that teachers of young children do one of the best things that there is to do in life; bring joy and beauty, mystery and mischievous delight into the hearts of little people in their years of greatest curiosity"* (Kozol, 2007, p. 8). Every teacher has a story about the joy he or she finds in teaching. Teachers treasure these moments and are always willing to share them. Ask a teacher you know what brings joy in teaching.

Video Case 1.1
The Joy of Teaching

1. Teachers in this video express ways of finding joy in teaching. What similarities did you find among their comments?
2. Not everyone decides to teach for the same reason. What are some of the reasons teachers in this video give for becoming teachers?

Intrinsic and Extrinsic Rewards

As Ms. Johnston expressed, joy in teaching can be found in a variety of ways. Most teachers experience **intrinsic rewards** when students grasp the concept or task they have been teaching. Students are as different as night and day. Some students may be successful in everything they pursue. Some are not. Some students are involved. Others are not. Some students actually resist learning. Teachers search for lessons that will engage all students, and they create ways to get all students to participate in discussions and projects. When teachers can do this they are rewarded for their efforts. The more teachers are able to bring students together in a learning community, the more they are rewarded. It is a positive cycle that excellent teachers strive to perpetuate. What is exciting is to try to meet the needs of each individual student. Teaching is never boring. It is different from minute to minute, and there is no formula that works for everyone.

Extrinsic rewards for teachers come in the form of acknowledgments from students, from other teachers, from parents, and from prestigious awards such as Teacher of the Year. Teachers receive visits and letters from former students thanking them for inspiration, comfort, and happiness. Sometimes teachers are surprised at the influence they have had on certain students, and when that mischievous student who made them want to tear their hair out, day after day, shows up in later years with a smile and a thank-you, the reward is clear. Parents write thank-you notes, volunteer to be a teacher's aide, and bake treats for special occasions. Other teachers ask for help with a specific problem, or ask to use a lesson that you have developed. Their appreciation of your skill as a teacher is rewarding. Teachers of the Year receive public accolades and have the opportunity to share their expertise with others through speeches and demonstrations. Some awards are even accompanied by money. Receiving payment for going an extra distance is rewarding, but most teachers will tell you it is not the money that brings them joy in teaching See Figure 1.1.

Teachers enjoy sharing the things that happen at school.

The Laughs

Every teacher has a funny story to tell. It is through the sharing of stories that teachers become aware of the strong ties they have to their professional community. Sharing stories also provides a venue for understanding the mysteries of teaching and why it is so rare and marvelous to be a teacher.

Figure 1.1 Why New Teachers Choose to Teach

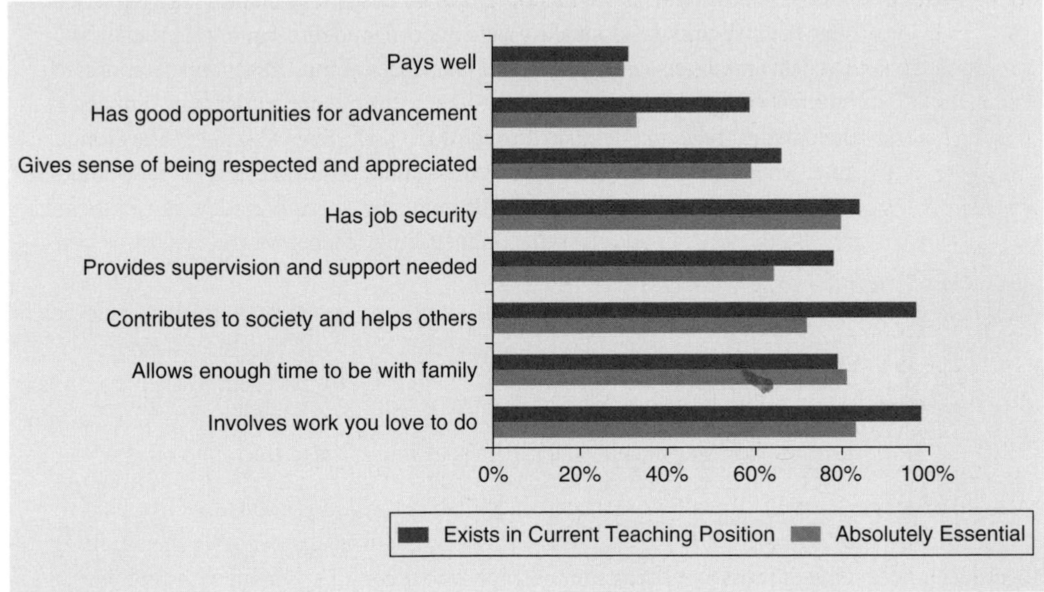

Source: Adapted from Farkas, S., Johnson, J., & Foleno, T. (2000). *A sense of calling: Who teaches and why* (p. 10). New York, NY: Public Agenda.

A Story: Mrs. Harper was a second-grade teacher in a rural school in Oregon. Due to a health problem, her doctor had put her on a special diet, and by the end of the first nine weeks Mrs. Harper had lost quite a bit of weight. One afternoon she donned her science apron and called her students to come stand around the science table for a demonstration. As was conducting the demonstration, the slacks she was wearing slipped past her hips and fell to the floor. Mrs. Harper was unaware of this but the students near her noticed and started to snicker. Mrs. Harper admonished them to behave and so they quieted down. When the demonstration was over Mrs. Harper turned to step toward the blackboard and stumbled over her downed slacks. "Oh, my," she exclaimed, "My pants have fallen off." And then she laughed. The shrieks and laughter from Mrs. Harper's classroom could be heard throughout the school. In no time at all everyone knew that Mrs. Harper had dropped her slacks. It was the highlight of the month. At the end of the year, Mrs. Harper's class held a going away party for her and the cake, made by a parent, was decorated according to the second-graders' directions. Atop the cake was an image of Mrs. Harper in her science apron with her slacks down around her ankles. The words "To our favorite teacher, Mrs. Harper, the day she dropped her slacks" said it all.

Audio Link 1.1
Listen to teachers who have made impacts on their students.

Ask teachers you know to tell you a story about something funny that happened to them while they were teaching. As their stories unfold, watch their faces and you will see the joy in teaching.

Making a Difference

Can you think of a teacher who made a difference in your life? It may be one who really cared about you, or a teacher who convinced you to apply for college, or one who challenged you to learn, or one who helped you develop self-esteem. Professional athletes, presidents of companies, and national leaders often attribute their success to a teacher. The teacher may not know until years after the student has left her classroom that she had such an impact.

Parents believe that teachers make a difference in their children's lives, especially when it comes to learning. Many parents know who the good teachers are in their schools and do everything they can to ensure their children are in those teachers' classrooms. According to the 2011 Gallop Poll of the public's attitudes toward the public schools, more than 50% of Americans gave either an *A* or *B* to the schools in their community (Bushaw & Lopez, 2011). Research validates parents' beliefs that effective teachers do make a difference in student learning. In the 1990s, Sanders and Rivers (1996) and their colleagues at the University of Tennessee compiled achievement data from standardized tests for students in Tennessee schools and followed the data through successive years of school. They found that two students who performed at the same level in the second grade could be separated by as many as 50 percentile points by the fifth grade if one of them had an effective teacher and the other an ineffective teacher for the next three years.

Students can create amazing things when they are allowed to express their talent.

Other researchers have found that the influence of teachers on student achievement is greater than any other observable factor such as small class sizes (Darling-Hammond, 1999; Rivkin, Hanushek, & Kain, 1998). Excellent teachers hardly ever stop thinking about the subjects they teach. When you discover a subject that you love, the best way to enjoy it for the rest of your life is to teach it to others.

Student Learning

One of most joyful parts of teaching is to see students achieve at high levels. This achievement could be physical, social, or creative as well as intellectual. All are important in the development of the whole child or person. During your teacher education program, you will learn how to develop lesson plans and deliver instruction. You will be expected to be creative in developing rigorous and engaging instructional strategies that draw on the cultural background and prior experiences of students. Your success will depend on students learning the concepts you are trying to teach.

How will you know that students are learning at the expected levels? One of the most superficial measures will be performance on standardized tests, which are required annually in most schools. Of course you will want students to perform well on those tests, but they measure only a narrow slice of the knowledge that students should be developing. Teachers are also helping students develop skills to use the knowledge required for doing well on a standardized test in real-life situations. Teachers provide opportunities for students to analyze and think critically about the subject. They help students develop **dispositions**, or attitudes and behaviors that will show they value learning. Joy is seeing examples of student learning in multiple forms that convince you that a student is ready for the next grade.

The Teaching Profession

Audio Link 1.2
Listen to an interview with a teacher advocate.

Most teachers consider themselves professionals. However, until recently, teaching was identified by many as a semiprofession as compared with the professions of law, medicine, architecture, engineering, and accountancy. One reason was that teaching had not provided the same monetary advantages or prestige as the traditional professional fields. Another reason was that teachers seem to have relatively little control over their work. Other professionals or policymakers select the curriculum, set rules, and develop learning standards. Most teachers have limited access to an office, telephone, and secretary. The structure of a teacher's day leaves little time to interact with colleagues to plan or challenge each other intellectually.

A profession is defined as "a calling requiring specialized knowledge and often long and intensive academic preparation" ("Profession," 2004). All states require at least a bachelor's degree to be eligible for an initial license to teach. Traditionally, states have required some specialized preparation in education that includes student teaching or an internship. A growing number of universities are requiring teacher candidates to have a bachelor's degree in a content area before they begin graduate work in education. Thus, over time a growing number of teachers are receiving their specialized preparation for teaching at the graduate level. Most teachers today have a master's degree and continue to participate in professional development activities throughout their careers.

Being a Professional

A profession sets standards for entry into the profession. In addition, its members apply standards and codes of ethics to themselves and others, disciplining one another when necessary by removing licenses from offenders. Professionals provide services to clients. Their work is intellectual, requiring specialized knowledge and skills. They are bound by an ethical code that guides their relationships with clients and colleagues. They also have an obligation to practice their profession in ways the public would find acceptable.

In other professions, standards and rules are set by the professionals themselves. School administrators, members of the school board, and state legislators usually set standards and rules for teachers. This practice is not likely to change unless teachers themselves become involved in the teaching profession beyond their own classrooms. Teacher unions provide an opportunity for teachers to negotiate contracts that outline salary and working conditions. Teacher organizations in most states conduct annual or semiannual statewide meetings for their members. These meetings provide professional development opportunities, a chance to network with other teachers, and a mechanism for becoming involved at the state level. You can stay engaged with your subject area and other educational interests by joining national organizations such as the National Council for Teachers of Mathematics (NCTM) or the National Council of Teachers of English (NCTE). Many of the national organizations have state affiliates in which you could be a member or become a leader. Through teacher organizations, teachers can serve on **accreditation** teams that evaluate schools and universities in their state or across the country. One sign of a true professional is active and continued involvement in professional organizations at local, state, and national levels.

Deeper Look 1.1
Read about criteria concerning teaching as a profession.

Setting and Upholding Standards

Throughout the past 20 years, teachers have worked with professors, parents, and the general public to set standards for students and teachers in their school districts, states, and national organizations. In some states, teachers have the majority control of professional standards boards that have the responsibility for developing licensure standards for teachers and other school professionals. When necessary, these boards withdraw licenses from teachers whose behaviors have led to malpractice. In states without professional standards boards, these functions are usually provided by a state board of education, whose members have been elected or appointed by the governor.

Accreditation

Both schools and teacher education programs are also held to professional standards. Most other professions require their members to graduate from an accredited program before they can take the state licensure examination. In the past, some states required teacher education programs to be nationally accredited by the National Council for Accreditation of Teacher Education (NCATE) or the Teacher Education Accreditation Council (TEAC). Recently these two accrediting agencies merged into one accrediting body with the new name Council for the Accreditation of Educator Preparation (CAEP). If you are in a teacher education program hosting a visit by an accreditation examination team, you may be asked to talk about your program and field experiences. The team may ask you about your **portfolio** and what you have learned about working with students from diverse populations. They may ask how you know that students are learning. They are also likely to ask you about the quality of teaching at the university, particularly by education faculty members. When you are teaching, you are likely to be involved every few years in an accreditation visit by the state and/or regional accrediting agency.

Licensure

To teach in a public school, teachers must be licensed by a state agency to teach a specific subject (for example, mathematics or social studies) at the middle or high school levels. Early childhood, elementary, special education, physical education, music, and art teachers are licensed to teach children in specific grades such as preschool, primary, K–6, or K–12. If you graduate from a state-approved program, which is connected to national accreditation, you have usually met the state requirements for a state license. You also will be required to pass a state licensure test in most states. Some states will grant a provisional license that allows you to teach for three to five years before meeting all of the requirements for licensure. Several years of successful practice and possibly completion of a master's degree is normally required to attain a professional license to continue teaching. Requirements are different when you apply for a license in a state other than the one in which you graduated. The second state may have additional requirements that you must meet and may have higher cutoff, or qualifying, scores on the required licensure tests. If you plan to move to a different state to teach, check the requirements for a license so that you can take the appropriate courses during your program.

National Board Certification

Teachers with three years of experience are eligible to apply for national certification by the **National Board for Professional Teaching Standards (NBPTS).** Applicants provide evidence in the collection of documents that are compiled in a portfolio to demonstrate meeting standards for their subject area at a specific age level. Each portfolio must include a videotape of the teacher teaching a lesson, **reflections** on teaching, and an analysis of student work. In addition, the teacher must complete assessment exercises at a testing center. Teaching performance is judged by experienced teachers using **rubrics** aligned with standards. Many states and school districts cover the costs for teachers to participate in this process, which could be $2,300 or more.

Video Link 1.2
Watch a video about National Board Certification.

What are the advantages of seeking national board certification? Most applicants report that the process helped improve their teaching and the performance of their students. They learned to reflect on their practice and make changes to improve student learning. A 2004 research study (Goldhaber & Anthony, 2004) of student test scores in North Carolina supports the perceptions of these teachers. The study found that the students of national-board-certified teachers are far more likely to improve their scores on state tests than students of non-national-board-certified teachers. In addition, many national-board-certified teachers receive annual bonuses or pay raises.

Specialized Knowledge

Teachers must know the subjects they will be teaching. The knowledge and related skills for teaching the subject are described in the standards of the national organizations that represent teachers in that field. You will be expected to understand the subject well enough to help young people know it and apply it to the world in which they live. If students are not learning a concept or skills, teachers must be able to relate the content to the experiences of students to provide meaning and purpose.

The professional and pedagogical knowledge needed by teachers is outlined in the widely accepted standards of the Interstate New Teacher Assessment and Support Consortium (InTASC), established by the Council of Chief State School Officers. In 2010 an updated version of the standards was vetted to educational organizations for public comment, and in April 2011 the new standards were adopted. The InTASC standards are used by most states as a framework for individual state standards, and it is likely that the revised edition of the InTASC standards will continue to guide what teachers should know and be able to do to be effective in today's schools. Visit **http://www.ccsso.org/Resources/Publications/InTASC_Model_Core_Teaching_Standards_A_Resource_for_State_Dialogue_(April_2011).html** to learn more about the new InTASC Model Core Learning Standards.

Reading about the effort behind the development and adoption of the new InTASC standards should make it very clear that teaching requires a great deal of specialized knowledge and skill. Teachers have to be some of the brightest people on the planet. Teaching may not be rocket science, but it is close.

Code of Ethics

Like members of other professions, teachers as a group have developed a code of ethics to guide their work and relationships with students and colleagues. Professional standards boards and other state bodies investigate teachers for infractions against the code of ethics adopted by the state. Ethics statements address issues such as discrimination against students, restraint of students, protecting students from harm, personal relationships with students, and misrepresenting one's credentials.

Obligation to Practice in Acceptable Ways

Being a member of a profession is more than showing up for work by 7:30 and not leaving before 3:30. The parents of students in your classroom expect that you will help their children learn. They expect their children to score at acceptable or better levels on achievement tests. They are counting on you to contribute to their children's literacy and to push them beyond minimal standards. Good teachers manage their classrooms so that students can focus on learning. The public and parents become very concerned when classrooms and schools appear out of control. As a teacher, it will be your obligation to model acceptable behavior based on the norms of the profession.

WHAT DO TEACHERS NEED TO KNOW?

When you watch teachers at work you may wonder why they do things in a certain way, or what motivates them to address one student's behavior differently from the way they might address another student's behavior. Since you can't get inside the teacher's head and they can't stop what they are doing to explain to you the reasons behind their actions, you have to accept the fact that they do know what they are doing and why they are doing it. Understanding and being able to articulate teaching practices is something that you will learn to do in your teacher education program. Becoming familiar with the teaching standards developed by InTASC will also help you understand the specialized knowledge, skills, and dispositions specific to the teaching profession.

Teacher Education Programs

Since teachers have to be well educated, the first step in getting into a teacher education program is to demonstrate your brightness by completing university core requirements with a grade point average (GPA) of at least 2.5. However, some colleges of education are requiring a GPA of 2.75 to be admitted to the professional course work teachers must take for licensure. The advising centers at most colleges of education have complete information on what is required before anyone can be admitted to a traditional teacher education program. Visit the website of your local institution of higher education and check out the steps you must take to be admitted to one of their licensure programs for teachers.

The college of education website at the California State University, Long Beach, presents a range of links to different programs, to different levels of professional work, and provides numerous links to career services and advising. It is easy to find out what you must do to earn a teaching degree. All the information you need to have a successful beginning is right at your fingertips.

Ways Programs Are Organized and Why

Teacher education programs are traditionally designed to move candidates along a path of acquiring knowledge of human development and behaviors, learning about laws affecting practice in schools, gaining understanding of counseling practices as well as the impact of cultural diversity on schools and classrooms, and gathering an understanding of working with children with disabilities in regular school classrooms. Candidates who are seeking a secondary license to teach in middle schools or high schools must, in addition to the general university core, complete a specified number of courses in their elected field. Since you are reading this text, you are no doubt already on the path to licensure as a teacher. Stay the course and you will discover a very rewarding future.

The Importance of Clinical Practice

Many teacher education programs include early clinical experience to provide the candidates opportunities to begin to learn what teaching involves (Darling-Hammond, Hammerness, Grossman, Rust, & Shulman, 2005). A policy brief on the clinical preparation of teachers by the American Association of Colleges for Teacher Education (AACTE) stresses the importance of clinical experiences as a key factor in candidates' success (AACTE, 2010). Lortie (1975) made it clear that observing teaching wasn't the ideal way to learn how to teach, that teacher education candidates had to be actively involved in the daily work of teachers. Now, nearly 40 years after Lortie's conclusions, teacher education programs are in the process of redesign to more closely align university course work with practice in the field. Field-based teacher education programs place cohorts of candidates in partnership or professional development schools, assign them site-based **mentors** and supervisors, and require evidence of reflection on practice to help the candidates develop cognitive frameworks for teaching. One such field-based program is the 21st Century Schools Partnership between the University Nevada, Las Vegas (UNLV) College of Education and the Clark County School District in Nevada.

Different Pathways to Licensure

Deeper Look 1.2
Read more about teacher certification in the United States.

The majority of teachers have completed bachelor's programs that prepared them for a license to teach. Most often, they began their preparation soon after high school. Although some education courses may be taken in the first two years of college, candidates are usually not admitted to education programs until they are juniors. Many education courses require candidates to complete field experiences in schools as a component of the course. Some programs require candidates to be observing and working in schools for several days a week, even offering the education courses at the school. Candidates student teach under the supervision of a teacher and college supervisor during the final year of their bachelor's program.

You can study to become a teacher through many routes. Programs are delivered in college classrooms and schools. Some programs can be completed via distance learning without stepping on a campus. A growing number of candidates begin exploring teaching as a career in community colleges, initially developing portfolios and working with children and youth in schools and community projects.

Most colleges and universities offer a number of pathways for becoming a teacher. Not all teacher education programs are traditional four-year undergraduate programs. Many colleges of education offer post-baccalaureate courses to meet state licensure requirements. School districts may negotiate professional development course work with state licensing agencies to provide on-the-job credit for individuals who have the expertise to fill high-need positions but do not have a degree in teaching or a state license to teach. A national debate regarding the credibility of differing routes to licensure is hotly contested in educational journals and the popular media.

The U.S. Department of Education provides funding incentives to colleges of education for creating specialized routes to licensure for high-need areas of teaching. An example of a U.S. Department of Education–funded program is the Project KNOTtT, Transition to Teaching Partnership led by The Ohio State University. This partnership is designed to recruit, select, train, coach, mentor, and retain teachers in high-need, hard-to-staff school districts. As a national initiative, Project KNOTtT addresses the teacher shortages in the subject areas of math, science, English/language arts, foreign languages, English as a Second Language (ESL), and special education (K–12). This project serves 545 new teachers pursuing nontraditional routes to certification in four states: Kansas, Nevada, Ohio, and Texas.

The Five-Year Teaching Degree

Some teacher education programs are five-year programs that begin at the undergraduate level and end with a master's degree or eligibility for a license after completing a sequence of graduate courses. These programs allow more time for candidates to study the art and science of teaching and learning. They sometimes require a year-long internship in schools, allowing candidates to practice under the guidance of professionals who provide feedback and support throughout the internship.

Many colleges of education offer teacher education course work once a student has completed an undergraduate program in a specific content area. The final or fifth year of a teacher education program generally places the candidate in a school as a teacher or co-teacher under the supervision of college faculty and school personnel. The fifth-year student gains practical experience during the day and attends classes in the evening. Once students finish their fifth year, they are eligible for licensure and also awarded a master's degree.

College graduates who decide after they have completed their bachelor's degree that they want to teach have several options for pursuing a teaching career. They could choose a Master of Arts in Teaching (MAT) program that provides in-depth study and an internship. Many colleges and universities have certificate or licensure programs in which candidates can complete the courses and student teaching required for a state license. These courses often can be used toward a master's degree, but you should check with a college adviser to ensure this is the case.

A Master of Arts in Teaching degree is offered through the University of Southern California Rossier School of Education. This program is offered completely online and to date is one of the fastest-growing teacher preparation programs online or on campus at a not-for-profit college or university. Candidates in this program participate in clinical experiences in their local area and become immersed in local school culture. Even so, according to Sharon Robinson, AACTE president, not all master's programs in education offer the value that should be expected of a master's degree (Robinson, 2011).

Alternative Licensure Plans

A number of new teachers are entering the profession through alternate routes that allow them to begin teaching without any specialized preparation in teaching and learning or field experiences in schools. Other professions such as medicine and engineering would never allow a person to work in the field without proper preparation and supervised experiences with professionals in the field. Opening the entry to teaching to anyone with a bachelor's degree challenges the status of a profession because no specialized training is required. However, most states require these alternate route teachers to take education courses and be mentored by experienced teachers.

In the past decade a number of nontraditional or alternate routes have emerged. Many of these programs are designed for adults beyond the traditional college age of 18 to 24. They build on the experience and background of candidates who often have worked for a number of years in a nonteaching field. These programs may be similar to traditional undergraduate and graduate programs, but they offer greater flexibility in scheduling courses and field experiences. Many candidates in these programs are working full time in schools or other jobs. Not all teachers complete programs at colleges and universities. School districts, state departments of education, and other organizations are also preparing teachers.

Military personnel may participate in Troops to Teachers, a program to assist men and women who have completed their military service in becoming teachers. Other programs help professionals in nonteaching fields to become teachers. These programs often place candidates in classrooms to complete their coursework and field experiences.

Teach for America (TFA), a nonprofit organization, recruits outstanding students from some of the nation's most prestigious universities to teach for two or more years in low-income communities throughout the United States. The TFA recruits spend a month in intensive preparation for their initial placement. During their years of teaching, they attend monthly professional development meetings conducted by TFA mentors and may also attend courses at a local college of education that will lead to a master's degree.

Graduate Licensure

Graduate licensure programs are generally limited to persons holding an undergraduate and/or graduate degree in a noneducation field. Licensure programs lead to an elementary or secondary teaching license and a Master of Education (MEd). Candidates in this type of program are required to complete courses that mirror the undergraduate teacher education courses and must complete all of the clinical practice required of undergraduates.

Where the Jobs Are

A projected 52 million students will be enrolled in U.S. public PreK–12 schools by the year 2018 (U.S. Department of Education, 2011), and a projected 4.2 million teachers will be teaching by 2016 (Hussar & Bailey, 2007). It would appear that in the near future there will be a need for your talent. Teaching jobs become available as current teachers retire, move to other schools, or leave the profession. Over the next decade, around 700,000 teachers—almost one of four current teachers—are projected to retire. Teachers leave the profession and move from school to school for a variety of reasons. The primary reasons for moving are layoffs, school closings, and other organizational changes in a school or district. Personal reasons include pregnancy, child-rearing responsibilities, moving to a new location, and health problems (Ingersoll, 2003). One in five beginning teachers are gone within the first three years.

The teacher turnover rate in urban high-priority schools is almost one-third higher than in other schools (National Commission on Teaching and America's Future, 2003), but the largest turnover rate is in small private schools. The rate of teachers leaving large private schools is fairly low, but small private schools suffer from a turnover that is often one-fourth of the staff annually. Although teachers in private schools report greater satisfaction and that their environments are more positive than public schools, they are much more likely to transfer to a public school than their public school counterparts are to transfer to a private school (Ingersoll, 2003).

Deeper Look 1.3
Read about teacher recruitment and retention.

Not all new hires in a school district are recent graduates. About half of them are teachers returning to the classroom or moving from another district. A growing number of new teachers are not recent college graduates. They are military retirees or people switching from business or other careers. They often complete alternative pathways into teaching in school-based graduate programs that build on their prior experiences.

You may not be able to find a teaching job in the community in which you grew up or near the university you are attending because the schools have few openings. However, jobs do exist if you are willing to move to a part of the country where there are shortages because of high turnover, a growing student population, or a move to reduce the teacher-to-student ratio in classes.

The demographics of the teaching force do not match the population at large. The majority of teachers are white females. The profession has a shortage of men and teachers of color. Other shortages exist in some areas of the country and for some teaching fields as described below. To attract teachers to areas with teaching shortages, some school districts offer signing bonuses, pay moving expenses, and assist teachers in purchasing homes. Wealthy school systems usually have a surplus of teachers who are applying for jobs. Some new teachers are willing to substitute in these school systems for a year or more until a job becomes available.

Opportunities are greater in urban high-poverty areas where high turnover exists. Generally, urban and rural areas have more openings than suburban areas, although acute shortages exist in high-poverty suburban areas as well. If you are willing to move to another state, your job opportunities will grow. Alaska, western states, and southern states are actively recruiting new teachers to staff the schools for a growing school-age population (National Commission on Teaching and America's Future, 2003). California, Texas, Nevada, North Carolina, and Florida are experiencing growth in their student populations, increasing the need for teachers.

Not all schools are the same, nor do they benefit from the same level of funding.

Teaching Fields

The first time the idea of teaching crosses our minds, we hold an image of teaching a certain age-group of children or a certain subject. Someone will imagine a kindergarten room full of brightly colored centers; another person will visualize herself at a board working equations with a group of serious high school seniors; someone else will imagine helping a group of students construct a model of the planets in Earth's solar system. Teaching is an endless display of possibilities, and for each aspiring teacher, its attraction is to a different reality.

Have you decided what subjects you would like to teach? Urban and rural schools are likely to have openings for all subjects, from elementary through high school. However, not enough teachers are being prepared or retained in schools to teach mathematics and science classes, English-language learners, and students with disabilities. Your chances of finding a job improve if you qualify for one of these high-need areas.

Many secondary schools report they have had to hire teachers who did not major in mathematics or science to teach their courses. These **out-of-field teachers** sometimes have not even minored in these fields and lack the knowledge and skills to help students learn these core subjects. The lack of qualified mathematics and science teachers in urban high schools has contributed to not offering advanced placement classes in these subjects and to the poor test performance of students in these schools. In 2000, the Recruiting New Teachers (RNT) organization reported that over 95% of the largest urban school districts had an immediate need for qualified teachers of mathematics and science. This remains true today, as many teacher education programs focus on recruiting teachers for math and science.

School districts report a shortage of culturally and linguistically diverse educators, especially in areas of the country with large numbers of Latino and immigrant students. Over the past decade, the schools with these needs have expanded from the Southwest, California, Florida, and large urban areas to smaller cities and communities in the Midwest and South where immigrants are employed and migrant workers have settled. Knowledge and skills in English as a Second Language and **bilingual education** will give a new teacher an advantage in many urban and rural areas today. Seventy-three percent of the large urban school districts in the RNT (Goldberg & Proctor, 2000) survey indicated they had an immediate need for ESL bilingual teachers.

Another major shortage area is special education teachers who are needed from preschool through high school. These teachers may work with a classroom of special education students, but often work as a resource teacher with regular teachers in inclusive classrooms. They teach students with mental, behavioral, sensory, physical, and learning disabilities. These jobs are usually very demanding, sometimes physically, but they can lead to great deal of joy as students become academically successful or learn to be independent. Many large urban school districts desperately need highly qualified special education teachers.

As mentioned earlier, it is not an uncommon desire among beginning teachers, to want to teach in the same community where they grew up and went to school. However, the types of communities that most beginning teachers have grown up in are not always the places that need the most teachers. If you want to be sure of beginning your teaching career when you graduate, you must go where the jobs are. Highly qualified teachers are always in demand. Make certain you meet the highest requirements for any job, and you will likely end up where you want to be.

Locations and Salaries

Deeper Look 1.4
Read more about teacher compensation.

Teachers do not select teaching because they expect to receive a high salary. According to the American Federation of Teachers analysis of teacher salary trends, the average teacher salary in the United States was $51,009 in school year 2006–2007 (DeCarlo, Johnson, & Cochran, 2008). It is expected that there will be a high retirement rate of teachers in the coming decades as baby boomers leave the profession, so it is encouraging that beginning teachers' salaries increased twice the rate of inflation in 2007 (DeCarlo et al., 2008).

The highest and lowest average teacher salaries are shown in Table 1.1. California tops the list with $63,640; at the other end of the scale is South Dakota, with $35,378. Salaries in most northeastern states are higher than in other parts of the country. Connecticut and school districts like Rochester, New York, view teachers as professionals, have high expectations for them, support them through mentoring and professional development, use multiple assessments to determine teacher effectiveness, and pay salaries commensurate with other professionals. Salaries in the plains states west of the Mississippi River fall disproportionately in the bottom 20%.

Most teacher contracts are for less than 12 months, but over 60% of the teachers earn additional income within the school or in summer or second jobs outside the school. Teachers report earning supplemental income above their contract by doing the following activities related to schools or their education:

- Serving as a mentor or staff developer
- Achieving additional teaching licenses or certifications
- Becoming national board certified
- Teaching in a subject area where there is a teacher shortage
- Improving student performance
- Working in a school more challenging to staff than other schools in the district
- Developing new skills/knowledge in non-university settings (NEA, 2003, p. 80)

Teachers also may receive supplemental income for chairing departments, being team leaders, sponsoring extracurricular activities, and coaching.

Table 1.1 Average Teacher Salaries in 2006–2007

TOP TEN	
$63,640	California
$61,039	Connecticut
$59,730	New Jersey
$59,557	New York
$58,420	Rhode Island
$58,275	Illinois
$58,178	Massachusetts
$56,927	Maryland
$55,541	Michigan
$54,977	Pennsylvania
BOTTOM TEN	
$42,816	Louisiana
$42,780	New Mexico
$42,379	Oklahoma
$42,044	Nebraska
$41,146	Montana
$40,384	Missouri
$40,182	Mississippi
$38,586	North Dakota
$37,775	Utah
$35,378	South Dakota

Source: DeCarlo, M., Johnson, N., & Cochran, P. (2008). *Survey and analysis of teacher salary trends, 2007.* Washington, DC: American Federation of Teachers. Printed with permission from American Federation of Teachers, AFL-CIO.

WHAT DO TEACHER EDUCATION CANDIDATES NEED TO DO?

The previous section of this chapter provided information regarding jobs, salaries, and expectations for being part of the teaching profession. This section will help clarify the purpose of teacher education programs and what you can do when you are enrolled. Knowing what is expected of you is one of the best ways to feel confident and to assure you get the most out of your classes and the clinical experiences you will have to complete.

How to Get Off to a Good Start in Your Teacher Education Program

Usually people spend some time planning and charting a path before they embark on a journey. There are maps to read and places of interest to check out to see if a side trip is warranted. Some folks even develop strategies for getting the most out of every mile. Not much forethought is required for a trip to the supermarket, though a list is always helpful. But when committing to something that might be a benchmark in your life goal of becoming a teacher, planning is certainly essential.

Test of Basic Skills

Teacher candidates are usually required to pass a basic skills test before they are admitted to a teacher education program. Every teacher should be competent in the basic skills of reading, writing, and mathematics. These tests are designed to determine that future teachers have the basic knowledge and skills in these areas. So in order to be admitted to the professional course work in a teacher education program, most states require that you demonstrate aptitude by achieving passing scores on basic skills tests. The Educational Testing Services (ETS) website at **http://www.ets.org/praxis** offers detailed information about taking a basic skills test. The ETS website also contains a drop-down menu for individual state testing requirements for licensure. The Pearson National Education Series website at **http://www.education.Pearsonassessments.com** provides detailed information about their test services and how you can take exams at their test centers. Some states have developed their own tests of basic skills and other tests required for teacher licensure. Individual state test requirements and passing scores also can be found at state departments of education websites.

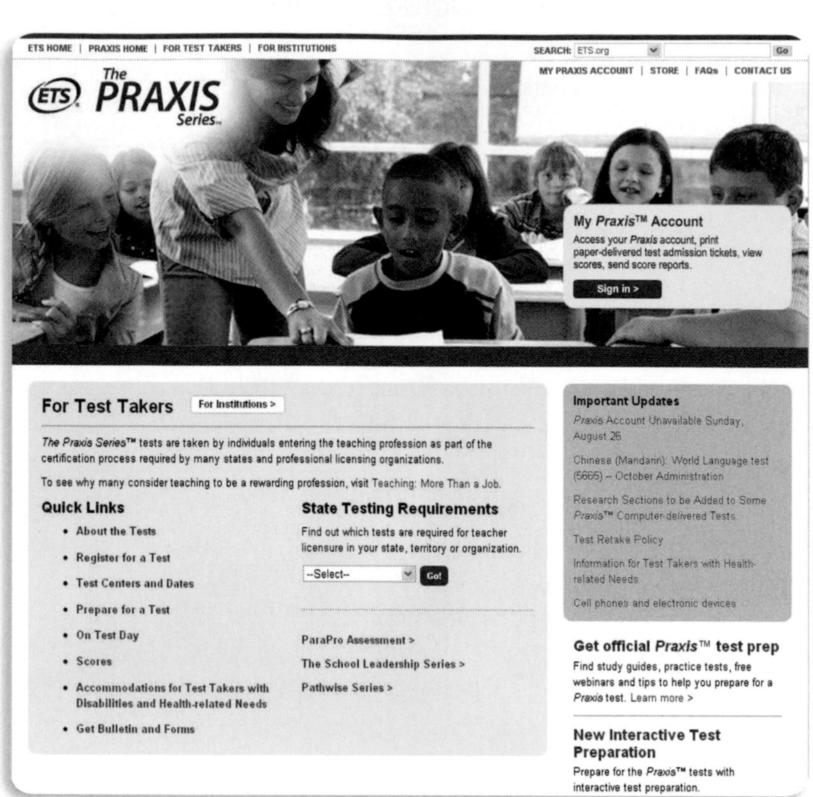

Teachers must demonstrate their knowledge of basic skills and their readiness to teach. Standardized tests provide states with evidence of a teacher's qualifications.

Learn About Assessment Practices

It is no longer enough to sit through the courses in a teacher education program to be eligible for a license to teach. You will be required to show evidence that you meet professional and state standards through a number of performance assessments throughout your program that demonstrate that you know your subject matter and can teach. These assessments are usually administered at admission to the program, before you can student teach, at completion of student teaching, and on completion of the program. The assessments include standardized paper-and-pencil tests, portfolios, case studies, evaluations of your student teaching or internship, comprehensive examinations at the end of the program, and projects. You will also be expected to show that you can help all students learn.

Your professors and field-based supervisors will evaluate your performance in the classroom on assessment rubrics that describe the areas you must reach to show you are proficient in the skills and knowledge to help all students learn. When you receive the feedback from the supervisors and professors, you will know where you need to improve your practice to meet the standards.

Pass Licensure Tests

Potential teachers in most states must pass one or more licensure tests to be eligible for a license to teach. States either develop their own licensure tests or contract with a major test company such as the Educational Testing Service (ETS) or Pearson National Education Series. A state board of education or standards board determines the **cut score** that test takers must achieve to pass the test. The score required to pass the same or similar tests varies from state to state. Your score could be high enough to be licensed in one state, but not in another. Ohio, Virginia, and Connecticut have set higher cut scores than other states as part of their effort to raise the quality of teachers in the state. Check with the state in which you plan to work to determine the tests you will be required to pass before you receive a license.

Content Tests

Content tests assess a candidate's knowledge of the subject or subjects they will be teaching or the field in which they will be working (for example, English as a Second Language or special education). These tests generally assess the knowledge outlined in the state and professional standards for the field, which is another reason to be familiar with the standards. You should develop the knowledge bases for your field in the courses you have taken in the sciences, humanities, arts, psychology, and social sciences. Secondary and middle-level teacher candidates often major in the academic discipline they plan to teach. Some states require elementary teacher candidates to major or have a concentration in one or more academic fields such as social sciences, mathematics, science, a foreign language, or English. Are you required to have an academic, rather than education, major to be licensed in your state? Check out the state department of education website for this information.

Most states require new teachers to pass content tests before they receive the first license to teach. Many institutions require candidates to pass this test before they are eligible to student teach. Knowledge of the subject you teach and how you teach it may seem like the same sides of a coin, but they are truly quite different. It is possible to be an expert in a field and not be able to explain one bit of it to a group of students in a classroom.

Knowledge, Skills, Dispositions, and Student Learning

Knowledge is one of the easier areas to assess. The most popular assessment of knowledge is a standardized, pencil-and-paper test, which now is often completed on a computer. Teacher-developed quizzes and tests provide information on what is known or understood. Grades and your performance on papers, projects, presentations, and case studies contribute to the overall evaluation of the knowledge needed to teach.

Skills or performances are usually demonstrated as you collaborate with your peers, interact with your professors, and work with teachers and students in schools. Your skills can be observed and measured by how successful you are in helping students achieve on tests and other assessments. Field experiences and student teaching provide opportunities for you to apply your knowledge about a subject and pedagogy. You and others will assess your effectiveness in these settings. Although standardized assessments exist, they are relatively expensive to implement.

A few states require beginning teachers to complete Praxis III, in which trained assessors evaluate their performance as a first-year teacher against standards using a scoring rubric. Teacher education programs in those states emphasize the development of the skills assessed by Praxis III. Other states, like Connecticut, require their new teachers to submit a portfolio after their first year of teaching as evidence they are meeting state standards. At the University of Nevada, Las Vegas, at the end of the student teaching practicum elementary teacher education candidates present an ePortfolio to an audience of their peers and professors. Artifacts collected for the ePortfolio are tied to the InTASC standards.

Many teacher education programs have identified the dispositions that you should demonstrate before you become a teacher. They might include proficiencies such as these:

- The belief that all children can learn at high levels, which requires persistence in helping all children be successful

Video Link 1.3
Watch a video about diversity.

- Appreciating and valuing human diversity, showing respect for students' varied talents and perspectives, and commitment to the pursuit of "individually configured excellence"
- Respecting students as individuals with differing personal and family backgrounds and various skills, talents, and interests

These proficiencies cannot be easily measured on a test. They come across in the papers that you write, the presentations that you make, the lessons you teach, and your interactions with students and parents in schools. Over time and in multiple ways, your dispositions are demonstrated and assessed.

In most teacher education programs, you are expected to learn how to assess student learning and how to respond when a student is not learning. During student teaching, you most likely will be required to collect data on student learning, analyze those data, and determine next steps if one or more students are not learning. Figure 1.2 provides an example of an assessment exercise you may be asked to complete during student teaching. See Figure 1.3 for an example of a rubric that accompanies the student learning assessment.

Figure 1.2 Assessment for the Analysis of Student Learning in a Teacher Work Sample

Teacher Work Sample Standard: The teacher candidate uses assessment data to profile student learning and communicate information about student progress and achievement.

Task: Analyze your assessment data, including pre-/post-assessments and formative assessments to determine students' progress related to the unit learning goals. Use visual representations and narrative to communicate the performance of the whole class, subgroups, and two individual students. Conclusions drawn from this analysis should be provided in the "Reflection and Self-Evaluation" section.

Prompt: In this section, you will analyze data to explain progress and achievement toward learning goals demonstrated by your whole class, subgroups of students, and individual students.

- **Whole class.** To analyze the progress of your whole class, create a table that shows pre- and post-assessment data on every student on every learning goal. Then, create a graphic summary that shows the extent to which your students made progress (from pre- to post-) toward the learning criterion that you identified for each learning goal (identified in your Assessment Plan section). Summarize what the graph tells you about your students' learning in this unit (i.e., the number of students who met the criterion).

- **Subgroups.** Select a group characteristic (e.g., gender, performance level, socioeconomic status, language proficiency) to analyze in terms of one learning goal. Provide a rationale for your selection of this characteristic to form subgroups (e.g., girls vs. boys; high vs. middle vs. low performers). Create a graphic representation that compares pre- and post-assessment results for the subgroups on this learning goal. Summarize what these data show about student learning.

Source: Elliott, E., (2003). *Assessing education candidate performance: A look at changing practices.* Washington, DC: National Council for Accreditation of Teacher Education. Reprinted with permission of the National Council for Accreditation of Teacher Education.

• **Individuals.** Select two students who demonstrated different levels of performance. Explain why it is important to understand the learning of these particular students. Use preformative and post-assessment data with examples of the students' work to draw conclusions about the extent to which these students attained the two learning goals. Graphic representations are not necessary for this subsection.

Suggested Page Length: 4 + charts and student work examples

Source: Hussar, W. J., & Bailey, T. M. (2011). *Projections of Education Statistics to 2020* (NCES 2011-026). Washington, DC: U.S. Department of Education, National Center for Education Statistics.

Note: You will provide possible reasons for why your students learned (or did not learn) in the next section, "Reflection and Self-Evaluation."

Figure 1.3 A Scoring Guide to Assess Student Learning

Teacher Work Sample Standard: The teacher candidate uses assessment data to profile student learning and communicate information about student progress and achievement.

Rating→ **Indicator↓**	**1** **Indicator Not Met**	**2** **Indicator Partially Met**	**3** **Indicator Met**	**Score**
Clarity and Accuracy of Presentation	Presentation is not clear and accurate; it does not accurately reflect the data.	Presentation is understandable and contains few errors.	Presentation is easy to understand and contains no errors of representation.	
Evidence of Impact on Student Learning	Analysis of student learning fails to include evidence of impact on student learning in terms of numbers of students who achieved and made progress toward learning goals.	Analysis of student learning includes incomplete evidence of the impact on student learning in terms of numbers of students who achieved and made progress toward learning goals.	Analysis of student learning includes evidence of the impact on student learning in terms of numbers of students who achieved and made progress toward each learning goal.	

Source: Elliott, E. (2003). *Assessing education candidate performance: A look at changing practices.* Washington, DC: National Council for Accreditation of Teacher Education. Reprinted with permission of the National Council for Accreditation of Teacher Education.

You might be asked to design an assessment that will help you know whether students are learning. You might be given a sample of student work and asked to analyze it and describe any concerns raised by the student's work. By the time you finish your program, you should be familiar with a number of assessments besides a test. You should also know that students learn in different ways, requiring that you teach using strategies that build on their prior experiences and cultures.

Pedagogical and Professional Knowledge Tests

Some states also require new teachers to pass another test that assesses general pedagogical and professional knowledge that teachers should have to manage instruction and students. This information is taught in courses such as educational foundations, educational psychology, multicultural education, tests and measurement, teaching methods, and the course that requires you to read this book. Your specialized knowledge about teaching and learning is assessed in this group of tests. They require you to know theories in education, the critical research that guides how to teach your subject, instructional strategies, the impact of diversity on learning, and the use of technology in teaching.

Schools are busy places full of happy people helping one another. New teachers should make a point to know and respect all the support staff at their school.

Spend Time in Schools

Most teacher education programs require candidates to observe and work in schools, often beginning with the first education course. You want to make sure you really like working with young children if you are planning to teach at the primary level or older adolescents if you are planning to teach high school. You can also learn whether you have the temperament to work with 30 students at a time or to maintain a schedule that requires you to be in a classroom with students for hours at a time without talking on your cell phone, texting, or having a snack. Field experiences confirm for most candidates that they really do want to teach. Others discover that teaching is not the job for them.

Learn to Be Comfortable in Schools

Most of us found the time we spent in school enjoyable and we liked going to school. That was probably one reason we were drawn to teaching. Most times we got along well with our classmates and with our teachers. Teachers must be at school most days of the school year. The teachers we remember fondly are the ones that appeared to enjoy being at school. They were the ones who greeted everyone with a smile and shared a kind word or two with everyone they came in contact with. They appeared generally happy and happy to be sharing their days with others in a school.

The people who work in schools alongside teachers also appreciate friendly greetings and encouraging words. It is important to know the people who support your role as a teacher as they are often the ones you call for help when something nonacademic goes amiss.

When you are comfortable in the schools you are assigned to, when you know the people who work at the school and what their jobs are, when you show a positive regard for each member of the school team and exude a happy character, you will be comfortable in schools and help the people who work with you feel comfortable too.

Professional Development Schools

Deeper Look 1.5
Read more about professional development schools.

You may be assigned to a professional development school (PDS) for your field experiences and clinical practice. Teachers, teacher candidates, and college professors in a PDS collaborate to support student learning. They may team teach and take turns teaching, planning together, and supporting each other. After a few weeks of working together, students and parents often are not able to distinguish between the teacher, professor, and teacher candidate. One or more professors may spend most of their time in a PDS, working with the teacher and candidate in the classroom and providing professional development for faculty as needed.

Having already completed my master's degree in elementary education, and not finding a permanent position in the previous summer, I turned my attention to working as much as possible in the schools of Johnson City as a substitute. In an attempt to meet and be known by as many people as possible, I accepted a several-day position as a kindergarten teacher. My teaching license covered grades 1 through 6, but I thought my experience and general training could be easily adapted to kindergarten. In addition, I thought that the small class sizes and presence of a teacher assistant could alleviate any potential problems that may arise.

For context, Johnson City had recently constructed one building to house its K–8 classes, eliminating the middle school and several aging neighborhood elementary schools. Within the school there were no male teachers in the 30+ sections of K–3, nor were there any male administrators or office staff. Additionally, Johnson City sits on the confluence of the Susquehanna and Chenango rivers in central New York. During the winter temperatures can easily dip below zero, and wind chills can cause dangerous situations if outside too long. As a self-preservation technique I used to grow a full, black beard each winter.

On my first day I was immediately ushered into the world of the little ones. Having a substitute immediately gets them into hyper-mode, and having a male teacher creates some form of irreconcilable conflict in their minds. As the day progressed we were having a productive experience, but one little boy kept referring to me as Mrs. G, instead of Mr. G. Normally, this isn't a big deal but he was a smart kid and was the only student to seem to have difficulty with the concept of his teacher being a man. The fact I was wearing a tie and had a full beard was of little consequence to him.

Finally, I pulled him aside and gently said "Buddy, I don't know about your family but in mine it is the men who have beards and we call them mister." After a few seconds of intense thought he motioned for me to come closer to him and responded with "But my grandma has a mustache." Out of sheer respect I let him call me Mrs. G for the rest of the time I was in the class.

Lloyd J. Goldberg, Teacher
Third grade, Schorr Elementary
Las Vegas, Nevada

School District/University Partnership Schools

These partnerships may appear similar to professional development schools given the collaboration that takes place between personnel in both institutions. The aim of a partnership between a university and a school district is to seek reform at all levels. This means that both members of the partnership have to learn to work in new ways. Institutional cultures may have to change, and while change is inevitable, it is not always welcomed. Forming a partnership is labor-intensive and not always perceived in the same way by all members of the partnership. The university teacher education curriculum may have to be revised to meet the specific needs of schools and students in a district. School structures may have to be redesigned to meet the goals of the partnership and the inclusion of teacher education candidates into the daily functions of the school. The achievement of K–12 students remains at the center of any reform effort of partnership schools as does the professional development of teachers and teacher candidates.

Challenging Assumptions

Are there special characteristics that are predictors of one's effectiveness as a teacher?

The Assumption

Many states allow some teachers to enter their first teaching job with little or no course work related to teaching and learning and no field experiences in a school setting. Is it really not important for teacher candidates to understand the professional and pedagogical knowledge that provide the foundation for teaching? Are there any teacher characteristics that influence achievement gains of students?

The Research

Andrew J. Wayne and Peter Youngs (2003) of SRI International and Stanford University, respectively, reviewed studies that examined teachers' characteristics and the standardized test scores of their students. The data reviewed were collected in the United States and accounted for students' prior achievement and socioeconomic status. The researchers found that a relationship exists between college ratings and student achievement gains. This relationship implies that factors beyond licensure tests should be used by states in determining who should teach. Institutional quality as determined by accreditation is a factor that should be considered. Studies indicated that

- students learn more from teachers with higher test scores (p. 100);
- high school students learn more mathematics when their mathematics teachers have additional degrees or coursework in mathematics (p. 103); and
- mathematics students learn more when their teachers have standard mathematic certification (pp. 105–106).

In the report of the National Commission on Teaching and America's Future, *Solving the Dilemmas of Teacher Supply, Demand, and Standards: How We Can Ensure a Competent, Caring, and Qualified Teacher for Every Child* (2000), Linda Darling-Hammond stated:

> One recent analysis found that, after controlling for student characteristics like poverty and language status, the strongest predictor of state-level student achievement in reading and mathematics on the NAEP [National Assessment of Educational Progress] was each state's proportion of well-qualified teachers (as defined by the proportion with full certification and a major in the field they teach). . . . A strong negative predictor of student achievement was the proportion of teachers on emergency certificates. (p. 15)

Teacher licensure or certification requirements, which Darling-Hammond and others have found to be critical to student achievement, outline the content, professional, and pedagogical knowledge and skills expected of teachers in the state. These are the proficiencies that teacher candidates should develop in their teacher education programs.

Sources:

Darling-Hammond, L. (2000). *Solving the dilemmas of teacher supply, demand, and standards: How we can ensure a competent, caring, and qualified teacher for every child.* Washington, DC: National Commission on Teaching and America's Future.

Wayne, A. J., & Youngs, P. (2003, Spring). Teacher characteristics and student achievement gains: A review. *Review of Educational Research, 73*(1), 89–122.

Shadow a Student or a Teacher for a Day

Before you receive your first clinical assignment, make a concerted effort to spend a day in a school shadowing a student or a teacher. Shadowing students will help you see the school day through their perspective. Observe what work they are engaged in and how they negotiate the physical, mental, and social demands of being members of a class group. Take note of the kinds of interactions they have with other students and with the teacher. Learn how they keep track of all that is expected of them.

Shadowing a teacher will help you begin to understand what will be expected of you during a typical school day. Make an effort to keep track of the number of decisions teachers make, and what those decisions entail. Note the special routines and management strategies they have in place to keep track of the students, student work, and class and school schedules. Listen to the conversations they have with the students and with other teachers. Watch their work with an eye toward the roles you will perform when you begin teaching. It could be an eye-opening experience. If you hear students, parents, other teachers, and administrators refer to effective teachers, ask if you can visit their class to observe their interactions with the subject matter and with students.

Volunteer as a Teacher's Aide or as a Tutor

To learn more about the work of teachers, volunteer to help out in a classroom or school. Teachers have scores of duties to address, before, during, and after class, and an offer of help from a well-meaning individual is always welcomed. Visit a school near your home, meet with the principal, and explain that you are studying to be a teacher and would like to have some experience working in a school as a volunteer. Your offer of help will certainly be met with enthusiasm.

There are many ways that you can develop skill when working with students. When starting out in your teacher education program, it is good to have experience working closely with one or two children. Tutoring is a great way to become familiar with students' learning styles and to understand the difficulties some students have learning specific content. Tutoring programs at reading centers in colleges of education or in public libraries seek tutors for a variety of programs. Working as a tutor can help build your confidence and competence as a teacher.

Become a Member of a Teaching and Learning Team

You will have ample opportunity to discuss educational issues in your teacher education courses. You will learn of the theories underlying practice and discuss ways theories are demonstrated through teachers' actions. While you are involved in your clinical practice, make an effort to join a teacher group and listen when teachers discuss teaching and learning issues and develop strategies for serving students. Take advantage of the expertise that can be gained from experienced teachers. Ask questions. When you visit schools as part of your field experience requirements, note effective teaching practices that you could incorporate into your own repertoire as you student teach and later have your own classroom.

To become effective teachers, we learn as we observe and practice. We test theories and strategies, expanding our repertoire of ways to help students learn. With time we become more familiar with the subjects we teach and the students with whom we work. We become more comfortable in the classroom as we understand the bureaucratic requirements of a school and become better managers of the classroom and learning.

UNDERSTANDING AND USING EVIDENCE

Licensure Test Scores

Each state sets the qualifying or cut score that test takers must achieve before they can receive a license to teach in the state. These scores differ across states as shown below.

Test	AR	CT	LA	MS	NV	OH	PA	VA
Biology: Content Knowledge	–	152	150	135	154	148	147	155
Elementary Education: Curriculum, Instruction, & Assessment	–	163	–	135	158	–	168	–
Elementary Education: Content Knowledge	–	–	150	–	–	–	–	143
English Language, Literature, & Composition: Content Knowledge	159	172	160	157	150	167	160	172
Mathematics: Content Knowledge	116	137	125	123	144	139	136	147
Social Studies: Content Knowledge	155	162	149	143	152	157	157	161

Your Task: Respond to the following questions:

1. What does this table tell you about becoming qualified in these eight states?
2. Why are scores not indicated for some states?
3. Why do some states require higher scores than others?

Source: Website of the Educational Testing Service (ETS) at http://www.ets.org/praxis/prxstate.html

The Power of a Support Group During Clinical Practice

Even though teaching involves being with groups of students every day, it can be a lonely profession if teachers don't make time to interact with one another in professional and personal settings. Sharing what works with colleagues and having them react and provide advice should be part of the culture of being a teacher. Other professions such as medicine and architecture require new graduates to practice as interns under the tutelage of experienced doctors or architects during their first years of practice. In many regards, field experiences and student teaching are intended to serve this purpose. Teachers who welcome teacher education candidates into their classrooms as co-teachers represent a special group who are not only experts in their profession but also eager give back to their profession by helping others succeed. These teachers will guide you through the myriad dimensions of teaching. They will give you feedback on your teaching assignments and actively listen to your concerns. They become your colleagues in learning to laugh when the unexpected happens and to cheer you onward when your steps may not be so sure. They are also responsible for making sure that you meet standards for clinical experience, so they will expect your best effort and may admonish you when your performance is not acceptable. Be ready to accept constructive criticism and also the praise that will certainly be yours to enjoy.

One way to analyze test scores across states is to look for patterns. In the table below, the red highlights indicate the state(s) with the highest qualifying score and the blue highlights indicate the state with the lowest qualifying score. In some cases, states have qualifying scores that are close, but the range between high and low scores can be as much as 33 for elementary education for the states shown below.

Test	AR	CT	LA	MS	NV	OH	PA	VA
Biology: Content Knowledge	–	152	150	135	154	148	147	155
Elementary Education: Curriculum, Instruction, & Assessment	–	163	–	135	158	–	168	–
Elementary Education: Content Knowledge	–	–	150	–	–	–	–	143
English Language, Literature, & Composition: Content Knowledge	159	172	160	157	150	167	160	172
Mathematics: Content Knowledge	116	137	125	123	144	139	136	147
Social Studies: Content Knowledge	155	162	149	143	152	157	157	161

Source: Website of the Educational Testing Service (ETS) at http://www.ets.org/praxis/prxstate.html

Understand the Role of Your Mentor or Cooperating Teacher

Many years ago the *Harvard Business Review* let the business community know that "Everyone Who Makes It Has a Mentor." The article went on to advise new members to business that if they didn't have a mentor they should go find one (Collins & Scott, 1978). Soon after this pronouncement, the teaching profession began to look at what roles mentors to new teachers could provide, and a formal construct for mentoring in teaching was developed. Of course experienced teachers who serve as mentors to beginning teachers have always been around even without being called mentors. Your cooperating teacher is one of the mentors you will encounter on your journey to becoming a teacher. Other mentors may come in the form of professors, relatives, colleagues, and friends. If you don't seem to have a mentor, ask questions and one will magically appear.

How to Set the Stage for Success in Your First Teaching Job

There is so much you need to know before you enter the classroom that first day. It has been said that if you desire a perfect ending then the beginning must also be perfect. Your teacher education course work and clinical experience will program you for success in your first teaching job, but the guarantee that you will be more than ready rests solely on your shoulders. To paraphrase Eleanor Duckworth, an emeritus professor of education at Harvard, you do not truly learn a thing until you understand it for yourself. All the lectures, all the assignments, all the visits to schools will have not prepared you at all if you have merely gone through your program with your eyes on the degree at the end of the line. The best way to be prepared for that first teaching job is to develop the habit of asking questions, reflecting on each new step you take, collaborating with others, and always trying to see the horizon through a perspective different from your own.

HOW DO YOU KEEP TRACK OF YOUR GROWTH AS A TEACHER?

As humans we are strangely programmed to keep track of changes in our environment and in ourselves. We track the weather, our weight, the stock market, and the standing of our favorite football team. We even use almanacs to help us track events that will happen in the future. Teachers use **benchmarks** such as "surviving the first year," "successfully completing a round of parent/teacher conferences," and "having students make adequate yearly progress on standardized exams," to track their progress and to set personal standards for their continuous professional development. Teaching is replete with standards of all types. In addition to setting personal standards, it is a teacher's responsibility to be familiar with school district, state, and national standards at all levels.

Know the Standards

You may feel overwhelmed with standards, but if you can't talk about standards during your job interview, you will not be the top candidate for the job. Most schools have adopted a **standards-based curriculum** and provide their teachers with power standards and common core standards. It is not only the standards for the students you will be teaching that affect your work. The teacher education program in which you are enrolled should be standards based. Your program should be preparing you to meet the InTASC standards mentioned earlier in this chapter. You are also expected to know the professional standards for your field (for example, mathematics or early childhood education). Are you familiar with any of these standards?

Student Standards

New teachers should know the student standards for the subject they will be teaching. All states have developed student standards that indicate what students at different grade levels should know and be able to do in a subject area. The tests that students are required to take annually in mathematics, reading, writing, science, and social studies are based on the state standards. Many state standards are based on national standards developed by national organizations such as the International Reading Association (IRA), National Council of Social Studies (NCSS), and American Association for the Advancement of Science (AAAS). These standards provide a guide for what you should be teaching in those core curriculum areas. They can be used to develop your own performance assessments to determine what students are learning. The state tests also provide feedback, although limited, on what students have learned. State standards can be accessed on the website of your state department of education.

Teacher Standards

National professional associations have also developed standards that describe what teachers should know and be able to do to teach a specific group of students (for example, English-language learners or students with disabilities) or a specific subject such as physical education. If teachers meet these standards, they should be able to help students meet the student standards.

After you have taught for three or more years, you may decide to apply for national board certification. The NBPTS standards expect accomplished teachers to do the following:

- Be committed to students and their learning.
- Know the subjects they teach and how to teach those subjects to students.
- Be responsible for managing and monitoring student learning.
- Think systematically about their practice, and learn from experience.
- Be members of learning communities.

In addition to these general expectations, the NBPTS has standards for teaching each subject area for specific age levels such as early childhood, middle childhood, early adolescence, and young adulthood. Your teacher education program will help you develop the foundation to meet these standards later in your career. A number of colleges and universities have redesigned their master's degrees to reflect these standards and help teachers become nationally certified.

There is no time like the present to start down the path toward successful teaching. Take advantage of the assignments and experiences you are required to complete, always thinking about how they relate to the subject or students you will be teaching next week or in a few years. In the activities at the end of each chapter in this book, you are provided opportunities to apply your knowledge to the realities of classrooms and schools. These activities can be incorporated into a portfolio of your work that will show your growth as you learn how to teach over the next year or two and can be used later during your interview for a job.

Begin a Portfolio

A portfolio is a collection of your work, including papers, projects, lesson plans, and assessments. It serves many purposes. During your program, the artifacts (that is, the documents and presentations) in your portfolio show your growth as a teacher from the first education course you take to completion of the program. Your written papers may have been submitted as part of your coursework, or they may be written reflections of your experiences working with students. They show that you understand a particular topic in your field and your ability to analyze issues and classroom situations as well as your writing skills.

Deeper Look 1.6
Read about how teacher portfolios support teacher growth.

Lesson plans, which you will develop later in the program as a detailed guide for your instruction of a topic, show that you understand the subject that you are teaching and that you can select appropriate instructional strategies for helping students learn. Evaluations of your field experiences and student teaching by your school and university supervisors provide evidence of your effectiveness in the classroom. Samples of student work related to the lessons you teach along with your analysis of the student work, and reflections on how effective your teaching was and what you would do differently the next time, provide evidence that you have the knowledge, skills, and dispositions critical to a teacher's work. The artifacts in your portfolio can serve as evidence that you meet state and professional standards that were discussed earlier in this chapter.

Like architects and artists, new teachers select examples of their best work for portfolios to be presented at job interviews. These portfolios should also include demographic information that present your credentials: a résumé, transcripts, child abuse clearance, criminal background clearance, and teaching license (Netterville, 2002). Any awards or honors that you have received should be added to this portfolio. Letters of recommendation from faculty and/or your

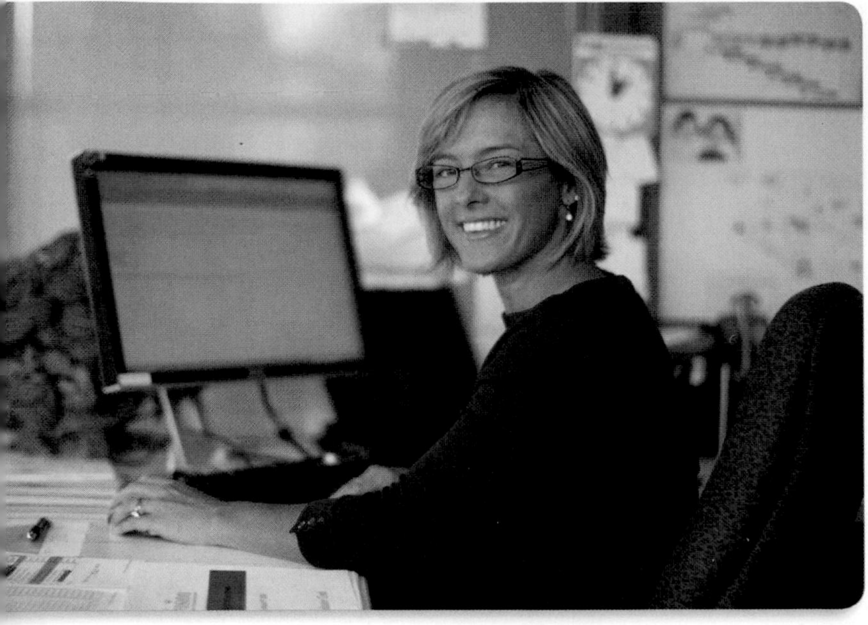

Maintaining a digital record of professional growth and achievements is one way teachers can document their careers and share information with others.

supervising teachers should be included along with any letters of appreciation or commendations from parents or students.

You may not be asked to present a portfolio until you are further along in your program. However, the task of compiling a portfolio will be much easier if you begin now to collect and organize your papers, projects, evaluations, and student work. You may be surprised to see your own growth over time. Technological advances have made the creation of digital portfolios commonplace. One advantage to the electronic portfolio is that it provides you the opportunity to highlight your technology skills—one of the requirements of many standards. To assist you in beginning your portfolio, each chapter in this book suggests one or two tasks for that purpose.

Reflect on Your Observations and Practice in Schools

Reflection, a valued skill in teaching, allows you to think about the effects of your choices and actions on students, parents, and other professionals in the learning community. According to Kottler, Zehm, and Kottler (2005), reflection is among the most important missions of a teacher. It is an extremely complex and demanding process that requires a lifetime of dedication. Portfolios may include papers in which teacher candidates reflect on their practice in the classroom. The papers show that candidates think about what works and what doesn't in the classroom. Reflective teachers can articulate why they chose one instructional method over another, analyze the effectiveness of the approach when they use it, and choose another approach for a student who did not learn.

Deeper Look 1.7
Read an overview of teacher reflection and teacher learning.

Early in your program, you will be observing teachers and working with small groups of students rather than teaching. However, you can begin to develop your reflection skills in both these school settings and activities in your college classroom. One popular process is the maintenance of **journals** in which you summarize your thoughts about and reactions to the major things you observed or experienced in a class or school. Journal entries should be brief, candid, and personal. You should record how you were affected by the events and why. You may be surprised, angry, puzzled, delighted, or apathetic. You may not believe what you are reading or seeing. You may want to step in and change something. You may have learned a new strategy for accommodating the needs of a student with disabilities. The journal allows you to regularly record (usually daily or weekly) your reflections on what you are learning. As you read your journal later, you will see how your thoughtful reflections helped you define your own teaching. The section at the end of each chapter, "Being Thoughtful About Becoming a Teacher," provides suggestions for topics you could address in journal entries related to the chapter.

Begin Collaborating With Peers and Professors

One way to help you determine whether you want to teach is to talk and work with teachers and other school professionals. You will begin to get a better sense of what it is like to be a teacher rather than a student. Ask them why they chose a particular lesson, responded to one student differently than all of the others, and used a particular assessment. Be helpful to the teachers you are observing when they ask for assistance.

You should begin to develop your collaborative skills as you work with other candidates and professors on campus. You are likely to be assigned to work with your peers on group activities. These activities provide you the opportunity to be a leader in planning and delivering papers and presentations. To be successful, you will have to work with people with whom you have many common experiences and others with whom you have little in common. You may have to assist others, and sometimes do some of their work for the good of the team. When you are in the classroom, you will find similar dilemmas as you work with other teachers. You may also have a better understanding of the group dynamics of students when you assign them to group work in the classroom. It is wise to begin now to learn to collaborate with professional colleagues. In a year or two or three you will be amazed at where your journey to become a teacher has taken you.

CONNECTING TO THE CLASSROOM

This chapter has provided you with some basic information about the need for qualified teachers, where the jobs are, how to become licensed, and some of the circumstances you might encounter during your first few years of teaching. Below are some key principles for applying the information in this chapter to the classroom.

1. Effective teachers make a difference in student learning.
2. Professional teachers are responsible for the well-being of their clients (students).
3. Mentoring of new teachers is a critical factor in the retention of teachers in the profession.
4. A school's curriculum will be guided by the state or school district's standards for students.
5. Teacher standards identify the key knowledge, skills, and disposition that teachers should demonstrate in the classroom.
6. The collection of your work in a portfolio should provide evidence that you have met standards and that you can help students in your classroom learn.

SUMMARY

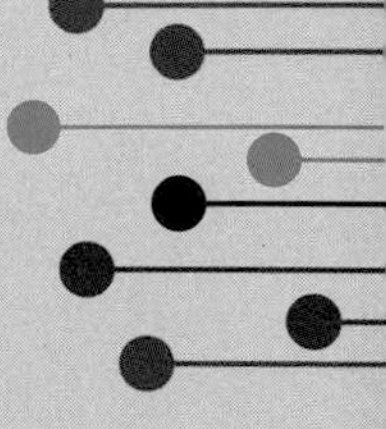

Five major points were discussed in this chapter.

- Teaching is a challenging profession that requires its members to be very knowledgeable, skillful, and in possession of the necessary disposition for working with students.
- The rewards of teaching can be both intrinsic and extrinsic, as teachers help students acquire knowledge and develop skills.
- Teacher education candidates need to become familiar with standards for PreK–12 students and standards for teachers, and to demonstrate competency in content areas through performance on standardized tests.
- Teacher education candidates need to spend time in schools observing experienced teachers and working with students.
- Activities that contribute to a teacher's development include the initiation of a portfolio, reflection on one's practice, and collaboration with colleagues.

CLASS DISCUSSION QUESTIONS

1. Some policymakers are attacking teachers as standing in the way of reforming schools. They argue that teachers do not want to be held accountable for student learning. Some teachers argue that the state and federal governments do not provide them adequate resources to make it possible for them to help children achieve academically and learn the skills they will need to be successful and productive citizens. Some teachers feel that the accountability measures imposed by policymakers stifle their creative abilities as teachers. Who do you think is to blame for students not learning? How accountable do you think teachers should be for student learning? How should teachers be held accountable?
2. This chapter suggests that teacher education candidates should be able to show evidence that they meet the InTASC standards. Why is it necessary for teachers to possess the knowledge, skills, and dispositions identified in these standards? Which of the InTASC standards do you personally find most important? Why?
3. Do you consider teaching a profession similar to law and medicine? Why? Why not?
4. Why is it important to track your professional growth during your teacher education program? How can tracking your growth as a professional help you in the future?

KEY TERMS

Accreditation 9
Benchmarks 27
Bilingual education 16
Cut score 18
Dispositions 8
English as a Second Language (ESL) 13
Extrinsic rewards 6
Field-based supervisors 18
Intrinsic rewards 6
Journals 30
Lesson plans 29
Mentors 12
National Board for Professional Teaching Standards (NBPTS) 10
Out-of-field teachers 16
Performance assessments 18
Portfolio 18
Profession 4
Proficiencies 19
Reflections 10
Rubrics 10
Standards-based curriculum 27

SELF-ASSESSMENT

WHAT IS YOUR CURRENT LEVEL OF UNDERSTANDING AND THINKING ABOUT BECOMING A TEACHER?

One of the indicators of understanding is to examine how complex your thinking is when asked questions that require you to use the concepts and facts introduced in this chapter.

Answer the following questions as fully as you can. Then use the Complexity of Thinking rubric below to self-assess the degree to which you understand the complexities of becoming a teacher.

1. How would you explain to someone who was not an educator why teaching is a profession?
2. Why is it important for teachers to possess specific knowledge and skills?
3. How can a teacher's competency in a content area be assessed?
4. When should someone who is a teacher candidate begin collecting artifacts about their professional growth? Why?

Complexity of Thinking Rubric

	Parts & Pieces	Unidimensional	Organized	Integrated	Extensions
Indicators	Elements/concepts are talked about as isolated and independent entities. Some important names are provided in isolation.	One or a few concepts are addressed, while others are under-developed, or not mentioned.	Deliberate and structured consideration of all key concepts/ elements.	All key concepts/ elements are included in a view that addresses interconnections.	Integration of all elements and dimensions, with extrapolation to new situations.
Becoming a teacher	Some reasons and necessary skills are provided with little or no connection between or among them	Discusses becoming a teacher in relationship to knowledge of content and classroom instruction	Describes multiple roles teachers perform	Offers a holistic view of the many facets of becoming a teacher	Describes becoming a teacher and teaching as professional, developmental growth

STUDENT STUDY SITE

Visit the Student Study Site at www.sagepub.com/hall to access links to the videos, audio clips, and Deeper Look reference materials noted in this chapter, as well as additional study tools including eFlashcards, web quizzes, and more.

Field Guide

for Learning More About Becoming a Teacher

A field guide is a book or pamphlet someone can take with them when they are exploring their surroundings. The term *field guide* is generally used to help people identify wildlife or other objects in nature. In biology, field guides are designed to help the reader identify specific birds, plants, or fish by studying their features and characteristics. Field guides can help people distinguish one object from another that might look similar but is not.

In this text, the term *field guide* is a metaphor. The activities described at the end of each chapter will help guide you through your investigations of the foundations and purposes of schooling in America. In a sense, you will be creating your own field guide of evidence of teaching and student learning. As a field biologist would do, you should take field notes as you complete the activities outlined for you at the end of each chapter. These notes should include facts and descriptions of your observations. Your field notes should also include date, time of day, the grade or group you are observing, and your reflections and aha moments. Keeping such detailed data is a form of journaling.

Persons engaged in field work also collect artifacts such as pictures and samples of what they are studying. John James Audubon (1785–1851), an American woodsman, completed more than 400 life-size paintings of birds in his expeditions into the field. You will not be expected to collect a specific number of items or even attempt paintings of the classrooms you visit, but you should have evidence of teaching behavior, student responses, and school organization and culture.

Once you have become comfortable in schools and in the classroom, you should begin to compile your field notes into a portfolio—a collection of evidence of your growth toward becoming a teacher. Each chapter in this text will introduce field guide activities such as observing the school and classroom environment, specific portfolio tasks, and journaling activities. When you complete each of the suggested activities you will have ample evidence that you have a thorough understanding of schooling in America.

Ask a Teacher or Principal

Ask one new and one experienced teacher to recall their first year of teaching. If they could start over, what would they do differently? What had they been well prepared to handle when they first entered the classroom? What were their greatest challenges? What recommendations do they have for making your first year successful? What amusing stories do they have to tell?

Make Your Own Observations

Both teachers and students are expected to meet standards in today's schools. The NBPTS states that teachers should be committed to students and their learning, know the subjects they teach and how to teach those subjects, be responsible for managing and monitoring student learning, think systematically about their practice, learn from experience, and be members of learning communities. For one of your next visits to a school, select one of these five expectations and record evidence that you see of teachers in the school demonstrating that expectation.

Reflect Through Journaling

Begin an entry in your journal about why you want to teach. Why do you want to teach a specific subject? Why do you want to teach at the preschool, elementary, middle, or high school level? Where would you like to teach when you complete your program? Why do you want to teach in a specific location? What adult, if any, had an influence on your decision to teach? As you observe and work in schools over the next few years, you may want to revisit your reasons for teaching and update them based on your new experiences.

Build Your Portfolio

Many people report that a teacher has made a great difference in their lives. Write a short paper on the influence one or more teachers have made on your life. Describe what the teacher did in the classroom that impressed you. Begin to develop a list of characteristics of teachers who made a difference. Later you can return to this paper to determine if you are developing the same characteristics in yourself as the teachers you admired.

Learn the standards for teaching in your state. Make a list of the proficiencies related to knowledge, skills, and dispositions that you are expected to demonstrate in the classroom. When, during your field experiences, you achieve one of these standards, place a check mark by the standard and indicate how you know that you have achieved the proficiency (for example, the assessment used and your score). As you progress through your teacher education program, continue to add check marks until all the standards are met. This exercise will help you become very familiar with the standards and will also be tangible proof of how much you have learned.

Read a Book

In *Why We Teach,* by Sonia Nieto (2005; New York, NY: Teachers College Press), experienced and new teachers share the reasons they find purpose and value in teaching. They discuss the kinds of learning that really matter and the kinds of lessons students can take with them for their entire lives. This inspirational book focuses on the quintessential values of teaching and challenges current issues of accountability and testing.

New and experienced teachers offer practical guidance for beginning a teaching career in *The New Teacher Book: Finding Purpose, Balance, and Hope During Your First Years in the Classroom,* edited by Terry Burant, Linda Christensen, Kelley Dawson Salas, and Stephanie Walters (2010; Milwaukee, WI: Rethinking Schools), a collection of writings. Teachers reflect on classroom management, curriculum, discipline, and the students.

Search the Web

Visit **http://www.ccsso.org/projects/National_Teacher_of_the_Year/National_Teachers/** to see examples of National Teachers of the Year.

For other reports of effective teachers, visit the website of Recruiting New Teachers (**http://www.rnt.org/channels/clearinghouse/whyteach/default.htm**).

State licensure requirements can be accessed from the state agency in which you are interested at the Recruiting New Teachers' (RNT) website (**http://www.rnt.org/channels/clearinghouse/deptedu.asp**) or from the National Association of State Directors of Teacher Education (**http://www.nasdtec.org**).

See the website of the National Education Association (NEA; **http://www.nea.org/code.html**) for an example of a code of ethics. You should become familiar with the code of ethics in your state and school district.

If you are not familiar with the standards that you must meet in your teaching field, you can access them at **http://www.ncate.org/standard/programstds.htm** or the website of your professional association.

For additional information on the licensure tests and study guides, visit the websites of the two major testing companies (**http://www.ets.org or http://www.nesinc.com/**). You will need to check with your state to determine the tests you will be required to pass.

Additional web resources include

http://www.nasdtec.org—Information on licensure requirements and state agencies responsible for teacher licensing are available on this website of the National Association of State Directors of Teacher Education and Certification.

http://www.edweek.org—The website of *Education Week* includes statistics on education and the latest news on educational practices and issues in schools and universities.

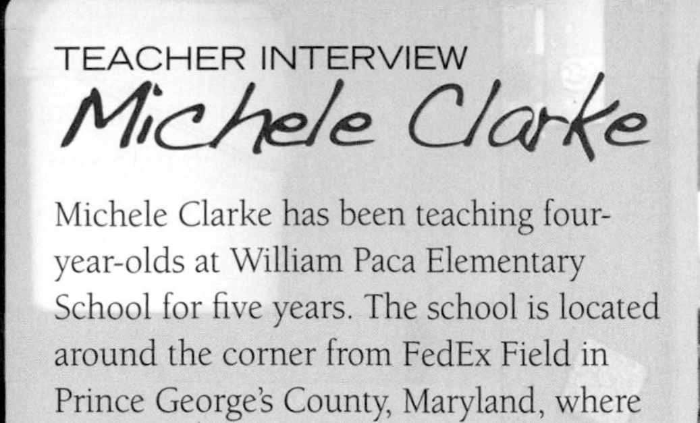

TEACHER INTERVIEW

Michele Clarke

Michele Clarke has been teaching four-year-olds at William Paca Elementary School for five years. The school is located around the corner from FedEx Field in Prince George's County, Maryland, where Washington's National Football League team plays its home games. Approximately 500 students attend this Title I school, with some students beginning as three-year-olds in Head Start and remaining through grade 6. Paca is a choice school to which parents can transfer their children if they are in a school that has not met adequate yearly progress (AYP). Four in five students qualify for free and reduced lunch, and the families are very transient, moving in and out of the school's boundaries. Ms. Clarke had previously worked in a school system where family incomes were fairly high. She chose to move to a school in which families had lower incomes because she believed that she could help young students develop the basic skills required for future success in school. In the next section she describes the diversity of her classroom and the challenges and joy of teaching students who are from a different racial group than her own.

CHAPTER 2

Today's Students

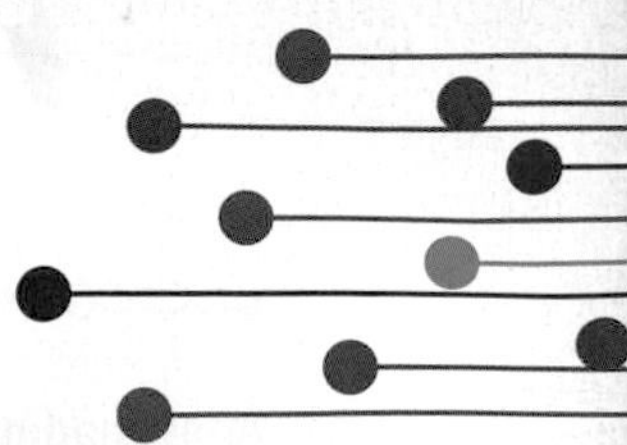

- **What is the diversity of your classroom?**

The students in my classroom are primarily African American, but 3 of the 31 students are Hispanic, and 1 student has parents from Nigeria. All students are income qualified and eligible for free and reduced-price meals. Two students have speech IEPs. For some reason, there are more boys in my two classes than girls. This year there are only four girls in each preschool class. Two of the Hispanic students are in families that use Spanish at home. In the past, I have had Muslim students, but not this year as far as I know.

What do you find most challenging about the diversity in your classroom?

It is a little bit more challenging to meet the needs of the children with the IEPs. Another challenge is making sure the English-language learners understand what I am teaching. Many of my students enter school with fewer academic skills than in schools where the families are more affluent. At the beginning of the year, I had five children who did not know their colors and shapes, let alone their letters. Many of the students do not have the prior knowledge to recognize their name in print.

What do you enjoy most about teaching students from diverse groups?

I enjoy seeing them learn new things to mark their improvement. I like the fact that your efforts are appreciated. For example, when I give the students books, both the students and their parents appreciate it; they don't take it for granted. I have had parents and grandparents tell me that I have helped their children and grandchildren learn and convinced them that they really want to come to school.

Questions to Consider

1. How does Ms. Clarke's class differ from schools with which you are familiar?
2. How prepared do you think you are to work in the setting where Ms. Clarke teaches?
3. What do you want to make sure you learn before you begin to work in a school with students from a number of diverse groups different from your own?

INTRODUCTION

The students you will be teaching may be very similar to you, coming from the same racial and ethnic group, from families with the same socioeconomic status as your own family, attending the same church, and speaking the same language. However, many new teachers find their first jobs in schools with students from groups and cultures with which they have little or no firsthand experience. The students may be very different from them, coming from a different racial or ethnic group, speaking a different language,

Learning Outcomes

After reading this chapter, you should be able to

1. Describe how students' race and ethnicity can be used by a teacher to develop effective instructional strategies for learning.
2. Identify ways that teachers demonstrate that they value and respect students regardless of the socioeconomic status of their families.
3. Explain at least three instructional strategies that are used with English-language learners.
4. Identify gender differences that will help teachers provide equitable instruction for both girls and boys.
5. List actions a teacher could take to stop the taunting and bullying of LGBTQ students in classrooms and schools.
6. Describe the impact of the religious beliefs of students and their families on classroom and school practices in your community and state.

and/or practicing a religion different from their own. Very few schools are segregated by **gender**, so it is likely that not all of your students will be the same sex as you. You are also likely to have one or more students with a **disability** in the classroom.

Both students and teachers are multicultural. We are all members of different groups in society. Our identities are influenced by our **race**, **ethnicity**, gender, socioeconomic status, language, religion, **sexual orientation**, mental and physical abilities, and age. Being a member of one of these group impacts on how we see ourselves as a member of another group. Religion, for instance, may have a great influence on how we think girls and boys are suppose to act. In our society, race and economics define power relationships. Our identities are also determined by others who define us based on their observations of who we are and their experiences or lack of experiences with members of our cultural groups.

One of the keys to being a successful teacher is to care about the students in your classroom. A part of caring is to know the students, their families, and the realities of their everyday lives. This task is much easier in a close-knit community in which most families know one another because they attend the same church, synagogue, temple, or mosque. It is more challenging in large urban and suburban areas in which the histories and experiences of families differ greatly. At the same time, learning about the cultures of your students and communities can be one of the joyful parts of teaching.

Video Link 2.1
Watch a video about diversity.

The growing diversity of the student population offers teachers the opportunity to learn new cultures and expand their cultural competencies. To help all students learn, regardless of their ethnic or racial identity, teachers should learn as much as possible about groups other than their own before they begin teaching. Learning about other groups can be very enlightening and should become a lifelong learning experience. This chapter will introduce you to the student diversity you may encounter as you prepare to be a teacher and in your subsequent jobs.

HOW RACIALLY AND ETHNICALLY DIVERSE ARE OUR SCHOOLS?

We are often asked to identify our race or ethnicity on applications and surveys. Our ethnicity is determined by the country or countries from which our families or ancestors have come. Race, on the other hand, is a term that groups people by biological traits such as the texture of hair, color of skin and eyes, and body stature. The United States census places the population into six pan-ethnic and racial groups: African American or black, American Indian and Native Alaskan, Asian American, Latino, Native Hawaiian and Pacific Islander, and white. We now can choose the category "Two or More Races" to indicate our parents or ancestors are from different races. Still a number of students find it difficult to classify themselves into one of these groups because they do not see themselves as a member of any of them. This section provides a brief introduction to the ethnic and racial diversity of students in schools today, but further study of this topic is strongly recommended to learn more about the history and experiences of the students you will teach in the future.

Race and Ethnicity of the Population

American Indians and Alaska Natives are the indigenous or original people who inhabited North America. Today, 2.4 million citizens identify themselves as Native American, American Indian, or Alaska Native only. Another 2.6 million indicate they are partially Native American or Alaska Native (U.S. Census Bureau, 2011). The American Indian population identifies with one or more of the 565 tribal governments recognized by the federal government (Bureau of Indian Affairs, 2011). Most American Indian students will identify with their tribal heritage such as Cherokee, Navajo, Choctaw, Sioux (that is, Dakota, Lakota, and Nakota peoples), or Chippewa. An important part of their identity is knowing the native language and culture, especially the old traditions and Indian worldview (Horse, 2001).

African Americans have developed their own culture out of their different African, European, and Native American heritages and their unique experiences in this country. Most African American students are greatly influenced by their group membership. They generally know about the discrimination faced by members of their group in the United States. By middle school, they have experienced racism firsthand or know families or friends who have.

Chinese Americans are the largest Asian ethnic group in the United States, followed by Asian Indians, Koreans, and Vietnamese (U.S. Census Bureau, 2011). California is home to the largest number of Asian Americans—over three times as many as New York, the next largest state. They account for more than 40% of Hawaii's population (U.S. Census Bureau, 2011).

Before 1965, the majority of immigrants to the U.S. were from Europe. Today, they are from Mexico and Asia, changing the diversity in the nation's schools.

Latinos come from many nations. The majority have ancestors or families from Mexico and the southwestern United States with roots in Spain, Mexico, and the indigenous tribes of the area. Others come from Central America, South America, Puerto Rico, Cuba, and other Caribbean islands. Many Latinos don't identify themselves by race. Instead they identify themselves as American or by their family's country of origin (e.g., Mexican American or Puerto Rican). They may or may not identify themselves by pan-ethnic terms such as Hispanic or Latino, which are used by the government to categorize the population from countries whose primary language is Spanish. Some families may refer to themselves as Chicano, especially if they are Mexican American and political activists. Maintenance of the Spanish language is important to many Latinos. Spanish is spoken at home by two in three Hispanic students, in part because it is the native language of a large number of their parents (Aud et al., 2011).

The Impact of Immigration

The immigration rate during the past decade has been 1 million persons per year (U.S. Department of Homeland Security, 2011). Over half of the foreign-born population is concentrated in four states, California, New York, Texas, and Florida, and around 20% of the population of Nevada and New Jersey is foreign born. Large cities attract immigrants, with the largest concentrations being in New York City and Los Angeles, where one in three people is foreign born (U.S. Census Bureau, 2011). Non-metropolitan areas are also becoming home to immigrants. For example, the Hispanic population more than doubled over the past decade in Alabama, Arkansas, Kentucky, Maryland, Mississippi, North Carolina, Tennessee, South Carolina, and South Dakota (Passel, Cohn, & Lopez, 2011). As a result, schools across the country include students from different cultures and with native languages other than English.

The nations from which immigrants come have changed over time, primarily because of immigration laws set by Congress. When the Johnson–Reed Act was abolished in 1965, immigration from the Eastern Hemisphere increased dramatically. The largest number of legal immigrants in 1960 came from Mexico, Germany, Canada, the United Kingdom, and Italy. By 2010, the largest number of immigrants came from Mexico (13%), China (7%), India (7%), the Philippines (6%), the Dominican Republic (5%), and Vietnam (3%) (U.S. Department of Homeland Security, 2011). Over 40% of the foreign-born population is from Mexico, 23% from other Latin American countries, 21% from Asia, and 9% from Europe (U.S. Census Bureau, 2011).

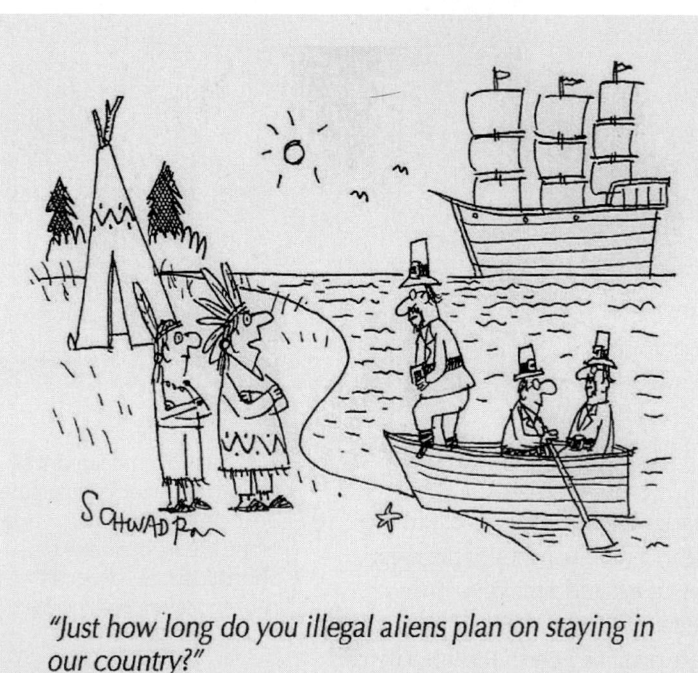

"Just how long do you illegal aliens plan on staying in our country?"

Another group of immigrants are **refugees** who have been recognized by the federal government as being persecuted or legitimately bearing persecution in their home country because of race, religion, nationality, or membership in a specific social or political group. More than 500,000 people were admitted as refugees between 2001 and 2010. The largest number came from Iraq, Myanmar (Burma), and Bhutan in 2010 (U.S. Department of Homeland Security, 2011).

The most controversial immigration issue in the country is that of unauthorized immigrants, who comprise nearly 4% of the nation's population (Passell & Cohn, 2011). Some of these immigrants will be eligible to have their status reclassified as legal when they meet the requirements for employment-based visas, refugees, or being sponsored by a family. Unauthorized immigrants are most likely to be from Mexico (58%), but other Central American countries account for 23% of the unauthorized immigrants, Asia for 11%, Europe and Canada for 4%, and Africa for 3%.

Although California and Texas are the homes to the largest number of unauthorized immigrants, they comprise 6% or more of the population in Nevada, New Jersey, and Arizona.

Children of unauthorized families cannot be denied a public school education. School officials cannot ask parents for their immigration status. They cannot be asked for Social Security numbers or other documentation that might expose their status. In 1975, the Texas legislature decided to withhold funds from local school districts for children who were not "legally admitted" into the United States. The act also allowed school districts to deny enrollment to unauthorized children. When the Supreme Court was asked in *Plyler v. Doe* (1982) to determine the constitutionality of the Texas statute, it ruled that unauthorized students have a right to seek a public education.

Race and Ethnicity in Schools

The United States population is predominantly white (65%), but less so each year. By 2050, less than half of the population will be white; the Latino population will nearly double, comprising 28% of the population (Hussar & Bailey, 2011). The school population reflects the growing diversity of the country more profoundly than the general population because a large number of immigrants are Latino or Asian, and the average age of those groups is younger than whites, resulting in a larger proportion of births. Students of color were 35% of the student population in 1995, but were projected to be 46% in 2010 and 49% by 2020 as shown in Figure 2.1 (Hussar & Bailey, 2011). The percentage of African American and American Indian students will remain about the same while the number of Latino and Asian American students will continue to grow over the next four decades.

Figure 2.1 The Changing Diversity of the School-Age Population

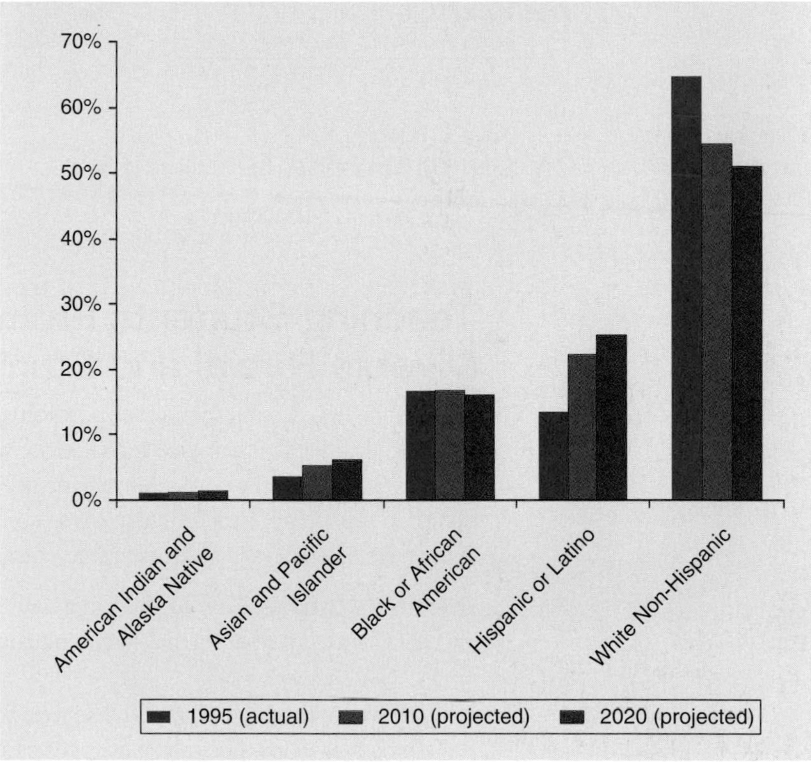

Source: Hussar, W. J., & Bailey, T. M. (2011). *Projections of Education Statistics to 2020* (NCES 2011-026). Washington, DC: U.S. Department of Education, National Center for Education Statistics.

The chances that you will teach students from diverse ethnic and racial groups depend on where your school is located. The largest concentration of students of color is in the western part of the United States; the least diverse part of the country is the Midwest. More than three in five students in California, the District of Columbia, Hawaii, New Mexico, and Texas are already students of color. Over half of the student population in Arizona, Florida, Georgia, Louisiana, Maryland, Mississippi, Nevada, and New York are students of color, and the number is approaching 50% in other states. The highest concentration of African American students is in the South at nearly 25% of the student population. They also comprise the majority population in many urban areas and the first ring of suburbs around large cities. Latino students make up 40% of the students in the West, and Asian American students 5% of the students in the Northeast and West (Aud et al., 2011). The majority of the population in many urban schools is comprised of students of color.

Figure 2.2 Diversity of Public School Teachers and Students in 2008 and 2009

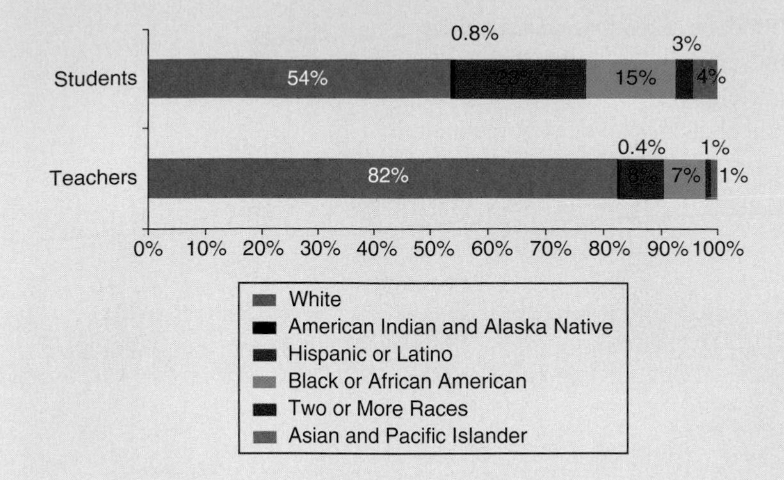

Source: Aud, S., Hussar, W., Kena, G., Bianco, K., Frohlich, L., Kemp, J., & Tahan, K. (2011). *The condition of education 2011* (NCES 2011-033). Washington, DC: U.S. Department of Education, National Center for Education Statistics.

The diversity of teachers in the nation's schools does not match the ethnic and racial diversity of the student population as shown in Figure 2.2. Over four in five public school teachers are white and three in four are women (Aud et al., 2011). Many teachers do not understand their students' cultures and have no or limited experience with them. In these cases, teachers and students may misunderstand each other's cultural cues. Teachers may believe stereotypes of students from ethnic and racial groups with which they have no experience. Students and parents may come to believe that the teacher does not respect or accept their cultures. They may feel that the only way to be successful in school is to adopt the teacher's culture, which may lead to the denigration of their own culture. Some adolescents of color resist the dominant culture of schools and label academically successful peers as "acting white." The incongruence between students' and teachers' cultures may contribute to students not participating in school in meaningful ways.

Teaching Students From Diverse Racial and Ethnic Groups

How should educators respond to the diversity in their schools? One approach is to treat all students the same regardless of their race and ethnicity, which is called color blindness. The problem with this approach is that the curriculum and activities of most schools predominantly reflect the culture of European Americans. In addition, teaching everyone the same does not seem to be working as shown in the great differences in academic achievement among groups as measured by standardized tests.

When asked "what is it like to teach in a school where the students are a different race than you?" Michele Clarke says that she has had minimal problems.

> However, there are cultural differences, particularly in understanding the district's PreK programs. Sometimes a parent appears to be uncomfortable talking to me. I give the parents my cell and home phone number and encourage them to contact me with any concerns. I try to build relationships not only with the child, but with the family by talking with them when they are at school and calling them if a child is having a problem.

The Achievement Gap

Audio Link 2.1
Listen to a clip about the achievement gap.

Disparities in the academic performance and achievement among groups of students are referred to as the achievement gap. Although some students from all groups perform at high levels, achievement data show that students from white and Asian American families are more likely than other students to score at high levels, graduate from high school and college, and attend professional schools. African American and Hispanic students, and students who live in poverty, suffer the most from the achievement gap. Their grade point averages (GPAs) are less than other students. Their performance on standardized tests is lower, they are less likely to take rigorous courses, and they are disproportionately placed in special education (Boykin & Noguera, 2011).

These gaps begin early in the lives of children when their families lack educational resources and suffer from poor health care and nutrition (*Education Week,* 2011). Peer pressure, student tracking, negative stereotyping, test bias, and many other factors also contribute to the achievement gap among students. Too often students in poverty and students of color attend high-poverty schools where most of the students are eligible for free or reduced-price lunch (Aud et al., 2011). They also end up attending the lowest-achieving schools (*Education Week,* 2011).

Figure 2.3 Performance on Eighth-Grade NAEP Reading Tests by Racial and Ethnic Group: 2009

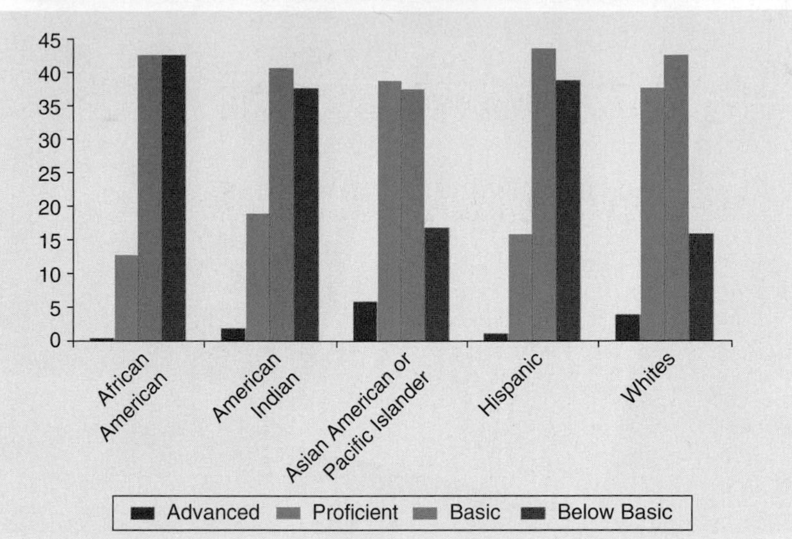

Source: National Assessment of Educational Progress. (2011). *NAEP data explorer.* Washington, DC: National Center for Education Statistics, Institute of Education Sciences, U.S. Department of Education. Retrieved October 17, 2011, from http://nces.ed.gov/nationsreportcard/naepdata/</bibliomixed>

One of the major challenges for educators is to close the achievement gap between students from different racial and ethnic groups. Schools are required by a federal law, No Child Left Behind (NCLB), to annually test public school students to determine if they are meeting state standards in reading and mathematics. To prevent receiving a sanction for not meeting adequate yearly progress (AYP), schools must meet the annual measurable objective (AMO) or fall within the confidence interval overall and in each subgroup (e.g., African American, American Indian, English-language learners) represented in the school. Students' achievement on standardized tests is the indicator most often used when the achievement gap is being discussed. Although the gap between students of color and white students decreased between 1970 and 1990, it then leveled off, not improving since 1990 (Howard, 2010). Today's African American and Hispanic fourth- and eighth-grade students are scoring an average of more than 20 test-score points—or two grade levels—less than white students on the reading and mathematics tests of the National Assessment of Educational Progress (NAEP) (*Education Week,* 2011). The differences among ethnic and racial groups of students are shown in Figure 2.3. The challenge for an educator is how to eliminate this achievement gap.

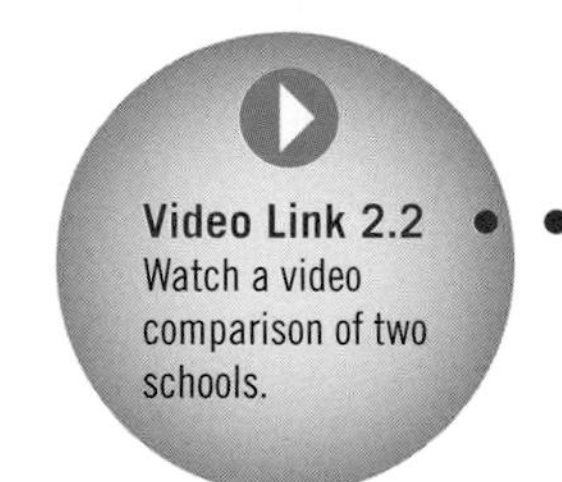

Video Link 2.2
Watch a video comparison of two schools.

The Children's Defense Fund (2011), an advocate group for poor and minority children, reports that many young African American children score lower on measures of cognitive development than white children beginning as early as nine months. They enter pre-kindergarten with lower levels of academic readiness. These gaps grow larger as students continue through school. By the 12th grade, 83% of the African American students who are still in school are not reading at grade level and 93% are not doing math at grade level (National Assessment of Educational Progress, 2011). Data are somewhat better for Hispanic and American Indian students.

To eliminate the achievement gap will require African American, American Indian, and Hispanic students to overcome a 20-point and more deficit. It will require a deliberate effort by educators to provide them additional learning time, better instruction, and more resources (Boykin & Noguera, 2011). Recommendations for reform to improve academic achievement have included "reducing class sizes, creating smaller schools, expanding early-childhood programs, raising academic standards, improving the quality of teachers provided to poor and minority students, and encouraging more minority students to take high-level courses" (*Education Week,* 2011, p. 3).

You are likely to be engaged in the work of eliminating the achievement gap, particularly if you teach in a high-needs school. You may be involved in writing a school improvement plan for your school. You

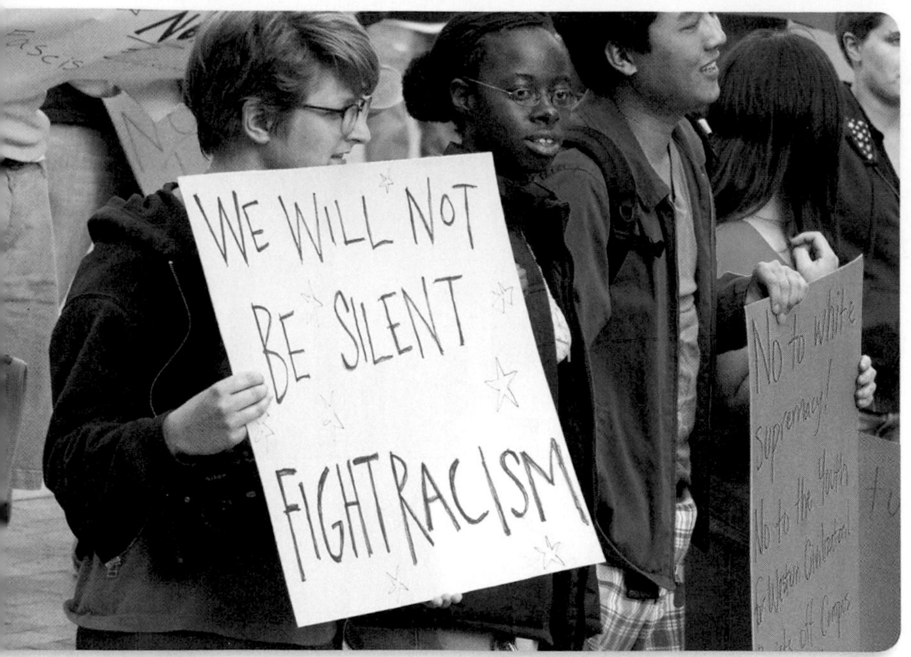

will work with other teachers and administrators to analyze the test scores for your school, and hopefully support each other in helping all students learn. In schools where the gap has been eliminated, educators stopped blaming students and parents for low achievement. Instead, they have taken responsibility for ensuring that students develop the expected outcomes (Boykin & Noguera, 2011). The school districts that have made the most progress in closing the achievement gap in recent years have had educational leaders who prioritize the learning needs of the most vulnerable students (Boykin & Noguera, 2011). Having such a positive impact on a group of students would be worth celebrating. When students aren't learning, the challenge is to figure out why and what can be changed to improve learning.

In the development of their European identity, many whites move from denying that racism exists to feeling guilt and shame about white privilege. Some youth and adults eventually move to the stage in which they fight against racism.

Race in the Classroom

Race has a profound effect on the life experiences of the U.S. population. The fact that African American and Hispanic students continue to achieve at grade levels behind their white peers has become so normalized that many educators have become comfortable with their underperformance, expecting no better. Even students of color become accustomed to failing grades and may avoid academic pursuits or rigorous courses. When failure becomes so normalized by both educators and students, it becomes extremely difficult to change the outcomes (Boykin & Noguera, 2011). The first step is recognizing the problem. Your job as a teacher will be to confront the ways that racial identity and the stereotype of failure are reinforced and reproduced in your classroom (Steele, 2010).

The inequitable educational outcomes for students of color are a function of the social context, in this case, their unequal access to key educational resources such as quality teachers and quality curriculum (Darling-Hammond, 2010). We need to understand "how race shapes the way in which many young people understand their worlds and how the world shapes their understanding of themselves as racial beings" (Howard, 2010, p. 121). Students of color do not always trust teachers from racially privileged groups because those teachers are more likely to not understand the impact of race on their lives (Howard, 2010). Racism's impacts on interactions in the classroom, the curriculum, and school policies have not often been confronted by educators.

Racism is not a topic that is easily discussed in most classrooms. Students of color have almost always experienced racism and discrimination while few white students have direct experiences with racism. Discussion can evoke emotions of anger, guilt, shame, and despair. Most students think of the United States as a just and democratic society. Therefore, it is difficult for many students to confront the contradictions that support racism. Nevertheless, we need to confront our own racism and students' racism to begin to overcome the racial gaps that exist in society.

Ethnic Studies

One approach to studying different racial and ethnic groups is **ethnic studies**, which provides in-depth examination of the social, economic, and political history and contemporary conditions of a group. Some high schools have ethnic studies courses, such as African American, Asian American, Native American, and Latino Studies. These courses help fill in the gaps in knowledge about a specific group. If you have little exposure to the examination of an ethnic group different from your own, you should consider taking some college courses or undertaking your own individual study.

Ethnocentric Curriculum

Another approach to incorporating students' ethnicity into classrooms is an **ethnocentric curriculum.** Some immigrant groups have historically established their own schools, with evening and weekend classes, to teach their children the values, traditions, and language of their native homelands. Today ethnic groups are establishing their own charter or private schools with curriculum centered on the history and values of their own ethnic group rather than the dominant Western European orientation of most schools. Some American Indian tribes, for example, have established tribally controlled schools in which the traditional culture provides the social and intellectual starting point.

Some African Americans have pushed for an **Afrocentric curriculum** to challenge Eurocentrism and "tell the truth" about black history. Proponents argue that centering the curriculum in the roots of Africa will improve their children's self-esteem, academic skills, and values, and encourage them to develop a positive African American identity. The African perspective of the world and historical events is at the core of this approach. These schools are now located in a number of urban areas with large African American student populations.

HOW DO ECONOMICS AFFECT STUDENTS AND SCHOOLS?

Preschool teacher Michele Clarke reported that the biggest challenge in teaching students from low-income families is the wide variety of skills that students bring to school. Some children know the alphabet and can write their first name. Others don't know colors or shapes. Being able to differentiate instruction and projects to help the students who lack skills achieve and still engage the students who have the skills is a challenge.

Schools are often described by the socioeconomic status (SES) of their students' parents or guardians. Students are distinguished by their family's income and wealth, in which more affluent families have more economic, social, and political resources. Even within a school, students are sometimes classified and sorted by their economic conditions, giving the advantage to students from higher-income families.

Economic Diversity of Students

The lack of family resources affects the quality of housing and environment in which students live, the food they eat, the way they dress, and the educational resources to which they have access. These economic conditions also can have a great impact on the quality of education they receive. Their schools may not have up-to-date laboratories and technology. Their teachers may not have majored in the subjects they are assigned to teach and have a higher absentee rate than those in schools that serve more affluent communities. With the disadvantages with which these students enter schools, as pointed out by Ms. Clarke, they need the best teachers and a great deal of support from school officials and the community to ensure they learn at the same levels as their more affluent peers.

Deeper Look 2.1
Read about the impact that neighborhoods have on education.

Students in Low-Income Families

Family members with low incomes may be temporarily unemployed or working at low wages because of a family illness or losing their jobs as a result of the 2008 recession. A very small portion

Figure 2.4 Persons in Poverty by Ethnic and Racial Groups in 2009

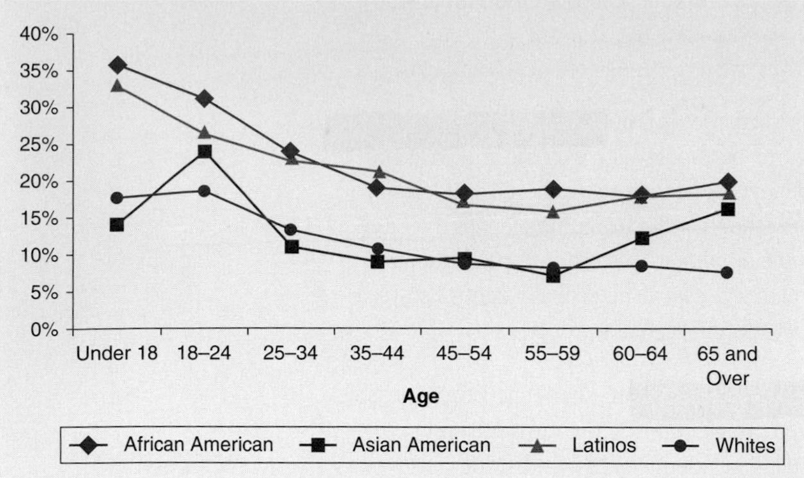

Source: U.S. Census Bureau. (2011). *Statistical abstract of the United States: 2012* (131st ed.). Washington, DC: Author.

of the population is persistently poor as measured by living in poverty for eight or more years. Other members of this group are the working poor. They often work more than one job at the minimum wage, which is $7.25 per hour or $15,080 annually, but still can't pull themselves out of poverty. Work in minimum wage jobs can be sporadic, and unemployment is unpredictably affected by the economy. Fringe benefits usually are not available, leaving many of these workers without health insurance or vacation time.

Poverty differs by age, race, and ethnicity as shown in Figure 2.4. The percentage of whites in poverty is less than people of color, with a larger percentage of Native Americans suffering more from poverty than any other group, followed by African Americans and Hispanics. Generally the poverty rate for Asian Americans is near that of whites, but some ethnic groups such as Vietnamese and other Southeastern Asian groups have greater poverty than other Asian groups. Children under eighteen are more likely to be in poverty than any other age-group, ranging from 14% for Asian American children to 36% for African American children (U.S. Census Bureau, 2011).

In 2010, the number of Hispanic students who were in families whose incomes were below the poverty level bypassed the number of white children for the first time in history. Because families of color earn less than white families, their children are more likely to be impoverished. Thus, the rate of poverty is greater for children of color, with 39% of African American and 35% of Latino children living in poverty as compared with 12% of white children (Lopez & Velasco, 2011). In addition, African American and Latino students are 2 to 3 times more likely than white and Asian American students to attend schools with large numbers of students in poverty (Aud et al., 2011).

Schools classify students as low income by the criteria that make them eligible to participate in the free or reduced-price lunch (FRPL) program. To be eligible for a free or reduced-price lunch, family income must fall below 130% of the federal poverty level or $28,540 for a family of four in 2009. For a subsidized lunch, family income must fall between 130% and 185% of the federal poverty level or between $28,541 and $40,615 for a family of four. In 2009, 48% of all students in grades 4 to 9 were eligible for FRPL ("College Participation Rates," 2010).

What does living in a low-income family mean for children and teenagers? For one thing, they are in poorer health than students in higher-income families. They have a greater incidence of vision and hearing problems, especially ear infections. They lack dental care, leading to toothaches. They have greater exposure to lead in water pipes, which affects their cognitive functioning and behavior. They are more likely to have asthma, especially when living in densely populated neighborhoods. They are less likely to have regular medical care and usually lack health insurance. Their nutrition is often poor. The lack of affordable housing results in their families moving from one school district to another. All of these factors affect school attendance and their ability to concentrate and attend carefully to their work when they are in school (Rothstein, 2008).

Students in low-income families are less likely than those in higher-income families to graduate from high school and pursue postsecondary education. The chances of youth attending college differ across states, from 8.3% in Alaska to 43.9% in New Hampshire. Attendance rates are higher in the Northeast and the uppermost states in the middle region of the country ("College Participation Rates," 2010).

Students from low-income families are concentrated in cities and rural areas, but they can be found almost anywhere. When children from low-income families are the majority of the students in a school, they are more likely to have low test scores, unsafe and unattractive schools, and less than stimulating schoolwork that has limited relationship to their lives. From the beginning of their school career, they are too often not expected to go to college. They are not picked to lead groups and are not encouraged to participate in extracurricular activities. It appears that these students are being prepared for jobs that more affluent people are unwilling to take.

Homeless Students

Some of the children in poverty are homeless. The U.S. Conference of Mayors (2010) reported a 9% increase in the number of families experiencing homelessness. Homeless people are not always unemployed. Some work at such low wages they are unable to afford housing. Others have lost their jobs or have become estranged from their families. Homeless women may have left home to escape violent relationships. Homeless teenagers have left home to avoid abuse and other family problems.

The Urban Institute (Pergamit, 2010) reports that 1.5 to 2 million young people are homeless and unaccompanied by an adult for at least one night each year. However, nearly a million homeless children and youth are enrolled in school and regularly attending classes (National Association for the Education of Homeless Children and Youth, 2011). Unfortunately some homeless students do not attend school for extended periods of time.

Many students identify themselves as middle class, which generally means that one or both of their parents are working and their family is buying a home.

Public schools must provide educational rights to homeless children and youth. The McKinney–Vento Homeless Assistance Act requires school districts to provide transportation for homeless students to stay in their schools of origin if their parents request it. Enrollment cannot be denied because homeless students do not have their school records, immunization records, proof of residency, or other documents. The school district's liaison for homeless students is expected to be an advocate for them, helping them access available services in the school system and community.

Middle-Class Families

Many Americans identify themselves as middle class. It is an amorphous category that often includes everyone who works steadily and who is not accepted as a member of the upper class. It ranges from service workers to well-paid professionals. This group includes white-collar workers who work in offices as secretaries, administrative assistants, and managers. It also includes many blue-collar workers who are involved in manual labor. Middle-class workers generally have greater job security and better fringe benefits than low-income workers. However, many families live from paycheck to paycheck, not earning enough to accumulate wealth. Both parents often work to make ends meet.

The number of African Americans and Latinos who are middle class has increased over the past five decades, but whites and Asian Americans have disproportionately high representation in this group. The upper middle class usually has high educational expectations for their children, expecting them to attend college or receive training after they finish high school. The parents are more likely to be involved with schools and their children's education than low-income families.

Families with higher incomes could choose to send their children to private schools or contribute to school funds to pay for art, music, and additional teachers. They not only have computers at home, but ensure that their children have access to the latest technology. When their children are not learning at the level expected, they hire tutors. Their children participate in enrichment activities such as academic summer camps when they are not in school. Income provides the advantages to ensure that the children of higher-income families are able to achieve at high academic levels and attend college.

Providing Equity in Schools

Most students who live in poverty have learned how to live in a world that is not imaginable to most middle-class students or teachers. However, their knowledge and skills do not always fit into the middle-class orientation of schools. Students should see ordinary working people as valued members of society. They should see low-income families as valued, contributing members of the school community, rather than as second-class citizens who are not expected to be involved in their children's education.

Schools that were serious about providing an equitable education to all of their students would develop instructional strategies to eliminate the achievement gap between students from low-income and affluent families. To participate with other teachers to ensure that your students are performing at high levels could make schooling much more meaningful for students and teaching a very rewarding career.

Teacher Expectations

Deeper Look 2.2
Read more about teacher expectations.

Sociologists have documented the classification and segregation of students based on their class and race beginning in their first days in school. Most teachers can quickly identify the **cultural capital** that students bring to school. At the same time, many teachers develop expectations for their students' behavior and academic achievement. Often unknowingly, they then develop instruction and interactions with their students that ensure they will behave as the teachers expect—a phenomenon called the **self-fulfilling prophecy**.

If a teacher's goal is to spend extra time with students who are struggling with academics with the goal of ensuring that they develop the academic skills necessary to move to the next grade, a grouping strategy might be successful. The problem is that too often students identified as having lower academic ability at the beginning of the year end the school year with little improvement in their skills, just as the teacher had projected early in the year. Unfortunately, their lack of academic growth during that year usually follows them throughout their school career.

When teachers make such judgments about students based primarily on their class status, they are preventing them from having an equal opportunity for academic achievement. In these cases, a teacher's expectations for student achievement lead to the confirmation of the self-fulfilling prophecy. The practice is not congruent with the democratic belief that all students deserve an equal education. One of the joys of teaching is to overcome the odds against students whose families are low income by guiding them to academic performance at the same level as their more affluent peers. You will need to expect all of your students to meet rigorous academic requirements regardless of the income of their families. If you require less of low-income students, they may think that you don't think they are as capable as the other students (Nieto, 2008).

Tracking

Tracking is an educational strategy that separates students for instruction based on their academic abilities. Students may be placed in a specific education track based primarily on their native language or disability. Students may choose or be assigned to a college, vocational, or general track that determines the courses they take. However, these assignments are sometimes based on teachers' or counselors' judgments of a student's future potential. Some students are placed in gifted programs and others in programs that are clearly designed for low-ability students.

Deeper Look 2.3
Read about the practice of tracking.

Socioeconomic status matters in tracking practices. Test scores, which may be used to track students, are more closely correlated to the education level, or social class, of students' parents than their academic potential (Burris, Wiley, Welner, & Murphy, 2008). The same pattern applies to placement of students in high-ability classes. Students in high-ability courses and programs are academically challenged with enrichment activities that improve their intellectual and critical-thinking skills. Courses for students classified as low ability are often characterized as uninviting and boring. They include oral recitation and structured written work that are related to low-status knowledge. In addition, many teachers in these classrooms spend more time on administration and discipline than actually teaching the subject matter, keeping students at the lowest level of academic achievement. These students are most likely to be taught by the least qualified and least experienced teachers. Students from low-income families are also disproportionately assigned to low-ability groups. They also are more likely to be classified as mentally challenged than their middle-class classmates.

Tracking has led to the resegregation of students based on race, class, and language into separate programs within the school. White middle-class students are disproportionately represented in gifted and talented programs while African Americans, Latinos, students from low-income families, and English-language learners are the majority of the students in low-ability classrooms and special education programs. Schools could be accused of discriminatory practice in placing these students in low-ability courses and programs because they are limiting students' educational opportunities and potential for later occupational and economic success.

WHAT IF STUDENTS' NATIVE LANGUAGES ARE NOT ENGLISH?

The goal of Michele Clarke's school system is to help students become fluent in English as soon as possible. With a few English-language learners in her preschool class, Michele Clarke ensures that

> some of our books are bilingual in English and Spanish. Sometimes I read the books using both languages to make the Spanish-speaking students more comfortable and introduce the English-speaking children to a second language. We sing songs in both languages, and there are posters in the classroom with both languages.

> **Video Case 2.1**
> **Bilingual Education**
>
> 1. What is the role of students' native languages in Mr. Frank's math class?
> 2. How does Mr. Frank's use of Spanish contribute to his students learning math?

Language diversity is valued in most countries of the world. The populations of many European, Middle Eastern, and African countries are bilingual or multilingual. In today's global world in which many companies operate internationally, employees who know more than one language and culture can be an asset to the company, especially in its interactions with other nations in the areas of commerce, defense, education, science, and technology. Bilingualism is also an asset for jobs such as hotel clerks, airline attendants, social workers, nurses, teachers, and police officers who may be interacting with individuals who speak little or no English.

More than 57 million residents of the United States speak a language other than English at home (U.S. Census Bureau, 2011). Most of them are recent immigrants from countries around the world. Many of their children will be learning English in school. They may speak no English, limited English, or fluent English. Three in four English-language learners speak Spanish. Other languages spoken most often at home by English-language learners are Chinese, Tagalog, French, Vietnamese, German, Korean, Arabic, and Italian. Between 30% and 40% of the population in California, New Mexico, and Texas speaks a language other than English at home, as shown in Figure 2.5. Other than Florida, most southern states have a limited number of non-English speakers.

Teaching English-Language Learners

Immigrants come to the United States with different levels of education. Almost as many of the foreign-born population holds bachelor's degrees as the native population. At the same time, three in 10 foreign-born adults do not have a high school degree—three times as many as the native-born population (U.S. Census Bureau, 2011). Immigrants come from different

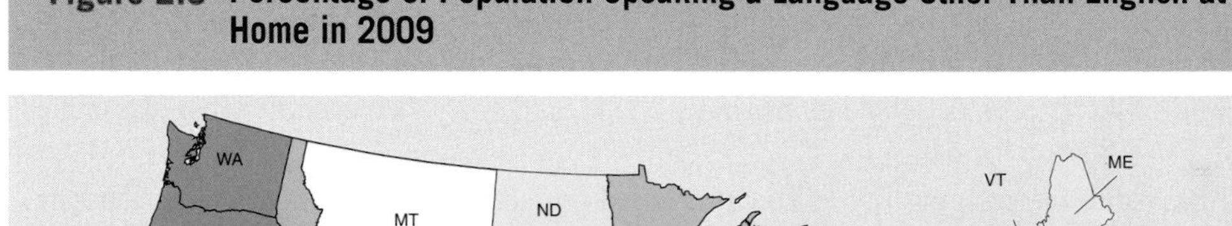

Figure 2.5 Percentage of Population Speaking a Language Other Than English at Home in 2009

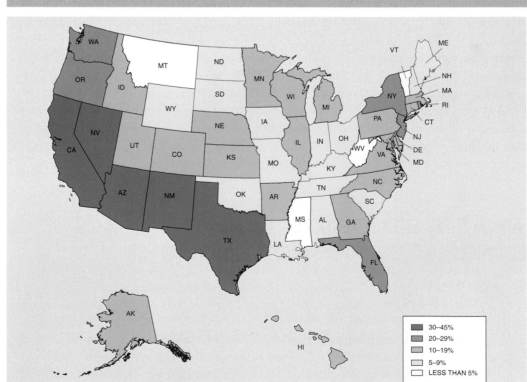

Source: Aud, S., Hussar, W., Kena, G., Bianco, K., Frohlich, L., Kemp, J., & Tahan, K. (2011). *The Condition of Education 2011* (NCES 2011-033). Washington, DC: U.S. Department of Education, National Center for Education Statistics.

UNDERSTANDING AND USING EVIDENCE

Making a Choice About the Diversity of Your Future School

You are nearly finished with your teacher education program and are ready to look for a teaching job anywhere in the United States. You think you would like to work in an urban area and are interested in knowing whether your diversity knowledge and skills fit with the population in the school districts you are considering. You find the following table that describes the diversity of the student population in the areas you are considering.

Area of Country	Enrollment	% Black	% Latino	% White	% Other	% FRPL*	% IEP**	% ELL***
Southwest	87,000	3.8	50.6	38.9	6.7	42.3	19.9	17.7
Mid-Atlantic	98,000	88.0	0.9	10.2	0.9	67.4	16.7	1.3
Midwest	21,000	72.4	1.0	27.5	0.5	73.7	20.1	0.0
North Central	32,000	15.3	9.8	69.6	5.2	44.5	17.4	9.8
South Central	211,000	31.3	56.1	9.6	3.1	72.7	9.9	28.4
South	37,000	67.4	2.4	28.0	2.2	59.8	13.1	0.2
Northeast	27,000	22.6	51.6	16.3	9.6	79.6	19.1	20.6
West	25,000	4.1	30.3	53.9	11.8	52.9	12.9	33.5
West Coast	59,000	15.2	21.3	10.3	51.7	54.5	11.9	30.8
Northwest	47,000	23.1	10.8	40.1	26.0	39.6	12.6	11.7

*FRPL = free or reduced-price lunch
**IEP = individualized education program
***ELL = English-language learner

1. Which area of the country has the greatest balance of ethnic and racial diversity?
2. Which area of the country has the fewest students from low-income families?
3. Which area of the country has the largest percentage of students with disabilities?
4. Which area of the country has the largest percentage of English-language learners?
5. Which area of the country would best match your knowledge and skills in diversity? Why?

socioeconomic levels, entering the country with limited economic resources or enough resources to invest or begin a business. Their education credentials and economic status in their home countries may give them the social and cultural capital that makes them acceptable to dominant society (Kubota & Lin, 2009).

The children in immigrant families also have different educational experiences. Some have never been in school and know no English. Metropolitan areas with large numbers of immigrant students may have established special schools or newcomer programs for those students to learn English and the United States culture. Other children have strong educational backgrounds and are fluent in English. Some families work hard to retain the native language from one generation to another, using their native language at home or sending their children to classes to learn their language and culture. They are helped in this process when they live in communities that value bilingualism.

Bilingual Education

Deeper Look 2.4
Read about ELL approaches.

The programs for English-language learners (ELL) vary across school districts, often based on the desires of the immigrant families or politics of the area. Bilingual education, which uses students' native languages and English in instruction, is the most controversial because it values the native language and supports its use in school. Bilingual programs require teachers or teachers' aides who speak the native language to ensure students are understanding concepts and developing academic skills while they learn English. The goal of two-way immersion, two-way bilingual, or dual-language programs is students' development of strong skills and proficiency in both the home language and English. Students may stay in these programs throughout elementary school (National Clearinghouse for English Language Acquisition [NCELA], n.d.).

Other programs that focus on students developing literacy in two languages include developmental bilingual or maintenance bilingual education programs. Instruction in these programs is in the home language in the lower grades. Although these students are gradually moved into English-only classrooms, they continue to receive support for their language development. Transitional bilingual programs also use the home language for teaching at the beginning of a student's experience in schools, but the goal is to move them quickly into English-only classrooms (NCELA, n.d.).

Two other programs are designed to support literacy in two languages. The heritage language and indigenous language programs provide assistance to ELLs with weak literacy skills in their home languages (NCELA, n.d.). The indigenous language program supports endangered languages and is used in American Indian, Native Hawaiian, and Native Alaskan communities.

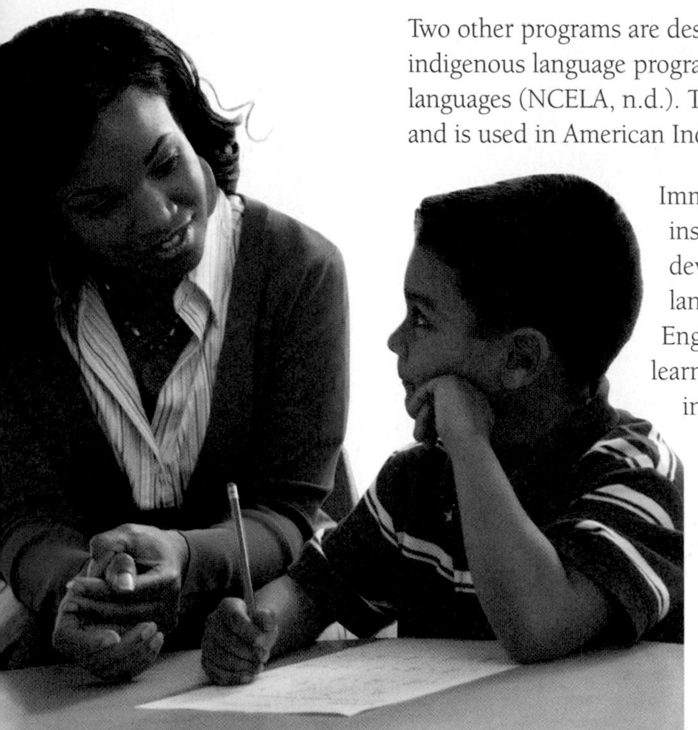

More and more classrooms across the country include students who are foreign born or have one or more foreign-born parents. A large number of students are Latino or Asian American.

Immersion classrooms use both the home language and English for instruction with the goal of students becoming bilingual. Students in developmental or maintenance bilingual programs share the same native language. In two-way immersion and two-way bilingual programs, English-speaking students are learning a second language while ELLs are learning English. Some school districts offer other immersion programs in elementary schools for English speakers to learn and use a second language such as Chinese, French, or Spanish.

English as a Second Language (ESL)

English as a second language (ESL) is the most common program used in schools. The home language is not used in ESL; instruction is provided only in English. Sheltered English instruction or content-based ESL programs usually include students from various linguistic and cultural backgrounds in the same class. Visual aids and the home language are used to help students learn English. Students in structured English immersion (SEI) programs are usually all ELLs who are trying to become fluent in English. Other programs for developing English fluency include the pull-out ESL or English language development (ELD) programs. Students are pulled out of the classroom for English instruction that focuses on grammar, vocabulary, and communication skills. In the push-in ESL program, ELLs are in a regular English-only classroom where an ESL teacher or teacher's aide translates if needed and uses ESL strategies to help students learn the content (NCELA, n.d.). Newcomer programs for immigrant students who know limited English use ESL to help students learn English, the content, and the common culture (Short & Boyson, 2012).

As the population of the United States becomes more and more diverse with larger numbers of people speaking languages other than English, teachers will need to know how to teach English as a second language. Most universities offer one or more courses on ESL that could expand your skills and make you more attractive to school districts with growing English-language learner populations. Speaking a second language that is common in the area in which you plan to teach should also provide you with an advantage when seeking a teaching position.

Video Link 2.3
Watch a clip about ESL teaching strategies.

WHAT IS THE RELATIONSHIP OF GENDER AND EDUCATION?

Men and women often segregate themselves at social gatherings and participate in gender-specific leisure activities. Most of our friends are of the same sex. Boys and girls generally choose different games to play. Sometimes they are segregated by sex in schools or school activities, especially sports. We often hold stereotypical perceptions of ourselves and the other sex. We disproportionately enter different occupations and have access to different financial opportunities. These differences are reflected in what is studied in school, how students interact with each other, and how teachers interact with students. In this section we will explore how education is affected by gender and how teachers can ensure they provide an equitable education for their female and male students.

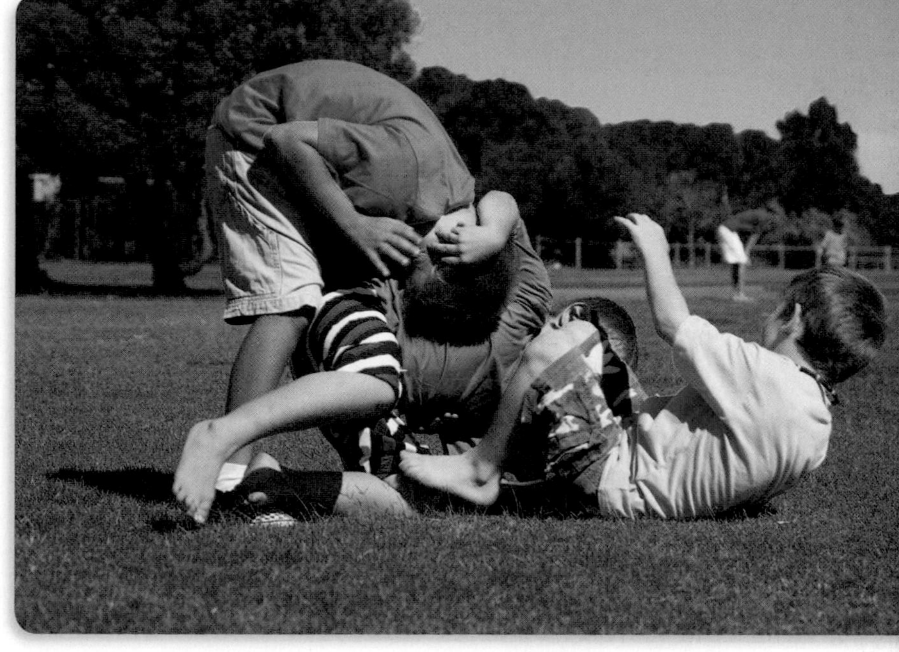

Some researchers believe that the differences between boys and girls are grounded in biology in which boys naturally behave differently than girls in classroom.

Differences Between Females and Males

Sex is the term used to identify an individual as male or female based on biological differences, while *gender* is used for the behavioral, cultural, and psychological traits typically associated with one sex. Physical differences between males and females can usually be determined by appearance alone. Before age eight, boys and girls have similar hormonal levels and similar physical development. During puberty, hormonal levels of estrogen and testosterone, which control the physical development of the two sexes, change. However, physical differences between the sexes can be altered with good nutrition, physical activity, practice, and different behavioral expectations (Eliot, 2009).

Intelligence tests show no differences in the general intelligence between the sexes, but many studies have found some gender differences in mathematical, verbal, and spatial skills. Spatial relations are controlled by the right hemisphere of the cerebral cortex. The left hemisphere controls language and other sequential skills. Females favor the left hemisphere associated with speaking, reading, and writing. Males tend to have greater right-hemisphere specialization, which leads to better performance on tests of spatial visualization and higher achievement in mathematics and science. However, not all boys and not all girls exhibit the inclination usually identified with their sex. Some girls achieve highly in mathematics and science, and some boys highly in language, reading, and writing. Therefore, academic, social, or physical ability based on a student's sex cannot be predetermined.

Proponents of brain-based differences based on sex argue that teachers who know these hemispheric differences have a better understanding of why boys and girls behave the way they do in classrooms. This research suggests that females and males are hardwired at birth to behave and think differently. These researchers argue that teachers design lessons and organize their classrooms based on the way that girls learn, which leaves boys behind (Gurian & Stevens, 2005). Boys do appear to be more engaged in lessons that support active, project-centered learning (Reichert & Hawley, 2010). They are stimulated by movement, requiring more physical space than many activities in which girls generally participate. Movement also helps boys manage and relieve impulsive behavior. Girls, on the other hand, are generally more social and prefer working together on a learning project.

Other researchers attribute most male and female differences to **socialization** patterns learned from their parents, relatives, teachers, and peers. They argue that girls and boys are socialized to use the skills associated with their gender or that are attributed to the right and left hemispheres of their brains. These debates focus on whether nature or nurturing is most important in determining the differences between the sexes. A balanced view gives credit to the interaction of both nature and nurture. Girls and boys can learn to use the hemisphere of the brain that is not being fully utilized. Gender-sensitive instruction helps boys and girls develop the knowledge, skills, and dispositions that may come more naturally to one than the other.

Schools historically reinforce society's view of gender. Girls are expected to be feminine and boys to be masculine. In school, girls are expected to be more quiet and better behaved than boys. Girls are more likely than boys to be encouraged to break out of their stereotypical modes. Many parents today tell their daughters that they can be whatever they want. They play on sports teams, are the leaders in many school activities, and attend college at higher rates than boys. Women and girls may struggle to develop a balance between their femininity and their participation in a masculine world.

Deeper Look 2.5
Read about gender bias in high school math education.

Young men are generally encouraged to be independent, assertive, leaders, self-reliant, and emotionally stable. They are pushed toward these characteristics, in part, to prevent them from being labeled gay or a sissy, which could lead to harassment by others. As a result, they sometimes go overboard in proving their masculinity (Kimmel, 2008). The problem is that not all males fit the masculine stereotype; some are empathic and caring, which are commonly recognized as feminine characteristics. Some critics of the women's movement declare that boys have been harmed by the focus on girls and women, which they believe has led to the lower participation of young men in academics and college. It is true that some young men are not adjusting well, as shown in the statistics on their high rates of suicide, binge drinking, and steroid use and as victims of homicide and car crashes. Psychologists do not always agree on the reasons that a number of boys and young men seem to be at risk today. Some argue that boys are programmed for a culturally determined masculine identity with little room for divergence.

Delivering an Equitable Education for Girls and Boys

When asked about differences she observes between boys and girls in her classroom, Ms. Clarke says that

> the boys are much more active and more hands-on learners than the girls. Both sexes need a lot of hands-on work when they are four years old. At this point most of the students do not yet have a strong gender identity. Once in a while, a student says that

Challenging Assumptions

Myth: Teachers interact with all students in the same way regardless of race and gender.

The Research

Drawing on 20 years of fieldwork in 11 elementary classrooms in the Midwest and South, a researcher traced the origins of school experiences for students of different races and gender. She also explored the implications of how teachers and students interacted based on their race, gender, and status.

White girls had the most positive interactions with teachers. They received frequent praise from teachers for their good behavior and academic work. In addition, teachers chatted with them about personal issues. For the most part, white girls understood the classroom routine and rules, followed the rules, and focused on the teachers.

Black males, on the other hand, had limited interactions with teachers, which were almost always negative and initiated by the teacher, not themselves. Teachers tended to monitor or criticize their behavior or academic work. Black boys were much more likely to interact with their peers than their teachers. White boys and black girls had a more balanced ratio of interactions with teachers and peers. Their relationships with teachers were cordial, but not as close as those of white girls.

The researcher concluded that schools do more to enhance than to diminish gender and race differences among African American girls, white girls, African American boys, and white boys. Although teachers do not appear to consciously intend to support white girls more than other students, such practices help ensure inequality in a classroom.

Source: Grant, L. (2004). Everyday schooling and the elaboration of race-gender stratification. In J. H. Ballantine & J. Z. Spade (Eds.), *Schools and society: A sociological approach to education* (2nd ed.; pp. 296–307). Belmont, CA: Wadsworth/Thomson.

> she cannot play with the blocks because they are for boys. In my classroom, both sexes like dramatic play, but they always choose the gender-appropriate role.

Teachers are expected to treat all students equally and encourage academic excellence in all of their students. Whether a student exhibits masculine or feminine characteristics or is transgender, a teacher has the responsibility to exhibit unconditional positive regard for him or her, to recognize the student's special talents and needs, and to provide a learning environment that fosters acceptance and understanding.

Federal legislation governing elementary and secondary education includes Title IX, which makes it illegal to treat students differently or separately on the basis of gender. It requires that all programs, activities, and opportunities offered by a school district be equally available to males and females. All courses must be open to all students, allowing boys to enroll in traditionally female courses, and girls to enroll in traditionally male courses.

You should be concerned about the academic performance of both boys and girls. You should be asking why so few girls are majoring in computer science and engineering in college and

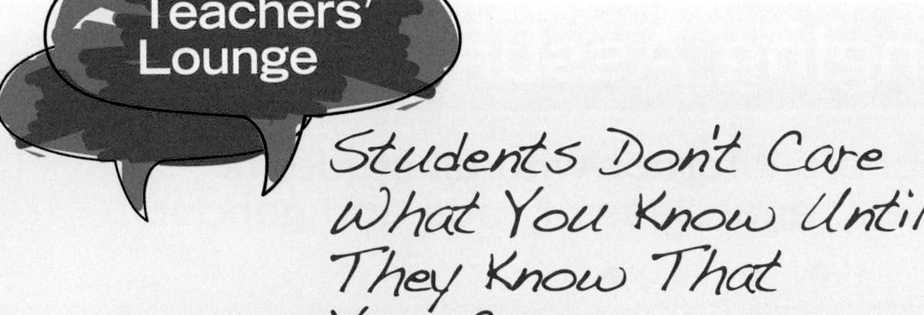

Teachers' Lounge
Students Don't Care What You Know Until They Know That You Care

It has been my experience while teaching middle and high school that students from diverse groups do not care what you have to say until they know that you care. Teaching is getting students to do what you want them to do while having them think it is their idea, because everybody loves their own ideas. Which takes me into my experience I had with two of my middle school students in Henderson, North Carolina. Teaching math to students when it is not their favorite subject can be a bit of a task. I had one student in particular who was having problems, and I tutored him after school. We began to develop a student–mentor relationship that was of significant importance because the student lacked any male guidance. His family welcomed my relationship with the student. As a result, I was granted permission to take the student and his brother for an afternoon out on the town. We went to the movies and had dinner in a nice restaurant and spent time enjoying each other's company at my expense. At the time this did not seem to be a big deal to me; however, it was a huge deal to the students. The students became ambassadors for me at the school and model students. The students realized that I really cared about them and that I wanted the best for them. The new challenge was that every student wanted to go to dinner and a movie with me now. You never know what you may be to a student and what need you fill. When you let them know you care, they will allow you to lead them where they need to go.

Peter M. Eley, PhD
Fayetteville State University
Fayetteville, North Carolina

developing strategies for increasing their participation in those fields. The fact that boys are not performing as well on reading tests suggests that new strategies for involving them in reading and language arts may be needed to ensure they are reading at grade level or above. You should wonder why boys are not graduating from high school and not enrolling or finishing college at the same rates as girls. Increasing the graduation rates of young men would be another challenge in which you could become involved when you begin teaching. Being engaged in activities that keep young men in school and open academic fields such as science, technology, engineering, and mathematics (STEM) to more girls and students of color is another way to bring joy to your teaching.

HOW IS SEXUAL ORIENTATION ADDRESSED IN SCHOOLS?

Michele Clarke, the teacher in the opening section of this chapter, indicated that she has a couple of parents with same-sex partners.

> When a student says that he or she has two mommies, it provides the opportunity to talk about different types of families. I have heard some of the students in the upper elementary grades call other students gay or a fag or queer, but have had no incidences of name-calling in my class.

Discussions about sexual orientation are no longer hidden in society. Over half of the population now views relationships between same-sex couples as morally acceptable (Jones, 2011), and half supports legal gay marriages (Newport, 2012). The problem is that we are divided about the right of an individual to have a sexual orientation other than heterosexism, with some people and religions calling anything else a sin. Nevertheless, the legal recognition of gays and lesbians has increased as shown in the repeal of "Don't Ask, Don't Tell," which did not allow military personnel to be open about their sexual orientation. The support for the equal rights of gays and lesbians has grown as cities, states, and school districts expand their policies on equality to include sexual orientation. Even with these changes, some school districts continue to struggle with how to handle diverse sexual orientations in the curriculum and in student clubs.

Gays and lesbians may continue to face discrimination in housing, employment, and social institutions in some communities, as evidenced when schools and universities prohibit the establishment of gay student clubs. Heterosexism, as expressed in harassment and violence against gays and lesbians, is still tolerated in many areas of the country. Society's prejudices and discriminatory practices result in many gays and lesbians hiding their sexual orientation and establishing their own social clubs, networks, and communication systems to support one another.

Sexual Identity

What is sexual orientation? The American Psychological Association (APA) (2008) defines it as an "enduring pattern of emotional, romantic, and/or sexual attractions to men, women, or both sexes" (p. 1), and further indicates that different sexual orientations are normal forms of human bonding. The sexual orientation of the majority of the population is heterosexual or straight, which has become the norm against which everyone else is measured. In a famous study of the sexual behavior of thousands of white adults in the 1940s and 1950s, Alfred Kinsey reported that 10% of the males and 2% to 6% of the females were homosexual (The Kinsey Institute, 2011). More recent data indicate that almost 4% of the population identifies themselves as lesbian, gay, bisexual, or transgender (Keen, 2011).

Deeper Look 2.6
Read about educational and psychological inequities of LGBTQ students.

LGBTQ is a popular term used to identify lesbian, gay, bisexual, transgender, and queer or questioning individuals. *Gay* is sometimes used more generically to refer not only to gay men, but also to lesbians and bisexuals. The Q in LGBTQ refers to *queer*—a term used to negatively label gays and lesbians in the past, but that is now used by younger people as a political term that rejects assimilation into a heterosexual world. The Q can also mean *questioning,* to include individuals who are not sure of their sexual orientation (Savage & Harley, 2009). Transgender persons psychologically identify their gender as different from their biological sex. For example, a man may feel like he is a woman or vice versa. Transgendered persons may dress and act like the opposite sex. In some cases, they surgically change their genitals and other physical characteristic to become the opposite sex, which is the definition of a transvestite or transsexual. It is appropriate to address a transgender student as a member of the sex to which he or she identifies.

Many LGBTQ adults report feeling different from their siblings or peers early in life. By the time they reach puberty, most students begin to feel an attraction to the same, opposite, or both sexes. Most students struggle with their identity during middle and high school. However, LGBTQ students usually have a more difficult time, especially with their sexual identity. They may question their sexual feelings but are not sure if they are LGBTQ. If they show signs of being LGBTQ, even if they are not, they may be subjecting themselves to harassment or bullying by their classmates. During this period, they may feel isolated and not know to whom they can turn for information and support, especially when their family will not accept their sexual orientation. LGBTQ students comprise a disproportionate percentage of homeless students on the nation's streets.

Supporting LGBTQ Students

As pointed out in the media and by many celebrities over the past few years, many students who identify their sexuality as different than heterosexual are harassed by other students. "That's so gay" appears to be the most common term in the hallways of schools. It is used as a derogatory term against heterosexual students as well as a reference to students perceived to be lesbian, gay, bisexual, transgender, or queer. As Ms. Clarke points out, this name-calling begins in elementary schools. It becomes more prevalent as students move through school, but it appears to be most prevalent in middle schools. Teachers and other educators can play a very important role in eliminating such harassment and bullying in schools as well as educating students to respect all students.

Most LGBTQ students fear for their safety in schools (Kosciw, Greytak, Diza, & Bartkiewicz, 2010). If gays and lesbians openly acknowledge their sexual orientation or appear to be LGBTQ, they are likely to be harassed and face reprisals from peers and, sometimes, school officials. Structures within the schools do not always provide the same kind of support to LGBTQ students that is available to other students.

Audio Link 2.2
Listen to accounts of LGBTQ students.

LGBTQ students feel more comfortable and safer in schools when faculty and staff are supportive, LGBTQ people are portrayed in the curriculum, gay–straight alliances or similar clubs exist, and a comprehensive policy on harassment is enforced (Kosciw et al., 2010). You may know little about this group and have had few or no contacts with LGBTQ people who are "out," or open, about their sexual orientation. Without a better understanding of sexual orientation, you may find it difficult to work effectively with LGBTQ students or the children of gay and lesbian parents. However, you always have the responsibility to provide a safe environment for students, which includes intervening when students are harassing their peers because of their sexual orientation, gender identification, sex, or other factors.

WHAT DO THE RELIGIOUS BELIEFS OF STUDENTS HAVE TO DO WITH SCHOOLS?

Asked how she handles religious diversity in her classroom during the holidays at the end of the year, Ms. Clarke replied:

> In eight years I have had only one student that celebrated Kwanzaa. I have books and stories about the holidays and how different families celebrate them. My goal is to expose the children to a variety of ways the season is celebrated. We usually do art projects around Hanukkah, Kwanzaa, and Christmas. Last year we took a field trip to the nearby Publik Playhouse to see *A Season of Miracles* so that my students could experience the stories of Christian, Jewish, and Kwanzaa celebrations.

Religion has a great influence on the values and lifestyles of families and plays an important role in the socialization of children and young people. Religious doctrines and practices guide how and when one worships, but they also guide beliefs about many aspects of daily life, including the roles of men and women, birth control, child rearing, friendships, and political attitudes. Most religions in the United States also promote patriotism, often displaying the American flag in their places of worship. A religious doctrine can also dictate a family's expectations for teachers and schools. When the religious perspectives and school expectations differ, numerous challenges arise for educators.

Religious Diversity

The United States has historically had strong Judeo-Christian roots. Some Christians believe that God led the European founders to establish this country as a Christian nation. With the increase of immigrants from Asia and the Middle East since the 1960s, other religious traditions have been introduced. Mosques and temples have been built in communities that were formerly all Christian. Most urban and suburban areas are home to numerous religious groups and beliefs. Metropolitan areas may have a number of megachurches with thousands of members and their own schools.

Approximately three in four Americans identify themselves as Christian (U.S. Census Bureau, 2011). Protestants have long dominated the U.S. population, currently representing half of the population (U.S. Census Bureau, 2011). Catholicism grew greatly over the past century as Southern and Eastern Europeans immigrated to the United States, now comprising one-fourth of the population (U.S. Census Bureau, 2011). Within all of these religious groups are liberal, moderate, and conservative or fundamentalist sects. The fundamentalist groups believe that their holy documents (for example, the Bible, Qur'an, and Torah) are the actual word of their God that must be followed to the letter of the law. Liberal religions, on the other hand, accept the validity of diverse perspectives that have evolved from different historical experiences. Two in five people describe themselves as **born-again** or **evangelical** (Gallup, 2011); they are also sometimes referred to as *fundamentalists* or the religious right. Some people do not participate in any organized religion, some declaring themselves as **atheist** or **agnostic**. The religious affiliations of the U.S. population are shown in Figure 2.6.

The families of students practice many different religions, including Islam. Educators should be sure that their practices do not discriminate against students whose families practice a religion with which they are not familiar.

Although Jews, Protestants, and Catholics once were expected to marry only members of their faith, marriage across those three groups is fairly common today. Time will tell whether the borders against intermarriage with members of nonwestern religious groups will also be permeable. Some religious groups such as the Amish and Hutterites continue to seek group cohesiveness by establishing their own communities and schools.

Addressing Religion in Public Schools

If you teach in an urban or metropolitan area, you can expect to have students from a number of different religious groups. Even smaller midwestern and western towns have had an influx of Asian, African, or Middle Eastern immigrants who are bringing their cultural version of Christianity, Islam, Hinduism, and Buddhism to communities that previously had only a few different Christian denominations.

Accommodations will be needed in schools to respect the religious diversity in the community. Christian holidays are already acknowledged through school holidays and the singing of Christian songs at some school convocations. Jewish students will not attend school during Rosh Hashanah and Yom Kippur. Islamic students will fast during the month of Ramadan and are expected to have daily prayers. Policies that prevent the wearing of a hijab or yarmulke discriminate against Muslim women and Jewish men. School officials should involve the parents of their religious communities in providing professional development about their religious traditions and

Figure 2.6 Religious Preference Among Americans

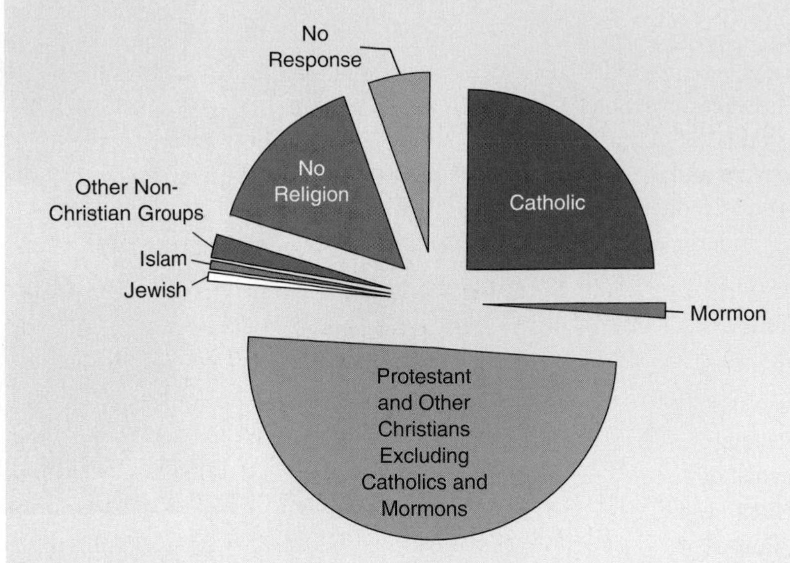

Source: U.S. Census Bureau. (2011). *Statistical abstract of the United States: 2012* (131st ed.). Washington, DC: Author.

cultures for educators and providing advice for guaranteeing that the civil rights of their children are not violated.

Religion is very important to some families and of little or no importance to others. Some communities' religion plays a major role in the lives of families, requiring attendance not only on Saturday or Sunday, but at services and activities throughout the week. Religious stories reinforce the values of the religion in Sunday school, bible classes, and other organized religious education programs. Parents in these communities may expect schools to reflect those same values, sometimes enrolling their children in private Catholic, Jewish, Islamic, or Christian schools that reinforce their values and teach their religious doctrine. They may decide to homeschool their children to ensure they are not exposed to values they disapprove of such as lack of respect for teachers, swearing by students, lack of discipline, and exposure to multiple perspectives.

Students whose religious beliefs differ from the majority in the community may be ostracized in school and social settings. Jews, atheists, Jehovah's Witnesses, Pentecostals, Muslims, and Sikhs are among the groups whose members are sometimes shunned and suffer discrimination. Educators must be careful that their own religious beliefs do not interfere with their ability to provide equal educational opportunities to students whose families are members of other religious groups.

CONNECTING TO THE CLASSROOM

This chapter has introduced you to the students who will be in your classrooms of the future. We have examined the diversity of their group memberships based on ethnicity, race, socioeconomic level, language, and religion. Below are some key principles for applying the information in this chapter to the classroom.

1. The curriculum and instructional strategies should be relevant to the lives of students, drawing on their ethnic and racial backgrounds and experiences to help them learn.
2. Teachers should have high academic expectations for all of their students.
3. Schools must provide language programs for English-language learners to assist them in becoming academically competent.
4. Girls and boys can be taught to develop the skills and behaviors that are usually attributed to the other sex.
5. Teachers should intervene when LGBTQ and other students are being bullied.
6. Teachers should be aware of the religious groups to which their students belong to make appropriate accommodations.

SUMMARY

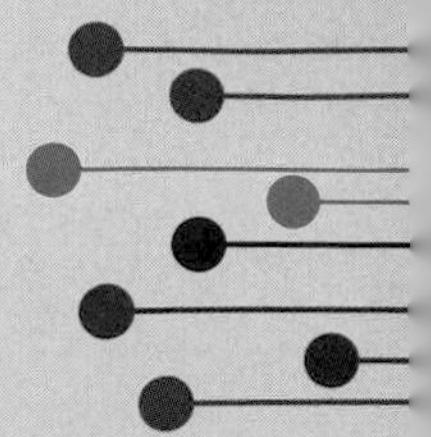

This chapter has explored the diversity of students who will be in your future classroom. The six major topics were addressed:

- Students come to your classroom with racial and ethnic heritages that can influence the many ways that they will respond to you and the lessons you create.
- Students' families experience very different levels of affluence that can affect their capacity to access resources needed to be successful within a specific school context.
- In some large cities in the United States more than 100 different languages are spoken.
- Attitudes about gender roles and responsibilities run deep in society, and teachers must constantly be careful not to reinforce stereotypes that might inhibit a student's chance of reaching his or her highest potential.
- Students whose sexual orientation is not heterosexual are often victims of bullying and do not feel supported in the school environment.
- Christianity has historically been valued in school, but today's student population is becoming increasingly religiously diverse, which impacts the curriculum and requires a climate that is supportive of students of all faiths.

CLASS DISCUSSION QUESTIONS

1. The curriculum of many schools privileges European American culture and history. How could a teacher ensure that the cultures and histories of other students in their classrooms are incorporated into the curriculum? Why should all students know about the cultures and histories of groups other than their own?
2. Over half of K–12 students are eligible for free or reduced-price lunch, indicating that their families have inadequate incomes. What impact does poverty have on the education of students? Should schools be charged with ensuring that the children of low-income families achieve at the same level as middle-class students? Why or why not?
3. More than one in five students have one or more foreign-born parents, many who speak a language other than English at home. Schools generally use bilingual education or English as a second language to help students learn English. Which strategy do you think more effectively serves the need of students and families? Which strategy is more cost-effective for school districts?
4. Boys are not completing high school and college at the same rates as girls. What are the reasons for this unequal participation in education? What could schools do to increase the participation of male students?
5. Many LGBTQ students feel very isolated in schools because teachers, students, and counselors do not understand them and provide little or no support for them. What should be the role of a teacher and other school professionals in supporting the psychological and emotional development of LGBTQ students?
6. Religion can influence what families think should be taught in schools. In some religious communities evolution and sexuality are taboo topics. How will you know how important a role religious groups have in the community in which you are teaching?

KEY TERMS

Achievement gap 42
Afrocentric curriculum 45
Adequate yearly progress (AYP) 43
Agnostic 59
Annual measurable objective (AMO) 43
Assimilation 57
Atheist 59
Born-again 59
Civil rights 60
Color blindness 42

Confidence interval 43
Cultural capital 48
Culture 37
Disability 38
Equity 63
Ethnic studies 44
Ethnicity 38
Ethnocentric curriculum 45
Evangelical 59
Gender 38
Heterosexism 57
Indigenous 39
LGBTQ 57
McKinney–Vento Homeless Assistance Act 47
Pan-ethnic 39
Race 38
Racism 39
Refugees 40
Self-fulfilling prophecy 48
Sexual orientation 38
Socialization 54
Socioeconomic status (SES) 37
Stereotype 42
Tracking 43

SELF-ASSESSMENT

WHAT IS YOUR CURRENT LEVEL OF UNDERSTANDING TODAY'S STUDENTS?

One of the indicators of understanding is to examine how complex your thinking is when asked questions that require you to use the concepts and facts introduced in this chapter.

Answer the following questions as fully as you can. Then use the Complexity of Thinking rubric to self-assess the degree to which you understand and can use the ideas presented in this chapter.

1. How can you bring the cultures of your students into the classroom?
2. What impact does the socioeconomic status of students' families have on teachers' expectations for the academic performance of students?
3. What is the teacher's responsibility for teaching students who are not authorized to be in the country?
4. How can boys and girls be damaged with education that focuses on the stereotypical roles of females and males?
5. What can teachers do to help eliminate the bullying of LGBTQ students?
6. What are some ways in which the religious diversity of a community can impact a school?

Complexity of Thinking Rubric

	Parts & Pieces	Unidimensional	Organized	Integrated	Extensions
Indicators	Elements/concepts are talked about as isolated and independent entities.	One or a few concepts are addressed, while others are underdeveloped.	Deliberate and structured consideration of all key concepts/elements.	All key concepts/elements are included in a view that addresses interconnections.	Integration of all elements and dimensions with extrapolation to new situations.
Relationships between the diversity of students and teaching and learning	Identifies the types of student diversity that exist without being able to explain the relationships to teaching and learning.	Describes a few of the impacts that diversity has on teaching and learning.	Provides examples of how student diversity can influence teaching and learning across cultural groups.	Analyzes the role of the teacher in using student diversity effectively to help students learn.	Explains how teachers can adjust their teaching to use student diversity positively to improve learning across cultural groups and develops a plan for increasing his/her knowledge about cultural groups with which he/she has limited knowledge.

STUDENT STUDY SITE

Visit the Student Study Site at www.sagepub.com/hall to access links to the videos, audio clips, and Deeper Look reference materials noted in this chapter, as well as additional study tools including eFlashcards, web quizzes, and more.

Field Guide

for Learning More About Today's Students

To further increase your understanding about today's students, do one or more of the following activities.

Ask a Teacher or Principal

Ask one or more of the teachers in the schools you are observing how they adapt their instruction to serve students from different ethnic, racial, socioeconomic, and language groups. What are their greatest concerns about providing **equity** across groups? What do they suggest that you do to prepare to work in a school with diverse student populations?

Make Your Own Observations

When visiting a school with English-language learners, observe two different classrooms. What are the home languages of the students in the two classrooms? What is the level of the ELLs' English proficiency? What ELL program is being used for instruction in the two classrooms that you observed? Ask the teachers why they are using this approach. Why has the school or school district decided on the approach that you have observed?

Reflect Through Journaling

This chapter indicates that some students are being better served by some schools than others as measured by achievement on the standardized tests required by No Child Left Behind. In your journal, write why you think students from low-income families do not perform as well on these tests. What difference do you think teachers can make in increasing the achievement of students from low-income families on standardized tests?

Build Your Portfolio

The degree of diversity at a school differs greatly across the country. Choose a school in the community in which your university is located or in which you grew up and describe the cultural makeup of the community and student population in the school, including their racial, ethnic, socioeconomic, religious, and language backgrounds.

Schools or school districts should have policies on the provision of safety for students. Review these policies in two school districts and determine what students are included in the policies. Identify how the policies incorporate LGBTQ students.

Read a Book

For advice from teachers that you may find helpful in your first years of teaching for equity, read *The New Teacher Book: Finding Purpose, Balance, and Hope During Your First Years in the Classroom,* by Rethinking Schools (2010).

For more information on the roles race and culture play in schools and on improving achievement outcomes for students of color, see *Why Race and Culture Matter in Schools: Closing the Achievement Gap in America's Classrooms,* by Tyrone C. Howard (2010; New York, NY: Teachers College Press).

To learn more about Islamic culture, religion, knowledge, and people to prepare you for working with Muslim students and families, read *Teaching Against Islamophobia,* by Joe L. Klincheloe, Shirley R. Steinberg, and Christopher D. Stonebanks (2010; New York, NY: Peter Lang).

Search the Web

To help you think about the issues raised in this chapter and read how teachers are addressing them in their classrooms, visit the website of Rethinking Schools (http://www.rethinkingschools.org/index.shtml).

For assistance on educational strategies for English-language learners, visit the website of the Center for Applied Linguistics (**http://www.cal.org/**).

To learn more about incorporating diversity into the curriculum and developing a classroom climate that supports students from diverse groups, go to **http://www.splcenter.org/what-we-do/teaching-tolerance**, which includes *Teaching Tolerance*, a magazine with ideas for addressing the issues discussed in this chapter.

TEACHER INTERVIEW

Brandy Donald

Brandy Donald is in her second year of teaching at Vista Heights Middle School in Saratoga Springs, Utah. She teaches seventh-grade Utah history, including a gifted section. She also is teaching a class called Student Success.

CHAPTER 3 Addressing Learners' Individual Needs

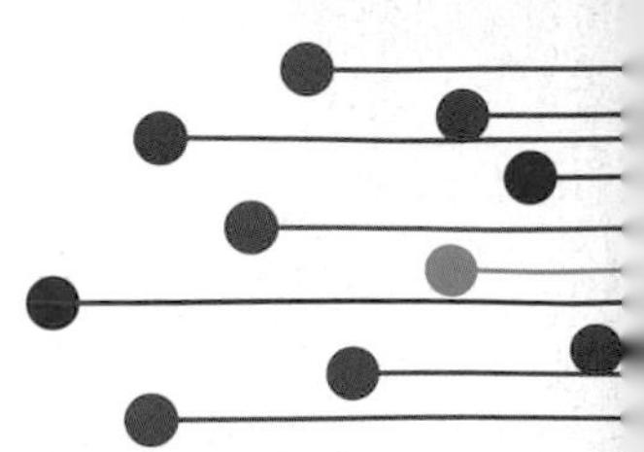

- *What is the Student Success class about?*

In Student Success we are catering to the needs of seventh-grade students. There is a huge jump from elementary school where you have one teacher who knows you and then you come to seventh grade where you have to keep track of eight different teachers and keep everything organized. This last summer two other teachers and I collaborated with the Counseling Department to develop this class. We talk about everything from using a planner, to time management, to testing strategies in different classes. It's really been an awesome course!

As a second-year teacher, how did it come about that you are teaching a gifted class? Typically this assignment is reserved for the most senior teachers.

It was part of my interview. "If you want the job you will get the endorsement (in Gifted and Talented)." In my interview one of the biggest focuses was on how my teaching was related to differentiating. I really like to find ways for every student to be successful, whether they are at the top, or the bottom, or somewhere in between.

You are teaching a wide range of students; how do you differentiate your teaching?

In my instruction I differentiate *process* in terms of how I deliver the lesson and how I deliver the information. Maybe by looking at different styles for presenting the information, and I vary it within my class. My hope is that it will connect with one student—that they are going to find some way to really tap into our curriculum and the content by my way of presenting it.

I like to differentiate *product,* whether it is an in-class assignment, or through an assessment, so that they can show me what they have learned. I want my students to have an understanding of how history makes a difference in the grand scheme of things. This is hard for seventh graders. So I like to make my assessments very authentic. They tend to be more project based than the more typical paper/pencil test.

How do you think about each student being different, or in what ways do you see each student being exceptional?

Across my classes I have both ends of the spectrum. I think each student comes with a unique set of skills and experiences and things to offer. When I teach, I really want to connect with that. If I just teach to the middle, I am missing a whole lot that is within each student. For example, in my 260 students this year I have 42 with IEPs. They have different skills within their

> **Questions to Consider**
>
> 1. In what ways do you see Mrs. Donald as seeing each student as being exceptional?
> 2. What tips did you pick up about how to teach to all the students in a class?
> 3. Based on Mrs. Donald's job interview experience, what did she say that could help you in preparing for your first interview?
> 4. Mrs. Donald is striving to have a balance between being a teacher and having a life outside of school. At this time, how good are you at doing this?

IEPs. My job is to find ways to include them in what's going on in class and for them to be an active part, rather than excusing them from parts is important.

What brings you joy in teaching?

I am always waiting for the moment when students make a connection to something in their own life. You know, history is interesting. There are a lot of great stories, but my philosophy in teaching history is that I want to make it matter to my students. When I see students making the connections, that is what makes me happy. Also, you see so many kids that just hate school. I think it really takes making that personal connection with whatever you are doing in class to make them enjoy the class.

What advice do you have for future teachers?

There are going to be moments when you are stressed out. Moments when you are challenged, or you are not quite sure how to handle something. Moments when you might think "Why am I doing this?" or "Why did I sign up for this job?" You have to go back to that place when you had thought in your head you wanted to become a teacher. Remember what motivated you to pursue this path in the first place.

Second, I think it is important that you become involved in your teaching, but you still need to be a well-rounded person. I am still a new teacher, but I tell first-year teachers to try not to take work home every night. In the end you can burn out. You will not be an effective teacher if there is not a place where you are a person outside of being a teacher. For example, I am a runner. I run half marathons. I don't place, I just do it for fun.

Learning Outcomes

After reading this chapter, you should be able to

1. Describe how students with different levels of understanding and skills, including those with disabilities, are identified and supported.
2. Describe at least four ways to view students in terms of their academic ability.
3. Understand different ways that students develop and implications for their learning.
4. Identify and provide examples of ways that family background and culture make each student exceptional.
5. Name the strengths and weaknesses of the more typical categories that are used to label students.

INTRODUCTION

What were your thoughts when you first read the title of this chapter? Did you think something like "Yeah, sure, another simplistic education slogan"? Or, in some way, did you think something like "Well, I suppose in some way(s) each student can be thought of as being exceptional." Thinking about student learning in terms of how each student is exceptional is essential to becoming an exceptional educator. As Mrs. Donald reflected in her interview, exceptional educators use their insights into how each student learns to continuously adapt instruction, thereby increasing the learning of all students. Note also that she finds joy in seeing her students make connections between what she is teaching and their lives. As you will discover toward the middle of this chapter, she also sees the humor in the antics of middle school students.

In this chapter we will introduce a variety of ways to view each student as being exceptional. Some of these ways come from research, some are based in laws, others are based on characteristics of students, and a few will be drawn from interesting ideas about how to best facilitate all students learning. Keep in mind that these really will be "introductions." Later on in your teacher education program and as your career unfolds you will learn more about different ways of seeing each student as exceptional.

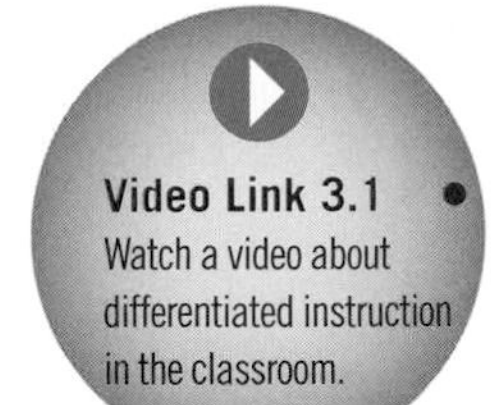

Video Link 3.1
Watch a video about differentiated instruction in the classroom.

The key objective for this chapter is to help you begin developing a repertoire of ways to see each student as unique. As you will hear often, teachers are supposed to **differentiate** instruction. This means customizing your teaching in ways that facilitate each of your student's learning. One important challenge for you will be determining the basis for differentiating. Will you only look at students' past grades? Will you consider their family backgrounds? Do you think that it makes a difference if the subject is reading, mathematics, or science? What about their performance in your class? Some students will grasp new ideas quickly and others will struggle. Which indicators will you emphasize as you come to see how each of your students is exceptional?

WHAT ARE KEY CHARACTERISTICS OF STUDENTS WITH DISABILITIES?

In my 260 students this year, I have 42 with IEPs in my general classes. Kinda of a lot to deal with. They have different skills within their IEPs. Finding ways to include them in what's going on in class and for them to be an active part of it, rather than excusing them from parts of it. I think that something that is best practice for IEP students is best practice for all students. So, I really try to teach with that in mind. I am not just making sure they get in, I am trying to make it the best for all students. There are students who learn in different ways. I think there are lots of ways they can get to the same results.—Mrs. Donald

Thirteen percent of the school population has an identified disability, which is defined as a long-lasting condition such as visual or hearing impairment or a condition that substantially limits basic physical, emotional, or mental activities (Aud et al., 2012). The nation's Individuals with Disabilities Education Act (IDEA), originally enacted by Congress in 1975 as the Education for All Handicapped Children Act, was established to make sure that children with disabilities had the opportunity to receive a free and appropriate public education. The law has been revised over the years, with the most recent amendments passed by Congress in December 2004. IDEA requires that students with disabilities be educated with regular students whenever possible and in as normal an environment as possible. IDEA guides how states and school districts provide special education and related services to 6.5 million eligible children between the ages of 3 and 21.

Students with disabilities will likely need accommodations at least some of the time.

All teachers are expected to implement the **individualized education plan (IEP)** for students with disabilities in their classrooms. The IEP is developed by parents, teachers, special educators, and other specialists such as a school psychologist or occupational therapist and indicates the accommodations and special services that must be provided to that student.

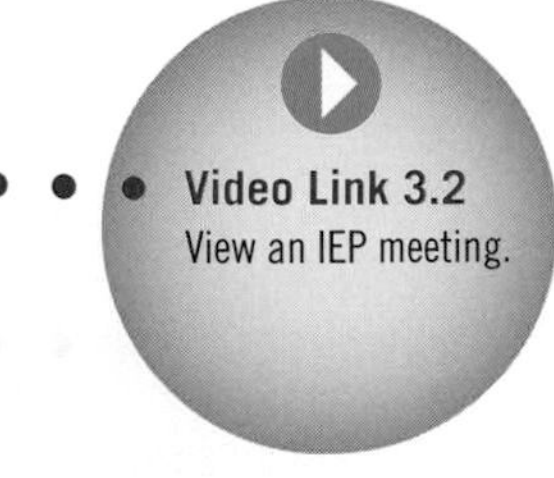

Providing services to these students usually involves a team of professionals and assistants, depending on the severity of the disability. The special educator may team teach a class with a regular teacher or serve as a resource teacher who works with students on the development of skills. Students with severe disabilities such as autism or physical conditions that require feeding tubes should be assigned a teaching or health assistant to help provide the necessary accommodations.

Established Disability Categories

School professionals categorize children with disabilities to determine the most appropriate services for students. Figure 3.1 shows the number of students being served for the different disabilities. Nearly two in five students receiving special education services have a specific learning disability, which makes it difficult for them to read, write, or compute. The number of students with speech impairments is nearly double the other categories. This section provides a very brief introduction to the categories with the largest number of students. You should take at least one course during your teacher preparation program to provide an overview of these disabilities and understand the accommodations necessary to help students with disabilities learn.

Figure 3.1 Percentage of Children and Youth Ages 3–21 Served Under the IDEA by Disability Type

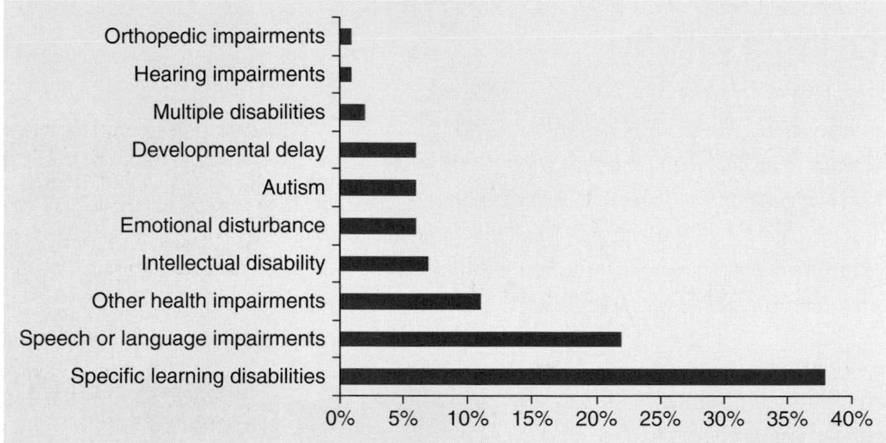

Source: Adapted from U.S. Department of Education, Office of Special Education Programs, Individuals with Disabilities Education Act (IDEA) database.

Learning Disabilities

Students with learning disabilities usually comprehend the material being studied, but it takes them more time or they need a different strategy. The problem is that they can't understand or use spoken or written language easily, which affects their ability to listen, think, speak, read, write, spell, or do mathematical calculations. These students are in regular classrooms with accommodations, which are purposeful additional supports or adjustments in instruction. Their IEP will specify the accommodation such as reading or writing for the student in testing situations. In mathematics, it could allow the student to use a calculator. Student work might be modified with fewer questions or a shorter reading assignment. Extra time may be required to complete an assignment or a computer used to write.

Speech Impairment

Speech impairment is a communication disorder. A student might stutter or be unable to produce certain words or sounds. Some students cannot process language (that is, they can hear directions but cannot repeat them), preventing them from following the teacher's directions for an assignment. Students may be able to comprehend at the same levels as other students, but they are not able to put their thoughts into words due to difficulties with word retrieval and recall. They may have trouble understanding directional prepositions such as *under* and *above*. These students should be receiving support from a speech pathologist. In the regular classroom, teachers will have to allow additional wait time for the student to process the question and to respond to it. Just because these students take extra time for processing or speaking does not mean that they do not comprehend and will not perform well academically.

Mental Retardation

Students with mental retardation have significant problems in intellectual functioning and in using socially appropriate behaviors for their age. The most severely affected of these students participate in life skills classes to prepare them to function independently as adults. The majority of these students are classified as mildly mentally retarded and spend most of their school time in regular classrooms. The IEPs for these students require work modified to skill level, more repetition of work, and shorter time periods for work with breaks built into their schedule.

Emotionally Disturbed

Students who are emotionally disturbed exhibit behaviors that impact on their ability to learn and cannot be explained by other intellectual, sensory, or health factors. They have trouble maintaining appropriate interpersonal relationships with their classmates and teachers. They may always be unhappy or depressed. They may develop physical symptoms and fears associated with personal or school problems. These behaviors may be diagnosed by professionals. The behaviors sometimes manifest themselves in outbursts in the classroom. They may indicate the need for therapy for abuse, family problems, or another traumatic incident that has affected their behavior. Students with severe behavior problems that interfere with their learning and the learning of their classmates may be removed from classrooms until they are stabilized.

Other Disabilities

As shown in Figure 3.1, the number of students in this category has tripled since 1991. This growth may be due to the greater move toward inclusion of all students with disabilities in regular classrooms. Another reason may be the increased knowledge and research that has led to increased diagnoses of many disabilities, especially attention deficit hyperactivity disorder (ADHD). This category includes students who are blind, are deaf, or have autism, ADHD, physical impairments, seizure disorders, or cerebral palsy. It also includes students who were crack babies, students with feeding tubes, and students with severe disabilities. The goal is for students to be a part of the regular classroom as much as possible. Students with the most severe disabilities may receive much of their instruction in a special education classroom, but join students without disabilities at lunch and during specials such as music, art, and physical education. The multiple disabilities included in this group are determined by medical evidence. They are not as subjective as the categories previously discussed.

Video Case 3.1

Addressing Learners' Individual Needs

1. Make a list of at least twenty different strategies these teachers identified for addressing all learners.
2. What are indicators of understanding these teachers look for in their students?
3. What can teachers learn from parents that will help their students learn?

Autism, a Spectrum

Rather than being a narrow set of factors that can be easily classified, the *autism* label represents a range of factors and variations in intensities that are referred to as a spectrum. Autism is a developmental disorder that appears in the first years of life. Parents may detect something when their two-year-old has difficulties with social interactions and/or with verbal and nonverbal communications. They may be slow to develop language and do not play with others. Autism is related to abnormal development of the brain. The causes are not understood at this time, although there are some indications of genetic factors being important. Although widely talked about, there is no research evidence that vaccines are a cause.

An early diagnosis is important, and treatment programs are intensive. If school-age children have atypical irritability or aggression, they may need to take a prescription drug. Teachers need to work closely with parents, and if the student is in a treatment program be sure to know about it and be sure to use complementary strategies in the classroom.

School Experiences for Students With Disabilities

Students with disabilities will be in your classroom. A critical factor in working with them effectively is to remember that they are more like regular students than unlike them. However, you are likely to have to make accommodations to promote their learning. Some will be challenged to learn quickly; others will have been formerly identified as having some type of disability. They will have a formal individualized education plan. Students with IEPs will more than likely have extra support such as an aide. There also will be a special education resource teacher with whom you will consult regularly.

The school should have special educators available to advise you on the implementation of students' IEPs. One of the problems is that most schools have not been designed for some of the needed accommodations. Whiteboards are too high and desks too low for students in wheelchairs; ramps are not always available. Computers, amplification devices, books in Braille, and other educational resources will provide students with disabilities the opportunity to learn at the same level as other students.

Inclusion

Inclusion is the integration of students with disabilities into the regular classroom. The goal is to have students with disabilities in regular education as much as possible with as much interaction with the regular teacher as possible. Students with disabilities and without disabilities are in the same class, but they do not always do the same work, depending on the nature and severity of the disability. Teaching and medical assistants may be assigned to work on skills development and accommodations with the students with disabilities in the classroom. Special educators may provide special services to the students at defined times during the school day.

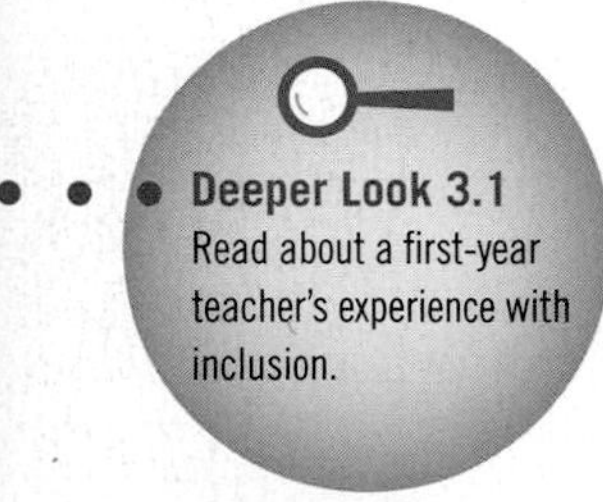

Deeper Look 3.1
Read about a first-year teacher's experience with inclusion.

Ninety-five percent of school-age students with disabilities are enrolled in regular schools (Aud et al., 2012). In full inclusion, students with disabilities and other special needs receive all of their education in the regular classroom; they are never found in segregated settings with only other students with disabilities. In reality, three in five students with disabilities spend most of their school days in regular classrooms (Aud et al., 2012), receiving special instruction or services from special educators, a speech-language pathologist, a school nurse, or a school psychologist. Students who are most likely to be placed in segregated classes are students with intellectual disabilities and students with multiple disabilities (Aud et al., 2012).

Audio Link 3.1
Learn more about inclusion in schools.

However, students should not be pulled out of the regular classroom during language arts and mathematics lessons. For example, if students are pulled out during reading instruction to be tutored in reading, they are not getting more reading instruction. Instead they are receiving alternate reading instruction. Because music, art, and physical education classes also provide the opportunity to develop social skills with students without disabilities, students with disabilities are almost always integrated into these classes. In the process of inclusion, students without disabilities become more tolerant of their peers who are disabled and learn to appreciate diversity and be more responsive to others' needs (Lipsky & Gartner, 1996).

Parental Involvement

Parents of students with disabilities must be involved with school personnel in the process of determining the best treatment for their children. Classroom teachers need to work closely with all the parents. In a survey of parents of special education students, parents indicated that their children were in regular classrooms most of the day. They strongly believed that their children were best served by being in a regular classroom to develop academic and social skills rather than being segregated with other students with disabilities. Parents believe that the social stigma attached to special education is declining. However, they do feel that parents of students without disabilities resent the special services and attention their children receive (Johnson, Duffett, Farkas, & Wilson, 2002).

Audio Link 3.2
Hear about parental involvement in schools.

Disproportionate Placement

There are continuing concerns that there may be overidentification of students with disabilities that is based in the students' ethnicity or family background. For example, students receiving special education services are disproportionately male, African American, Latino, American Indian, English-language learners, or whites from low-income families. Twelve percent of students in special education are African American as compared with 5% who are Asian American (National Center for Education Statistics [NCES], 2010). White and Asian American students are overrepresented in gifted classes. Educators should monitor their consideration of making referrals of students to be tested for placement in these classes to be sure that there is a clear learning need and that there is not an underlying bias of some sort.

WHAT ARE SOME WAYS OF DISTINGUISHING STUDENTS IN TERMS OF ACADEMIC ABILITY?

Obviously, students can be differentiated based on academics, advanced or not. There are some other ways, for example I think students can be exceptional socially. Some kids know how to interact with adults. They are great with other kids, and really get along with others. They tend to do well on my group projects. I don't know if this is recognized at school a lot. Typically, they are expected to sit down, be good and listen.—Mrs. Donald

For better or worse, most teachers probably first think about students being exceptional in terms of their "intelligence." They may think of some students as being "smarter" than others. This really is too simplistic a view. Think about your own academic ability and that of some of your classmates. Some will be better with language arts while others will be better with math or science. Each has strengths in terms of learning certain subjects. There will likely be some other areas where learning is more difficult. Simplistically these differences can be talked about in terms of intelligence. However, as we describe next, the meaning of intelligence is more complicated.

Sometimes an effective strategy for increasing learning is to group students with similar interests and assign them a special project.

Intelligence as a Basic Ability

In the past there was a tendency to see intelligence as a single score on a special test. For example, when the authors of this textbook were in school we had to take an **intelligence quotient (IQ) test**, which was the dominant way of determining a student's ability to learn. Neither we nor our parents were likely to be informed of the results, but schools would group students based on the score. We and our parents would speculate about our IQ score based on what we thought of the other students in the same class. Today scholars and teachers have in mind several different meanings of intelligence. It can refer to how easy it is for particular students to learn new material. Or it could refer to how much a student knows. Other aspects of intelligence could refer to creativity and problem solving, or one's ability to be reflective about his or her learning.

Intelligence as One Ability

Video Link 3.3
Learn more about the IQ test.

Over the years psychologists have examined intelligence in many ways and in relation to many types of tasks. Those who view intelligence as a single ability refer to it as general intelligence. This ability entails information processing and would be used with all types of cognitive tasks. However, for any particular tasks there will likely be specific abilities such as language development, memory, and auditory perception. Measuring general intelligence as it relates to learning in school is done with standardized tests.

The story of how these tests became a part of our system of education dates back to the early 1900s. The Minister of Public Instruction in Paris wanted to determine a way to identify students early on who would need extra help in their schooling. The result was Alfred Binet developing a battery of tests for students between the ages of 3 and 13. The scores for any student taking these tests could then be compared with how well other students of the same age had done.

The label of IQ or intelligence quotient was added when the tests were revised at Stanford University and became known as the Stanford–Binet Intelligence Scales. IQ then became a comparison of a student's score with that of their age-group, multiplied by 100. Interestingly, in its original forms this test was administered orally, rather than by having students read and write. In general, a higher IQ score does correlate with higher achievement in school. Contrary to what you might think, when the number of years of education and IQ scores are compared with accomplishments as an adult the correlations are not very high. Other abilities can play a major part in success in the real world.

Multiple Intelligences

As you can quickly see, the construct of intelligence is more complicated than will be of use to teachers. More than 70 specific abilities have been identified by research psychologists. For teachers, a more useful approach is the Multiple Intelligences (MI) theory of Howard Gardner (Table 3.1). Gardner has theorized that there are seven abilities. Each person will have strengths with some abilities and weaknesses with others (Gardner, 2005).

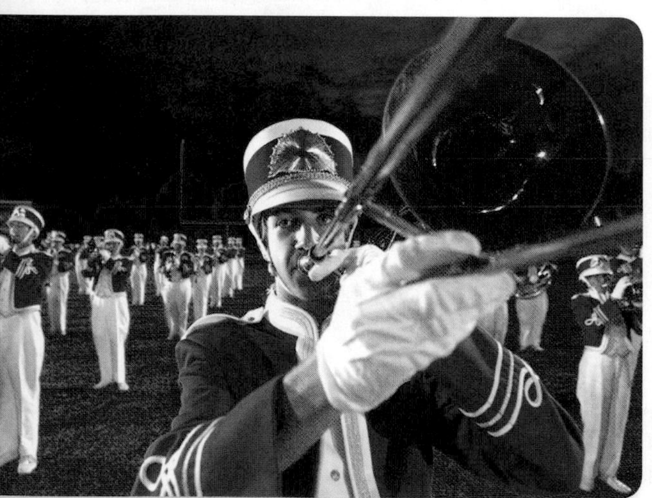

Musical ability is one of Gardner's Multiple Intelligences that teachers can use to increase student learning.

Gardner's theory has not been accepted widely by psychologists. However, teachers see the seven intelligences providing a useful framework for seeing each student as exceptional in one or more ways. Students will vary in the degree of ability they have in each of the seven areas. Just as Mrs. Donald pointed out in the interview for this chapter, students will not be equally successful in learning if only one, or two, types of instructional strategies are used.

A good beginning point is to be sensitive to the possibilities of each student being more ready to learn with particular ones of the Multiple Intelligences. As Mrs. Donald observed, when she has a class with more "bodily-kinesthetic" students she needs to make sure to use instruction and assessment strategies that "get them up and moving around."

Table 3.1 Howard Gardner's Theory of Multiple Intelligences

Linguistic intelligence involves sensitivity to spoken and written language, the ability to learn languages, and the capacity to use language to accomplish certain goals.
Logical-mathematical intelligence consists of the capacity to analyze problems logically, carry out mathematical operations, and investigate issues scientifically.
Spatial intelligence involves the potential to recognize and use the patterns of wide space and more confined areas.
Bodily-kinesthetic intelligence entails the potential of using one's whole body or parts of the body to solve problems. It is the ability to use mental abilities to coordinate bodily movements.
Musical intelligence involves skill in the performance, composition, and appreciation of musical patterns.
Interpersonal intelligence is concerned with the capacity to understand the intentions, motivations, and desires of other people. It allows people to work effectively with others.
Intrapersonal intelligence entails the capacity to understand oneself, to appreciate one's feelings, fears, and motivations.

Source: Gardner, H. (2011). *Frames of mind: The theory of multiple intelligences.* New York, NY: Basic Books. Copyright © 1993 Howard Gardner. Reprinted with permission of Basic Books, a member of the Perseus Books Group.

There are several simple-to-use tests of MI that can be found easily on the Internet. Several of these are free for you to use, as long as you are not copying them for publication. You will immediately see the logic behind each test question, for example, asking whether you have music going on in your head, or if you like to be physically active. Two words of caution in regard to these tests: There is little research evidence to support their validity, and the responses are simple ratings along a continuum, from low to high. In your teaching, you can more accurately check your students' intelligences through interviewing and observing them at work and play.

Deeper Look 3.2
Read more about Multiple Intelligences.

Implications of Academic Abilities for Teaching and Learning

Most assuredly intelligence and academic ability are important factors for teachers to consider. Just be sure not to think about intelligence as one simple idea or score on a test. In terms of Gardner's Multiple Intelligences, each of your students will have a different profile. Many will be excellent at speaking and writing (Linguistic Intelligence), some will be good at understanding mathematics and science (Logical-Mathematical), and others will be fully engaged with music (Musical). Your challenge will be to devise instructional approaches that take advantage of this rich diversity of exceptional students. Do not teach as your authors regularly find teachers doing: students seated in a block, the teacher standing and talking at the front, short teacher questions followed by right or wrong student answers, and students then completing desk assignments. This might be all right once in awhile. Unfortunately, we see too many teachers doing only this approach and doing it the same way every day. Exceptional students should have exceptional teachers.

UNDERSTANDING AND USING EVIDENCE

Using Multiple Intelligences to Develop an Instructional Match

Although there are criticisms of Howard Gardner's Multiple Intelligences Model, it provides a way of thinking about the importance of teachers matching their instructional approach to the different ways that students learn. There are several free questionnaires on the web that can be used with students to determine which of the MI they would appear to prefer.

Learning Styles of Students in One Class

Part I:
Study the data presented in Table A with this question in mind:

1. What do you see as the overall distribution of students in terms of their learning styles?

Table A Distribution of Student Multiple Intelligences (1 Being Low and 5 Being High)

Student	Linguistic	Logical-Mathematical	Visual-Spatial	Bodily-Kinesthetic	Musical	Interpersonal	Intrapersonal
Anne	4	5	3	3	4	2	1
Bill	5	4	2	4	5	4	4
Charlie	1	3	4	4	4	5	4
Elizabeth	2	3	1	3	3	3	4
Fran	2	3	2	5	2	3	4
Juan	2	2	3	5	4	5	4
Maria	3	4	1	3	5	4	4
Roberta	2	4	3	2	4	3	2

Do not read further until you have developed your answer to the question.

DO ALL STUDENTS DEVELOP IN THE SAME WAY?

Teaching middle school is really funny. I find myself laughing constantly—such a contrast from teaching high school. There are times when middle school students are just goofy! They don't get what is going on. They fall out of their chairs. I don't know how teachers could stay in middle school if they didn't see the humor.—Mrs. Donald

In her interview, Mrs. Donald described some of the behaviors that she sees being characteristic of middle school students. High school teachers and teachers of elementary school will offer different

Part II: Read after you have developed your analysis of the MI distribution in Table A

One way to summarize the student information is to count how many of the students had high and low scores for each intelligence. For example, in Table B there is a count of how many students scored high (4 or 5) and how many students scored low (1 or 2) on each intelligence.

Table B High and Low MI Scores for Students in One Class

Number	Linguistic	Logical-Mathematical	Visual-Spatial	Bodily-Kinesthetic	Musical	Interpersonal	Intrapersonal
High	5	1	4	1	1	1	2
Low	2	4	1	4	6	4	6

Matching Instruction to MI

The underlying importance of using the Multiple Intelligences Model is to have teachers think more carefully about the extent to which their instructional strategies match up with their students' learning styles. When there is a match there should be greater learning. Now that you have studied the students in Table A, consider the following questions.

2. In developing several weeks of instruction, which styles would you want to strive to match more and which less?
3. What would be characteristics in the design of your instructional strategies to have a greater match?

Do not read further until you have developed your answer to these questions.

Matching Instruction to MI Scores

One place to start your lesson planning would be to look for those intelligences where the students scored lowest. Of the eight students, six scored lowest on Musical and Intrapersonal, which would strongly suggest that matching instruction to these intelligences would be less likely to be successful.

Five students scored highest on Linguistic and four scored highest on Visual-Spatial. Having lessons that are based in reading, writing, and talking would match up. In this case, having students active and moving around would seem to be less important.

Another important consideration is the subject being taught. These students would be ready for language arts and English classes. However, if these students were in a math class there would likely be difficulties since only one indicated that she was "logical mathematical." It would be very important to take advantage of the higher scores on Visual-Spatial by using many manipulates, charts, diagrams, and pictures.

This discussion is only meant to be illustrative. In your teaching it will be important to be aware not only of how your students score in terms of intelligences, but of how you score. For example, for the students presented here, if you are predominantly Logical-Mathematical you would need to be careful not to have your main approach to instruction always be based in this intelligence.

descriptions of how they see students at their level of schooling. Each of these stereotypes will emphasize certain characteristics. However, as with all generalizations, you need to be careful with applying them to individual students. At the same time, to what extent do you think that these descriptions of "typical" students are valid? What these descriptions reflect is a developmental model of how children grow and how they learn (Hart & Risley, 1995). In other words, there are predictable phases and stages to child development that represent another way to see each student as exceptional.

Stages of Cognitive Development

In your psychology courses you will have studied different models and theories about how thinking develops as children grow up. Probably the model that you will be most familiar with is that of Jean Piaget. In his model the way children think changes in major ways as they develop from infancy through adolescence. Two of his main ideas are important to consider here: maturation and activity.

Maturation

According to Piaget, the way that thinking changes as a child grows older is genetically programmed. Parents and teachers cannot have much affect on this programming. Providing safety and keeping children healthy are important supports, but basically how children think will develop at the pace that their biology sets.

Activity

Deeper Look 3.3
Read more about the Cognitive Stages of Development.

Children learn by interacting with their environment. Infants, for example, will be limited in their ability to interact due to not having developed muscular control and having limited eyesight. As their neuromuscular system develops, their interactions with their environment become more dynamic and their thinking changes as a result.

As you should recall from your psychology courses, Piaget identifies four stages of cognitive development: sensorimotor, preoperational, concrete operational, and formal operational. Within each stage, the way in which children reason and think is different. It is important to keep in mind that Piaget sees that all children will go through these four stages in sequence. They will not skip a stage. Also, there are age ranges associated with each stage.

Sensorimotor Stage (0–2 years)

This is the stage where infants rely on their basic senses to learn. Seeing, hearing, touching, tasting, and smelling are the main sources of information. At the earliest part of this stage infants only think of objects as existing when the object is present. Later on in this stage children are able to purposefully interact with objects in their environment. These are physical interactions. In other words, they can "reach out and touch something."

Preoperational Stage (2–7 years)

Being able to recall what happened in the past, keeping track of information, and planning for the future are important parts of thinking. These skills have to be learned. These are mental processes, not physical ones. Developing the ability to use words and gestures is part of the preoperational stage. Using words that represent objects happens in this stage. The tendency is to focus on one element only, such as height and not width. At this stage children's thinking is mainly self-centered, often holding the assumption that others feel as they do.

Concrete Operational Stage (7–11 years)

The indicators of students at this stage include their coming to understand that changing the shape of a material still keeps the material the same. They also understand that such changes can be reversed. Another aspect of student thinking at this stage is the ability to classify such as placing cities within states, and states within countries. Further, they can see different ways to classify objects such as by shape or color.

Formal Operational Stage (11 years to adult)

At this stage students continue to have all of the ways of thinking that they developed during the earlier stages. Now they can imagine what might happen. They can do deductive reasoning;

"If college graduates make more money then I should go to college." They can think inductively, such as constructing generalizations: "The kids in theater and band are doing things besides going to subject classes." At this stage they can do "thought experiments." They can imagine what an experiment would entail and what would happen if it were conducted.

Human Brain Development

There are other developmental models that we could consider. A useful contrast is to turn to the findings from neuroscience research. Not that long ago this area of research had little that teachers could apply. Now, the topic of brain development has significant implications for thinking about teaching. This field of research represents another way to think about teaching and learning. The findings from neuroscience research also represent new ways to see each child as exceptional.

The basic metaphor in neuroscience for talking about thinking and learning is called brain architecture. At its simplest, we are talking about how the brain is "wired." It turns out that brain architecture is not just a matter of genetics. Researchers have established that characteristics of developing brain architecture in young children are heavily shaped through interactions with the environment and personal experiences.

Another basic finding from the studies is that there are certain developmental stages or "sensitive periods" where certain experiences have specific effects on how the brain develops. With infants, for example, basic sensory, social, and emotional experiences are necessary. Further, at each sensitive period development of different parts of the brain are more affected. As stated by the National Scientific Council on the Developing Child, "That is to say, the quality of a child's early environment and the availability of appropriate experiences at the right stages of development are crucial in determining the strength or weaknesses of the brain's architecture, which, in turn determines how well he or she will be able to think and to regulate emotions" (National Scientific Council on the Developing Child, 2007).

Different Neural Circuits Develop at Different Ages

Brain architecture is composed of neural circuits. Interestingly, these circuits are organized in hierarchies. In other words, some neural circuits have to be in place before others can develop. Also, the circuits within each hierarchy process certain kinds of information. For example, one hierarchy has the set of circuits for analyzing visual information. Another set of neural circuits processes auditory information. There are other circuits for learning a language, planning next steps, and interpreting emotions. Within each hierarchy those that process lower-level information develop earlier.

Again, within the process of brain development there are sensitive periods, and for different parts of the brain these periods come at different ages. In other words, the development of particular neural circuits occurs at different ages. For example, low-level circuits such as analysis of sensory stimuli develop around the time of birth. High-level circuits such as those that process complex information develop much later.

The research findings related to brain architecture have been organized around three mental capacities. The first to develop are the neural circuits related to visual and auditory interactions. Second is development of networks related to learning and speaking languages. The third area of learning has to do with higher-order thinking and problem solving. A visual summary of the findings about development of brain architecture in relation to these capacities is presented in Figure 3.2. Notice how significant the early years are for the developing brain.

Figure 3.2 Human Brain Development

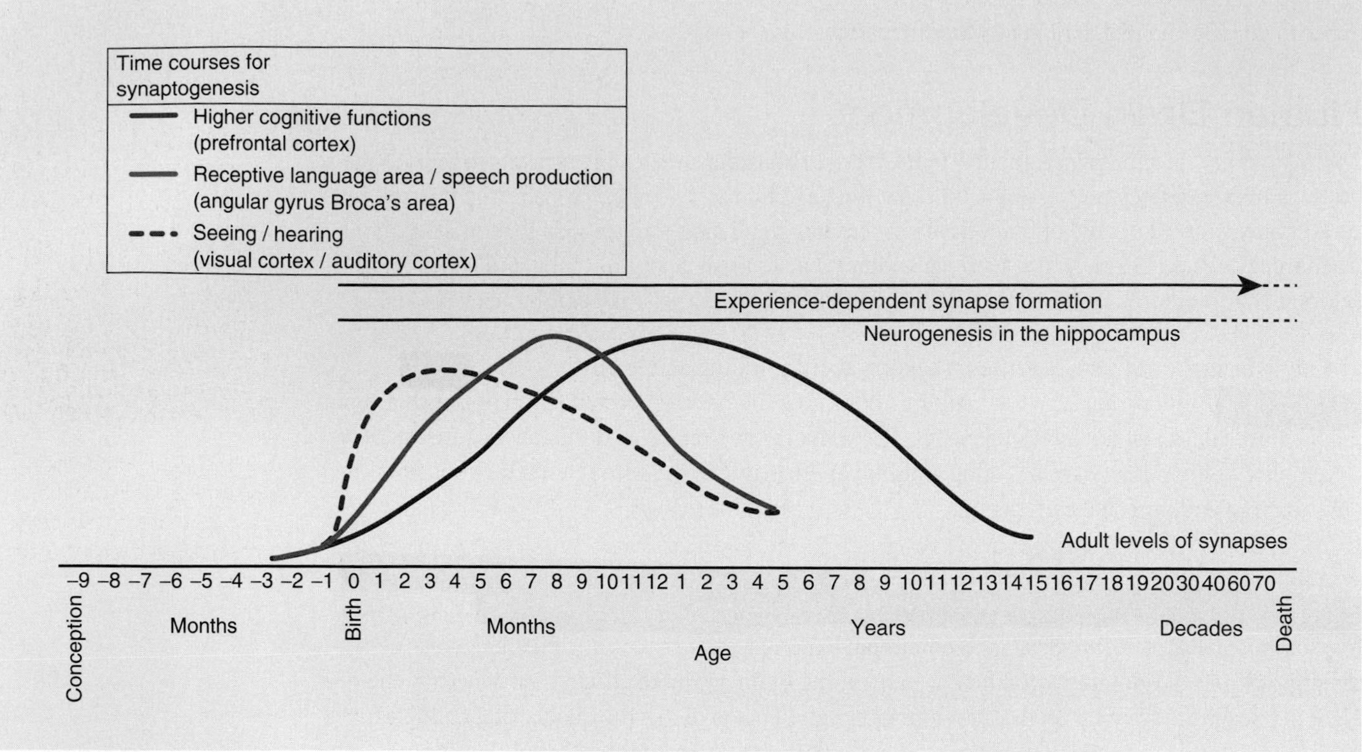

Source: Charles A. Nelson, University of Minnesota.

Impoverishment Effects Can Be Long Lasting

The findings from brain research document that when the environment for early development of the brain is impoverished the effects are long lasting. When there is not a positive and appropriately stimulating approach to social, cognitive, and language development, neural networks may not develop fully or in the same ways. This risk is especially problematic during the sensitive periods. At those ages, the neural networks are growing even more rapidly. If there is extreme stress, for example, the functioning and architecture of particular neural circuits can be altered. The result can be that the brain does not process basic information as well or completely. In a hierarchical model, if the foundation is not strong, the functions further up will be less efficient, or perhaps not work well at all. When limited or incorrect information is being produced at the lower levels then the higher levels of brain functioning may not receive complete information or accurate information. This can result in higher cognitive functions not working well or efficiently.

The Brain Has Plasticity

Contrary to what was thought for a long time, the brain architecture and its neural circuits continue to adapt throughout adulthood. In other words, even when there was not an optimal environment during the sensitive periods there is a continuing capacity to learn. However, at these later times the experiences have to be customized more carefully and targeted toward the particular neural circuits. Another way to think about this is that the architecture of each student's brain is exceptional. When teachers strive to address each student's way of functioning, more learning will be possible. This is not always easy, but teachers most certainly need to understand that learning always is possible and learning can be a lifelong process.

Contrary to what many people have believed, the adult brain has the capacity to continue to learn.

Implications of Developmental Models for Teaching and Learning

Hopefully you are seeing some of the similarities across the developmental models. Each has phases. Each has a predictable sequence and assumes that these sequences cannot be skipped. Development is related to chronological age, and development is based in interactions with the environment. Also, there is extensive research behind each model.

Often policymakers, administrators, parents, and even some teachers will start pressing for ways to speed up a child's development. The story is often told that when Piaget was asked this question his response was to label it as "the American question." Regardless of the developmental model, the experts will state that little can be done to accelerate development. What they will emphasize is that children who have caring, supportive, and rich environments in their early years will be ready for school and progress well.

These developmental perspectives offer important ways for teachers to see each student as exceptional. Each student is developing at his or her own rate based on experience and age. Past experiences affect development, and if those experiences included toxic stresses, such as extreme poverty or abuse, then the brain architecture will be different. As a teacher you need to appreciate that your students will bring different cognitive, emotional, and social capabilities to school based on their past experiences. Your task is to understand where each of your students begins and to differentiate your instruction in ways that build from there. Do not assume that any of your students cannot continue to develop. They may be ahead or behind in terms of developmental perspective, but as the neuroscience findings indicate, our brains have plasticity. It is our task to provide a supportive and rich instructional environment so that each student can continue to develop.

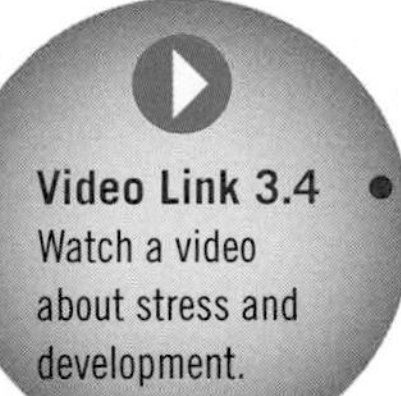

Video Link 3.4
Watch a video about stress and development.

HOW DO CLASS AND CULTURE AFFECT TEACHING AND LEARNING?

Students have so many things they are dealing with. Maybe sometimes I know, maybe sometimes I don't. When students are having trouble at school, it is not always due to academics. There could be a lot of other things going on in their lives. If teachers don't recognize that, or don't think about that, it is almost a disservice to their students. They are people too. Yes, they are kids but they are still people. They have emotions, feelings, and things they have to deal with.—Mrs. Donald

In Chapter 2, social class and other forms of diversity were reported and described. By now you should understand that many different factors can be used in describing the diversity of students, families, and communities. There also is diversity in consideration of culture. Religion, the country of origin of ancestors, political parties, and each state can be characterized in terms of certain values and beliefs. Culture reflects differences in "how things get done around here." Even when there are formal policies, rules, and procedures, there also will be informal ways of accomplishing desired ends.

For teachers, one of the significant consequences of social class and culture is that in addition to describing demographic differences, these same ideas represent significant ways that each student is exceptional.

Socioeconomic Status as a Way to See Each Student as Exceptional

Teachers need to be very careful to not have low academic expectations for students because their families are poor. Although there are identified characteristics of low-, middle-, and high-income families as a group, teachers should be very careful in applying these stereotypes to individual students. From the very first day of their school experience expectations are set. Too often, for example, the middle- and upper-class kids are expected to go to college. The same expectation is not presented to poor students, or those who have recently arrived from another country. They are not picked to lead groups and are not encouraged to participate in extracurricular activities. It appears *without saying* that these students are being prepared to take the jobs that most other people are unwilling to take.

At the same time there are some very real differences in students based on class and culture. The excellent teacher seizes on these differences as keys for helping each student learn, rather than as levers to discount each student's potential. This is not meant to say that students will not have deficits. They most certainly will. This is true regardless of class and culture. Students of higher socioeconomic status (SES) will have learning challenges as will students from poor families. It is the job of the teacher to identify needs, deficits, and keys to learning for each student and to address these in ways that lead to each student learning the most. Several of the themes about differences based in social class and culture are highlighted next.

Students from different socioeconomic backgrounds bring different prior knowledge and experiences to the classroom. Children from very affluent families will likely come to school with larger vocabularies.

Relationships Between Family Status and the Quantity of Words Heard

Earlier in this chapter we introduced findings from neuroscience about brain development. A major theme in that field is emphasizing the critical importance of the first five years in a child's development (see Figure 3.2). Researchers in other fields have identified related patterns that are important indicators of a child's cognitive development that also are indicators of their readiness for school. One of the most important of these is vocabulary.

The findings from studies about the size of vocabulary of young children have been summarized in Table 3.2. The overall patterns and themes that emerge from these studies are profound. Again, the caution for you to keep in mind is that these studies are for groups of children. The findings may, or may not, apply to each of the individual students you teach.

In Table 3.2 one of the first themes to recognize is the enormous differences in the quantity of words heard depending on family status. Children in welfare families are exposed to significantly fewer words than are children in working-class families. The number of words heard doubles again for children in professional-class families.

Look at the last column in Table 3.2. The accumulating effect is that across the first four years of life, children from higher economic classes hear millions of words more than their poorer-class

Table 3.2 Vocabulary Development in the Early Years

In a typical hour, the average child hears:

Family Status	Actual Differences in *Quantity* of Words Heard	Actual Differences in *Quality* of Words Heard	Words Heard in 4 Years
Welfare	616 words	5 affirmations, 11 prohibitions	13 million
Working Class	1,251 words	12 affirmations, 7 prohibitions	26 million
Professional	2,152 words	32 affirmations, 5 prohibitions	45 million

Source: Adapted from tables in *Big Ideas in Beginning Reading.* (n.d.). Eugene, OR: Center on Teaching and Learning, University of Oregon. Retrieved from http://reading.uoregon.edu/

peers. This is a characteristic of how each of your students is exceptional that requires you to develop in-depth understanding about how best to design instruction. Please keep in mind that the implications of these differences apply all the way through high school. Size of vocabulary is not a factor that only needs to be considered by teachers in elementary schools.

Relationships Between Family Status and the Quality of Words Heard

Take another close look at Table 3.2. The significant differences in the quantity of words heard is not the only pattern in the data. Depending on family status there are significant differences in *what is said* to children. Distinctions are made between affirmations, offering positive comments and supports, and prohibitions, rebukes, and telling the child not to do something. Notice how the proportions of affirmations and prohibitions change across the three family statuses. The quantity changes, but the real significance is that the ratio changes to where prohibitions are a relatively small proportion of the words heard by children in the professional families.

The Vocabulary Gap Continues to Widen

You might think that even if some students begin school with a more limited vocabulary they will catch up. Unfortunately, the vocabulary gap based on family status does not shrink as students move through elementary school. Instead it increases. It is estimated that a child's vocabulary doubles between grades 3 and 7. The problem is that if some third-grade students begin the year with a vocabulary size that is half of that of others, doubling it does not lead to their catching up. Instead, they are falling further behind.

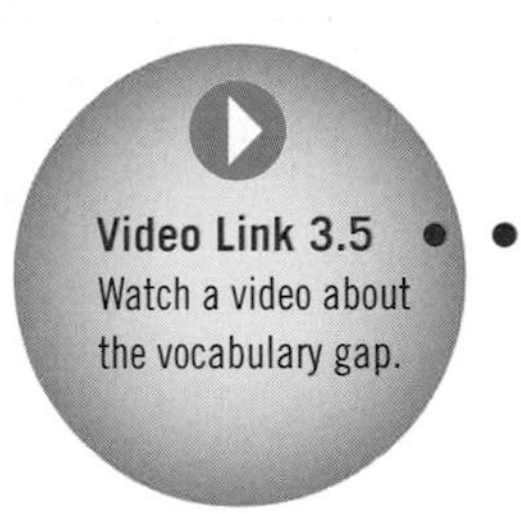
Video Link 3.5
Watch a video about the vocabulary gap.

Implications of Vocabulary Development for Teaching and Learning

An obvious first implication from the data presented in Table 3.2 is that you will need to be cautious in making predictions about the size and type of vocabulary your students will bring to your classroom. Regardless of family status, each of your students will have heard a different quantity of words. They also will have heard words of different quality. It will be very important for you in some way to estimate the size of vocabulary each of your students brings to class.

Those of you who plan to teach in middle and high school cannot escape the vocabulary gap and its consequences. Students who leave elementary school with half the size of vocabulary of their peers will most certainly have trouble keeping up during their time in secondary school. Without adequate vocabulary size students cannot solve mathematics problems, read literature, or engage in safe science laboratory investigations. All teachers need to post key vocabulary for each lesson and need to continuously work on reducing the vocabulary gap.

One example of success by one high school: One year in a high school in Douglas County, Colorado, all of the teachers agreed to work together on increasing the vocabulary size of all their students. A list of words was established for each week and all the teachers engaged in helping students understand and use the words. They did this because the previous year students scored lower on the verbal part of the SAT than the staff thought they should. What do you think happened? Yes, the following year SAT verbal scores were up.

Culture as a Source of Student Exceptionality

Let's think about culture in some ways that makes each student exceptional. Probably your first thought is to think more about the concepts introduced in Chapter 2. There students were described in terms of their race and ethnicity, their gender, and as was done earlier in this chapter their socioeconomic status. In reality, each of your students will represent a combination of these factors. For example, one of your students could be a Latino boy whose middle-class family has been ranching in New Mexico for several hundred years. Next to him sits a girl, Caucasian, from Appalachia, whose father lost his job in the coal mines and whose mother is a teacher. Each of these students represents a unique combination of many factors that makes each exceptional in his or her own way.

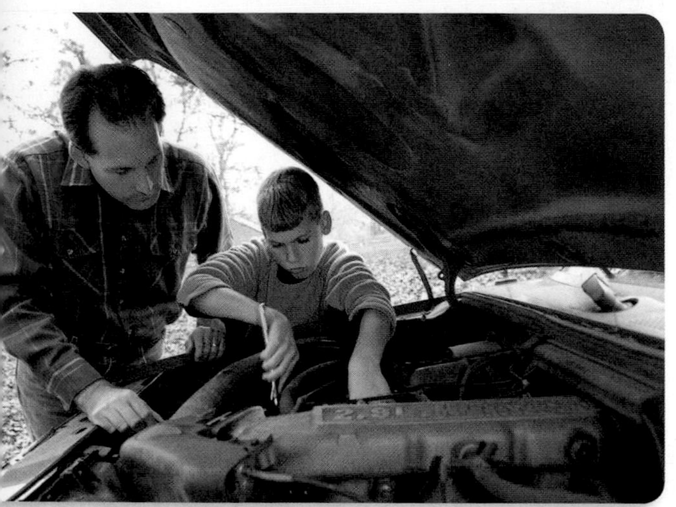

When parents share knowledge and skill with their children, both gain.

In terms of culture, as a teacher you need to understand that each of your students comes to class with a different set of experiences, values, and perspectives. The challenge for you as a teacher will be to devise ways of incorporating each student's experiences and perspectives into your instruction. Here we will use a broad definition of culture to represent the rich ways that each student's family and community backgrounds interconnect with their experiences and perspectives to make them exceptional. To help in this exploration, we begin with a brief review of basic ideas about culture.

Elements of Culture: A Quick Review

Much is said about culture, but often little is defined. In a simple way culture can be thought of as a combination of beliefs, values, and norms. **Beliefs** are those fundamental tenets that a person or a group holds to be true. Beliefs are not easily challenged or changed. **Values** are those elements of behaviors and principles that reflect what is viewed as important. Values are more open to change than are beliefs. **Norms** are the shared guidelines that define which actions and products are acceptable for a particular group. For example, one school had a norm of beginning each staff meeting with celebrating one teacher's success in helping a struggling student succeed. In another school there is a norm of being sarcastic about a particular district office staff person.

The indicators of culture can be found through examination of symbols, assumptions, and ceremonies. As was stated above, beliefs are not amendable to change. For example, in most high schools a widely shared belief is that only the "best" of students will participate in sports, theater, music, yearbook, and so on. What do you think would happen if this belief were challenged and changed? The staff in one large high school in Riverside County, California, made this change. They believed that all of their students should be involved in at least one extracurricular activity. This meant that all teachers had to help create additional clubs and supervise one or more of the before- and after-school activities. They expanded the size of the pep squad and marching band, and added club sports. The school became known for its success in regional and state competitions, as well the percentage of students who graduated on time.

Symbols reflect core beliefs and values through the meaning that is ascribed to various icons. The types of displays in the entrance to the school, in the main office, and in classrooms tell all what is valued. Ceremonies range from the topics that are, and are not, announced on the PA system each day to the many activities that unfold around a football game or graduation. Each of these activities and many others have meaning for the participants.

The Meaning in the Symbols

As one way to illustrate how you can learn about the culture of a school, consider a return visit to your high school. What would a visitor see first on entering the front lobby? In most high schools it would be displays of trophies! Most likely these will be from athletic events. The meaning behind this symbol is clear: Athletics is important. If the school also displays trophies from debate or theater competitions, then a different message is being sent: All co-curriculum activities are valued equally. The same analysis of symbols can be done in elementary and middle schools. Are there displays of student work? Is there some sort of reference to the school mascot? What is the message in what is there?

Determining the meaning behind things, actions, and events is important to understanding culture. For example, in some communities, such as Portland, Oregon, Washington, D.C., and Boulder, Colorado, there are many bike paths. The meaning is clear: Riding bicycles is a shared and supported value. In some communities there are up-to-date and sparkling school facilities. Which part of the curriculum has the most and most up-to-date supplies? In which part of the community are the "best" schools located? What does the placement of each of these mean? Does the poor neighborhood have the same quality of facilities as the well-to-do? Again, from a culture perspective, each of these symbols conveys a message about who or what is important.

Another important indicator of culture has to do with "how things get done around here." Regardless of the formal rules and procedures, the members of a particular school will know "who to call." There will be certain people and steps that can be taken to get a window repaired, or to get that extra computer. Often submitting the correct requisition form will be the long way around. "Why didn't you just tell Jo Ann (the assistant principal) what you needed?" In most schools the head school secretary is the one who knows how to get things done.

Probably you have had experience with this informal way of getting things done as part of your time in college. By now you know which steps to take when you are having a problem getting registered for the courses you want. There also will be shared information about which instructors you want (and don't want). These informal ways of working are important aspects of culture.

Communities, families, schools, and, yes, classrooms, have a culture. There are shared beliefs, symbols, and unwritten ways of getting things done. As a teacher it will be important for you to be able to detect and interpret of each of these elements of culture. In particular, what kind of culture will you strive to establish in your classroom? What elements of school culture do you anticipate making a difference in your effectiveness? What about the unique cultural background of each of your students? Do you plan to learn about each student's heritage? To what extent will you draw upon the background of your students to help them learn?

Culture in the Classroom

Each classroom has its own "feel." For example, some classrooms will be overflowing with posters, charts, bulletin boards, and book displays. Other classrooms will be barren. Before judging these different classrooms, it is important to discover the meaning behind each. One easy starting point to understanding the "full" classroom is to examine the source of the displays. Are the displays primarily the teacher's? Or are they primarily the work of the students? The meaning will be different depending on the answer to this question. You could also check to see which subject(s) is represented. In elementary schools aspects of language arts most certainly will be on display. But, is there equal representation of mathematics? Are there any indications of science or the performing arts?

Teachers must be vigilant in their monitoring for safety in their classrooms and throughout the school.

In many high school classrooms there are apt to be only a few posters or charts on display. Here too, what about student work? In the science classroom are there clear signs related to lab safety? Are there any symbols to suggest that one content area can be related to another? For example, are there writing activities in physical education, or do English classes connect with mathematics problems?

There are many other aspects of classroom culture. Another that is important has to do with norms of student behavior. Is the teacher addressed as Ms., Mr., Mrs., or Dr., or by first name? Speaking of symbols, how is the teacher dressed? Jeans and scuffed-up shoes give one meaning. Men wearing ties and women wearing dresses yield a very different meaning. When one of the authors was teaching high school science, all the science teachers wore white lab coats. There could be lots of meanings and interpretations related to this symbol.

The research related to classroom culture offers some guidance to teachers. As you would expect, certain characteristics of the classroom environment are associated with higher levels of student learning. Classrooms that are perceived to have greater cohesion, clear goals, and less disorganization and conflict are associated with greater student learning (Freiberg, 1999). Interestingly, these characteristics of classroom culture appear to be more important for low-income students, which again points out the interconnectedness of all these factors.

Safe and Caring Classroom Environment

An important consideration for you as a teacher will be safety in your classroom. There are two major components to classroom safety: physical and cultural. **Physical safety** is about the potential for students (and you as a teacher) to be injured. Accidents can happen at any moment. Teachers need to organize their classrooms in order to *prevent* injuries. They also need to be *prepared* to respond if an injury occurs.

Begin by checking your classroom for the placement of wastebaskets, electrical cords, uneven carpet, open desk drawers, situations where students might be tempted to climb, stacks that could fall on students, and access to dangerous materials such as scissors. As a teacher you are responsible for the physical safety of your students.

There is another type of classroom safety that you may have not thought as much about—cultural safety. Cultural safety is based in the unique background and experiences that each student brings to the classroom. A classroom is culturally safe when each student feels safe in terms of being who they are. There is shared respect, there is learning together, and the teacher and students listen to each other.

There are several elements that you can employ in developing cultural safety. One obvious strategy is to incorporate instructional strategies that reduce language barriers. With so many students coming to school speaking languages other than English, an important step is to use strategies that do not isolate them. Leaving non- or limited-English-speaking students out of instruction has to be avoided. Instead think about strategies that can take advantage of the other language. For example, engage yourself and your students in learning the other language by listing key vocabulary on the board in both languages. Have other students help the limited English student to understand and accomplish instructional tasks.

Other elements to consider in assuring cultural safety include anticipating and respecting religious differences, holidays, and the many different symbols of respect and disrespect. As you should be aware, in different cultures the same action or symbol can have very different meanings. For example, in some cultures eye to eye contact is avoided. In others you do not touch a person with the left hand. In the Chinese culture teachers are held in very high regard. The dates of major holidays will be different. All of these values and related symbols can be important resources for you to help each student learn.

Bullying Can Come in Two Ways

Another component of the classroom environment is the many ways that students can be victims of bullying. You probably already have in mind the first way that bullying occurs, which is some threat to physical safety. We have become more aware of incidents such as students hitting and shoving others, and their damaging books and clothing of other students. There also are the unsafe toilet areas and the gang fights after school.

However, don't forget about the other major type of safety—cultural. Students can be bullied based on their clothing, their limited skill in speaking English, or their being "too white" or too much of a "geek." Jocks often bully band members, or vice versa. When any of these types of behaviors occur, students will feel less safe and there will be less learning.

Implications of Class and Culture for Teaching and Learning

Each of your students in some ways will be exceptional within each of the elements of culture and the various situations that have been introduced in this section. As a teacher you will need to establish ways of respecting these differences while at the same time reflecting on how each can be used as a resource to help each student learn. In other words, as a teacher one of your tasks is to create a learning-centered classroom culture. This means that the students feel safe physically and in terms of their culture. The classroom culture is one of respect, and there is a shared belief in the importance of having all students learn. Table 3.3 provides a list of suggestions that you can use to check on the extent to which the culture in your classroom is learning centered.

Table 3.3 Elements and Characteristics of a Learning-Centered Classroom Culture

Physical Safety
1. Chairs, electrical cords, drawers, and other items will not trip students.
2. Supplies and tools, such as scissors, are stored in appropriate containers and kept in secure locations.
3. Chemicals and other dangerous materials are stored in secure areas. This is especially critical for science classrooms and labs.
4. Immediate emergency aid supplies are available.
5. Appropriate levels of lighting cover all areas of the classroom.
6. Classroom safety rules are posted.
7. The physical environment is attractive and supports learning.
Cultural Safety
1. There is a welcoming and caring atmosphere.
2. Students have a say in planning for instruction.
3. There is a shared respect for differences in religious views, holidays, and dress.
4. Instruction takes into account the unique knowledge and experiences of each student.
5. Metaphors and examples are based in student knowledge and experiences.
6. There is not only hope but a clear expectation that each student can and will learn.
7. Student work is shared and displayed.

Each student brings a unique set of knowledge and experiences to the classroom that can be used to enrich learning.

One neat example of linking students' cultural background to instruction can be seen in the movie *Stand and Deliver.* This movie is about an exceptional high school math teacher, Jaime Escalante. Mr. Escalante was teaching algebra in a high school in East Los Angeles. An important instructional tactic is to use metaphors. In other words, to use something in the students' background of experiences that can be connected to the content of a lesson. In the movie Mr. Escalante is explaining negative numbers. He uses the metaphor of going to the beach and lifting up a handful of sand. This leaves a hole in the sand and he has the equivalent amount of sand in his hand. In other words this action illustrates minus one.

This metaphor works with these students since there is a cultural match. The students have had related experiences (going to the beach), and it is an accurate representation of the concept being taught. Too often teachers use examples and metaphors that their students have not experienced. One that may help illustrate the problem of mismatches with you is the platypus. Assuming you have never seen a platypus, how big do you think they are? The size of a medium-sized dog? Bigger still, or do you think they are very small? Actually they are much smaller than most think, perhaps 12 to 18 inches long. The point here is that you need to carefully select examples and metaphors so that they match the background and knowledge of your students.

CHARACTERISTICS OF STUDENTS AS LEARNERS

Before I got my teaching job at Vista Heights I was out of a job for a year. History teaching jobs are hard to come by. In the meantime I got a job doing what they call "Academic Coaching" at another junior high. That is where I got to work with students more on a one-on-one basis. If they were failing their classes I would pull them out. I would help them figure what it was in their habits or their previous schooling that was preventing them for getting good grades.—
Mrs. Donald

"Eddie is a very ambitious child."

Another all too frequently used strategy to characterize students is to label them as being representative of a certain stereotypic group. "She should be in the GATE program." "He is homeless. You know he is living in a car!" Other students will be labeled as "at risk" or limited English proficiency (LEP) or IEP. All too often these labels are used as rationalization for a student not doing well in school. At the same time, these labels represent another set of categories that can be useful in considering ways that each student is exceptional. Let's review some of these labels in relation to how they can help us see each student as exceptional.

What Are Some of the Most Common Ways of Categorizing Students?

While learning about some of these commonly used categories we need to be mindful of not using them as excuses for why some students are not learning. The following is a brief introduction to some of the major categories. Others, such as ELL, have been introduced in other chapters, so we won't return to them here. As your teaching career unfolds you will discover that your colleagues, as well as administrators, researchers, and policymakers, are always creating new stereotypic categories. Be careful not to be trapped into seeing any of these as more than superficial generalizations.

One of the authors of this text had an experience related to this type of simplistic labeling. While studying implementation of a standards-based approach to teaching mathematics in one of the U.S. Department of Defense school districts (based in Germany) he heard teachers refer to "those Abrahams children." Several teachers went on to exclaim, "Well, you know those kids can't learn this way." Not knowing if these children were from a particular part of Germany, or who they were, a colleague was asked to explain who/what were Abrahams kids. It turns out that there is a type of armored vehicle that is called the Abrahams tank. Some teachers had decided that the children of the military personnel who worked with these tanks were not able to learn through a standards-based approach. They were categorized as being less able to learn simply because of the work of their parents.

Gifted and Talented Education (GATE)

One of the major challenges facing each teacher, school, and community—as well as the nation—is how to enhance learning for the brightest students. In a recent synthesis of surveys of teachers reported by the National Association for Gifted Children (n.d.), the pattern is clear. The more able children are not receiving the learning opportunities they need. Four major themes were identified:

1. Academically advanced students are not a priority at their schools.
2. Curriculum is not appropriately challenging for advanced students.
3. Teachers are not trained to meet the needs of advanced students,
4. There is a lack of accountability and reporting.

Responses to some of the survey items illustrate the seriousness of the problem. For example, "77% of teachers agree that 'getting underachieving students to reach proficiency has become so important that the needs of advanced students take a back seat." This condition is likely a direct consequence of the No Child Left Behind statute, which focused schools singularly on bringing test scores of low-achieving students up. Schools were not sanctioned if the performance of students at grade level did not increase.

Audio Link 3.3
Learn more about programs for under-achieving students.

"Only 10% of teachers report that advanced students are likely to be taught with curriculum and instruction specially designed for their abilities." Here is another opportunity for you as a teacher to have joy in your teaching. Be sure to implement instructional approaches that engage and challenge the gifted students in your class.

All students will struggle at times. Teachers need to be ready to reach out with support and encouragement.

What do you think happens when gifted students are not challenged? Many of them drop out of school. In a major study using national databases, Renzulli and Park (2002) examined the reasons for gifted students dropping out and what they did after dropping out. Study the Challenging Assumptions box to learn about the findings from this study.

Struggling Students

There will be times as a teacher when you will have a student who should be learning, but she or he is not. This can be perplexing and frustrating. Based on what the student has done in the past, you are certain that she or he should be doing well now. Something has changed. Students can be struggling for many reasons. If adjusting instruction doesn't work, then you need to look further afield.

Some students struggle due to not having the required prior knowledge. Students who are new to the school, or new to your classroom, may struggle. In other cases a family situation such as a parent losing a job can be a cause. Students from low-income families may struggle not only because they are poor but perhaps because they are being pressured by fellow students from more economically well-off families. At some time most students will struggle. When you detect that a student is struggling, you should strive to find out what's going on.

Students at Risk

Another major grouping of students is those that are at risk. Behind the label is the suggestion that for one or another reason these are students who may fall behind in learning and may drop out of school. The reasons that a student may be at risk come right back to the ways outlined in this chapter that each student can be seen as exceptional. Students from low-income families

Challenging Assumptions

Are gifted students at less risk of dropping out?

The Assumption

Much has been written about the risk of students from lower socioeconomic backgrounds dropping out of school. They have more limited vocabulary. They are likely to have less support from family members. Expectations will be lower about the possibility of their going to college. Gifted students certainly are smart enough to do well in school, so it would seem that they are less likely to drop out. Of those that do drop out, are their reasons the same or different as for the less academically able?

Study Design and Method

To examine this question, Joseph Renzulli, a leading scholar of gifted education at the University of Connecticut, and a coauthor, Sunghee Park, examined a major national database called the National Education Longitudinal Study of 1988. These data are for 25,000 students who were in the eighth grade in 1988. The study includes surveys of parents, teachers, and administrators. Follow-up surveys have been conducted every two years. The researchers analyzed the surveys to find out the reasons that gifted students dropped out.

Study Findings

Contrary to what one might expect, the study findings should sound familiar. "Many gifted students left school because they were failing school, didn't like school, got a job, or were pregnant." Many participated less in extracurricular activities. Parents were not actively involved in their child's decision to drop out. Almost half (48.2%) were from the lowest quartile of SES while only 3.6% were from the highest SES quartile. A high percentage of the fathers (40%) and the mothers (25.6%) had not finished high school.

Two of the more unique findings were these: (1) Gifted students who dropped out had higher self-concept than nongifted students who dropped out, and (2) gifted students who dropped out had used marijuana more than gifted students who completed school.

Implications

The first very important implication for teachers is to not assume that just because one of your students is bright she or he will not be at risk of dropping out. In most ways the same indicators of being at risk that have been identified for regular students seems to apply for gifted students. Developing supportive relationships, knowing family backgrounds, and establishing a classroom climate that is safe will be effective for all of your students.

Source: Renzulli, J. S., & Park, S. (2002). *Giftedness and high school dropouts: Personal, family, and school-related factors* (RM02168). Storrs, CT: The National Center on the Gifted and Talented, University of Connecticut.

are more likely to be at risk. Students who move a lot and do not stay in one school are at risk. Students in schools where there is not physical and/or cultural safety are at risk. Very bright students may be bored with the level of assignments.

A key time of risk is when there are **transitions** from one school to the next. The move from elementary school to junior high/middle school is a risky time, as is the transition to high school. When one of the authors was working with a high school in California, they were able to identify 108 students who disappeared between the spring of eighth grade and the following fall's beginning of ninth grade. No one had any idea about what happened to those students.

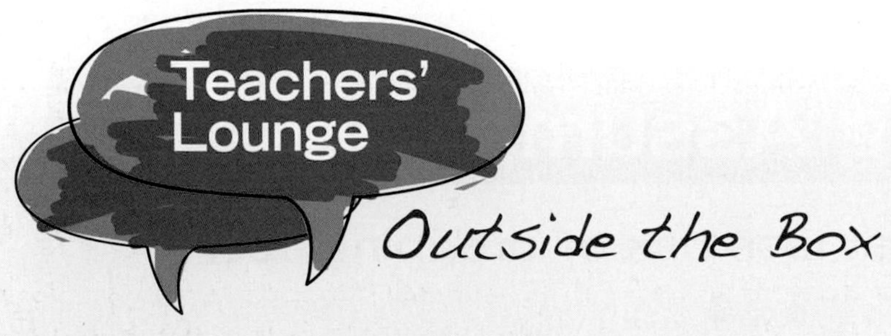

Gifted and advanced students often think "outside the box," and it's important to be flexible and open-minded when working with them. As a seventh- and eighth-grade language arts teacher, I had a class of gifted students. We were reading William Golding's *Lord of the Flies* as part of an interdisciplinary unit on Law and Society. During a discussion in which we were reviewing several essay topics from which students could choose for their culminating essay, one of the young men in my class said, "I wonder how this book would have been different if it had been all girls . . . or a mixed group." In all the years I had taught this novel, this topic had not occurred to me! It gave rise to both some wonderful essays (since I immediately added it to the choice of topics) and discussion about gender and sex-role stereotyping—perfect for the real-world developmental issues of middle level students.

Susan R. Rakow
Cleveland State University
Cleveland, Ohio

Again, keep in mind that students who have had good grades may also be at risk of struggling. Family issues, threats in their communities, missing meals, and health problems can place students at risk.

Early Warning Indicators of Students Dropping Out

Deeper Look 3.4
Read about dropout prevention.

There is widespread concern about the problem of low high school graduation rates and the correspondingly high rate of dropouts. Depending on which statistic is used, one third or more of the students who begin high school fail to graduate. For you as a teacher, another way that some of your students may be exceptional is that they will be at risk of dropping out. Do not assume that only secondary teachers are responsible for preventing kids from dropping out. As you will read here, it is in the elementary school years where much of the problem begins.

Many opinions are offered to explain why the graduation rate is not increasing, and many solutions are proposed for fixing the problem. Most of these address some characteristic of schools ("High schools are too large."), or blame someone else ("Well, if they had learned to read in elementary school we wouldn't have this problem."), or advocate for a particular solution (e.g., small learning communities, homeschooling, more or less technology). The contributing factors can be different for each student; however, for students in general there are several predictors that you should keep in mind.

Researchers at Johns Hopkins University have identified four indicators that predict a student's potential to not graduate on time. The study was done by examining the records of students in the Philadelphia public schools. The records of the students were studied from the time they were in sixth grade until one year after high school graduation (Neild & Balfanz, 2006).

The researchers identified four indicators that if in place for sixth-grade students would likely lead to their not graduating from high school on time:

- Attending school 80% or less of the time
- Receiving a poor final behavior mark
- Failing math
- Failing English

You might think that students would need to score poorly on a combination of these four indicators to be at risk. However, the researchers concluded that a sixth-grade student with any one of the four indicators has only a 10% to 20% chance of graduating high school at the same time as his or her peers.

Implications for Teaching and Learning From Placing Students in Categories

The findings from the Johns Hopkins/Philadelphia study along with others, including the Renzulli and Park study, make it clear that students can be exceptional in some ways that are not good. Gifted students can be at risk as well as those who are struggling. There are many possible factors that can contribute to students failing to achieve at grade level. Still, just because a student is experiencing one or more of the risk factors does not guarantee their being a failure, but it sure increases the likelihood. You as a teacher need to use all of the indicators, possible disabilities, SES, culture, GATE, performance in earlier grades, and your own observations and assessments to identify the different ways that each student is exceptional. Regardless of their entering profile, it is your job to devise ways to reduce their at-risk indicators and to increase their learning.

Developing a classroom culture that facilitates positive relationships between students and teachers, and between students, is a good place to start. Acknowledging their skills, learning about their interests and aspirations, and being sensitive to their worries is important. Teachers also need to learn about the community and different neighborhoods surrounding the school. Devise ways to reduce the perceptual gap between the community and your classroom. Students and their families want to be connected to the school. When possible link the curriculum to community resources including businesses, historical sites, and leaders. At all times see each student as exceptional in his or her own way and set expectations that each student will be a successful learner in your classroom.

CONNECTING TO THE CLASSROOM

In this chapter, we discussed ways to view each student as exceptional. These are the major topics discussed:

1. Become very familiar with the different types of disabilities and implications for teaching and learning.
2. Teachers should not think of there only being one kind of intelligence.
3. Physical activity is an important component of brain development, which means students should have plenty of opportunities to move.
4. For all ages the brain is plastic and can change through experience.
5. Vocabulary development should be a key component of lessons for all students, and especially students from lower SES families.
6. Poverty does not mean that a student cannot learn.
7. Developing a classroom culture that is physically and culturally safe will also be one that celebrates each student being exceptional.

SUMMARY

The major theme in this chapter has been the importance of seeing each student as exceptional. It is very important for teachers to figure out how each students is exceptional in some way(s).

- Many different categories, labels, and concepts can be used to describe students.
- Each of your students will represent a unique combination of these categories.
- Some students will have identified disabilities.
- There are multiple forms of intelligence.
- Developmental models can be used to see each student as exceptional.
- Neural science is providing ways to understand how the architecture of the brain relates to learning.
- Do not use the various concepts and labels to judge students poorly.
- Use the unique ways each student is exceptional to design instruction so that all of your students are learning.

CLASS DISCUSSION QUESTIONS

1. A sampling of the different ways that students can be categorized as exceptional has been introduced in this chapter. Which of these can be used to describe you as an exceptional student?
2. What do you see as implications of the various developmental models for how the curriculum should be organized, the design of instruction, and the structure of schools? In other words, are schools and the curriculum organized in ways that reflect what is known about child development?
3. What have you seen teachers do to establish classroom cultures that are physically and culturally safe?
4. What do you see as implications for you as a teacher of the various factors associated with students dropping out of school? What can elementary and secondary school teachers do to compensate for the potential harmful effects of these factors?
5. In this chapter, one of the topics was developing an understanding of the risk factors associated with lower SES families. What do you know/think about possible risk factors that would be more closely associated with students from high SES families?

KEY TERMS

Accommodations 70
Activity 78
Affirmations 83
At risk 90
Beliefs 84
Brain architecture 79
Ceremonies 85
Cultural match 88
Cultural safety 87
Developmental 77
Differentiate 69
General intelligence 74
Inclusion 72
Individualized education plan (IEP) 69
Intelligence quotient (IQ) test 73
Learning-centered 87
Maturation 78
Multiple Intelligences (MI) 74
Norms 84
Physical safety 86
Prohibitions 83
Specific abilities 74
Stereotypes 77
Symbols 85
Toxic stresses 81
Transitions 91
Values 84
Vocabulary 83

SELF-ASSESSMENT

WHAT IS YOUR CURRENT LEVEL OF UNDERSTANDING AND THINKING ABOUT ADDRESSING LEARNERS' INDIVIDUAL NEEDS?

One of the indicators of understanding is to examine how complex your thinking is when asked questions that require you to use the concepts and facts introduced in this chapter.

Answer the following questions as fully as you can. Then use the Complexity of Thinking rubric to self-assess the degree to which you understand and can use the organization ideas presented in this chapter.

1. Use several of the concepts introduced in this chapter to describe ways that you see yourself as exceptional. How have teachers used, or ignored, these factors in relation to your learning?
2. Four risk factors have been identified as strongly predictive of students not graduating from high school. What are implications of these factors for instruction and different levels of schooling?
3. There are two kinds of classroom culture. How will these come to be in your classroom?
4. Two developmental models were introduced in this chapter. What are some of the implications of these in regard to organization of the curriculum and design of instruction?
5. You can expect that you will have several students in your classroom who have a recognized disability. In order for you to be effective in instruction, what will you need to know about the way each of those students is exceptional?

Rate your responses to each of the questions using this rubric.

Complexity of Thinking Rubric

	Parts & Pieces	Unidimensional	Organized	Integrated	Extensions
Indicators	Elements/concepts are talked about as isolated and independent entities.	One or a few concepts are addressed, while others are under-developed.	Deliberate and structured consideration of all key concepts/elements.	All key concepts/elements are included in a view that addresses interconnections.	Integration of all elements and dimensions, with extrapolation to new situations.
Identifying characteristics of exceptional students	Names one or two indicators, such as low-income family, or failing a subject, without placing them into an overarching category.	Only describes one way that a student could be exceptional, such as gifted.	Describes and compares several ways that students can be exceptional and compares one to the other.	Describes and compares several ways that students can be exceptional and compares one to the other, and suggests implications for classroom culture and instruction.	Presents an integrated view of different ways that each student can be exceptional, describes related characteristics of classrooms and instruction, and identifies areas where s/he plans to develop more in-depth understanding.

STUDENT STUDY SITE

Visit the Student Study Site at **www.sagepub.com/hall** to access links to the videos, audio clips, and Deeper Look reference materials noted in this chapter, as well as additional study tools including eFlashcards, web quizzes, and more.

Field Guide

for Learning More About Addressing Learners' Individual Needs

To further increase your understanding of the different ways to see each student as being exceptional, engage in the following field activities.

Ask a Teacher or Principal

Ask a teacher or principal to describe the different ways that they see students being exceptional.

Talk to a well-regarded teacher about the ways that she or he strives to learn about the learning-related background of each student. Then inquire about examples and strategies she has used to engage students who have brought an unusual set of prior experiences to the classroom.

Make Your Own Observations

When you visit classrooms for your clinical experiences ask students to describe for you ways that each of them sees themselves as exceptional. Ask how their background of experiences is helping them learn. Have there been aspects of their background that have hindered their learning? Follow up by asking in what ways their teachers take advantage of their special strengths. Or do they?

Reflect Through Journaling

The premise in this chapter is that exceptional teachers need to see each student as being exceptional. In other words, each student is special, unique, and brings to learning a particular set of background knowledge and experiences. A good place for you to start your journaling following the reading of this chapter is to address this question: *How do you feel about the assertion that teachers should teach each student as being exceptional in unique ways?*

Many teachers will not be comfortable with this idea. Also, many teachers will be at a loss to think of a broad spectrum of ways to consider each student as exceptional. Therefore, the second part of your journaling task is to make your own list of indicators and categories for seeing each student as exceptional. Along the side of each indicator, keep note ideas for how you could take advantage of each student's "exceptionalities" to facilitate their learning.

Build Your Portfolio

With a teacher education classmate, find two or three students who recently dropped out of school. Interview them about their reasons for leaving. Do their reasons relate to the four factors identified in the Johns Hopkins study? What do they suggest would be necessary to facilitate their returning to school?

Develop a classroom culture observation guide that could be used to assess physical and cultural safety. Try the guide out in one or two classrooms. Develop a short presentation about your findings.

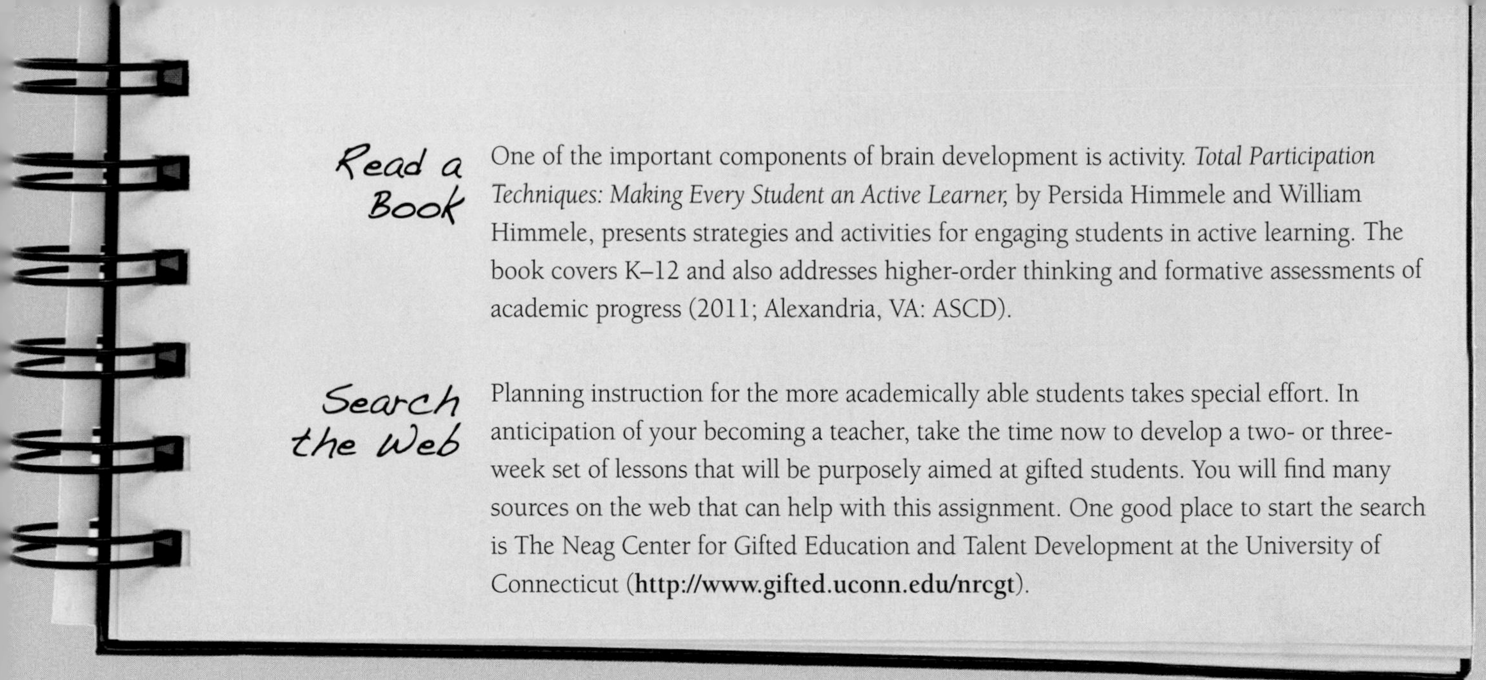

Read a Book

One of the important components of brain development is activity. *Total Participation Techniques: Making Every Student an Active Learner,* by Persida Himmele and William Himmele, presents strategies and activities for engaging students in active learning. The book covers K–12 and also addresses higher-order thinking and formative assessments of academic progress (2011; Alexandria, VA: ASCD).

Search the Web

Planning instruction for the more academically able students takes special effort. In anticipation of your becoming a teacher, take the time now to develop a two- or three-week set of lessons that will be purposely aimed at gifted students. You will find many sources on the web that can help with this assignment. One good place to start the search is The Neag Center for Gifted Education and Talent Development at the University of Connecticut (**http://www.gifted.uconn.edu/nrcgt**).

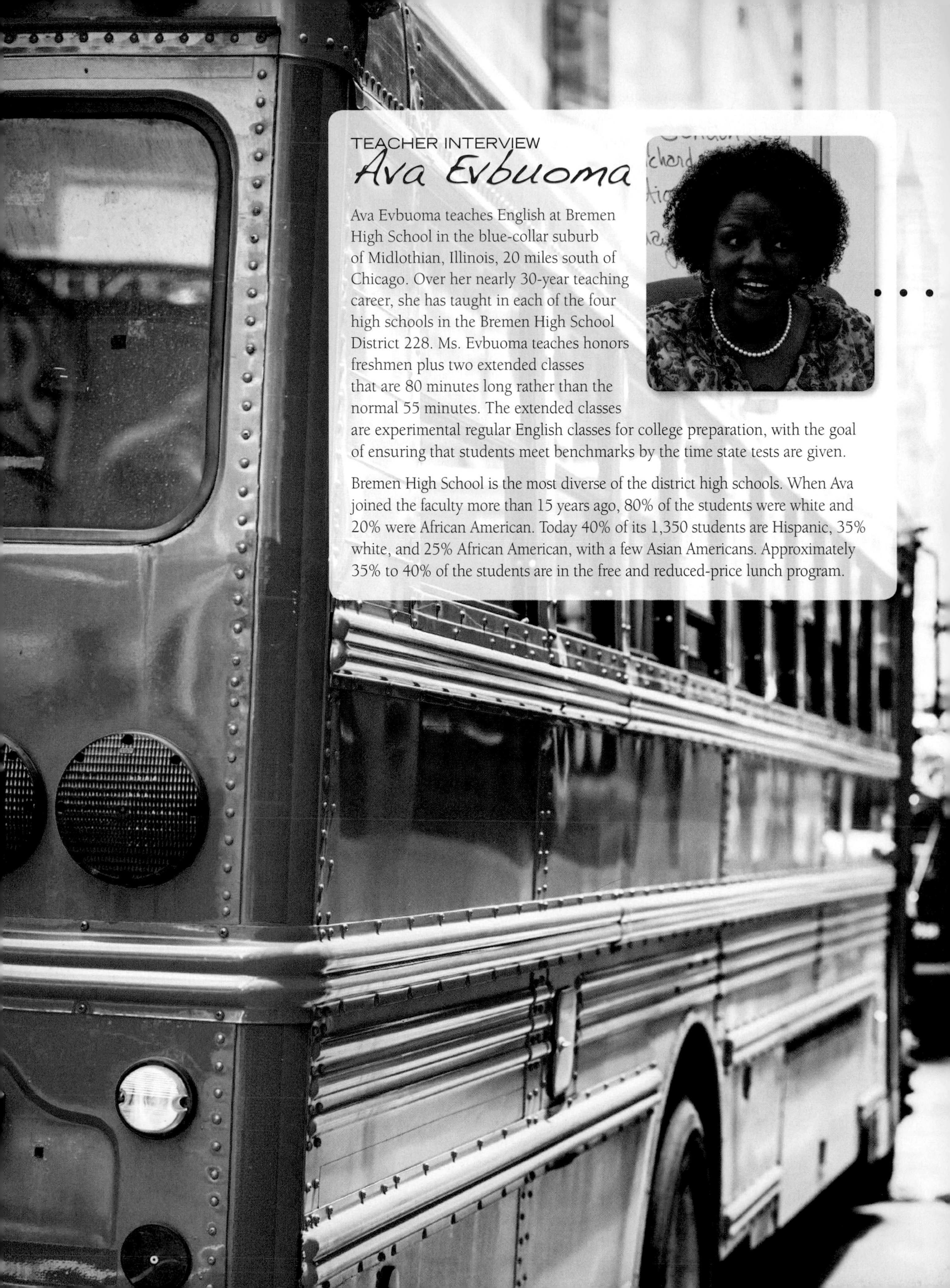

TEACHER INTERVIEW

Ava Evbuoma

Ava Evbuoma teaches English at Bremen High School in the blue-collar suburb of Midlothian, Illinois, 20 miles south of Chicago. Over her nearly 30-year teaching career, she has taught in each of the four high schools in the Bremen High School District 228. Ms. Evbuoma teaches honors freshmen plus two extended classes that are 80 minutes long rather than the normal 55 minutes. The extended classes are experimental regular English classes for college preparation, with the goal of ensuring that students meet benchmarks by the time state tests are given.

Bremen High School is the most diverse of the district high schools. When Ava joined the faculty more than 15 years ago, 80% of the students were white and 20% were African American. Today 40% of its 1,350 students are Hispanic, 35% white, and 25% African American, with a few Asian Americans. Approximately 35% to 40% of the students are in the free and reduced-price lunch program.

The Social Context of Schools

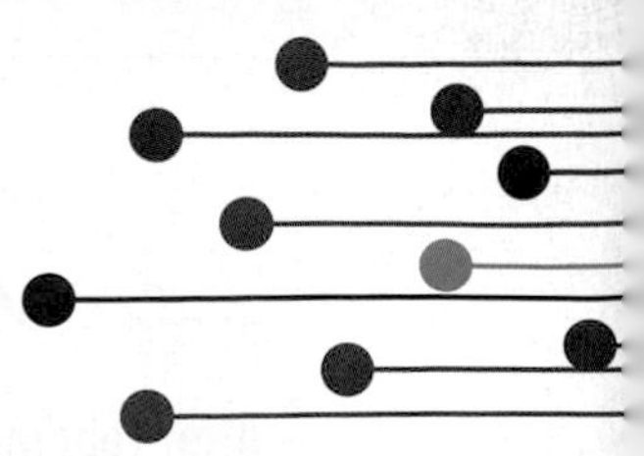

- *How do social contexts that challenge your students impact your teaching?*

This year we had two pregnant ninth graders, which was probably our biggest problem. We are in a unique situation in that the mayor of the city of Midlothian is a science teacher at our school. We couldn't ask for more support as far as watching the drugs and the gangs. Only four students have been suspended from our school this year because of substance abuse. Until this year we had a thriving program with a counselor who worked for all four high schools to combat drug substance abuse. All we have left is a skeleton program with no counselors.

What do you find joyful about teaching?

To see the kids actually grow and love literature, to love writing, and to love being risk takers on their own. When I come into a class, and the kids take over the class, I am just like "Wow, this is pretty wonderful." They're in charge of each other's behavior. For the most part, all I can do is introduce the subject area and give them the necessary information and support. They are so proud of themselves. You say, "how do you know a kid is proud? How can you measure that?" You can measure it in their behavior—the looks on their faces and the quality of their work. At some point they realize they have actually taken over the class. They are so comfortable with what is going on. They want more, and they are willing to take it on themselves to make it happen. That's when I know that I've done a good job.

Questions to Consider

1. What are some of the social challenges that the high school students at Bremen and other high schools across the country face as teenagers?
2. What are some of the challenges that teachers face as they try to engage students in school and help them learn?
3. How does Ms. Evbuoma's description of joy in her classroom compare to the reasons that you are considering teaching for your career?

INTRODUCTION

Knowing the social context in which our students live should help us better serve them. Social contexts affect not only our lived experiences but also our learning, behavior, and participation in society. Social contexts or social organizations are "patterns of human relationships and intersections that characterize social life" (Zusman, Knox, & Gardner, 2009, p. 5). They have "a powerful impact on who we are and the choices we make" (Zusman et al., 2009, p. 4). When we have limited understanding and experiences with the social contexts in which our students live, it may be more difficult to engage them in learning and help them become partners in their own learning.

The social contexts of communities and society provide opportunities for some students and reinforce the status quo for others. They impact the performance and outcomes of both educators and students (Milner, 2010). What are some examples of social contexts that affect learning? The economic well-being of students' families is one example. High-poverty schools in which most students are from low-income families, some

Learning Outcomes

After reading this chapter, you should be able to

1. Identify some of the most pressing social context issues challenging educators in today's schools.
2. Analyze how the curriculum is influenced by the social context of teachers, communities in which the school is located, and politics.
3. Discuss some of the nonacademic challenges faced by children and youth as they make their way through school.

in abject poverty, are more likely to have a disproportionate number of new teachers who may not have majored in the subject they are teaching. Students who live in high-income families are much more likely to attend elite private schools at all education levels. Students who live in poverty are much more likely to attend high-poverty schools, score below proficiency levels on standardized tests, not finish high school, and not attend college. In this chapter we will explore other social contexts that can have a powerful impact on choices made by educators and students.

HOW DOES SOCIAL CONTEXT CHALLENGE EDUCATORS?

Social context can open students' opportunities for academic, financial, and social success in society or it can limit their opportunities. The social context of a family, community, or school can provide many examples of the payoff for graduating from college or few models of the advantages of studying hard and finishing college. The challenge for schools and educators is how to engage students in learning even when their social contexts may be working against their academic success. In this section we will explore some of the challenges that you and your colleagues may encounter as you try to help all students learn at higher levels.

Academic Performance

Although the goal of teaching has always been to help students learn, today's teachers are being held accountable for the level of their students' learning. It is no longer enough to ensure that all of your students learn enough to pass to the next grade. They must show evidence of meeting state or national standards as measured on a number of assessments, but most important by their performance on state tests in reading, mathematics, and sometimes science. In a growing number of states, your evaluation will be based partly on how well your students perform on these tests. In some school districts and states, your salary increment also will be based on these scores. As a result, student learning, at least in some subjects, has become more important than ever in the lives of teachers. A positive outcome is improved student learning.

To improve student learning, students need to become invested in their education (Boykin & Noguera, 2011). Too often they do not see the payoff in working hard, studying hard, doing their homework, regularly attending school, being on time to class, and participating actively in academic work. Our challenge as teachers is to help them become invested in their education.

The Federal Mandate

The federal legislation for PreK–12 education, No Child Left Behind (NCLB), was first passed by Congress in 2001 and is expected to be reauthorized in 2013, with a number of changes and possibly under a different name. For the first time, the federal government held schools accountable for student achievement as measured by state tests. The focus of the legislation was on improving the academic achievement of children, especially those who had historically not performed well on standardized tests. To accomplish that goal, schools and districts were required to disaggregate student test scores by the student characteristics of race, socioeconomic status, language, gender, and disability. Scores had to be published, and schools that were not making progress at improving student scores were labeled as "not meeting adequate yearly progress (AYP)." If a school did not meet AYP for three years, students in that school could transfer to another school in the district.

The Importance of a Teacher

Good teaching matters. You can make a difference in a student's academic and social success in school by attending to the students who are struggling with learning. These students should not be left behind because they entered your classroom with less knowledge and skill than other children. Turning around their performance and seeing the glee on their faces when they get it is an important payoff in teaching.

Teacher quality has a great impact on the academic achievement of students.

What difference does a high-quality teacher make? Studies have found that when a high proportion of the teachers in a school or school district are inexperienced, underprepared, or unlicensed, the impact on student achievement is negative (Darling-Hammond, 2010). Among the factors that contribute to high-quality teachers are their academic backgrounds, the quality of their teacher preparation program, higher scores on licensure tests, more than two years of teaching experience, and national board certification (Darling-Hammond, 2010).

In a study of data from 46 countries whose students had participated in the Trends in International Mathematics and Science Study (TIMSS), researchers found that the countries with highly qualified teachers had higher mathematics achievement outcomes for students. The quality indicators that produced significantly higher math scores were teachers who were fully certified, had a mathematics education major, and had at least three years of teaching experience (Akiba, LeTendre, & Scribner, 2007). One of the prominent teacher education researchers, Linda Darling-Hammond (2010), concludes from her research that "the achievement gap would be much reduced if low-income minority students were routinely assigned such high-qualified teachers rather than those they most often encounter" (pp. 43–44). You are taking the first step in becoming one of those highly qualified teachers who help students learn regardless of the social contexts that may impact their progress. You can make a difference to the children you teach.

The Sociopolitical Context

Schools are controlled by the sociopolitical context in which they operate. When English is the only language respected by political and educational leaders, a school district will adopt immersion programs

UNDERSTANDING AND USING EVIDENCE

Using Test Scores

The review of proficiency test scores across gender and ethnic/racial groups can help educators know possible reasons for the achievement gap. The scores in the table below are from the National Assessment of Educational Progress (NAEP), which is given to a sample of students at the fourth, eighth, and 12th grades. This information can help a faculty decide areas that they need to attack to eliminate the gap among students. Examine the data below on scores at different ages in reading and mathematics.

							Education of Parents				
		Sex		**Race/Ethnicity**					**More Than High School**		
Age/Grade Level	**Total**	**Male**	**Female**	**White**	**Black**	**Hispanic**	**Less Than High School**	**High School**	**Total**	**Some College**	**College Graduate**
Reading											
9-year-olds	212	209	215	221	186	193	199	206	220	(NA)	(NA)
13-year-olds	259	254	265	267	238	244	238	251	270	(NA)	(NA)
17-year-olds	288	282	295	295	264	271	265	274	298	(NA)	(NA)
Mathematics											
9-year-olds	232	233	231	239	211	213	214	224	(NA)	237	240
13-year-olds	276	277	275	283	251	259	256	264	(NA)	279	286
17-year-olds	308	310	307	315	283	293	289	299	(NA)	308	317

1. What patterns do you see in the NAEP scores for reading? What groups score highest on the test?
2. What differences exist between the mathematics and reading scores?
3. What do the data suggest to teachers?
4. Why should teachers and school administrators review how their students are scoring on NAEP and state tests?

The disaggregation of test data has shown that not all students in our schools are performing at grade level. Even schools whose overall performance on state tests has been very high have learned that they have not ensured that their African American, Hispanic, and American Indian students; students from low-income families; English-language learners; and students with disabilities are learning at the same high level. Many schools across the country are struggling to identify strategies that will improve learning for all students and dramatically reduce or eliminate the gap among groups of students. When you begin working in a school, you will be expected to analyze your students' test scores and improve their achievement on required state tests.

rather than bilingual programs for its English-language learners. If a school district values the diversity of its students, it will support multicultural education and learning about the histories and experiences of ethnic and racial groups in the community. If ethnic studies are viewed as divisive and threatening to the status quo, the school district may ban them as has recently occurred in Tucson, Arizona.

Deeper Look 4.1
Read about the urban social context and the achievement gap.

Many schools are influenced by a meritocracy ideology in which students are believed to begin school with an equal opportunity for academic access. There is little acknowledgment of the cultural capital that students bring to school with them. Pierre Bourdieu introduced the term *cultural capital*, as the endowments we gain from our families such as cultural and linguistic competence. He claimed that schools are not as neutral and objective as many people think because they value and reinforce the cultural capital of middle- and upper-class families, placing the children of working-class families at a disadvantage. The language, ideas, and knowledge of "the arts" that are learned in many upper- and middle-class homes provide children an "important exchange value in the educational and cultural marketplace" (Sadovnik, 2004, p. 17). Thus, families who do not adopt the language, ideas, and arts of the dominant group are at a disadvantage in schools. Their cultures are not generally valued or rewarded in schools. In most instances, their children must adopt the dominant culture or become bicultural to be successful in schools. The problems that occur when students lack the cultural capital that will make it easier to be successful in school can be overcome when educators recognize them and make adjustments in the school climate and culture.

Audio Link 4.1
Listen to a clip about teacher expectations.

Deficit Ideology

When we think about people or groups of people in terms of their weaknesses rather than their strengths, we are projecting a deficit ideology. When educators hold a deficit ideology, they think that people who are ethnically, racially, or economically different from them or who behave differently from them are deficient or inferior, which can have a negative impact on learning. Some teachers do not respect the nonstandard dialects of students and families, thinking that these students are less likely to learn at high levels than those students who speak the Standard English that is used in schools. When teachers have low academic expectations of students because they come from broken homes or are foster children, they have developed a deficit perspective of those students, which is likely to influence how they interact with them and how much they will work with them to help them learn at high levels.

Students whose families have cultural capital are much more likely to attend schools that are attractive, have nationally board-certified teachers, and are rich in resources to support learning.

The deficit ideology is reflected in the notion of a "culture of poverty" in which low-income students and families are described by negative generalizations such as fun-loving, loud, inherently criminal, sexually deviant, and not valuing education (Redeaux, 2011). It is reflected in the belief that students of color and English-language learners are not achieving at grade level on standardized tests because they are intellectually inferior (Milner, 2010). It justifies inequalities in schools by the perceived deficiencies of students and their families (Gorski, 2011). The deficit ideology is reflected in the language that educators sometimes use to describe students: "at-risk," "remedial," "culturally deprived," and "disadvantaged" (Gorski, 2011). Recognizing when a deficit ideology is dominating the work of a teacher or a school is a first step toward changing dispositions and behaviors toward students.

Deeper Look 4.2
Read about stereotyping in society.

Stereotyping

Stereotyping is one of the outcomes of a deficit ideology. Stereotypes are an exaggerated, and usually biased, view about a group based on prior, and often wrong, assumptions. When teachers hold stereotypes about a group, they tend to think every member of that group is like the stereotype. Stereotypes can sound positive, such as labeling Asian American students as the **model minority** because they achieve at higher levels than other groups. The problem is that not all Asian American students perform at high levels, and those who do not may be neglected by teachers. However, most stereotypes are negative portrayals of groups, labeling their members as lazy, on welfare, cheaters, terrorists, troublemakers, sexually active, or dumb. One of the dangers of stereotyping by teachers is that they may not give students from stereotyped groups the opportunity to develop their potential because they believe they are intellectually inferior to other students in the class. Teachers should be alert to the stereotypes they have developed over time to ensure they do not interfere with their ability to help all students learn.

It is not just the teacher's stereotype about students that affects behavior and learning. The common stereotypes in society influence how we see ourselves and perceive our own identity. Social psychologist Claude Steele (2010) has identified this **stereotype threat** as impacting the academic performance of students of color, female students, and other disenfranchised students. Today's students know the common stereotypes about their group memberships. Unfortunately, some students of color meet the stereotype of not performing at high levels by underachieving even when they have the cultural capital for academic achievement. In other cases, they may not want to reinforce the stereotype, placing such pressure and stress on themselves that they do not perform at the levels at which they are capable. The good news about this research is that teachers can change students' negative stereotypical perceptions of themselves simply by treating students as capable and talented.

Dr. Steele and his research team have found that educators can have a positive impact on students by removing the threat of the stereotype from the way they see themselves. Strategies that will help you accomplish this goal include

- Providing critical feedback to students, especially students of color
- Improving a group's critical mass of students from the same group in a setting
- Fostering intergroup conversations among students from diverse groups
- Allowing students to affirm their sense of self
- "Helping students develop a narrative about the setting that explains their frustrations while projecting positive engagement and success in the setting" (Steele, 2010, p. 216)

These strategies will help students improve their comfort, sense of belonging, trust, academic achievement, and grades in the classroom. By not reinforcing the negative stereotypes and letting students know that they can perform at high levels, you can begin to change the academic performance of students who have believed they weren't capable of higher performance.

Students Leaving School Early

In 1990 the nation's governors joined President George H. W. Bush in developing six National Education Goals for 2000. One of the goals was to increase the high school graduation rate to 90% and eliminate the high school graduation gap between white students and students of color.

Not only did we not meet that goal, we learned that many students, especially for students of color, were not completing high school in four years, as shown in Figure 4.1. African Americans and Latino males in some urban areas have only a 50–50 chance of graduating from high school in four years (Swanson, 2011). English-language learners and students with disabilities are also more likely to drop out of high school than are other students (Thurlow & Johnson, 2011).

The socioeconomic status of families also impacts high school graduation. Students whose parents finished high school are more likely to complete high school than those whose parents did not graduate (Rumberger, 2011). Students from low-income families are five times more likely to drop out of high school than students from high-income families (Rumberger & Lim, 2008). Children who are in poverty at birth are three times more likely to drop out of school than children who have never been poor (Ratcliffe & McKernan, 2010). Another study by the Annie E. Casey Foundation confirmed the link between family income and high school graduation, finding that children who live in poverty and read below grade level by third grade are three times as likely not to graduate from high school as students who were born into families with incomes above the poverty level (Hernandez, 2011).

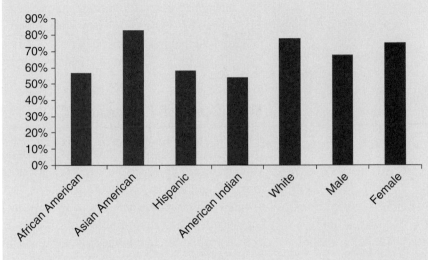

Figure 4.1 Graduation Rates for the Class of 2008

90%
80%
70%
60%
50%
40%
30%
20%
10%
0%

African American | Asian American | Hispanic | American Indian | White | Male | Female

Source: Swanson, C. B. (2011). Nation turns a corner: Strong signs of improvement on graduation. *Education Week Diplomas Count, 30*(34), 23–25. As first published in *Education Week*, June 9, 2011. Reprinted with permission from Editorial Projects in Education.

The dropout crisis appears to be turning the corner. The most recent graduation rates indicate that 72% of the students in the class of 2008 graduated from high school within the four years after they entered the ninth grade—the highest graduation rate since the 1980s. However, the Editorial Projects in Education (EPE) Research Center projected that 1.2 million students in the class of 2011 would not graduate with diplomas. Although graduation rates are projected to continue to improve, we have a way to go to meet the goal of 90%.

Why Students Drop Out of School

Students drop out of school because of individual and contextual factors. Individual factors include students' "attitudes, behaviors, school performance, and prior experiences" (Rumberger, 2011, p. 7). Some students report that they leave school because of school, family, or work responsibilities. Absenteeism, low educational aspirations, moving from school to school, not passing a grade, suspensions, and pregnancy are among the contributors to the decision to leave school (Rumberger, 2011). However, these reasons do not account for the social contextual factors that may have contributed to the decision. As you would expect, schools have a powerful influence on student achievement; they have a similar influence on dropout rates. For one thing, they create the conditions for student engagement with the subjects being taught, teachers, and their peers. Some students choose to withdraw from school because they are bored or not performing well. Other students are pushed out of school by the policies and decisions of

Hear about the lives of student drop-outs.

educators that lead to suspensions and expulsions. Peers and conditions in the community and family can also influence a student's decision to drop out of school (Rumberger, 2011).

Ms. Evbuoma reports that her school district has examined the data on suspensions and determined that they needed to keep students in schools:

> We've almost eliminated suspensions in our district. Kids are spending too much time out of school being suspended, and you have to be in school. So we moved to a loss of privilege (LOP) program where they aren't allowed to go to a school dance. They have silent lunch periods where they sit at a table in silence for maybe up to a month. They are not allowed to talk at all, just get their lunch for an entire hour because we saw those numbers. Unfortunately Hispanic and African American males were being suspended at a startling number at our school. So students are not put out of school anymore unless it is for drugs or an occasional fight. We don't have many fights anymore because of programs such as peer mediation. We are doing everything we can think of to keep kids in school. At first we wondered how this was going to work, but teachers supported the change wholeheartedly.

The Cost of Dropping Out

Students who do not finish high school greatly limit their ability to find a job that will allow them to earn enough to support a family and live comfortably. Annual earnings increase significantly with postsecondary education, as shown in Figure 4.2. Of course, our individual earnings differ based on our job or career choices. For example, the opportunity for the chief executive officer of a major corporation and a private equity investor to be wealthy is much greater than a teacher's. The amount of education required for a specific job varies. A lawyer must have a J.D., a physician must have an M.D., and public school teachers must have at least a bachelor's degree. The educational requirements are more flexible in other occupations. Many firefighters, medical technicians, and aircraft mechanics/service technicians have postsecondary education, but they are generally not required to have a bachelor's degree. In some occupations, earnings may not differ much based on the worker's educational level (Sparks, 2011).

Figure 4.2 Median Income by Educational Attainment in 2009

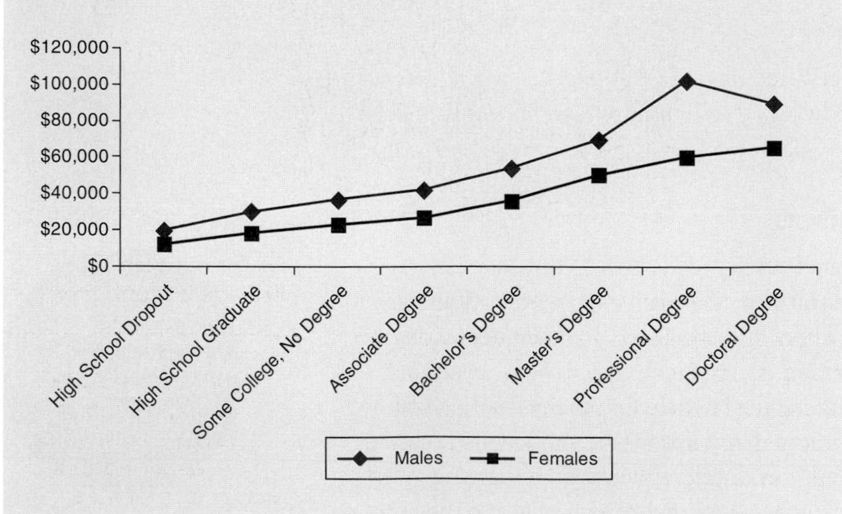

Source: U.S. Census Bureau. (2011). *Statistical abstract of the United States: 2012* (131st ed.). Washington, DC: Author.

The U.S. Department of Education expects high schools to prepare all students for college or career readiness, which does not always require a four-year degree. President Barak Obama proposed a goal that every U.S. student have at least one year of postsecondary education. The intent is to prepare young people for the jobs needed in a changing world economy. High schools and community colleges are designing academic and career programs that reflect local and regional job markets. A growing number of school districts are establishing career-themed academies (Sparks, 2011). The problem is that students generally must finish high school or have a GED to enter postsecondary education, and 3 in 10 students are not earning a high school diploma.

School-to-Prison Pipeline

High school dropouts are more likely to be incarcerated than their peers who earn a diploma (Orfield, 2004), in part, through a process labeled as the school-to-prison pipeline. In many schools that are primarily attended by large numbers of students of color and students from low-income families, "students are required to wear uniforms, to be scanned by metal detectors and frisked by security guards, to use clear plastic bags and backpacks so that their items are visible at all times, and more" (Meiners, 2007, p. 143). These schools have become mirrors of prisons with similar rules, police as guards, surveillance, and a belief that students are inherently dangerous (Meiners, 2007).

Deeper Look 4.3
Read more about zero-tolerance policies.

What is viewed today as a nonviolent crime in school may have been considered a teachable moment in the past (Rethinking Schools, 2011–2012). Students were not automatically punished for first minor infractions, but the event was used as a learning experience in which a lesson could be taught. Zero-tolerance policies call for punishing any infraction of a rule. They are generally used to punish students for the possession of drugs or weapons in school, and allow for no excuses, innocent mistakes, or ignorance of the rules. The policies have led to a significant increase in the number of students being suspended and expelled since the 1970s (Losen, 2011). Although suspensions or expulsions are required by law for infractions such as bringing a gun to school, many infractions are for less serious rule breaking such as possessing over-the-counter drugs such as Advil or Midol.

Students from low-income families and low-achieving students are disproportionately the students who are punished by school authorities (Gregory, Skiba, & Noguera, 2010). These practices have contributed to the disproportionate number of African American males who are suspended and expelled from school, often on their way to prison where they are 36% of the total prison population (Lewix, Simon, Uzzell, Horwitz, & Casserly, 2010).

In most schools, there is a relationship between the achievement gap and the discipline gap, which has the greatest negative impact on students from low-income families and African American and Hispanic students (Boykin & Noguera, 2011). In a study at the Public Policy Research Institute at Texas A&M University (2005), researchers found that students involved in disciplinary incidents at school were 23 times more likely to be referred to the juvenile system. As Ms. Evbuoma indicated, the major problem with suspensions and expulsions is that they interrupt learning, often for the students who are already struggling (Losen, 2011), and start them down the road that could lead to prison. Knowing that these students are at risk should lead to the identification of interventions that could change the direction for students in this pipeline.

Police officers provide security for many schools to support educators in maintaining discipline. However, the resulting disciplinary policies and practices of a school district sometimes lead to students being arrested even for minor infractions.

Challenging Assumptions

The discipline and achievement gaps

● ● ● ● ●

The Assumption

School disciplinary actions are applied equally across students regardless of their socioeconomic status, race, ethnicity, or achievement status.

Study Design

Researchers conducted a synthesis of the research on school discipline patterns for racial and ethnic groups and their impact on student achievement to determine "the degree to which low-income, low achievement, and rates of misconduct contribute to why Black, Latino, and American Indian students are overselected and oversanctioned in the discipline system" (Gregory et al., 2010, p. 59).

Study Findings

When a student breaks school rules or is disrupting a classroom, he or she can be removed from the classroom and suspended or expelled from school. Research studies over the past 30 years show that African American students consistently are more than twice as likely as their white or Asian American peers to be disciplined. Latino and American Indian students are also differentially and disproportionately suspended in some schools. Males of all racial and ethnic groups are more likely than girls to be suspended.

One of the most consistent research findings is the correlation of academic achievement and being engaged in academic learning. Engagement in learning occurs when students are actively participating in classroom work, completing homework, and studying on their own. When students are suspended from school, they may be removed from one class period to two weeks or longer. "Frequent suspensions appear to significantly increase the risk of academic underperformance" (Gregory et al., 2010, p. 60). They also are a moderate to strong predictor of dropping out of school. Other research has found that "suspended students may become less bonded to school, less invested in school rules and course work, and subsequently less motivated to achieve academic success" (Gregory et al., 2010, p. 60).

Part of the gap in disciplinary actions across groups may be due to family income. Low-achieving students from low-income families who live in

HOW DOES SOCIAL CONTEXT INFLUENCE WHAT IS TAUGHT?

Parents send their children to school to learn the knowledge, skills, and dispositions that will prepare them to be good citizens and earn a decent living as adults. Although imparting knowledge is one of the goals of schools, children have been learning since birth from their parents and siblings. They have also been learning from their friends, religious mentors, television, books, and games they play. They are learning as they experience life. That is why parents care about who their children's friends are and where they spend their time. What students learn when they are not with their parents leads to decisions to homeschool children or select a private or charter school in which parents are comfortable with what their children will learn and with whom they will interact.

high-crime/high-poverty neighborhoods are at a greater risk of being disciplined. However, income alone does not account for the disparities in the disproportionate suspensions of African American, Latino, and American Indian students. Researchers have also explored the possibility of greater misbehavior among groups of students, but have generally not found evidence to support this explanation.

What explanations account for the discipline gap? One hypothesis is "differential selection," in which students of color are more likely than their peers to be selected for disciplinary action by a teacher or school administrator. In observing urban classrooms, Vavrus and Cole (2002) found that students who questioned classroom practice or the teacher's authority, which they called "violation of implicit interactional codes," could face suspension. The students most often singled out were students of color. Other explanations for male students of color being disproportionately disciplined have included the cultural mismatch, implicit bias, or negative expectations between students and the school. In some cases teachers appear to rely on "stereotypes to interpret Black students' language and physical expression" (Gregory et al., 2010, p. 63) and overreact to what they perceive as negative student interactions, leading to an office referral for discipline.

Implications.

Although more carefully designed research on the reasons for the discipline gap is needed, it is clear that African American, Latino, and American Indian students are more likely to be suspended than their classmates. Because suspensions and other disciplinary actions remove students from the classroom, they are also not engaging with academic work, which negatively affects their academic achievement. To reduce the compounding effect of the discipline and achievement gaps, the authors of this article recommend that teachers and administrators recognize the potential for bias in their disciplinary actions, develop a range of responses to student misbehavior, use expulsion as a last resort, learn more about the cause of the behavioral problems, and identify ways to reconnect misbehaving students to the school.

References:

Gregory, A., Skiba, R. J., & Noguera, P. A. (2010, January/February). The achievement gap and the discipline gap: Two sides of the same coin? *Educational Researcher, 39*(1), 59–68.

Vavrus, F., & Cole, K. M. (2002). "I didn't do nothing": The discursive construction of school suspension. *Urban Review, 34,* 87–111.

Social Construction of Knowledge

What is knowledge? It is knowing information, facts, and ideas about someone or a topic that has been learned through education or lived experience. However, the knowledge valued by one group may be viewed by another group as inaccurate, unimportant, or not relevant to their lives. The dilemma for educators is whose knowledge should be taught in the curriculum. Traditionalists argue for the focus to be on the Western canon, which privileges the country's Northern and Western European heritage, experiences, literature, and scholarly work. Multiculturalists, on the other hand, argue that the curriculum must also incorporate the experiences of people of color, the labor class, women, and non-Christian religions. They believe that the curriculum should more accurately reflect the histories and cultures of the many groups that populate the nation and should value their multiple perspectives,

It is not just educators and scholars who debate what should be taught in schools. Some parents lament that public schools do not reflect their religious values. They may even think their religion is purposefully denigrated in the curriculum. Some parents report that their cultures or languages are not valued by their children's teachers. Parents of students with disabilities or students who are gifted may complain that the curriculum does not challenge their children. These differing perspectives on what should be taught lead to controversies about the teaching of ethnic studies, class difference, evolution, sex education, and other controversial topics. Some families may protest readings and books assigned to students because they do not reinforce their values. Other families may demand more coverage about their cultural heritages or more stimulating higher-level coverage of the content. As a teacher, you should understand the history, experiences, and values of the community as you develop lessons.

Whose Knowledge

What is taught in schools is generally determined by standards adopted by the state. State or local school districts select a curriculum and textbooks that they think will help students meet the standards as well as reflect their own values and beliefs. Some state legislatures set parameters on the content that can be taught in public schools. For example, a few states require that creationism be taught alongside evolution. Some states allow the inclusion of lesbian, gay, bisexual, transgender, and queer (LGBTQ) identity and issues only if presented in a negative way that indicates that such an identity is wrong.

We generally think that what we are taught in schools is objective and true, that it has been codified through a process with which most experts agree. What a surprise to learn that knowledge is actually socially constructed. It is influenced by the ideas, values, experiences, and interpretations of the teachers and authors of textbooks and scholarly documents. In some cases, authors have removed content from or added it to their books at the request of a state so that their book would be adopted by the state, even though the requested changes may omit events such as lynching that are embarrassing to the state or do not accurately reflect events or the diversity of the nation. In the 1960s the state of Mississippi, for example, adopted a social studies textbook that misrepresented the role of African Americans in the state's post–Civil War history over another textbook because the majority of state board members believed the second text would be controversial and focused too heavily on racial issues. When the authors of the second book sued, a federal court ruled that the state did not have justifiable ground for not adopting the book (*Loewen et al. v. Turnipseed et al.*, 1980).

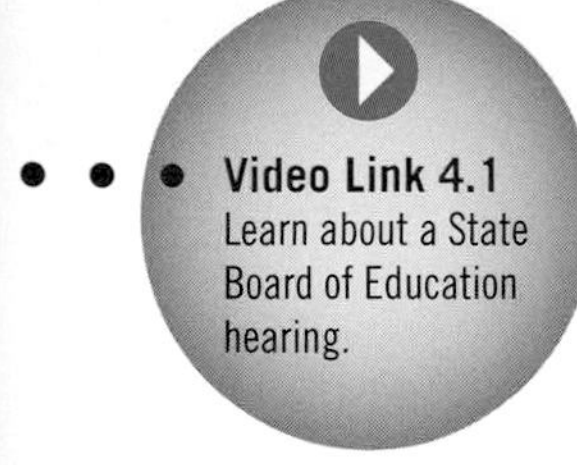

Video Link 4.1
Learn about a State Board of Education hearing.

In 2010 the Texas Board of Education pitted Democrat and Republican board members against each other in the debate about the curriculum standards that would guide the adoption of social studies textbooks that would be used by 4.7 million high schoolers. They disagreed about the portrayal of the separation of church and state; the portrayal of the role of discrimination in society; the prominence given to civil rights leaders of color, including Cesar Chavez and Thurgood Marshall; and hundreds of other details (Robelen, 2010).

Because most recognized scholars who codified what is known about an academic discipline over the centuries in the United States were white, upper-middle-class, Protestant males, the perspectives of the powerful in society are reflected in their work. Scholars from different racial, class, and religious groups or from other countries have developed their own, and sometimes different, conceptualizations of the world from their own perspectives, experiences, and world views. Thus, the Western canon, which has been the core curriculum throughout most of U.S. history, is labeled by these nontraditionalists as limiting and exclusive with its focus on the history, literature, and arts of Northern and Western Europe. In this section we will explore what is being taught in schools.

Multiple Perspectives

We live in a multicultural nation in which our students may have very different lived experiences. Some students' families have recently immigrated. Some could be refugees who have spent periods of time in refugee camps. Some students may be living in a car or homeless shelter. The quality of the housing and nutrition for some children may be very inadequate, affecting their school behavior and performance. Other children may live in comfortable homes with two parents, but one parent has just lost a job, which is affecting their standard of living. Students come from different racial and ethnic groups that constantly feel the brunt of racism. Some are struggling with their sexual identity. Some may be bullies or their victims. Even if the students in your classroom appear to belong to the same ethnic group, they may not share the same religion, and some may be more financially secure than others.

How this diverse group of students and their families see the world is likely to differ. Their cultures and experiences impact their perspectives, which could be different from those of their teacher, especially when the teacher is from a different culture and lives in a different community. How can those multiple perspectives be integrated into a curriculum that serves all students well?

As a teacher, you should listen and learn from your students, their families, and their communities. You should encourage multiple perspectives in your classroom by validating student voices. During class discussions, students can be helped to think about how people from different groups might view the topic or event based on experiences and histories that are different from the students. Current events, for example, could be explored from the perspectives of American Indians, Afghans, Muslims, labor unions, or people who have recently lost their jobs.

A diverse group of students provides a rich resource for incorporating multiple perspectives into the curriculum.

Multicultural Education

Multicultural education embraces the diversity of students, strives to help all students learn regardless of their group memberships, and promotes social justice. It is concerned with equity in the curriculum, relationships between teachers and students, the school climate, staffing patterns, and the school's relationships with parents and communities. Multicultural educators are able to view all aspects of the educational process through a critical lens that has the needs and learning of students at the center. The content of a multicultural curriculum could include human relations, the study of ethnic and other cultural groups, the development of critical-thinking skills, and the examination of issues such as racism, power, and discrimination. Education that is multicultural requires educators to

1. Place the student at the center of teaching and learning.
2. Establish a classroom climate that promotes human rights.
3. Believe that all students can learn.
4. Acknowledge and build on the life histories and experiences of students and their families through culturally responsive teaching.

5. Analyze oppression and power relationships in schools and society to understand racism, sexism, classism, heterosexism, ableism, and ageism.
6. Model social justice and equality in the classroom and in interactions with students, families, and the community. (Gollnick & Chinn, 2013)

Deeper Look 4.4
Read more about multicultural education.

The curriculum, bulletin boards, resource books, and films should incorporate accurate and positive references to diverse groups. The specific content about groups will differ based on the course being taught. Students should study the racial and ethnic diversity of the United States and world along with their own ethnic group. Although time will not allow you to discuss every ethnic group in a single course, you should ensure at a minimum that you include the groups represented in the community or state. If textbooks do not include information about these groups, you need to find supplementary materials. You could invite experts from the community to make a presentation or assist with lessons. Multicultural teachers become acutely aware that they need to intervene when the curriculum is focusing solely on the dominant group.

Multicultural education is important for all students regardless of their group memberships. Unfortunately, many educators have thought that it is only for students of color, believing that white students did not need to explore the issues that are so disruptive to society (for example, racism and discrimination) or to know about other groups and perspectives that help explain the different conclusions reached by groups about history, events, and subjects. Most textbooks today refer to diverse ethnic and racial groups, and most teachers include information about groups other than their own in lessons, particularly during the months that have been highlighted for African American, Latino, or women's history. However, in some schools attention to multiculturalism begins and ends with tasting ethnic foods and participating in ethnic festivals organized by parents, which provide only a superficial understanding of differences. Multicultural education, on the other hand, goes much further by integrating diversity and equity throughout the curriculum and school environment.

Culturally Responsive Teaching

The real-life experiences that students bring to the classroom are often given little credibility in the curriculum and instruction. However, school behavior and prior knowledge are related to what is learned to survive and thrive in their community environments. Students have rich cultural experiences grounded in their ethnic and racial backgrounds that are expressed in community and religious events and family traditions. They have histories that differ based on how long their families have been in the United States, their native and immigrant experiences, and the discrimination their ethnic and racial group has suffered. Bringing students' cultures into the curriculum is one way to make schooling more meaningful to students.

Video Case 4.1
Reaching Diverse Communities

1. What are the advantages of knowing the cultures of students and their families in the delivery of education? What advantage does Mr. Frank have in working with his students from the Dominican Republic and Ecuador?
2. Why does Principal Carol Conklin-Spillane think it is important to do "it on their terms, not our terms" as educators work with families from cultures different than their own?

Culturally responsive teaching is based on the premise that culture influences the way students learn (Gay, 2010; Hollins, 2011; Nieto, 2010). Culturally responsible teachers affirm the cultures of students, view the cultures and experiences of students as strengths, and reflect the students' cultures in the curriculum. Students learn to be proud of their ethnic and cultural identities. Teachers build on the students' diverse ways of knowing as they teach. The curriculum expands beyond the traditional canon grounded only in the knowledge and experiences of Western and Northern Europeans. It helps students learn about cultures other than their own with a goal of respect for and acceptance of differences as the natural state of a diverse society.

Learning is enhanced when teachers use representations from the experiences of students. Students should be encouraged to expand their knowledge about others as they read novels and short stories about people from diverse groups. They should examine current and historical events from the perspectives of European Americans and other ethnic and cultural groups. Students in the sciences, mathematics, the arts, and physical education should learn that persons from many different cultures have contributed to these fields. The examples used to teach lessons should be drawn from the experiences of diverse groups, not just the group to which the teacher belongs. Schooling should help expand students' knowledge of the world, not hide them from the unpleasant realities that exist because of class discussions. Students of all racial and ethnic groups should develop critical-thinking skills that push them to question and investigate what they read, see, and hear in textbooks, the mass media, and discussions with friends. A curriculum for equality encourages them to identify inequities across groups and ask why.

Video Link 4.2
Watch a video about culturally responsive teaching.

At Bremen High School, Ms. Evbuoma has adjusted to the changing demographics in her school and community, where the number of Hispanics has greatly increased over the past 10 years. She decided to learn more about the Hispanic culture and Spanish.

> When you look at the students, you try to include as much as possible to make them feel comfortable. I teach English, but I have taken more Spanish classes than I ever thought I would. Although I took three years of Spanish in high school, I never thought how much I would need it. Over the past few years, professional development has played a great part in my life. When I began teaching Hispanic kids, I realized that I needed to know more. I started going to *cencerras* so that I could see the Hispanic young ladies. This was not part of my culture. Twenty years ago I knew nothing about the Hispanic culture. Now I have a better understanding.
>
> I spend two months on Hispanic heritage. One is for Hispanic heritage month. Students give speeches for Cinco de Mayo and we celebrate it by having students bring in foods from their countries; the parents also come to school. Oh, just the warmth of it. I am always surprised at how much the parents contribute, but when the Hispanic parents had a chance to show their heritage, it was quite overwhelming.
>
> The school district curriculum infuses African America literature so you have to look at it. For us that was a groundbreaking move when it occurred some years ago. Slowly, we are putting more focus on the Hispanic population, but not so much in the literature that we teach overall.

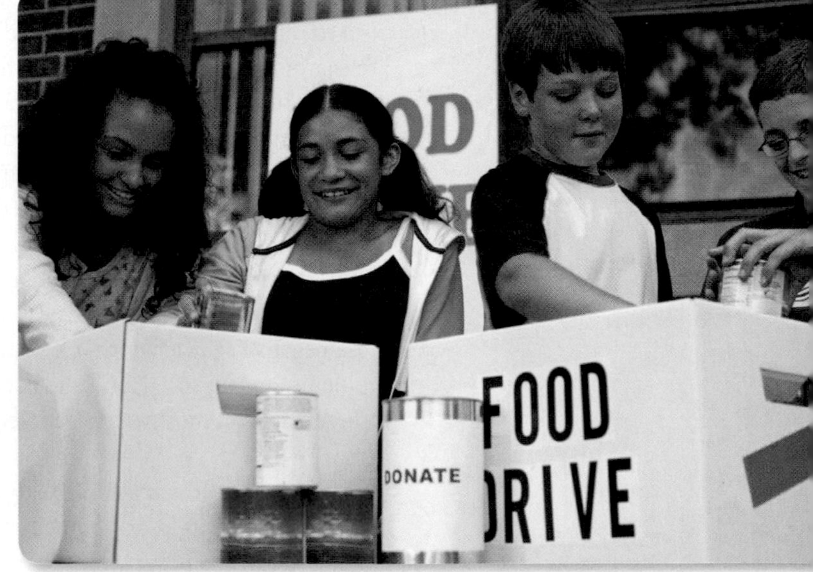

Social justice education encourages students to interact with and assist people who are more disadvantaged than they.

Social Justice Education

The principle of social justice expects us to provide for those persons in society who are not as advantaged as we are. It is a value in most religions, suggesting that all people be treated equitably and with dignity. The philosopher and educator John Dewey (1997) called for social justice in education when he said, "What the best and wisest parent wants for his [or her] own child, that must the community want for all of its children" (p. 3).

Providing a socially just education requires taking steps to eliminate inequities within the classroom and school. Teaching for social justice requires what Marilyn Cochran-Smith (2004), former president of the American Educational Research Association, calls "teaching against the grain." It is more than teaching the literature and history of one's own group along with that of the dominant society. It also means confronting the inequities of society and working toward eliminating them. Socially just teaching examines and critiques equity across groups. It confronts the social and economic inequities that prevent students from learning and participating effectively in schools (Burant, Christensen, Salas, & Walters, 2010).

Teachers for social justice feel a social responsibility for persons who are not advantaged. They believe that everyone has a right to decent housing, health insurance, education, and adequate food and nutrition, regardless of their ethnicity, race, socioeconomic status, sexual orientation, or disability. They develop classrooms in which students are involved in community projects for improving living conditions, and sometimes become engaged in the political process.

HOW ARE STUDENTS AFFECTED BY SOCIAL CONTEXT?

Learning is affected by many factors other than intelligence. The behavior of students may be influenced by the conditions they encounter in their families and communities that can have positive or negative impacts in the classroom. They face numerous societal challenges as they mature to adulthood. Children are dependent on their caregivers who may or may not be very supportive of their growth and development. Teenagers are figuring out their own identity and their place in the family, neighborhood, school, and larger world. They are searching for answers, but in their own unique ways. Friends, family, religion, and inner strength help them resist being drawn into negative responses to life's challenges. Adults are very important in helping children and young people travel safely through childhood and adolescence. Parents, caretakers, educators, and youth workers can help students make sound choices among the unlimited possibilities while avoiding excessive interference.

The portrayal of youth in the media is often negative, suggesting that today's youth are violent, overly sexed, and amoral. However, the attitudes and behavior of most teenagers do not support these negative exaggerations. Of course, schools do include some students who have emotional problems, are antisocial, and shock adults with inappropriate behavior, but they are not representative of most young people.

Students have been impacted greatly by the 2008 recession that led to an increase in unemployment and loss of homes, resulting in an increase in the number of students from families below the poverty level. Students in these families often do not have adequate housing, nutrition, or medical and dental care, which affects their well-being. They also are more likely to engage in the risk-taking behaviors discussed in this section. Research shows that "the younger they are and the longer they are exposed to economic hardship, the higher the risk of failure" (The Annie E. Casey Foundation, 2011). The challenge for educators is how they can best contribute to the educational success of these students. The joy comes in engaging students in increasing their knowledge and skills along with their social abilities. Helping them enjoy learning and encouraging them to come to school are goals of many teachers.

Many young people are very busy, participating in extracurricular, religious, and community activities as well as sports. Sixteen percent of high school students work part time while attending school (U.S. Census Bureau, 2011). Unfortunately, activities that they share with adults are more limited, in part, because of their own schedules and their parents' work schedules. They may be left to socialize and seek assistance and approval from their peers. Their behavior can also be influenced by media and their stereotypical images of youthfulness.

Audio Link 4.3
Learn about nutrition and school performance.

Adults' fear of youth violence and drug use has led to policies of zero tolerance, tougher sentencing requirements for young people, and abusive corrective camps to straighten them out. The inattention and lack of support by adults has made children and youth feel devalued by a society that often resents or fights governmental support for their well-being and safety. School, on the other hand, is often a haven for children and youth. It is generally seen as a place with supportive adults who care about their growth and potential. As a teacher, you can be one of those adults whose caring for students helps make their transition to adulthood make sense. In this section, we will explore some of the social contexts that influence choices students make on this path.

Health and Fitness

The nation is at risk of raising unhealthy children and youth. When teachers are asked to concentrate almost solely on the subjects on which students' academic achievement will be tested, little time is left in the school day for what some policymakers call frivolous activities related to nutrition and physical education. And yet, healthy children perform better in school.

Nutrition

Beginning as early as elementary school, some students, especially girls, worry about their looks and weight. Some young people are just not happy with how they look. They equate thinness with popularity and strive to look like the models and movie stars they see on magazine covers, in music videos, and on the screen. This need to be thin can turn into an obsession that leads to eating disorders such as anorexia and bulimia (Bainbridge, 2009). Some youth develop poor eating habits that include eating binges and fad diets. A growing number of them seek plastic surgery such as breast implants and liposuction to change their bodies. Some have plastic surgery to look like someone else, usually a movie star or popular singer.

The concern with how one looks does not stop with girls. Rather than being obsessed with thinness, boys are more likely to be concerned with muscles. They concentrate on weight lifting to improve their attractiveness or athletic ability. Some young men end up abusing weight control medications or steroids in their effort to be muscular.

Girls are not the only ones concerned with how they look. Rather than worrying about being thin, boys are more likely to be concerned with lifting weights and exercising to develop the body they desire.

At the other end of the continuum, obesity has tripled over the past 30 years, from 13% to 40% for adults and from 5% to 17% for children. The U.S. Surgeon General reports that nearly one in three children are now overweight or obese (Benjamin, 2011). Schoolmates taunt overweight and obese peers in very hurtful ways. They often feel rejected, develop low self-esteem, are depressed, and become isolated from their peers. In addition, the condition increases their lifelong risks for high blood pressure, diabetes, depression, and low self-esteem.

Improper nutrition and lack of physical activity are the main culprits that have led to the obesity epidemic. Most children are not eating the recommended five or more fruits and vegetables

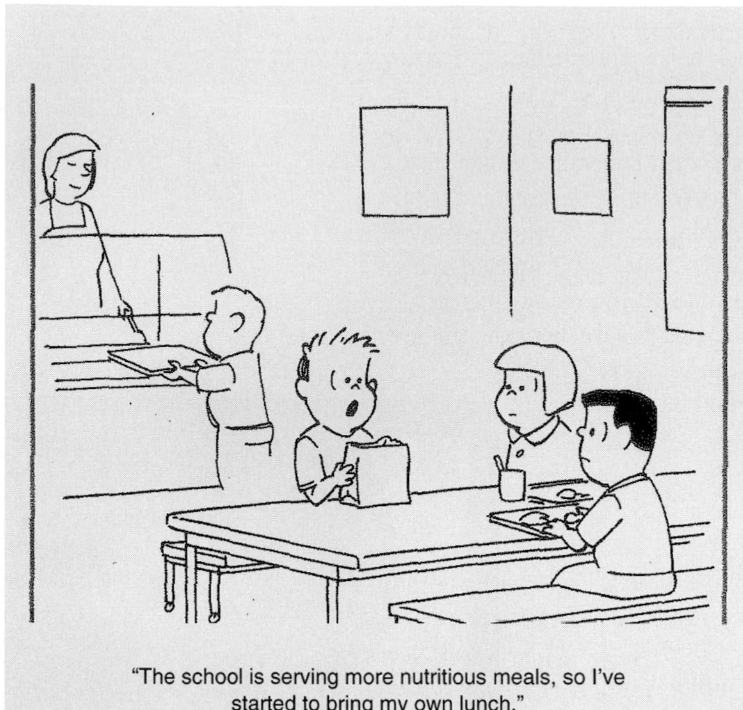
"The school is serving more nutritious meals, so I've started to bring my own lunch."

every day (U.S. Department of Health and Human Services, 2011b). School lunches are not always models of healthy choices for students, but many schools are making an effort to provide more healthy school lunches by improving the nutritional value and eliminating foods that are saturated with fat. It is not just school lunches that do not provide adequate nutrition. Many schools have snack foods and sugary soft drinks available in vending machines. Fast-food chains aggressively market their products to children and young people. Fast food has become the common meal for many families who are too busy to prepare their own meals. In many families, adults and children are eating at different times, and older children may be on their own to select their meals.

The U.S. Department of Health and Human Services is calling on educators to "make schools healthier places to learn by providing quality nutrition, integrating physical activity during the day and teaching children about the importance of embracing a healthy, active lifestyle" (Let's Move, n.d.). The Department has recommended that schools take the following five steps:

1. Create a School Health Advisory Council.
2. Join the HealthierUS School Challenge.
3. Set a good example. Make your school a healthy workplace.
4. Incorporate nutrition education and physical education into the school day.
5. Plant a garden. (Let's Move, n.d., p. 1)

Some schools are removing vending machines or replacing them with ones that dispense more healthy food. Some school officials have notified parents that their children are at risk of being obese. Schools and teachers can take proactive approaches to reducing childhood obesity.

Physical Activity

Good nutrition is only a part of being healthy as a youngster. Another critical aspect is regular physical activity. The U.S. Department of Health and Human Services recommends that young people (6–19 years old) engage in 60 minutes of moderate to intense exercise daily. However, only one in four students are regularly meeting this objective (U.S. Department of Health and Human Services, 2011b). Instead, they are spending over 7½ hours in sedentary activities such as watching television, using computers and cell phones, and playing video games (Benjamin, 2011).

Researchers have found that participation in team sports and athletics has a positive benefit for youth. There is good and bad news on this front. Over half of high school students are playing on a sports team. However, physical education is no longer a requirement in many schools. Only one in three high school students participate in physical education on a daily basis (U.S. Department of Health and Human Services, 2011b).

Low-income students are more likely to live in neighborhoods without adequate facilities for physical activity. Their families can't afford membership in gyms and recreational facilities, which are usually not located in their communities. Even their parks may be used for drugging, drinking, and illegal activities, making them unsafe for children and youth. Without school programs or community centers, many of these students have little opportunity to be engaged in regular exercise or individual or team sports. Because being healthy contributes to readiness to learn, we need to attend to those needs of our students as well as to their academic achievement.

Sexuality

One of the major challenges for youth is figuring out their sexuality. During puberty, students' sexual curiosity is natural and developmentally appropriate. Young people can become confused by the mixed messages they receive from their parents, their friends, and the diverse media to which they are exposed. While one medium glamorizes sex, others condemn it as sinful and immoral unless you are married. As a result, schools face a dilemma about how to help students understand their sexuality. How should it be addressed in the curriculum and what services or support should be provided to students? It is often left to the students to sort through the mixed messages from their peers, their parents, the media, and religious leaders.

Sexual Behavior

Whether or not to have sex is one of the major dilemmas most young people encounter. High school students may not be as wild as they are sometimes portrayed. Less than half (45%) have had sexual intercourse (U.S. Department of Health and Human Services, 2011a). Most teens (61%) who are sexually active are being responsible about sex by using contraceptives (U.S. Department of Health and Human Services, 2011a). Teenagers are giving the credit for these reductions in sexual activity to the messages they receive at home, in school, and elsewhere. Almost 90% of them reported that they had been taught about AIDS or HIV infection. Health education courses appear to be the major source for information on preventing pregnancy, HIV, and sexually transmitted diseases. Nearly 90% of the required health education classes taught abstinence as the most effective method to prevent pregnancy (U.S. Department of Health and Human Services, 2011a).

Teen Pregnancy

Becoming pregnant as a teenager is not always a choice that a young woman consciously makes. Most female (87%) and male (80%) teens report that they would be upset if they or their sexual partner became pregnant. As young people become more knowledgeable of contraceptives and their use becomes more acceptable among their peer group, fewer pregnancies occur. In fact, the number of teenage pregnancies has decreased since its high in 1990. Nevertheless, the United States continues to have the highest teen birthrate in the industrial world (Guttmacher Institute, 2011a).

Almost 750,000 U.S. women between the ages of 15 and 19 become pregnant annually with 18- to 19-year-olds being the majority (two thirds) of those who are pregnant (Guttmacher Institute, 2011a). Not all of those pregnancies result in birth; only 4% of female teenagers gave birth in

Because teenage mothers are less likely to complete high school and college than other teens, efforts to assist these mothers in finishing their education will have benefits to both their children and society.

2009 (Centers for Disease Control and Prevention, 2011a). Pregnancy has much less to do with age and ethnicity than with poverty (Males, 2010). Teenage mothers are sometimes forced to fend for themselves under poverty conditions. Their families can provide little or no financial support, and the fathers of their children are often absent and either are unable or choose not to provide financial support. Staying involved in school is very important to the future economic stability of teenage mothers. Unfortunately, they are much less likely to finish high school or obtain a GED by age 22 than their peers who are not mothers. Only 2% of the mothers who have their baby before they are 18 earn a college degree (Guttmacher Institute, 2011a).

Sex Education

Many teenagers lack accurate information about sex and its possible consequences of pregnancy, AIDS, and sexually transmitted diseases (STDs). Most adolescents report that their preferred source for information on sex is their parents (Guttmacher Institute, 2011b). The majority (65%) of the nation's high schools do provide information about condom use (Guttmacher Institute, 2011b). School programs such as sex education and health clinics are helpful to young people in learning to use contraception if they are going to be sexually active. However, families and communities do not always support such programs. High school and middle school educators should be aware that defining their sexuality can be stressful on a number of their students. Their apprehensions and activities related to sex may affect their school behavior and academic performance.

Violence

Young people do commit crimes, but fewer than most people think. They are much more likely to commit crimes related to property such as arson, burglary, car theft, and larceny than to commit violent crimes. Automobile accidents are three times as likely to kill young people as are homicides (The Annie E. Casey Foundation, 2011).

Children are being criminalized at younger and younger ages as they are arrested for minor charges by police in schools (Rethinking Schools, 2011–2012). As was suggested in the section on the school-to-prison pipeline, the prison population has a disproportionately high representation of persons of color. For example, the imprisonment rate of African American males is seven times that of non-Hispanic white males; Hispanic males are incarcerated at a rate three times that of whites. Hispanic and African American females are in prison at a rate two to three times that of white females. Persons of color comprise nearly 70% of the prison population (Guerino, Harrison, & Sabol, 2011). Students with disabilities are also overrepresented (Meiners, 2007). Although most people in poverty do not commit crimes, crime is more directly related to poverty than to the age and ethnicity of the criminal. People with low incomes are also more likely than higher-income people to be the victims of violent crimes.

Child Abuse

Children and young people are most often the victims of crime, not the perpetuators of crime. One in every 50 children is the victim annually of neglect by parents, caretakers, or relatives (Finkelhor, Turner, Ormrod, & Hamby, 2010). The abuse suffered by these children is shown

Figure 4.3 Child Abuse by Selected Characteristics

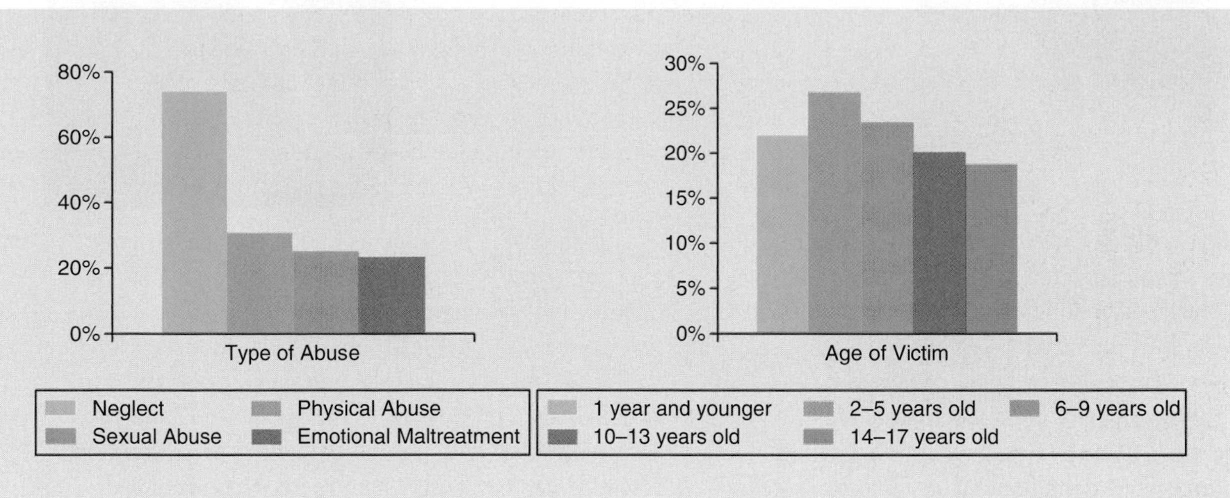

Source: U.S. Census Bureau. (2011). *Statistical abstract of the United States: 2012* (131st ed.). Washington, DC: Author.

in Figure 4.3. Eleven percent of female and 5% of male high school students (grades 9–12) report being physically forced to have sexual intercourse (Youth Risk Behavior Survey, 2011). Perpetrators of both physical and sexual abuse are more likely to be males than females.

Abused and neglected children and youth may arrive at school hungry, bruised, and depressed. They may find the school a safe haven, arriving early and staying late. They sometimes blame themselves for the abuse they receive and are reluctant to acknowledge the abuse by their parents or caretakers. Many abused youth run away from home, choosing to be homeless or seek assistance in a shelter. These childhood experiences become the foundation for mental health problems and delinquent behaviors for a number of young people. A large proportion of the adults seeking psychological and mental health treatment are formerly abused children. Teachers should be caring and supportive of these students. At the same time, teachers are expected to report abuse to school officials.

Bullying

Bullying is an imbalance of power in which bigger, older, or more aggressive students intimidate or belittle others. Bullies typically begin to hone their skills in elementary school as they push other students, force them to give up money, verbally abuse them, or threaten them. Bullying reaches its peak in the middle school years (Office of Justice Programs, 2011). Bullies are more likely to carry weapons to school and be involved in fights in and out of school (Robers, Zhang, & Truman, 2010). Sometimes the result of bullying is assault or murder. While the majority of bullies are males, the victims include both males and females. Nearly half of the students who admitted to sexually harassing others didn't think it was a big deal. Most students who admitted to sexually harassing another student had been the target of harassment themselves (Hill & Kearl, 2011).

Many students with disabilities, gay students, female students, obese students, and others who are different from the majority of students report harassment by peers, and sometimes teachers. Unfortunately, harassment is a common occurrence for many students. A national survey found that 48% of the students had been sexually harassed at school. Thirty percent had been cyberbullied through texting, e-mail, Facebook, or other electronic means. Many of

Mordida!

My second year of teaching was a busy one. I was teaching two courses at two different levels, both below the college preparatory level, in an inner city school with about 2,000 students. The students I taught were often very diverse culturally but were traditionally low achievement and high-risk groups. Many of my students were English-language learners trying to struggle through complex science courses while just beginning to learn the language. One particular class of mine was made up mostly of these students and we learned very quickly that science is especially difficult when you don't understand the basic language. To help my students I purchased resource books to translate scientific terms from English to Spanish, used an online program to make loose translations of the notes, and practiced conversational Spanish with them so that I could speak with their families when needed. The whole time I just thought I was doing my job, but I didn't realize I was doing more. On my birthday, our school posted teacher birthdays; I came into the classroom after lunch to a big surprise. The students in that class had arranged a special "party" to celebrate, bringing balloons, snacks, ribbons, and a home-made *tres leches* cake—a great deal since so many of them had so very little. To make it even more special, when cake time came, I was asked to "bite the cake," or *Mordida!* as they chant. In Latino and Hispanic culture, this is a tradition where when you lean down to bite, they push your face into the cake! I later learned that this is something you do with family, and their inclusion of me in this tradition was something very special. Most of their teachers had simply given up on them because of the language barrier, but I had reached out to them and their families and not tried to take their culture out of the learning experience. In return for simply caring for them, they brought me into their culture with a birthday experience I will never forget!

Amanda L. Glaze
Jacksonville State University
Jacksonville, Alabama

Audio Link 4.4
Learn about electronic aggression.

these cyberbullied students had also been harassed in person. Girls and young women are most commonly verbally harassed with unwelcome sexual comments, jokes, and gestures. Girls were more likely than boys to report that the harassment had a negative effect on them, causing them to have trouble sleeping and not want to go to school. Being called gay or lesbian in a negative way is experienced equally by boys and girls (Hill & Kearl, 2011).

Lesbian, gay, bisexual, and transgender (LGBT) students are often targets of bullies. Eighty-five percent of these students report verbal harassment; 40% report physical harassment; and 19% have been physically assaulted. Both boys and girls were harassed when their gender identity did not match traditional norms (Kosciw, Greytak, Diaz, & Bartkiewicz, 2010).

As she was preparing for her interview, Ms. Evbuoma asked her honors students about some of the issues addressed in this chapter.

> I asked the kids how the community had influenced them. The students were surprised, especially the honor students, at how much harassment they had experienced because they want to be the best and the brightest. We never knew that they were being harassed until you gave me these questions. I don't know why this question wasn't asked in our teaching community. We discovered some of them are bullied because they carry books and they want be the brightest.

> I shared the students' input with the English teachers and math teachers at my school. It began to be a conversation in our group that maybe the students who are being bullied and harassed were the stereotypical nerds, and that is what they call themselves. We needed to look at the issue because there is something in the culture that still makes it not cool to be a nerd. And we were disturbed by it. We took our findings to the principal who took them to the superintendent responsible for curriculum. So teachers need to be on the lookout and realize what is going on in the students' lives from day to day. When they come into the classroom, sure, it may be a safe harbor for them, but we need to know what is going on in the halls, and in their homes and in the community that they have to combat in order to get the quality education that we want them to have.

Schools should be safe for children and youth. However, some students find schools unsafe and dangerous. Educators play an important role in limiting and eliminating bullying, and other youth violence in schools. Many schools have adopted antibullying programs, but successful strategies require a commitment by teachers, administrators, and parents to change the school climate and norms related to bullying.

Gangs

A number of students have had to make a decision about belonging to a gang. Membership provides a strong identity for many of its members. It may help a young person feel important. Although some female gangs exist, young men are more likely to participate in gangs. In 2009, 28,100 gangs with 731,000 members existed in the United States (Egley & Howell, 2011). More high school students (24–28%) than middle school students (15–21%) reported that street gangs were present in their schools (Robers et al., 2010).

Suicide

One in four of the nation's high school students report that they feel so sad or hopeless almost every day for at least two weeks in a row that it interferes with their usual activities (Centers for Disease Control and Prevention, 2010b). This feeling of sadness or a stressful event in a student's life leads some students to consider suicide. Suicide accounts for the third leading cause of death for all 15- to 24-year-olds, behind automobile accidents and homicides. Many more young people consider and try suicide than actually kill themselves. Although 14% of high school students report that they have seriously attempted suicide, 6% of them actually attempted suicide (Centers for Disease Control and Prevention, 2010a). Eight of every 100,000 juveniles actually commit suicide, which is one of every 25 attempted suicides (U.S. Census Bureau, 2011).

Female teenagers are twice as likely as males to attempt suicide, but males are four times as likely to commit suicide. The suicide rate is higher for American Indians and Alaska Native young people ages 15 to 34 than for other groups. Hispanic and African American girls are more likely to attempt suicide than other groups (Centers for Disease Control and Prevention, 2010b). Suicide attempts are often calls for help. Teachers should be alert for signs that may suggest the need for a referral to other professionals.

Video Link 4.3
Watch a video about substance abuse.

Substance Abuse

Young people begin to consider experimenting and using alcohol, cigarettes, and drugs as early as middle school. They tend to associate these risky behaviors with adult behavior and independence from their parents. Biological predispositions or psychological problems might trigger drug use. Social pressures, family problems, or self-hate sometimes become an excuse for trying these substances.

Figure 4.4 Use of Alcohol, Cigarettes, and Drugs by Age

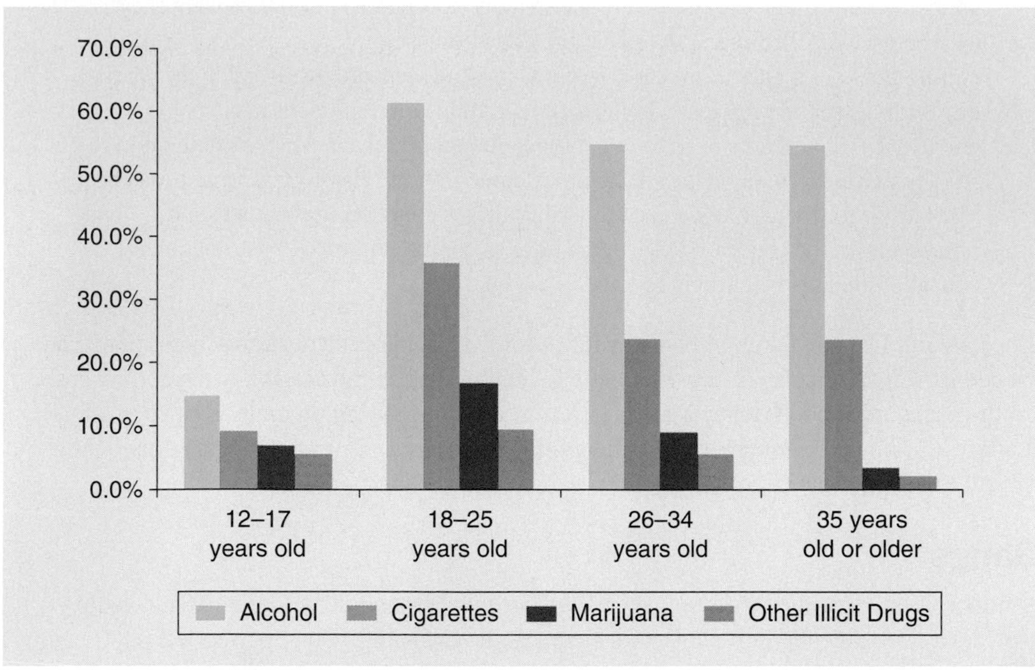

Source: U.S. Census Bureau. (2011). *Statistical abstract of the United States: 2012* (131st ed.). Washington, DC: Author.

Students who plan to attend college are less likely to use drugs. Male teenagers are more likely than females to smoke, drink, and use drugs. A larger portion of American Indian, Native Hawaiian/Pacific Islander, and multiracial/biracial teenagers use illicit drugs and marijuana than teenagers in other ethnic groups. Alcohol is by far the favorite drug of teenagers as shown in Figure 4.4 and is more popular among white teenagers, with over half of them drinking in the previous month as shown in Figure 4.5.

Figure 4.5 Use of Alcohol by Race and Ethnicity by 12- to 17-Year-Olds

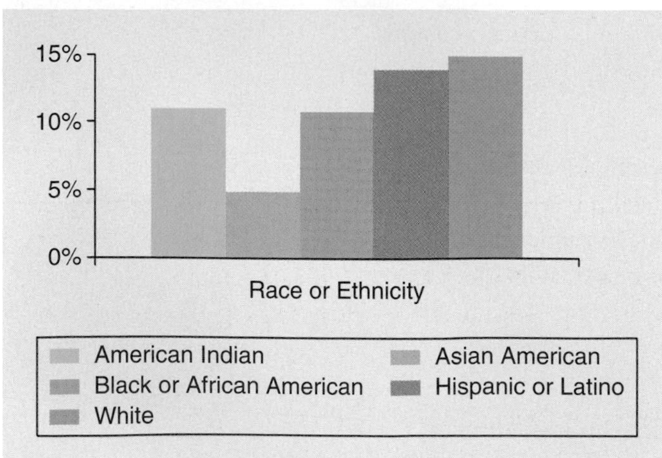

Source: Substance Abuse and Mental Health Services Administration. (2011). *Results from the 2010 national survey on drug use and health: Summary of national findings,* NSDUH Series H-41, HHS Publication No. (SMA) 11-4658. Rockville, MD: Author.

The public believes that drugs are the fifth greatest problem that public schools face behind the lack of financial support for schools, overcrowding, lack of discipline, and fighting/violence/gangs (Bushaw & Lopez, 2011). Parents legitimately worry that drug use could lead to future chemical dependency in which the need for the chemical substance is constant and use can no longer be controlled. Overcoming dependency can be difficult and often requires professional treatment.

As you can see in Figure 4.4, teenagers smoke cigarettes, drink alcohol, and use drugs less than almost any other age-group. Their use of most of these substances has decreased since the 1980s except for marijuana. Nevertheless, it will be important for educators and parents to continue to help young people know the dangers and long-term effects of using these substances.

CONNECTING TO THE CLASSROOM

This chapter has provided you with some basic information about the role of social context in understanding schools and students. Below are some key principles for applying the information in this chapter to the classroom.

1. Teachers should be aware of the social contexts that can have very positive or negative influences on student behavior and learning in the classroom and be able to establish an environment that engages students in their learning.
2. When teachers hold high expectations for the academic achievement of students, students can overcome the negative influence of stereotype threat.
3. Teachers should be aware of the social context of the community and its politics, as they determine how to teach controversial and meaningful lessons to students.
4. Culturally responsive teaching incorporates the culture and experiences of students and their families in developing curriculum and instruction to make the content relevant to students' lives.
5. Teachers and parents can have a positive influence on the choices that students make about sex, drugs, and other potentially harmful choices.

SUMMARY

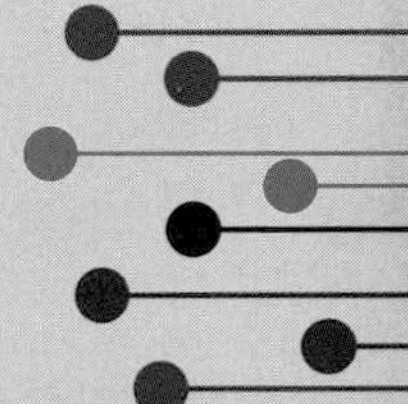

This chapter focused on the social contexts in which teachers, students, and communities interact. Three major topics were addressed in this chapter:

- Recognizing that many factors in and outside of school contribute to students' academic performance and behavior in classrooms can help educators choose appropriate instructional strategies.
- Whose history, values, and experiences make their way into the curriculum of a school is often controlled by decisions made at the state level, often influenced by politics and beliefs.
- At an individual level, often with the influence of peers, families, and the media, students struggle with developing their own identities around issues related to taking care of their body and mind; sexuality; being a bully or victim in their interactions with other students; and use of alcohol, drugs, and cigarettes.

CLASS DISCUSSION QUESTIONS

1. How can stereotype threat impact student performance on high-risk activities? How can a teacher turn around the potential negative impact of stereotype threat?
2. What is the role of multiple perspectives in the curriculum? What changes could you make to the curriculum if you find that multiple perspectives are not included in the textbook or curriculum package that you have been assigned to use?
3. What should be your role as a teacher when you hear a student verbally or physically harassing another student? How could you appropriately support the victim of abuse?

KEY TERMS

Bullying 119
Canon 109
Cultural capital 103
Culturally responsive teaching 111
Deficit ideology 103
Knowledge 101
Meritocracy 103
Model minority 104
Multicultural curriculum 111
Multiple perspectives 109
School-to-prison pipeline 107
Social justice 111
Stereotype threat 104
Zero tolerance 107

SELF-ASSESSMENT

WHAT IS YOUR CURRENT LEVEL OF UNDERSTANDING AND THINKING ABOUT THE SOCIAL CONTEXT OF SCHOOLS?

One of the indicators of understanding is to examine how complex your thinking is when asked questions that require you to use the concepts and facts introduced in this chapter.

Answer the following questions as fully as you can. Then use the Complexity of Thinking rubric to self-assess the degree to which you understand and can use the organization ideas presented in this chapter.

1. What social contexts challenge teachers as they try to engage students in school and their academic work?
2. How can social contexts be reflected in multicultural education?
3. How can teachers support students in making appropriate decisions about issues such as their health and fitness and sexuality—decisions that can have a long-lasting positive or negative effect on their lives?

Complexity of Thinking Rubric

	Parts & Pieces	Unidimensional	Organized	Integrated	Extensions
Indicators	Elements/concepts are talked about as isolated and independent entities.	One or a few concepts are addressed, while others are underdeveloped.	Deliberate and structured consideration of all key concepts/elements.	All key concepts/elements are included in a view that addresses interconnections.	Integration of all elements and dimensions, with extrapolation to new situations.
Social contexts	Lists a few social contexts that can impact on student learning.	Identifies social contextual characteristics that generally support student learning and students' engagement in school.	Describes how educators can support students whose social contexts work against positive educational engagement.	Analyzes educational strategies that improve school attendance and keep students engaged in school and learning.	Develops and tests lesson plans that are culturally responsive and designed to engage students from diverse groups actively in the content being taught.

STUDENT STUDY SITE

Visit the Student Study Site at **www.sagepub.com/hall** to access links to the videos, audio clips, and Deeper Look reference materials noted in this chapter, as well as additional study tools including eFlashcards, web quizzes, and more.

Field Guide

for Learning More About the Social Context of Schools

• • • • •

To further increase your understanding about schools and social contexts, do one or more of the following activities.

Ask a Teacher or Principal

Ask an experienced teacher in one of the schools you are observing which of their students are having difficulty learning the lessons being taught. What social contexts does the teacher think may contribute to the problems in the student's engagement with the subject matter? What instructional strategies is the teacher using to improve the student's performance? What noninstructional strategies have the teacher or other personnel in the school used to engage the student? What impact are these strategies having on the student's learning?

Make Your Own Observations

One of the goals of culturally responsive teaching is to connect the concepts being taught to the students' real lives. The teachers that you are observing may use different strategies to make the curriculum authentic and meaningful to their students. As you visit classrooms, look for evidence of how the teachers you observe are connecting the curriculum to students' lives by using the following rubric from the *Five Standards for Effective Pedagogy and Learning* of the Center for Research on Education, Diversity & Excellence. Begin the process by identifying the school and the group memberships of the teacher and students being observed.

School:				
Location of School:				
Race and Gender of the Teacher:				
Race, Gender, Native Languages, and Class of Students:				
Standard	**Emerging**	**Developing**	**Enacting**	**Integrating**
Making Meaning—Connecting School to Students' Lives	The teacher (a) includes some aspect of students' everyday experience in instruction, OR (b) connects classroom activities by theme or builds on the current unit of instruction, OR (c) includes parents or community members in activities or instruction.	The teacher makes incidental connections between students' prior experience/knowledge from home, school, or community and the new activity/information.	The teacher integrates the new activity/information with what students already know from home, school, or community.	The teacher designs, enacts, and assists in contextualized activities that demonstrate skillful integration of multiple standards simultaneously.
Comments:				

Reflect Through Journaling

Think about the last three fiction or nonfiction books that you have read. Whose knowledge did they reflect? Were the stories grounded in the United States' dominant society or did they introduce you to other cultures? How could you increase your knowledge about groups other than your own?

Build Your Portfolio

When you begin teaching, you may have a class with students from ethnic or racial groups with which you are not familiar. You should be able to incorporate information about your students' culture into the curriculum and draw on their cultures to provide examples to help them learn. To provide you a beginning, identify instructional resources on African Americans, Asian Americans, Latinos, or American Indians that can be incorporated into lesson plans for the future.

The sexual harassment of students by teachers or other students is illegal. Gay and lesbian students report fairly regular harassment from other students, particularly verbal abuse. How will you respond if students in your class or within your hearing are verbally taunting gay or lesbian students? How will you help the gay and lesbian students in your classroom handle the harassment? Develop a plan for confronting harassment in your classroom.

Read a Book

To learn about successful practices in schools and classrooms that are improving students' engagement in learning and their academic performance, read *Creating the Opportunity to Learn: Moving From Research to Practice to Close the Achievement Gap,* by A. Wade Boykin and Pedro Noguera (2011; Alexandria, VA: Association for Supervision and Curriculum Development).

For an analysis of the myths taught in U.S. history and a discussion of how textbook decisions are made, see *Teaching What Really Happened: How to Avoid the Tyranny of Textbooks & Get Students Excited About Doing History,* by James W. Loewen (2010; New York, NY: Teachers College Press).

Search the Web

Teachers are required to report child abuse if they suspect it. Check **http://www.childwelfare.gov/pubs/usermanuals/educator/index.cfm** or **http://www.scholastic.com/teachers/article/what-should-you-do-when-you-suspect-child-abuse** for assistance on identifying and reporting child abuse.

For information on the U.S. Department of Health and Human Services' Let's Move program, visit **http://www.letsmove.gov/schools** to learn more about raising a healthier generation of children and activities in which schools can participate.

TEACHER INTERVIEW

Arlene M. Costello

Arlene M. Costello is a teacher on special assignment in the English for Speakers of Other Languages (ESOL) program in the school district of Escambia County in Florida, where Pensacola is the county seat. Located in the westernmost corner of the Florida Panhandle on the Pensacola Bay, which connects to the Gulf of Mexico, Pensacola has a population of more than 52,000. Although she has taught in ESOL classrooms for many years, Ms. Costello has also worked in gifted education programs and now manages the ESOL programs for her county.

Ms. Costello grew up in the Philippines, receiving her bachelor's degree there. She began her teaching career in the Philippines, but soon wanted to explore the world, accepting a position at an international school in Okinawa, Japan, teaching Japanese students and the children of diplomats who spoke a language other than English. These students had to be proficient in the English language in order to be admitted to the international school.

> During the summer, I taught Chinese students in the American School in Taipei, Taiwan. Those were great experiences because the Taiwanese people were very focused on education and liked their children to learn English. After I married a Navy man, we moved to Italy where I taught on the Navy campus for achievement into the University of La Verne.

When her family moved to Pensacola, she began teaching in a Catholic school, moving to the Escambia County schools when an ESOL position became available.

Families and Communities

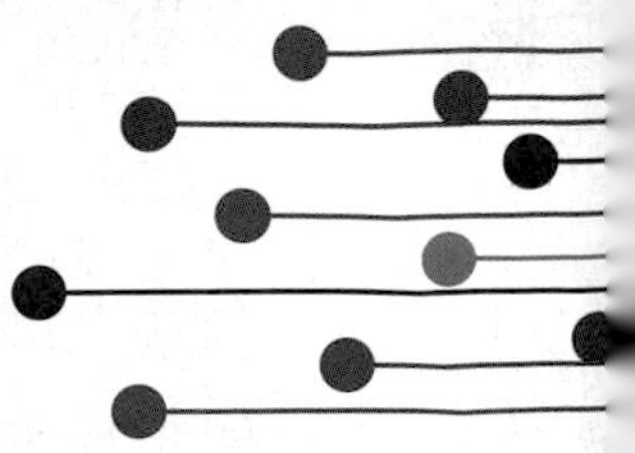

- *Why did you choose to work in ESOL?*

  I was very interested in diversity and also language as well as the education of English-language learners (ELLs) and their being successful in the American educational system. Because I knew that a number of the ELLs were also gifted, I developed an interest in that field as well. After years of experience working with ELLs, I was asked to manage the training and certification of ELL teachers.

Who are the students in your ESOL programs?

Our students are Vietnamese, Hispanic, Spanish, South American, and some from European countries. We have Asian students from many different countries. Although Asians are classified as one national pan-ethnic group, they come from many different countries with different languages. We have a total ESOL population of 450, more or less, depending on the season of the year.

How have you engaged parents in the schools that their children attend?

In ESOL we realize the different challenges in the cultural background of parents. What we have done is organize parent leadership councils for the district. We meet about three times a year to formulate our plans on what programs we need for our parents. They have said they need information on health services. They need information on how they can use technology. We use technology in our schools, but not all parents have access to technology and the Internet.

We hold parent training sessions about three times a year. We connect with Title I and Migrant Programs. We send the communications to all the parents. We hold English classes for parents. We also hold training sessions for parents who are interested in resources in the community. For example, we had someone from the public library come and explain to the parents how to apply for library cards, the library hours, and how to use computers in their libraries. We have Spanish and Vietnamese translators. We had visitors from the immigration office for parents who are interested in applying for U.S. citizenship. Right there and then, we help them complete the form. That is really helpful. Visitors from the school district explain our school system to them and provide them with telephone numbers, exposing them to the way our system works so that they can make use of resources for their children. Our system is very friendly to them, but very challenging. The system depends so much on our office to get translators and help parents with the needs of their children. We work very closely with Title I and the Migrant Program to make sure our parents are informed.

Questions to Consider

1. What is an ESOL program? Would you be interested in teaching in an ESOL program? Why or why not?
2. What are the advantages of parents being engaged with their children's teachers and schools?
3. What ways would you engage families in the classroom and school that are not listed among the approaches used in Escambia County?

Learning Outcomes

After reading this chapter, you should be able to

1. Analyze public perspectives about the quality of schools and teachers.
2. Respect a student's family and understand the importance of not stereotyping students based on their family structure and size.
3. Discuss how culture is another social context that influences teaching and learning.
4. Examine the influence that the culture of students and their families can have on curriculum and instruction in schools.
5. Practice several strategies for effectively involving parents in your classroom.

INTRODUCTION

The school is much more than the educators and students who populate it. A good school contributes to the health of a community by taking care of its children and preparing them to contribute to society in the future. Families, of course, are critical in the education of their children, which is enhanced when families and educators work together to help students learn. The community is represented by the people who live there, the public agencies and officials who serve the community, and the businesses and other organizations that inhabit it. They all play a role in making schools successful.

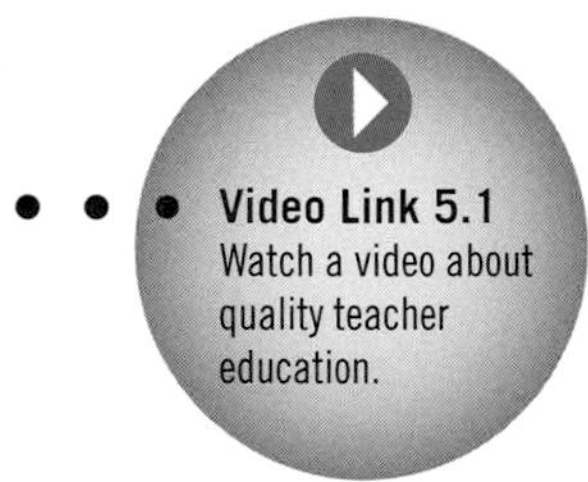

Video Link 5.1
Watch a video about quality teacher education.

When they have a choice, families choose to live in communities that are known to have good schools. These schools provide safe environments for their children, have qualified teachers who are committed to student learning, and have a record of preparing graduates who are successful, contributing adults. They value the input of parents and both encourage and support family involvement in the schools. Yet, most communities have some schools that have become isolated from the community. These are schools in which it feels that no one cares about the children who attend them. They do not provide pleasant or engaging environments; they too often are not safe havens for the students who attend them. Many of their teachers are not fully qualified or may not appear to care about their students' social, psychological, or academic growth. In some cases it may seem that the community has given up on its schools and their inhabitants. In this chapter we will explore the involvement of families, communities, and educators in making schools work for students.

HOW DO THE PUBLIC AND EDUCATORS VIEW EDUCATION?

Almost everyone has an opinion about schools and how they could be improved. Public attitudes about schools can influence educational policies and practices. When the public is upset with the quality of schools, politicians may respond with demands on teachers and school administrators for reform. The most common way to determine what the public thinks is to conduct surveys by pollsters. Educators and policymakers use survey results to determine agreement or disagreement with current and proposed policies and practices. In this section we will examine some of the public's, educators', and parents' views of education that may impact your work in schools.

The quality of schools is important to families when they choose the community in which they want to raise their children. Half of the respondents to the annual Phi Delta Kappa/Gallup poll grade their community schools as an *A* or *B*, which is slightly higher than they rated them 10 years earlier. Parents grade their community schools higher than the general public, with four in five giving an *A* or *B* to the school of their oldest child, as shown in Figure 5.1. Interestingly, the public believes that their community schools are better than other schools in the United States, with fewer than one in five giving an *A* or *B* to the nation's schools (Bushaw & Lopez, 2012).

Figure 5.1 Percentage of Public Awarding *A*s and *B*s to Schools

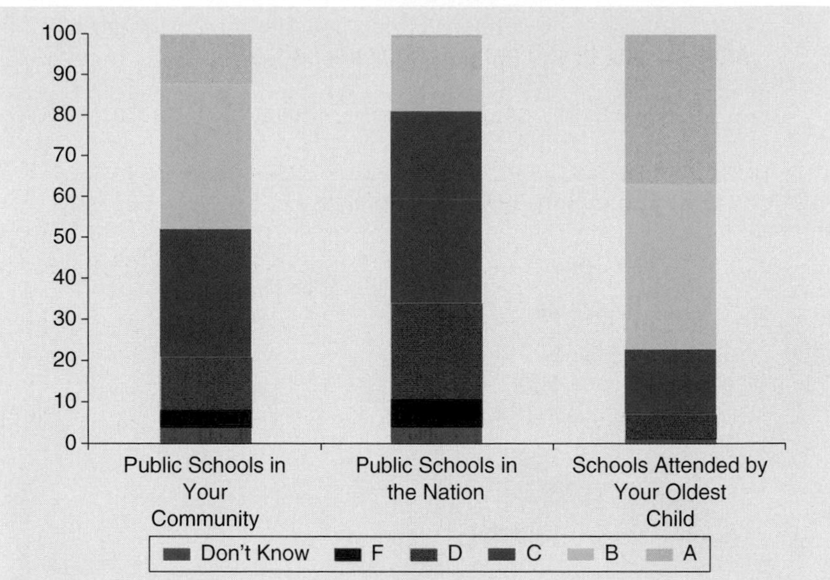

Source: Bushaw, W. J., & Lopez, S. J. (2012, September). Public education in the United States: A nation divided. *Phi Delta Kappan, 94*(1), 9–25.

Teacher Quality

In his January 2011 State of the Union address, President Barack Obama said that "after parents, the biggest impact on a child's success comes from the man or woman at the front of the classroom." Parents and community leaders agree that the quality of schools is measured, in great part, by the quality of the teachers in the schools. Parents and students know who the effective teachers are. A number of parents do everything possible to ensure their children are in those teachers' classes and steer their children away from classes taught by ineffective teachers. They clearly know the value of an effective teacher to the potential academic success of their children. How does the public view teachers? Seven in 10 respondents in the Phi Delta Kappa/Gallup (Bushaw & Lopez, 2012) poll reported that they trust and have confidence in public school teachers. In another nationwide survey, the Harris Poll found that teaching is ranked as the fifth prestigious occupation, as shown in Figure 5.2. Although teacher pay is lower than for most other professions, two in three Americans indicate they would support a child of theirs in becoming a public school teacher (Bushaw & Lopez, 2011).

Figure 5.2 Occupations by Highest and Lowest Rankings by the Public

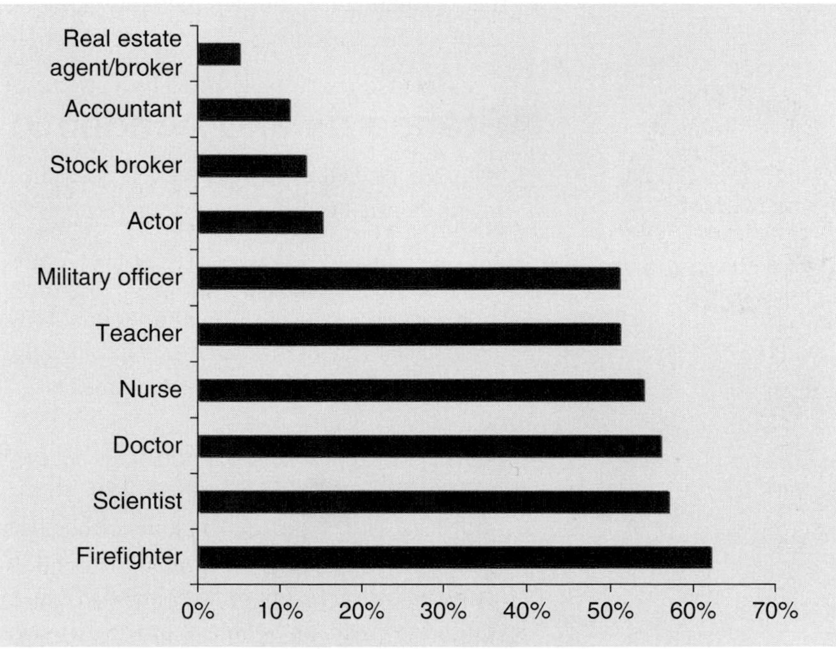

Source: Harris Interactive, Inc. (2009a, August 4). Firefighters, scientists, and doctors seen as most prestigious occupations. Retrieved February 5, 2012, from http://www.americanbar.org/content/dam/aba/migrated/marketresearch/PublicDocuments/harris_poll.authcheckdam.pdf

Problems With Schools

The public also has views about what they think are the problems in schools. In the Phi Delta Kappa/Gallup poll they identified the lack of financial support six times more often than any other problem, as shown in Figure 5.3. However, groups have a different set of concerns based on their own experiences and needs. A study of African American and Latino families found that they are most concerned about the high school drop-out, low college attendance, and graduation rates that their children face (Hart Research Associates, Brossard Research, & the Insights Marketing Group, 2011). Latino and African American parents are not supportive of closing schools as is the practice in many school districts. They would prefer that the schools be fixed and that teachers be supported in improving their teaching (Hart Research Associates et al., 2011).

Figure 5.3 Public View of School Problems

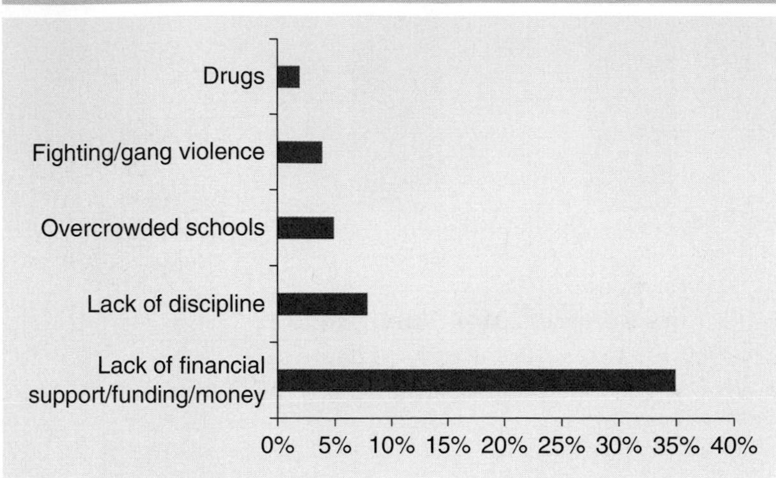

Source: Bushaw, W. J., & Lopez, S. J. (2012, September). Public education in the United States: A nation divided. *Phi Delta Kappan, 94*(1), 9–25.

Teachers report that the main challenges they face are related to the increasing number of students who are English-language learners, the growing inclusion of students with disabilities, and children of poverty in their classrooms. These challenges are more extensive in urban schools. Half of the teachers report that parents do not provide adequate support for their children's learning, but the majority of principals and teachers think that relations between parents and schools have improved in recent years (MetLife, 2009). Other problems that teachers think interfere with students' academic success are poor health, poor nutrition, and violence in schools (Harris Interactive, Inc., 2009b).

Standards and Academic Success

Many reports on the quality of schools decry the low academic achievement of students, particularly when compared with students of other nations. You may have seen television commentators discussing what they perceive as the poor state of education and schools. These reports sometimes lead to local, state, and federal policies for improving U.S. students' performance on international tests and closing the achievement gap among groups of students. Schools have responded by adding more days to the school year, hiring only highly qualified teachers, and providing tutoring for students. How do parents and the public perceive these problems?

The majority of teachers and principals believe that all children should meet high standards (MetLife, 2010). The public agrees. Most states have adopted standards for every subject and grade level, but employers think that schools have not yet set high enough expectations for meeting the standards. They would like schools to push students harder. African American and Latino parents also support high standards and expectations for their children, but they worry that schools may not be able to provide enough support for their children to learn at those high levels. They also want their children to take rigorous courses for college preparation even if they may struggle in those classes (Hart Research Associates et al., 2011).

Students don't always think their teachers are holding them to high standards. More than one in three admit that they only do enough work to get by in school; 71% of their secondary teachers don't think students are working hard (MetLife, 2010). Although teachers think that all students should meet standards, only one in three actually believes that all students have the ability to be academically successful. The rate is even lower in schools with high proportions of students from low-income families, where only 3 in 10 teachers believe their students can learn at high levels. Even worse, fewer than one in five of the teachers and principals believe that all students are motivated to be academically successful (MetLife, 2010). A high expectation for academic learning is not a disposition held by the majority of teachers.

Video Link 5.2
Watch a video about common core standards.

IN WHAT TYPES OF FAMILIES DO STUDENTS LIVE?

Audio Link 5.1
Learn more about the role of parental involvement in the classroom.

The population is getting older as large numbers of baby boomers retire, which means that the percentage of children and young people continues to decrease. In 2010 nearly one in four persons in the United States was under the age of 18, down 4% from 1980. Less than half of U.S. families have children under the age of 18 (U.S. Census Bureau, 2011). These changes in the demographics of age impact educational policy. Families without school-aged children are not always advocates for education and social programs for children, especially when it comes to providing additional financial support.

Diversity of Families

Families today are different than those in which your grandparents and great grandparents were raised. Sixty years ago couples married within a few years after they finished high school. The typical family included both mother and father and two or more children, with the father usually working while the mother stayed at home to raise the children. Children were more likely to be born to married women, and divorce was rarer than today.

Families in the United States today are very diverse. They include mothers working while fathers stay at home with the children, stay-at-home mothers, single-parent families, two working parents, remarried parents, married couples without children, families with adopted or foster children, gay and lesbian parents, extended families, grandparents raising grandchildren, and unmarried couples with children. Most children live with two parents, even though one of them may not be their natural parent. However, single mothers, single fathers, grandparents, and other guardians raise approximately one in three children in the United States, as shown in Figure 5.4. African American students are less likely to live with two parents than students from other ethnic or racial groups, with over half of them in families with a single mother (U.S. Census Bureau, 2011).

Figure 5.4 Structures of Families in Which Children Live

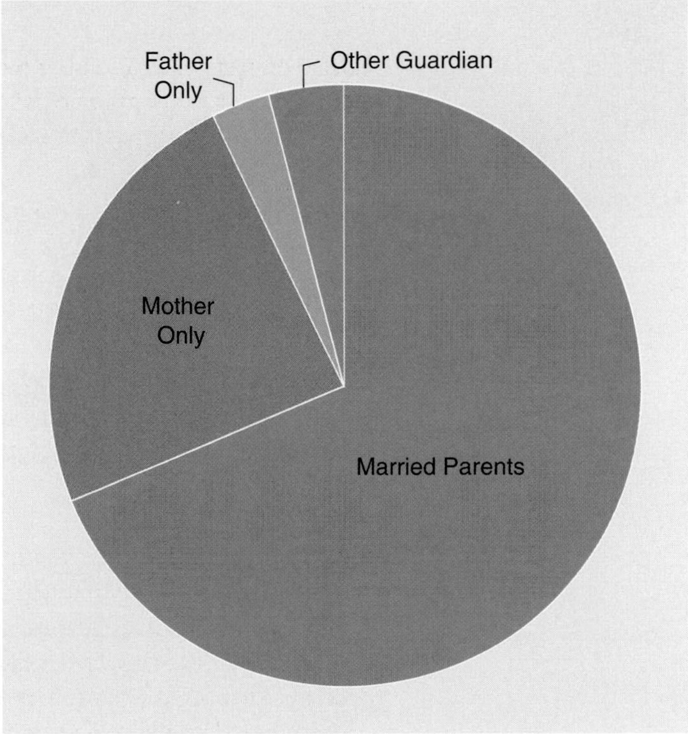

Source: Federal Interagency Forum on Child and Family Statistics. (2011). *America's children: Key national indicators of well-being, 2011.* Washington, DC: Author.

Deeper Look 5.1
Read about family diversity and education.

Today there are more unmarried women than ever before, and they are having more children than in the past. Two in five children are born to an unmarried mother (Federal Interagency Forum on Child and Family Statistics, 2011). Although children are advantaged when they live with two caring and loving parents, living with two parents is not essential for success in school and life. Problem behavior and lack of academic success are more directly related to poverty, conflict, and instability in families (Furstenberg, 1999) than family structure.

Unfortunately, poverty is a prevalent factor in families headed by single mothers. Their income is only 42% that of a married couple, making single mothers five times more likely to be below the official poverty line (U.S. Census Bureau, 2011). Poverty leads to children suffering from inadequate health care and hunger that results from poor housing conditions and not enough money to support basic needs. In addition, three in five children now live in communities with poor environmental conditions such as air quality (Federal Interagency Forum on Child and Family Statistics, 2011).

Children in single-parent families are more likely to be in poverty than those in two-parent families. A good education is critical to them for an economically independent future.

During your career in schools, you may also have students whose parents are gay or lesbian. Most of these parents are married or have made a commitment to their partner and have decided to raise children. Because of the prejudice against lesbians, gays, bisexuals, transgenders, and queers (LGBTQs) in some communities, young students may not understand a family with parents of the same sex and ask you questions about why a student has two mommies or two daddies. Some heterosexual couples with children in your classroom may ignore the gay or lesbian couple or refuse to work with them. In other communities, families will be very acceptant of the diversity of students and families that comprise the school. Nevertheless, you should be prepared to help students understand and accept families that are different than their own and be welcoming to all parents and guardians who will be your partners in helping their children learn.

Ms. Costello reports that families in Escambia County reflect the diversity of family structures described above. Because a navy base is located in the county, the school system also has families in which one or both parents may be deployed to Afghanistan or other areas of the world for extended periods of time.

Size of Families

Although a few families have many children, most married couples with children under 18 years old in the United States are small, with one or two children; 21% of families have three or more children (U.S. Census Bureau, 2011). The birth rate now is lower than it has been since the government began keeping records, with the greatest drop among African American teenagers (Centers for Disease Control and Prevention, 2011b). However, birth rates are higher for women of color, in part because the median age of persons of color is younger than for whites. Therefore, a larger percentage of women of color are of childbearing age, leading to higher birth rates.

HOW DOES CULTURE INFLUENCE FAMILIES AND THEIR CHILDREN?

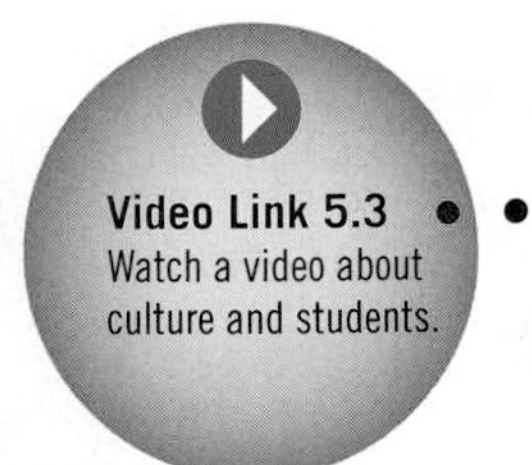

Video Link 5.3
Watch a video about culture and students.

Our culture defines us. It guides our way of thinking, feeling, and behaving in our family and community. Members of a group develop behavior patterns that help them understand each other and be able to live together in relative harmony. Our cultural identity is not innately based on the culture in which we are born. For example, Chinese infants adopted by Polish American, Catholic, middle-class parents will share a cultural heritage with middle-class Polish American Catholics, rather than with Chinese, because they were raised in the Polish American culture.

We are comfortable with the members of our cultural group because we know the meaning of their words and actions. However, we may misunderstand the cultural cues of members of a different cultural group. We grow up thinking that everyone thinks and acts like us, not realizing that the experiences and conditions of other groups could lead to different **values**, behaviors, and knowledge. As a result, we may respond to differences as personal affronts, rather than as cultural differences. These misunderstandings may seem insignificant, but they can carry important cultural meanings to members of groups. These differences vary from how loud is too loud to how close to stand to someone without being rude or disrespectful to how to raise children. You can gain respect or offend a parent by raising your palm to greet them or raising your eyebrow. These are culturally determined behaviors with meaning to members of a group.

Ms. Costello, who was profiled at the beginning of the chapter, recognizes the importance of the family's culture, especially when working with English-language learners whose families are recent immigrants. One way that she and other ESOL teachers in her school district have focused on the cultures of their families is through heritage days in the schools with an ESOL center. She works with ESOL teachers to design heritage days that are more than ethnic foods and dances. She meets with the teachers and asks them what their ideas are and then leads them in developing knowledge and learning activities as well as involving the parents and others.

> We started by involving the hallway where the Centers are located and studying the cultures represented in the ESOL program. They study about the countries; they use technology; they use research; and they use parent and community resources. I help in getting those resources and help the teacher know how to put those resources together. Just like the science fair, we have a culture fair. The kids put together their presentation boards and practice how to make their presentations. They learn about dances and teach other students the cultural dances. The students use the school announcement system to announce the heritage day and explain what it is.
>
> The next year, we broadened the approach, but we had to communicate and coordinate with the administrators in the school. I made a presentation of the plan and put together a plan. We now involve the whole school with each classroom choosing a country. The heritage day was held on Saturday so that the community could be involved. The presentations were really beautiful. The whole school was involved in the presentations of the research and dances. We had food. The students sold their food for their internal account so that they could use it for their awards program at the end of the year. The parents were invited to the awards program, and they bought medals and certificates and all that. We have done that in several schools. It has been very successful.

Where we don't have success is at the high school level. It is a different world at the high school level. We have had to modify this. We do it during lunch hour. The ESOL teacher organizes a cultural club. She started with placemats of different countries based on the students' research and had presentations by students. The high school students seemed to enjoy that a lot.

Characteristics of Culture

Our culture has a great impact on how we interact with each other in our everyday living. We do not always realize that different patterns exist in other cultures.

Culture is learned, shared with others, adapted to the circumstances, and dynamic. We learn our culture from our parents and caretakers. It is reinforced at places of worship, community events, and ethnic celebrations. We acquire our culture and become competent in its language and ways of behaving and knowing through a process called **enculturation.** We learn the social norms and expectations of society through the process of **socialization.** Thus, we learn what it means to be a mother, husband, student, or friend as well as the meaning of occupational roles such as teacher, businessperson, custodian, or politician. Nurses, physicians, teachers, neighbors, and religious leaders assist parents in enculturating and socializing children by modeling appropriate behavior and rewarding children and youth for acceptable behaviors.

Over time cultures have had to adapt to environmental conditions, available natural and technological resources, and their relationship to the larger society. Thus, the Eskimo who lives with extreme cold, snow, and ice develops a culture different from that of the Pacific Islander, who has limited land, unlimited seas, and few mineral resources. The culture of urban residents differs from that of rural residents, in part, because of the nature of the resources available in the different settings. Cultures adapt as technology forces changes in available jobs and communication. The cultures of groups that suffer discrimination in society respond to the power relationships within society differently than the dominant group.

Cultural Relativism

Cultural relativism requires that we not judge other cultural groups by our own cultural standards, but see the second culture as one of its members sees it. We might come to understand that the way of doing things in that culture has validity. As countries and cultures around the world become more interdependent, we can learn to respect other cultures and avoid relegating them to an inferior status. This stance is particularly important in schools as students with foreign-born parents enter our classrooms.

The principle of cultural relativism is not limited to cultures outside the United States. The cultures of many groups in the United States have been judged as inferior to the dominant and privileged Western European culture. We are likely to find children of immigrant parents, students of color, and students from low-income families in our classrooms. What do we really know about their cultures and lived experiences in the community? When we expect students from diverse cultural groups to act, think, and know as we learned in our own culture, we are placing a burden on the students to learn our culture. Your respect in the community will improve as you learn the cultures of the students and their families and begin to understand why they behave and think differently than you.

Biculturalism and Multiculturalism

We are all multicultural because we are members of more than one identity group within our culture. We behave and think differently about ourselves and the world based on our gender, ethnicity, race, language, religion, socioeconomic status, and abilities. We may act and speak differently in a professional setting than when we are interacting in the community in which we grew up. Males and females, for example, often exhibit different behaviors in social settings. As we grew up, we learned the competencies appropriate in our multiple identity groups. We can also learn the history, experiences, and cultures of other groups. As we learn to function effectively in two or more cultures, we become border crossers. We become bicultural or multicultural and often bilingual or multilingual as well.

Because most schools reflect the dominant society, students may feel forced to adopt the dominant culture to be academically successful. In contrast, other students find almost total congruence between the culture of their family, schooling, and work. Persons of color, immigrants, and persons with low incomes generally have to become bicultural to fit in at work or school, maintaining their own cultural patterns at home and the cultural patterns of the dominant group at work and in school.

When our cultural differences result in one group being treated differently from another, **cultural borders** are erected between groups. Crossing these borders can be difficult, especially when behavior valued on one side of the border is denigrated or not tolerated on the other side. Borders are sometimes drawn in schools around speaking one's native language or dialect in school or wearing a hijab as expected for one's faith. Cultural borders are established in classrooms when teachers ground all activity and communications in their culture alone. Being able to function comfortably in different cultures allows educators to cross cultural borders, incorporating the students' cultures and experiences into the curriculum and classroom activities. It also allows teachers to model respect for cultural differences and the cultural borders some students must cross on a daily basis.

School Culture

Schools have their own culture with rituals, rules, academic and social expectations, teaching practices, dress codes, and social interactions between students and teachers and among students. The school culture gives a school its own unique look and feel. It could be friendly, competitive, caring, elitist, inclusive, or intolerant and racist. The culture can support academics, sports, bilingualism, or the arts. Some schools have established nurturing environments that value and care about their students as individuals. Others are very authoritarian with strict rules and hierarchies to reinforce the rules (ASCD, 2012). The school culture can impact student learning, helping to improve it or dampen it. Schools that are successful in helping students learn have positive school cultures that care about students, families, and the communities in which they are located.

Deeper Look 5.2
Read about the relationship between school culture and student achievement.

Traditions

Although they differ across schools and communities, students and educators practice many common rituals in athletics, extracurricular clubs, graduation exercises, and school social events. The signs and emblems of the school culture are displayed in school songs, colors, and cheers. Traditions in the school culture are associated with regional influences, the social structure of a

Most schools participate in competitive sports events. These events are used to develop school spirit that brings students and the community together.

community, and location in a rural, urban, or suburban area. Some schools are influenced greatly by the religion of the children's families, others by the presence of a large military base.

Schools develop histories that are transferred from generation to generation. Extracurricular activities, proms, awards and graduation ceremonies, fundraisers, school plays, bands, clubs, football games, and school trips take on different degrees of importance from one community to another and from one familty to another. Some graduates retain lifelong feelings of pride about their schools. Others have less lofty memories.

Hidden Curriculum

In addition to the formal curriculum of academic and career courses, schools include a **hidden curriculum** that maintains the power relations between teachers and students and reinforces existing differences between socioeconomic levels through practices such as tracking and self-fulfilling prophecies. A problem with the hidden curriculum is that it generally privileges the cultural values and patterns of the dominant group and does not positively acknowledge the cultural differences that exist in many schools. As a result, white middle-class students adapt easily to the school culture because it reinforces the behaviors they have learned from their families. Students from other cultures may find school practices different and sometimes contradictory to what they have learned at home. One example is a school's emphasis on competition over collaboration in academic work. In a collaborative mode, students work together on assignments and assist each other as needed. In a competitive mode, students are individually responsible for their work and compete for the best grade and the teacher's praise. As educators, we can confront the discriminatory practices that are often inherent in the hidden curriculum in our own classrooms and ensure that the cultural patterns of all groups are respected and drawn upon to help all students learn.

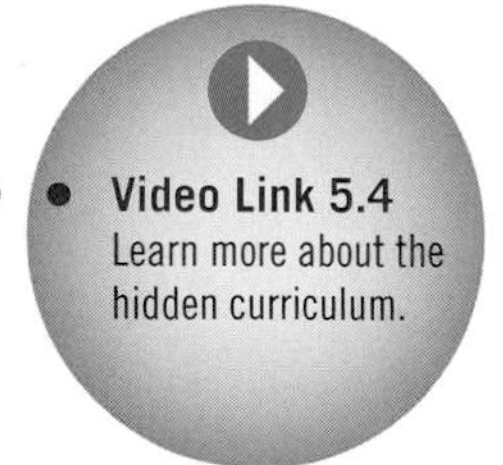

Video Link 5.4
Learn more about the hidden curriculum.

The hidden curriculum also contributes to moral and character development as teachers reward some student behaviors over others. These lessons are reinforced as students study real and fictional characters in English language arts and social studies. Lessons sometimes deal with issues of social injustice such as racism, homelessness, and inequities, supporting stereotypes or developing empathy, understanding, and sometimes social action. The rituals and ceremonies of schools also provide nationalistic lessons as the Pledge of Allegiance is recited and patriotic songs are sung.

WHAT HAPPENS WHEN STUDENTS' CULTURES COME TO SCHOOL?

Students appear at the school door with the cultures of their families. They come with the values, beliefs, and languages or dialects that they use in their families. Their cultures may conflict with the cultural patterns of the school, sometimes leading to conflicts between families, teachers, and school officials. As a teacher, you will need to be aware of these possible conflicts as you choose what to teach and how to teach it. In this section we will explore a few of the cultural clashes you may face in the communities in which you teach.

Religious Beliefs

Many Americans believe that religion is losing its influence on Americans. Religious leaders find this very worrisome. They and their adherents blame many of the problems in families and schools on the lack of the morals that are taught. Their frustration with student drug use, premarital sex, gang violence, and undisciplined students has led some groups to pressure schools to incorporate character education. They have campaigned to elect school board members who will push schools to return to what they perceive as the Christian values of the past. They may reject the introduction of multiple perspectives that give equal weight to the knowledge and experiences of religions other than Christianity. These issues can cause tension in a school about curriculum, student behavior, and school activities.

Prayer in School

In 1963 the Supreme Court ruled that prayers could not be said in school. However, the law allows voluntary prayer by teachers and students. A private prayer can be said before a meal, between classes, and before and after school. Generally, students can initiate prayer at school events as long as school officials have not endorsed or encouraged it. Schools cannot support a moment of silence because the motivation for the moment of silence has been to encourage prayer. Public group prayer is unlawful in school or at school events such as a convocation or football game.

Deeper Look 5.3
Read more about the legal aspect of prayer in schools.

Books to Read

Some families are concerned that the books their children are assigned to read in school are immoral or inappropriate. For example, parents of some religious groups do not want their children to read the Harry Potter books because they are perceived as promoting witchcraft and wizardry. However, the most frequent reasons for requesting that a book be banned are based on sexually explicit content, offensive language, or the belief that the book is not suited to the age-group to which it is assigned (American Library Association, 2012). Some people or groups pressure school libraries, video stores, or art galleries to remove books, music, videos, or artwork from their shelves or walls. The American Library Association reports that efforts to ban books are on the decline. In 2000, 646 books were challenged, as compared with 348 in 2010 (American Library Association, 2012).

Schools and school libraries are the most vulnerable for challenges by parents who question books more often than all other individuals and groups together (American Library Association, 2012). However, the Supreme Court ruled in *Board of Education v. Pico* (1982) that books could not be removed from school libraries simply because someone does not like the ideas in the books. Families have also sued school districts because the curriculum or textbooks were reflective of secular humanism or the content was offensive to their religious beliefs, but the courts have ruled that the curriculum includes important secular values such as tolerance and self-esteem and does not have to be revised to accommodate specific religious beliefs.

Calls for censoring books often split communities. Not all families agree with the request not to use a book, leading to caustic relationships in communities. Both sides are very sincere about their cause. One side believes the censorship is just and moral. They believe that the objectionable materials will contaminate the minds of their children and contribute to the moral decay of society. On the other side, opponents want their children exposed to the real world and multiple perspectives. They do not find the materials objectionable to their religious beliefs. They may not want their children to learn the lessons that they believe promote a religion other than their own. Instead, they find that they help their children explore reality and think critically about important issues in society. Educators should share with families the objectives of new curricula and materials. Communication with families is critical in reducing possible alienation between educators and parents over the inclusion of what might be viewed as controversial content in the curriculum. You will need to know your community and gauge their reactions before introducing a book or curriculum such as sex education or evolution that might be controversial.

Religious Beliefs in Schools

Audio Link 5.2
Learn more about religion in public schools.

Our religious orientation may strongly influence our perception of objectivity, fairness, and legality in schools. While some families believe that schools should reflect their religious values, others believe that public schools already reflect Christian perspectives, denigrating their own religious beliefs if they are not Christian. Some families have removed their children from public schools because they don't feel that the school reflects their values of appropriate student dress, language, and behaviors. Some families support prayer in school and at school events. Some complain that the curriculum and assigned readings are too secular, not acknowledging their beliefs. Non-Christians accuse schools of not respecting religious diversity, scheduling important assignments and celebrations on their religious holidays, singing Christian hymns during convocations and concerts, and expecting their daughters to attend coed physical education classes.

Understanding the importance of religion to students and their families provides an advantage to educators in developing effective teaching strategies for individual students. Educators should avoid stereotyping all students from one denomination or religion. Within each religious group are differences in attitudes and beliefs. Members of the same religion may be a part of a liberal or moderate group, whereas others would be identified as very conservative or fundamentalist. Educators must periodically reexamine their own interactions with students to ensure that they are not discriminating against students because of their religion. Although teachers have a right to their own religious convictions, they cannot **proselytize** or promote their religion in the classroom.

Use of Native Languages

More than one in five students in K–12 schools speak a language other than English at home. Although 95% of them speak English without difficulty, speaking English fluently does not necessarily mean that students can function effectively with academic work that is written and discussed in English. Most students can become conversationally fluent within two or three years, but they may require five to seven years to reach the proficiency necessary for success in academic subjects such as social studies and English (Thomas & Collier, 1997). Students who are conversationally fluent may be assigned to English-only classrooms without appropriate support to ensure they can function effectively in academic work. In this case, these students may fall further behind their classmates in conceptually understanding the subjects being taught.

The Supreme Court ruling in *Lau v. Nichols* (1974) requires school districts to offer language programs to help English-language learners learn English. This case was brought on behalf of Chinese American students in San Francisco who argued they were being deprived of equal education because they could not understand the English that was being used for instruction. To help ELLs learn English and progress through school, schools most often offer either bilingual education, **English as a Second Language (ESL)**, or **English for Speakers of Other Languages (ESOL)**. Teachers are expected to use the approach to teach English-language learners that has been adopted by the school or school district.

You might ask how the use of native languages to help students learn could be controversial. The reason is that a number of citizens believe that English should be the only language used in public places or for government documents. Adherents to this approach proposed a referendum in California to replace bilingual education with a program to teach English in sheltered English-immersion programs of no more than one year in length. Proposition 227 was approved by 61% of California voters in 1998 and provided the impetus for similar referenda in Arizona and Massachusetts. Discussions about how best to teach English to immigrant students continues today with different views and actions from one community to another.

Learning English

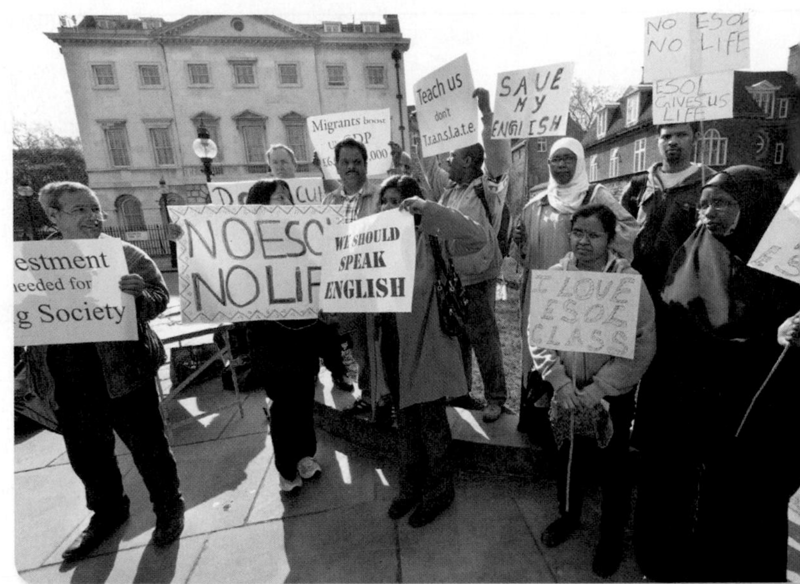

Strategies for teaching immigrant students are influenced by local and national politics related to the use of languages other than English for instruction in schools.

When children speak little or no English when they enter a classroom and neither the teacher or teacher assistant speak their native language, they may feel alienated and can become quite frustrated. Usually other children become their first allies as they try to communicate with ELLs using signs. When you enter your classroom as a teacher, you may have a number of students who speak languages other than English. School administrators and other resource people in the school district should help you know the approaches you should use to help these students learn both English and the academic content.

Bilingual education uses both English and the students' native language as the mode of instruction. It requires either the teacher or an assistant teacher to be bilingual. In bilingual education, the academic subjects are taught in the native language, giving English-language learners the opportunity to learn at the same pace as their English-only classmates. Most schools offer transitional bilingual programs that move students from their native languages to English as soon as possible, usually in one to four years. Over time more and more of the instruction is conducted in English.

Blanca Estela Carbajal Rodriguez, a fourth grade teacher in a Colorado school, reports that English-language learners in her school district are suppose to have transitioned into English by the end of the third grade.

> However, most of my students have some basic knowledge of English at the fourth grade, but they are not ready for transition into English-only classrooms. One of four of them are still Spanish dominant. Some of my students were born in the United States, but their parents only speak Spanish. Some lack the confidence to transition to English, in part, because their peers ridicule them when they mess up. My class is bilingual in the morning with only English-language learners. In the afternoon the instruction is in English. Once a week I teach an enrichment class in Spanish for English-only students.

Asked how she knew that she had made a difference in student learning, she responded:

> It is when the kids take a risk and speak in English or write in English. At beginning of the school year, you can't tell whether writing samples are English or Spanish because they are so afraid of English. By the middle of year, I can read what they are writing. When they begin to use the tricks I have taught them to remember the spelling and writing of English, I know they are learning. By end of year, kids who were reading at the first grade level are now reading at fourth grade level. Students also have good attitude about learning and how they feel about themselves in the classroom.

English as a Second Language (ESL) or English for Speakers of Other Languages (ESOL) promotes English proficiency and is used extensively in the United States to move English-language learners into English-only classrooms. Unlike bilingual education, ESL is conducted totally in English; the native language is not used at all for instruction. ESL is used in newcomer and sheltered programs for new immigrants who have limited or no experience with English and sometimes have limited literacy skills in their native language.

Families should be involved as a school decides the appropriate approach for teaching English. Educators and parents together should decide whether they want to promote bilingualism so that ELLs become competent in both English and their native language. Families may want their children to move into English-only instruction as soon as possible, requiring a different program. Some English-only families may advocate for an immersion program in which their children become fluent in a second language and culture.

Ms. Costello reports that the Escambia County school district offers sheltered English programs for its ELLs.

> It is English for Speakers of Other Languages (ESOL), focusing on teaching English for second language learners. We align our goals with the state of Florida schools for them to be able to acculturate into the American educational system and be successful with that so that we can transition them to the general education program. We don't have a dual program in Escambia County. In south Florida they do. Florida has approved models of English for second language learners, but we choose to have a sheltered model and inclusion model as well depending on the population of students in the different schools.
>
> So we have ESOL Center schools where students are bused to the Centers. Some parents choose to remain in their old schools. We serve those children with ESOL itinerant teachers who work with the teachers in those schools. We serve six elementary schools, two middle schools, and two high schools.

Maintaining the Native Language

Although the majority of bilingual education programs for English-language learners are transitional, some bilingual programs are designed to help students maintain their native language. These maintenance programs promote the use of both languages and cultures as students become bilingual and bicultural with neither language being the dominant one. This approach values the language and cultures of the students' families and promotes the development of a positive self-image as a bicultural individual. These programs support bilingualism and literacy in both English and the native language. In these programs, both English and the native language have equal status, and both are used interchangeably for instructional purposes. One approach is an immersion program in which English-only students are in classes in which the second language is used for instruction. Two-way immersion helps both English-only and English-language learners develop bilingualism as language training is integrated with academic instruction. These classes usually have an equal number of English speakers and speakers of another language.

HOW SHOULD TEACHERS WORK WITH PARENTS AND COMMUNITIES?

Teachers are encouraged to work as partners with families in helping students learn. In some schools, a high percentage of families are involved with their teachers and their children's

Challenging Assumptions

Do English-language learners (ELLs) achieve at academically higher levels when they are in bilingual or English-only classrooms?

The Assumption

ELLs learn English more quickly if they are immersed into classrooms in which only English is used for instruction.

Study Design and Method

Two researchers followed every ELL in grades K–12 in five urban and rural school districts for five years. The school districts were located in the northeast, northwest, south-central, and southeast United States. The students represented 80 different languages, but the data analysis in three of the sites focused on Spanish speakers. Findings were tracked by the type of program in which the ELL participated. The programs available to students in these five school districts included approaches that ranged from English-only without bilingual or ESL services to two-way bilingual immersion in which ELLs and students whose native language is English received instruction in the two languages.

Study Findings

The researchers found that the reading and mathematics achievement of ELLs in English-only classrooms without bilingual or ESL services decreased by the fifth grade. The largest number of dropouts had been enrolled in these English-only classrooms.

The ELLs in the one-way developmental bilingual education program with four years of instruction in English and their native language in two high-achieving school districts outperformed the ELLs in all other programs and remained above grade level at the seventh grade. The one-way and two-way developmental bilingual education programs were the only programs that assisted ELLs in reaching grade level and maintaining it through the end of their schooling. These programs also had fewer dropouts.

When ELLs enter English-only elementary classrooms after ESL or bilingual education, they do not perform as well on tests given in English as their counterparts who were in English-only classrooms. However, the bilingually educated students reach the same level of achievement by middle school and outperform the monolingually schooled students during high school. Native English–speaking students in two-way immersion programs equaled or outperformed on all measures their comparison group who was in English-only classrooms. The highest-quality ESL programs closed only about half of the achievement gap.

Implications

The findings of this and similar studies are important to policymakers and educators as they try to determine the best strategies for increasing the academic achievement of English-language learners in PreK–12 schools. The results of this research suggest that ELLs should be placed in bilingual education programs to improve long-term academic achievement and reduce drop-out rates. The researchers also found that students who do not speak English need to be placed in bilingual programs for four years or more. For best results, bilingual and ESL programs must meet students' linguistic, academic, cognitive, emotional, social, and physical needs.

Source: Thomas, W. P., & Collier, V. P. (2001). *A national study of school effectiveness for language minority students' long-term academic achievement.* Santa Cruz, CA: Center for Research on Education, Diversity & Excellence.

"I'VE FOUND THAT WHEN YOU HAVE GOOD TEACHERS AND LOVING, CARING PARENTS AND RELATIVES, YOU CAN DISAPPOINT A LOT OF PEOPLE."

learning. In other schools, involving families can be a challenge because of their lack of babysitters, lack of transportation, and work schedules that do not allow them time to meet with teachers. Parents or other caretakers may feel insecure in meeting with teachers who are usually better educated and speak standard English. They may not be proficient in English, and translators may not be provided. As you observe and work in schools over the next few months or years, ask to observe meetings with families, noting successful practices that support the involvement of families in their children's education.

Working With Families as Partners for Student Learning

Parental support is perceived by teachers and principals as a major contributor to student learning. However, half of the nation's teachers report that one in four of their students lack the necessary parental support to be academically successful; 64% of urban school teachers report the lack of parental support (MetLife, 2008). While parents report that their lack of time is a major reason for their lack of participation in school, more than one third of them identified the disconnect between them and the school as a contributor to their lack of participation (Bridgeland, Dilulio, Streeter, & Mason, 2008). Nevertheless, teachers think that relationships with parents have improved over time (MetLife, 2008).

Deeper Look 5.4
Read about the effects of parental involvement in schools.

Regardless of their race, ethnicity, or socioeconomic status, families share a belief about the importance of education for their children (Bridgeland et al., 2008). Even more than white parents, parents of color strongly support the goal for their children to be college and career ready by the time they finish high school; the majority expect their children to attend college (Hart Research Associates et al., 2011). African American and Latino parents and caregivers know that their local schools have problems, but fewer than one in five blame the schools directly. Half of them still have confidence in their local public schools. They think that academic success can be improved with "parents taking more responsibility, students working harder, and schools providing more individual attention" to the students who need it (Hart Research Associates et al., 2011, p. 10).

The percentage of parents who report being involved in their child's education varies by school, as shown in Figure 5.5. Families at high-performing high schools were more likely to indicate having good conversations with teachers than families at low-performing schools. High-performing high schools were almost twice as likely to communicate effectively with families about the academic performance of their children (Bridgeland et al., 2008). The parents of high school students recommend that schools provide them

1. Prompt notification of academic or other problems their children are experiencing,
2. Information about what constitutes academic success when their children are in the eighth or ninth grades,
3. More information about requirements for graduation and college admission, and
4. A faculty advisor who would be the single point of contact, homework hotlines, and flexible conferences (Bridgeland et al., 2008).

As you work with families, remember that the parents or guardians were the children's first teachers. They have the welfare of their children in mind when they push for services and attention to their children. In many cases, they are anxious to help their children do well in school. Family involvement in schools and with teachers has proven to be an important variable in supporting student learning and successful school experiences. The largest organization for families and teachers in the United States, the PTA (2009), has found that families' involvement in education at both home and school leads to students achieving higher grades and test scores, attending school more regularly, liking school better, behaving better at school, and being more likely to graduate and attend postsecondary education. Family involvement contributes to better teacher morale, an increase in teacher effectiveness, improved job satisfaction, improved communications with families and students, and increased community support. It also improves parents' relations with their children and teachers and improves their attitudes toward school and teachers.

Figure 5.5 Parent Satisfaction and Involvement by School Type and Student Performance

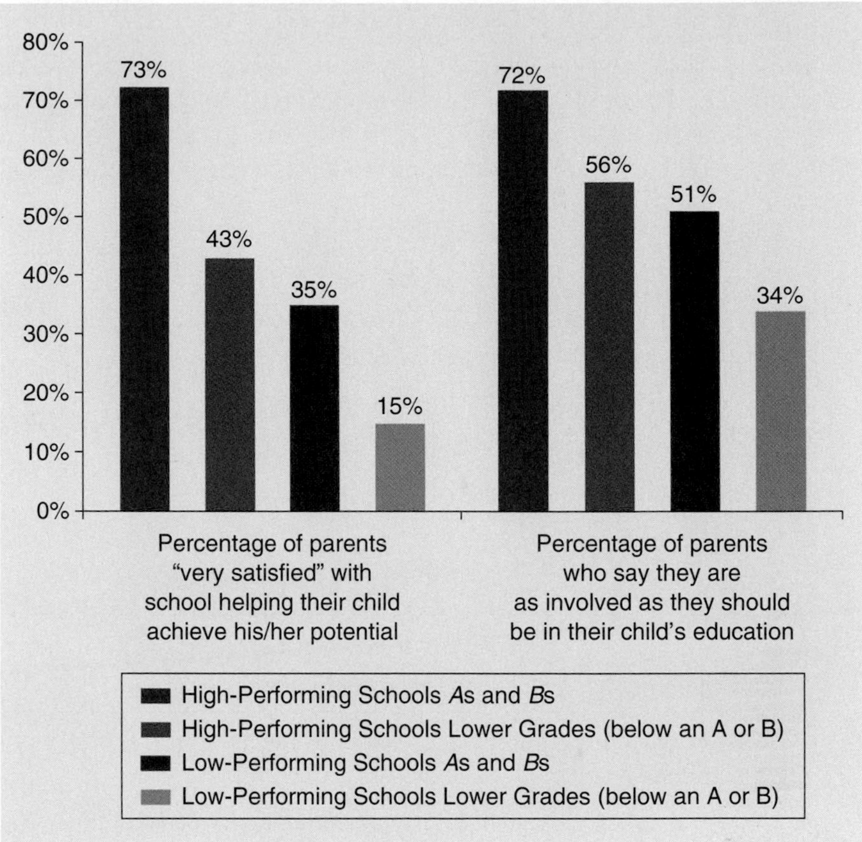

Source: Bridgeland, J. M., Dilulio, J. J., Streeter, R. T., & Mason, J. R. (2008, October). *One dream, two realities: Perspectives of parents on America's high schools* (p. 10). Washington, DC: Civic Enterprises. © Civic Enterprises

The following PTA (2009) standards, which are written for family–school partnerships, outline the key components of successful relationships with parents and caretakers:

1. Welcoming All Families Into the School Community—Families are active participants in the life of the school, and feel welcomed, valued, and connected to each other, to school staff, and to what students are learning and doing in class.
2. Communicating Effectively—Families and school staff engage in regular, two-way, meaningful communication about student learning.
3. Supporting Student Success—Families and school staff continuously collaborate to support students' learning and healthy development both at home and at school, and have regular opportunities to strengthen their knowledge and skills to do so effectively.
4. Speaking Up for Every Child—Families are empowered to be advocates for their own and other children, to ensure that students are treated fairly and have access to learning opportunities that will support their success.
5. Sharing Power—Families and school staff are equal partners in decisions that affect children and families and together inform, influence, and create policies, practices, and programs.

UNDERSTANDING AND USING EVIDENCE

Parental Involvement in Homework

Survey data can help educators think about their own practices and perspectives and test them against the perspectives of others. In a survey of parental involvement in schools, Public Agenda asked teachers to consider parental involvement in their children's homework. Parents were asked how they actually handled their children's homework. The following two tables show how the two groups responded.

	TEACHERS	
	What parents *should* do:	**What parents do:**
Check the work to make sure it was done, and done correctly	57%	10%
Get involved in helping them do the work	30%	6%
Ask the student if the work has been done, and leave it at that	9%	34%
Leave it up to the student	2%	44%

% of parents saying they have done the following:	
Have had serious arguments with child where there was yelling or crying over schoolwork	50%
Have walked away and let child deal with the consequences of not doing their schoolwork rather than dealing with child's constant stalling	49%
Have done part of child's homework because it was too difficult for them or because they were too tired	22%

Your Task: As you examine the responses about homework from teachers and parents, what do you learn?

1. What do the tables tell you about the perceptions of teachers and parents regarding parental involvement in students' homework?
2. What other information do you wish you had about parental involvement?
3. Why do teachers think that parents are not assisting their children appropriately with their homework?
4. What do the data suggest about parent and teacher relationships and communication?
5. How might teachers be involved in improving parental support on homework assignments?

Source: Farkas, S., Johnson, J., & Duffett, A. (1999). *Playing their parts: Parents and teachers talk about parental involvement in public schools.* New York, NY: Public Agenda.

6. Collaborating With Community—Families and school staff collaborate with community members to connect students, families, and staff to expanded learning opportunities, community services, and civic participation. (p. 6)

We will discuss a number of these standards in this section as we explore ways to involve families as partners in the education of their children.

Communications

A major challenge for new and many experienced teachers is communicating with parents and involving them in the formal schooling of their children. One of the keys is that the communication be two-way, meaning that family members are equal partners in the conversations with teachers and other school officials. This means that teachers cannot do all of the talking; you will need to ask questions and listen to the answers. The focus of communications should be their child's learning. Families should know the academic expectations for the class and how they can help their child meet them. If family members do not speak English or have limited proficiency, you should have a translator with you during the conference. Your school may have translators who can assist you. Parent or community volunteers often serve in this role as well.

Gail Tillery (2011), a National Board Certified high school teacher, says that the first rule to remember is "Your students' parents are not your enemies. Ultimately, they want the same thing you want, which is the best for their children. By maintaining respectful and productive communication, you can work together to help students succeed" (p. 1). Her second rule is to remember that the parents are probably more nervous about talking with the teacher than you are about talking with them. If you keep the student and her or his needs as the focus of the conversation, you will begin to develop a common goal with the parent as well as beginning to establish trust. Ms. Tillery shares the following tips for effective communications with parents:

- Contact parents at the beginning of the year.
- Be proactive in contacting a parent when a student's grades or behavior has changed.
- Reach out immediately when you have a conflict with a student that leads to an event such as removal from the classroom.
- Return calls from parents promptly.
- Be cautious when you respond to negative e-mails by having colleagues review your response.
- Admit to mistakes when you make them.
- Don't be intimidated and don't accept verbal abuse.
- Notify school officials immediately of situations of which they are likely to become aware and may need to take action.

Parents can be involved in the schooling of their children by volunteering to help the teacher in the classroom, helping at school events, or assisting their children with homework.

It will be important to be in touch with families on a regular basis. Contact with parents can be more than face-to-face conversations. Phone and e-mail messages, short newsletters, and written notes can also be used. You will also have to be attentive to the native languages of your students. Communications may need to be written in the home language to facilitate positive communications and show respect for the language and culture of students' families. In some programs such as Head Start and special education for preschoolers, teachers or school social workers visit families in their homes to support student learning. Some schools have expanded home visits beyond these preschool programs. For example, The Parent Teacher Home Visit Project in Sacramento has conducted thousands of home visits that have led to improved student achievement and parent–teacher communications (Ferlazzo, 2009).

When I first started teaching second grade in Tulsa, Oklahoma, I was incredibly intimidated by the parents and families of my students. I lacked confidence in my own teaching abilities and as a result I sought to isolate my classroom from the rest of the world . . . literally! There was a small window in the front door of my classroom and parents would often congregate outside to watch morning activities. This made me so nervous that I covered the window with a poster and effectively sealed the parents out. However, I soon realized that I didn't need to be intimidated by these parents because they desperately wanted me to succeed. After all, I was the one who was working with their children. I came to appreciate the critical role that parents played in my success as a teacher. They made sure that their children were well rested and ready to learn, they helped reinforce the values that we sought to instill in the classroom, they often provided an extra set of hands during school activities, they helped their children with homework and supplemented the curriculum with their own expertise, and they were invaluable resources in terms of better understanding the needs of each individual child. By the end of the first semester I had taken the poster down and opened the door of my classroom to the broader community. As a new teacher, this simple act made a tremendous difference. Teaching is often portrayed as an isolating profession, but in reality effective teachers have the potential to serve as critical boundary spanners between families, schools, and communities.

Michael P. Evans
Miami University
Oxford, Ohio

Some schools expect parents and guardians to volunteer to be in the classroom on a regular basis. However, employers do not always allow employees time off of work for such volunteer activities. Therefore, the school should ensure that parents who can't volunteer during the day have other opportunities during school or weekend activities. Sometimes the only volunteerism to which a family member can commit is to provide assistance to their children at home. When parents are volunteering, they should be made to feel welcome and valued. When family members do volunteer in a classroom, it is important to have specific tasks to assist with when they are there.

Regularly scheduled parent–teacher conferences are the most common format employed by schools to arrange for teachers to meet parents, share the academic and social progress of their children, and discuss strategies for improving student learning. If your school does not require parent–teacher conferences, you may want to schedule them yourself to learn more about your students from their parents' perspectives and to develop partnerships for students' growth. Parents may also initiate the request for a conference to check on their children's progress.

You may find it helpful to know what parents' organizations suggest to parents to prepare for and participate in conferences with their children's teachers. Before the conference with a teacher, parents should talk to their child about what they like and dislike about school; gather input on their child from doctors, counselors, or others who could provide information that would be helpful in serving their child well; and make a list of the topics to discuss with the teacher (PTA, n.d.). The PTA suggests that during the conference parents establish rapport with the teacher, ask questions about their child's success in the classroom, address any problems their child is experiencing, and develop an action plan for addressing academic or behavioral issues.

Because some parents have a difficult time arranging to meet with teachers about their children's progress, some schools have tried various strategies to support the attendance of low-income families. For example, providing transportation, child care, and a meal may increase attendance. Provision of translators for parents who have limited English skills may make the school setting more comfortable for some parents. There may be cases in which meeting the parent in a neutral spot will contribute to effective communications.

Working With Diverse Families

Socioeconomic differences among families can influence their interactions with educators. For example, middle-class families are more likely to volunteer at the school, becoming known to teachers as supportive, caring parents. They also monitor the progress of their children and encourage them to develop their academic skills and may ask school officials to test their children for the academically talented program. Low-income families also know they should volunteer, but their economic conditions may make it more difficult to be actively engaged in school activities. Yet, schools can encourage and facilitate their involvement by proactively reaching out to them. Some schools are providing resource rooms for parents in which they have access to computers and classes such as parenting, learning English, and helping their children with their math homework. Teachers might invite parents to visit their classrooms at any time and ask them to assist with classroom work in meaningful ways. By engaging parents in this way, you become a partner with the parent in supporting student learning.

Deeper Look 5.5
Read about cultural differences in parental involvement.

Most families of color have a history of discrimination in society and schools that makes them cautious of the treatment that their children receive. African American families have a long and recent legacy of segregation that prevented them from attending schools with white students and limited their access to equal educational resources. American Indian families have a history of their children being removed from their families to attend boarding schools where their heritage was not respected or promoted. Latino families recall the times that they were punished for speaking Spanish in schools. As a result, many parents are distrustful of educators who do not recognize that racism pervades their experiences. Some parents may directly criticize or attack educators, accusing them of discrimination against their children. In other cases, they quietly rebel against the school establishment, convinced that their children are not being supported at the same levels as other students. At times, parents may even raise their voices as they talk with teachers and other school officials. Such aggressive behavior usually does not meet the school's standards of positive and supportive parents, leading to them being rebuked or ignored by teachers and school administrators.

White middle-class parents generally have the advantage in schools because they accept the school's standard of positive parental involvement. They also may be more willing to defer to school officials. Although white working-class families do not have the cultural and economic capital to privilege their children in schools, they usually do not have to worry about racism affecting the school's treatment of their children and are able to focus on their children's experience in classrooms when they interact with teachers and other school officials (Lareau & Horvat, 2004).

Strategies to develop successful partnerships with parents will require a transformation of the power relations between families and schools, including actively removing the legacies of racism and social inequality that have historically shaped schools and their interactions with students and families (Hong, 2011). It will be critical that you monitor your relationships with families based on socioeconomic status, family type, race, or ethnicity to ensure that you are not privileging families from the same cultural group as your own. All families should have the same access to and support from teachers.

Video Case 5.1
Partnering With Families

1. In what ways do teachers in this video clip try to become partners with the families of their students?
2. How can educators engage parents and guardians who may be reluctant to volunteer in schools?

Family and Teacher Organizations

The relationship between families and schools is not always positive and supportive, especially when trust is lacking and families do not agree with the decisions being made about their children, the curriculum, or other school policies. Over time, however, families have allowed most of these decisions to be made by professional educators rather than parents. At the same time, most parents want to be involved in their children's education. They also know that their children's education is not just the responsibility of schools. Most parents believe that what happens at home also affects student achievement. The problem is that many parents do not get involved in schools on their own, requiring educators to figure out how to involve them.

In many areas of the country the families of students are unauthorized or undocumented, which could make it more challenging to involve parents in school activities. One structured way of involving some parents is a parent–teacher organization. African American and Latino parents trust the advice of parent organizations on the public education system and school reforms more than other sources such as the news media and other community organizations. They are also more likely to attend meetings of a parent organization than other activities to support schools, although volunteering in them is not far behind.

The most well-known parent organization is the PTA, which was founded in 1897 by Alice McLellan Birney and Phoebe Apperson Hearst as the National Congress of Mothers. In its early days the organization led efforts to create kindergarten classes, establish child labor laws, initiate hot lunch programs, develop a juvenile justice system, and require mandatory immunization (PTA, 2012). Anyone who is an advocate for students may join the National PTA. Local chapters can be found in many of the nation's schools, with the goal of promoting partnerships between educators and families to advocate on behalf of children. Another option for parents is a PTO, which is an independent organization at the local school level that is not connected to a national organization.

Audio Link 5.3
Listen to how parents involve themselves in schools.

Ms. Costello found the following activities very effective in working with the diverse families in her ESOL programs.

> I sent a very short letter to parents to introduce myself, my educational qualifications, and my goals for the year. I put my educational qualifications in the letter because they are very important in some cultures to show they have a teacher who is qualified to teach their children. I plan my parent activities and the projected dates for those activities so that parents can put them on their calendars and allow parents to talk to their bosses or superiors about taking off those times. I have letters translated into different languages. Our department has different samples of letters to parents. We have translated our field trip permission slips into different languages.
>
> I send newsletters to parents and have them translated into other languages. I provide a telephone number where parents can reach me. I don't do this, but some teachers provide cell phone numbers. Some teachers like to text parents about homework. Our most recent college graduates who teach at the high school level like to use technology to communicate with parents. You have to be very careful about what you publish using technology and need to know the

policy of the district about using technology to communicate with parents or students.

I call parents for good news, not just when their children get in trouble. They are very thankful about that. I try to build the confidence in the students and the confidence of the parents to be able to communicate with me. What I found the least helpful is calling parents at the last minute to talk about meetings and conferences or their kids getting in trouble. Parents sometimes feel that it is the teacher's responsibility to take care of what is going on in the classroom. Why are you asking me when you are the expert? That can cause a conflict about what your role is as a teacher and the role of the parents.

Relationship of Schools to the Community

The saying "it takes a whole village to raise a child" applies to the communities in which schools are located. When the community cares about and is actively involved in education, schools serve the community, families, and students well. When schools and communities work together,

- Families are strengthened, resulting in better support for student learning.
- Families access community resources more easily.
- Trust is built among the community partners and schools.
- Businesses help connect education programs with the realities of the workplace.
- Students serve and learn beyond their school involvement.

When the community becomes actively involved in its schools and with the students in those schools, education programs can be strengthened and student learning improved.

Partnerships

The goal of school–community partnerships should be to improve the academic achievement and positive development of young people in the community. Partners should make an investment of time, money, people, and expertise as appropriate. Potential partners include businesses, the Chamber of Commerce, charitable organizations, churches, civic groups, foundations, local government, local media, museums, military groups, nonprofit associations, senior citizens, and youth groups. The partners provide support to schools in a number of ways, including assigning some employees or volunteers to work with the school, encouraging employees to assist teachers and administrators, and contributing equipment and other resources.

School and community partnerships should be two-way. While the community contributes resources and expertise to schools, the school should help families know more about available resources in the community. Schools could distribute to families information about activities and agencies in the community. They could encourage community members besides parents and guardians to volunteer in schools. Finally, they could encourage both students and their families to be more involved in community service.

Bringing the Community Into the School

As a teacher, you could bring the community into your classroom in a number of ways. The parents and grandparents of your students are resources and assets for their children (Hong, 2011). They can be excellent teachers of their own traditions and histories. You might consider asking a Muslim parent to explain to the class the meaning of Ramadan or a Jewish parent to talk about Rosh Hashanah and Yom Kippur. Immigrant parents could talk about their country of origin and why they immigrated to the United States. Parents can be invited to talk about their jobs or a community project. Parents, of course, are not the only community resources. Grandparents, employees at local businesses, museum staff, and staff at community agencies have valuable information to share in classrooms. Public officials such as firefighters and police officers might be invited to talk about their roles, safety issues, or community involvement.

Field trips provide another opportunity to know the community. Many students don't have the opportunity to attend concerts or visit museums, fire stations, the zoo, or historical sites except through field trips. A school district should have guidelines for selecting and conducting field trips. Families must be made aware of field trips and give permission for their children to participate.

Through school projects, students can learn to be involved in community projects that range from planting trees to cleaning up a park to assisting elderly people and young children. Students, especially older ones, might conduct research on a community need that could lead to action by a city council or state legislature. Some schools require students to provide community service by volunteering in a nursing home, child care center, nonprofit association, health clinic, or governmental agency. These projects help students understand their responsibility to the larger community.

CONNECTING TO THE CLASSROOM

This chapter has introduced you to public perceptions of schools and the importance of understanding the influence of culture on teaching and learning. Understanding communities and working with your students' families will be important in supporting learning. Below are some key principles for applying the information in this chapter to the classroom.

1. Being aware of the public's perception of public education helps educators reflect on their own practices.
2. All students can achieve at high levels regardless of the structure of their families.
3. Language and cultural diversity can be assets in the teaching and learning process.
4. Teachers who are multicultural, bilingual, and bidialectal function effectively in a number of cultural groups.
5. Teachers cannot promote a religion in their classroom or school activities.
6. Bilingual education encourages ELLs to be literate in both English and their native language while ESL immerses ELLs into English for all instruction.
7. Partnerships between teachers and families can improve student learning.

SUMMARY

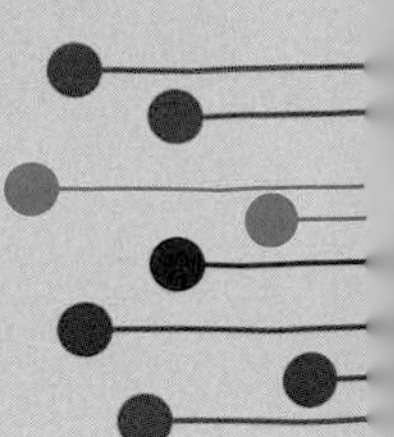

This chapter focused on how the public and parents view schools and can be involved in schools, supporting students and the community. Five major topics were explored in this chapter:

- Public perceptions of schools, teachers, and standards. Half of the public rates public schools in their communities as an *A* or *B*, but fewer than one in four rate schools nationwide as high.
- Structure of students' families. Two in three students live in a family that includes two parents. Most other students live in single-parent families, most often with their mother. Other students have gay or lesbian parents; some are living with their grandparents or other relatives, and others live in foster homes.
- Influence of culture on students. Culture provides the blueprint for how people live, which is different from one region of the country or world to another. It is learned from parents and the community in which we live and includes behavior, communication patterns, language, values, and the way we think.
- Students' cultures in schools. The religious beliefs of families and communities sometimes lead to cultural clashes around issues such as prayer and assigned readings. Schools are required to provide language programs for English-language learners, but the type of program differs from one community and school to another.
- Involvement of parents and communities in schools. Positive and supportive communications with the families of students increase the chances of students having productive experiences in schools. Businesses and community agencies can also support schools and students through formal or informal partnerships.

CLASS DISCUSSION QUESTIONS

1. The Phi Delta Kappa/Gallup poll found that the public generally supports public school teachers. However, teachers feel besieged as their unions are being attacked by governors and education critics as the obstacle to student learning. How do you think teacher unions could partner with students and their parents to improve student learning? (For information on what the public thinks of teacher unions, visit **http://www.pdkintl.org/poll/docs/pdkpoll43_2011.pdf**).

2. Although a growing number of states are allowing same-sex partners to marry, not all communities are supportive of LGBTQs. How will you respond when you meet your first set of lesbian or gay parents at a parent–teacher conference? How will you react when one of your students points out that another student has two mommies or two daddies?

3. There are many similarities and differences across cultures that bind us together and make us unique. What are some of the similarities and differences across the cultures that exist in the community in which you were raised? How can teachers become familiar with the cultures of their students?

4. Religious diversity in the United States is expanding beyond the Judeo-Christian heritage that has long been reflected in textbooks. How will Muslim, Buddhist, Hindu, and other non-Christian families impact on a community and the schools their children attend? What changes may you have to make to respect and include the diverse religions of students in your classroom?

5. Research reported on the website of the PTA indicates that the involvement of parents in the education of their children is important for student achievement. What is the appropriate role of teachers in contacting parents about the behavioral and academic performance of their children? How can teachers prevent the interactions with parents from being adversarial?

KEY TERMS

Bilingual education 141
Cultural borders 137
Cultural relativism 136
Enculturation 136
English as a Second Language (ESL) 141
English for Speakers of Other Languages (ESOL) 141
Hidden curriculum 138
Proselytize 140
Secular 139
Secular humanism 139
Socialization 136
Values 135

SELF-ASSESSMENT

WHAT IS YOUR CURRENT LEVEL OF UNDERSTANDING AND THINKING ABOUT FAMILIES AND COMMUNITIES?

One of the indicators of understanding is to examine how complex your thinking is when asked questions that require you to use the concepts and facts introduced in this chapter.

After you answer the following questions as fully as you can, rate your knowledge on the Complexity of Thinking rubric to self-assess the degree to which you understand and can apply the ideas presented in this chapter.

1. What are the differences between becoming partners with families and meeting with parents or caretakers periodically at parent–teacher conferences?
2. What components of effective partnerships with families are most supportive of student learning?
3. What is the value of developing positive relationships with the community? How and with whom would you initiate community contacts and interactions?

What is your current level of understanding the effective engagement of families and communities as partners in student learning and becoming effective partners?

Complexity of Thinking Rubric

	Parts & Pieces	Unidimensional	Organized	Integrated	Extensions
Indicators	Elements/concepts are talked about as isolated and independent entities.	One or a few concepts are addressed, while others are underdeveloped.	Deliberate and structured consideration of all key concepts/elements.	All key concepts/elements are included in a view that addresses interconnections.	Integration of all elements and dimensions, with extrapolation to new situations.
Identifies components of effective communications with parents and caretakers	Identifies components of effective communications with parents and caretakers.	Knows how to set up a parent–teacher conference but is not comfortable interacting with parents and caretakers, especially when they are from different cultural groups than your own.	Is comfortable interacting with parents and caretakers on a regular basis about the academic and social progress of their children.	Is proactive in establishing positive partnerships with parents and caretakers from diverse cultural groups to promote student learning.	Is not only interacting with diverse parents and caretakers to support student learning, but also works with community members and agencies to provide additional support of students and their families.

STUDENT STUDY SITE

Visit the Student Study Site at **www.sagepub.com/hall** to access links to the videos, audio clips, and Deeper Look reference materials noted in this chapter, as well as additional study tools including eFlashcards, web quizzes, and more.

Field Guide
for Learning More About Families and Communities

• • • • •

Ask a Teacher or Principal

Religious diversity in a community may have an impact on the curriculum, books assigned to students, and school events. Check the impact of religious beliefs on one or more of the schools you visit. Ask one or more teachers how the religious beliefs of families in the community impact schools. What accommodations does a teacher or school make for religious holidays, religious songs, and so on? Has the school had any clashes related to religious differences in the community? If a parent expresses concern about the curriculum or assigned readings, what would the teacher do? What advice does he or she have for you to prevent clashes with parents based on their religious beliefs?

Make Your Own Observations

New teachers report that communicating with families is one of their most challenging tasks. Being able to observe parent and teacher interactions in your field experiences should reduce your fear of working with parents. Ask the teacher or principal in one of the schools in which you are observing for permission to observe a parent–teacher conference and a PTA or PTO meeting. Determine how the contact with families was made and by whom. In your notes, describe the structure and focus of the conference or meeting. Also record how active the family members were in the conference and the nature of the interchange with the teacher. What strategies did the teacher or principal use to make the conference or meeting helpful to parents? What would you have done differently? How closely did the conference or meeting reflect the recommendations discussed in this chapter?

Reflect Through Journaling

A critical part of working with students from diverse cultural backgrounds is to know oneself. In your journal, describe your own cultural background. For example, what influence has the ethnic background of your family had on your choices of food, entertainment, sports, books you read, where you live, and so on? How does your culture influence your politics or religious beliefs? How were the child-rearing practices of your family different than those of another family you know? What do you particularly like about your cultural background? What do you wish you could change?

Build Your Portfolio

Some families choose to send their children to private religious schools for part or all of their elementary and secondary education. What occurs in these schools that is different from a public school? Compare the curriculum and instruction in a Catholic, fundamentalist Christian, Jewish, Islamic, or other religious school to a public school by visiting the schools for several days and reviewing their websites and promotional information. Write a paper with your observations of the similarities and differences.

Public and parental perceptions of the quality of their public schools influence state and local policies on issues such as support of teachers, teachers' unions, charter schools, school vouchers, teacher evaluations, and merit pay. Search the local papers for articles related to the quality of public schools in your community. Prepare a table that indicates the stance of different members of the community on school quality and reform efforts that they support. Write an analysis of your findings and the policy changes that could result from the public's perceptions of schools.

Read a Book

For portraits of the positive, challenging, and sometimes conflicting experiences of parents and teachers in the low-income, non-English-speaking community of the Logan Square Neighborhood Association in northwest Chicago, read *A Cord of Three Strands: A New Approach to Parent Engagement in Schools* by Soo Hong (2011; Cambridge, MA: Harvard University Press).

Read stories of how well-respected educators became biliterate, often in spite of the odds against them in their schools, in *Words Were All We Had: Becoming Biliterate Against the Odds,* by Maria de la Luz Reyes (2011; New York, NY: Teachers College Press).

Learn about fifth graders in Chicago who initiated a project to replace their dilapidated school, requiring research, speeches, and meetings with governmental officials that became their curriculum for the year, in *Spectacular Things Happen Along the Way: Lessons From an Urban Classroom,* by Brian D. Schultz (2008; New York, NY: Teachers College Press).

Search the Web

To see guidelines and resources for teachers on religion in the classroom, go to the First Amendment Center website (**http://www.firstamendmentcenter.org/**).

To learn more about bilingual education, two-way immersion, immigrant education, dialects/Ebonics, and English as a second language, visit **http://www.cal.org**, the website of the Center for Applied Linguistics.

For assistance in working with the families of the students in your classroom, check the *PTA National Standards for Family-School Partnerships: An Implementation Guide* (**http://www.pta.org/Documents/National_Standards_Implementation_Guide_2009.pdf**), which provides examples of how schools have successfully implemented the PTA standards.

The Foundations of Education

Chapter 6 History of Schools in the United States

Chapter 7 Developing a Philosophy of Teaching and Learning

Chapter 8 Organizing Schools for Learning

Chapter 9 Governance and School Finance

Chapter 10 The Law as It Relates to Teaching and Learning

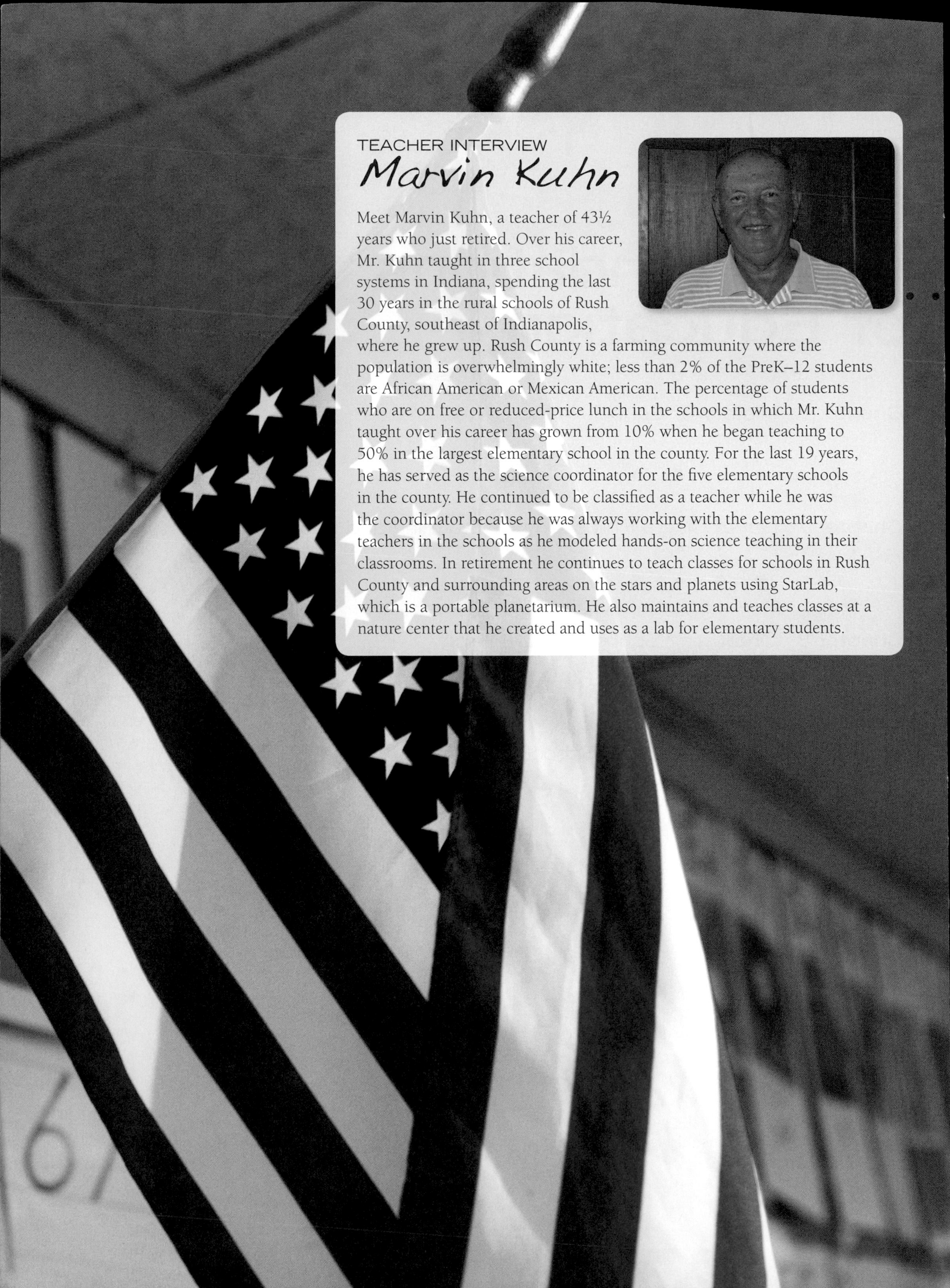

TEACHER INTERVIEW

Marvin Kuhn

Meet Marvin Kuhn, a teacher of 43½ years who just retired. Over his career, Mr. Kuhn taught in three school systems in Indiana, spending the last 30 years in the rural schools of Rush County, southeast of Indianapolis, where he grew up. Rush County is a farming community where the population is overwhelmingly white; less than 2% of the PreK–12 students are African American or Mexican American. The percentage of students who are on free or reduced-price lunch in the schools in which Mr. Kuhn taught over his career has grown from 10% when he began teaching to 50% in the largest elementary school in the county. For the last 19 years, he has served as the science coordinator for the five elementary schools in the county. He continued to be classified as a teacher while he was the coordinator because he was always working with the elementary teachers in the schools as he modeled hands-on science teaching in their classrooms. In retirement he continues to teach classes for schools in Rush County and surrounding areas on the stars and planets using StarLab, which is a portable planetarium. He also maintains and teaches classes at a nature center that he created and uses as a lab for elementary students.

History of Schools in the United States

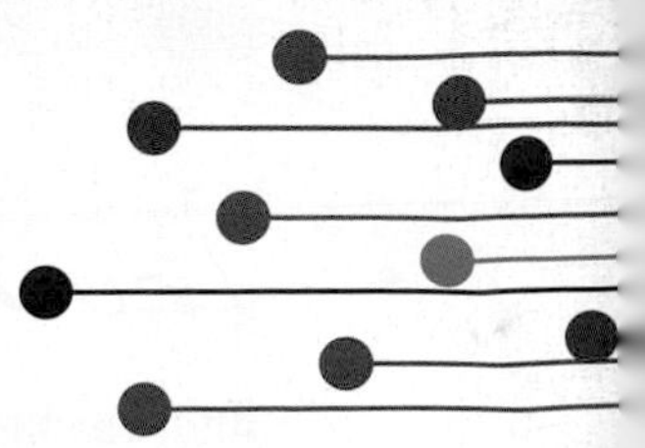

- ***What can teachers learn from the history of education that will be helpful in their work?***

  Interestingly, I was not crazy about history when I was in school, but I now love teaching history and making it fun for students. Knowing where we have been can be very helpful in looking forward. You should not be afraid of trying something new, but I have learned over four decades of teaching that not everything is new. Many teaching strategies that we have been expected to implement are refinements of methods developed earlier in our profession.

What does excellence in teaching look like?

The more enthusiasm you show in what you do and the more excited you are, the more excited the kids become. From the beginning of schooling, students have been asked to read and then discuss what they read and answer questions. You need to be much more creative than that to engage students in the lesson. I also find that hands-on activities help students remember what is being taught because they are actually doing it. Years after students have left my classroom, they remind me of a hands-on activity they did when they were in my classroom.

What do you find joyful about teaching?

Seeing the kids succeed and seeing them go from not doing something to being able to do something and say "look what I did." It is the kids that always kept me going each and every day. Just to see the smiles on their faces, to see their accomplishments. I would say, "This is what you need to do; I want to see you do it." And when they did, I was proud of them, and they were proud of themselves.

Questions to Consider

1. What are some of the lessons from history that can help you reflect on your own work in schools?
2. What reforms are being discussed today that have been tried in one form or another in the past?
3. What are some creative and hands-on strategies that you can use to engage students in learning and being excited about learning? What do we know from history about this approach to learning?

INTRODUCTION

Knowing the past helps us plan the future. Since the Boston Latin School was established in 1635, the nation has adopted universal schooling for all children, established a public education system, desegregated schools, and opened post-secondary education to almost any student who desires it. In studying the history of education, we find that some educational practices appear cyclical, reappearing in a different form every few generations. Movements such as progressivism have had a lasting effect in some aspects of schooling even though it fell out of favor as a movement by the 1950s. Reforms of schools come and go as school administrators and policymakers strive to find the magic curriculum, teaching strategies, and system that will ensure that students learn at high levels.

Learning Outcomes

After reading this chapter, you should be able to

1. Identify reasons that the states established free and universal education.
2. Describe the practical and pedagogical reasons for the establishment of schools by the age of children.
3. List some of the people and events that have been influential in determining school curriculum in the nation's schools.
4. Analyze some of the historical events that have resulted in different educational experiences among students from diverse racial and ethnic groups.
5. Identify changes in the professional lives of teachers between the 19th century and now.

Audio Link 6.1
Listen to the ways teaching has changed over the years.

HOW DID PUBLIC SCHOOLS COME TO BE?

The United States has had a long history of providing a **free and universal education** for its children. Many hard-fought political and legal battles over the past four centuries have led to universal education for all students regardless of their race, ethnicity, socioeconomic status, or native language. However, this has not always been the case. In colonial times access to schooling in basic literacy and numeracy was available only to the affluent. Critical themes in these early debates were around the rights of individuals to decide for themselves whether to attend school and the basic requirements necessary for all citizens in a democracy.

As with many other aspects of early society in the Colonies, the Puritans transferred their views and expectations for education from England to the United States. Who should be educated and the purposes of education were hot topics across Europe in the 1600s. Citizens were asking whether all children should attend school and whether girls as well as boys should attend. They were also asking what students should learn, how long they should attend school, who should pay, and whether school attendance should be compulsory.

Schools in the Colonies

Before communities built schools, children were often taught by women in their neighborhoods who established "dame schools" in their homes. Most schools were established and controlled by churches, where religion was taught along with reading, writing, and arithmetic. Locally controlled schools were first established in the New England colonies where the *New England Primer* was the first widely used textbook. It included the Lord's Prayer, the Ten Commandments, and a list of the books of the bible. Students were asked to memorize the primer's **catechism**, which was a series of questions and correct answers that taught the Protestant faith (Spring, 2011).

The Massachusetts Bay Colony is credited with first requiring all children to receive formal education. The Massachusetts Law of 1642 called for children to learn to read so they could understand the bible and the country's laws. A 1647 statute, the Old Deluder Satan Law, established schools by requiring towns with 50 or more families to appoint a teacher and collect taxes to support schools. In 1650, Connecticut established its own school statutes. Other colonies were slower to engage with these core issues, and the South continued to resist the establishment of schools for anyone other than aristocrats.

Although the early Massachusetts and Connecticut statutes made reference to the importance of reading the Scriptures, they also implied that the state would be better off with educated citizens. This view had been championed by leading philosophers, scientists, and politicians in Europe for several centuries. Jean-Jacques Rousseau, Francis Bacon, Thomas Hobbes, René Descartes, and John Locke argued in the 18th century that there was a public interest in having all citizens educated. They believed that citizens had to have skills in literacy and numeracy for a democracy to thrive and that education should be available to all children and youth (Urban & Wagoner, 2009). Most leaders in the United States agreed that a free and universal education was a cornerstone of democracy.

Around the time of the Revolutionary War, the concept of secular schools emerged. Some leaders were concerned that religious control of schools could limit political freedom and the scientific revolution. Thomas Jefferson, for one, believed that freedom of thought and beliefs was key to a republican society. This concern led to the adoption of the First Amendment to the Constitution, which prevents the establishment of a state religion. The focus on freedom of ideas during this period opened the door to teaching more than religion, **morals,** and civil obedience. Education began to be seen as providing intellectual tools based on science that would help create a better society (Spring, 2011).

Creating a System of Public Education

That the states should be responsible for education was seen as important even before the Constitution was written. During the Revolutionary War, the Continental Congress passed several ordinances related to the opening up of lands in the West. The Land Ordinance of 1785 required each new state to form a central government and address education as a component of its founding laws. It also required each township in the new territories north and west of the Ohio River to designate one section (one square mile) of its 36 allocated township sections for public schools. Two years later the Northwest Ordinance encouraged the establishment of schools because religion, morality, and knowledge were critical for a good government (Urban & Wagoner, 2009).

When the U.S. Constitution was adopted in 1789, it made no reference to education. Even though some of the founders wanted education to be a federal responsibility, the responsibility for education was clarified in the Tenth Amendment, which states that "(t)he powers not delegated to the United States by the Constitution, nor prohibited by it to the States, are reserved to the States respectively or to the people." State legislatures became responsible for establishing education policies and financing a public education system.

As the 1800s unfolded, school debates focused on whether attendance should be compulsory and how schools should be supported and managed. Gradually a consensus emerged that each state would set expectations for public schools, that towns were responsible for the operation of schools, and that schools would be financed through taxation. Concerns about the quality and rigor of education across the states led to a system of education that was somewhat uniform in the organization and operation of public schools. By the 1830s, children were attending public primary schools to learn reading, writing, and arithmetic in what were called **common schools.** Important dates in the development of a system of education are outlined in Table 6.1.

Table 6.1 Significant Events in the Development of the American System of Education

1635	Boston Latin Grammar School established.
1647	Massachusetts's Old Deluder Satan Law required establishment of schools.
1785–1787	Northwest Ordinances passed to support schools in new territories.
1789	United States Constitution adopted without reference to education.
1821	The English Classical School, the first high school established in Boston. The Troy Female Seminary first prepared teachers for certification.
1825–1826	First known child care center opened in New Harmony, Indiana.
1827	Massachusetts law established high schools.
1837	Massachusetts established first state board of education; Horace Mann appointed the first secretary.
1839	First public normal school for preparing teachers opened in Lexington, Massachusetts.
1848	Quincy School, based on grades, was established in Boston.
1852	Massachusetts establishes first compulsory attendance law.
1872	Kalamazoo Decision made public high schools legal.
1873	St. Louis opened the first public kindergarten in the United States.
1918	Compulsory education required in all states.
1965	Elementary-Secondary Education Act (ESEA) passed.
1979	The U.S. Department of Education established by President Jimmy Carter.
2001	ESEA reauthorized as No Child Left Behind Act.

Although public schools have long been a reality in the United States, critics of today's schools question their ability to prepare students for the global world in which we live. When asked how important public schools are today, retired teacher Marvin Kuhn replied,

> It is just as important as back then. Everybody needs an education. If you don't have the money, where else are you going to get your education but through public education? One of the things I've seen in the past few years is the creation of charter schools and vouchers. Even though they may be available to low-income students, charter and private schools pick who they want in their schools, and if those students do not perform at the expected level, the school does not have to let them come back.

HOW DID SCHOOLS BECOME DESIGNED BASED ON THE AGE OF STUDENTS?

Early in the 18th century educators and policymakers envisioned schools as a way to overcome poverty and crime by inculcating a good moral character into students who the reformers believed lacked appropriate parental guidance. **Charity schools,** which were the forerunner of the common school, were developed for this purpose (Spring, 2011). Although some students from low-income families attended the schools that existed during this period, many, including African American students in the north, attended charity schools while more affluent children attended private or public schools (Spring, 2011).

"Take out your iPhones, open the American History app, and turn to the page about George Washington."

The elementary school curriculum in the first half of the 19th century was influenced greatly by the spellers and textbooks written by Noah Webster. His influence was not only on schools; he wrote an American dictionary with which many of you may be familiar. Webster was a schoolmaster who, in 1779, had an idea for a new way of teaching that included a spelling book, grammar book, and reader. When he finished writing the books five years later, he became an itinerant lecturer, riding through the country selling his books. He was a good salesman, selling 1.5 million copies by 1801 and 75 million by 1875. Webster's books contained catechisms, but he did not limit the recitation to religion. He included a moral catechism and a federal one that stressed nationalism and patriotism (Spring, 2011).

The first schools built in many rural communities were one-room schools with a teacher who taught all subjects to students who sometimes ranged in age from five to 17. These schools generally had desks or long benches on which students sat together. A popular instructional method was recitation in which pupils stood and recited the assigned lesson. Values of punctuality, honesty, and hard work were stressed in these rural schools (Howey & Post, 2002).

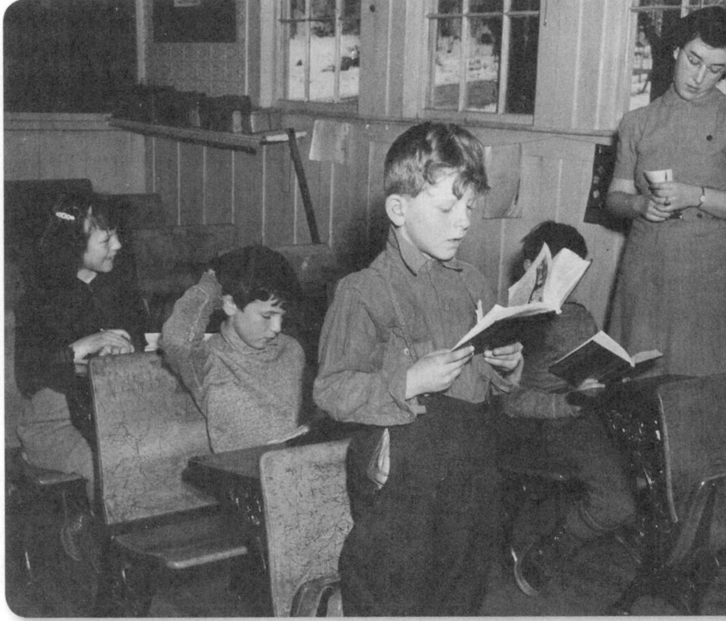
Teachers in the one-room schools of the past and today serve not only as the teachers, but also as the custodian, nurse, secretary, and principal.

In the 1830s and 1840s, the father of common schools, Horace Mann, was concerned with divisions between social classes and saw mixing the social classes in the common school as one way to reduce the tensions between groups. Mann applied his ideas to schools when he became the first secretary of the Massachusetts Board of Education in 1837. His concept of the common school became the tax-supported, locally controlled elementary schools that dominated U.S. education in the industrial era.

The curriculum of the common school included the skills needed for everyday life, ethical behavior, and responsible citizenship, with standardized subject matter in reading, writing, arithmetic, spelling, history, and geography (Cremin, 1951). Common schools were also expected to create conformity in American life by imposing the language and ideological outlook of the dominant Anglo American

UNDERSTANDING AND USING EVIDENCE

Public School Statistics for 1879

The federal government has collected data on the population and institutions for more than 100 years. These data provide demographic information, but they also assist policymakers and other leaders in planning for the future. The following statistics on the school populations by selected state were reported by the federal government in 1879.

States	School Age	School Population	Number Enrolled in Public Schools	Average Daily Attendance	Average Duration of School in Days
Alabama	7–21	376,649	174,585	112,374	84
California	5–17	216,404	156,769	98,468	149
Colorado	6–21	29,738	14,111	10,899	89
Florida	4–21[a]	72,985[b]	36,964[a]	23,933[a]	105.8[a]
Illinois	6–21	1,000,694	693,334	404,479	150
Kentucky	6–20[c]	539,843	*227,607*[d]	160,000[d]	110[d]
New York	5–21	1,628,727	1,030,041	570,382	179
Pennsylvania	6–21	1,200,000[e]	935,740	587,672	149
Texas	8–14	208,324	192,616		80
West Virginia	6–21	206,123	135,526	90,268	100.76

[a]In 1878. [b]In 1876. [c]For colored population, the school age is from 6 to 16. [d]In 1877. [e]In 1873.

Source: U.S. Census Bureau. (2006). *Statistical abstract of the United States: 2006.* Washington, DC: U.S. Government Printing Office.

Your Task: Using these statistics, answer the following questions to compare attendance and length of school years in 1879 to today.

1. How do the ages of students in 1879 compare with the ages of students in schools today?
2. What percentage of the school-aged population was enrolled in schools in 1879 in the states above?
3. How many months did students in schools in 1879 attend school? How does the length of the school year compare with the time spent in schools today?
4. What percentage of the enrolled students in 1879 attended school daily?

Protestant group that governed the country. Education in common schools was seen as a venue for upward social and economic mobility for native whites and European immigrants in the United States. Both girls and boys attended the common schools, usually together.

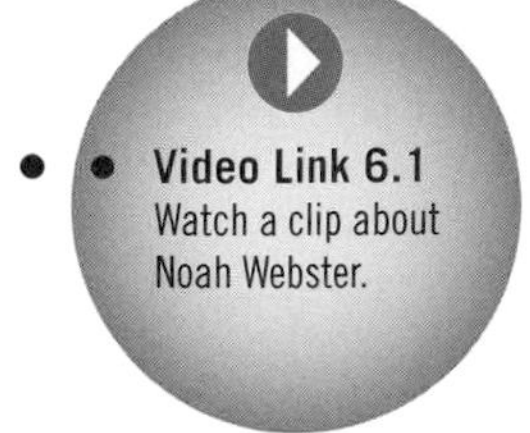

Video Link 6.1
Watch a clip about Noah Webster.

Elementary Schools

The first school based on grades was established in Boston in 1848 as Quincy School. Teachers had their own separate classroom, and each student sat at a desk in classrooms designed for 56 students. Within seven years, all Boston schools were graded. Other cities and communities soon adopted the Quincy model, setting the stage for the graded schools of today (Spring, 2001).

Many urban schools prior to 1850 had classrooms for more than 100 students. One teacher managed the classroom with the assistance of student mentors who were selected from the better students. In this Lancasterian method, developed by Englishman Joseph Lancaster, students sat in long rows and the teacher sat at a desk on a raised platform at the front of the room. When it was time for instruction by the teacher, students marched to the front of the room. Afterwards, they were replaced at the front of the room by another group. The first group of students moved to another section of the classroom for recitation and drill with one of the mentors. Throughout the day, students moved from one part of the room to another to work with different mentors with several recitations occurring simultaneously in the room. Many educators and politicians of this era saw this very structured and orderly learning environment as the panacea for efficient schooling of the masses (Spring, 2011).

The Lancasterian classroom was designed for one teacher to manage the education of as many as 100 students at one time in the same room.

By the beginning of the 20th century, the standard classroom had rows of desks bolted to the floor. As the century progressed, many educators moved from lecture and recitation to student-centered activities, which called for smaller classes that allowed experimentation and flexibility. New York City classrooms, for example, averaged 50 students around World War I; by 1930, the average was 38 students (Spring, 2001).

The Webster spellers were replaced in the last half of the 19th century by the McGuffey Readers, which were written by William Holmes McGuffey. The readers provided moral lessons for an industrialized society. The leading characters in the readers were stereotypically male (Spring, 2011). Although the stories were more secular than those in earlier textbooks, religious selections were included along with stories focusing on moral character and the importance of charity. The McGuffey Readers sold more than 120 million copies between 1836 and 1960 (Urban & Wagoner, 2009). Textbooks in the last third of the 20th century became much more secular to the chagrin of some church leaders, who sometimes suggested that the nation would be better off if textbooks and schools returned to their Puritan roots. The "Dick and Jane" readers, which were popular from the 1930s through the 1950s, reflected white middle-class lifestyles and behaviors (Kaestle & Radway, 2009).

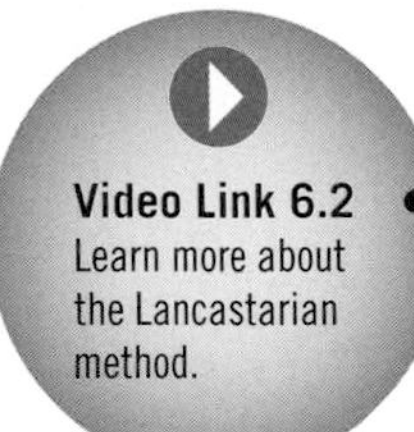

Video Link 6.2
Learn more about the Lancastarian method.

In response to the question about changes that have occurred in the elementary school since 1968 when Mr. Kuhn began teaching, he said:

> One of the things that is different is the mass amount of paperwork you have to do. Yes, you had to do paperwork when I first started teaching, and you were accountable for your work, but you now have to document everything you do. You're basically teaching more to the standards than anything else. If you are not teaching to the standards, you are supposedly not on the right track.

High Schools

During the colonial period, a struggle for intellectual freedom was under way in England to expand education beyond the classical study of Latin and Greek. Dissenters believed that schools were limiting the freedom of ideas by teaching students to be obedient to a church or the government. The scientific revolution fueled the debate, and intellectuals such as Francis Bacon argued that education should provide the intellectual tools and scientific knowledge required to create a better society. This movement led to the development of what was called dissenting academies (Spring, 2001).

When the idea crossed the Atlantic Ocean, the academies became a popular alternative to the Latin grammar schools. An early model of a high school, the academies taught ideas and skills related to the practical world, including the sciences and business. They provided useful education and transmitted the culture that helped move graduates into the middle class. Sometimes the academies were considered small colleges, at other times high schools (Spring, 2001).

The English Classical School was founded in Boston in 1821 as an alternative to boarding schools and the Boston Latin School, which provided a classical education. The curriculum included English, geography, arithmetic, algebra, geometry, trigonometry, history, navigation, and surveying. A few years later, it was renamed English High School, becoming the first high school in the United States (Spring, 2001). Within a few years, Massachusetts passed a law to establish high schools across the state. Other states followed suit, but not without resistance. One of the most famous cases against public high schools was the Kalamazoo decision in the 1870s, brought by three prominent citizens who believed that high school should not be supported with public funds. The courts did not agree, settling the question about taxes supporting high schools.

Massachusetts enacted the first **compulsory attendance** law in 1852, requiring 12 weeks of school. By the end of the 19th century, 27 states had compulsory attendance laws, but all 48 states had passed them by 1918 (Urban & Wagoner, 2009). However, the establishment of attendance laws did not come about without objections. There were competing interests for what children should be doing at a specific age, which sometimes meant working instead of attending school.

By the end of the 19th century children were a large component of the rapidly growing industrial labor force, especially in the textile mills. Three in 10 mill workers in the South were under 16 years of age and 75% of the spinners in North Carolina were 14 or younger (Woodward, 1971). They worked long hours in dark, dirty, and dangerous conditions, which eventually led to child labor laws. However, this was slow to happen, especially in the South. It was not until 1912 that southern states prohibited night work for children and set age and hour limits that were as low as age 12 and 60 hours per week.

By the beginning of the 20th century, most 7- to 13-year-old children attended school. However, only 10% remained in school beyond age 14, and less than 7% of the 17-year-olds graduated from high school (Olson, 2000). As the 20th century unfolded, the combination of child labor laws and compulsory attendance laws were increasingly effective in pushing young people into school.

As high schools were established in small towns and cities, debates about the purpose of high schools were similar to those that led to the development of academies during the colonial days. Some people argued that the high school should develop a well-disciplined mind in the tradition of the old grammar schools. Others believed that the curriculum should prepare students for the practical world and occupations. Most of the early high schools ended up focusing on advanced science, math, English, history, and the political economy, but the curriculum was generally determined by the textbooks of the period. Admission required passing rigorous examinations; only 4% of eligible students were enrolled in a high school in the 1870s. Less than one in three of the admitted students completed high school. Those who didn't complete the four-year curriculum entered business or taught elementary school (Cuban, 2004).

The National Education Association (NEA), which today is the largest teachers' union, formed the Committee of Ten on Secondary School Studies in 1892 to develop uniform requirements for college admission. Instead, its final report identified goals for secondary education, recommending that the children of wealthy and low-income families take the same course of study, regardless of whether they would attend college. The Committee called for at least four years of English, four years of a foreign language, and three years each of mathematics, science, and history (Spring, 2001). The number of high schools grew dramatically at the turn of the century. Seventy percent of the students entering college in 1872 were graduates of academies; by 1920, 90% were high school graduates (Alexander & Alexander, 2001).

High schools at the turn of the 20th century were beginning to sort students for specific roles in society. The NEA's Commission on the Reorganization of Secondary Education published its report, *Cardinal Principles of Secondary Education,* in 1918. Its attempt to redesign the high school to meet the needs of the modern corporate state impacted the high school curriculum for the next 50 years. The proposed comprehensive high schools were to teach English and social studies to promote unity among students from different socioeconomic, ethnic, and language backgrounds, but also included vocational programs in agriculture, business, industry, fine arts, and the household. The purpose of high schools was expanded from a narrow focus on academics to also attend to the socialization of students by encouraging their involvement in common activities such as athletics and extracurricular activities such as student government, the student newspaper, and clubs. The report also called for high schools to promote good health through physical and health education (Spring, 2011). During this period, high schools developed an academic track for students who were encouraged to attend college. All other students were guided into general or vocational tracks that would prepare them for jobs immediately after high school. Over time, fewer and fewer students took the academic courses, as shown in Figure 6.1.

Figure 6.1 Percentage of High Schoolers Taking Academic Courses: 1928 to 1961

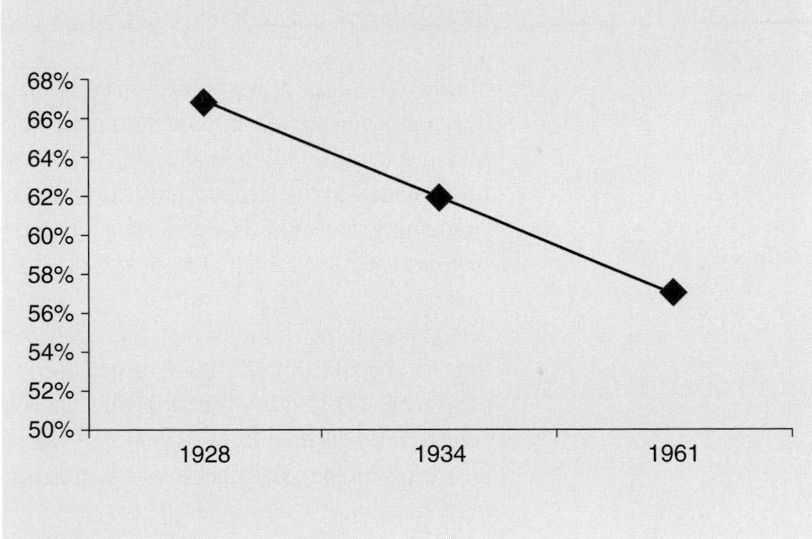

Source: The failed promise of the American high school, 1890-1995 by Angus, David I.: Mirel, Jeffrey E. Copyright 1999. Reproduced with permission of Teachers College Press in the format of Textbook via Copyright Clearance Center.

It was not until after World War II that the need for a high school education became widespread. By the 1950s, a majority of teenagers were earning high school diplomas. Although more students were attending high school, not all of them were happy with the curriculum and the way they were treated. By the end of the 1960s and into the 1970s, students of color were disrupting many high schools as they confronted discrimination and demanded that their cultures be included in the curriculum. High schools entered the 1980s more peacefully, but with more rights for students, in part, due to a number of court cases. The curriculum and textbooks began to incorporate content on the experiences and history of people beyond the white, Anglo-Saxon, Protestant male.

Middle Level Education

At the beginning of the 20th century, psychologist G. Stanley Hall argued that early adolescents were neither children nor adults. He believed that separate education would better serve the students between elementary and high school (Beane, 2001). A second reason for the creation of this new level of schooling was to prepare young people for the differentiated comprehensive high school in which they would be sorted into academic and vocational tracks (Urban & Wagoner, 2009). Table 6.2 lists some of the educators who have influenced U.S. education.

The first junior high school was established in1909 in Columbus, Ohio, followed by one in Berkley, California, in 1910. Although some educators and psychologists were calling for the creation of schools between elementary and high school, the number of junior high schools grew over the next few decades primarily in response to social conditions. Elementary schools were overcrowded with the large influx of immigrant children and the increasing number of students not being promoted to the next grade (Beane, 2001). Four in five students were attending junior high school by 1960 (McEwin, Dickinson, & Jenkins, 2003). For the most part, they had become miniature high schools that were not effectively serving young adolescents.

Still believing that early adolescents deserved an education that was different from that provided in elementary and secondary schools, middle level educators proposed a new structure. Like junior high schools, middle schools evolved, in part, because of the practicalities of the times. By the late 1950s, the baby boom generation was overcrowding elementary schools, which suggested building more elementary schools. Another option was to add a wing to the high school, move to it the ninth grade from the high school, and grades 6–8 from the elementary school. Some communities built a new high school and remodeled the old one for grades 6–8. Sometimes the fifth grade was moved into the new intermediate schools.

Middle school advocates argued that schooling for young adolescents should focus on their developmental as well as academic needs. Rather than a large, departmentalized school like high school, their vision was smaller clusters of teachers and students. Teachers and other school professionals in these schools were to provide guidance to help students maneuver though their changing social and physical development. Educators were to be more affectionate and sensitive to young people.

As the popularity of junior high schools declined, the number of middle schools grew quickly to more than 11,000 by 1999 (Snyder & Dillow, 2011) and more than 15,000 today (McEwin & Greene, 2011). With the national focus on academics in the 1990s, middle level educators pushed for a curriculum that would provide access to academic subjects in a positive and nurturing climate. Teachers were encouraged to use collaborative and cooperative learning with interdisciplinary teams of teachers and block scheduling. Advocates promoted eliminating the tracking of students and creating heterogeneous groups in which cultural diversity was celebrated and diverse learning styles were recognized.

How to best serve preadolescent students remains an unsettled issue. Critics charge that the middle school philosophy focuses on the self-exploration, socialization, and group learning to the detriment of academics. These charges are fueled by poor showings of eighth graders on national and international tests where they rank lower than fourth graders, suggesting that they are losing ground as they progress through the middle grades. Some research suggests that these students would be better served in K–8 schools (Meyer, 2011). You are likely to be engaged in discussions about the value of middle schools as you proceed through your teaching career.

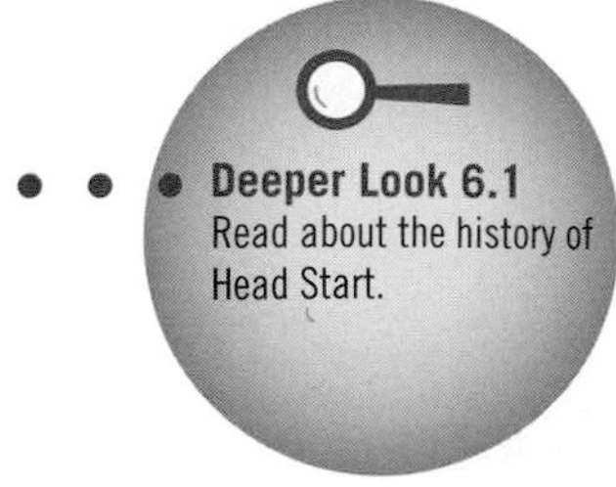

Deeper Look 6.1
Read about the history of Head Start.

Early Childhood Education

Throughout history, some mothers have had to work to support their families. Almost always, they have had to leave their children with someone, often a relative or a neighbor. Some women in the neighborhood watched several children, but organized schools with child care providers

Table 6.2 Who's Who in U.S. Education

Noah Webster	Author of spellers and textbooks that influenced the elementary school curriculum from 1783–1875.
Emma Willard	An early feminist who opened the Troy Female Seminary in 1821 where women prepared for a certificate to teach.
Reverend Samuel Hall	Established the Columbian School in Vermont in 1823 for preparing teachers.
Robert Owens	Welsh social reformer who opened the first known child care center at a mill in New Harmony, Indiana, in 1825–1826.
Horace Mann	First secretary of the Massachusetts Board of Education and father of the common school movement.
William Holmes McGuffey	Wrote the McGuffey Readers that were used between 1836 and 1960.
Friedrich Froebel	Established the first kindergarten in 1837 in Germany that served as the model for early kindergartens in the United States.
Samuel Chapman Armstrong	Founder of Hampton Institute in 1868 to prepare African American teachers who paid for their education through manual labor.
Booker T. Washington	Educator and author who served as the first president of Tuskegee Normal and Industrial Institute in 1881 and promoted preparing African Americans for the trades and their appropriate roles in the Jim Crow South.
W. E. B. Du Bois	Sociologist, historian, professor, author, and civil rights activist who challenged the oppressive southern economy and argued that African Americans should have a classical education to prepare them to be leaders.
John Dewey	Philosopher and professor who established a laboratory school in Chicago in 1896 to test his progressive ideas about a child-oriented curriculum. His ideas have been very influential in education and social reform.
William James	Harvard philosopher and psychologist who found that the stimulus-response concepts of learning could be used to help children develop desirable habits.
G. Stanley Hall	Psychologist who established child development and child psychology as fields that influenced education at the end of the 19th century.
Margaret Haley	Activist teacher who was an early member of the Chicago Federation of Teachers and later an organizer for the American Federation of Teachers.
Catherine Goggin	Along with Margaret Haley, she helped affiliate the Chicago Federation of Teachers with organized labor.
Edward Thorndike	Professor at Teachers College, Columbia University and author of *Educational Psychology* (1903). He promoted behaviorism and testing, which was widely used by the military.
Mary McLeod Bethune	An educational leader who opened a school for African American girls in 1904 in Daytona Beach, Florida, that evolved into Bethune-Cookman University. Also served as an adviser to President Franklin D. Roosevelt.
William Chandler Bagley	Professor and author of *Classroom Management* (1907), which was the primary guide for preparing effective teachers for many years.
William Heard Kilpatrick	Teachers College, Columbia University professor who supported progressive education and introduced in 1918 the "project method" in which students direct their own learning.
Thurgood Marshall	U.S. Supreme Court justice who had argued *Brown v. Board of Education* in 1952–1953.
Theodore Sizer	Education reformer who wrote *Horace's Compromise* and founded the Coalition of Essential Schools in 1984 to create a group of high schools based on the progressive tradition.

were not available until the 19th century. Robert Owens opened the first known child care center at a mill in New Harmony, Indiana, in 1825–1826 with more than 100 children (Ranck & NAEYC's History & Archives Panel, 2001).

Early nursery schools were developed in the 1920s and 1930s on what was known from the emerging field of child development and psychology.

The first kindergarten was opened by Friedrich Froebel in 1837 in Germany for three- and four-year-old children. He believed that the kindergarten teacher should not be **authoritarian**, but instead would guide children's learning through their own play, songs, stories, and activities (Gutek, 2012). The first public kindergarten in the United States opened in St. Louis in 1873 to serve children in poverty. Children were to learn the virtues and manners, moral habits, cleanliness, politeness, obedience, promptness, and self-control that would prepare them for elementary school. By the 1880s, Froebelian kindergartens had become popular in the United States (Spring, 2001).

By the beginning of the 20th century, about 6% of the kindergarten-aged population was enrolled in kindergarten. It was at this time that the work of G. Stanley Hall established child development and child psychology as fields of study. He defined childhood as the years between four and eight, which remains the general range for primary education today. The focus of a kindergarten class focused on creating order and discipline in the child's life, but continued to encourage children to play and be creative. During this period, the age for kindergarteners in public schools was raised to five. Approximately 90% of five-year-olds were attending kindergarten in the 1980s at the time that the curriculum was beginning to shift from being child-centered to academics (Berg, 2003).

WHAT HAS INFLUENCED THE SCHOOL CURRICULUM?

Audio Link 6.2
Learn more about global education.

Curriculum has gone through some major changes since the first schools were established in the Plymouth colony. It no longer has the religious and moral overtones of the past. Educators today are concerned about the academic performance of their students and providing equal access for all students to learn. In his reflections on curriculum changes over his 43 years of teaching, Mr. Kuhn reports that

> you used to use the textbook to develop curriculum guides that reflected the current state standards. State standards existed, but they were not emphasized as much as now. At that time, the basic test taken by almost all Indiana students was the Iowa Basic Skills Test. Now it is the ISTEP, which all Indiana students take at exactly the same time of the year.

In addition, the curriculum has been influenced by the changing needs of businesses and evolving new technologies. The intensity of debates among educators, politicians, and the public about what should be taught and how it should be taught continues as reflected in numerous national and state reports about the state of education. In this section we will examine how the curriculum changed in different historical periods.

The Industrial Revolution

As industrialization took hold in the cities of the Northeastern United States at the end of the 19th century, schooling was greatly influenced by the need to help new immigrant populations become literate and disciplined workers. Education was becoming more standardized, compartmentalized, and centralized. The Lancasterian system was promoted as an inexpensive solution for the education of the masses.

The move toward preparing young people to contribute effectively to the industrial revolution was assisted by the work of psychologists at the turn of the century. Harvard philosopher and psychologist William James found evidence that the stimulus–response, or behavioral, concepts of learning could be used to help children develop desirable habits. His ideas were expanded by Edward Thorndike, whose ideas of teaching as a science and behaviorism in which rewards and punishment were used to control student behavior influenced education for the next few decades (Spring, 2011). He also promoted testing as a way of determining which people are suited for which social roles. Thorndike's principles were applied to schools in the popular textbook *Classroom Management* by William Chandler Bagley, who believed that schools should help students develop the industrial habits needed for the assembly line.

Progressivism: Curriculum for Reform

In *Emile,* published in 1762, European philosopher Jean-Jacques Rousseau questioned the focus of education on memorization and the subordination to authority. He thought that learning occurred through experience and discovery. He also believed that moral education should occur in adolescence, not childhood (Urban & Wagoner, 2009). Influenced by Rousseau, Johann Pestalozzi of Switzerland introduced a teaching approach in 1781 that used teaching objects from the real world, learning by doing, and activities rather than seat work (Urban & Wagoner, 2009).

A philosopher who integrated psychology and pedagogy into his thinking about education, John Dewey opened his laboratory school in Chicago in 1896 to test his progressive ideas about a child-oriented curriculum. His classrooms had movable tables rather than individual desks to encourage group work and learning (Spring, 2011). Unlike most of his colleagues, Dewey saw education as critical to changing society and preparing students to participate in a democratic society (Urban & Wagoner, 2009).

A colleague of Dewey's at Columbia University, William Heard Kilpatrick, introduced in 1918 the "project method" that was widely adopted by school districts. The project method developed school activities that were meaningful to students and relevant to society (Urban & Wagoner, 2009). In the eyes of progressives, traditional curriculum with its emphasis on lecture and recitation could not possibly address students' individual needs and learning styles. They believed that curriculum must be moderated through activities directed by the learner.

Student-centered instruction had become good practice in the 1940s, and schools were more humane by the 1950s. As progressives pressed for reformed schools that they believed could solve societal problems, they became more vulnerable to criticism for neglecting academic subjects (Urban & Wagoner, 2009). Not to be kept down, progressive thought reappeared in the 1960s and early 1970s, but it was confronted by the back-to-basics movement at the end of the 1970s. Nevertheless, it continues to reappear. For example, Theodore Sizer founded the Coalition of Essential Schools in 1984 to create a group of high schools along progressive lines. The progressive ideology was adopted by hundreds of schools across the country

The progressive movement led to moveable furniture, small-group work, and more hands-on work in classrooms.

(Coalition of Essential Schools, 2012). The progressive ideology continues to be reflected today in charter schools and other schools of choice that have some freedom from the central-office-driven culture. Many of the practices of the progressive movement are now taken for granted by educators as they use movable furniture, place students in small work groups, and teach an integrated curriculum.

Sputnik I

An urgent demand for new curriculum and teaching techniques emerged after the Soviet Union launched the first satellite, Sputnik I, on October 4, 1957. U.S. leaders were bound to do whatever it would take to regain their nation's scientific and technological supremacy over the Soviet Union during this Cold War period. Congressional resistance to financially supporting education disappeared with passage of the National Defense Education Act (NDEA) in 1958 to improve the curriculum and teaching of science, mathematics, and foreign languages. The law also included support for guidance, counseling, testing, and the identification of the brightest students. The development of more scientists, mathematicians, and engineers was seen as critical to U.S. prominence in the world, and the federal government began to take its first step toward a national curriculum (Kliebard, 2004).

The National Science Foundation (NSF) was charged with developing curricula for science and mathematics. Professors in major research universities, rather than professional educators, designed the new curricula that would transform the teaching of science and math in the nation's schools. "New mathematics" was one of the outcomes of this work that changed how math was taught in schools. Math teachers participated in professional development workshops to learn the new math and how to teach basic concepts such as set theory and functions. Although the public generally supported the new focus on reforming schools, they questioned the need for the new math as they tried to help their children with their homework (Spring, 2011).

New formats for textbooks and ideas for the presentation of relevant subject matter emerged from these projects. Teachers were suddenly presented with an avalanche of choices regarding what and how to teach. There were Attribute Games and Tangrams. Elementary school science packages offered Petri dishes full of fungi and amoebas on order from the local science laboratory (Spring, 2001). Reading texts were organized around literary themes and generalizations relating to the students' own lives. Many teachers benefited from the programs that taught new math and introduced them to new curriculum materials.

The curriculum reforms after Sputnik I continue to resurface in the nation's discourse about improving education. Today's critics once again are concerned that the United States is falling behind other countries in scientific and technological advances. As a result, achievement on standardized tests is of utmost importance to the public and policymakers. The federal government has called for the recruitment of more bright students in science, technology, engineering, and mathematics (STEM). Finally, common core standards for mathematics and reading have been adopted by most states to improve the academic achievement of students and the prominence of the United States in these fields.

HOW HAS THE EDUCATIONAL SYSTEM CONTRIBUTED TO EQUALITY?

An examination of how different groups have been treated in our educational system over the past four centuries provides insights into the importance of education in the struggle for equality in the United States. All groups have fought for quality education for their children. The progress toward ridding the nation of inequality and providing equal education for all students has involved committed people of color as well as whites. The joy in this sad history of discrimination and inequality is that much has changed, especially in the past 50 years. In addition, teachers are key in providing a quality and equitable education for all students. Our understanding of how we got to where we are today should encourage us to make a commitment to ensure that all of our future students have every possible opportunity to learn. A chronology of significant events in providing equality for students is shown in Table 6.3.

First Americans

European colonists thought that American Indian leaders should be educated in the schools of the colonists for the purposes of learning Christianity and the Anglo-Saxon culture, with the goal of replacing their native cultures and languages. When Virginia's William and Mary College was established in 1693, a part of its mission was the education of Native American students (Glenn, 2011). New Hampshire's Dartmouth College had the same goal when it was established in 1780, but most of its students were white (Spring, 2011).

Deeper Look 6.2
Read more about the history and current state of Native American education.

Resistance to Conversion

The conversion of American Indians to the Anglo-Saxon culture met with great resistance from tribes and their members. The conversion that did occur was most often among the families formed by marriages of whites and American Indians. Because the government's plans for **deculturalizing** Native Americans were ineffective, Congress passed the Civilization Act of 1819 with the explicit purpose of culturally transforming the native population, especially the southern tribes. To move the effort forward, the Superintendent of Indian Trade, Thomas L. McKenney, encouraged the establishment of tribal schools with missionary teachers. The Protestant churches that joined this effort believed that the spread of Anglo-Saxon culture around the world was part of the nation's **manifest destiny.** Most Native American families who participated in the missionary schools had a different goal than the federal government. They were interested in literacy, not the extinction of their cultures or the adoption of Christianity (Spring, 2011).

One of the federal government's goals for the tribes in the south was to convince tribal members to divide tribal lands into private property that could then be sold to Anglo settlers—a goal that was reinforced by missionary schools. When few Native Americans were willing to sell tribal lands, Congress passed the Indian Removal Act of 1830, authorizing the president of the United States to set aside land west of the Mississippi River for Native Americans who then were living in the southern states east of the Mississippi River. Within a few years, the Cherokees, Creeks, Choctaw, Chickasaws, and Seminoles were forcibly moved to the new "Indian Territory." In the Trail of Tears one in four Cherokees died on the trek west from their ancestral homeland in Georgia. In the new territory, which is now Oklahoma, tribes established their own schools. By 1848 the Choctaws had nine boarding schools with many Choctaw teachers. The Choctaws also established segregated schools for the children of freed slaves after the Civil War and a system of schools that included academies for boys and girls (Spring, 2011).

Table 6.3 Significant Events in the Movement Toward Educational Equality

1693	William and Mary College established with mission to educate Native Americans.
1855	Massachusetts outlawed the segregation of schools.
1896	Supreme Court finds "separate but equal" laws constitutional in *Plessy v. Ferguson.*
1905	San Francisco schools are desegregated, allowing Chinese youth to attend regular high schools.
1915	Student strike in Puerto Rico supports instruction in Spanish.
1918	Texas makes it a criminal offense to use any language other than English for instruction.
1928	Meriam Report attacks government's policies of removing American Indian students from their homes.
1934	Padin Reform restricts English instruction to high schools.
1940	Federal court requires equal salaries for African American and white teachers in *Alston v. School Board of City of Norfolk.*
1947	Federal appeals court strikes down segregated schooling for Mexican Americans in *Méndez v. Westminster School Dist.*
1951	Puerto Rico gains greater control of their school systems after being granted commonwealth status.
1954	Supreme Court makes school segregation unconstitutional in *Brown v. Board of Education,* overturning *Plessy.*
1956	Virginia legislature calls for "massive resistance" to school desegregation.
1958	In *Cooper v. Aaron* the Supreme Court rules that fear of social unrest or violence does not excuse state governments from complying with *Brown.*
1959	Officials close public schools in Prince Edward County, Virginia, rather than integrate them.
1964	Congress passes the Civil Rights Act, which prohibits discrimination in school programs and activities that receive federal assistance.
	Supreme Court orders Prince Edward Country, Virginia, to reopen its schools on a desegregated basis.
1965	In *Green v. County School Board of New Kent County* the Supreme Court orders states to dismantle segregated facilities, staff, faculty, extracurricular activities, and transportation.
	Congress passes the Handicapped Children's Early Education Assistance Act.
1968	Title VII of ESEA supports bilingual programs in Indian languages and English.
1971	In *Swann v. Charlotte-Mecklenberg Board of Education* the court approves busing, magnet schools, compensatory education, and other tools as appropriate remedies to overcome the role of residential segregation in perpetuating racially segregated schools.
1972	Congress passes Title IX Education Amendment outlawing discrimination based on sex.
1973	Court rules that education is not a "fundamental right" and that the Constitution does not require equal education expenditures within a state in *San Antonio Independent School District v. Rodriguez.*
1974	Supreme Court blocks metropolitan-wide desegregation plans to desegregate urban schools with high minority populations in *Milliken v. Bradley.*
	In *Lau v. Nichols* the Supreme Court stipulates that special language programs are necessary to provide equal educational opportunity to students who do not understand English.
1975	Congress passes Education for All Handicapped Children, Public Law 94-142.
	Congress passes Indian Self-Determination and Education Assistance Act.

1978	Supreme Court rules that race can be a factor in university admissions, but it cannot be the deciding factor in *Regents of the University of California v. Bakke.*
1982	Supreme Court rejects tax exemptions for private religious schools that discriminate in *Bob Jones University v. U.S.* and *Goldboro Christian Schools v. U.S.*
1986	Federal court finds that a school district can be released from its desegregation plan and returned to local control after it meets the *Green* factors in *Riddick v. School Board of the City of Norfolk, Virginia.*
1988	Tribally Controlled Schools Act gives grants for tribal schools.
1990	Native American Languages Act promotes preservation of Native American languages.
1996	Federal appeals court prohibits the use of race in college and university admissions, ending affirmative action in Louisiana, Texas, and Mississippi in *Hopwood v. Texas.*
2003	Supreme Court upholds diversity as a rationale for affirmative action programs in higher education admissions but declares point systems inappropriate in *Gratz v. Bollinger* and *Grutter v. Bollinger.* Federal district court case affirms the value of racial diversity and race-conscious student assignment plans in K–12 education in *Lynn v. Comfort.*
2007	Supreme Court strikes down the use of race in determining schools for students in *Parents Involved in Community Schools Inc. v. Seattle School District* and *Meredith v. Jefferson County (Ky.) Board of Education.*

Boarding Schools

Still trying to convert American Indians, the 1867 Indian Peace Commission said that American Indians could become citizens if they gave up their native religions and ways of life. Again, education was to play an important role in this process. The charge to schools was to replace native languages with English, destroy tribal customs, and develop allegiance to the federal government. The new strategy called for boarding schools, requiring the removal of children from their families at an early age to isolate them from the language and customs of their parents and tribes. Between 1879 and 1905 a number of boarding schools were located far from the reservation. Thousands of young Native Americans from the Dakotas were boarded at the Carlisle Indian School in Pennsylvania (Glenn, 2011). Parents and tribes continually complained about the boarding schools, how their children were being treated, and how their native cultures were being denigrated.

Federal policies removed many American Indian children from their homes to attend boarding schools into the 20th century.

Children continued to be removed from their homes and placed in boarding schools at the time citizenship was granted to Native Americans in 1924. Not until then did concerned citizens seriously investigate the horrible conditions in these schools. Red Cross investigators found that children at the Rice Boarding School in Arizona were fed "bread, black coffee, and syrup for breakfast; bread and boiled potatoes for dinner; more bread and boiled potatoes for supper" (Szasz, 1974). The poor diet and overcrowded conditions contributed to the spread

Video Link 6.3
Watch a video about boarding schools.

of diseases such as tuberculosis and trachoma (Spring, 2011). Investigators found that boarding schools were supported by the work of students who attended classes half the day and worked the other half. The 1928 Meriam Report by Johns Hopkins University attacked the government's policies of removing Native American children from their homes. Following the release of this report, the government began to support community day schools and native cultures (Spring, 2011).

American Indian Control

When John F. Kennedy was elected to the presidency in 1960, the Bureau of Indian Affairs began to involve American Indians in policy decisions. The Office of Economic Opportunity and the Bureau of Indian Affairs supported the creation of the Rough Rock Demonstration School on the Navajo reservation, in part to preserve the Navajo language and culture. In addition, Navajo parents were again able to control the education of their children.

As the Civil Rights Movement grew in intensity in the 1960s, America Indian tribes began to participate in a Pan-Indian movement that recognized that tribes shared a common set of values and interests. The American Indian Movement (AIM) and the Indians of All Tribes led demonstrations demanding self-determination. At the same time, a Senate report, *Indian Education: A National Tragedy—A National Challenge,* condemned previous federal educational policies for Native Americans. The report said "a careful review of the historical literature reveals that the dominant policy of the Federal Government toward the American Indian has been one of forced assimilation. . . . [because of] a desire to divest the Indian of his land" (Senate Committee on Labor and Public Welfare, 1969, p. 9).

Federal policy began to change. Title VII of the Elementary and Secondary Education Act of 1968 provided support for bilingual programs in Indian languages and English. In 1975, Congress passed the Indian Self-Determination and Education Assistance Act, which gave tribes the right to operate their own schools. The 1988 Tribally Controlled Schools Act gave grants to tribes to operate their own schools. In a complete switch of earlier policy for assimilation and the destruction of native cultures and languages, the 1990 Native American Languages Act promoted the preservation of traditional Native American languages.

African Americans

The education of African Americans is also built on a history of discrimination, but their relationship with the European colonizers was different than that of the American Indians. They were not the native inhabitants of the United States. For the most part, they had not chosen to immigrate to the United States, but entered involuntarily by force. They did not own land that the settlers wanted, but they were a critical source of labor necessary for the southern economy. Most African Americans were owned and sold, and had little control over their own lives. Until the early part of the 20th century, most African Americans lived in the South where before the Civil War it was illegal to attend school. Although literacy was a punishable crime for African slaves in the South, at least 5% of them were literate by the outbreak of the Civil War (Anderson, 1988).

Participation in Schools After the Revolutionary War

African American children in the North most often attended segregated and inferior schools. Charity schools for freed slaves opened at the end of the 18th century in Philadelphia, New York City, and Baltimore (Kaestle, 1983). African American children could attend Boston schools at that time, but most did not because of their poor economic situations and the hostile reception of them in schools. In 1798 a group of black parents petitioned the School Committee for a separate school to protect their children from the hostile environment. The School Committee did not accept the parents' proposal at first, but it changed its position in 1806 and opened a segregated school with public funds and money from white philanthropists (Spring, 2011).

By the 1820s black parents decided that the segregated school was providing an inferior education for their children and began to demand better conditions and teachers. They petitioned the Boston School Committee in 1846 to desegregate schools. Even though the School Committee found the segregated schools unacceptable, it took no action to change those conditions or to require its public schools to be open to African American children. In response, Benjamin Roberts sued the city for excluding his daughter from all-white schools near their home. He lost his case before the Massachusetts Supreme Court when it ruled that the city had provided "a separate, but equal" school for his daughter. Not long afterwards, in 1855, however, the state legislature passed a law that prevented the segregation of schools based on race or religion, becoming the first state to outlaw school segregation. The Boston schools were integrated that year (Spring, 2011).

Education in the South

Before the end of the Civil War, former slaves in the South were fighting for universal education. They craved literacy but were unwilling to wait for the government to provide schools. They established and staffed their own schools with African American teachers throughout the South. The African American teachers, school officials, and other leaders adopted the common school ideal with the New England classical liberal curriculum. The curriculum in elementary schools included reading, spelling, writing, grammar, diction, history, geography, arithmetic, and music. In the black colleges, students studied Latin, Greek, mathematics, science, and philosophy (Spring, 2011).

Deeper Look 6.3
Read about segregated schools in the South.

To pursue the goal of universal education, the former slaves sought the help of Republican politicians, northern missionary societies, the Union army, and the Freedmen's Bureau, which had been created by Congress in 1865. However, it was very important to them that they control their own education, which was sometimes difficult as northern missionaries moved into the South to establish schools. When John W. Alvord was appointed the national superintendent of schools for the Freedmen's Bureau in 1865, he discovered a system of at least 500 "native schools" as he traveled across the South (Anderson, 1988). These schools had been established and were being managed by ex-slaves who were committed to ensuring that African American children and adults would learn to read and write as soon as possible. In some communities, black churches developed Sabbath schools that offered literacy instruction in the evenings and on the weekends. In these schools, the speller was as prevalent as the bible (Anderson, 1988).

Most planters resisted universal education for former slaves and impoverished whites. Their opposition was, in part, due to economics. The planters needed a workforce that would work for low wages; it depended heavily on child labor, which led to schools being opened as late as December. They supported low taxes, opposed compulsory school attendance, and discouraged universal public education. Eventually, they began to provide schools for low-income white students, but they failed to provide schools for black children in most communities. The gains made by African Americans in the 1860s were quickly stymied and the proportion attending school began to drop (Anderson, 1988).

Education at the Beginning of the 20th Century

Although ex-slaves had founded their schools with a classical curriculum, some leaders questioned the need for such advanced study. They argued that black children would be better served with training for the trades and learning their appropriate role in the Southern culture. With this goal in mind, Northerner Samuel Chapman Armstrong founded Hampton Institute in Virginia to prepare teachers. Most of Hampton's early students had completed only the eighth grade. They were required to work long hours in a sawmill, on the school's farm, or in the school's kitchen or dining room to develop the ethic of hard work that Southern landowners expected of their laborers. One of Armstrong's top students, Booker T. Washington, founded Tuskegee Normal and Industrial Institute in 1881 to extend Armstrong's pedagogy.

Most African Americans had a different vision for their education. They saw Washington giving in to the white demands of industrialists who wanted a steady, complacent workforce at low wages. The primary spokesperson for a different vision, W. E. B. Du Bois, wanted no compromises with the powerful white elites. Instead, he wanted to challenge the oppressive southern economy. He argued that black education should be about preparing the African American leaders of the future. He supported the classical education that was available in black colleges like Atlanta and Wilburforce. While Washington supported segregated schooling, Du Bois became one of the founders of the National Association for the Advancement of Colored People (NAACP)—the organization that spearheaded the effort to desegregate schools later in the century. By 1915, the Du Bois supporters had prevailed; the Hampton-Tuskegee model began to lose favor among its previous supporters (Spring, 2011).

At the beginning of the 20th century, most African American children did not attend elementary school because no schools existed for them, and they were not allowed to attend the schools that white children attended. If they wanted a school, African American families in the South often had to build their own schools even though they paid local and state taxes to support white segregated schools (Spring, 2011). When African American children could attend school, their schools were usually inferior to those attended by white students. The schools lacked equipment and supplies. They were allocated textbooks after they had worn out their usefulness in the white schools. Families and leaders in the African American community turned to the courts for support in accessing resources for the education of their children.

School Desegregation

Nearly 100 court cases from 20 states and the District of Columbia were filed for equal education in the 19th century. African Americans in the North won a majority of their cases, prohibiting segregation in their public schools (Hendrie, 2000). Nevertheless, segregation continued in the South. After Homer Plessy was arrested for refusing to ride in the "colored" section of a train in Louisiana, he protested that his **Fourteenth Amendment** rights had been abridged. The United States Supreme Court disagreed, ruling in its 1896 *Plessy v. Ferguson* decision that "separate but equal" facilities were legal. This decision supported the segregation of schools for the next six decades.

Audio Link 6.3
Listen to a clip about freedom rides.

The NAACP decided to pursue a legal path toward desegregating public schools. Five cases from South Carolina, Virginia, Delaware, Kansas, and the District of Columbia were percolating in the lower courts in the mid-1940s. The first four cases were argued before the U.S. Supreme Court in 1952 and 1953 by Thurgood Marshall, who later became the first African American Supreme Court justice. In 1954 the Court declared that "[i]n the field of public education the doctrine of 'separate but equal' has no place. Separate educational facilities are inherently unequal" (*Brown v. Board of Education of Topeka,* 1954). The fifth case, *Bolling v. Sharpe* (1954), declared that the federal government could not segregate schools in the District of Columbia.

Most school districts did not respond to this mandate until after the passage of the 1964 Civil Rights Act. Many white families fiercely resisted the desegregation of their schools. In cities like Little Rock, Arkansas, the National Guard protected African American students who were entering white schools for the first time. Virginia's Prince Edward County School Board resisted desegregation, closing its public schools for five years. White families established private Christian schools or moved to the suburbs where the population was primarily white to avoid integration. The 1971 *Swann v. Charlotte-Mecklenburg* decision moved desegregation efforts to another level when it upheld district-wide busing to overcome segregation.

As schools were desegregated, many African American teachers and principals who had worked in segregated schools were not invited to teach in the integrated schools, leaving many of them without jobs. However, the race of the students in schools did change in the three decades following the *Brown* decision. In the mid-1960s only 2% of black students attended integrated schools; by the late 1980s, 45% of them were in integrated schools (Frankenberg, Lee, & Orfield, 2003). During this period, rural and small-town schools across the South were integrated. The achievement gap between black and white students closed substantially, students of color had greater access to quality schools and college admission, and students were better prepared to work and interact in a multicultural society (Boger & Orfield, 2005). Even more dramatic than the desegregation of schools during this period was the dismantling of *Plessy v. Ferguson* and its resulting **Jim Crow laws**, which did not allow African Americans to use the same facilities as whites.

By the mid-1980s federal court sanctions for integration began to be lifted. After the Supreme Court allowed federal courts to end desegregation plans with *Board of Education of Oklahoma City v. Dowell* in 1991, many federal courts prohibited school districts from voluntarily using race-conscious assignment policies to maintain diversity in their schools (Boger & Orfield, 2005). Because of **de facto segregation** in many communities, neighborhood schools were often comprised of students of the same race. Segregation in schools began to return to pre-1970 levels. At the beginning of the 21st century African American and Latino students were again much more likely than other students to attend schools that are characterized by poverty and their peers are predominantly other students of color. Half of the nation's schools are highly segregated white schools, but the degree of poverty in those schools is considerably less. Although the ability to attend less impoverished schools provides all students a better chance at being successful in school and life, the one-time goal of integrating schools has been abandoned (Boger & Orfield, 2005).

African American students often had to be protected by the National Guard as they desegregated schools in the 1960s.

Latinos

Whether Mexican American students could attend the same schools as whites depended on whether they were classified as white. There was no common agreement on the race of Mexican Americans. In 1897, Texas courts ruled that Mexican Americans were not white. However, California classified them as Caucasian until 1930 when the Attorney General categorized them as American Indians (Spring, 2001). As a result of not being white, most Mexican American children attended segregated schools through the first half of the 20th century. The same separate but equal laws applied to them as to African Americans.

The Battle for the Use of Spanish

In addition to being in segregated schools, Mexican American students often were not allowed to speak Spanish in school. To ensure that teachers would deliver instruction in English, states passed laws to that effect. In 1918 Texas made it a criminal offense to use any language other than English for instruction. Often, students were forbidden to use Spanish at any time while they were in school. In the last half of the 19th century, Mexican Americans sent their children to Catholic or nonsectarian private schools, both of which were more likely to provide bilingual instruction, to escape the anti-Mexican attitudes of public schools (Spring, 2011).

Many Mexican American children were not attending school at the beginning of the 20th century, in part, because farmers were not willing to release them from work in the field to attend school. On the other hand, many school officials wanted them in schools to Americanize them and rid them of their cultures and language (Spring, 2011).

Deeper Look 6.4
Read more about Latino education.

Concerned about discrimination against Mexican American students in public schools, the League of United Latin American Citizens (LULAC) called for bilingual instruction and the maintenance of Mexican cultural traditions in schools as early as 1929. However, the English-only laws were not repealed until 1968 when the federal government supported bilingual education as an option for teaching English-language learners (Spring, 2011). As the federal policy has moved away from support of bilingual education in recent years, some states have now returned to laws prohibiting bilingual education and the use of any language other than English for classroom instruction.

Mexican American families were fighting for the right to attend white schools at the same time that African Americans had turned to the courts for assistance. In the 1930s the Texas courts upheld the right of school boards to provide segregated education for Mexican Americans. The first breakthrough for integration occurred with the 1947 *Mendez v. Westminster School District* decision that required a California school district to allow a Mexican American girl to attend the white school. The Mexican American Legal Defense and Education Fund (MALDEF) was established in 1967 to continue suing for the civil rights and equality of Mexican American students. Court cases since then have focused on discriminatory practices in the funding of schools, the sole use of English in classrooms, and the disproportionate placement of Spanish-speaking children in special education classes as a result of biased tests or tests being given in English.

Equity for Puerto Ricans

Education for students in Puerto Rico has been interrelated with a history of occupation by the United States. Puerto Rico had just received its autonomy from Spain when it came under the control of the United States as part of the spoils (along with the Philippines and Guam) from the Spanish-American War at the end of the 19th century. With the 1900 Foraker Act, Congress established a colonial government to replace military rule in Puerto Rico and appointed the first U.S. Commissioner of Education for Puerto Rico. Just as with American Indians, the federal policy was to Americanize Puerto Ricans through education. Because the language of instruction was to be English and many Puerto Rican teachers spoke only Spanish, teachers from the United States were hired. Not only were students expected to learn English; they were also supposed to learn American ways. Educational policies required celebration of the U.S. patriotic holidays, such as the Fourth of July. Students were required to pledge allegiance to the U.S. flag and study U.S. heroes. Local textbooks were replaced with U.S. textbooks. When new teachers applied for a teaching certificate, their test included an English examination (Spring, 2011).

Puerto Ricans were not interested in becoming Americans and losing their own native language and culture. In 1912, the Puerto Rican Teachers Association began to defend Spanish as the language of instruction. When a student at San Juan's Central High School was expelled in 1915 for collecting signatures in support of instruction in Spanish, a student strike was sparked (Spring, 2011). Calls for nationalism and independence were common. Congress granted Puerto Ricans citizenship in 1917, which obligated them to serve in the military, but did not grant the right to vote in elections.

Tensions increased in the 1920s when a Puerto Rican who supported the United States' assimilation policies became the Commissioner of Education. He pressed his predecessor's policies even further. He required seniors to pass an English examination before they could graduate. He banned school newspapers in Spanish. Teachers were required to use English in teacher meetings and informal discussions with students. Protests by teachers, professors, and college students expanded. College students were expelled for participating in anti-American marches and professors were warned to stop supporting student protests (Spring, 2011).

The efforts to change U.S. educational policies in Puerto Rico resulted in the Padin Reform of 1934, which restricted English instruction to high schools. Spanish could be used at other levels. However, textbooks continued to be printed in English. After the Teachers Association had successfully lobbied the Puerto Rican legislature to pass a bill requiring the use of Spanish, President Harry Truman vetoed it. After Puerto Rico was granted commonwealth status in 1951, Puerto Ricans gained greater control of their school systems, restoring Spanish as the language of instruction (Spring, 2011).

Asian Americans

The first Chinese migrants arrived in California in the 1850s to join the gold rush as free laborers. They faced a great deal of hostility and discrimination from the dominant white population. The courts considered Chinese immigrants as having the same status as American Indians, and policies related to citizenship continued to discriminate against Asians. It was not until 1943 that the Chinese Exclusion Law was rescinded, allowing Chinese immigrants the right to become naturalized citizens (Spring, 2011).

When the court ruled in 1885 that native-born Mamie Tape had equal access to public schooling, the California legislature responded by allowing school districts to establish segregated schools for Asian Americans. By 1905, the segregated system in San Francisco was broken as Chinese youths were admitted to the regular city high school (Spring, 2011). Southern courts retained Asian American children in segregated schools attended primarily by African Americans. The family of a Chinese American girl argued that she was not black and therefore should be able to attend the white school. However, the court ruled in 1924 that she was not white and gave schools the authority to determine the race of their students (Spring, 2011).

After the passage of the 1965 Immigration Act, the number of Asian immigrants began to grow. Schools in cities like San Francisco were faced with a growing number of students who spoke languages other than English. Because the language of instruction was English, parents worried that their children were not able to achieve at the high academic levels they expected. They sued the San Francisco school system and, in 1974, won the right to have their first language used in instruction in *Lau v. Nichols.* The court said "under state imposed standards, there was no equality of treatment merely by providing students with the same facilities, textbooks, teachers, and curriculum; for students who do not understand English are effectively foreclosed from any meaningful education" (*Lau v. Nichols,* 1974).

HOW HAS TEACHING EVOLVED?

Asked about the teaching profession itself, Mr. Kuhn, who has served on negotiating teams for the teachers' union, indicated that "teachers are generally highly respected in my community. You have to earn their respect. Once you have gained that respect, students and the parents will respect you."

This story was told to Dr. Sturgeon in 2003. The information was gathered as part of an undertaking to document the teaching experiences of 1930s and 1940s one-room school teachers in Mason County, West Virginia.

OK, I'll tell you about fun things in the one-room school. The children liked it when we played "button, button, who has the button" because they always seemed so excited. They also looked forward to playing "I Spy." When we played "I Spy" you would hide these scissors so that maybe only the tip end would stick out. Then they would have to hide their eyes; all but the one that was hiding the scissors was up and around. He would walk around and around inside the school and then after he had hidden the scissors somewhere he would pretend he was putting them in other places so that they wouldn't know just where you were. So, OK they are hidden and the kids get up out of their seats and then the teacher would say "Wayne, you're getting hot, you're getting hot." The closer you got to it, the hotter you'd get. Or, "Oh, Thelma, you're cold, you're just so cold it's a wonder you wouldn't be freezing," you know, stuff like that. Anyway, then whoever found it got to hide it then from the rest of them. Then, "Button, Button, Who Has the Button?" you'd seat them all; you had these front seats, you know, where the kids came up to recite, and so there would be a long row of just people sitting and they would have to hold their hand. Then you had a button, and it would slide through their hands. Only one person got the button up there. So you had to make, pretend like you were dropping it when you weren't so that when you got through then finally you'd open your hand and show it to someone else. Then the teacher would say, "OK, button, button, who has the button?" Then she'd say, "Carla May has it." Then she'd say, "No I don't." "Fred. Fred has it." "Nope." So finally they'd get it and whoever had it last, they got to be the button hider. They were fun, because we didn't have any toys or playground equipment or computer games, you know. We were all together in the school, in one room. We had a baseball bat and softball. And that's about all we had. A lot different from today. But I loved every day. That school was the center of those little communities.

Dr. Douglas Sturgeon
Shawnee State University
Portsmouth, Ohio

The role of women in teaching defines the profession. Because of their traditional roles as nurturing mothers, women have been seen as the natural teachers of children. Historically, they have provided a stable, inexpensive, moral teaching force for the country. Women have not always been the majority of teachers. During the colonial period, teachers were men except in the dame schools. After the Revolutionary War, females began to be recruited as teachers. Teachers today are even more likely to be women than in the 19th century, which may contribute to the lower status attributed to teaching.

The emerging pattern in the 19th century was men administrators managing women teachers. The leadership of the NEA was male school administrators, college presidents, and professors throughout most of its first 100 years. Women teachers had to seek permission from the male leadership to speak at the business meetings of the annual conference. The American Federation of Teachers (AFT), on the other hand, evolved from the Chicago Federation of Teachers, where two activist women teachers—Margaret Haley and Catherine Goggin—joined forces with organized labor because they felt they shared the same interests as workers (Spring, 2011).

Although teachers are held responsible for preparing students to meet national standards, they have not always been represented in the groups developing those standards. The expertise and knowledge of teachers are not yet valued by the policy-makers, business leaders, and think tanks as reflected by their limited involvement on many national and state committees on education reform. The Center for Teaching Quality asserts that "teachers must be seen as solutions, not problems" to raise student achievement and serve students effectively (Berry, 2011, p. 20).

Women teachers in the 19th century were expected to be single and follow strict codes of behavior set by local school boards.

Teacher Preparation

To ensure that teachers taught the curriculum that educational leaders desired, teacher education programs were developed. Reverend Samuel Hall is credited with establishing one of the first institutions for preparing teachers in 1823 in Concord, Vermont, but Emma Willard had opened the Troy Female Seminary in 1821, in which women earned their certification, which many school boards required. However, certified teachers were not readily available in many rural areas for another century (Spring, 2011).

Normal schools were established in 1839 in Lexington, Massachusetts, to prepare teachers for elementary schools. Most students in normal schools were women who had completed elementary or common schools, but had not completed high school. Curriculum in the normal schools required one to two years of study in which the elementary school curriculum was reviewed, classroom management studied, and teaching methods taught. Many of today's state colleges and universities began as normal schools. They changed their names and expanded their missions beyond the preparation of teachers in the mid-1900s. Today, they continue to prepare the majority of teachers in the country.

Teachers of children in the 1700s had not always finished elementary school although teachers of adolescents may have attended college. The amount of education increased in each century that followed. In the 1800s, a growing number of elementary school teachers completed high school and began to attend teacher institutes and normal schools to further develop their knowledge of the subjects they were teaching as well as their teaching skills. It was not until the mid-1900s that most teachers completed a four-year college, which is now required for a teaching license. Into the mid-1900s teachers had more education than most members of their community. However, by the beginning of the 21st century, a larger proportion of the population had a bachelor's degree than in previous centuries.

Teacher Behavior

Teachers have long been under the control of school boards and administrators. Not only did administrators oversee the work of teachers and select their textbooks; they also monitored their personal behavior. Teachers were expected to live exemplary moral lives. Their social activities were monitored by school officials throughout the 19th century and into the 20th. Horace Mann in 1840 indicated that a teacher should have "perfect" knowledge of the subject being taught, an aptitude

Challenging Assumptions

Are college students preparing to be teachers as academically strong as college students preparing for other jobs?

• • • • •

The Assumption

Some teacher candidates are not as academically talented as other college students, contributing to the lower than expected academic performance of PreK–12 students.

Study Design and Method

A researcher at the Educational Testing Service (ETS) examined college students' performance on the SAT, Praxis II licensure tests of content knowledge, and undergraduate GPAs to determine whether this assertion was true.

Study Findings

Teacher candidates today have stronger undergraduate GPAs than their predecessors with over 80% of them reporting a 3.00 or higher GPA. A smaller proportion of candidates taking Praxis II are passing it, primarily because states have raised their licensure requirements. Both candidates who have completed teacher education programs and those in alternate route programs have stronger academic profiles than in the past across ethnic, racial, and gender groups.

The research data indicated that candidates in secondary programs had verbal SAT scores at least as strong as other college students and sometimes stronger. Teacher candidates in math and science had math SAT scores well above other college graduates. Although scores on the verbal and math portions of the SAT are improving, candidates in elementary, special, and physical education score lower than other college students. The academic profiles of middle level teacher candidates are more like elementary teachers than secondary teachers.

Implications

To ensure that more candidates pass the content test for licensure, colleges and universities may consider raising requirements such as GPAs for admission into teacher education. An analysis of candidate performance on licensure tests, their performance on authentic assessments such as performance in student teaching, and the achievement of their students during the first years of practice could provide valuable information about the predictability of current assessments for determining successful practice in classrooms.

Source: Gitomer, D. H. (2007). *Teacher quality in a changing policy landscape: Improvements in the teacher pool.* Princeton, NJ: Educational Testing Service.

for teaching, which he believed could be learned, the ability to manage and govern a classroom and mold moral behavior, good behavior as a model for students, and good morals (Spring, 2011).

Even though morals were only one of Horace Mann's five qualifications, it appeared to be one of the most important to school superintendents and school board members. Contracts for women teachers did not allow them to socialize with men or be married. The emphasis on high moral character continued into the 20th century as teachers were warned that they should be very careful about their dress and behavior. Although moral character is not included in today's teacher contracts, teachers are still expected by the public to be models of high moral character.

CONNECTING TO THE CLASSROOM

This chapter has provided you with some basic information about how schools and the education of different students have evolved to the schools we know today. Below are some key principles for applying the information in this chapter to the classroom.

1. The history of education helps us understand teaching practices that have been tried previously by educators, the reasons for their falling out of favor, and the possibility of their recycling again as desirable practice.
2. Teachers in primary, middle, and high schools are expected to provide age-appropriate education for students based on research on child and adolescent development.
3. Good teachers are able to analyze and evaluate the different curriculum packages their school districts are likely to impose on them during their careers and make wise, pedagogically sound decisions about their use in their classrooms.
4. The Civil Rights Movement of the 1960s and 1970s was the foundation for ensuring that an equal education could finally be accessible to all children regardless of their race, ethnicity, socioeconomic status, language, gender, and abilities.
5. Expectations for the high academic achievement of teachers continues to rise in these times of accountability.

SUMMARY

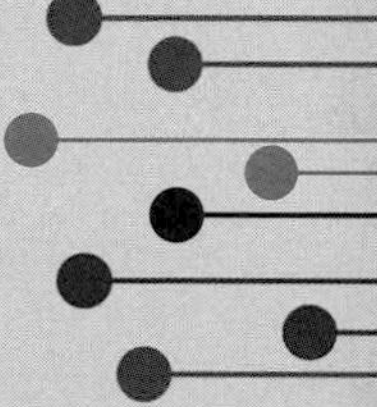

This chapter reviewed key developments over the past four centuries that established public schools and influenced the schools you know today. The following five major topics were discussed:

- Establishment of public schools in the United States. The Constitution gave the responsibility for education to states, which were expected to provide schools for their children.
- Schools designed by students' age. As scholars learned more about child and adolescent development, schools were divided into grade levels to meet the needs of early childhood, elementary, middle level, and high school students.
- Historical influences on the school curriculum. The curriculum has been influenced by strong religious and nationalistic themes, the industrial revolution in the 1800s, the progressive movement in the early 1900s, and the launching of the first satellite by the Soviet Union in 1957.
- Education and equality. When students of color began attending school, they were enrolled in segregated schools, which did not change until schools were desegregated in the 1960s.
- The evolution of teaching. The preparation of teachers has evolved from the requirement for completion of elementary school in colonial days to a college degree today.

CLASS DISCUSSION QUESTIONS

1. Today Americans assume that a free and universal education is a "right," but that has not always been the case. If you had been a participant in the various debates of the past three centuries, why would you have argued for, or against, the state establishing common schools? How would you have argued

about citizens being taxed to pay for public schools for all children? What is the relationship of these issues to debates today about vouchers to attend private schools, charter schools, and decreases in state support of public education?

2. You have probably decided that you want to teach students of a specific age. How long have schools for this group of students existed and what makes students of this age different from students at a different level? Why have you chosen to work with children of this age, and how will you learn the age-appropriate strategies for these students?

3. The Industrial Revolution, progressiveness, and Sputnik I are among societal changes that have impacted the school curriculum over the past 200 years. What remnants of these events and the early emphasis on religion and nationalism are reflected in today's schools?

4. Historically, not all children have had access to the same quality of education, sometimes legally not being allowed to either attend school or attend school with white students. What factors led to the changes in equal educational opportunity that occurred in the 1960s and 1970s? How has education changed for students of color since the 1954 *Brown v. Board of Education* decision by the Supreme Court?

5. The education level of today's teachers is much higher than in the past. In what other ways have the conditions of teaching changed over the past two centuries? What conditions appear to remain little changed from the past?

KEY TERMS

Authoritarian 170
Catechism 160
Charity schools 163
Common schools 161
Compulsory attendance 166
Deculturalizing 173
De facto segregation 179
Fourteenth Amendment 178
Free and universal education 160
Jim Crow laws 179
Manifest destiny 173
Morals 161

SELF-ASSESSMENT

WHAT IS YOUR CURRENT LEVEL OF UNDERSTANDING AND THINKING ABOUT THE HISTORY OF SCHOOLS IN THE UNITED STATES?

One of the indicators of understanding is to examine how complex your thinking is when asked questions that require you to use the concepts and facts introduced in this chapter. After you answer the following questions as fully as you can, rate your knowledge on the Complexity of Thinking rubric to self-assess the degree to which you understand and can apply the ideas presented in this chapter.

1. Who are some of the key educators and scholars who contributed to the establishment of the common schools in the 1800s and the early childhood and middle school movements in the 1900s?
2. How has the field of child development contributed to the types of schools that exist today?
3. Why were high schools initially established? Why and how have they changed since those early days?

What is your current level of understanding of why schools developed into educational settings for students of different age levels?

Complexity of Thinking Rubric

	Parts & Pieces	Unidimensional	Organized	Integrated	Extensions
Indicators	Elements/concepts are talked about as isolated and independent entities.	One or a few concepts are addressed, while others are under-developed.	Deliberate and structured consideration of all key concepts/elements.	All key concepts/elements are included in a view that addresses interconnections.	Integration of all elements and dimensions, with extrapolation to new situations.
Understanding of history of school development	Identifies some of the key people involved in establishing common schools, early childhood education, and middle level education.	Identifies the role of child development in creating the type of schools that exist today.	Describes the development of schools based on the age of students.	Discusses the development of schools based on the age of students and the work of the scholars and educators who contributed to their development.	Explores the major developments over time of the level of the school in which he/she plans to teach and discusses the major issues faced at that school level today.

STUDENT STUDY SITE

Visit the Student Study Site at **www.sagepub.com/hall** to access links to the videos, audio clips, and Deeper Look reference materials noted in this chapter, as well as additional study tools including eFlashcards, web quizzes, and more.

Field Guide

for Learning More About the History of Schools in the United States

Ask a Teacher or Principal

Identify a teacher who has been teaching for more than 10 years and ask him or her to describe some of the curriculum packages or programs the school system has asked teachers to use over the years. How long did most of them survive? Why were they successful or not successful? What does the teacher think are keys to a curriculum package being successful?

Make Your Own Observations

When you begin teaching, you will probably work in a preschool, kindergarten, or primary, elementary, middle, or high school. Your teaching license may allow you to teach at two or more levels. The levels are different not only in the curriculum taught, but also the organization of a school day and the interactions of students and teachers. As you observe teachers in schools at two different levels (for example, middle and high school), make notes of the similarities and differences between the levels. You could organize your notes into a table or narrative. Write a brief paper on what level you would prefer to teach and why.

Reflect Through Journaling

Expectations for education have changed greatly since colonial times. Take a few minutes to reflect in your journal on what has changed and remained the same since the primary goal of education was to learn to read the scriptures and be a moral and patriotic person. In your opinion, what should be the goals of education today?

Build Your Portfolio

What is the largest group of color in your community or state? What do you know about the historical educational experiences of this group in your community or state? Write a brief paper on the historic and current segregation or integration of schools in your area.

Teachers have a history of not being included as members of committees or panels developing policies to reform education. Why are they not included? How could teachers become more involved in these activities? Prepare a brief paper about the importance of teacher involvement on policy groups that are making recommendations for improving teaching and public schools.

Read a Book

For more information on the issues, trends, and personalities that have shaped education in the United States since 1900, check these articles by *Education Week* staff: *Education Week, Lessons of a Century: A Nation's Schools Come of Age* (2000; Bethesda, MD: Editorial Projects in Education).

To learn more about the court cases that led to *Brown v. Board of Education of Topeka* and the ones that stopped desegregation later in the 1900s, read the Spring 2004 issue of the Southern Poverty Law Center's magazine *Teaching Tolerance.*

Search the Web

Check out the references to the Constitution of the United States and the amendments mentioned in this chapter (**http://www.archives.gov/exhibits/charters/constitution.html**).

Listen to National Public Radio's discussion and background on the historic Supreme Court case *Brown v. Board of Education of Topeka* by historians, political leaders, and educators (**http://www.npr.org/news/specials/brown50/**).

To review the 200-year history of education in the United States with images of schools, classrooms, and students, visit **http://www.pbs.org/kcet/publicschool/**, a part of the website of the Public Broadcasting System (PBS).

TEACHER INTERVIEW

Heather Cyra

Heather Cyra has been a teacher at Guild Gray Elementary School for four years. Approximately 600 students attend kindergarten through fifth grade at Guild Gray. The school is located between an older, well-established neighborhood and low-rent apartment complexes. Student enrollment fluctuates at the school, and teachers may be asked to change grade levels when populations at specific grade levels decrease or increase. Ms. Cyra began teaching first grade but after one year she was moved to fifth grade. For as long as she remembers, she wanted to be a teacher. She knew that there would be challenges and rewards in teaching, but teachers make a difference in the world. She wanted to be creative and use the natural skills she possesses for helping people learn.

Developing a Philosophy of Teaching and Learning

- ***What do you see when you see excellence in teaching?***

  I see someone who is organized and has created an enjoyable, engaging environment—teachers who keep the students engaged in learning and also help everyone learn. I see excellence in teaching when I see teachers who have "fun" with their students; teachers who listen to their students and keep the students from being bored. Excellence in teaching is also surprising the students with unexpected activities, rewards, or information.

How do you know when your students are learning?

There are many ways to know that students are learning. You can often tell just by the looks on their faces that show whether they are confused or enlightened. You can tell by verbal cues from how the students respond to the questions you ask or how they contribute to class discussions. You can tell from a written assessment or merely a show of hands. If they are not responding the way I expect them to then I realize I have to reteach a concept or go back over something that may not have been explained in a way that they can understand. If you are tuned in to your students it is quite easy to tell when students have checked out by the way they look at you or don't and by the responses they give you.

What brings you joy in teaching?

When I see how far the students I started out with grow in a year. By keeping track of their stages of development, I can see how much they have learned and how their attitudes and behavior have developed. When my students tell me at the end of the year that they don't want to leave, I know that I have created a warm, nurturing environment. I feel like I am doing something right. It's not entirely about what the tests say. As long as they're learning, showing growth, and enjoying themselves in school and have enjoyed their fifth-grade experience I am happy and feel like I have done my job.

How did you develop a personal philosophy of teaching?

I constructed my philosophy one course at a time through integration of the most prominent and influential pieces of knowledge from each professor and textbook. During the course in special education my attitudes about special education students were formalized when I thought about what kind of an educator I would be if I did not accept the challenge of working with special needs students to the fullest extent of my abilities to positively influence people.

My philosophy was also formulated by my personal experiences as an elementary school student. I have always been passionate about learning, so I look back at what I loved about being at school, what I admired about my teachers, and what lessons and activities provided me with the best experiences to prepare me for the future.

Questions to Consider

1. Ms. Cyra said she constructed her philosophy of teaching throughout her teacher education course work. Would such an approach to developing a philosophy of teaching work for you? Why? Why not?
2. Is the enjoyment one gets from learning as important as scores on standardized tests? Explain.
3. What other ways, besides the ones Ms. Cyra mentioned, can teachers use to know if their students are learning?
4. How do you anticipate finding joy in teaching?

How do students learn?

Students learn in many different ways. I pay attention to the individual differences among my students and use differentiated instruction to focus on individual needs. I balance instruction with mini lessons, group activities, and individual practice. When students are engaged, they are learning, and I vary my instruction in an attempt to keep them involved.

Learning Outcomes

After reading this chapter, you should be able to

1. Identify specific events that may help you develop an educational philosophy.
2. Draft a personal philosophy of teaching.
3. Understand how an educational philosophy influences instructional practices.
4. Summarize the relationship between philosophical perspectives, educational psychology, and approaches to teaching.

INTRODUCTION

A beginning step in becoming a teacher is to examine the attitudes and assumptions you have about teaching and learning through developing an educational philosophy.

Knowledge about teaching and learning is most useful to teachers when past knowledge is constantly rearranged and integrated with new ideas and new experiences. The knowledge, skills, attitudes, and opinions we all bring to any situation have a powerful influence on our behavior and expectations. What we have learned and practiced, and what we have gained from experiences both favorable and not so favorable, has caused us to create a personal perspective toward life (*isms* if you will) that influence everything we think and do. Naturally what teachers know and are able to do have changed over time, but like all of us, teachers are motivated by their assumptions (i.e., Do you think technology diminishes personal interaction?, Do you believe there is some knowledge that all students should learn?, Do you believe competition is a great motivator?).

Learning to teach and how to apply this knowledge in the classroom is truly a developmental process. In this chapter you will begin to understand why it is important for teachers to confront the assumptions that guide their behavior and practice in classrooms.

HOW DO TEACHERS DEVELOP PERSONAL PHILOSOPHIES TOWARD TEACHING AND LEARNING?

Heather Cyra, the teacher interviewed at the beginning of this chapter, was required to write multiple statements of her philosophical perspective toward teaching and learning during her education course work.

Formulating a philosophical perspective on teaching and learning gives you a chance to reflect on what you want to become. And then when you become a teacher you can look back on what you wrote and make sure that you are not being a hypocrite. I find myself reflecting on my experiences as a learner and who were the teachers who had the greatest influence on me, and who were the teachers I most admired and wanted to learn from and try to be like.

Everyone operates from a personal philosophy. We know what makes sense to us, what is important, and what is good. When you become a teacher you take your personal vision of the world into the classroom with you. This personal vision affects everything you do in your classroom and with your students. It is necessary to understand your philosophical perspectives so that you can understand and reflect on what you are doing and why you are doing it. Teachers who do not know or understand themselves can be of little service to the students in their classrooms. Or as Confucius put it, "What has one who is not able to govern himself to do with governing others?"

Video Link 7.1
Watch a video about personal teaching philosophy.

Developing a Personal Philosophy of Teaching

An educational philosophy consists of the beliefs and principles that guide teaching and learning practices. Teacher education candidates are usually asked to draft a statement that organizes their thinking about how students learn and how teachers should teach. Revisiting this original philosophy statement over time throughout your program is one way you can keep track of your growth as a professional. As you acquire more wisdom and encounter new ideas you will develop new attitudes and opinions that will cause changes to your personal philosophy. Understanding can be achieved only through an examination of what you have learned about teaching and learning and how well you are able to articulate your perspectives. Figure 7.1 provides an example of one teacher's effort to identify a philosophical perspective on teaching.

I know an English composition teacher who requires students to attach all previous drafts of a composition to the final copy that is being submitted. This allows the teacher to evaluate students' growth in writing ability and also to see whether students have incorporated or learned from the teacher's editorial comments. The final packets can be rather substantial, but they do represent effort and the process of coming to a final, publishable paper. Keeping copies of your original and subsequent philosophy statements will provide you with a graphic representation of the changes in your thinking as you become more knowledgeable about teaching.

Whether it's fair or not, you will be expected to do the same job on your first day of work as a veteran of five or 10 years. Logically, this doesn't seem possible, but who can argue with the fact that the children in your classroom deserve no less than the children in Mrs. Z's room who has been teaching for 20 years. Beginning teachers may react to this dilemma by performing certain actions that make them appear capable of keeping up with the more experienced teachers, even when those actions don't exactly mesh with their own personal philosophy of teaching. Nothing can be more exhausting than maintaining a false front or upholding the assumptions of others. Ideas need time to percolate in the reality of full-time teaching.

Dr. Mark Bailey of Pacific University School of Education (2003) offers eight critical dimensions of an educational philosophy. In order to build an educational philosophy, Bailey poses the following questions for teacher education candidates to consider.

1. What is knowledge and understanding?
2. What is worth knowing?
3. What does it mean to learn?
4. How do you know that learning has taken place?

5. What should be the role of a teacher?
6. What should be the role of the student?
7. What is the ultimate purpose of education?
8. What are your core educational values?

Respond to these questions when creating your personal philosophy of teaching statement. During your teacher education course work, reread your personal philosophy and revise it according to any changes in your philosophical perspective. If you are in a practice teaching situation, examine how your philosophy of teaching is enacting through your teaching behaviors.

There are always more questions than answers in life, but as your answers to the above questions begin to take shape, your idea of who you will be as a teacher will fall into place. You will also begin to understand the many ways your opinions can shape your teaching behavior and practice. Having a firm belief regarding your place in the teaching profession will provide you a solid foundation from which to try out new ideas—something teachers are always challenged to do. Advice from experts to anyone attempting to cross a rushing stream on rocks is to make sure your footing is secure before taking the next step. Believe it or not, sometimes classrooms can resemble rushing streams.

The Influence of Stories in Building a Personal Philosophy of Teaching

There are defining moments in everyone's life. We tell stories about them. Stories are powerful. We all remember a good story whether true or not. Stories can alter our perception of things. That's one reason the news media and television are so powerful. The stories we hear and tell can frighten us or evoke courage. Sooner or later the stories we tell about our lives become our lives. We can make the stories we tell about our lives healthy or destructive. The choice is ours. Stories provide us with ideas, actions, and tools for working toward goals. Stories are what Robert Coles refers to as "reservoirs of wisdom" (Coles, 1989, p. xii).

Many of the professors where you are preparing to be a teacher have been classroom teachers or still are. They may work in classrooms, serve as mentors for new teachers, or work with teachers in professional development seminars. They have had the benefit of experience to help them mold their philosophies of teaching. They have no doubt kept track of their professorial careers through portfolios and tenure and promotion files. Talk to them about the defining teaching moments in their lives that helped them construct a specific approach to teaching. Teaching is a people profession. People like to talk and tell stories about their lives.

Researchers and writers have looked at teachers and listened to their stories of teaching to unravel the mysteries of the profession (Lieberman & Miller, 1984; Lortie, 1977). Clark and Peterson (1986) listened to teachers talk about planning. They then mapped their stories into flowcharts for new generations of teachers to follow and learn from. Ester Wright (1999) says, "There is a moment when the struggle to master an activity or subject ceases and the action becomes familiar and regimented. Teaching is hundreds of such moments, strung together to create a career" (p. 11). As you try out your ideas, you will become more familiar and therefore comfortable with what works in a variety of contexts. You are fortunate to be learning to teach in this period of time. Life is full of choices, and many of those choices add depth and breadth to your ultimate practice in the classroom. What happens in classrooms will continue to accommodate evolving ideas and trends about which learning is of most worth.

Figure 7.1 A Personal Philosophy Example

Prior to completing this assignment, I had not given much thought to my own teaching philosophy nor taken a reflective analysis of myself as a teacher. Because I have only been in the classroom for five months, I feel like I am just now "getting it" and discovering the type of teacher I am and want to be. Just like our students, the diversity among teachers guides each individual classroom. The values that I hold with high importance will be displayed throughout my instruction, regardless of curriculum. In my initial teaching experience, I have held an eclecticism viewpoint due to gathering as many resources and as much advice from peers as possible. However, as a scientist, I also strongly relate to the experimentalism philosophy and always try to incorporate an element of discovery for my students.

Experimentalism draws from the notion that we are constantly adapting our viewpoints and collaborating with one another to make discoveries (Kurtus, 2001). As a science teacher, this is an idea I am constantly trying to promote with my students. Science is always changing and with this change comes the opportunity to make discoveries and collaborate with peers to find answers. I believe experimentalism closely connects with science in a way that other philosophies do not. Existentialism and realism promote more abstract and individualized viewpoints, in my opinion.

With increasing advances in technology and communication, scientists are able to experiment and collaborate with peers easier than ever before. As I try to incorporate an integration of science, technology, engineering, and math (STEM) into my curriculum, I promote student-centered learning and self-discovery for my students. The research has shown that true understanding of concepts comes from individual internalization rather than oral or written reception of material. In my recent science methods class, my professor discussed her "three touch method" with instruction. She pulls out the main concepts and subconcepts from the curriculum documents and plans to instruct on each topic at least three times and with three different styles (verbal, written, kinesthetic, etc.). This is a practice I have started to integrate into my lesson planning. Taking curriculum documents and pulling out the main concepts that unite all objectives from within a unit is a necessary skill that helps connect all parts of my instruction back to the original goal.

Experimentalism also connects to the scientific inquiry process. Student-centered learning and inquiry-based activities give students the opportunity to discover for themselves by going through a problem-solving and critical-thinking process that leads to retention. I also stress to my students that there are many answers to a given problem, and that problems and failures are often a necessary pathway to success. In connecting teaching with epistemology, I try to foster a meta-cognitive process within my classroom as well. As I encourage my students to make their own discoveries, I try to guide their cognitive processes to work through their own assumptions on their way to understanding.

A deeply rooted understanding through a process of experimentation and analysis is the key to learning science. I encourage my students to embrace change, ask questions, and then go on a journey to answer them. While reflecting through this paper, I realize that my teaching philosophy does pull from a variety of sources. I aim to encourage individualization in my students through identifying problems and discovering solutions for themselves. I constantly have to stop myself from giving every answer or explanation; even though the processing might take much longer, it is more beneficial to my students to individualize my instruction through their own personal experimentation. Reflection is a crucial part of teaching and something I will aim to work on throughout the next school year. Through changes in curriculum, I will always use my own philosophies and interpretations to serve my students to the best of my ability.

Angie Marsden
Philosophical Perspective Paper
June 19, 2012

Defining Events in Building a Personal Philosophy of Teaching

Certainly, high-profile events on the education scene affect the type of teaching and the content you are required to study. Knowing the effect certain events have had on teaching and learning when you were a student will help you better understand your own philosophical perspectives toward schooling. There have been defining moments in society as well as in our own lives. We learn about defining moments in the world of education in history and foundations of education courses. Defining moments change the way we go about our business. In many ways the launch of Sputnik in

1957 was a 9/11 of the mind. It changed the ways Americans thought about the future. It initiated a reexamination of the purpose of schooling and school curriculum. The National Science Foundation (NSF) made millions of federal dollars available for the development of modern science and mathematics programs and materials. Another defining moment was the publication of *A Nation at Risk: The Imperative for Educational Reform* (National Commission on Excellence in Education, 1983), which prompted a renewed focus on student achievement and the condition of schooling in America.

Keeping a record of your own stories of teaching and events in a journal or diary can also help you build a data reference system for comparing new ideas you encounter with the old ones you have used. The act of looking back to remember which way you've come is a device that has been used by travelers and learners for centuries. From time to time you need to revisit your journey to becoming a teacher with a critical eye. By checking where you've come from you will have a better idea where you are headed. Looking back can help you to assess the defining moments in your professional development and to prepare for the future.

Taking Stock of Your Beliefs

Teachers can become exhausted operating under expectations counter to what they believe. For many first-year teachers, discouragement raises its ugly head about mid-December when they begin to realize that the theories they have put into practice are not working. Formulating who you are going to be as a teacher will prepare you to act on your beliefs and assumptions rather than someone else's. When you do this, you increase your chances of success and happiness as a teacher.

Using tenets of known philosophies as keystones for developing your own philosophy about teaching and answering some of the questions these philosophies pose can help you decide who you will be as a teacher. Do you think that the world is an orderly, logical place, or do you see it as chaotic and random? Obviously these two views would have a strong influence on how, for example, you arrange your classroom and lessons. Do you learn by repetition or by connecting new information to what you already know? Do you prefer to discover information for yourself or have it delivered to you in an organized outline? What senses do you find most important? In other words, how do you learn about the world around you?

All teachers create mental images of how their future classroom will appear in reality.

Do you believe there are clear rights and wrongs in life (black and white) or is life a series of slightly differing shades of gray? Do you feel it is possible to understand everything if enough intelligence and logic is applied, or do you believe some things must simply be taken on faith? Are you an abstract or random learner?; linear or global? There is so much to learn and so little time.

Taking Stock of Your Students

Every child is an individual, a smaller-sized person than most of the people you socialize with, but no less individual in opinions and thinking. We all have a friend who can't follow the simplest directions, or one who asks the same question over and over until you answer it in a way that makes sense to her, or one who never shows up on time and may even forget the day he was supposed to meet you. Frustrating, at times, yes, but we try to understand them and help them understand us. Humans (friends, relatives, and students) have so much to learn that any single theory or simple approach to helping them just won't do. Teacher-focused and student-focused approaches to teaching and learning combined can encompass the spectrum of philosophical perspectives that underpin decision making and curriculum in education. It is the teacher's responsibility to continuously question what to teach and how to teach it, and to learn about and develop skill in using methods that have their roots in philosophical approaches to teaching that may differ from your own.

Video Link 7.2
Watch a video about taking stock in your students.

When classroom teachers puzzle over which educational goals should be met and how these goals might be achieved through teaching practices, they are dealing with questions about knowing, learning, and teaching. In Plato's discussion of epistemology, he argued that in order to grasp reality or know, individuals use understanding, reason, perception, and imagination. Visit **http://www.e-torredebabel.com/History-of-Philosophy/Summaries/Plato-Summary.htm** for a summary of Plato's ideas.

Teachers implement Plato's ideas of knowing when they plan and structure lessons and decide which methods are most appropriate to a specific learning task. As you progress in your teacher education course work, you will no doubt become very familiar with the theory of constructivism or constructivist teaching. When you study this approach to teaching and learning, think of it as an epistemological view. Constructivist approaches to teaching take into account the ways that children learn and what conditions are necessary to promote such learning. The theory of constructivism ponders how knowing is achieved.

HOW DO STUDENTS LEARN?

When asked how students learn, Ms. Cyra replied, "Students learn best in a nurturing environment—one in which they have fun and can work together to solve problems. I do not allow bullying or other forms of meanness from students and encourage my students to show respect for others. I learned all the ways of delivering instruction in my classes in the university but I never realized, until I started teaching, how important it was to vary instructional strategies."

Few modern educators would argue that there is but a single way to learn, or a single way to teach the skills, facts, and concepts deemed essential to a contemporary education. However, there are those who would argue that one particular way of teaching is inherently better or more efficient than another. Listen to teachers talk about how they teach their students to read or spell, and chances are that you will hear quite different philosophies regarding learning, methods, and materials. Such discussions often generate more heat than enlightenment and provide proof of the value we place on our own firmly held assumptions.

Understanding ways students construct meaning from what they see and hear can provide teachers insights into how students learn.

Ideas about how students learn are in abundance, and since not all ideas are of equal value, it can be difficult to weed out the good from the bad. Some ideas are priceless. Some are not. Some are in direct conflict with one another. Ideas germinate in knowledge and are driven by opinions, beliefs, assumptions, and experiences, and the context in which the ideas blossom. Unfortunately, in education, as in all areas of life, some good ideas are stamped out before they have a time to blossom, while some bad ideas flourish in unguarded cultures.

As you progress through your teacher education program you will encounter many ideas about how students learn. Such ideas are often based in one or another of the established philosophies of life. There will be more about this later in the chapter. Good ideas about how students learn can come out of educational research conducted by professors and research centers dedicated to the study of teaching and learning. Good ideas also emerge from teacher educators and teachers practicing their craft, collecting data, and making grassroots changes in practice. Some of the teachers who have generated great ideas for future generations of teachers and learners are famous. Some are not, but all have, through thinking about teaching and learning, contributed to the profession.

Ideas About How Students Learn

Great minds in American education wrestle with ideas of what should be taught in America's schools, how it should be taught, and when it should be taught. As American education has evolved, a number of approaches and programs to promote students' learning have been tried. Nearly everyone you talk to has some idea about what should be happening in school. The popular press has nearly as much to say about teaching and learning as educators. The range of ideas teachers are confronted with is staggering.

Deeper Look 7.1
Read about educational models and methods.

Numerous ideas about structuring curriculum and methods for delivering the curriculum have been tried, revamped, and re-tried. The Old Testament Book of Ecclesiastes says that there is nothing new under the sun. Teachers who have been around for any length of time and have experienced the ebb and flow of programs and approaches to teaching will tell you that many of the new programs they are asked to implement are really only revamped versions of tried and true methods. The fact is that data collected on some of these tried and true methods is frequently used to improve them. Constant thinking about teaching can lead to new ideas that will improve education for teachers and learners alike.

While educators know an informed populous helps build a democratic society, they do not know exactly what skills a six-year-old of today will need 30 years down the line in order to be successful and to contribute to the well-being of the society. The constant generation of ideas about teaching and learning is one way educators attempt to imagine and prepare for the future. The following sample of individuals who have generated ideas about teaching and learning ranges from the recent past to the present and from the famous to those who may be known only to a local community or school district. Their ideas provide a cross section of ways thinking about education has affected schooling and how students learn.

The Western world's first great philosophers came from Athens, Greece. The names of three of these philosophers are no doubt familiar to you: Socrates (470–399 BCE), Plato (427–347 BCE), and Aristotle (384–322 BCE). Socrates is famous for creating the **Socratic method** of teaching still used by many teachers today who ask a series of questions that lead the student to a certain conclusion. Plato believed that each person's abilities should be used to serve society and should be developed to the fullest capacity. Aristotle favored the scientific, the practical, and the objective in learning, and believed that the quality of a society was determined by the quality of the education that society promoted.

John Dewey (1859–1952)

It would be folly to try to adequately cover the contributions of Dewey's ideas to how students learn best in this chapter. Suffice it to say he was a giant among the thinkers of the 20th century. For more than 50 years, Dewey's ideas helped shape the destiny of education in America. Dewey's thoughts on pedagogy and epistemology (knowing) and his pragmatic approaches to ethics and aesthetics remain influential in education today. You should become familiar with John Dewey's ideas as you progress through your teacher education course work. His ideas can provide a basis for you to establish your own pedagogical vision. Visit http://dewey.pragmatism.org/ to view a comprehensive coverage of Dewey and his accomplishments.

Many of John Dewey's educational theories were tested at the Chicago Laboratory School.

Dewey established the Chicago Laboratory School for the purpose of testing the sociological implications of his educational theories and the effect his theories had on student learning (http://johndewey.org/). Dewey called his laboratory school a "miniature society," an "embryonic community," in which children learned collaboratively by working together to solve problems (Martin, 2002, pp. 199–200). Dewey described "the fundamental factors in the educational process as (1) the learner, (2) society, and (3) organized subject matter" (Dewey, 1974).

Dewey's ideas in *The School and Society* (1943) have remarkable significance to the field of education as we now know it. His ideas about the needs, the problems, and the possibilities of education are detailed in *Experience and Education* (1963), perhaps the best concise statement on education ever written.

Dewey devised a five-step, process-oriented method for students to approach problem solving that involved

1. Encountering a problem that needed to be solved;
2. Defining the problem, asking questions that would help clarify exactly what needs to be solved;
3. Collecting information about the problem;
4. Making tentative hypotheses and reflecting on possible actions and outcomes; and
5. Acting on a hypothesis that is likely to solve the problem.

Problem solving using the scientific method, action, and empirical testing is considered by many to be the most effective strategy to help students learn. Dewey believed that schools should teach children not what to think but how to think through "continuous reconstruction of experience."

Hilda Taba (1902–1967)

This Estonian-born U.S. educator spent much of her professional career contemplating ideas concerned with the development of thinking skills in students. She believed that information must be organized for students to understand it. She developed concept development and concept attainment strategies to help students learn. She based her teaching model on three main assumptions:

1. Thinking can be taught,
2. Thinking is an active transaction between the individual and data, and
3. Processes of thought evolve by a sequence that is "lawful" (Joyce & Weil, 2000, p. 131).

According to Taba, "efforts to develop thinking take a different shape depending on whether the major function of education is seen as fostering creative thinking and problem solving or as following the rational forms of thinking established in our classical tradition. As such, differences in these concepts naturally determine what are considered the essentials and the dispensable frills in education" (Taba, 1962).

Taba was famous for her work in concept development in social studies. Visit the Global Connections for Elementary Students website at **http://www.globaled.org/curriculum/tomcollins.html** for a look at how Taba's ideas on concept attainment can be applied in a classroom to promote student learning.

Ralph W. Tyler (1902–1994)

Ralph W. Tyler's innovative ideas made him one of the most influential men in American education. Tyler believed that successful teaching and learning could be determined by scientific study, but he stressed that evaluation should start with objectives and not rely entirely on a statistical process. His insights into educational evaluation affected the lives of generations of students whose performance and potential are frequently tested. As director of the Eight-Year Study (1933–1941), he helped convince the educational community that schools that offer programs that are interesting and useful to their students can help students become successful in college (see **http://www.8yearstudy.org/projectintro.html**).

Tyler's 83-page book, *Basic Principles of Curriculum and Instruction,* published in 1949, made an indelible mark on teaching practices in the American public schools. This short text was originally the syllabus for one of Tyler's courses at the University of Chicago. In the text Tyler espoused four basic ideas for developing a curriculum that would promote student learning. These four basic ideas, listed here, remain as relevant for teachers today as they were 60 years ago, and they serve as a framework for selecting appropriate strategies to use to connect the learner with the content:

1. Define appropriate learning objectives.
2. Establish useful learning experiences.
3. Organize learning experiences to have a maximum cumulative effect.
4. Evaluate the curriculum and revise those aspects that do not prove to be effective.

Through Tyler's ideas teachers became scientific observers of student behavior, checking for evidence of student learning and making modifications to plans when necessary to guarantee results. Tyler's ideas were so powerful, functional, and easy to apply that they are still widely implemented in public schools today.

Paulo Freire (1921–1997)

Paulo Freire's idea that the process of education can never be neutral and that education should provide nontraditional educational opportunities grew out of his efforts among illiterate poor workers in Brazil. Helping the workers learn to read and write led him to recognize the ways education can result in powerful changes among people and governments. In 1967, Freire published *Education as the Practice of Freedom*, and in 1970 he published the *Pedagogy of the Oppressed* in English. Briefly stated, Freire posits that education is a political act—the way students are taught and what they are taught serves a political agenda. The purpose of education should be the liberation of the "oppressed" (those not currently in control of the political agenda) through nontraditional forms and through their own examples, not the models presented by the oppressors. Education can help the oppressed overcome their status as long as they play a role in their own education. Freire's ideas encouraged educators to consider the political aspects of the institution of education, thereby bringing a new perspective to teaching and learning in the form of critical pedagogy. Critical pedagogy presents a philosophical perspective toward teaching and learning that seeks to empower the student to "recognize authoritarian tendencies, and connect knowledge to power and the ability to take constructive action" (Giroux, 2010).

Eleanor Duckworth (1935–)

Eleanor Duckworth is a professor at Harvard Graduate School of Education. She has grounded her work in Piaget's (1896–1980) insights into the nature and development of intelligence, and she has developed Piaget's research methods into a critical exploration approach to helping students learn. According to Duckworth, ideas are the essence of intelligence. Through her research she has demonstrated that there are many ways of knowing and that different paths can be taken to understanding similar concepts (Duckworth, 1996).

Duckworth's ideas on teaching and learning provide exceptional insight into the blossoming of ideas, how they are nurtured, and how they grow. She discusses the detrimental effect teachers who view learning from only one perspective can have on the wonderful ideas of their students. She encourages teachers to explore their students' intelligence rather than turn it off in the pursuit of conventions and standardized ways of thinking. This may seem difficult to teachers, given the current standards-based assessment culture in American education. Duckworth's ideas require that teachers engage in intellectual conversation with their students—that teachers make time to listen to students' explanations so they may recognize the students' wonderful ideas.

Howard Earl Gardner (1943–)

Audio Link 7.1
Listen to an interview with Howard Gardner.

In his 1993 text, *Frames of Mind: The Theory of Multiple Intelligences,* Howard Earl Gardner presented the idea that intelligence cannot be determined by only one measure. He created a list of seven intelligences and demonstrated how some are typically valued in school, while some are usually associated with the arts and some are what he termed "personal intelligences." In brief, the seven intelligences defined by Gardner are

1. Linguistic intelligence: the ability to learn, understand, and use language
2. Logical-mathematical intelligence: the ability to think logically and scientifically
3. Musical intelligence: the ability to recognize musical patterns and compose music
4. Bodily-kinesthetic intelligence: the ability to direct bodily movements through mental abilities
5. Spatial intelligence: the ability to recognize dimensions of large and confined spaces
6. Interpersonal intelligence: the ability to understand and work effectively with others
7. Intrapersonal intelligence: the ability to understand oneself and to regulate one's life

By helping educators think about the many ways intelligence can be understood and demonstrated, Gardner provided teachers a rationale for designing lessons in ways that would engage all students in learning. Visit **http://www.infed.org/thinkers/gardner.htm** to learn more about Gardner's ideas.

Grant Wiggins (1950–)

Grant Wiggins, president of *Authentic Education* in Hopewell, New Jersey, is perhaps most famous for his ideas on curriculum expressed in *Understanding by Design* (2005), which he coauthored with Jay McTighe. Understanding by Design (UbD) presents a framework for improving student learning. UbD helps teachers create learning goals, build engaging activities, and develop authentic assessments. Four ideas to improve student learning inherent in UbD are (1) that topics taught should be covered in depth rather than breadth, (2) that goals and assessments should be established prior to instruction, (3) that teachers should collaborate in planning lessons and units for students, and (4) that materials should be adjusted according to student success. One of the subcomponents of UbD is "backwards design," encouraging teachers to consider the end goal in deciding what is most important for students to learn. Wiggins's ideas encourage teachers to improve student learning by exploring essential questions and big ideas.

Diane McCarty (1954–)

Diane McCarty, a former classroom teacher, now a professor of education at Wartburg College in Waverly, Iowa, has been a source of great ideas throughout her teaching career. As a classroom teacher, McCarty was trained as a consultant at the National Geographic Headquarters in Washington, D.C. There she met other teachers with great ideas, and working together they developed numerous projects. One of the projects McCarty promotes, "Travelmates: Geography for Kids" (1993), is essentially a way of letting students travel around the world without ever leaving home. More information on Travelmates can be found in the article "Travelmates . . . One More Time," in *Teaching PreK–8* (2003). Other projects McCarty has created from good ideas include, The Great Bike Ride Across Iowa (McCarty, 1997), Kids Writing for Kids (McCarty, 1994), and A Literacy Luncheon (McCarty, 2004).

Effective teachers provide learning opportunities for students by creating curricula such as "Travelmates."

McCarty's projects provide opportunities for students to learn through participation in places and ideas outside of their daily environment. By developing multidisciplinary curricular experiences for her students, she translates her great ideas into activities that enrich the lives of students and their families at home and around the world. McCarty is one of those hero teachers—a teacher who has good ideas, puts them into practice, and shares them with others. This is not always the easiest thing to do when working on the front lines of teaching, but good ideas should be disseminated to inspire learning and more "good" ideas.

Conflicting Perspectives in Teaching and Learning

There is a back and forth nature to the struggle to educate. Perpetual controversy over one or another reigning educational philosophy and the give and take regarding ideas about classroom practices often create a cyclical effect. Ideas in education have been batted back and forth like ping-pong balls, falling out of favor only to be, at some later date, re-embraced as brilliant. Education is neither here nor there, one way or another. It is what works, and what actually works is not always most commonsensical.

During the 1960s, a period of unprecedented upheaval and change in the field of education in America, two men in particular, Jerome S. Bruner and David P. Ausubel, came to symbolize a dichotomy of viewpoints regarding the methods and means of teaching and learning, and, between them, defined the terms of a debate that continues unabated to this day.

For his part, Jerome Bruner theorized that by categorizing one's environment, a learner is better able to comprehend it. Bruner's learning theory, which emphasized the structure of disciplines and the use of inquiry—or what came to be called the discovery method—stressed the importance of teaching the sort of thinking skills necessary to the development of problem-solving abilities. His concept attainment theory was based on the technique of combining rules learned by discovery into a concept the learner is desired to understand. This discovery or experience of the learner is the "moving force" Dewey described as central to learning.

Deeper Look 7.2
Read a comparison of popular theories.

It was David Ausubel's view, on the other hand, that the teacher's major task is to transmit large bodies of already organized knowledge to the learner through a reception-receptive method—the relationship between the way knowledge is organized and the manner in which the mind works to process such information. Ausubel, considered the more traditional of the two thinkers, was opposed to most learning activities that could be described as discovery, and felt "discovery" was not an indispensable condition for the occurrence of meaningful learning (Ausubel, 1967).

Bruner was attempting to find new answers to basic questions of how students learn, and from there to lead learners to construct models of reality on their own terms (Bruner, 1966). Ausubel was adamantly opposed to passive learning on the part of the student, and unyielding in his insistence that receptive learning could be meaningful, arguing that just because learning by reception implies the material is "presented" rather than "discovered" does not make it inherently less meaningful (Ausubel, 1963).

Bruner's and Ausubel's contrasting theories came into prominence on the education scene as Dewey's progressivism entered its final stage, and there was a felt need for some sort of orderly guidance, some sort of basic adjustment to the entire education system, from top to bottom. As American education got busy flexing its newfound muscles during the early sixties, Bruner and Ausubel found their models of learning increasingly at the center of debate over how to best help students become processors of information. Oddly enough, within their theories are many broad areas of agreement, which have never been of much interest to the "warrior-pedagogues" of the continuing methods wars.

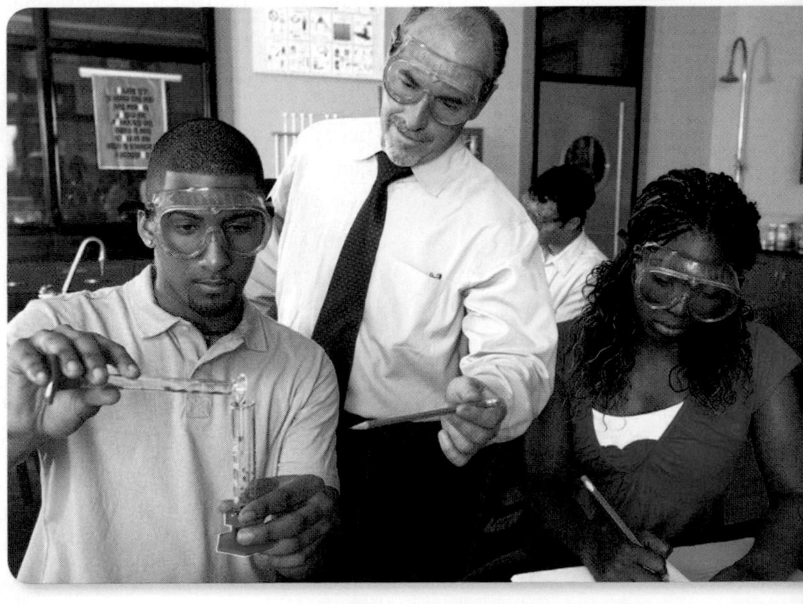

According to Jerome Bruner, when students take an active role in their learning, they construct meaning from the experience.

Their ideas were well founded, based on research and clear thinking. Both men supported the necessity of the teacher as director in the classroom, although from Ausubel's point of view the most efficient arrangement for the acquisition of knowledge involved the teacher "telling" the student what needed to be known. Ausubel did not consider discovery a prerequisite for understanding, believing instead that it was possible to teach students to think deductively. Though Ausubel did not deny the usefulness and practicality of problem-solving skills, he regarded "knowing" as a substantive phenomenon, not a problem-solving capability.

The Necessity of Evaluating Ideas

What could be better than always having the correct answer? Right? A quick, right answer in the classroom and on timed standardized tests is always appreciated. Unfortunately, quick, right answers measure what students have already mastered, not what they are in the process of figuring out. Learning is, however, the process of understanding concepts and for many of us the understanding of complex concepts does not take the form of quick, right answers. Think about the process you have gone through in your teacher education course work. Facts and concepts that you learned early in your program will take on more meaning as your experiences with the concepts in action increase. You may have been able to recite back ideas expressed by your professors, but ideas do not become part of your teaching schema until you have figured them out through thoughtful action.

Schooling as we know it today appears to focus more on a right answer than how the student came to that answer. This may be in part that schools have so much to teach and so little time to teach it. It may also be in part that society seems more concerned with how a world-class golfer thinks through a shot to the green or a putt, or how cyclists prepare for different legs of the Tour de France, than how a seventh-grader comes to appreciate the elements of literary style in a compelling story about the death of a favorite pet. Your mission as a teacher, should you chose to accept it, is to help your students recognize the routes they have taken to finding the right answers, and that those paths represent learning as much as a right answer does.

Having a Research-Based Perspective

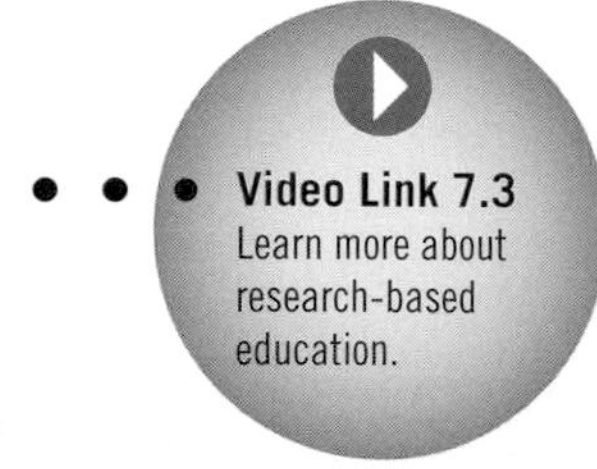

Video Link 7.3
Learn more about research-based education.

Some ideas that seem good have been held through long-standing beliefs. They are what we have come to know through experience, and they stick with us regardless of how the facts or our environment change. Jerome Kagan's book *Three Seductive Ideas* (1998) challenges some basic assumptions the social sciences have held about intelligence, child development, and motivation. His arguments are based on research and give teachers, both new and experienced, some ideas to ponder about the way we conduct business in classrooms. William James, a 20th century pragmatist, said that new knowledge derived from new experiences is absorbed slowly into firmly held prejudices and beliefs so that old knowledge is maintained and unaltered as much as possible to maintain one's equilibrium of thought (James, 1975).

Theory and practice are fundamental to how we organize and think about our intellectual and practical world. Ideas and theories sometimes prevail and sometimes take a backseat to the driving force of practicality. It may be an unfortunate fact that many teachers consider application the only relationship between theory and practice when, in reality, the relationship is ever more complicated. When teachers test ideas, they have a better chance of detecting those that contain flaws based on beliefs and assumptions. Each one of us could probably make a list of the bad ideas we have had. Sometimes we're lucky not to put our bad ideas into action; sometimes, after the fact, we have proof that they were bad ideas and we don't try them again.

Great ideas and grand plans for educating the children and young adults of this country can come from a variety of sources. Such thoughts may spring forth from the minds of the country's leaders as they did from Thomas Jefferson, or from the minds of business executives such as Andrew Carnegie, or from the minds of thoughtful teachers, or from the minds of leaders in the field of education like John Dewey. While tried and true ideas are being implemented, newer and seemingly more radical ideas are being proposed. The continuous flow of refreshing ideas is part of the reason many of us have been drawn to the profession. Teachers constantly work with ideas. Teachers also represent a rich pool of creative thinking that has the power to stimulate major changes in education as well as in student learning. Everyone has an opinion, though sometimes the ideas that reach popularity are not of the highest caliber. Regardless of where the ideas about education come from, they are put into play by a classroom teacher. Translating ideas into practice is a heavy responsibility and takes a courageous heart. In order to fulfill this responsibility, teachers must be knowledgeable of the ideas of numerous others who have encountered the same concerns and have established theories that have practical application in teaching and learning.

HOW DOES EDUCATIONAL PSYCHOLOGY HELP TEACHERS UNDERSTAND STUDENT LEARNING?

Teacher Heather Cyra shares how educational psychology helps teachers understand student learning:

> Knowing stages in a student's development is important to understanding ways students can learn. Teachers have to adjust their teaching practices in order to meet the students at their level of understanding. When my fifth-graders start the year they exhibit behaviors that would be considered immature for fifth-graders. However, after about six weeks I can see a big change in the way they act in class; they are more responsible about their work and demonstrate the attitudes and behavior expected of fifth-graders. When they come back from Christmas vacation they have grown so much, and by the end of the year they are truly ready to go on to middle school.

Since you are studying to be a teacher you will no doubt take a course in educational psychology. How students learn in school is what educational psychology is mainly about, and it underlies all that teachers do. The role of research in educational psychology is to carefully examine certain questions about factors that may contribute to learning. Such research can help you interpret your experiences and understand why you teach and learn the ways you do. Educational psychology is concerned with the behavioral and social development of an individual and is a branch of applied psychology that studies children in educational settings. It deals with the psychological aspects of teaching and learning processes of early childhood, adolescence, and adulthood. One focus of educational psychology is the assessment of ability and aptitude, the evaluation of teaching and learning (Lucas, Blazek, Raley, & Washington, 2005).

Research on Teaching and Learning

Perhaps the first research on learning occurred when people began to ask *why?* Why do I know how to do that? How did I learn that? What do I need to know now? Or when philosophers began to ask questions related to the state of knowing. Research that attempts to explain what we know and learn is deeply ingrained in the history of learning. Some important events in the establishment of educational research include, but are not limited to, the following list. Many of the names will be familiar to you.

Audio Link 7.2
Listen to a clip about child development and education.

- 1690, John Locke publishes *An Essay Concerning Human Understanding*
- 1802, Johann Pestalozzi publishes *How Gertrude Teaches Her Children*
- 1896, John Dewey establishes the laboratory schools in Hyde Park, Chicago
- 1917, First large-scale IQ testing of American adults
- 1921, Jean Piaget publishes his first article on the psychology of intelligence
- 1956, Benjamin Bloom publishes *Taxonomy of Educational Objectives*
- 1962, Vygotsky's Social Development Theory published in the United States
- 1969, Carl Rogers publishes *Freedom to Learn*

A glance at this short list makes it clear that as schooling in America developed it was accompanied by researchers documenting its growth through studies and assessments of teaching and learning. Knowledge of past findings can help you understand teachers' roles and responsibilities toward student learning, and it can often illuminate the path of education so past mistakes are not repeated.

Translating Educational Psychological Perspectives Into Teaching Practice

Theories of learning translate into teaching practices as organization of information, creation of environments to promote student access to this information, and ideas about human development come together; and through this combination echo Dewey's ideas of the learner, society, and organized subject matter (1974). Theorists often differ in their perspective on what provides the optimum setting for student learning; hence the variety of programs and activities that exist in schools today.

Deeper Look 7.3 Read more about Maslow's Hierarchy of Needs.

Johann Pestalozzi (1746–1827), Jean Piaget (1896–1980), and Abraham Maslow (1908–1970)

Pestalozzi's theories emphasize group and participatory activities. His ideas on recognizing individual differences and grouping students by ability rather than age were considered radical for his time. He felt teachers should allow students freedom to express themselves and develop naturally. He envisioned children learning through observation of the "real" world rather than from books.

Piaget is best known for his epistemological studies (how we know what we know) of the intellectual growth of children. Piaget concluded from his studies that human knowledge is "constructed" through interactions with reality. Piaget's work has had a profound effect on educational theories regarding when students are ready to learn specific information.

Maslow developed the theory of human motivation now known as Maslow's Hierarchy of Needs. He described the power of human needs and organized these needs into five general categories, from most urgent to most advanced. Maslow's Hierarchy of Needs became a framework for considering the individual needs of students as indicators of what they were capable of learning when constrained by personal needs.

Piaget studied the ways children come to know the world about them; for very young children, knowledge of "what's in the box" can only be constructed if it can be seen.

These different, yet somewhat similar, perspectives have promoted self-actualization and developmental and motivational approaches to instructional practices.

Ivan Pavlov (1849–1936), Edward Thorndike (1874–1949), and Burrhus Frederick Skinner (1904–1990)

Pavlov demonstrated a form of conditioning in 1927, with the help of a dog and a bell. His experiments on stimulus and response led him to posit that learning required a dependent relationship between an unconditional stimulus (presenting a stimulus to elicit a reflexive response) and a conditional stimulus to create a conditional response.

Thorndike developed the Law of Effect principle suggesting that responses closely followed by satisfaction are more likely to elicit similar responses when the situation is repeated. However, when a situation is followed by discomfort the response to the situation will be less likely to occur or will become weakened over time. Thorndike helped lay the scientific foundation for modern educational psychology.

Skinner based his theories of operant conditioning on the work of Thorndike. He studied observable behavior by looking at an action and its consequences. Skinner believed that the best way to understand behavior is to look at the causes of an action and the consequences of that action and so be able to predict and control behavior.

Each of these theorists believed that behavior can be modified, controlled, or directed when specific stimuli are present or when a behavior is rewarded or depressed. Behavior modification practices are widely used in classrooms today that affect instructional practices and classroom management strategies.

Lev Vygotsky (1896–1934)

Lev Vygotsky presented the Social Development Theory, viewing cognition as the end product of socialization and social behavior. Interactions with more knowledgeable others help students learn. His theories support the foundations of constructivism. Three major themes in Vygotsky's social development theory are that (a) development in a child appears first on a social level with others and then inside the child, (b) the child learns from a more knowledgeable other, and (c) learning occurs in a zone of proximal development between the learner's ability to learn with the support of others and the ability to learn independently (Vygotsky, 1978).

Deeper Look 7.4
Read more about Vygotsky's Theory.

It would be foolish to suggest that the complex theories of these educational psychologists can be explained and discussed in such succinct terms. Detailed information about their contributions to the ways educators perceive student learning is available through the references listed at the end of this book. It is necessary that as future teachers you begin to understand the many ways their ideas have influenced different modes of instruction in schools.

HOW DO PHILOSOPHICAL PERSPECTIVES HELP TEACHERS UNDERSTAND STUDENT LEARNING?

Ms. Cyra believes that teaching and learning are a social process and should be shared by everyone in the classroom. In her classroom everyone is a teacher.

> By developing a mutual respect with my students and creating an environment that is comfortable and relaxed, my students are eager to share information and stories. I wish there were more time to just have conversations with my students about what they think, what they know, and what they know how to do, but the pressure of standardized testing limits how much time teachers have to truly get to know their students. I know there are days that I learn as much from my students as they learn from me.

You no doubt took a philosophy or logic course as part of the core requirements for your degree. Understanding philosophical thought prepares teachers for critical thinking and reasoning and constructing logically sound arguments. The study of philosophy helps teachers sift through ideas and articulate thoughts in ways that others can follow. Understanding the practices of philosophical perspectives helps teachers learn how to look and listen, how to engage in meaningful discussions, and how to recognize the many ways of thinking about teaching.

We all seek answers to questions in order to make sense of our worlds. In translation, the word *philosophy* can be defined as "love of wisdom," though it's clear we don't all have the same questions or view wisdom in the same way. Philosophers have thought long and hard about their philosophies and about the implications their perspectives have for learning and teaching.

Metaphysics, Epistemology, and Axiology

Three different branches of philosophy are concerned with seeking answers to different types of questions. **Metaphysics** is concerned with questions about the nature of reality and humans' attempts to find coherence in the realm of thought and experience. Questions on teaching and learning examined from this perspective explore the relationship between learners and teachers.

Epistemology examines questions about how and what we know, and how knowing takes place. Questions dealt with in the study of epistemology may include "Where do ideas come from?" and "How do we pose and solve problems?" The **axiology** branch of philosophy deals with questions concerning the nature of values. Questions examined from the axiology perspective deal with what should be or what values we hold: "What is good for students?" "How should students behave?" As you can see, the questions that are the focus of each branch of philosophy are related to different aspects of education. Such questions posed by the different branches of philosophy can be found in educational concerns over curriculum, methods, and teaching behaviors.

Teachers must engage in critical thinking to be able to translate ideas so their students can understand complex problems and begin to make sense of the world.

The Metaphysical Questions of Content or Child

In 340 BCE, Aristotle declared that metaphysics involves intuitive knowledge of unprovable starting points (truths) and demonstrative knowledge of what follows from them. Teachers want to know why some students are successful at particular tasks while other students struggle with them. Can a child choose whether to learn or not to learn? Is the ability to learn determined by factors outside of a student's control? Is understanding of specific content necessary to a successful life, or is the way in which the content is learned of utmost importance to the learner. The manner in which a teacher approaches the content and how the child interacts with the content depends somewhat on the teacher's attitudes about human nature. Diann Musial, from Northern Illinois University, believes that a teacher's classroom approach is linked to the teacher's metaphysical beliefs: "If the teacher believes that very specific basic knowledge is crucial to the child's intellectual development, it is likely that this teacher will focus on the subject matter. If, on the other hand, the teacher holds that the child is more important than any specific subject matter, it is likely that this teacher will focus on the child and allow the child to provide clues as to how he or she should be instructed" (J. A. Johnson, Dupuis, Musial, Hall, & Gollnick, 2005, p. 308). Children are real. How they develop and learn is, at times, metaphysical.

Ways of Knowing, Learning, and Teaching

In the concern over how students learn, what they should learn, and how they should learn it, educators connect epistemology and education. Epistemology is the study of the origin, nature, methods, and limits of knowledge. Epistemology is the science of how we learn and teach, and encompasses the range of questions educators face in designing the very best schooling for children. Education is focused on how students best learn the knowledge they must have and how teachers learn the necessary behaviors to facilitate student learning.

When classroom teachers puzzle over which educational goals should be met and how these goals might be achieved through teaching practices, they are dealing with questions about knowing, learning, and teaching. In Plato's discussion of epistemology, he argued that in order to grasp reality or know, individuals use understanding, reason, perception, and imagination.

You will also learn about Jean Piaget in your course work and how his program of naturalistic research helped teachers understand child development. Piaget was primarily interested in how knowledge developed in human organisms, and he termed his general theoretical framework "genetic epistemology."

The Role of Values and Ethics in the Classroom

There are many reasons that parents care a great deal about who teaches their children. Certainly parents hope for a teacher who is knowledgeable. They hope for one who will be sympathetic to any idiosyncratic behaviors or learning styles their particular child might possess. But probably nothing concerns parents more than the moral values, or ethics, the teachers of their children demonstrate. Parental concern over the moral values of individual teachers as well as those expressed by schools has given rise to an increased interest in homeschooling and school vouchers. As one example, the National Character Education Center (**http://www.ethicsusa.com/**) relates core values to human anatomy and gets at the heart and mind of values in action. In this approach, the seven virtues attributed to respective body parts are respect (eyes and ears), integrity (mouth), compassion (heart), perseverance (stomach), cooperation (hands), initiative (feet), and positive mental attitudes (mind).

Another initiative to accomplish the teaching of core values is the Institute for Global Ethics (**http://www.globalethics.org**). This institute provides guidelines for ethical literacy through ethical fitness. The Ethics Resource Center, a character education website at **http://www.ethics.org**, discusses the questions of whether schools should be teaching values and if so, whose values should be taught. Ethics is a way of processing behavior. Teachers weight different elements of their own behavior and the behavior of their students differently depending on their own set of ethics and values.

While ethics might provide food for thought, not everyone has the same beliefs that public institutions should dictate to individuals what should be considered an acceptable form of conduct. Teachers must negotiate the omnipresent conflict between societal values and individual values in the classroom. A well-informed teacher understands and respects the diversity of cultural and ethnic thought in any community and uses this knowledge to help all students learn. Teachers faced with questions about values are dealing with the axiology branch of philosophy.

Thirty-one years ago I walked into school with a set schedule, set class list, set curriculum, and set lesson plans . . . or so I thought. Within the first hour, I realized that I would need to change a "few" things. As the day wore on, then the weeks, the months, and then years, I have come to understand that ideas, students, methods, expectations, and anything else related to education is anything *but* set. The commonality for all these things is change. You can't fight it. You can't worry about it. You can only be flexible and open-minded and know too that change will be the one constant in your teaching career. I have experienced changes in students, families, changes in discipline, changes in standards, changes in technology, and, well, you get the idea. Sometimes we think we have found a "better way" only to revert back to the way we did things a decade earlier. Flexibility is being capable of being "bent without breaking." There were many times I thought I would break but didn't. We are a unique group in that way. We contort, give, change, and bounce back. Students need us to be that way and hopefully by doing so they will learn a very valuable lesson about life through us. I honestly believe that as an educator, my philosophy of education has a direct impact on my students' lives. Our greatest responsibility as educators is to be everything we can be, learn everything we can learn, and to find and capitalize on the strengths of our students—not for our own benefit, but for the lives of students we touch on a daily basis.

Mary Ella Bauer as told to Dr. William Bauer,
Marietta College, Marietta, Ohio

Philosophical Perspectives' Influence on Teaching and Learning

Various **schools of philosophy** seek to answer the broad philosophical questions posed through metaphysics, epistemology, and axiology from differing perspectives. The schools of philosophy most often mentioned in terms of the implications they have for education are idealism, realism, perennialism, pragmatism, progressivism, essentialism, and existentialism. These philosophies represent a broad spectrum of influence on educational practice and thought, and ways of knowing. Some schools of philosophy give rise to compatible educational theories, while others generate quite opposite and competing points of view. Some of the philosophical perspectives listed below may not be considered schools of philosophy in the truest sense. However, their impact on teaching and learning has given them a relevant stature in the realm of thinking about education. Observance of one or another of these philosophical perspectives, or a combination of two or more, could produce differing school structures, curriculum, instructional methods, and classroom practices for teachers and students. What follows is a succinct description of some of the schools of philosophy teachers should be familiar with as they undertake construction of their own personal philosophy of teaching.

Confucianism

Confucius (551–479 BCE) is in many cultures regarded as the world's foremost and greatest philosopher. Confucius's teachings, a source of perennial good sense, encourage people to lead good lives by doing what is right. At some time in your preservice teacher education course work and during inservice professional development you will no doubt see or hear one of Confucius's many axioms. One of the most frequently displayed is, "I hear, I know. I see, I remember. I do, I understand." Here is another: "If you think in terms of a year, plant a seed; if in terms of ten years, plant trees; if in terms of 100 years, teach the people." Confucius taught that there are three methods to gaining wisdom. The first is reflection, which is the highest. The second is imitation, which is the easiest. The third is experience, which is the bitterest. As a teacher education candidate, you will have the opportunity to use all three methods to gain wisdom.

Idealism and Realism

Idealism, the oldest of the Western philosophies, originated with Plato (427–347 BCE). Idealism refers to a rational world of the mind where ideas or concepts are the essence of all that is worth knowing. The idealism philosophy guides behavior or thought based on the theory that the objects of external perception consist of ideas. Universal and absolute truths offer examples of the ideal to strive for. Since ideas are consistent in an ever-changing world, they should be learned and understood. The ideal should be sought and emulated when found. Hegel's (1770–1831) absolute idealism posits that since ideas about reality are products of the mind, there must be a mind at work in the universe that establishes reality and gives it structure. Idealism is used to refer to any metaphysical theory positing the primacy of mind, spirit, or language over matter.

Ancient philosophical ideas are present in current teaching practices.

Realism describes a world in which material objects exist in themselves apart from the mind's awareness of them. Aristotle (384–322 BCE) built upon the ideas of his famous teacher, Plato, to describe the realistic world. That world is real and exists whether or not a mind is there to perceive it. Remember the question of the tree falling in the forest that you discussed in your first philosophy class? If a tree falls in the forest and no one is there to hear it, does it make a sound? Imagine the answer from both an idealist and a realist perspective. In realism, laws of nature and the order of the physical world override the idealist notion that ideas are the ultimate reality. In a realist's world we respond to what is seen and sensed. According to John Locke's (1632–1704) *tabula rasa* theory, we all begin as blank slates and our senses help us fill the void with knowledge. Plato's idealistic perspective has us full of ideas at birth and life's experiences help us eventually know these ideas. Is it the teacher's responsibility to bring out the knowledge students already possess or to engrave it on their blank slates?

Perennialism and Essentialism

The roots of **perennialism** lie in the philosophies of Plato and Aristotle and also of St. Thomas Aquinas. Perennialism offers a conservative and traditional view of human nature. In this school of thought, humans do not change much, but they are capable of analytical thinking, reason, and imagination, and should be encouraged along these lines. Through reason lies revelation. When certain perpetual truths are learned, individuals will develop rationality. While human nature is somewhat predictable, it is possible to improve the human condition through understanding of history, the great works of literature, and art.

Essentialism became a popular educational philosophy in the United States in the 1930s following what was considered an excess of progressive education. Essentialists believe there is a fundamental core of knowledge that any functioning member of society must possess. Such knowledge is absolutely essential for an individual to lead a productive life. Learning takes place through contact with the physical world as well as with specific core disciplines. Goodness lies in acquisition of certain essential knowledge. E. D. Hirsch clearly delineated the finer points of essential knowledge in his 1987 book, *Cultural Literacy,* making clear the exact information that every literate person should possess. Teaching the essentials has since colonial times been the dominant approach to American education. The testing frenzy of the current No Child Left Behind movement would attest to the staying power of essentialism in American education. "While essentialism reflects the traditional view that the 'real' world is the physical world we experience with our senses, perennialism is more open to the notion that universal spiritual forms are equally real" (Sadaker & Sadaker, 2000, pp. 400–401).

Pragmatism and Progressivism

Pragmatism was first introduced into philosophy by Charles Peirce in 1878. The term *pragmatic* is derived from the Greek word *pragma,* meaning action, which is also the source for the words *practice* and *practical.* The universe of pragmatism is dynamic and evolving. Change happens and humans are constantly in the process of becoming, evolving to reach ever-greater understanding. Truth is what works in one place and time, and even if it worked once it might not work again given different variables. Concepts and outcomes should be tested by their practical results. Maybe your university professor who answers "Depends" to your questions about what works best is taking a pragmatic point of view. Pragmatism shares some views with Aristotle's realism but is less rigid since in pragmatism experience is of utmost importance. Because of the changing nature of truths, individuals must be flexible and be capable of dealing with change. America was founded on pragmatic ideals. Since the arrival of the first explorers and settlers, Americans have spent a large portion of their energy adapting to one another and to ever-changing environments.

Libraries around the world, such as this one at Trinity College in Dublin, Ireland, contain the wisdom of the ages.

Progressivism, marked by progress, reform, or a continuing improvement, became popular in the 1920s through the work of John Dewey. The tenets of progressivism demonstrate respect for individuality, a high regard for science, and receptivity to change. According to Dewey, humans are social animals that learn through interaction with one another. Learning increases when we are engaged in activities that have meaning for us (Dewey, 1963). The influence of progressivism helped American educators take a closer look at the role of the learner in any acquisition of knowledge.

Existentialism

Existentialism rose out of the cult of **nihilism,** a philosophical position that argues the world, and especially human existence, is without objective meaning, purpose, comprehensible truth, or essential value, and **pessimism,** a general belief that things are bad and tend to become worse. The rise of this view followed the destruction of European civilization in World War I. Existentialism presents a world in which individuals determine for themselves what is true or false. Only through free will can individuals oppose hostile environments. The first principle of existentialism, according to Jean-Paul Sartre, is "Man is nothing else but what he makes of himself." When the caterpillar in *Alice in Wonderland* asks, "Who R U?" had Alice been an existentialist she might have answered, "Yes, who am I and what should I do?"

Maxine Greene, a long-time professor at Columbia Teachers College, contends that living is philosophy and that freedom means overcoming obstacles that obstruct our attempt to find ourselves and fulfill our potential (1988). The writings of Friedrich Nietzsche (1884–1900) offer a framework for cultivating a healthy love of self. He wanted to help liberate people from the oppression of feeling inferior.

Carl Rogers (1902–1987), the founder of humanistic psychology, made outstanding contributions to the field of education. His writings focus on empowering individuals to achieve their full potential, that is, becoming self-actualized. According to Rogers, existential living means living in the here-and-now, being in touch with reality, while learning from the past and dreaming of the future (1969). Though the ideas of existentialism seem radical to many people, Donald Kauchak and Paul Eggen (2005) point out that "existentialism makes a contribution to education because it places primary emphasis on the individual, and in doing so, it reminds us that we don't teach math, science, reading, and writing; rather, we teach people, and the people we teach are at the core of learning" (p. 214).

There are far more philosophical perspectives than have been mentioned here. When you read of the naturalists or of scholasticism, humanism, or social reconstructivism, you will increase your knowledge of the ideas that have influenced how you may be expected to perform in the classroom. Most philosophical perspectives hold increased knowledge or understanding as good. For more details on schools of philosophy and their implications in education visit the website of the Sophia Project of the Molloy College Philosophy Department (**http://www.xmarks.com/site/www.molloy.edu/academic/philosophy/sophia/plato/republic/contents.htm**). The Sophia website lists numerous links to the thinking and writing of educational theorists.

Knowledge of teaching and learning is always incomplete even though there is a wealth of theories to support many of the practices and policies that exist. Knowledge and attitudes about education grow and change as the physical and social world changes. Teachers construct a personal philosophy toward teaching and learning in order to make sense of the complexities of their craft.

Teachers may not be able to name a specific school of philosophy if you ask them to tell you which philosophy they adhere to in daily practice, but they will certainly be able to give you their thoughts on how children learn, what they should learn, and how they should be learning it. Most teachers select ideas from a number of schools of philosophy and apply what works best for them given the requirements of their teaching situation. In order to maintain a sense of humor and hope in teaching, most teachers are pragmatic and operate from a philosophical viewpoint of eclecticism. They select ideas from various systems in the same way they gather materials from various sources. Such is the practical world of teaching.

The Presence of Educational Philosophies in Classrooms

All teachers have moments in the classroom when they are captivated by the topic they are teaching, only to be caught up short by blank stares or student questions from left field. It is at such moments that teachers begin to realize that their perspectives on what is important to know may not be universally shared. The knowledge one person believes fundamental, from say a perennialist's point of view, may seem like so much intellectual domination to another. Any personal philosophy of teaching sets the stage for plans and actions. Teachers, by nature of the profession, must make decisions that incorporate a range of philosophical perspectives that are doable and that "work" given a variety of contexts. Figure 7.2 provides a comparison of ways some philosophical perspectives might be apparent in classrooms and teaching practices.

Teacher-Focused Classrooms

Room arrangement may not be the best clue as to a teacher's views on what and how children should learn, but it is an indicator. Picture students seated in individual islands separate from other

Figure 7.2 The Influence of Philosophical Perspectives on Teaching and Learning

	Learning Focus	Teaching Methods	Educational Goal	Curriculum	Assessment
Perennialism	Students will be prepared for their futures through learning the essential truths identified in idealism and realism.	Teachers use didactic instruction and questioning strategies. The Socratic method.	Students will develop intellectual skills and demonstrate rational behavior.	Liberal arts. The Great Books. The basics.	Objective tests. Essay exams.
Essentialism	Teach knowledge and skills. Focus on literacy. Teach the past as a way to understand the present and prepare for the future.	Through lecture instruction will focus on learning competencies. Teachers use detailed lesson plans.	Students will develop disciplined minds. Become literate.	Reading, writing, and mathematics as the basis for achieving a basic body of knowledge. A focus on common core standards.	Standardized tests. Mastery learning.
Progressivism	Engage students in cooperative learning experiences. Provide opportunities for students to interact with the environment in solving problems.	Teacher as a guide and collaborative partner. Child-centered classroom. Lessons engage students in group work and projects.	Students will become productive citizens in a democratic society.	Subject matter relevant to social experiences. Foster group work. Integrated lessons that model life.	Formative assessment. Student progress is closely monitored. Feedback is frequently provided.
Existentialism	Subject matter of personal choice. Reality exists in the eye of the beholder. Meaning constructed by learner.	Community projects to identify and rectify social problems. Examine the hidden curriculum.	Students exercise critical inquiry. Become citizens to challenge established constructs in society.	Curriculum presented as a model for questioning, critiquing, and analyzing social values and political culture.	Self-assessment. Journaling. Writing samples. Portfolios.

Source: Adapted from Webb, L. D., Metha, A., & Jordan, K. F. (2013). *Foundations of American education* (7th ed.). Upper Saddle River, NJ: Pearson.

students with eyes directed toward a teacher at the front of the room explaining or demonstrating something the students are expected to remember. The students are quiet. The teacher is talking. We've seen examples of this style of teaching in movies and on television. Unfortunately, in most of these examples, the teacher is oblivious to what the students are doing or thinking. Watching *The Amanda Show* on the cartoon network with my youngest grandson, Kai, I was struck by the parody of a teacher-focused classroom. The teacher was writing questions on the blackboard while the students were being turned into frogs and mice by a witch, and Mark, Amanda's friend, was trying to explain to the teacher, who was totally in outer space, what was going on.

Teacher-focused approaches to teaching, in which the teacher is master of the knowledge to be learned and dispenses it to all students at a specified rate over a specified period of time, adhere to the essentialism school of philosophy in which learning the content is of major concern.

UNDERSTANDING AND USING EVIDENCE

Changing Values

From 1950 to 1990, American values experienced radical change. Consider the following, and then discuss with your classmates the consequences such changes may have had on American education. How do current American values compare now in 2013?

1950	1990	2013
delayed gratification	instant gratification	
middle class	underclass	
"We"	"Me"	
heroes	cover girls	
value-added	charge cards	
Ozzie & Harriet	latchkey kids	
unionization	bankruptcy	
equity	renting/leasing	
public troubles	private issues	
"Do what you're told"	"Do what you want"	
public virtue	personal well-being	
achievement	fame	
regulation	deregulation	

One way to process the ideas presented in the Understanding and Using Evidence feature of this chapter is to first consider the major events in American life now and compare them with ideas present in the 1950s and 1990s. How are current events different from or similar to events that took place for past generations? How might these differences affect American values? What is on YouTube, Facebook, and Twitter? How might what we watch on TV influence American values? How has technology changed the ways students think about their world? What potential does it have to change American values?

Consider the public nature of a person's private life given the reality aspects of media programming. In what ways can reality TV possibly change the ways that students and teachers react in a classroom or think about education in general?

Make a list of your own ideas about the state of American values today. To get you started, here are some ideas.

Your Task:

Corporate Fraud
Terrorism
Social Networks
Animated Movies
Childhood Obesity
Graying Baby Boomers
Health Care

Challenging Assumptions

Is one method of teaching reading skills universally better than another?

• • • • •

The Assumption

Teacher-focused direct instruction is not as effective as a child-centered, constructivist method in helping children learn, retain, and apply reading skills. Teacher educators, teachers, and school administrators have long debated the effectiveness of a whole language approach versus the direct instruction approach to teaching early reading skills. Critics of the whole language approach blame colleges of education for continuing to advocate a teaching method that does not seem to be working for all students, while proponents of the whole language approach argue that the direct instruction approach constrains a child's learning style. According to educators who advocate the whole language approach, the child-centered focus of this method introduces students to reading in a way that makes them enjoy reading and become lifelong readers.

The Research

Schug, Tarver, and Western (2001), of the University of Wisconsin–Madison, examined the issue of direct instruction in their study, Direct Instruction and the Teaching of Early Reading. Their goal was to conduct research on direct instruction in authentic settings using methods that would capture the rich complexity of classroom experience. Six schools in Wisconsin participated in the study. The researchers observed and conducted interviews related to the use of direct instruction programs in these schools. In this qualitative study, teachers and principals reported positive effects from use of direct instruction for both regular education and special education students in reading decoding, reading comprehension, and attitudes toward reading. Teachers also reported other positive effects that included improved writing skills, improved capacity to focus and sustain effort, and, generally, improved student behavior. Teachers also reported no evidence of the various negative effects critics have attributed to direct instruction methods.

Implications

Since not all individuals learn, retain, and apply information in the same way, it is important for teachers to use a variety of instructional methods to meet the needs of all students. One approach to teaching reading may gain popularity to the detriment of other equally effective methods. It is important for teachers to be aware of the role of academic fashion in instructional programs, and to examine research results.

There are more sites on the Internet for constructivist lesson plans then there are for teacher-focused lesson plans. Does this mean that student-focused approaches to teaching are more popular than teacher-focused approaches in the nation's schools? Or is this an idea that sounds excellent in theory but is difficult to put into practice? Visit http://www.interventioncentral.org for suggestions using teacher-focused strategies to increase student learning. Then go to **http://www.thirteen.org/edonline/concept2class/constructivism** to learn about teaching strategies in student-focused classrooms. Is one type of lesson more appealing to you than the other? What do you think that might be?

Source: Schug, M. C., Tarver, S. G., & Western, R. D. (2001). Direct instruction and the teaching of early reading: Wisconsin's teacher-led insurgency. *Wisconsin Policy Research Institute Report, 14*(2). Retrieved from http://www.wpri.org/Reports/Volume14/v0114n02.pdf

The teacher-focused approach also follows a perennialist perspective, believing that education serves to inform students of knowledge that will remain constant through life (Oliva, 2005). In education, essentialism and perennialism perspectives dictate basic and prescribed subject matter. Learning is transferred in a programmatic fashion from teacher to students.

Student-Focused Classrooms

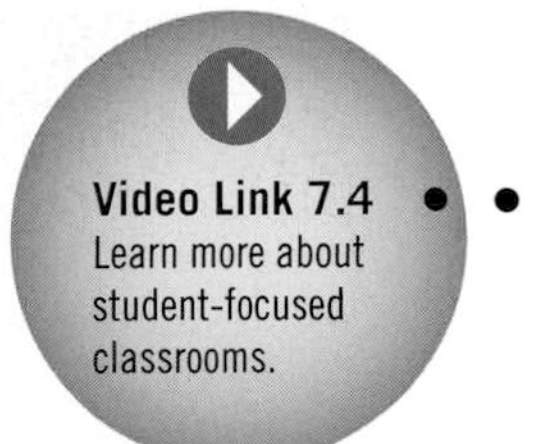

Video Link 7.4
Learn more about student-focused classrooms.

Student-focused approaches to teaching correspond to pragmatism and progressivism. In education, these philosophical perspectives view the major role of schools and teachers as being to create learning opportunities that will allow students to construct knowledge relevant to a specific task or situation through self-interest and dialogue with others. The tenets of a constructivist teaching style are closely associated with progressivism, emphasizing hands-on, activity-based learning. The room arrangement in a student-focused classroom is open and flexible. Students can easily interact with one another. Motivation is encouraged through intrinsic rewards. Teacher and learners share control of behavior and the learning environment. Inquiry is promoted and divergent points of view are respected. The teacher models participatory evaluation through questioning and student-led discussions of results. The students value themselves as learners and welcome the active role they have in directing their education along the lines of their own interests. In a student-focused classroom, the curriculum should take into account students' interests. Students construct knowledge through interaction with others.

The Changing Focus

In any given day in a classroom, the focus shifts from teacher to students and back again. This is not wishy-washy. It is merely a fact of the profession. In much the same way a world-class photographer will shift the focus on a scene to emphasize or pick up an unusual feature, an effective teacher is able to view the classroom as a vibrant life form, taking note of all movement and features. In doing so the teacher may find it necessary to redirect student attention, or perhaps momentarily call a halt to all activity. Learning how to combine parts of different educational philosophies for the benefit of all of the students may be one of the hardest tasks a new teacher must learn.

Using Philosophy to Problem Solve

Thinking and trying to find answers to questions is much of what teaching is about. A teacher perplexed by certain student behaviors or by the content of the textbooks mandated by the school district administrators can find comfort in the teachings of philosophers. With a little effort teachers can use the great ideas from different philosophical perspectives to help them understand human learning, behavior, and value systems. As your knowledge of teaching practices increases, so must your understanding of the basis for such practices. Do not take anything on hearsay. Seek the answers to your questions and build a cognitive framework of theory and practice to rival the architecture of the Taj Mahal. The mind should be a beautiful thing.

Deeper Look 7.5
Read about the importance of an educational philosophy for first-year teachers.

Our opinions about public school teaching and learning begin with the very first moment we enter schools as students. Every beginning teacher's knowledge of teaching is more memory than schema. Beliefs are the frameworks that all subsequent knowledge is incorporated into. It is necessary for teachers to categorize their thinking and understand the traditions of practice and the historical circumstances out of which certain kinds of thinking arise.

There are many ways to think about teaching and learning, and because of this, identifying one particular philosophical perspective for your approach to teaching can be like looking for a needle in a haystack. Don't worry. Be happy that there are so many possibilities and ideas. It is important for you to become familiar with a variety of philosophical perspectives in order to organize your own thinking and develop a personal wellspring of original and useful ideas to help your students learn. The more you think about teaching and the more you hear how others think about it, the easier it will be for you to construct your very unique personal philosophy of teaching.

CONNECTING TO THE CLASSROOM

This chapter has provided information on some of the widely held philosophical perspectives that influence attitudes about what and how children are to learn and how teachers are to teach. It is likely that during your teaching career you will have firsthand experience with more than one philosophical perspective. Below are some ways to recognize and become familiar with different philosophical perspectives in instruction and in interactions with students, their families, and teacher colleagues.

1. Keep a list of the questions teachers ask during instruction. Do the questions seem to ask for recall of facts or are the opinions of students considered? Are students often asked to make inferences or does that teacher provide conclusive statements for the students to record and remember? At what point do the students seem to be most engaged in answering the teacher's questions?
2. In a previous chapter, it has been suggested that you take part in a parent–teacher conference. You can learn much about the philosophical perspective of teachers and parents when observing a parent–teacher conference. Pay close attention to how the teacher conducts the conference. In what ways does the teacher express his or her personal philosophy of teaching? Are the parents given equal opportunity to express their attitudes about what their child is learning in school?
3. When teachers agree with one another and with their administrators, the school climate is pleasant and productive. On the other hand, when there are glaring differences among colleagues regarding content, conduct, and teaching strategies, discord may permeate the school. What actions have you seen teachers and administrators take to alleviate the disagreement among colleagues that stems from belief in the tenets of different schools of philosophy?

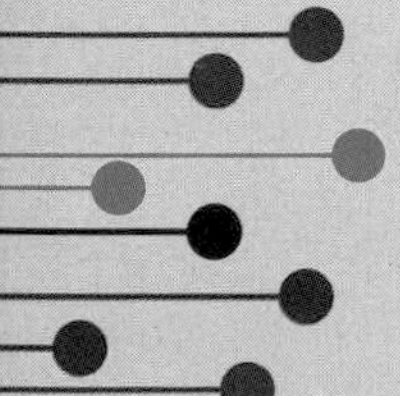

SUMMARY

Four major topics were covered in this chapter:

- Developing a personal philosophy toward teaching and learning: Knowing your beliefs and attitudes toward teaching and learning is an important first step in understanding your influence on student learning.
- Student learning: There are a variety of ways students learn and a variety of ways teachers can support student learning.
- Recognizing the connection between educational psychology and student learning: When teachers understand the tenets of educational psychology they have an improved chance of helping all students learn.
- Philosophical perspectives toward teaching and learning: Using different approaches to teaching and learning is necessary to help students with a variety of approaches to learning succeed in school.

CLASS DISCUSSION QUESTIONS

1. Experiences you have had as a student quite likely will shape your attitudes and beliefs as a teacher. Discuss one experience that stands out from the rest. Refer to particular schools of philosophy to explain why this experience was so important to you.
2. Describe stories from your experiences that have shaped your philosophy of teaching. What critical events have given rise to strongly held opinions?
3. In schools where teachers follow the same philosophical perspective as their colleagues or

students' families, there is probably agreement with the curriculum that is being taught and the instructional methods that are used to teach it. What issues might arise, however, if many of the teachers followed the tenets of the progressive school of philosophy, while many of the families of the students followed the tenets of essentialism, and the administration mainly expressed a perennialist's point of view?

4. Pick a philosophical perspective. What role might reflection on student achievement play for a teacher from that perspective?

KEY TERMS

Axiology 208
Epistemology 208
Essentialism 211
Existentialism 212
Metaphysics 208
Nihilism 212
Perennialism 211
Pessimism 212
Pragmatism 212
Progressivism 212
Schools of philosophy 210
Socratic method 198

SELF-ASSESSMENT

WHAT IS YOUR CURRENT LEVEL OF UNDERSTANDING AND THINKING ABOUT DEVELOPING A PHILOSOPHY OF TEACHING AND LEARNING?

One of the indicators of understanding is to examine how complex your thinking is when asked questions that require you to use the concepts and facts introduced in this chapter.

Answer the following questions as fully as you can. Then use the Complexity of Thinking rubric to self-assess the degree to which you understand and can use the ideas presented in this chapter.

1. What are three issues related to developing a personal philosophy of teaching and learning?
2. Why is it important for teachers to have a working knowledge of educational psychology?
3. What are the common educational philosophies teachers should know?
4. Name three ways educational psychology perspectives and educational philosophies can be apparent in classrooms.

Complexity of Thinking Rubric

	Parts & Pieces	Unidimensional	Organized	Integrated	Extensions
Indicator	Elements/concepts are talked about as isolated and independent entities.	One or a few concepts are addressed, while others are underdeveloped.	Deliberate and structured consideration of all key concepts/ elements.	All key concepts/ elements are included in a view that addresses interconnections.	Integration of all elements and dimensions, with extrapolation to new situations.
Relationships between educational psychology, educational philosophy, and teaching and learning	Names a few educational psychology approaches without mentioning relationship to schools of philosophy.	Describes only one or two approaches to teaching and learning.	Describes how educational psychology and philosophical perspectives can result in specific teaching practices.	Learner can categorize educational psychology perspective with educational philosophies to provide examples of ways a teacher might plan, implement, and assess lessons.	Explains ways past knowledge and experiences can influence the development of a personal philosophy of teaching and learning.

STUDENT STUDY SITE

Visit the Student Study Site at **www.sagepub.com/hall** to access links to the videos, audio clips, and Deeper Look reference materials noted in this chapter, as well as additional study tools including eFlashcards, web quizzes, and more.

Field Guide

for Learning More About Developing a Philosophy of Teaching and Learning

• • • • •

At this point in the text you should have quite a collection of artifacts to add to your personal field guide of learning to teach. Refer back to Chapter 1 for a detailed description of what your field guide should contain and how it can provide opportunities for reflection on your professional growth.

Ask a Teacher or Principal

Ask two separate teachers to share with you their opinions of how students learn. Ask how they know when their students have actually learned the information being taught. Do they believe that learning one piece of information automatically leads to learning a subsequent piece of information? In their opinion, is all learning of equal value? Will "knowing" help students lead a better life?

Make Your Own Observations

Classrooms are different. They come in different sizes and shapes, and they are populated by people who also come in different sizes and shapes. It is interesting to compare the way classrooms are arranged, what is being taught, how the teacher interacts with the students, and how the students are expected to interact with one another. Can such observations provide a clue as to the attitudes and beliefs of the teachers regarding how children learn? Is it possible for only one observation to present a clear picture of a teacher's beliefs? How might someone who watched you teach identify your personal philosophy of teaching?

Reflect Through Journaling

Think about the teachers you have encountered over your years as a student in classrooms. Explain why you believe that a specific teacher had a specific philosophy of teaching and learning. What do you remember of their actions in the classroom that would lead you to this conclusion? Did you find their teaching methods compatible with your style of learning?

Build Your Portfolio

In order to recognize the influence of life events on the adoption of a personal philosophy of teaching, create an educational autobiography by documenting at least three critical events that had an impact on your schooling. Here are some questions you might consider: What were the major events taking place in the world during your childhood years? What were some of the learning experiences you had in school that are still vivid memories? Which of your teachers did you like or dislike the most? Why? Who were your heroes? What was of major importance when you graduated from high school? What did your family expect you to do with your life? At the end of your autobiography, reflect on how your experiences might be alike or different from your students' experiences.

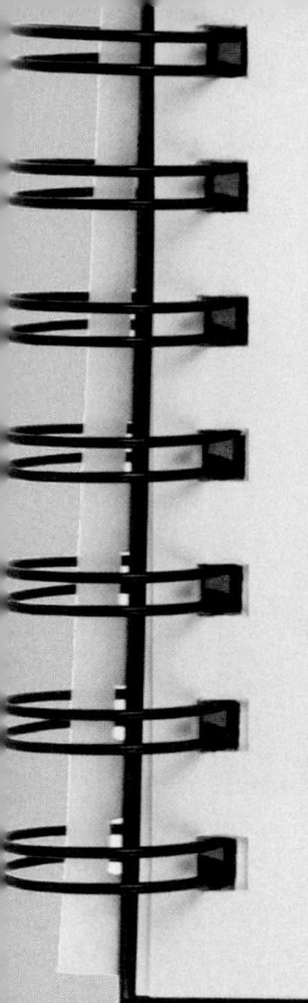

Read a Book

On Knowing: Essays for the Left Hand, by J. S. Bruner (1962; Cambridge, MA: Harvard University Press), takes a fascinating look at the influence of intuition, feeling, and spontaneity in determining how we know what we do know, and how we can teach others what we know.

In his book *The Courage to Teach: Exploring the Inner Landscape of a Teacher's Life* (1998; San Francisco, CA: Jossey-Bass), Parker Palmer discusses emotional and social aspects of the profession that have a tremendous effect on the ways a teacher might understand and approach the art and science of teaching and learning.

Search the Web

Visit **http://www.school-for-champions.com/education/philosophies.htm** for Ron Kurtus's overview of five basic philosophies of education.

Visit **http://oregonstate.edu/instruct/ed416/sample.html** for two sample philosophy of education statements from Oregon State University education candidates.

TEACHER INTERVIEW

Dr. Kim Friel

Dr. Kim Friel is principal of Sawyer Middle School in Las Vegas, Nevada. She has been principal of Sawyer for nine years. The school has 1,300 students in grades 6 to 8. The students' families range from very wealthy to some who live in cars. There are 232 ELL students, 118 special education students, and 45 languages spoken. There are 53 teachers and 27 support staff, including secretaries, custodians, teacher aides, and cafeteria workers.

Organizing Schools for Learning

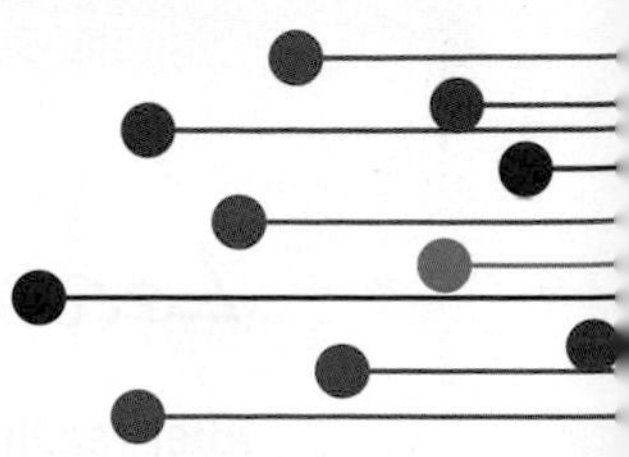

• For you as a principal, what is excellence in teaching?

I look for a teacher who engages students in the subject and convinces students that this is the most exciting thing they have ever learned in their entire life. If I find that, then I know that that teacher is being successful. Also, it is pretty funny, but often teachers who are most successful with students are not so successful in working with adults.

At times we have talked about schools as a workplace for teachers and students. Does this metaphor "work" for you?

It depends on how you define *work*. If you are only going to define work as an 8 to 5 job then it doesn't work for me, because schools are more than an 8 to 5 job. It is much more for a child and for a teacher. A teacher takes the work home with them, regardless of whether they want to. An educator will always take home that child that bothered them that day. They will tell someone about the child that was funny that day. Students have homework and will be thinking about that teacher who encouraged them. Or, when they are walking down the street and they see something and think, "Huh! I learned about that today."

When you are hiring a beginning teacher, what do you look for?

I am looking for someone who was involved in service, coaching, or something else. They could have worked. I also want to see an energy and that they know what they are getting into when they are working with kids. When I interview, I am looking for that energy. At the interview I have a question I ask: "If a student came into the classroom eating an ice cream cone, what would you do?" Their answer shows me what they think about kids and what they will be like on a day-to-day basis. I lean toward the person who says "Hey, did you bring enough for everybody? If not, throw it away." If they can't find humor in working with middle school kids, then they don't belong.

Given all that is involved in being a principal and all that is going on at Sawyer Middle School, what brings you joy?

The students, actually! When I walk into a classroom and a student who has been struggling all of a sudden gets it. You see that, and you see that they got it, it is the best feeling ever. Another thing is when our students leave us they go to the high school across the street. They come back the first week of high school and tell us all about high school and say "you helped us." Or when we get those graduation cards, we know our job was complete. That brings me the joy. That is why we keep doing what we are doing. Because you know you are helping the future.

Questions to Consider

1. What do you hear as key themes in the expectations that Dr. Friel has for teachers and students?
2. What were you thinking you would say in response to Dr. Friel's teacher interview question about a student eating ice cream?
3. In what ways would you expect to see joy in Sawyer Middle School?

Learning Outcomes

After reading this chapter, you should be able to

1. Explain the organizational relationship between teachers and the school principal.
2. Understand who has the final say about what happens in schools.
3. Describe the important functions of school districts and state government as they affect teachers.
4. Recognize how the federal government influences what teachers do.
5. Understand the key issues about the way that schools are organized, and how the role of the school district, and state and federal government, affect the work of teachers and students.

INTRODUCTION

Becoming a successful teacher entails understanding teaching, standards, students, and parents. Becoming successful also requires beginning teachers to understand how schools are staffed and organized, and to be clear about the principal's expectations for students and teachers.

You may not have ever thought about schools being organizations, but they are. Just like businesses, schools are comprised of employees that produce a product or service. To be successful all organizations must structure the work and arrange employees so that their product or service can be produced efficiently and effectively. However, a unique characteristic of schools as organizations is that all of the "workers" are not paid a salary. Teachers, principals, custodians, cafeteria works, and other adults receive pay checks. Students are workers too, but their "pay" is in a different form. Rather than receiving money, students are rewarded in other ways, including the joy of learning, the satisfaction of participation, feedback on assignments, grades, and ultimately earning a diploma.

Another special characteristic of schools as organizations is that the largest component of the labor force is composed of professionals: teachers. Professionals have higher levels of education and expect to have more autonomy in organizing and doing their work than would be acceptable for other types of workers. Professionals also expect to have strong input into how the whole school is organized and which tasks they will do. Since they are staffed by professionals, schools are unique organizations in many ways. The organizational structures, the degree of employee involvement in decision making, and the way the work is done, as well as how the money is spent, are done differently than would be true of a manufacturing business or a bank.

In this chapter, learning about schools as organizations is the topic. One way of understanding schools as organizations is learning about their structure. The differences in authority of teachers, principals, teacher leaders, and other personnel can be described and charted. Schools should not be thought of as isolated and autonomous. Instead schools are clustered into school districts. In addition, schools are accountable to their state and the federal government. Each of these ways of understanding schools is presented in this chapter. The final major section of this chapter will introduce a number of issues and implications of viewing schools as the workplace for students and teachers.

HOW ARE SCHOOLS STAFFED AND ORGANIZED?

We asked this follow-up question of Dr. Kim Friel: How is your school organized? For example, do you have an assistant principal (AP) and department chairs (DCs)?

> I have all of them. There is one assistant principal (AP), one dean, and three counselors. The AP is in charge of curriculum, testing, special education, and awards. The dean is responsible for the mentoring program, attendance, the discipline program, and whatever positive things we can give her, so that she is just not always dealing with the bad kids.
>
> In addition, I have department chairs (DCs) and team leaders (TLs). The departments are organized by subject area. The DCs are responsible for communication with the nine other subject teachers such as English, mathematics, science, and social studies. Team leaders are responsible for the teams within each grade level. Each team has an English, math, science, and social studies teacher. In addition, they are assigned a PE teacher, an art teacher, and a special education teacher. Each team has a cohort of 150 students that they are with all day.

When thinking about schools as organizations, the first place to start is with identifying the different roles of the adults including teachers, principals, secretaries, and department chairs. There are structural concepts that are important for you to understand, including areas of responsibility, line and staff relationships, and chain of command. In its purest form, the structural view of schools does not deal with workers' feelings and perceptions. Instead, the focus is entirely on the work at hand, how tasks are organized, who does what, and who is responsible.

Roles of the Adult Workers in Schools

Role differentiation is the primary way to understand the organizational structure of schools. All of the adults do not do the same things. Instead roles are defined in relation to the accomplishment of organizational tasks. The two most obvious roles for the adults in schools are administrators and teachers. However, there are a number of other important roles to know about including resource teacher, curriculum specialist, counselor, secretary, cafeteria worker, and custodian. There are a number of additional roles outside of the school that directly impact what teachers do, for example school psychologist and coordinators of special programs such as those for English-language learners (ELLs) and school–community liaison. School bus drivers and the human resources (HR) personnel are important too.

Deeper Look 8.1
Read more about the impact of principal leadership and teachers.

Principal

The administrator with final authority over everything that goes on in a school is the principal. In most schools principals have major say in who is hired. They supervise all teachers and the other school-based personnel. The principal is the person who is charged with the responsibility for evaluating all teachers, especially beginning teachers. Earlier in their careers nearly all principals were teachers. Therefore it is assumed that principals are experts in curriculum and instruction, as well as knowing about all of the other aspects of running a school organization. In addition, principals are in charge of discipline, enforcing rules of student behavior, and making sure that all of the employees and students obey all laws, statutes, policies, rules, and regulations. Principals also work with parents, community groups, and the various committees that are established for involving teachers, students, parents, and others in doing the work of the school.

Assistant or Vice Principals and Deans

As the brief summary of the principal's role suggests, the job expectations cover more areas and tasks than one person can do. The organizational structure solution to this problem has been to create another administrator role: assistant or vice principal. Depending on the size of the school there may be one, two, or no assistant/vice principals. For example, elementary schools will typically need to have more than 600 students before they will have an assistant principal. As high schools increase in size from under 1,000 to 2,000 or 3,000 students, the number of vice principals and other administrators such as deans will increase from one to three or more. Typically, the individuals in these roles share in accomplishing the tasks that are formally the responsibility of the principal. Assistant/vice principals and deans may evaluate teachers, although normally not probationary teachers. Assistant/vice principals and deans may have full responsibility for certain tasks, such as discipline or managing the school's budgets. They also will assume authority for the school during times when the principal is out of the building.

Teachers

The other obvious role in the organizational structure of schools is that of teachers. Here too, there is differentiation within the role. One form of differentiation is by the level of schooling where the teacher works. Elementary and secondary teachers are viewed as specialists within that level of schooling. There are other ways that the teacher role is differentiated. For example, elementary teachers are classified as **primary** (grades K/1–3) or **intermediate** (grades 4–5/6), while **secondary** teachers are either junior high (grades 6–8), middle school (grades 6–8/9), or senior high school (grades 9–12). Teachers also may specialize in other ways:

On a regular basis school staffs meet to review data about student progress and to refine Action Steps in the School Improvement Plan.

- Subject(s) Taught: Specializing in terms of subject(s) taught is the regular pattern in secondary schools. For example, teachers are specialists in teaching mathematics, English, social studies, science, physical education, music, or technical areas. Increasingly there is specialization in elementary schools; for example, some teachers become literacy specialists and work across grade levels to teach the language arts.
- Types of Students Taught: Teacher roles may be specialized according to the needs of particular students, such as resource teachers (for students with special needs), bilingual or ELL teachers for students whose first language is not English, and Title I teachers who teach students who are from low-income families and may be at risk of falling behind.
- In most schools teachers will have additional responsibilities. For example, in most secondary schools teachers will be expected to supervise an **extra-curricular** activity such as yearbook, pep squad, theater, or a music program. Elementary school teachers may be expected to offer tutorials before or after school, do "bus duty" during the morning arrival and afternoon departure of students, or supervise the lunchroom.

Department Chairs and Teacher Leaders

This was another follow-up question we had for Dr. Friel: In addition to the assistant principal, dean, department chairs, and team leaders, are there teacher leaders in your school?

> Yes. I have teacher leaders who are responsible for our Restructuring Plan. Since we have not made satisfactory growth in test scores for five years, our school

needs to be restructured. We have 11 teachers serving as a committee to help us write our Restructuring Plan.

As schools have grown in size and as more has been expected, another important teacher role has developed: department chair and team/grade-level leader. The widespread staffing pattern in secondary schools is to have teachers organized into departments by subject matter. One of the teachers will serve as department chair. At a minimum this way of structuring work facilitates communication between teachers within the subject area. Typically the department chairs will meet regularly with the principal and serve as a communication channel by passing on to teachers information that is received from the principal. In most schools department chairs are teachers, not administrators. In other words, they have no role in the evaluation of teachers; their primary tasks are to facilitate communication and coordination of teacher work within the particular subject area. Department chairs also are important sources of ideas and assistance for new teachers. A similar coordination and communication role will be assumed by grade-level teacher leaders in elementary schools.

Other School-Based Staff

It takes more than teachers and administrators to run a school. In addition to making sure all the necessary forms are completed, office managers and secretaries greet students, staff, parents, and district office visitors. Custodians keep the campus clean and the plumbing/heating/cooling working. Cafeteria workers not only prepare meals; they also see students daily. Another position increasingly found on school staffs is for individuals who provide security. They may be district employees or representatives of the local police force.

Organization Charts

This was another question for Dr. Friel: Is there an organization chart for Sawyer Middle School?

> Yes. Actually, we have two! I have the official one the district wants with me as the principal, the AP, you know, da da da. Then we have the flowchart of all the different leaders we just talked about. And for that one, I am not at the top of that chart; I am in the mix of the flowchart.

An **organization chart** is a graphic that depicts the formal relationships between different roles and positions in a particular organization. An organizational structure for a typical school is presented in Figure 8.1. A number of the important characteristics of organizational structure are represented in this type of chart. One that is very important for beginning teachers to understand is the difference between line and staff relationships. **Line relationships** are those where one position has direct supervisory authority over another. In the organizational structure of schools, the principal is in a line relationship with all teachers, the assistant/vice principals, and all other school-based personnel. **Staff relationships** are those where one position does not have direct authority over another but there is an expectation that the two positions will communicate, coordinate, and work together. For example, in secondary schools there will be a staff relationship between the various department chairs, and in all schools assistant/vice principals are in a staff relationship with teachers. Teachers are in staff relationships with other teachers.

School secretaries and other noninstruction staff are important to teacher and student success.

Audio Link 8.1
Listen to a clip about school-based staff.

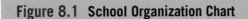

Figure 8.1 School Organization Chart

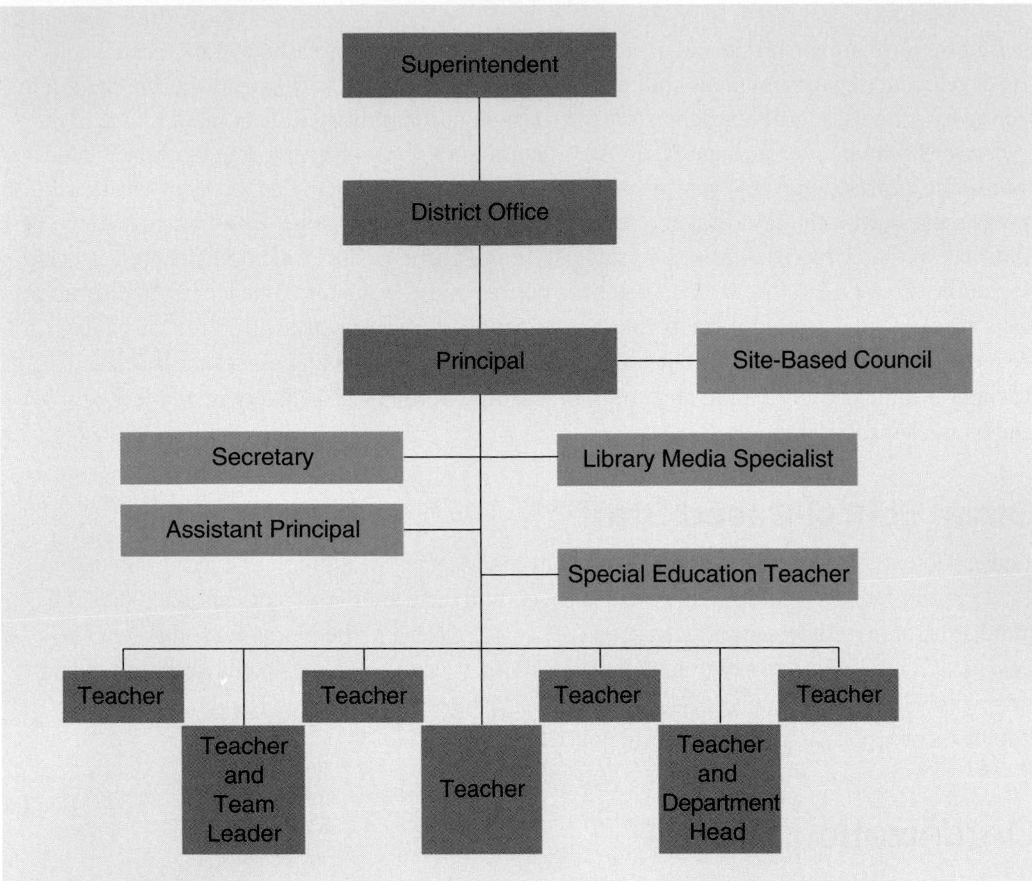

Source: Adapted from Johnson, J. A., Musial, D., Hall, G. E., Gollnick, D. M., & Dupuis, V. (2005). *Introduction to the foundations of American education* (13th ed.). Boston, MA: Allyn and Bacon.

Communication Is Important

One of the reasons schools are structured as they are is to facilitate communication. There is a continual risk that teachers will become isolated within their classrooms, grade levels, or departments and not be aware of schoolwide needs and district initiatives. The reverse risk also is very real: one teacher, a team, or a department may be doing something very wonderful but without communication the rest of the organization does not learn about it. Two types of communication are built into the structure of the school organization chart, vertical and horizontal. **Vertical communication** is communication that moves down, and up, the organization chart. This is where the phrase "the lines of communication" comes from. An important responsibility of people in each role is to initiate and facilitate communication up and down the lines of authority. In business and military organizations a frequently used phrase to refer to the up/down line relationships in an organization chart is **chain of command.** As a teacher you will need to follow this chain one level at a time when you have a question, a concern, or a suggestion.

In most organizations, including schools, vertical communication is not sufficient, so there also needs to be communication *across* the various levels in the organization chart—in other words **horizontal communication.** One example of horizontal communication is when a veteran fourth-grade teacher tells a first-year fourth-grade teacher about an upcoming professional development workshop. Another example would be when a department chair tells another about an interesting idea that the principal proposed in an informal conversation. In schools that are more successful there will be more vertical *and* horizontal communication.

"Since we initiated regular staff development sessions, we've turned the school around 360 degrees."

Organizing for Horizontal Communication

In her interview, Dr. Friel pointed out that she had two organization charts. *One that is the official one the district wants.* This chart would be similar to Figure 8.1. *Then we have the flowchart of all the different leaders we just talked about.* This chart is presented as Figure 8.2. How is this chart different than the official one? What does this type of flowchart suggest about coordination and communication?

Variations in the Teachers' Role

We also asked Dr. Friel: Do you have expectations for teachers that go beyond their classroom?

> Oh, yes. Ninety percent of our staff have the same shared belief that we will do whatever it takes to make the kids successful—whether it is stay after school, work with them at lunch time, attend trainings, or whatever it is we can do to make these kids successful. One of the ways of having this value shared is through the distributed leadership of the DCs, the team leaders, and many teacher leaders. Another way is by having some teachers become expert with one program and then have them teach the others.

Up to this point the description of the organizational structure of schools has been about the typical way schools are staffed and how the different roles relate to each other. There are many interesting variations to this typical pattern, some of which are presented next.

Variations in Teaching Responsibilities

There are many variations in the assignments of teachers. For example, secondary school teachers will be expected to teach more than one grade level and perhaps more than one subject. A few of the other variations are introduced below:

Departmentalization

One variation that is increasingly being tried in the intermediate grades in elementary schools is departmentalization. Instead of each teacher being responsible for one group of 25 to 35 students for all subjects, teachers will specialize by teaching one subject to all students. For example, one teacher teaches mathematics, while another teaches social studies, and another specializes in language arts. A variation on this staffing model is to have one teacher lead in the preparation of the instruction for a subject and each teacher then uses the same lesson plan and materials to teach his or her class.

Looping

Deeper Look 8.2
Read more about looping in education.

An interesting staffing variation used in some elementary, junior high, and middle schools is **looping.** In looping, teachers follow their students to the next grade. For example, the teacher of a first-grade class one year moves to teaching second grade the next year and keeps the same students. An obvious advantage is that the teacher knows the students and the students know the teacher, which means less time lost to diagnostic assessments at the beginning of the year. Of course looping also requires teachers to develop new preparations for use in the second year.

Figure 8.2 Flowchart for Sawyer Middle School Designed to Distribute Leadership and Increase Communication

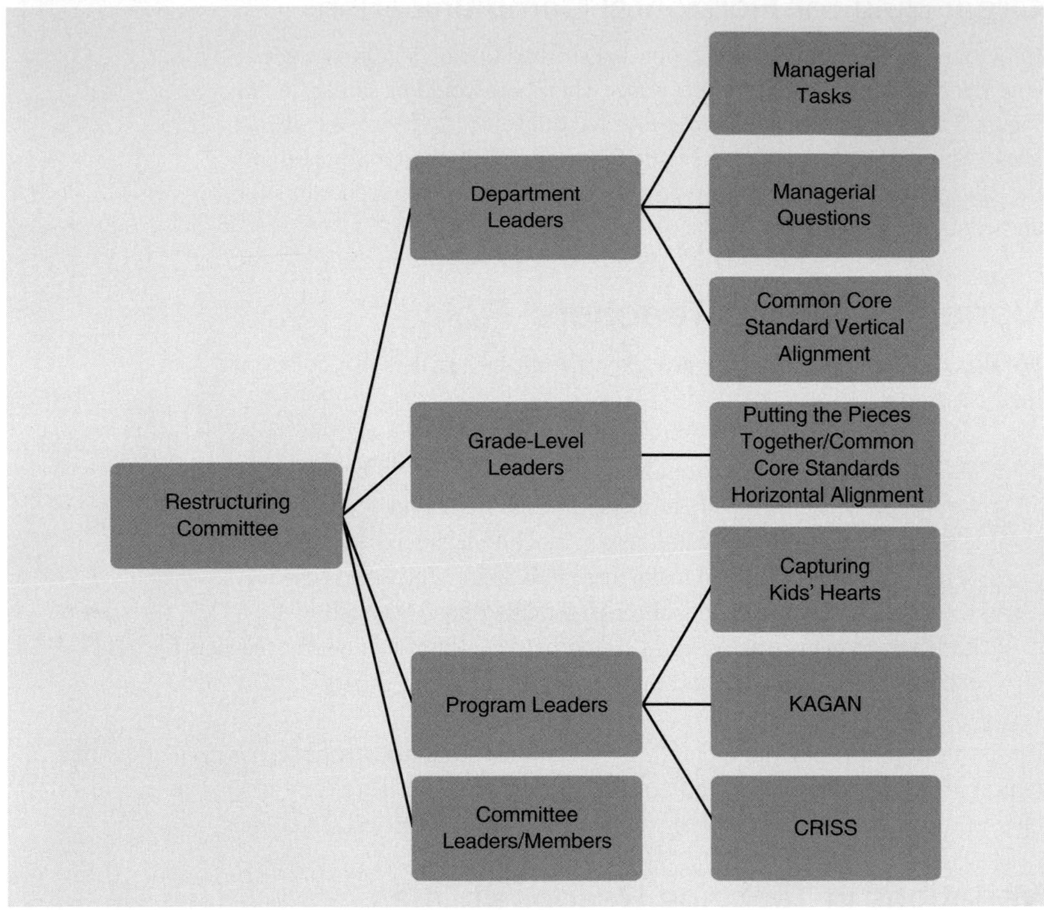

Team Teaching

Team teaching is a staffing plan that has two or more teachers working together to plan and teach a common group of students. Team teaching is used in many configurations in both elementary and secondary schools. For example, Dr. Friel described how teachers in Sawyer Middle School are members of a department and also members of a grade-level interdisciplinary team. Each team is assigned a large block of students, and they are responsible for all of the instruction and for most of the day. This configuration is frequently applied in elementary schools.

Another frequently found variation is to have teachers team part of the day and for the remainder of the day they teache their "own" students. The organizational support of teachers to team will vary too. In some schools teams have to do their planning before and after school. In other schools there will be a scheduled team planning period. Another variation is to have an "early release," which means that on certain days students leave school early in order to provide time for teacher teams to plan.

On-Site Staff Developer

Some school districts will have another important role that can be especially important for beginning teachers. This role is that of an **on-site staff developer.** They are master teachers who serve as mentor, model teacher, peer coach, and teacher trainer within a school. Often they specialize in supporting the teaching of a particular subject such as literacy or mathematics. They will teach another teacher's students in order to model an instructional strategy, but they will not have a class assigned to them full time. They do not have a teacher evaluation role. Instead their primary responsibility is to serve all teachers by helping them increase their knowledge and skill in ways that will lead to increases in student learning.

Professional Learning Communities

A new approach to organizing the adults in a school is through what are called **Professional Learning Communities (PLCs).** There are two general approaches to PLCs: (1) A scheduled time is set each week for teachers to meet as PLCs, and (2) a schoolwide effort is focused on developing a collaborative culture around student *and* adult learning. In the last 15 years there has been extensive study of PLCs, their characteristics, and what it takes to develop and sustain such an ideal organizational culture. One of the researchers, Dr. Shirley Hord (2004), has identified five themes or dimensions of PLCs (see Table 8.1).

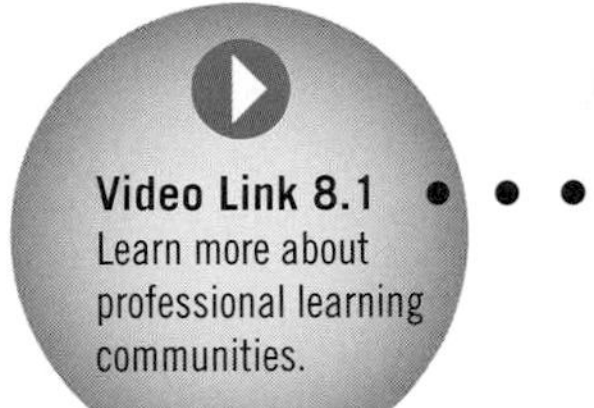

Video Link 8.1
Learn more about professional learning communities.

As important as each of these themes is individually, additional importance comes from the ways that they become intertwined in a live PLC. For example, without supportive leadership it is very difficult for teachers to be collegial and collaborative. Collective learning of the adults in the organization is only possible when there is shared practice. Developing and sustaining a PLC is hard work. All of the adults and students in the school must participate. In her study of school organizational culture in Belgium, Dr. Katrine Staessens (1993) identified a culture that is very similar to the PLC, which she named "the school as a professional organization." Dr. Staessens also described the importance of the principal in this type of school:

> In this type of school, the teachers characterize the principal as an architect. He [sic] is a well-read person, is well-informed about the recent developments in the different domains, and often talks about these with his staff. . . . The norm is created whereby the school is a place where teachers can learn something, and can become better teachers by bringing up professional concerns. To be isolated in one's classroom is not accepted. The proposition that everything can always be improved appears to be a fundamental belief of this principal. (p. 119)

Table 8.1 Themes in Professional Learning Communities

Supportive and shared leadership requires the collegial and facilitative participation of the principal who shares leadership—and thus, power and authority—by inviting staff input and action in decision making.
Shared values and vision include an unwavering commitment to student learning that is consistently articulated and referenced in the staff's work.
Collective learning and application of learning requires that school staff at all levels are engaged in a process that collectively seeks new knowledge among staff and application of the learning to solutions that address students' needs.
Supportive conditions include physical conditions and human capacities that encourage and sustain a collegial atmosphere and collective learning.
Shared practice involves the review of a teacher's behavior by colleagues and includes feedback and assistance activity to support individual and community improvement.

Source: Hord, S. M. (2004). *Learning together, leading together: Changing schools through professional learning communities* (p. 7). New York, NY: Teachers College Press.

Organizing Students for Learning

Organizing the adults in the school seems relatively easy in comparison to organizing the students. A variety of organizational structures, methods, and groupings have been tried. (For many of these structures there are continuing debates about their effectiveness. For example, study the Challenging Assumptions box about student grouping.) Curiously, some of the structures for organizing students seem to have become fixed in concrete.

Think about it: What is the first step in organizing school students for doing their work? What characteristic of students is determined first in deciding their placement? This characteristic of students is not used in any other type of organization as the basis for organizing the workers. It is their age! Students cannot begin schooling until they have passed a certain birthday. Students cannot leave school until they have reached a particular birthday. At its simplest, grade levels are groupings of students by their age.

There are a number of additional ways that should be considered when organizing students to do their work.

Self-Contained Classroom

In most settings **self-contained classroom** means that one teacher stays in a classroom and is assigned responsibility for teaching one set of students all subjects. The self-contained classroom continues to be the dominant structure for U.S. elementary schools. However, an interesting variation on the meaning of self-contained classroom was tested recently in some high schools in New York City. In this variation, the students stay in one classroom and the teachers change rooms. This variation seems to be reducing the isolation that so many students experience in high schools, especially those with thousands of students.

Chairs, tables, storage, and the walls of a classroom can be used to group students in a variety of ways to facilitate group work.

Organizing Students for Work

Continuing the use of the metaphor of students as workers leads to examination of how they can be organized for learning. Table 8.2 presents a brief summary of the range of ways that students can be grouped. At different times in your career as a student in schools you will have experienced each one of these, and you probably prefer some ways over others. Each of these ways brings with it important consequences for the teacher, as well as for student learning. For example, presenting a lecture to the whole class provides the teacher with a way to "cover" the content, but brings with it very limited opportunity to check for individual student understanding.

As another example, think about the different ways of organizing small groups. The teacher role needs to change dramatically from being a dispenser of information (or giving directions), to monitor and facilitator of group work. Each time a lesson is planned, the teacher has to decide how the student workers will be organized. Table 8.2 will be of help to you as you begin thinking about how you want to organize the "workers" in your classroom.

WHAT IS THE RELATIONSHIP OF SCHOOLS TO SCHOOL DISTRICTS AND THE STATE?

Dr. Friel shares some answers to questions about the relationship of schools to their local district and the state.

You are in one of the largest school districts in the country; to whom do you report?

> I report to an Academic Manager, who reports to an Area Superintendent, who reports to the Superintendent. It is not so much the people that are above the principal, you know they are your boss. It is all the support people who work for those people who think they are the principal's boss.

Table 8.2 Ways of Organizing Students to Do Their Work

Structure	Description	Advantages	Teacher Challenge
Whole class	All students are taught as a single, intact group	The lesson is presented at the same time to all students	Difficult to address individual differences in understanding
Small groups	Typically three to five students per group	More opportunity for each student to participate	Some students may do most of the work; difficult to determine each student's effort
Dyads/pairs	Two students work together	Each student has opportunity to participate	Managing and monitoring all dyads at the same time
Individuals	Each students does own work without dialogue with others	Students can learn at their own rate	Managing and monitoring each student closely
Homogeneous	Grouping like students together	Students can progress at the same rate	Risk of labeling and neglecting "fast" and "slow" groups
Heterogeneous	Groups composed of mixed levels	Helps all students learn	"Slow" students may be neglected
Fixed groupings	Keeping the same students together over extended time	Students and teachers know what to expect	No adjustment for different students' rates of progress
Flexible groups	Routinely changing group membership	Provides fresh opportunities	Monitoring to know when to regroup
Cooperative groups	An organized process where each group member has a prescribed role, e.g., facilitator or note taker	Students learn roles for facilitating group work; some research suggests students learn more	Students have to be trained in doing roles

Challenging Assumptions

Should gifted students be grouped together?

Student Grouping: Which Is Best, Tracking or Mixed Ability?

Teachers, parents, school leaders, and policymakers have long debated which is best, homogeneous or heterogeneous grouping of students. The debate can focus on what a teacher should do in grouping students for a day's lessons, or how students should be grouped for an entire school year. When students are grouped according to ability for a semester or longer it is called **tracking.**

What is your current position about this important question? Do you believe that students will make greater progress if they are placed with like students so that all can move at the same pace? Or do you believe that students can learn from each other and that it is not fair to label some as being in the "slow" group?

Findings From Research

Although there have been literally hundreds of studies there still are not definitive answers, but a set of subquestions has become clear: (a) In which grouping pattern do students learn more? (b) What difference do grouping patterns make in students' attitudes about learning and self-perceptions? and (c) What difference do teachers make in determining the effects of grouping arrangements?

Well over two decades ago, Oakes (1985) and Slavin (1987) argued for all students being placed in heterogeneous classes. A main theme in their position is that a democratic ideal is not to create different categories of people, and there needs to be equal opportunity for all students. They also reported that there was no clear pattern of gains in student learning with homogeneous grouping.

The grouping question is so important that it is a continuing topic of inquiry in other countries and is a component of the TIMSS research as well. For example, in a study of grouping of fifth- and eighth-grade students in Canada, Shields (2002) reported that the academically talented self-contained classes had higher student achievement. However, there was "considerable overlap (from 46% to 88%) in the scores of the two groups." In other words, students in both the gifted and heterogeneous classes were achieving. (An important contextual factor to keep in mind is that Canada has offered self-contained programs for elementary school academically able students since 1934.)

Although the findings about perceptions and attitudes were more complicated, Shields concluded:

> These data do not suggest that the needs of all students would be better served if they had all been grouped in a single heterogeneous class; rather, in this study, homogeneous grouping for academically talented and gifted students was associated with positive student perceptions of themselves as learners and of their total school experience. Likewise, students placed in a heterogeneous classroom demonstrated similarly positive attitudes and perceptions. (p. 118)

Across the many studies of student grouping a key factor that is emerging as probably the most significant is that of the teacher's attitudes and teaching approach. When the teacher sets high expectations for learning and presents all students with the same curriculum, students learn in either grouping arrangement. Student attitudes and perceptions can be positive in either grouping arrangement, again dependent on the teacher's attitudes and expectations. Still, much of the research indicates that placing more academically able students in a homogeneous group advances their level of achievement while not diminishing other students having success in heterogeneous groups.

Sources:

Oakes, J. (1985). *Keeping track: How schools structure inequality.* New Haven, CT: Yale University Press.

Shields, C. M. (2002, Spring). A comparison study of student attitudes and perceptions in homogeneous and heterogeneous classrooms. *Roeper Review, 24*(3), 115–120.

Slavin, R. E. (1987). Ability grouping and student achievement in elementary schools: A best-evidence synthesis. *Review of Educational Research, 57,* 347–370.

This would seem to be a failure of line and staff relationships.

> Very much so.

How do you relate to the school district, and the state and the federal levels?

> For principals, right now, sometimes it is a juggled mess. For example, you get a directive from the district, then something comes from the state, and then something comes from the federal government. And then you wonder about which one to do. The federal government will say, "Oh that is just how we wrote it. The states are to interpret it." But the federal level holds the money back. Then the district has to interpret what comes down from the state.

As you hear in Dr. Friel's descriptions, schools are not isolated and autonomous organizations. Instead schools are clustered to form school districts, also called **local education agencies (LEAs)**; above them is the **state education agency (SEA)**; and above the state(s) is the federal government. The primary factor for determining an LEA is geography. School districts typically encompass all of the public schools within a certain area such as a town or city. In a few states, such as Nevada and Florida, the geographic area of the school districts is the same as for the counties.

All of the schools and school districts within each state are accountable to the state. At the same time, as Dr. Friel observed, the SEA is the interpreter and transmitter of the directives from the federal government.

Organization of School Districts

Mapping the geographic area covered by a school district is one way of understanding its size. Another is the levels of schooling that are covered. For example, most school districts encompass all public elementary and secondary schools within a certain geographic area. However, in some states, such as Arizona, some school districts are responsible for elementary schools only. A separate school district will be responsible for the secondary schools. Another way to understand the size of a school district is to find out the number of schools within the school district. Very small districts may have as few as one or two schools. The largest school districts will have 200 or more schools.

School District Organization

An organization chart for a typical school district is presented in Figure 8.3. One of the first impressions from studying this chart should be the fact that there are many roles and functions that are not directly related to teaching and learning. As is true for organizations in business and industry, a number of support functions must be addressed and staffed. A **human resources (HR)** department is needed to hire employees, to see that they are paid, and to see that they have health and retirement programs (benefits). Organizations need specialists to manage and audit the budgets. (As you will learn in Chapter 9, school districts' budgets are very large. Even small districts will have budgets in the tens of millions of dollars.) Other typical school district departments include maintenance/facilities and grounds, a transportation department to operate the buses, and legal counsel.

There are a number of functions that are unique to schooling such as the various special services for students and their families. Another unique district department will be for federal programs. School districts receive federal funds through grants and to support different functions. There also are many required reporting tasks. Of course, the instructional support function must be staffed as well. A function that has grown significantly in importance is the research and evaluation office. With

Figure 8.3 School District Organization Chart

Board of Education
Community
Attorney
Superintendent
Associate Superintendent

Assistant Superintendent for Elementary Schools
Assistant Superintendent for Secondary Schools
Business Services
Facilities and Transportation
Personnel Services
Special Services

Auditor
Budgeting
Accounting
Purchasing
Food Services

Maintenance and Operations
Transportation
Architectural Planning
Property/ Energy

Payroll
Retirement
Recruitment/ Employment
Staff Development
Negotiations

Health Services
Psychological Services
Guidance
Attendance
Student Records
Adult and Community Education
Vocational Education

Principals
Principals

Assistant Principals
Teachers
Librarians
Counselors

Nonteaching Personnel

Assistant Principals
Teachers
Librarians
Counselors

Nonteaching Personnel

Students
Students

Source: Adapted from Parkay, F. W., & Stanford, B. H. (2004). *Becoming a researcher* (6e). Boston; Allyn & Bacon.

the heavy focus on testing, experts are needed to organize test administration and for analyzing test data. As never before, teachers, administrators, parents, policymakers, and the public are demanding quick turnaround and understandable reporting of data about student achievement.

School District Superintendent

Deeper Look 8.3
Read about women superintendents.

The chief executive officer (CEO) of the school district is the **superintendent.** This person has the overwhelming responsibility of leading the entire school district. As is reflected in the organization chart (Figure 8.3), all of the district office and school personnel are in a line relationship with the superintendent. As President Harry Truman was known to say, "The buck stops here." In the end the superintendent is accountable for everything that happens, should happen, and should not happen within the school district. In a large school district, with many layers to the organization chart, holding the superintendent responsible for everything is very unrealistic; however, in the structural view of organizations that is the reality.

Most superintendents are appointed and will have a contract for one to three, and in some cases four or five, years. There are some exceptions, such as occurs in Florida, Indiana, and a few other states where some superintendents are elected through a community-wide vote. One of the consequences of their being elected is that the individual may not have any background in education as either a teacher or administrator. In some cities the superintendent is appointed by the mayor.

Superintendents do not have tenure in the position and may be removed at any time. One unfortunate consequence of this fact is that there is a large turnover in the superintendency each year. Some years a state will have one third or more of the school district superintendents change. In urban school districts the average longevity of superintendents is under three years. One important consequence of this rapid turnover is that with the arrival of each new superintendent the strategic directions and priorities within the school district change. This leads to another consequence: District and school administrators, as well as teachers and families, are unable to develop and sustain initiatives and directions across the three to five to eight years it takes to make meaningful changes. This places significantly heavier responsibility on principals and teachers to maintain a focus on the most essential long-term efforts that will benefit students the most.

District Office–Based School Support Personnel

In most school districts there will be a number of education professionals whose role is to support instruction across all schools and classrooms. Curriculum specialists in literacy, mathematics, science, and ELL provide districtwide leadership in their specialty area. They also develop professional development sessions. Many not only will visit schools but are willing to model instructional strategies and coach teachers. School district support staff increasingly include data analysis specialists who assist school leaders and teachers in making sense of test scores and help in drawing connections between standards and individual student performance. Experts in special education are another important district office resource. You will work with them when you have a student with an IEP, or refer a student for testing. The testing will be done by a licensed school psychologist, who also is based in the district office.

The superintendent must communicate well with teachers, the school board, the public, and the media.

School Boards

The school district governing body is the **school board** or **board of trustees.** School boards typically consist of five to seven members. (The reasoning behind having an odd number of members is to reduce the chance of having tie votes by the board.) In most communities school board members are elected by voters in a designated geographic part of the community or by the community at large. In some cities, such as Chicago, Illinois, and Hartford, Connecticut, the mayor or the city council will appoint some or all of the school board members.

In 1988, Downey identified two major obligations for school boards, which hold true today:

1. To process the values, needs, and demands of society and, in so doing, to determine which of these are to be accepted as the official guidelines for the educational system
2. To set the guidelines for action which are, in effect, the directions or general rules for the operation of the school system (Downey, 1988, p. 18)

This important role of school boards, and other governing bodies, is to establish policy.

I had told my district office supervisor about several teachers that were weak. One in particular (whom we will call Ms. Jones) was a problem that affected the whole school. I had not told my supervisor the names of any of these less effective teachers. However, one day the supervisor was visiting the school and requested that we visit Ms. Jones's classroom.

So we walked down there. Sure enough, in true weak teacher form, she turned it on for the thirty minutes we were in the classroom. Even the kids were looking around indicating "Wow, this was an unusual class!" My supervisor and I then decided to visit some other classrooms so that it would not look like we were picking on Ms. Jones.

We went across the hall to an English teacher's classroom where the students were doing a hands-on assignment. The supervisor went to one side of the classroom and I went to the other side. We were looking at student work and asking the students about what they were doing, and why.

All of a sudden I look up, and my supervisor is shaking; trying to hold back a laugh. I am watching a conversation take place between her and a student. Later, the supervisor gives the signal to meet out in the hallway.

The supervisor couldn't wait to tell me what happened. "As we walked in, the student said 'Who are you?'" She answered that she was Ms. White, and asked "Who are you?" The student introduced himself and said "We know who she is (pointing to me). That's our principal and we have to behave when she is here. Do I have to behave when you are here?"

Ms. White replied, "I am her boss, so yes." And he goes "OK. I have a question for you." "What is it?" "I saw you across the hallway in Ms. Jones's classroom. What ya think of her?" "Ahm, I thought she was OK. What did you think?"

"I think she is just *delightful* (while rolling his eyes and shaking his head)." Ms. White replies "I catch a hint of sarcasm there." The student replies, "It is more than a hint, it is a dump truck full of sarcasm."

It takes special principals and teachers to see the humor in middle school students. As this anecdote illustrates, they see more than many adults expect. The teacher (Ms. Jones) thought she had pulled one over on the kids and me, yet everyone on campus including the kids knew she was not invested in improving students' learning.

Kim Friel, Principal
Sawyer Middle School
Las Vegas, Nevada

School Boards as Policy Bodies

Policies are the official stated overarching parameters for what can, and cannot, be done within an organization. Policies are guidelines that can be **prescriptive** by setting limits and specifying the procedures that are to be used, or they can be **empowering** by identifying the target or vision and leaving open the means for achieving the desired end.

For example, a school board could set in policy that the school district should achieve a 10-point increase in the percentage of high school graduates that go on to some type of postsecondary education. This would be an empowering policy, as district administrators and teachers would be expected to devise the steps to be taken to achieve the goal. If the school board established a prescriptive policy they would specify the approach to be used, such as "no-pass-no-play," or that all eighth-grade students must take algebra I. With prescriptive policies administrators and teachers have little or no say in the strategies to be used and instead are charged with implementing the policy mandate.

School boards set polices for the district as long as these are not inconsistent with state and federal policies. For example, a school board could require a longer school year, but they couldn't set a minimum number of days that is less than what is required by the state.

School Board Responsibilities

One of the most important school board responsibilities is hiring the superintendent. Another is approving the employment of all district personnel, including teachers. Beginning teachers will turn in their signed employment contract to the district office of human resources, but the contract is not official until it has been approved by the school board. School boards are responsible for oversight of all administrative and educational matters, including review and approval of the district budget, large purchase orders, student band trip travel support, and review of test scores. Boards also evaluate the performance of the superintendent. In the ideal setting the board will turn to the superintendent, as the chief executive officer, and trust him or her to lead the day-to-day operations of the district.

Audio Link 8.2
Hear how school boards impact policy.

Unfortunately, in too many instances school board members are not satisfied with limiting their role to establishing policy and oversight of district operations. Many board members seem to be most interested in pushing a pet agenda, such as a particular curriculum approach or "trying to get" a particular district employee. Many boards also have a tendency to become overly involved in the day-to-day operations of the district, that is, **micromanaging.** This is a significant contributing factor to the high rate of superintendent turnover.

Organization of Education at the State Level

In the distant past the governance of schools was primarily a matter of **local control.** School boards set most policies and obtained financial support locally. In the last 60 years much of the control has shifted to the states. This shift has come about in part because the funding of public schools has become a very large part of state budgets. Also, state policymakers have a right to take an active interest in education. In fact, all state constitutions have articles related to the responsibility of the state to assure that all citizens have access to education. Some examples follow.

> Arkansas:
>
> Intelligence and virtue being the safeguards of liberty and the bulwark of a free and good government, the State shall ever maintain a general, suitable and efficient system of free public schools and shall adopt all suitable means to secure to the people the advantages and opportunities of education. . . . (Arkansas, State Constitution, Article 14, Education, Sec. 1, Free school system)
>
> California:
>
> The Legislature shall provide for a system of common schools by which a free school shall be kept up and supported in each district at least six months in every year, after the first year in which a school has been established. (California Constitution, Article 9, Education, Section 5)
>
> Vermont:
>
> The right to public education is integral to Vermont's constitutional form of government and its guarantees of political and civil rights. Further, the right to education is fundamental for the success of Vermont's children in a rapidly-changing society and global marketplace as well as for the state's own economic and social

prosperity. To keep Vermont's democracy competitive and thriving, Vermont students must be afforded substantially equal access to a quality basic education. However, one of the strengths of Vermont's education system lies in its rich diversity and the ability for each local school district to adapt its educational program to local needs and desires. Therefore, it is the policy of the state that all Vermont children will be afforded educational opportunities which are substantially equal although educational program may vary from district to district. (Vermont: Added 1997, No. 60, 2, eff. June 26, 1997)

Figure 8.4 Organization Chart for State Government

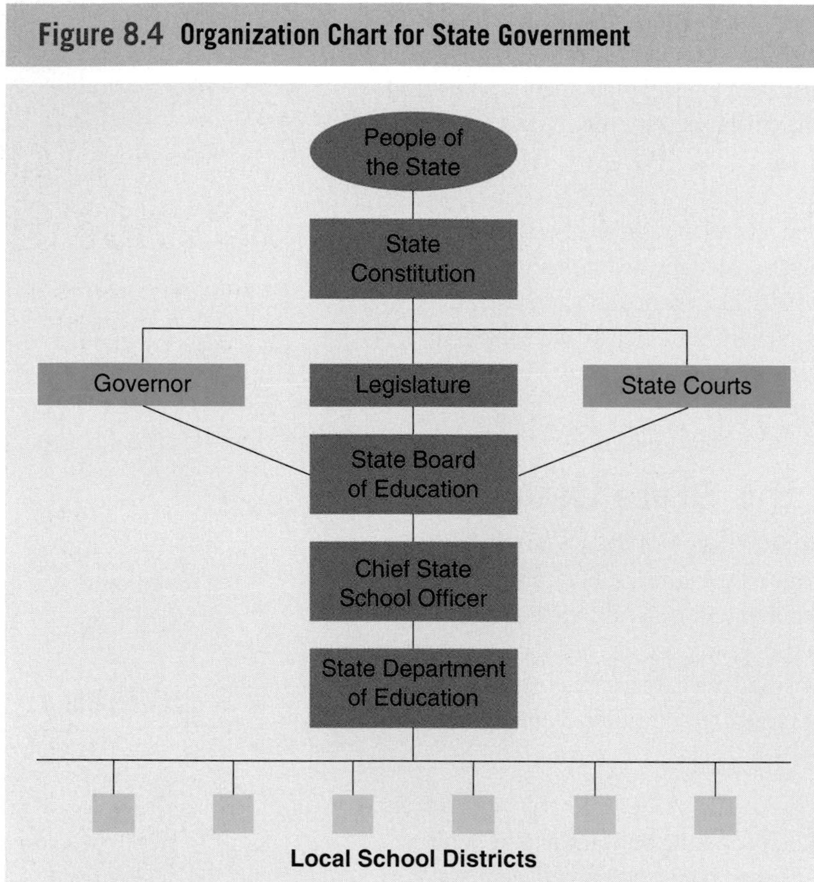

Source: Adapted from Johnson, J. A., Musial, D., Hall, G. E., Gollnick, D. M., & Dupuis, V. (2005). *Introduction to the foundations of American education* (13th ed.). Boston, MA: Allyn & Bacon.

Today, all three branches of state government—legislative, administrative, and judicial—are extremely active when it comes to public education. Figure 8.4 is an organization chart for state government.

Executive: State Governors

Since citizens are concerned about the quality of schools and the costs of education, it is logical that political leaders would be attending to education problems and needs. In the past the phrase *education governor* was applied frequently. Now, with the economic problems across the United States, many governors have cut the support for public education. Recently, in states such as Wisconsin, Ohio, and Florida, the governors have openly attacked teachers and other public employees. This is a new phenomenon in the United States, and unlike how teachers are held in high esteem in some communities and other countries.

Governors are able to establish aspirations and visions for a state's education system. In some states they have a major say over the state budget and in all states can propose changes in state policies that they believe will improve schools. In some states the governor appoints members of the state board of education and/or the state superintendent. In other states the legislature may appoint or will need to approve appointment of the state superintendent and state board members.

Legislative: State Legislatures

The primary policy-making body for education is the state legislature. State legislatures can create new education policies in any area from student discipline, to curriculum, to standards for hiring teachers and administrators. A very significant responsibility of state legislatures is to establish the state budget for education, which necessarily is linked to state sources of funds such as income and sales taxes. Within whatever limits have been set by a state's constitution, the legislature can prescribe what the state board of education and other education agencies can and should do.

Judicial: State Courts

State legislatures have major responsibilities in setting education policy.

As the cost of public education has increased and as concerns about the adequacy of schools has grown, the courts have become more instrumental in shaping the directions of education. In the past the courts were turned to mainly to address contractual issues and to make determinations about the rights of students. In the last 20-plus years the courts have been asked to address issues of funding adequacy and equity. In fact, most of the states have had, or have, lawsuits related to the funding of education.

The precedent-setting case was filed in the 1980s in Kentucky. Using the wording in the Kentucky Constitution, the state supreme court ruled in 1989 that the entire system of public education in Kentucky was "inadequate." Going even further, the court ruled that the entire system and organization of the State Education Agency (SEA) and the Local Education Agencies (LEA) were "unconstitutional." The court then directed the governor and the legislature to develop a new system of education.

The result was the Kentucky Education Reform Act (KERA), which was passed in 1990. KERA identified a number of important reforms including Integrated Primary, School-Based Management Councils, major changes in high schools, and a system of annual standardized testing of students. Since then, many other states including Arkansas, Kansas, Ohio, and New York have had state courts review and rule on the quality and adequacy of the state's education system. However, to date no other state has been as ambitious in its attempts to redress past inadequacies and to implement dramatic changes in practice.

State Boards of Education

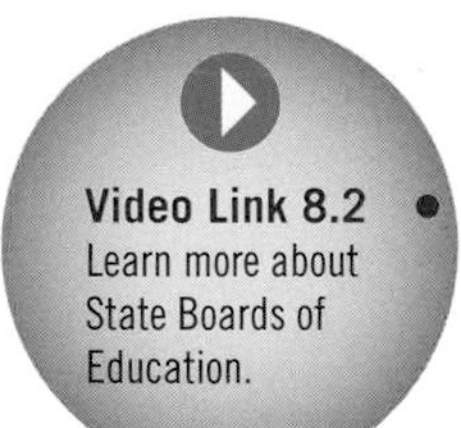
Video Link 8.2
Learn more about State Boards of Education.

State boards of education have become very important bodies. As the legislators and governors have become more engaged with education issues, the state boards of education have been given more authority and charged with greater responsibilities. The state board and the staff of the state education department must ensure that all school districts and schools are performing in compliance with state policies and statutes. Other responsibilities include setting standards for teacher licensure, establishing processes for developing and approving curriculum standards, and organizing test data and other data from schools in order to prepare reports about school and student performance for the legislature, the public, and the federal government. State boards also are the body to review cases of teacher malpractice and the revocation of teacher licenses. Most states board members are either elected or appointed by the governor.

Chief State School Officer

The **chief state school officer**, state superintendent of public instruction, or commissioner of education, is the chief executive officer (CEO) for the state board of education. This person is responsible for supervision of the staff and work of the state education department. He or she also plays a key leadership and advocacy role for education with the legislature, the governor, school districts, and the state at large. In some states "chiefs" are elected at large; in others they are appointed by the state board of education or the governor.

Over the last 60 years the federal government has played an ever-increasing role in setting directions for schools.

The Role of the Federal Government

In the United States, the federal government has a special and in many ways unique role in relation to public education. The first half of Chapter 9 describes how the federal government relates to public education in the states and ways that it is impacting schools. The consequences for teachers are immense.

One activity for you to do before beginning to read Chapter 9 would be to study the U.S. Constitution. Can you find the word *education*? Is it in the preamble, the Constitution itself, or any of the Amendments? Does the word *education* appear in the Declaration of Independence?

WHAT ARE TODAY'S ISSUES IN THE WORKPLACE CALLED SCHOOLS?

In this chapter the workplace called a school has been described and analyzed in terms of organization and structure. We also have described schooling in terms of roles, authority, and responsibilities. We used organization charts to show how schools are placed inside the larger organization of school districts, and the importance of the state's ultimate responsibility for education of all its citizens was described. What was not done within each of these descriptions was to point out some of the many related tensions, debates, and unresolved issues. In the remainder of this chapter a number of these are introduced.

Audio Link 8.3
Learn more about the federal government and public education.

Questions About the Organization of Schools

The structure of schools, school districts, and state education departments is well established and has been pretty much the same for the last 100 years. Still there are questions, issues, and debates about the best ways to organize schools.

Class Size: What's Best?

Teachers and parents regularly express concern about the number of students in classes. The general belief is that smaller classes are better. In fact this belief is so widespread that between 1990 and 2008 all but six states adopted some form of class size reduction policy (Mitchell & Mitchell, 2003). It is believed that with smaller classes teachers will be able to spend more time with each student. One obvious consequence of going to smaller classes is that the cost of staffing the school will go up; smaller classes mean more teachers. At some point the school will not have enough classrooms and there would be the added cost for constructing more classrooms. Due to the Great Recession of 2008 and the significant budget cuts that have followed, the trend toward smaller class sizes has now been reversed. Class sizes are increasing dramatically.

UNDERSTANDING AND USING EVIDENCE

Differences in School Staffing

There are a number of readily available statistics that you might want to consider as you look ahead to your first teaching position. How important to you is the size of the school? What about class size? Would you prefer to be teaching smaller classes, or does it really matter that much? Also, what about the diversity of students?

Study the table below. What information can you draw from the data? Based on these data, which school would you expect to be most challenging? In which school would you most want to teach?

Descriptive Statistics for High Schools

School	No. of Students	No. of Teachers	Student/Teacher Ratio	Free Lunch	Reduced-Price Lunch
Adams High School	2,572	114	22.6	1,212	127
Jefferson High School	2,583	102	25.3	1,074	121
Lincoln High School	1,636	80	20.3	182	64
Washington High School	1,038	97	10.5	28	53

These data were from the National Center for Education Statistics website (http://neces.ed.gov/globallocator/). Within this site there is a tab "Search for Schools, Colleges, and Libraries." The author of this chapter pulled up these statistics for the high school he attended and for three other schools where he has conducted research.

In which of these schools would you want to teach?

Be careful about drawing conclusions about each of these schools based on these data alone. Still these are the facts, as far as they go. Here are some guiding questions:

- Which school is the largest? Which the smallest?
- An important indicator of diversity is socioeconomic status (SES). The federal government indicator for poverty is how many students are eligible for free or reduced-price lunch. What does this indicator suggest about these four high schools?
- If you want small class sizes, which school would you pick?

One of the patterns within these data is that the two largest high schools have the highest student/teacher ratios. You might expect that larger schools would have more teachers and could have lower student/teacher ratios. In this case the two largest schools also have the highest student/teacher ratios. A factor that is not reported in this table is the funding for each school. A useful statistic for comparing funding, which will be described in Chapter 9, is the amount of dollars per pupil. If you were to know that Adams and Jefferson High Schools are in a state that is relatively low on funding, how would this make a difference in your thinking?

There are other questions related to this good idea. For example, if it were possible to organize schools with classes of ideal size, what would that size be? The general conclusion from the various research studies is 17 or fewer students with one teacher.

This leads to other questions; for example, at which level(s) of schooling will small class sizes provide the most return on investment? Going to ever smaller class sizes leads to increasing costs. Another question: How do teachers' instructional strategies change as class sizes go down? In their summary of the research, Mitchell and Mitchell (2003) concluded, "a broad consensus has been reached that (class size reduction) has a statistically significant, small to moderate impact on achievement and a slight, though not necessarily inconsequential, influence on teacher instructional behavior" (p. 139). In other words, there can be gains in student learning, but how teachers teach may not change that much. Another question: Are smaller class sizes more important at some grade levels? The studies also show that small class size is most important in the primary grades and when it obtains for at least two years.

Deeper Look 8.4
Read about research concerning class size.

Why Are Schools Organized the Way They Are?

In many ways the organization of schools at this time is a direct result of the Industrial Revolution. Think about the photos you have seen of factory workers standing at their stations on the assembly line that produces the Model T Ford, or textiles, or soft drinks. For the assembly line to work well, each worker has a prescribed job. There are supervisors/managers too. Even the timing of tasks and the workday are specified. Many of these ideas about how to structure an organization are now institutionalized in schools. Line and staff relationships, organization charts, position descriptions, and 50-minute class periods with bells ringing are well-defined components of nearly all schools.

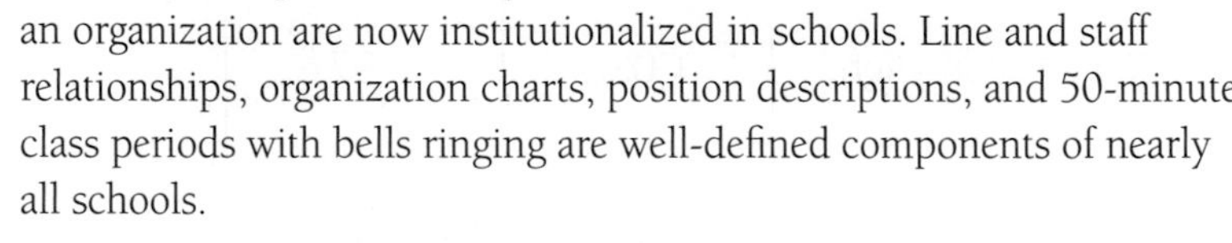

Think about the typical middle/junior high school and high school. Each teacher is a specialist in a subject, the bells ring at specified times, and the students are on conveyor belts moving to their next workstation. The principal and assistant principals monitor the movements and press to make sure everyone is "at their station" for the next 50-minute period. The structural view of schools continues on. Is this industrial model best for adult and student workers in the 21st century?

What Should Be the Role of School Boards?

In the past school boards were the major policy bodies for governing their school district. Today, much of the governance role has been assumed by governors and state legislatures. An important question now is, What is the appropriate role for school district school boards? In most communities they no longer are responsible for determining local taxes for schools, as they receive most of their funds from the state. Curriculum, standards, and even many personnel and student behavior policies and procedures are dictated by the state and federal governments.

So what should school boards be doing? Or do we need local school boards any longer? It is easy to find individuals to argue on all sides of these questions. Some strongly believe that school boards are essential as representatives of the citizens in local government. Others are concerned about the willingness of many boards to engage in determining the details of day-to-day operations of the school district, in other words micromanaging. Many believe that school boards are no longer needed and that they should have no role beyond selecting the superintendent and approving the annual district budget.

What About School Safety?

One of the most challenging problems for today's schools is safety. Before learning can take place schools need to be safe and secure places for students and adults. The concern and challenges related to violence, bullying, and disasters are so complex that all levels of the education system are pressed to address the problem. Teachers have responsibilities to have a safe classroom. School facilities including the grounds must be safe. Many school districts now have their own police forces, and all have to coordinate closely with the local police agencies. State-level policy-makers are engaged by passing laws such as the ones that require a student that brings a weapon to school to be expelled. No matter the circumstances, teachers, principals, and school district personnel have no option—state law mandates the response.

Video Link 8.3
Watch a video about school safety.

Being prepared and knowing what to do ahead of time is essential. One important response is for schools to have established procedures for what to do in the case of an emergency. Figure 8.5 is illustrative of the kinds of steps that teachers, students, and administrators should have in place and practice—just in case.

In summary, there are a number of additional issues and points of debate about education and the best way to organize schools. The four introduced here—class size, the industrial model, the role of school boards, and safety—are significant and directly relevant to teachers. The number of students teachers teach is of personal as well as professional concern. Having more students means less time to know and help each one individually. Can teachers teach with quality and students learn best within the 20th century model? The way a particular school board goes about its work in the end affects teachers. And all have to assume responsibility for the safety of children and adults.

Figure 8.5 School Emergency Action Plan

Fire Drill	Lockdown	Shelter-in-Place
• Students exit room with no talking and proceed to designated area • Teachers take Emergency Folder • Turn out lights • Close and lock door • Take roll at assigned area • Immediately report any missing student by holding up red card • Administrator will announce when clear • Students return to classroom quietly	• Everyone moves inside to safe location • If students are with special teachers they stay there • Lock all doors and DO NOT OPEN FOR ANYONE • Take attendance • Report any missing students to the office • Stay away from doors and windows • Use intercom for emergencies only • Wait for "ALL CLEAR"	• FOLLOW EXACT SAME PROCEDURES AS LOCK-DOWN • Plus • For drill: Place a piece of masking tape on classroom window • Locate plastic sheets and flashlight • In emergency, use plastic to cover and tape all vents and doors • DO NOT USE CELL PHONES • Wait until an administrator has given the "all clear"

CONNECTING TO THE CLASSROOM

The organization of schools, school districts, and state education systems has been described in this chapter. Learning about organization structures may seem remote for candidates that are at the beginning of their teacher preparation program. However, each of these organizations will become increasingly important as you begin having clinical and field experiences, and as you have conversations with parents and community members. Understanding these organizations will be critical as you seek out your first-time employment as a teacher.

1. In many ways schools are professional organizations. One consequence is that teachers have more autonomy and greater responsibility than is possible for workers in most businesses. Teachers must be very careful to demonstrate that they are ready and able to be effective given this higher level of self-responsibility.
2. Keep in mind that teachers and schools are not autonomous; they are subparts of school districts and each state's education system.
3. Local control can be talked about in the abstract but is quite limited at this time.
4. The principal is the one administrator that is in a line relationship with teachers.
5. Line and staff relationships are especially important in a professional organization, such as a school. There are many high-quality professionals in schools to support teachers and students, and in terms of structure all are in staff relationships.

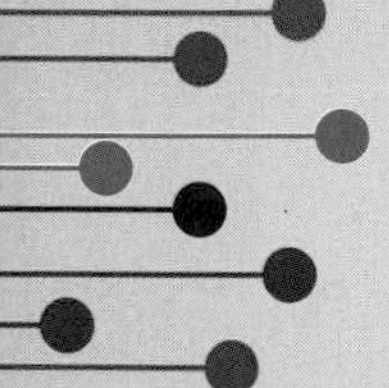

SUMMARY

This chapter has presented different ways that schools are viewed as organizations. Of course, the work of teachers is teaching, and the work of students is learning. But teachers and students do their work in an organizational setting. Key topics that have been addressed include these:

- The adults and the children in a school have to be organized in effective ways to do their work.
- Schools are organized into districts (LEAs) with school boards and a superintendent.
- Each state has ultimate authority for its public education system.
- Issues and problems include class size, the role of school boards, and safety.

CLASS DISCUSSION QUESTIONS

1. When you are a beginning teacher and you have a concern about a student or some problem within the school, whom do you talk to?
2. As a teacher, how important will it be to you to know who the superintendent is and to learn about what she or he thinks is important?
3. Who is the chief state school officer in your state? Who are state school board members? What issues are they grappling with at this time?
4. The role of school boards has been reduced in many ways. Some argue that local school boards are no longer needed. Others argue that school boards are an important component of democracy and having local citizen representation is very important to the process. What do you say?

KEY TERMS

Board of Trustees 237
Chain of command 228
Chief state school officer 241
Empowering 238
Extra-curriculum 226
Horizontal communication 228
Human resources (HR) 235
Intermediate 226
Line relationships 227
Local control 239
Local education agencies (LEAs) 235
Looping 229
Micromanaging 239
On-site staff developer 230
Organization chart 227
Policies 238
Prescriptive 238
Primary 226
Professional Learning Communities (PLCs) 231
School board 237
Secondary 226
Self-contained classroom 232
Staff relationships 227
State education agency (SEA) 235
Superintendent 236
Team teaching 230
Vertical communication 228

SELF-ASSESSMENT

WHAT IS YOUR CURRENT LEVEL OF UNDERSTANDING AND THINKING ABOUT ORGANIZING SCHOOLS FOR LEARNING?

One of the indicators of understanding is to examine how complex your thinking is when asked questions that require you to use the concepts and facts introduced in this chapter.

Answer the following questions as fully as you can. Then use the Complexity of Thinking rubric to self-assess the degree to which you understand and can use the organization ideas presented in this chapter.

1. How would you explain the authority of the school principal to a friend?
2. What is the difference between line and staff relationships?
3. What is the relationship of teachers to the school district superintendent?
4. What role do you think school boards should have?
5. What education problems would you like to see your state address in policy that could significantly improve student learning?

Complexity of Thinking Rubric

	Parts & Pieces	Unidimensional	Organized	Integrated	Extensions
Indicators	Elements/concepts are talked about as isolated and independent entities.	One or a few concepts are addressed, while others are underdeveloped.	Deliberate and structured consideration of all key concepts/elements.	All key concepts/elements are included in a view that addresses interconnections.	Integration of all elements and dimensions, with extrapolation to new situations.
Organization structure	Names a few roles and organization concepts, without explaining relationships.	Describes school-based role and line relationships for the principal, but not LEA or SEA; no ideas about what the state policy-makers should do.	Describes school-based, LEA, and SEA roles and relationships; provides very general idea for needed policy.	Describes role, line, and staff relationships at all levels and issues related to communication; identifies one education problem that state policymakers should address—the identified problem may have limited implications for student learning.	Describes role, line, and staff relationships at all levels and issues related to communication; identifies one education problem that state policymakers should address—the identified problem may have limited implications for student learning.

STUDENT STUDY SITE

Visit the Student Study Site at **www.sagepub.com/hall** to access links to the videos, audio clips, and Deeper Look reference materials noted in this chapter, as well as additional study tools including eFlashcards, web quizzes, and more.

Field Guide

for Learning More About Organizing Schools for Learning

• • • • •

To further increase your understanding about schools as organizations and workplaces, do one or more of the following activities.

Ask a Teacher or Principal

Ask a veteran teacher about the relationship with his or her principal. When is the principal clear about there being a line relationship? How much autonomy as a professional does the teacher have?

Study the organization chart for a school. Are the various relationships clear? Are there roles named that you had not thought of?

Make Your Own Observations

When you are visiting a school, seek out the school's organization chart. How does it compare with the one pictured in Figure 8.2? Is it drawn so that line and staff relationships are clear? Ask different staff members where they see themselves within the school's organization. Are they clear about who is in a line relationship to them, and who have staff relationships? For example, many teachers will see the assistant principal as their supervisor. However, in most schools the AP is officially in a staff relationship with teachers. How do they relate to people with these different formal relationships?

Reflect Through Journaling

In the past, local control was an important argument against state and federal governments intruding on what were seen as local issues, such as selection of curriculum and determining the qualifications of teachers and principals. Now, the state and federal governments are making most of the decisions about schools. For you as a teacher, what do you see as being gained? What is lost with the current trend toward increasing centralization?

Build Your Portfolio

Find the website for the school district where you would like to teach. Review the organization chart for this district. Note the name of the superintendent. Also, check within the HR office for directions about applying for a teaching position. You should keep copies and make notes about information you need to have when you apply for that teaching position. Also, develop a checklist of things you need to work on so that you will be well qualified for a teaching position.

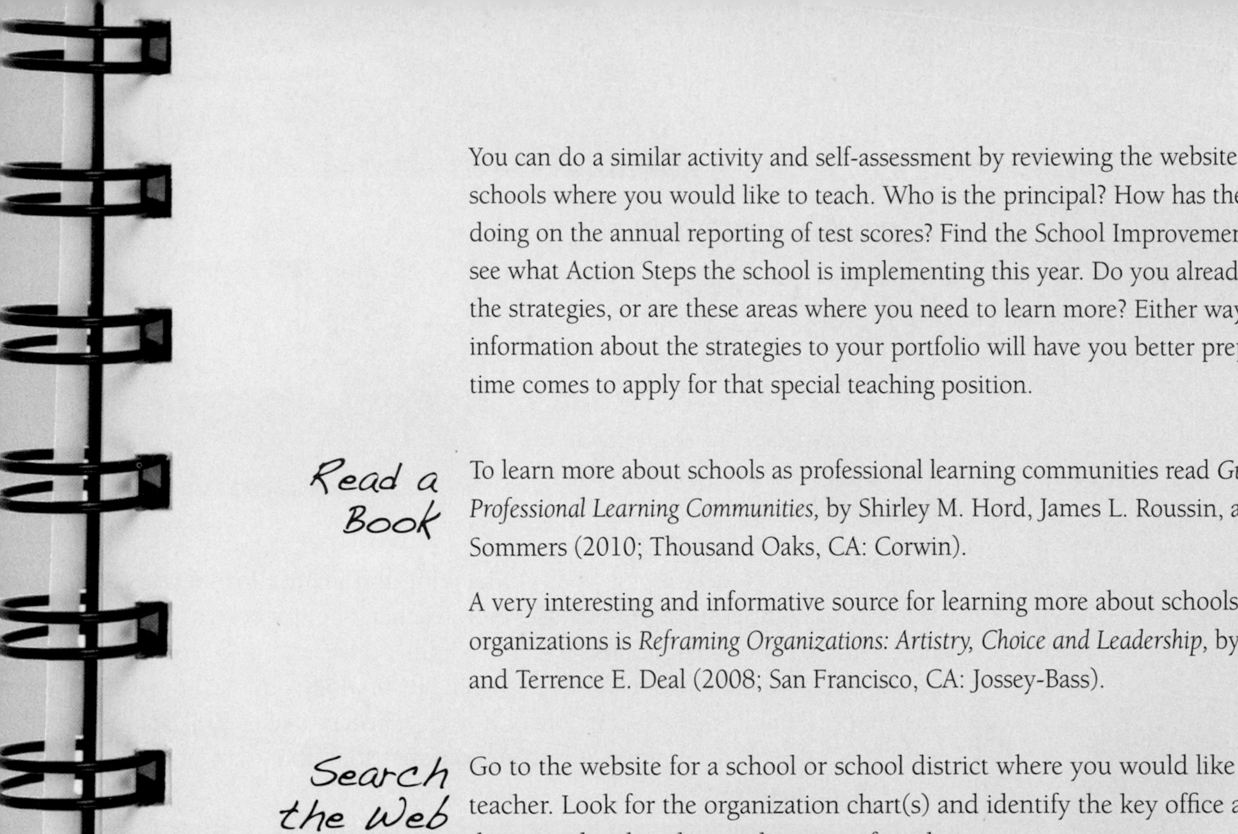

You can do a similar activity and self-assessment by reviewing the website for particular schools where you would like to teach. Who is the principal? How has the school been doing on the annual reporting of test scores? Find the School Improvement Plan and see what Action Steps the school is implementing this year. Do you already know about the strategies, or are these areas where you need to learn more? Either way, adding information about the strategies to your portfolio will have you better prepared when the time comes to apply for that special teaching position.

Read a Book

To learn more about schools as professional learning communities read *Guiding Professional Learning Communities*, by Shirley M. Hord, James L. Roussin, and William A. Sommers (2010; Thousand Oaks, CA: Corwin).

A very interesting and informative source for learning more about schools as organizations is *Reframing Organizations: Artistry, Choice and Leadership*, by Lee G. Bolman and Terrence E. Deal (2008; San Francisco, CA: Jossey-Bass).

Search the Web

Go to the website for a school or school district where you would like to become a teacher. Look for the organization chart(s) and identify the key office and individuals that are related to the employment of teachers.

Review the website for the SEA in your state. Find the name of the chief state school officer/state superintendent. What are the person's professional background and qualifications for this important position? Also, review the qualifications of the members of the state board of education. How do their qualifications compare?

TEACHER INTERVIEW

Dr. Italia Negroni

The professional career of Dr. Italia Negroni, assistant superintendent in Norwalk, Connecticut, has taken place across several of the school districts in Connecticut. Before working in public education she was in banking and finance for six years. Her first teaching assignment was as a PreK teacher. She has been a library media and technology specialist, a grants administrator, and more recently senior director for Professional Development, Technology, and NCLB with the Hartford Public Schools. Her breadth of experiences makes her the perfect district office administrator to answer questions about governance and school finance.

Governance and School Finance

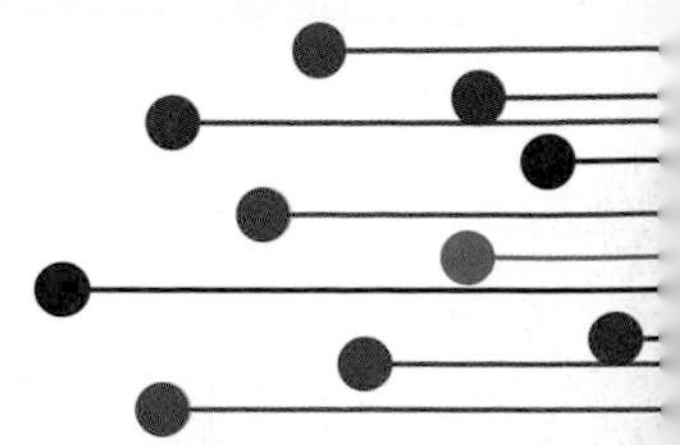

- *In your experience what does governance mean?*

I see three levels: federal—the president and congress that establish a lot of the policies and procedures for the states; state—the governor and legislators that make laws that districts have to abide by; and then you have the district—boards of education. Governance means a body of people elected or appointed who establish the district's values, vision, and expected outcomes. They are supposed to create the conditions to make those things happen.

What do you see being the role of the school board when things are working well (and not well)?

Their membership can come from different combinations. They can be elected by the community at large. In some cities, for example Bridgeport and Norwalk, the mayor sits on the board. Mayors bring a lot of power. It makes the governance much more political. Unfortunately, there may be ulterior reasons for them wanting to be on the board. It could be a political reason, a personal vendetta, or a stepping stone toward higher office.

I thought of five things boards should do: Develop policies, govern the use of fiscal resources, engage the community in the schools (which is a big part of the job), sustain a strong relationship with the superintendent and his/her cabinet, and approve contracts.

Where does the state and federal government fit in?

The feds give us money and the state gives us money. That's important. Also, they lay out certain policies nationally, for example NCLB. The states have to abide by the feds and the districts have to abide by the states. Both have a very strong impact on what schools and teachers do.

What brings joy to your work as it relates to teaching and learning?

The kids bring me a lot of joy. They are adorable. Especially the ones who can show you what they have learned. If they can demonstrate what they have figured out about a problem. If they can show how they figured it out and why they think they have the right answer. I love seeing kids taking responsibility for their own learning and their own behavior.

Also, I get joy out of working with teachers and helping them improve their practice. We have a bunch of teachers here that are really phenomenal. They really are!

What advice do you have for teacher education candidates?

Oh, my gosh. Stay focused. Find good mentors. It is really important to reach out. You can learn so much from other people who have been in the profession

Questions to Consider

1. What were the distinctions Dr. Negroni made between the structures of government and governance?
2. It is clear that Dr. Negroni grants special importance to the role of the school board. Why would she do this?
3. When she was asked about what brings her joy she immediately described behaviors and understandings that she expects to see in students. How well does her answer match with what you would expect school district office administrators to say?
4. Dr. Negroni emphasized the importance of mentors for beginning teachers. What will you look for in a mentor?

longer. Connect with the positive people in the building—and don't get caught up in the toxic cultures that may exist. New teachers should not be afraid to reach out and ask questions. New teachers need to understand that they are not going to know it all in one year or two years.

Learning Outcomes

After reading this chapter, you should be able to

1. Describe key characteristics of governance and what the processes of good governance entail.
2. Examine some of the major ways that the federal government influences states, districts, schools, and classrooms.
3. Compare the pros and cons of the different sources of funds that are used to pay for public education.
4. Analyze issues related to how education funds are spent in schools, districts, and states.
5. Identify, describe, and evaluate some of the current issues and challenges related to governance and financing of education.

INTRODUCTION

In Chapter 8 the organizational structures of education were described. It may be somewhat of a surprise to have this chapter returning to talk of school boards, states, and the federal government. This is because understanding the structures of government is only half of the picture. How well the various governmental structures operate on a day-to-day basis makes an enormous difference. Just because the structures are presented in organization charts, and policies and procedures are published, doesn't mean that the actual way governing bodies accomplish their work will be productive, efficient, or effective. Each level of government has its own ways of working. In addition, all of these structures and operations have to be paid for. The money has to come from somewhere, and there always will be disagreements about how the funds should be spent. These are the major topics in this chapter.

HOW IS GOVERNANCE DIFFERENT FROM THE STRUCTURES OF GOVERNMENT?

Dr. Negroni shared some insight about school boards.

> The meetings should be short and regular. They should have goal-setting meetings and annual retreats. It is important that they get on the same page as the superintendent. It is important especially for the chair of the board and the superintendent. I have seen it work well, and I have seen it deteriorate. When there are good connections and communication, they make good decisions. You have to have policies, money, people, and support. If they have good control of those areas, they should be able to implement their vision.

Governance is what a government does. It is the functions, the processes, and various roles that lead to decisions and actions. Although we are talking about governmental entities, such as school boards and the Congress here, the idea of governance also can be applied to a family, a church, or some other agency such as a bank or manufacturing company.

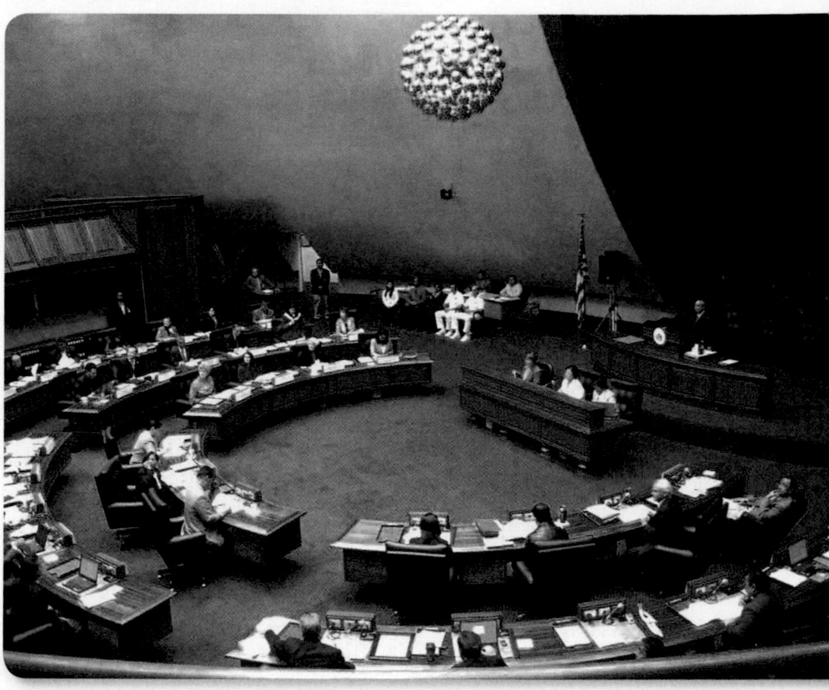

Governance is the process of involving a variety of interests in making decisions.

How well a school board meeting runs, who gets to speak, whether there is consensus, and how public the discussion is are all elements of the processes of governance. In other words the quality of the decision making, as well as the consequences of the decision, are related to governance. Surrounding the governance process is politics. This last point makes many teachers uncomfortable. They do not want to think about politics being a part of education. But it is an inescapable component of educational governance, just as politics is infused within any other governing body.

Governance Can Be Good or Bad

In and of itself the idea of governance is not good or bad. At the same time we tend to think more about our experiences with a governmental body that is not working well. Do you remember how in recent years Congressional Republicans and Democrats have come so close to shutting down the government over finances? In the summer of 2011 there was ongoing disagreement about raising the debt ceiling. In December of 2012 it was over addressing the "fiscal cliff." These were not positive processes. A governing body cannot function well unless there is dialogue and compromise.

On the good side are the many examples of governing bodies working well together, debating openly, and in the end developing powerful decisions for the better. One clear example from the recent past would be how so many governmental agencies and corporations from several countries worked together in 2010 to rescue the Chilean miners. Thirty-three miners were trapped one half mile underground. Various long-established governmental entities, national and international corporations, and other national governments—each with their own structures (policies, procedures, and leaders) and politics—worked across their structures and together committed experts and resources to address a serious problem. The whole world watched over the two months it took to drill a new hole more than a half mile into the ground. In the end all of the miners were rescued. This story is a wonderful example of how the processes of governance can be used to work through the many rules, regulations, and silos of different government entities to solve a pressing problem.

Video Link 9.1
Learn more about governance.

Characteristics of Good Governance

What was Dr. Negroni saying above about the characteristics of a good school board? It isn't just a matter of structure, or a district having a certain number of board members, a chair, and a superintendent. What's important is how they work together. Efficiency in use of time is important. Having both short-term objectives and long-term strategic goals is important. Having clear and

Figure 9.1 Characteristics of Good Governance

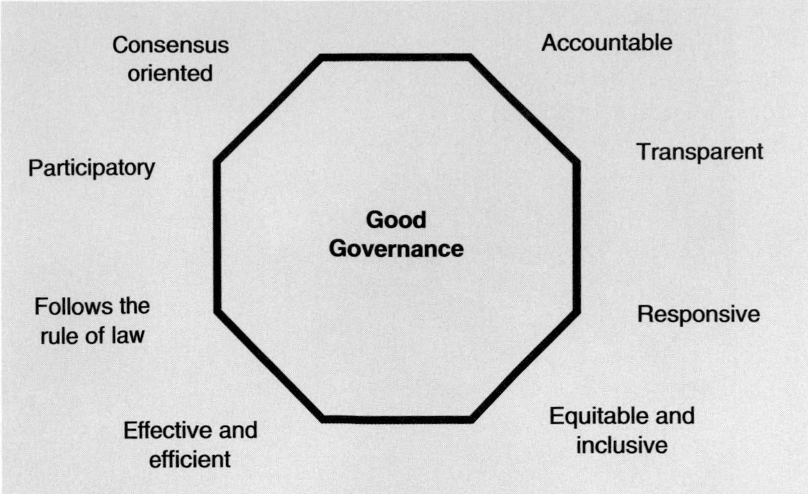

Source: United Nations Economic and Social Commission for Asia Pacific. (n.d.). What is good governance? Retrieved from **http://www.unescap.org/pdd/prs/ProjectActivities/Ongoing/gg/governance.asp**

open communication between the board and superintendent is important. Being able to listen as well as advocate are important skills. All of these are indicators of good governance, which entails conducting affairs in public, managing resources well, and keeping in mind core values and what will be best for the people in the long term. These characteristics can be applied to state legislatures, the Congress, and boards of corporations. In many ways they are universal indicators.

The universality of the interest in and concern about the need for good governance is reflected in Figure 9.1. This figure is from a United Nations document, but each of the characteristics is directly applicable to a school board, a state legislature, and to Congress. As you read each of these, keep in mind that they also apply to well-functioning committees and other kinds of meetings.

- **Participation** includes men and women, and there is freedom to express one's views.
- **Rule of law** is enforced equally for all.
- **Transparency** means that the decision-making process, the reasoning, and the output are open to the public and freely available.
- **Responsiveness** entails establishing time frames that are reasonable and at the same time sufficiently long so that all necessary information is available.
- **Consensus oriented** in decision making through open dialogue, rather than resorting to ultimatums and refusals to negotiate.
- **Equity** and **inclusion** mean ensuring that all groups have open access.
- **Effectiveness and efficiency** so that time and resources are used purposefully and well.
- **Accountability** through decisions, actions, and evaluations that demonstrate to the various constituencies that there has been careful consideration of the alternatives and that there is wise use of public resources.

Achieving and maintaining each of these characteristics is a major responsibility of all governing bodies. As you can quickly see, these characteristics ask a lot of the participants, whether they be state legislators or teachers serving on a school-based council. Achieving and sustaining good governance is not easy.

Characteristics of Bad Governance

Oh, the stories people tell. You heard hints of some of these in our interview with Dr. Negroni. Another observation of hers was this:

> Often politics and personal interest get in the way with the result being that we don't always do what is best for kids. When I am in schools I see the inequities between

classrooms. And across districts there will be inequities from school to school. I am sure there are inequities from state to state. There should be better ways to address these problems without causing such turmoil.

When one or more of the characteristics of good governance are violated there can be loss of the strategic vision and increasingly narrow focus on short-term actions and reactions. Trust gets lost. As the tensions increase there is greater impatience to fix things, which usually results in the agency establishing short-sighted directives and narrow mandates. In recent years this consequence is regularly observed in education. Instead of supporting teachers, several state governors have led initiatives to cut their bargaining rights. Federal legislation mandates tests for all students whether or not from the teachers' perspective it makes sense. **No pass no play** laws are passed by state legislatures. School boards ban certain books, movies, and websites. The increasing polarization within so many governing bodies and the failure to come together and make important decisions most certainly illustrates the absence of many of the characteristics of good governance.

There Are Politics

By now you are probably thinking, but what about politics? As we said earlier, there is no escaping politics, which is the means through which the governance process operates. For example, in most governing bodies the final decision is made by a vote. A key step that effective leaders take before there is a vote is "vote counting." How do you project that each member will vote? Does your side have enough votes?

The idea of "sides" hints at another aspect of politics, **interest groups.** These are individuals who have joined together around a shared agenda that they want to see implemented. For example, a teachers union may want more planning periods built into their contract. At the same time a business association doesn't want to pay more taxes. The school board has to decide. It is time for vote counting. Which board members are friends of the teachers and which are business owners?

Debate and passion are two important characteristics of politics in government, education, and elsewhere.

Frequently interest groups will join together to form a **coalition.** By joining forces with one or more other interests groups they will have larger numbers and can have more influence on how the board votes. Keep in mind that quite often coalitions are made up of interest groups that in general have different and even opposing purposes. This can result in strange marriages of convenience, such as Ducks Unlimited (who want more ducks) forming a coalition with the National Rifle Association (who wants more hunting). What could possibly be their shared agenda? Having Congress protect more wetlands will provide more habitats for ducks, and more ducks to hunt. It is a win-win situation.

Deeper Look 9.1
Read more about interest groups.

This is not a far-fetched example. Interest groups form coalitions all the time. In a high school the science teachers join with the math teachers to get more computers, while the coaches join with the theater and band directors to change the end of the school day. Teachers must understand that politics is not about right or wrong—it is about getting what you want through the governance process. Teachers have to not only accept that education is politics, but also develop the knowledge and skill to be political. Hopefully, you will engage in politics for the right reasons.

Audio Link 9.1
Learn more about politics and education.

WHAT IS THE ROLE OF THE FEDERAL GOVERNMENT IN EDUCATION?

Feds give us money and the state gives us money. That's important. They lay out certain policies nationally, for example, testing. The states have to abide by the feds, and the districts have to abide by the states. They have a very strong impact.

The teacher has her classroom of kids, the administrator has his or her school of teachers and employees, the state has their districts, and the feds have their states.—Dr. Negroni

Audio Link 9.2
Listen to a clip about federal funding for schools.

In Chapter 8 the overall structure of the federal government was described. At one point in that chapter it was suggested that you look for the word *education* in the U.S. Constitution. Did you do this? Did you find any reference to education? It is not there! Yet since World War II the federal government has had increasing influence over education. In the following pages we will explain how this has happened.

Where does the federal government fit into the overall scheme for education? This is an increasingly important question. Although the federal government provides a very small proportion of the funds (just over 9%), its influence over states, districts, and schools has been steadily increasing. Each of the three federal branches of government—the executive, legislative, and judicial—is influencing schools. The president can give a speech with the intent of influencing education. Legislation, such as NCLB, when passed by both houses of Congress and signed by the president, can have major implications for schools. Also, when the U.S. Supreme Court rules on a case, such as it did in *Brown v. Board of Education of Topeka*, there can be major implications for schools.

As with all political processes, even writing the Constitution included debate, passion, and compromise.

The U.S. Constitution and the States' Responsibility for Education

For any level of government the role and authority of all bodies (executive, legislative, and judicial) is derived from what is stated in the related constitution. Curiously, the U.S. Constitution includes no statements about expectations or responsibilities for education. Through interpretation of what is said, the states have been assigned responsibility for education. As a result, each state's constitution sets the beginning expectations for education. However, over the last 60 years the federal government has increasingly become engaged with and increasingly directive about what states, school districts, and schools should be doing.

The U.S. Constitution is composed of six "articles." Shortly after it was approved the Bill of Rights was added. The Constitution itself has been stable over time. However, over the last two centuries 26 "amendments" have been added. As is frequently stated, the U.S. Constitution is "the law of the land." All other laws, statutes, each state's constitution, and the actions of governments at all levels must be consonant with the U.S. Constitution. Since the U.S. Constitution does not directly address education or schooling, several of its amendments have been interpreted by the U.S. Supreme Court and various governing bodies in ways that assign responsibility to the states. The Tenth Amendment is the key.

The Tenth Amendment—Grants Responsibility to the States

The Tenth Amendment was adopted in 1791 in order to make clear that the civil rights of citizens would be protected against state actions. The Bill of Rights protected citizens against actions of the federal government, but not necessarily a state's. The Tenth Amendment states:

> The powers not delegated to the United States by the Constitution, nor prohibited by it to the States, are reserved to the States respectively, or to the people.

Since education is not mentioned in the U.S. Constitution, it is "reserved to the states."

The First and Fourteenth Amendments of the U.S. Constitution also continue to be of major importance to schools, teachers, and students.

The First Amendment—Freedom of Speech and Religion

Video Link 9.2
Learn more about freedom of religion in schools.

Passed in 1791, the First Amendment states:

> Congress shall make no law respecting an establishment of religion, or prohibiting the free exercise thereof; or abridging the freedom of speech, or of the press; or the right of the people peaceably to assemble, and to petition the Government for a redress of grievances.

Two clauses in the First Amendment have become central to the role of schools, and the rights of teachers and students:

- The interpretation of the establishment clause, "Congress shall make no law respecting an establishment of religion," has today taken center stage as various individuals and groups advocate for prayer in schools and use of public dollars to fund educational activities in buildings and programs sponsored by religious groups. The Founding Fathers had serious concerns about the possibility of government supporting a religion or punishing citizen participation in a religion. There is a continuing debate about how to balance what government can do with the need to provide educational opportunities for all students without it being seen as government support of a particular religion.
- The "free speech" clause has been used to challenge a variety of topics such as the extent of teacher academic freedom, the amount of freedom of school-sponsored student newspapers, and dress codes. Since there have been a number of past court decisions there are fewer questions in this area at this time.

The Fourteenth Amendment—Due Process

Passed in 1868, the Fourteenth Amendment states in part:

> No State shall make or enforce any law which shall abridge the privileges or immunities of citizens of the United States; nor shall any State deprive any person

State governments have the responsibility for educating their citizens.

of life, liberty, or property, without due process of law; nor deny to any person within its jurisdiction the equal protection of the laws.

Due process is an important right granted to all citizens, including students in public schools. There are two components: substantive due process and procedural due process. **Substantive due process** has to do with protection against the loss of the rights granted in the Constitution, such as freedom of expression. Government cannot be arbitrary, capricious, or unreasonable in their actions relative to the rights of all citizens, including educators and students. Administrators can enforce rules of behavior, but all students must be treated similarly. **Procedural due process** deals with whether or not a person has been treated fairly and that proper procedures have been followed. Procedural due process has been at the center of many student suspension cases. We will delve into specific court cases and questions of teacher and student rights in Chapter 10. For now, the important point is that the increasing involvement of the federal government in education has been based in interpretations of what is stated and not stated in the U.S. Constitution.

Three Parts of the Federal Government: Three Sources of Education Policy

Deeper Look 9.2
Read about the role of the federal government in education.

As you learned in social studies, the U.S. Constitution specifies that the federal government is comprised of the executive, legislative, and judicial branches. The architects of the Constitution wished for balance and equality in power between the three. Although at times in history there have been imbalances, in general the three-way approach has been maintained. Even with no direct mention of schools or education in the Constitution, today, all three branches play activist roles in regard to what should, and should not, occur in public schools.

Executive: President of the United States

In the last 60 years each president has had a strong interest in public education. For example, in 1965, as one of the major pieces of legislation within his Great Society program, President Lyndon B. Johnson led the passage of the first **Elementary and Secondary Education Act (ESEA)**. This act established a number of national priorities for improving schools and education. Federal funds were targeted to improving libraries, teacher professional development, improving teacher education, support for bilingual and special education, the development of national statistics about education, and, through the **National Assessment of Educational Progress (NAEP)**, regular study of student learning within each state. ESEA has been reauthorized every four to five years since that time. For example, in 2001 President George W. Bush took the lead in that reauthorization of ESEA, which was called No Child Left Behind (NCLB). Since then, the Obama administration has followed through with other major education initiatives including Race to the Top, which provided multimillion-dollar grants to selected states to bring about statewide reforms.

Legislative: U.S. Congress

Many members of the House of Representatives and the Senate have very strong interest in schools and education issues. Both the House and the Senate have committees with responsibilities related to education. As a result, each year there are a number of education bills and statutes initiated and approved by both houses. Of course each does not become law until signed by the president.

An important understanding related to legislative bodies, such as the Congress, is that two pieces of legislation are needed to accomplish a change. First, a bill must be passed to **authorize** the program or activity. This bill does just what its name implies: It places into law authorization for schools, or any other body, to engage in a specified activity. No dollars are provided with authorization, although frequently the bill will set a limit on how much can be spent. Funding for an authorized activity or project comes through separate **budget** legislation. Although the major budget bills for the federal government are supposed to be approved by Congress early in the year, it seems to be typical to have them not approved until well into fall. A regular occurrence in the budget process is that an education activity that was authorized earlier will not be funded, or the budget bill will include funding far below what was authorized and desired.

The U.S. Supreme Court has the final say when there are legal questions that pertain to the educational system.

Judicial: U.S. Supreme Court

At the top of the judicial branch is the U.S. Supreme Court. This court is the highest court in the nation and has the last word on any legal issue in the United States. The justices are appointed for life and really are the "court of last resort." Over the years the Court has reviewed many cases and made a number of significant decisions that have had a direct and long-lasting impact on schools, students, teachers, and communities. We will go into detail about Court decisions in Chapter 10.

U.S. Department of Education

Another important component of federal government comprises the various departments and offices that, in theory, are part of the executive branch. We say *in theory* because in many ways these departments develop their own directives through the establishment of regulations, rules, and procedures, which are called **administrative law.** When the Congress and president pass a bill, it becomes federal law. Implementation of the law becomes the responsibility of the various federal agencies and departments. The same is true when the Supreme Court makes a decision. One or more offices of the federal government will be responsible for drawing up the steps to be taken to implement the decision. The Education Department, for example, will develop the rules, procedures, and guidelines for implementing each newly passed statute. In many ways developing administrative law is more important than is the official passage of the statute. It is these rules and procedures that specify what states, schools, teachers, and others must do.

A number of federal agencies have authorities and responsibilities related to schools, but the largest and most visible is the U.S. Department of Education (ED). Major Program Offices of ED include the Office of Civil Rights, the Office of Safe and Drug-Free Schools, the National Center for Education Statistics, and the Office of Special Education and Rehabilitative Services. Each of the offices, initiatives, and institutes has its own home page and all can be found within the home page for ED (**http://www.ed.gov/**).

ESEA Past and Future

The 2001 reauthorization of ESEA, commonly referred to as NCLB, represented the most significant federal intrusion into public education. Within its 2,100 pages the statute set expectations for levels of teacher qualifications, student performance, and activities by each state. The statute backed these expectations with an array of mandates to states, school districts, schools, and teachers. The overall aspiration was admirable: To have all children proficient by 2013–2014. NCLB included penalties and sanctions for schools, districts, and states that did not reach this goal. No American wants to see any of our children left behind and not equipped to participate in society and contribute. At the same time, NCLB represented a new high in terms of federal involvement in public education. Also, as the school year 2013–2014 got closer, everyone had to face the facts. All children, schools, districts, and states were not going to reach the goal.

Elements of No Child Left Behind (NCLB)

Deeper Look 9.3
Read more about NCLB.

NCLB was the education legislative initiative of President George W. Bush. Many of the ideas were derived from his earlier initiative in Texas when he was the governor. The expressed intent was to raise student achievement, increase teacher quality, and make schools safer. The bill was passed by both houses of Congress in 2001 and signed into law in January 2002 by President Bush.

Three important areas of NCLB mandates continue to have direct consequences for states, schools, and even teacher education candidates. These are Highly Qualified Teacher, Adequate Yearly Progress, and School in Need of Improvement. Within each of these components were many expectations and explicit directives that have had all of the nation's schools, teachers, and administrators struggling to comply. An added observation about NCLB, which is true of many other pieces of federal and state legislation, is that the act was not funded at anywhere near the level that would be necessary to make total compliance a reality. In other words, in part it was an **unfunded mandate.**

Highly Qualified Teacher (HQT)

NCLB set specifications for what it means to be a **Highly Qualified Teacher (HQT).** Note that the term is *highly qualified,* not *high quality.* The intent was to assure that all classrooms would be staffed by teachers who have met a set of minimum criteria. The HQT criteria are now reflected in what you have to do to receive a teacher license. Teachers should

- Be fully licensed by the state and must not have any certification requirements waived on an emergency or temporary basis.
- Have at least a bachelor's degree and demonstrate competency equivalent to a major in a graduate degree or advanced certification.

In addition are are these further requirements:

- New teachers must pass a state test of subject matter knowledge and teaching skill.
- School districts must notify parents of the availability of information on the professional qualifications of the student's classroom teachers and whether a particular teacher meets state qualification and licensing criteria. In other words, when you become a teacher, if parents ask, your district has to inform them of your professional qualifications.

"They meet in there. Some kind of support group."

As with many other parts of NCLB, the states were mandated to determine the details of what HQT meant. For example, in most states before being licensed aspiring teachers must pass a test. In many states there is a test upon entering the teacher education program and another at the time of program completion. However, the test score that a candidate needs to make can vary by state, since each state can set its own **cut score.** A few states do not rely on a single "high stakes" test and instead use multiple measures, such as teacher portfolios or work samples. If you have not already done so, very soon you should seek out the criteria that have been established for teacher licensure for the state in which you plan to teach.

Adequate Yearly Progress (AYP)

Another significant NCLB component had to do with student achievement as measured on standardized tests. The **Adequate Yearly Progress (AYP)** mandate included these stipulations:

- All grade 3–8 students must be tested annually in math and reading/language arts, and students in grades 10–12 must be tested at least once.
- For each school and school district, student test performance must be "disaggregated" using a number of demographic factors, for example, boy/girl, ethnicity, special education, and ELL.
- Students in each of the subgroups must make progress each year.
- 95% of all students in a school must be tested.
- In addition to states implementing statewide annual testing programs, each year between 2002 and 2014, all students who have scored below the proficient level will make progress toward scoring at the proficient level, that is, the students will make AYP. As was mentioned above, this admirable goal turned out to be unachievable.

Schools in Need of Improvement (SINOI)

Another continuing element of what was established in NCLB is what would happen to schools that failed to have the mandated increases in test scores. These became **Schools in Need of Improvement (SINOI)** and faced a set of escalating consequences for each year

Working as an administrator in Tulsa Public Schools, I observed hardworking teachers at multiple school sites receive incentive pay for improved test scores—the payout for each teacher $2,000.00 before taxes.

The *Tulsa World* came and wrote an article about the pay and several teachers commented that they would use the money to pay off student loans, pay down credit card debt, pay for graduate school, or other bills. Many teachers talked about using their money to buy more resources for their classrooms. However, one lone soul was completely honest and said she'd always wanted a Coach purse, and by golly, that was the first place her money was going! I appreciated her honesty!

In spite of all of this coverage, one significant detail was missing from the article. The support staff of the schools did not receive any incentive pay. This upset the teaching staff at one particular site, and a meeting was called to determine the best way to handle the situation. An envelope was passed, and when all was said and done, each support staff member walked away with $200.00.

Generosity and service seem to go hand-in-hand in this profession. This episode has always stood out to me as a true testament of the caring, competence, and commitment of excellent teachers who recognize that without the aid of their colleagues they wouldn't be in a position to help their students learn.

Jennifer Holloway, PhD
Cameron University

that the test scores did not increase by a sufficient amount. The NCLB expectations included these:

- Students in all schools must make AYP in each of the subgroups that have been identified.
- Failure to make AYP in any one category means that the school will be placed on the list of SINOI.
- A report card must be prepared and disseminated to parents and the public that
  - Names each SINOI.
  - Provides the number and percentage of SINOIs and how many years they have been on the list.
  - Compares the SINOI student achievement to the district and the state.

If a school does not make AYP for five or more years, then the district is required to send a letter to all the parents indicating that they are free to choose to send their children to another school that has been making AYP.

Although the aspirations in NCLB were admirable, the act required a great deal of additional work on the part of teachers, administrators, states, and students. There has been significantly increased pressure on teachers, administrators, and students to do well on each year's tests. Then the 2013–2014 school targets were missed. As has happened each time in the past, with the next reauthorization of ESEA a different set of expectations and mandates will be established. Using test scores in the evaluation of teachers is one of the critical items that will affect you as a teacher.

High-stakes testing is now mandated by the federal government and most state governments.

As the Realities and Consequences of NCLB Came to Fruition There Were Waivers

As admirable as the aspirations of NCLB may have sounded in 2001, the approach of the 2013–2014 school year brought a certain reality. Probably the largest fact that had to be acknowledged was that if the mandate of AYP was held to more than 80% of the schools, most of the school districts across the United States would be labeled as failing.

This reality and the associated political pressures forced the federal government to act. However, as with all issues at this time, Congress was split along Republican and Democrat lines and unable to act. As a result, in September 2011 President Obama issued an executive order that allowed states to apply for an "NCLB Waiver." There were some conditions, however:

1. States must adopt "college and career-ready standards" and assessments that include growth measures.
2. States must develop and implement a system of differentiated recognition, accountability, and support for all districts.
3. States must commit to develop and support effective instruction and leadership.

Together these conditions forced states to implement a refined set of initiatives that bring together the setting of standards, support to districts and schools, and sustained professional development of teachers and school leaders. But **test-based accountability** remains; annual state testing continues to be driving the evaluation of schools as well as teachers and administrators.

Growth Scores: A Different Way

One of the significant changes that has emerged out of the NCLB experience is a different approach to the way that student test scores are compiled and interpreted. In the early years of NCLB, determining AYP was done by using an annual snapshot. The test scores in reading and mathematics for all the students in a school for this year were compared with the test scores for all the school's students who took the test last year. The school was judged based on whether the average scores in all categories went up or down. Remember that the mandate was that all the scores should go up each year. It was a comparison of all the students for this year against all the school's students from the previous year. It didn't matter if there was a 30% turnover in students or no turnover. In most schools some students move out and others move in. This was not a fair way to evaluate whether or not the school was making a difference.

Now a new approach is being implemented for judging AYP. **Growth scores** compare the test scores for each student from year to year. In this new approach the expectation is that students will show growth in each subject from year to year. The calculations determining AYP are more complicated but more closely based on the individual students that attended the school.

Audio Link 9.3
Learn more about school accountability.

A related element within President Obama's waiver was the requirement for states to develop a **differentiated system of accountability.** In the past a single test was the basis for judging a school's effectiveness. The new requirement set an expectation that there will be multiple assessments and that there will be accommodations for some students such as ELL and special education students. Each of these themes foreshadowed key elements of the next reauthorization of ESEA.

Reauthorization of ESEA, 2012 and Beyond

Historically, ESEA has been reauthorized every four to six years. However, the reauthorization that would follow NCLB has dragged on much longer. In response to the experience with NCLB, several new themes are being addressed. Each of these will have direct implications for you as you become a teacher.

Rewarding School Success

One of the criticisms of NCLB was that it was punitive. Schools, districts, and states could be punished for not improving. But there were no incentives for increasing student outcomes, other than avoiding the punishments. The new thinking is to have rewards and incentives for success.

Graduating Every Student

An area of increasing concern has been the high school graduation rate. Depending on the school and how this indicator is calculated, the rate can range from 35% to 90%. In addition, there are increasing expectations for high school graduates to be ready for college and/or a career. This is where the emphasis on adopting "college and career-ready standards" has come from. The widely adopted Common Core State Standards go hand in hand with the intention to increase the graduation rate.

Placing Effective Teachers and Leaders

The new goal is to place effective teachers and leaders in every school and classroom. Of particular concern is to have more effective educators in schools with more poverty and lower student performance.

Improving STEM Education

STEM stands for science, technology, engineering, and mathematics education. Historically, these disciplines have been important. They now are an increasing priority due to concerns about international economic competitiveness.

Teacher Incentive and Evaluation Pay

Although less visible than the elements identified above, there is heavy emphasis on different ways to evaluate and pay teachers. In the past teacher pay was uniform and increased from year to year solely based on how many years one had taught. There now are a variety of teacher pay models that are based in performance. A principal factor in these models is to have a large proportion of increases in teacher pay based on student test scores. One argument in opposition is the difficulty of identifying the differences in student learning that are single-handedly due to what a teacher does. However, teacher pay based on some type of performance measurement system is here to stay. The only questions will be about which measures and how much weight will be given to each.

HOW ARE SCHOOLS PAID FOR, AND HOW IS THE MONEY SPENT?

In Connecticut, schools are funded through local property taxes. In addition, we have a formula called ECS (Equal Cost Sharing). It is based on a number of factors including wealth, single-family households, and some other SES factors. Each school system has an ECS score calculated for them. This formula is the basis for receiving funds from the state. For example, districts with more low-income families will have a higher ECS score and receive more money from the state. However, given the current financial situation there is the threat of getting less from the state.— Dr. Negroni

There are two important questions for you to consider:

1. Where does the money come from to pay for schools?
2. How is the money spent?

As obvious as these questions may seem, as you might expect, the answers are complicated. Here we will sketch the big picture of school finance. We will leave the details for you to study in graduate school.

As Dr. Negroni indicated, the funds for schools come from three main sources: the local community, the state, and the federal government. There are other sources of funds, but these tend to provide much smaller proportions of school budgets.

Paying for all of the schools and school districts requires that a large amount of money be found each year. In the last year for which the statistical analysis has been done, 2008–2009, approximately $593.1 billion in revenue was collected. These funds were for elementary and secondary education only. Of course, as can be seen in Figure 9.2, the amount of revenue raised within each state varies depending on a number of factors, such as the size of the state, the health of its economy, and the political party in power. For example, the high was California, which had revenues of around $70.687 billion, while the low was North Dakota, with revenue of $1.102 billion.[1] Once the funds are raised, states, school districts, and schools spend the money, with most of it being spent on instruction.

---

[1] Table 1. Revenues and percentage distribution of revenues for public elementary and secondary education, by source and state or jurisdiction: Fiscal year 2009. Washington, DC: National Center for Education Statistics, ED.

Finding the Money to Pay for Schools

The money for the funding of schools comes from a number of different sources. The obvious sources are income, sales, and property taxes. There are several other sources including estate taxes and lotteries. In addition, as schools' need for funds has increased, a number of additional sources are being tested. In most states half of the funding for local schools comes from the state.

Income Tax

The first thought by most of us when we hear the word *taxes* is income tax. Implicitly we are thinking about **personal income taxes**, which are the taxes individuals pay to the federal and state governments based on their level of income. What is not thought about is that businesses also pay a **corporate income tax.** Governments rely heavily on these two forms of income tax. One of the important features of income taxes is that those with higher levels of income pay

Figure 9.2 State Revenues for Public Elementary and Secondary Schools as a Percentage of Total School Revenues, by State: School Year 2007–2008

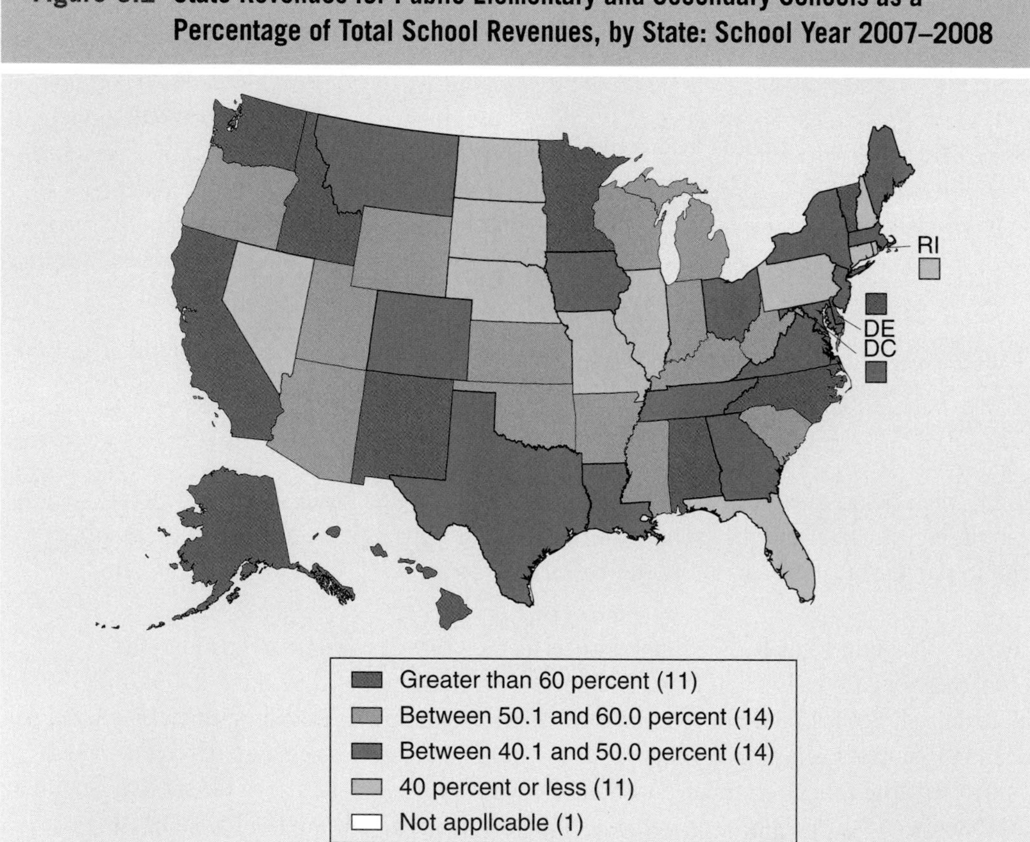

Note: Both the District of Columbia and Hawaii have only one school district each; therefore, neither is comparable to the other states. For more information about revenues for public elementary and secondary schools, see http://nces.ed.gov/programs/coe/supnotes/2011-n10.asp. For more information about the Common Core of Data, see *Supplemental Note 3* (http://nces.ed.gov/programs/coe/supnotes/2011-n03.asp).

Source: U.S. Department of Education, National Center for Education Statistics, Common Core of Data (CCD). (n.d.). National Public Education Financial Survey, 2007–08. Retrieved from http://nces.ed.gov/

more. The term for this is **progressive.** In other words, the income tax is graduated, with those having a higher level of income paying a larger amount. The assumption is that a progressive tax is correlated with the ability to pay, and that there will be less impact on those with less income.

Property Tax

Property taxes are those paid on tangible and intangible property. Tangible property includes real estate, vehicles, boats, computers, livestock, and equipment, while intangible property consists of those forms of wealth that do not have a physical existence such as stocks, bonds, and savings. Property taxes, especially real estate, have been a primary source of funds for public schools. Advantages of this form of taxation are that the property can be objectively evaluated and a tax rate determined. It also doesn't move away or have its value change very rapidly. So there is a predictable evenness to the revenue over time. A disadvantage is that only those who own property pay the taxes. For example, apartment renters do not directly pay property taxes.

Another very significant disadvantage of the property tax is that the value of real estate is not the same for every community, which limits the ability of each school district to raise the money that it needs. For example, a school district that has a popular shopping mall in its tax district will have a significant source of revenue in addition to the property tax on homes. But a school district that has a high proportion of older homes and the only local industry is a closed manufacturing plant will not have the same ability to raise revenue through a local property tax. As will be discussed at the end of this chapter, these local differences in ability to pay for schools have led to school finance lawsuits in most states.

Sales Tax

Sales taxes are based on consumption. When various products and some services are purchased a certain percentage may be added on to the price as a sales tax. The dollars from sales tax typically go to the state; however, in some localities, a proportion will become a source of local or regional revenue. For example, the total of the sales tax may be 7% with 5% the state sales tax and 2% a local city tax. This form of taxation is **regressive,** which means that it proportionately costs more for those with lesser ability to pay.

Federal Government Sources of Funds

We asked Dr. Kim Friel, whom you met in Chapter 8, if any of the Sawyer Middle School budget came from federal funds.

> We are 67% free and reduced-price lunch (FRPL), which qualifies the school for Title I funds. Interestingly, in our state, the state education department pretty much told us how the funds could be spent. These funds can be spent on tutoring, staff development, and we were able to hire two additional staff to make class sizes smaller.

As can be seen in Figure 9.3, about 10% of their funding for schools comes from the federal government. The Education Department, the Department of Labor, the National Science

Figure 9.3 Sources of Revenue for Public Schools: School Year 2005–2006

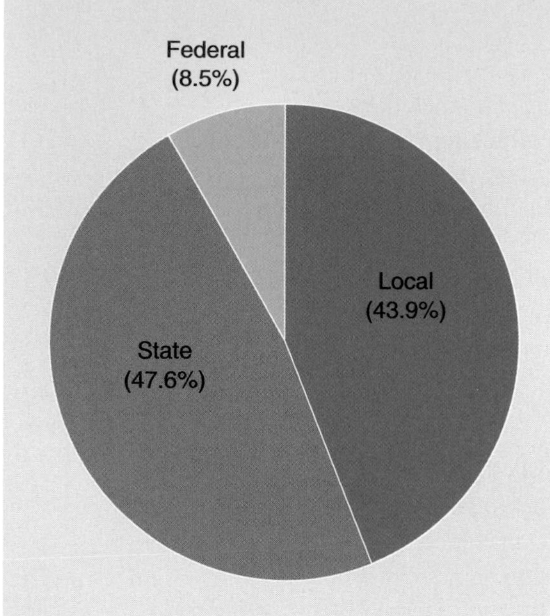

Source: U.S. Department of Education, National Center for Education Statistics, Common Core of Data (CCD). (n.d.). National public education financial survey (NPEFS), fiscal year 2006, Version 1a. Retrieved from http://nces.ed.gov/ccd/

Foundation, and other federal agencies provide funding. Most of the funds are tied to particular needs such as providing more instructional supports and free meals to children of poverty. Other programs provide grants to obtain technology, provide in-service training for teachers, and support the needs of special education and ELL students.

Citizens Fight Back

Given all of the forms of taxation, including a number not mentioned above, such as the federal excise tax on car tires and phone calls, it is not surprising that many citizens are unhappy with the current tax system. As a result, various forms of tax rebellion such as citizen referenda and the underground economy have been growing. The now infamous Proposition 13, which was passed by the voters of California in 1978, has since been replicated in a number of other states, such as Colorado with its Tax Payer Bill of Rights (TABOR).

Citizen initiatives begin by seeking signatures and placing on the ballot a constitutional referendum that if approved by the voters sets a cap on tax rates and/or government spending. Typically these initiatives sound very good to frustrated tax payers and in the short term appear to work well. Depending on the size and rate of growth of a state's economy, as well as the restrictions in the referendum, a state may be able to continue for quite some time before the unintended consequences become visible. For example, it has taken some 30 years for the long-term consequences of California's Prop 13 to become visible. A key reason for California's current serious financial problems and the sad decline in the quality of its schools can be traced back to the reductions in property tax revenues that resulted from passage of Prop 13. The consequences were observed sooner in Colorado, where recently there have been local and statewide efforts to override the TABOR caps.

In many communities there have been tax payer revolts that have raised questions about how to pay for public institutions such as schools.

Seeking Additional Sources of Funding for Schools

Even with the funding provided by the established sources, education systems across the United States are short of dollars. Costs keep going up, buildings need maintenance, and class sizes have gotten as large as can be tolerated, but growth in revenue has not kept pace. This has been an increasing problem not only due to the recent economic struggles, but also due to conservative politics and the unwillingness of many taxpayers to pay more.

Income, property, and sales taxes are direct forms of taxation. Everyone has to pay them. So policymakers have been turning to sources of revenue that are "voluntary." In other words, the financial situation has led policymakers to seek additional forms of "revenue enhancement," especially ones that would be less direct and more open to citizen discretion.

"Before we begin our student concert, note that, due to budget cuts, the role of the drum will be played by banging on inverted paint cans and the role of the flute will be played by blowing breath across half-filled soda bottles."

Lotteries and Gambling

Lotteries and gambling have become additional sources of revenue. Beginning in the mid-1960s, New Hampshire and New York established lotteries. Over the 55-plus years since, nearly all of the states have their own or participate in a multistate lottery. In lotteries a portion of the funds received through sale of tickets is used to pay for the prizes. There also are administration costs. The remainder becomes revenue for the state.

Initially, in each state the proponents of lotteries promised new funds for schools and other well-thought-of needs. For example, the original intent in Florida was that the lottery profits would be used for add-on and special projects in schools. However, very quickly in a tight budget year the legislature rolled lottery revenues into the base funding for schools, leaving no more funding for special projects. This has been the trend across the country. Very quickly the promised extra revenues from lotteries and gambling became absorbed into the regular budgets and were used to offset, or even reduce, past levels of spending. In addition, although the revenues from lotteries sound large, in terms of the overall budget for schools the revenue is at best 1% or 2% of the total budget.

In the last decade, many states have turned to gambling as another source of revenue. More and more states are opening up casinos, and others have approved riverboat gambling. This is another form of revenue gain that is voluntary. People do not have to buy lottery tickets, and they do not have to gamble in casinos or play video poker. For those that do, there is a tax on the casino's "take" and a licensing fee for each machine. In addition, in states with an income tax, "winners" must pay state as well as federal income taxes.

Critics argue that lotteries and gaming are played most by those who can least afford to spend their money that way. Low-income adults play more than the well-to-do. Other critics are concerned about the many who become problem gamblers. Also, the odds of winning are infinitesimally small. People have a much higher probability of being hit by lightning than winning a lottery. Still, the states have become addicted to these indirect sources of revenue and the direct forms of taxation have not had to be raised as much to cover the level of services provided.

Finding the funds to maintain schools is a continuing challenge.

Creative Sources of Funds for Schools

Given how tight school district budgets have become, educators too have become creative about fundraising. Bake sales are no longer sufficient. Now there are fees for participating in athletics, and product advertising will be painted on the sides of school buses. Even the Cola

War is being played out in school districts with the decision to only allow one or the other brand to be available. Of course each of these decisions has a price.

School Carnivals, Field Events, and Parent–Teacher Organizations

As schools seek additional funds, one activity is to have a carnival or special field day. The activities and events may be entirely organized by the school staff and students. Or an outside vendor may be contracted to organize and manage the day. **Parent–teacher organizations (PTOs)** may also be major organizers of fundraisers. Parents also will join booster clubs that raise funds for extracurricular activities such as football, baseball, and band.

Schools have had to seek a variety of new sources for funding; some have even begun placing advertisements on school buses.

School–Business Partnerships

Neighborhood businesses and branches of national companies are partnering with specific schools. Too often these partnerships seem to be one-way, with the business partner providing resources and services to the school. At the simplest, a business pays for an advertisement in a school publication or for a sign on the athletic field. More serious partnerships will have the business providing employee time to help students learn to read or to paint a classroom. When it is a two-way partnership the staff and students will be engaged in service to the business. For example, a high school history class could take on a project of developing a written or oral history of the business. Students could shadow business employees and perhaps coach on the use of a new technology.

Each of These Fundraising Activities Has a Price

Critics of these innovative approaches to fund-raising have some serious concerns. The school is no longer objective or independent of particular commercial interests. The particular products or services that are advertised on campus will have an edge over those that are not present. Business partners might expect favoritism in the assignment of students to teachers. And parents may be concerned about the too ready availability of junk food.

A Possible Source of Revenue That Was Never Considered Before

As the demand for better schools continues to be in conflict with the pressures to not raise taxes, more states are turning to consideration of even more extreme sources of revenue. When it comes to conflicts between the need for more revenue and traditional values, a majority of policymakers—and voters—seem to be willing to take the money. A frequently used euphemism for this is **sin taxes.** For example, in the 1930s, Prohibition was ended and along with alcohol consumption came the revenue from taxing it. There have been sin taxes on tobacco for a long time. Fifty years ago lotteries and gambling were illegal everywhere except Nevada. Now there

Challenging Assumptions

Are disadvantaged students less ready to succeed in doing critical-thinking activities?

The Assumption

One of the major themes in the Common Core State Standards is rigor. The standards set the expectation that all students need to be challenged and engage in higher-order problem solving. At the same time, as is being described in this chapter, there are major differences in funding for schools. In addition, many students come from poor families and broken communities.

These conditions lead many teachers to question whether students from disadvantaged families and communities are ready to do critical thinking. The consequences of this belief are easily observed in schools and classrooms where the instruction norm is extensive teacher talk—much of which is giving directions. The implicit teacher expectation about the level of disadvantaged student performance is also seen in the tightly scripted lessons and the large number of assignments using fill-in-the-blank worksheets. When disadvantaged students are doing computer-based assignments, these typically will be more drill and practice, and be based on lower-level expectations for what disadvantaged students can do.

Research Findings

Contrary to the assumptions of many teachers, the findings from research are that disadvantaged students benefit as much as the more advantaged students when they have the opportunity to engage with high-level critical-thinking instruction (Zohar & Dori, 2003). In another study, Torff (2006) found that expert teachers did not hold beliefs that were supportive of lower expectations for disadvantaged students in terms of critical thinking. A comparison sample of randomly selected teachers did hold different beliefs about which students are ready for problem solving and higher depth of knowledge instruction.

A related concern that Torff identifies is the difficulty of changing teachers' beliefs. Even preservice teachers' beliefs can be strongly set. Only through having this assumption talked about, reflection through journaling, and learning about models of instruction that work can teacher beliefs be changed.

Torff (2011) has identified six factors that contribute to teachers "opting for less rigorous curriculum for disadvantaged students" (p. 23). These factors are students' level of prior knowledge, time constraints, influence of parents, influence of colleagues, students' level of motivation, and students' level of academic ability.

Implications

In summarizing the research, Torff (2011) points out that a "rigor gap" emerges when disadvantaged students are given a less rigorous curriculum. If they only experience "watered-down lessons," there is little option but less academic growth. The research studies have documented that disadvantaged students can succeed when they have the opportunity to experience a more rigorous curriculum. It is important for you to consider your own beliefs. How many of Torff's six factors do you now use to set lower expectations and to design less challenging lessons? It is important for you to start thinking more about how you will make sure that through unstated beliefs your instruction will not further disadvantage some of your students.

Sources:

Torff, B. (2006). Expert teachers' beliefs about critical-thinking activities. *Teacher Education Quarterly, 33,* 37–52.

Torff, B. (2011, November). Teacher beliefs shape learning for all students. *Phi Delta Kappan, 93*(3), 21–23.

Zohar, A., & Dori, J. (2003). Higher-order thinking and low-achieving students: Are they mutually exclusive? *The Journal of the Learning Sciences, 12,* 145–182.

Figure 9.4 Percentage Distribution of Current Expenditures for Public Elementary and Secondary Education in the United States, by Function: Fiscal Year 2006

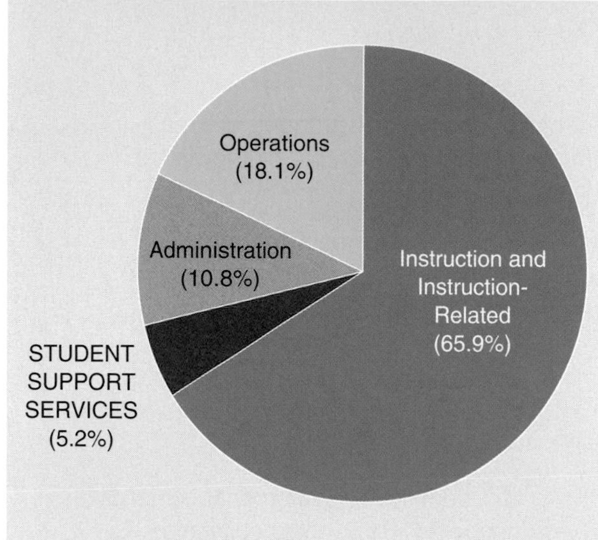

Source: U.S. Department of Education, National Center for Education Statistics, Common Core of Data (CCD). (n.d.). National public education financial survey (NPEFS), fiscal year 2006, Version 1a. Retrieved from http://nces.ed.gov/ccd/

Key:

Administration: School principal's office, the superintendent, and board of education and their immediate staff

Instruction and Instruction-Related: Teacher salaries, textbooks, librarians, etc.

Operations: Operation and maintenance of schools and district facilities, student transportation, and food services

Student Support Services: School maintenance, administration, nurses, library, psychological services, etc.

are only two states where neither of these sources of revenue is legal.

A newly emerging source of sin tax funds is the legalization of marijuana. Although it is illegal at the federal level, as of the beginning of 2012 some amount of it was legal, "for medicinal purposes," in 16 states and Washington, D.C. In the same year, 12 other states had initiatives to make it legal. Whether this additional source of tax revenue will be a gain or just offset other expenditures remains to be seen.

HOW DO SCHOOLS SPEND THE MONEY?

Dr. Friel, principal of Sawyer Middle School, described some of the parts of her school's budget, when asked, "Does your school have a budget?"

> We have several. The budget for personnel salaries is kept by the district. The school receives a set amount from the district based on the number of pupils. This budget is for teacher supplies, books, janitorial supplies. Within this budget I can determine how it is used. For example, if I get $150,000 for textbooks I sit down with the staff and we decide what to buy. Another budget is Student Generated that come from fundraisers, vending machines, etc. These funds are spent on students for awards, field trips, and teacher incentives.

Once the funds have been collected and allocated to school districts and schools, budgets are constructed and the funds are spent. There are several ways to analyze and summarize the way that the money is spent. One is to compare how much is spent on instruction versus for administration. Another commonly employed statistic is to compare the amount of money spent per pupil.

Distribution of Revenue: By Different Levels of Government

Deeper Look 9.4
Read about school finance and school infrastructure.

Clearly the most important component of spending should be directly related to instruction. Teacher salaries, curriculum materials, technology for instruction, and school library resources are some of the direct costs for instruction. Figure 9.4 represents the national averages for **current expenditures** by function, which are the funds spent during the 2005–2006 school year. Don't forget that there are other expenditures, such as payment on school construction bonds, which are in addition to those identified in Figure 9.4.

In Figure 9.4 the category of Instruction represents more than three fifths of the budget. Although this is a large proportion it actually is a conservative estimate since the definition of what is included in this category is very restrictive. It only relates to teachers and resources for classrooms. The principal's salary and that of the school secretary, as well as the cost of the library are included under Support Services. Other items included in Support Services are student counseling and transportation, which most school and community members see as having a direct influence on instruction and student learning. Thus the Instruction and Instruction-Related statistic is very conservative. Overall it is clear that at least 90% of a school district budget is directly related to teachers and what they do in the classroom. From this perspective, another way to summarize the information in Figure 9.4 is to say that very little of every education dollar is spent on something that is not related to instruction.

Deeper Look 9.5
Read about commercialism in public school finance.

Per-Pupil Expenditure

One very useful statistic for comparing school funding is **per-pupil expenditure.** This ratio can be used to compare how much different districts and states spend for each student. Basically this statistic is derived by dividing the total number of dollars spent by the number of students. Per-pupil expenditure is used regularly as an indicator of a community's commitment to and support of public education. As can be seen in Figure 9.5, per-pupil expenditure also is useful in comparing each state's investment in its schools.

Figure 9.5 Per-Pupil Expenditures for Elementary and Secondary Schools: School Year 2009–2010

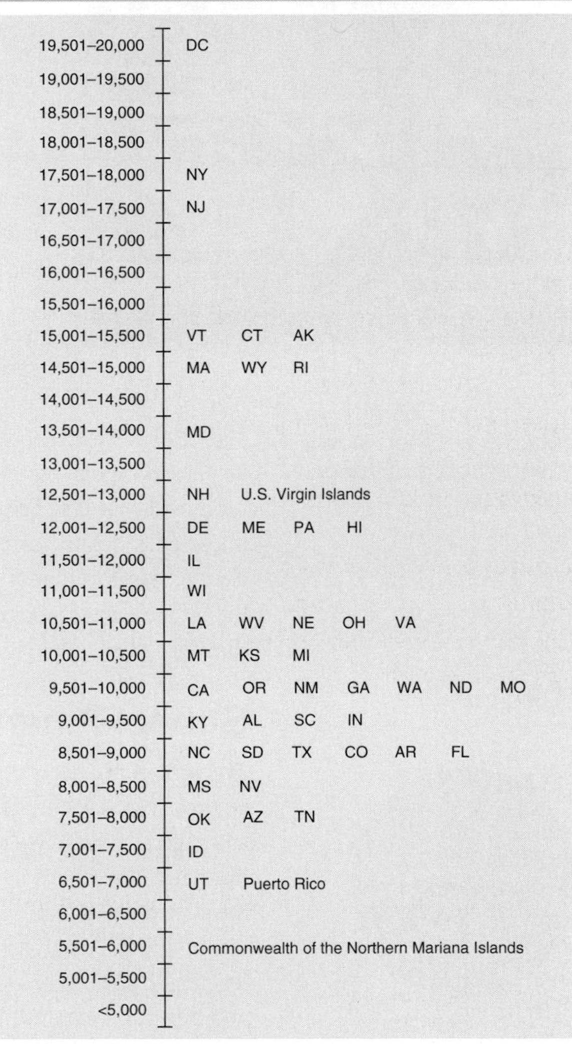

Note: Detail may not sum to totals because of rounding.

Source: U.S. Department of Education, National Center for Education Statistics, Common Core of Data (CCD) (n.d.). "National public education financial survey (NPEFS)," fiscal year 2009, Version 1a.

Balancing the Budget in Tight Times

School districts, and states, are required to balance their budgets each year. In times of tight budgets and tax limitations very difficult choices have to be made. Districts may increase class size. Increasing the average class size by one student across all schools will save significant dollars by reducing the number of teachers that need to be employed. Building maintenance may be deferred, and computers kept for another year. In extremely difficult financial times districts will turn to a number of other money-saving strategies.

Outsourcing/Privatizing

Instead of having district employees do a particular function, such as cleaning buildings or driving school buses, contracts are made with outside companies to provide these services. The district then can reduce the size of its payroll and hold the outside contractor accountable for the quality of service. Unfortunately, this strategy, as well as across-the-board budget cuts, likely means that a number of district employees will lose their jobs. Another consequence is that the quality of service is not of the same level as before. For example, the district-employed high school custodian will note when an outside door is left open at the end of the day and know that it needs to be closed. The outsourced employee understands that his or her job description is to sweep the floor. Nothing is in the contract about keeping doors closed.

Unpaid Furlough Days

Following the beginning of the Great Recession in 2008, many states, school districts, and municipalities required employees to take one

Student fees to participate have become another widely used source of funds.

or two days a month off without pay. At the same time there was an unwritten expectation that there would not be interruptions in services. For school and college teachers there has been no way to accommodate both of these conflicting expectations.

Reduction in Force (RIF)

As a last resort, balancing the budget has been done by giving some employees "pink slips." These are official letters informing certain employees that due to budget cuts they may not have a job for the next school year. Unless there has been a different agreement, in most school districts the teacher contract will specify that the last person hired will be the first to be fired. There may be exceptions for certain areas such as for mathematics and special education teachers, which are always in short supply.

WHAT ARE SOME OF THE SCHOOL FINANCE ISSUES AND CHALLENGES?

When I am in schools I see the inequities between classrooms. And across a district there will be inequities from school to school. I am sure there are inequities from state to state, but there should be betters ways to address these problems without causing such turmoil.—Dr. Negroni

Securing sufficient funds for schools and deciding how the available dollars will be spent are serious activities. Many actors are involved and many more have opinions about what should be the major sources of funds (e.g., no increases in [my] taxes), and in what ways schools should spend the funds (e.g., too many administrators). Table 9.1 is a list of key questions that have to be answered in relation to finding the funds and deciding how the obtained funds will be spent. The debates and final decisions related to each of these questions requires becoming informed and participating in the decision-making processes—which is why the first major topic of this chapter was governance. No individual has the final say. Many individuals and agencies contribute to the debates, and in the end schools and teachers have to live with the final decisions. There are many pressing issues related to governance and school finance. A few key ones are introduced here.

School Finance: Equal and Enough

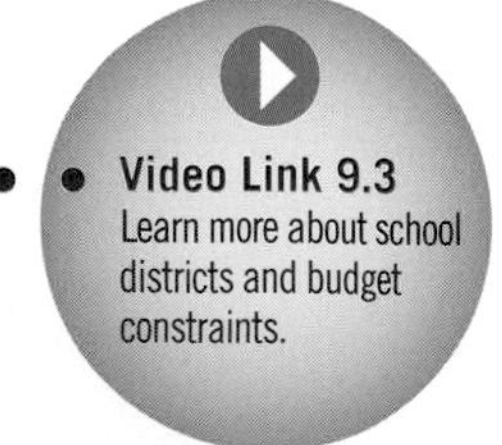

Video Link 9.3
Learn more about school districts and budget constraints.

The school finance suit in Kentucky was only the first. Since that time more than 40 states have experienced lawsuits related to the funding of schools, and others are under threat of having suits filed. You do not have to look very far in a community, across a large city or a state, to see dramatic differences in the quality of school facilities. Some districts, typically in the suburbs, have brand-new buildings, while other school districts, typically inner city and rural, will have old buildings. As an aspiring teacher, you likely already can name those school districts that pay teachers higher salaries. These dramatic discrepancies in the quality of facilities, teacher salaries, and per-pupil expenditures provide ripe conditions for school finance lawsuits.

Two Fundamental Finance Questions

One form of accountability that clearly is a state responsibility has to do with how schools are financed. When some perceive that the state has not been doing its job they may turn to the

Table 9.1 Key Questions About School Finance That Policymakers, School Administrators, Teachers, Parents, and Community Members Need to Consider
1. How much funding per pupil is really enough?
2. What sources of funds should be used to pay for increasing quality?
3. Should high-stakes test scores be the only determinant of teacher and/or school quality?
4. When there is a low level of performance, should there be sanctions or should there be additional investment?
5. Who should decide how schools are financed? Should it be mainly policymakers at the state or federal level, or should it be experts at the local level? To what extent should citizens have a role?

courts. The exact basis for the funding lawsuits has varied by state. Each is carefully crafted to take advantage of whatever that state's constitution says about that state's responsibility for education.

Two general models are being used to test the constitutionality of school finance: equity and adequacy:

> Equity school finance suits test whether there is equal funding given to all schools or students.
>
> **Adequacy** suits argue that the needs are different in different districts and for different students. The question is raised as to whether or not sufficient funds are being provided so that all students have a reasonable opportunity to learn.

In the 1980s and 1990s, most of the finance suits were based in questions of equity. It was clear that within each state there was unequal funding of school districts. Now, most of the finance suits are based in questions of adequacy. One main theme in these court challenges is that simply providing the same number of dollars to each school district and school does not provide the same level of opportunity for students to learn. Plaintiffs argue that it costs more to educate students from poor families, students with special needs, and those that are English-language learners. In other words, there is not adequate funding of schools that have higher proportions of needy students, and they therefore do not have an equal opportunity to learn.

Opponents of this view argue that it is not the state's role to determine how the funds are spent. As long as all school districts receive the same number of dollars per pupil, that is, equity, it is the district's responsibility to use those funds in ways that will help their particular mix of students succeed. Key policy questions about the financing of education are listed in Table 9.1. What do you see being good answers to each of these questions?

Different Levels of Government: Roles and Consequences

Since education is of such importance, every level of government has a role. Issues arrive when it comes to balancing the amount of power and influence each entity brings to the table. In the past the local community had major say. Over the last half century the federal government has had increasing say. Determining the appropriate balance of the different levels of government is never easy. Also, there is a many-year delay between a decision being made by a particular governmental entity and seeing the results in student learning.

Centralization Versus Local Control

An important theme and source of debate through the last 100 years concerns the balance between having decisions made by those people close to home versus having decisions made by those who are more removed but have a broader view. **Local control** is the term used when the authority for decision making is in the hands of those nearest the site, whether it is the district or a school. At this time, local control has been eroded not only by the states, but also by the federal government.

As was described above, as the state proportion of the education budget has increased, so has the interest of state policymakers in making education decisions. Over the last 60 years there has been increasing involvement of the federal government in making decisions about education for the whole nation, in other words increasing **federalism.** NCLB was by the far the most far-reaching and, many would say, "top-down" education policy initiatives ever for the federal government. The pattern over the last 60 years is clear: Local control of schools and education has been dramatically diminished. In some states there still is an expectation for local communities to have more say. For example, note the excerpt presented earlier in this chapter from the Vermont state constitution that expressly preserves some local control. Also note that Vermont was identified as one of states with the highest proportion of school funding coming from the state level.

Widespread Variations or a National Curriculum?

Another area for debate is whether the United States, like many other counties, should have one curriculum for all states and schools. In the past each state and most school districts decided what the curriculum would entail. Districts made the decision about whether or not to use a standardized test each year. Teachers and college faculty would become a state curriculum committee. These committees would suggest what content would be taught at each grade level, and each district would then adopt the textbook they desired. Also, in general teachers were free to use and adapt these curriculum "guidelines" and materials as they developed units.

Now there is what seems to be an inextricable trend toward establishment of a national curriculum. NCLB mandated testing and publishing the results for each school and district. By 2011–2012 nearly all states had adopted the same set of learning standards, the **Common Core State Standards.** During the same period the U.S. Department of Education funded two consortia (the Partnership for Assessment of Readiness for College and Careers [PARCC] and SMARTER Balanced Assessment Consortium [SBAC]) to develop new forms of tests that are aligned with the Common Core State Standards.

Those that advocate for a national curriculum see it being necessary to compete globally. They also argue that a national curriculum, including standards and testing, is necessary to bring up low-performing students, teachers, schools, districts, and states.

Others question the trend toward having a national curriculum. Countries that have had national curricula, such as China and the United Kingdom, are trying to move away from them. Their concern is that the national exams reduce students' abilities to problem solve. They also are pushing for teachers to help their students become creative thinkers. Some critics of the trend toward a national curriculum are concerned that it will reduce the opportunity for local creativity and entrepreneurial innovation in education, and that it will result in there being a "one size fits all" system that does not allow for individual differences.

UNDERSTANDING AND USING EVIDENCE

Parents are not the only ones who need to understand the basic financing of schools. Teachers also need to understand where the money goes. The table presented here is a summary of the budget for one school.

Gold Flake School Enrollment: 1,657	**Amount**
Instruction	$5,876,265
Instructional Support	$1,923,388
Operations	$2,524,402
Other Commitments	$0
Leadership	$772,706
Total School Expenditures	$11,096,761

Tables of numbers are easily understandable for some people. For others it is easier to understand a summary number, such as a ratio. An even easier way to understand numbers, for those who are visual, is to present the same information in a graph. For example, the budget numbers for this school could be presented in some other ways that might make more sense. The ways data have been displayed in the figures in this chapter provide good models.

Per-Pupil Expenditure

One very common statistic that is used to understand and compare the funding for schools is to determine how much is spent for each student in the school. There are 1,657 students in Gold Flake School. Simply divide the total dollars in each budget line item by the number of pupils and the per-pupil expenditure is determined.

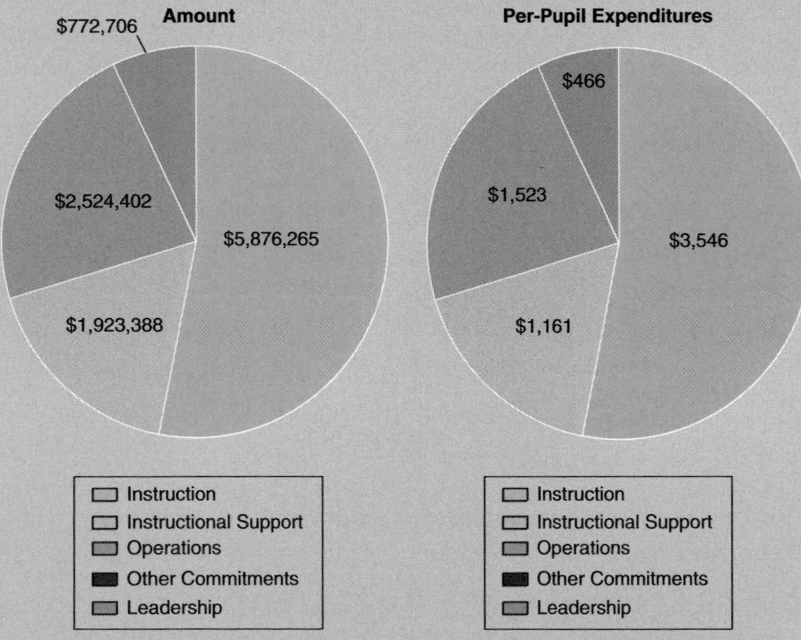

Graphing the School Budget

The budget for Gold Flake School can be displayed just as was done in Figure 9.4. A pie chart was used, and we have done the same here. The information could be placed in a bar graph too, but it would not be as easy to "see" the whole.

CONNECTING TO THE CLASSROOM

School finance, taxation, and how the money is spent are three of the main topics in this chapter. Another is the importance of having good governance. These topics may seem remote for candidates near the beginning of their preparation program. However, each of these topics will become increasingly important to understand as you begin having clinical and field experiences, and as you have conversations with parents and community members. You need to be ready to explain where the money for schools comes from. You also need to be ready to describe how the money is well spent. And you will have many opportunities to observe and participate in committees and other governing bodies.

1. Governance is the process through which government works. Good governance is transparent, it is participatory, and it follows the rule of law.
2. The three main sources of funds for schools are income, property, and sales taxes. In most states approximately half of the funds for schools come from the state.
3. The federal government is playing an increasing role in public schools as was demonstrated in the NCLB legislation. However, only around 10% of the funds for schools comes from the federal government.
4. Be respectful of the fact that a large proportion of the taxes you and others pay are used to fund schools. People work hard and want to be assured that their taxes are being spent wisely and well.
5. Continuing issues include the ever-present need for more funds, which is leading to tapping new sources, increasing federalism with the concomitant loss of local control, and changing criteria for determining accountability.

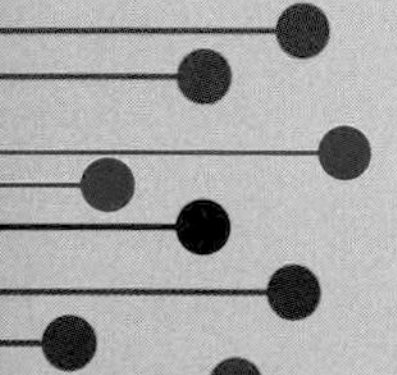

SUMMARY

Five major topics have been addressed in this chapter:

- Governance: The processes by which agencies make, implement, and evaluate decisions.
- The federal government influences education by tying funding with requirements to implement certain activities.
- Revenue: The funds that pay for schooling come from several sources including income, property, and sales taxes.
- Expenditures: By far the largest item in the education budget is for instruction and instruction-related expenses.
- Current issues: Tighter definitions of accountability and who pays are two of the most challenging questions.

CLASS DISCUSSION QUESTIONS

1. Look back at Figure 9.1; what are some examples in your experience that illustrate what happens when some of the characteristics of good governance are missing?
2. Accountability for schools, teachers, students, and school districts is not going away. The form that accountability will take is where the debate is taking place. What indicators and processes do you think should be used to hold teachers, students, and schools accountable? Are test scores sufficient? Should test scores for students be the basis for teacher pay increases?

3. The funding of schools is heavily dependent on property taxes. Do you think this is fair? What other sources of revenue for schools do you think should be used instead?

4. Budgets for schools have been tight and, due to the downturn in the economy, are shrinking. What do you see school districts and schools doing in response to this condition? Do you see other sources of funds? In which areas would you cut spending? What do you see as the long-term consequences of the budget cuts?

5. One of the embedded themes in this chapter has been the need to accept and understand politics. How do you feel about this recommendation? Are you ready to engage in politics with your current activities? What about in your future life as a teacher?

KEY TERMS

Accountability 254
Adequacy 275
Adequate Yearly Progress (AYP) 262
Administrative law 260
Authorize 259
Budget 259
Coalition 255
Common Core State Standards 276
Consensus oriented 254
Corporate income tax 267
Current expenditures 273
Cut score 261
Differentiated system of accountability 264
Effectiveness and efficiency 254
Elementary and Secondary Education Act (ESEA) 259
Equity 254
Federalism 276
Governance 253
Growth scores 264
Highly Qualified Teacher (HQT) 261
Inclusion 254
Interest groups 255
Local control 276
National Assessment of Educational Progress (NAEP) 259
No pass no play 255
Outsourcing/privatizing
Parent–teacher organizations (PTOs) 270
Participation 254
Per-pupil expenditure 273
Personal income tax 267
Procedural due process 258
Progressive 267
Reduction in force (RIF) 274
Regressive 267
Responsiveness 254
Rule of law 254
Schools in Need of Improvement (SINOI) 262
Sin taxes 270
STEM 265
Substantive due process 258
Test-based accountability 264
Transparency 254
Unfunded mandate 261
Unpaid furlough days 273

SELF-ASSESSMENT

WHAT IS YOUR CURRENT LEVEL OF UNDERSTANDING AND THINKING ABOUT GOVERNANCE AND SCHOOL FINANCE?

Answer the following questions as fully as you can. Then use the Complexity of Thinking rubric to self-assess the degree to which you understand and can use the organization ideas presented in this chapter.

1. Use the characteristics of good governance to describe what happens when the process is working well.
2. What are the key sources of revenue for schools, and what are the strengths and weaknesses of each?
3. What's wrong, and right, about relying on property taxes to pay for public schools?
4. What do you see as implications of the trend toward increasing federalism in education?
5. Given the tight financial times, what additional sources of funds for schools would you propose be tapped? What would be the strengths and potential pitfalls?
6. What do you see as being the most pressing issues related to the governance and financing of education? Why do you see these as being significant?

What is your current level of understanding? Rate yourself using this rubric.

Complexity of Thinking Rubric

	Parts & Pieces	Unidimensional	Organized	Integrated	Extensions
Indicators	Elements/concepts are talked about as isolated and independent entities.	One or a few concepts are addressed, while others are underdeveloped.	Deliberate and structured consideration of all key concepts/elements.	All key concepts/elements are included in a view that addresses interconnections.	Integration of all elements and dimensions, with extrapolation to new situations.
Organization structure	Names one or two elements of the topic, but fails to describe with any depth.	Describes one idea in depth, such as the pros/cons of property taxes, but only offers superficial reference to other constructs.	Identifies key ideas, issues related, and their interrelationships. Provides clear examples that illustrate meaning and implications.	Describes key ideas, their interrelationships, uses clear examples, and extends the description to potential implications and consequences.	Describes vertical and horizontal relationships and provides examples of how these affect the place of teachers and draws implications of student learning, schools, and society.

STUDENT STUDY SITE

Visit the Student Study Site at **www.sagepub.com/hall** to access links to the videos, audio clips, and Deeper Look reference materials noted in this chapter, as well as additional study tools including eFlashcards, web quizzes, and more.

Field Guide

for Learning More About Governance and School Finance

To further increase your understanding about governance and school finance, do one or more of the following activities.

Ask a Teacher or Principal

Ask a principal to share with you the budget for the school. Where do most of the dollars come from? In what areas of the budget does the principal have major say in how the funds are spent?

For a school district where you would like to be a teacher, take a look at the district's budget. Which items are the largest? Are there budget items that you had not expected to see?

Make Your Own Observations

When you are visiting a school, seek out the school's budget. Inquire about how decisions are made to spend the funds. What are the sources of funds? To what extent are teachers involved in making the spending decisions? Listen for the characteristics of good governance that are embedded in the allocation process.

Attend a school board meeting and observe the processes of governance firsthand. How many of the characteristics of Good governance (Figure 9.1) do you see in action? Is there a characteristic that seems to be employed less?

Reflect Through Journaling

Summarize your notes about governance and finance. What are the key themes for you? What are the implications for you in terms of what you need to learn more about before you enter your classroom as a first-year teacher?

In the past the value of local control was a very important argument against state and federal governments intruding on what were seen as local issues, such as local communities and school districts selecting curriculum and determining the qualifications of teachers and principals. Now, the state and federal governments are making most of the decisions about schools. Develop a file of your current position. Outline what you see as being gained, and what is lost, with the current trend toward increasing centralization?

Read a Book

A key component of good governance is the quality of meetings. *Leading Effective Meetings, Teams, and Work Groups in Districts and Schools,* by Matthew Jennings (2007; Alexandria, VA: ASCD), provides a wealth of information that you can use whenever you are a participant in a meeting and especially when you are the leader. The information will be useful in teacher team meetings, in schoolwide staff meetings, and when serving on committees at the district and state levels.

School finance is a very important and complex subject. *School Finance: A Policy Perspective,* by Allan Odden and Lawrence Picus (2007; New York, NY: McGraw Hill), is a good source if you want to go into depth about any school finance topics. The authors are leading school finance scholars. Each chapter goes into detail about one of the important topic areas, including evolution of finance policy, legal issues, equity and adequacy, and different approaches to adjusting for student needs. The chapters in the last half of the book address how the funds can be spent to improve results.

Search the Web

This chapter has included many statistics about revenue, expenditures, and the size of schools and school districts. A useful resource for finding statistical information related to your state, and to compare your school district or school to national norms is the National Center for Education Statistics of the U.S. Department of Education (**http://nces.ed.gov/**). As a first activity, click "Fast Facts," then "Elementary/Secondary." Within each item on the list that appears will be an array of statistical information. Explore a topic that is of particular interest to you. Prepare a short report to share with your classmates. Hint: Depending on which you are more comfortable with, you can view either the "tables" or "figures."

Go to the website for a school or school district where you would like to become a teacher. Find the minutes of the school board meetings. Which budget topics seem to be most discussed?

TEACHER INTERVIEW

Assistant General Counsel Michael Simpson

The exceptional educator interview for this chapter comes from a different part of the education system and the person has a different job. Michael Simpson is assistant general counsel for the National Education Association in Washington, D.C. Each state affiliate will have lawyers to do legal work for NEA members. "Primarily, I am an adviser to all of our attorneys around the country," explains Mr. Simpson. In addition to offering advice to attorneys for more than 30 years, his current position requires him to maintain a private electronic database of legal materials for affiliated attorneys and to publish a bimonthly electronic newsletter about important legal developments. He also is the organizer of a two-and-a-half-day annual meeting of NEA attorneys.

CHAPTER 10 The Law as It Relates to Teaching and Learning

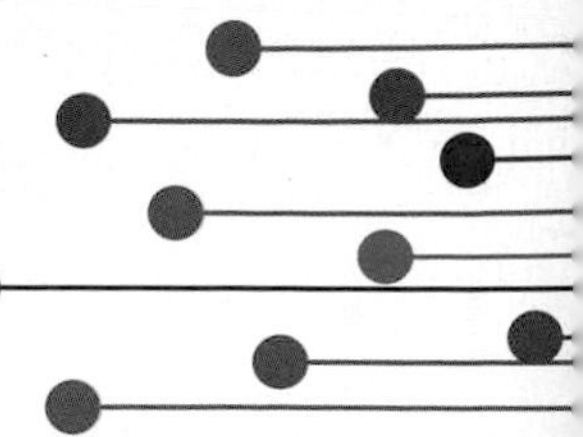

- ***You have a lot of major responsibilities; is it fun?***

  People ask me that. There is an old saying from Confucius, "find a job that you love and you will never have to work a day in your life." I learn something new every day I come to work because the law is constantly evolving; there always are questions I don't know the answer to. I love figuring those things out. I always have enjoyed my job very much.

What do teacher education candidates need to know about the law?

Number one is the proper use of social media. If you read the papers, virtually every day there is a story about some school employee getting fired for posting something inappropriate on Facebook or MySpace. These are not just teachers, but principals and other staff as well.

So many of the young teachers in particular are so active in using social media that they think nothing of putting up stories about themselves on their own Facebook pages. My step-daughter has more than 2,000 Facebook "friends." Her page might as well be open to the public.

Using social media responsibly is really important. The irresponsible use of such media can cause an uproar in the community, which can and has caused the termination of school employees. For example, there was a case from Georgia a couple of years ago where a probationary teacher posted a picture of herself having a glass of wine in France. She certainly was of age. She got fingered by a parent; the administration told her to "resign now or we will fire you." So she resigned.

What other topics are important for future teachers to know about?

They need to know how to identify and put an end to sexual harassment in schools. We have had a number of our members sued for damages because they witnessed instances of harassment and didn't step in and stop it. This includes harassment based on sexual orientation and not just gender-based harassment. The courts are quite sympathetic to students who are bullied at school or harassed, when the adult has the power and the obligation to step in and stop it and doesn't do anything at all. Future teachers need to know their responsibilities about intervening when they witness harassment or bullying.

What about the contractual part of teaching, probationary teachers, student teachers, their rights, responsibilities?

I work for a teachers' union, and we also have support personnel as members. I do think it is important for a number of reasons that beginning teachers join a professional association. If it is not the NEA it could be the AFT, or some other organization. There's been a real shift in the focus of NEA over the last 15 years away from what I would call hard-line unionism to professional

Questions to Consider

1. How aware have you been of the fact that there are legal aspects in teaching?
2. What examples have you seen in the social media that if done by a teacher could cause a problem?
3. What do you know already about the rights of students?
4. What do you know about the rights of probationary teachers?

development. Unions now are taking on the task of helping beginning teachers do better in their teaching. It could be something as simple as negotiating in the collective bargaining agreement to establish a system of master teachers who are assigned to beginning teachers who are often thrown into the classroom with nothing for support. There now is an understanding that the turnover of teachers is so high that we need to do a better job of helping beginning teachers excel and not to be left alone in the classroom.

In your experience how do you see joy in teaching?

Very interesting question; it did give me pause. I come from a family of teachers. My mother was a teacher for 46 years. Both of my aunts were teachers. My grandmother was a teacher. My great aunt was a teacher and has a school named for her in Statesboro, Georgia.

I am "old school." I know that teaching is more than a profession; it is a calling. It is very hard to be a teacher, and a beginning teacher will know in a year or two whether it is something she or he is cut out to do. If a fourth-grade teacher gives a kid a hug, it may be the only hug that kid gets all day. If a secondary school math teacher says "good job," it may be the only time that child hears encouragement. If schoolchildren get a free lunch because they are so poor, it may be the only decent meal they get that day.

I have found that the best teachers are the ones who are empathetic with students and who have the capacity to engage them. As we know, student engagement is the single most important factor in learning. A teacher who understands her role, which is more than just providing information, and enjoys that role, certainly will get a joy out of teaching.

At this point you likely have a very limited understanding of how the legal system relates to your developing career. However, now is the time for you to learn the basics, especially since, if not already, very soon you will be in schools and classrooms as part of your professional preparation.

Teacher education candidates must consider legal aspects of their activities every time they are in field settings and whenever they are in contact with students, parents, other teachers, and administrators. They most certainly must be understanding of student rights and the protection of student records, as well as your responsibility for their safety. Also teacher education candidates need to learn about the liabilities and protections accorded to beginning/probationary teachers. Although first-year teachers have the same professional responsibilities as tenured teachers, they do not have all of the same protections, especially related to nonrenewal and dismissal.

Learning Outcomes

After reading this chapter, you should be able to

1. Describe laws and court decisions related to education, such as the appropriate uses of social media, which is now being addressed in the legal system.
2. Describe the themes within major issues that although addressed in the past continue to be major topics within the legal system.
3. Identify and describe key aspects of students' rights.
4. Identify, describe, and provide examples of the responsibilities and rights of teachers.

INTRODUCTION

Probably your beginning thought about the legal system is an image of the court as seen on television, with a judge and jury. Actually, much is done before an issue is the subject of a court case. The first step is for a legislative body, such as the Congress or a state legislature, to pass a **statute.** This law then becomes the formal statement of what is not, or in some cases what is, permitted. The wording in most statutes sets the general boundaries and some of the limits, but not the specific details. Normally, developing the details for implementing the statute is done by the executive branch of government. For education law at the national level, the U.S. Department of Education would develop the rules and procedures, which are called **administrative law.** In your state, the state education department will most likely establish the rules underlying new education statutes.

The courts do not become involved until there is a disagreement. An individual or a group may take an action that is seen by others as a violation of a statute, or its related rules and procedures. In other instances some may disagree with any or all of a particular legislative agenda and question its correctness. When there is a dispute the courts become the decider. The resulting decisions through the courts are called **case law.**

The U.S. Supreme Court's nine justices have the final say when there are legal questions with regard to the educational system in the United States.

In this chapter we will introduce the findings from selected court cases, especially from the U.S. Supreme Court. Since America is a nation of laws, the final decision in regard to any issue is made by each state's highest court and ultimately the U.S. Supreme Court. All decisions made by the courts begin with first considering what is stated in the U.S. Constitution, and when relevant state constitutions. Then past case law and related statutes will be taken into consideration. In the end, what the Supreme Court decides is final. We also will reference selected pieces of legislation, since in many instances these statutes become important bases for determining what teachers, students, and schools should do.

CONTEMPORARY LEGAL ISSUES AND THEIR DELIBERATIONS

I have given a number of presentations around the country on the social media problem. I tell them upfront: Do not ever text your students unless you are using your school district server, your school district e-mail account, and you are only talking about class work, or study questions, or something like that. Don't ever "friend" students on social media and certainly don't text them. Maintain a professional relationship.—Mr. Simpson

The rapid development of new technologies most certainly is an area where teachers, school administrators, and parents need to think carefully about what is appropriate use. Use of technology is but one of many contemporary problems that are being addressed through legislation and the development of new rules and procedures, and tested through court challenges. Bullying of students and school safety in general is another important problem area. Also, the increasing ease with which technology makes it possible to access information is generating new questions related to protection of copyrights and fair uses.

These topics illustrate the continually evolving need for new legislation and emerging questions that have to be addressed by the courts. Social media, bullying, and copyright protections are examples of important questions that are now being considered by the courts. Many other questions have been decided in the past and need to be understood by today's teachers. Keep in mind that different lower-level courts may reach different decisions. Until the U.S. Supreme Court decides, and ultimately, each state's statutes reflect what is prohibited and permitted, it is very important for you to be extra careful in what you do and don't do.

Social Media: Uses, Misuses, and Issues

Teachers and administrators need to consider carefully acceptable uses of new technologies as well as "older" technologies such as cell phones, digital cameras, and the Internet. Recently courts have been addressing various questions related to rights of privacy, consequences of distributing certain types of information, and legality of searches.

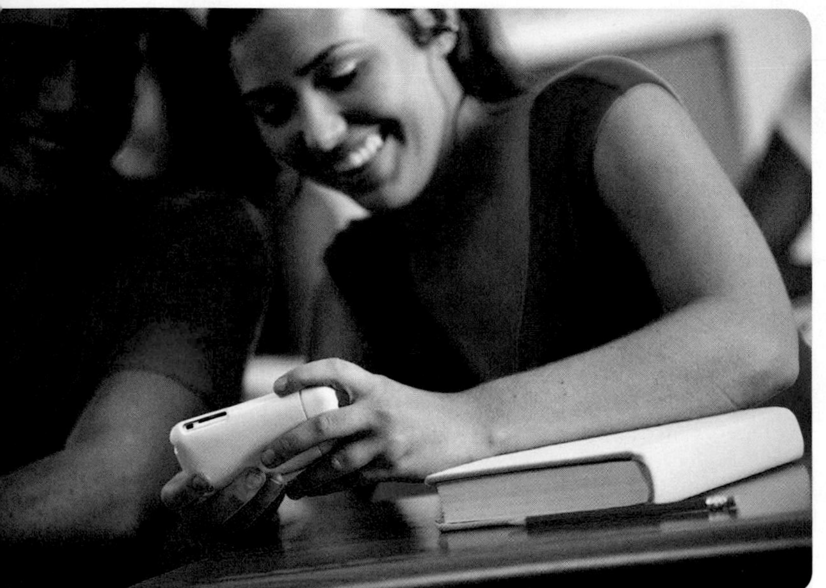

Teachers and students should be very careful about what they share through social media.

Teachers' Use of MySpace

Do teachers have guaranteed First Amendment free speech rights to establish MySpace profiles and make these available to students? No. In the fall of 2005, Jeffrey Spanierman, a nontenured English teacher in Connecticut, set up a MySpace website called "Mr. Spiderman." He used the account to communicate with students about homework and also more personal issues including casual comments and pictures of naked men. Several students complained to a counselor, who referred the matter to the principal. An administrative investigation was conducted with the conclusion being a letter from the assistant superintendent that the teacher's contract would not be renewed. Mr. Spanierman filed suit in federal court. The federal district court's decision supported the school district's decision in seeing the MySpace profile as disruptive and that it was "reasonable for the Defendants to expect the Plaintiff, a teacher with supervisory authority over students, to maintain a professional, respectful association with students" (*Spanierman v. Hughes, Druzolowski, & Hylwa,* 576 F. Supp.2d 292 (D. Conn. 2008).

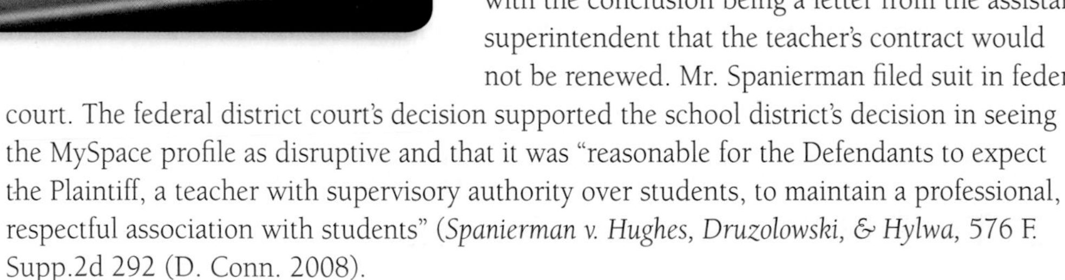

Cyberbullying

Are there any limits on what students can create and distribute about school officials and students from home? Yes. Two of the major questions related to cyberbullying are (1) When does the exercise of free speech become bullying? and (2) Under what conditions can a school district suspend a student for cyberbullying? Each of these questions is being addressed by lower courts. Ultimately, it is likely that the U.S. Supreme Court will be asked to provide final answers.

Cyberbullying can be directed toward adults as well as students. For example, in 2010 two cases in Pennsylvania (*J.S. v. Blue Mountain School District* and *Layshock ex rel. Layshock v. Hermitage School District*), students were suspended for having created offensive MySpace fake profiles of school officials. One eighth-grade student had called her principal a "hairy sex addict" and a "pervert." In the other case a high school senior had called his principal a "whore" who used drugs. In both cases the students had been using home computers. Both cases were appealed to three-judge panels of the U.S. Court of Appeals for the Third Circuit. The two panels rendered opposite decisions. The J.S. case was seen as proper while the Layshock case was not seen as having established a sufficiently close connection to be disruptive. Since then the full Third Court is rehearing the cases.

Video Link 10.1
Watch a clip about teachers and social media.

In a recent case in West Virginia, the Fourth Circuit Court of Appeals ruled that a school district had the right to suspend a senior who online had called another girl a "slut" with venereal disease. School officials labeled this a "hate website" that violated school policy against harassment and bullying.

As you can see, different courts are making different decisions. As the process continues to unfold, one or more cases will be appealed to and accepted by the U.S. Supreme Court. Also, as the process unfolds there will be gradual clarification of what is considered cyberbullying and under what conditions school officials can suspend students. One possible emerging direction from the cases cited here is that school officials may have more authority to suspend students when the victim is a fellow student. They may have less authority when the offensive activity is done away from school. Another element to be tested is the extent of disruption of school activity.

Sexting

Is it OK for students to take and share explicit photos of themselves? No. **Sexting** is the act of using a cell phone or other technology to send or receive sexually explicit pictures, video, and/or text. This act can be consensual or nonconsensual. One of the earliest sexting cases (*Miller v. Skumanick*, 2009) developed in Pennsylvania. Teachers discovered pictures of three topless 13-year-old girls on the cell phones of boy classmates. School district officials confiscated the phones and turned them over to the district attorney who determined that the images were provocative and that the girls were accomplices in the production of child pornography.

The district attorney threatened charges against the girls as well as the boys for distribution unless they participated in a counseling remediation program. The boys agreed but the girls refused and filed a lawsuit (*Miller v. Mitchell*, 2010) alleging violation of their First Amendment right to free expression. Following two years of legal procedures the Third Court of Appeals ruled that the photographs did not constitute child pornography and the girls were protected under the First Amendment.

Although in the case cited here the students were not taken to criminal court for either the production of pornography or its distribution, in other states and other school districts the same challenges are wending their way through the courts. Fortunately, state legislatures are now developing laws that distinguish between crimes related to child pornography, that is, a felony, and the unwitting behaviors of minors, which in many cases can be considered a misdemeanor. Regardless of the intent, teachers and their students need to be sensitive to the action that can be constructed as sexting as well as the legal and emotional consequences.

Table 10.1 Contemporary Questions Being Considered by the Courts

Question	Case	Decision
Do teachers have First Amendment protections in their use of MySpace?	Teacher Free Speech *Spanierman v. Hughes* (2008)	Not when what they do is considered to be disruptive.
Are students protected when they post uncomplimentary descriptions of school personnel or students from home?	Cyberbullying *Blue Mountain School District* and *Layshock v. Hermitage School District* (2010)	No, when it is about students; may be OK when it is about school personnel.
Is sharing photos of topless girls the production and distribution of pornographic material?	Sexting *Miller v. Skumanick* (2009)	Yes, in some states, maybe in others.
Can teachers take and use whatever they find from the Internet?	Taking Material off the Internet *U.S. Copyright Law*	Be careful when thinking that you are covered by "fair use." Check the source carefully.

Copying Documents and Other Material From the Internet

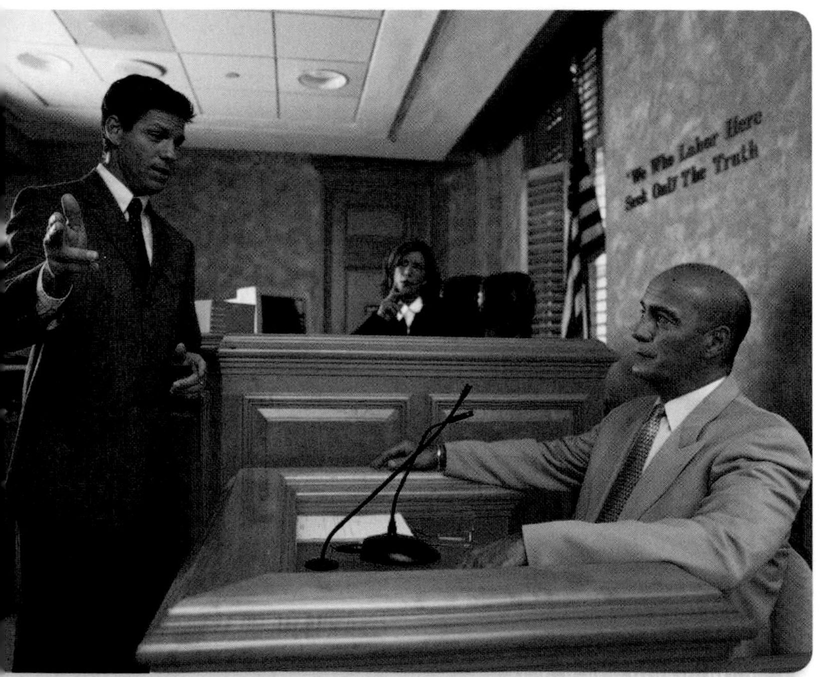

Everyone, including teachers, can be prosecuted for violating copyright laws.

Uses, and misuses, of social media is just one of the areas currently being examined by the courts. Table 10.1 is a summary of selected court cases related to social media and a number of other contemporary legal questions. As you will read below, many of the current questions have to do with uses of the Internet, which has most certainly brought us into the Information Age. Teachers and students can access all sorts of documents, pictures, sources, and resources by simply hitting a few keys and accessing a search engine. Students today seem to think nothing of downloading for free music and videos. Teachers can be all too casual about copying text and other resources. But what about downloading and using digital material that is protected and/or has a copyright? By law a potential user, teacher, or student, is required to seek permission from the source before distributing said material.

Accessing Material on the Web That Has a Copyright

Searching for and finding a juicy piece of information to complement any work in progress is a satisfying process. The accessibility of the web even makes it convenient. What is not so clear, given the ease of downloading artifacts or evidence from the web, is just how closely protected are web-based sources, and what are the requirements for using such sources in your own work.

Is all information on the Internet considered public domain? No. There are federal, state, and international laws that govern copyright practices. In general, they are designed to protect the rights of scholars and artists while preserving the public's right to benefit from the works of those same creators. Copyrights protect the imagination of individuals.

Federal law *(U.S. Copyright Law {Title 17 U.S.C. Section 101 et seq., Title 18 U.S.C. Section 2319)* protects copyright owners from the unauthorized reproduction, adaptation, performance, display, or distribution of copyright-protected works. Penalties for copyright infringement differ in civil and criminal cases. Civil remedies are generally available for any act of infringement without regard to the intention or knowledge of the defendant, or harm to the copyright owner. Criminal penalties are available for intentional acts undertaken for purposes of "commercial advantage" or "private financial gain." Private financial gain includes the possibility of financial loss to the copyright holder as well as traditional "gain" by the defendant.

Is there information regarding copyright that will help teachers understand what they can and should do? Yes. For example:

- Given the easy access to digital media by students and teachers, one important resource is the website of the Recording Industry Association of America (RIAA; **http://www.riaa.com/**). Two important tabs to check out are "Information for Parents" and "Programs for Educators."
- Commonsense media (**http://www.commonsensemedia.org/educators/curriculum**) offers a variety of curriculum resources for teachers and information for parents about how to use media in safe and responsible ways.
- At **http://www.templetons.com/brad/copymyths.html** 10 myths about copyright are explained in ways that teachers and students can understand.
- Among the teacher resources of the U.S. Library of Congress is a page titled "Copyright and Primary Sources" (**http://www.loc.gov/teachers/usingprimarysources/copyright.html**), which addresses the importance of teachers using primary sources in legally correct ways.
- The Electronic Frontier Foundation (**http://www.teachingcopyright.org/**) has developed a unit, "Teaching Copyright," that consists of five 60-minute lesson plans including quizzes, handouts, and notes for the teacher.

Video Link 10.2
Learn more about copyright laws for educators.

Copyright Guidelines for Teachers and Students

Are there some exceptions to copyright laws on the Internet? Yes. **Fair use** criteria can create some exceptions to copyright laws for teachers and students. However, keep in mind that there are no absolute guidelines for fair use in educational settings. According to the Stanford University Libraries website (http://fairuse.stanford.edu/), the only way to get a definitive answer on whether a particular use is a fair use is to have it resolved in federal court. Judges use four factors to resolve fair use disputes:

1. The purpose and character of your use
2. The nature of the copyrighted work
3. The amount and substantiality of the portion taken
4. The effect of the use upon the potential market

Additionally, guidelines have been established for uses and copying of information in educational settings. These guidelines are not part of the Copyright Act but should be studied carefully before embarking on any major use of copyrighted material.

According to a Smartype.com info sheet, "many newcomers to the Internet may perceive it as a lawless space where communication is ungoverned and anything goes." This is not necessarily so. Internet users are accountable to copyright laws in the same way that they are when accessing and using information in the real world. Since April 1, 1989, every communication (words, photos, music, or art) produced on the Internet is copyrighted by default.

Is it true that as long as you don't use the material for commercial purposes you are not breaking any laws. No. Be safe. Ask for permission when using any material produced by anyone else.

Finding Out If Something Has a Copyright

You may not be in the habit of scrolling down to the bottom of any webpage that you access, but in the future click on the disclaimer and copyright information posted at the bottom of nearly every webpage. You'll find out quickly how much of the information on that website is available for public use. In most cases it's zilch, but there is usually a place where you can contact the designers or owners of the website to see if they will let you use some of the information they have organized. Most would be more than happy to give permission to educators.

CONTINUING LEGAL DILEMMAS RELATED TO EDUCATION

Given the hundreds of years of history related to the identification of problems, development of laws to address each problem, and the arbitration of disputes by the courts, you might think that all the questions from the past would have been addressed and solutions established. However, this is not the case. There are a number of questions for which there have been no final answers. Several of these related to education are highlighted next.

There are continuing questions and challenges related to the separation of church and state when it comes to education. For example, can tax dollars be used to pay for student transportation to Catholic schools?

One idea that might help you understand why each of these areas has been so enduring is to make a distinction between something that is a **problem** and something that is a **dilemma.** By definition a problem has a solution. Once a problem is defined, one or more solutions can be devised to fix it. Most of the time when something stops working on your car a mechanic can fix it. A problem is identified (it won't start), there is a diagnosis, and a new part installed (a starter motor). Sometimes the car still won't start and all are puzzled—in other words, a dilemma. Dilemmas do not have simple solutions. In fact, dilemmas are so complex that there is no single solution. The enduring legal topics described herein are dilemmas. Although there have been legislative actions, statutes approved, and court cases conducted, the "problem," that is, dilemma, persists. It is likely that each of these enduring topics will still be in debate at the end of your teaching career.

Separation of Church and State

One of the reasons taught in school for the Puritans to travel in tiny boats across the Atlantic to a new country was to escape religious persecution. When the U.S. Constitution was written this concern was addressed directly in two clauses within the First Amendment.

> Establishment clause: "Congress shall make no law respecting an establishment of religion.
>
> Free exercise clause: "or prohibiting the free exercise thereof"

These two clauses would seem to be straightforward. At the time, Thomas Jefferson talked about a wall of separation between church and state. Until some 70 years ago this view was pretty much accepted—in other words, no problem. A 1947 Supreme Court decision *(Everson v. Board of Education)* is now seen as the beginning of the creation of a dilemma.

Using Public Funds to Pay for Transportation to Catholic Schools

New Jersey had a statute that allowed for reimbursement of public bus transportation costs to parents who sent their children to Catholic schools. The question asked in *Everson v. Board of Education* (1947) was whether or not these payments were a violation of the establishment clause. A divided Court ruled that it was not a violation. The reasoning was that the payments were not direct support to parochial schools but a "general program" of support to assist parents of all religions.

Two Continuing Questions

In many ways *Everson v. Board of Education* broke a logjam. Since 1947 there have been continuing debates, actions that challenge the boundaries, development of various statutes, and publication of various rules and procedures, all of which were intended to either stay clear of or test where the boundary now is between church and state.

Two questions that can be used to understand elements of what is now a dilemma are these:

1. In what ways and to what extent can public funds be used in association with religious schooling and not be in violation of the U.S. Constitution?
2. What types of religious activities can and cannot be done, within and around public schools, and not be seen as a violation of the U.S. Constitution?

Since 1947 there have been many court challenges and decisions relative to the ways that public funds can be used in association with nonpublic schools. Table 10.2 includes a summary of selected cases. Each decision has provided more guidance but also led to new questions.

Can public funds be used to pay for teachers in nonpublic schools? No. In *Lemon v. Kurtzman* (1971) the Court was asked to decide whether public funds could be used to pay for teachers and textbooks for secular subjects in nonpublic schools. The Court ruled 8–0 that state financial aid of this type was a violation of the establishment clause. Additionally, Chief Justice Burger stated a three-part test for laws to be constitutional. This test has become known as the "Lemon Test." The three parts are that (a) the statute must have "a secular legislative purpose," (b) it must neither advance nor hinder religion, and (c) it must not encourage "an excessive government entanglement with religion."

As you can see in studying Table 10.2, there has been a continuing circling around the central question of to what extent and in what ways public funds can be used in conjunction with nonpublic schools and not run into violation of the establishment clause.

Table 10.2 Legal Dilemmas That Continue to Be Addressed by the Courts Have Major Impacts on Schools, Students, Teachers, and Communities

U.S. Supreme Court Decisions Related to Separation of Church and State		
Question	**Case**	**Decision**
Can state funds be used to reimburse parents for bus travel to Catholic schools?	*Everson v. Board of Education* 1947	Yes. The law did not pay money to parochial schools, nor did it directly support them.
Can public funds be used to pay for teachers in nonpublic schools?	*Lemon v. Kurtzman* (1971)	No. This would be a violation of the establishment clause.
Can student-led prayer be a part of school activities?	*Santa Fe Independent School District v. Doe* (2000)	No. This would be a violation of the establishment clause.
Can religious holidays be observed in public schools?	*Florey v. Sioux Falls School District* (1980)	Yes, if the celebration is secular.
Can religious student groups meet at a public school?	*Board of Education of the Westside Community Schools v. Mergens* (1990)	If one noncurriculum-related student group is permitted to meet at a public school then the school may not deny other clubs.
	School Finance	
Can local property taxes be used to pay for schools?	*San Antonio (Texas) Independent School District v. Rodriquez* (1979)	Yes.
Do the states have to fund all schools efficiently?	*Rose v. Council for Better Education* (1989)	Yes, in Kentucky. Many other states also have had to reconfigure their funding of schools, based on how education is addressed within each state's constitution.
	Desegregation and Integration	
Is separate but equal constitutional?	*Plessy v. Ferguson* (1896)	Yes.
Is separate but equal constitutional?	*Brown v. Board of Education of Topeka* (1954)	No.

The Place of Religious Activities in Public Schools

Tests of the free exercise clause have been equally extensive. A year does not go by without reports in the news in which another student at his or her graduation ceremony prays, or a teacher is reported to be proselytizing, or a governing body mandates that the Bible or a topic such as creationism be part of the public school curriculum. The central question then becomes, is not permitting the activity prohibiting the free exercise of religion? Of course allowing it may be seen as a violation of the establishment clause. Table 10.2 is a summary of selected cases and Court decisions related to religious activities in public schools.

Video Link 10.3
Learn more about religion and public schools.

Prayer at School Events

Can students lead a prayer at athletic events, graduation ceremonies, and other school-sponsored events? No. Before 1995 an elected student council member at Santa Fe (Texas) High School delivered a prayer over the public address system before every home football game. It was described as overtly Christian. A Mormon and a Catholic family filed suit. In *Santa Fe Independent School District v. Doe* (2000) the Court ruled 6–3 that the policy of permitting student-led prayer at football games violates the establishment clause.

But what if there is a period of silent meditation and prayer set aside in public schools? Here too, the answer is No. In *Wallace v. Jaffree* (1985), the Court ruled that an Alabama statute that authorized a minute of silent prayer, and another authorizing silent meditation, were unconstitutional. The Court concluded that there was no secular purpose and that the intent of the Alabama legislature was to establish prayer in the schools.

Celebration of Religious Holidays in Schools

Can religious holidays be observed at school events? Yes, if the celebration has a secular basis. In *Florey v. Sioux Falls School District* (1980) the Court based its decision on the historical and cultural significance of Christmas and the fact that the holiday was not being observed for the purpose of promoting Christianity. A federal district court in New Jersey allowed a school district to include on the school calendar holidays such as Christmas and Hanukkah "to broaden students' sensitivity toward religious diversity and their knowledge of the role of religion in the development of civilization" (Cambron-McCabe, McCarthy, & Thomas, 2004, p. 38). The courts have ruled that school choirs and assemblies may sing holiday carols, for instance, as long as the performances are not organized for religious purposes.

Some parents have charged schools with promoting the religion of Wicca when they observe Halloween with pictures of witches and goblins. However, a Florida court ruled that such displays did not promote a religion. The U.S. Supreme Court has declined appeals of cases related to the observance of holidays that are perceived by some parents as promoting religion.

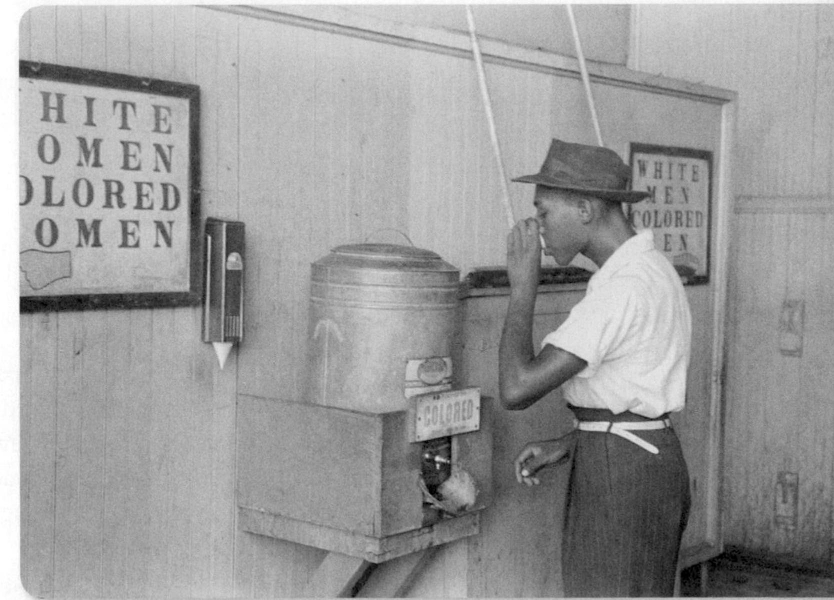

Separate but equal was not equal.

Funding of Public Schools: Equity and Equality

Another continuing dilemma has to do with the funding of schools. Over the last 30 years more than 40 states have had court challenges related to the amount of funding support and/or whether the available funds have been distributed fairly. In *Rodriguez v. San Antonio Independent School* (1971) the U.S. Supreme court deferred to the states questions about the funding of schools. Thus since then challenges about funding have been based in the wording and way the provision of schooling has been addressed in each state's constitution.

What the U.S. Constitution Says About Funding

Is the funding of schools a U.S. Constitution issue? No. The Mexican American Legal Defense and Education Fund (MALDEF) filed a class action suit on the behalf of a group of Mexican American parents against the inequitable funding of Texas schools. In 1971, the federal district court ruled in *Rodriguez v. San Antonio Independent School* that the Texas school finance system was unconstitutional based on the equal protection clause of the Fourteenth Amendment. In 1973, the United States Supreme Court ruled that school finance was not a constitutional issue, pushing the cases back to state courts for resolution.

View of the States About the Funding of Schools

Could a state supreme court declare the whole system of public education unconstitutional? Yes. This is exactly what happened in Kentucky in the early 1990s. In *Rose v. Council for Better Education* (1989) the Kentucky Supreme Court ruled "... it is crystal clear that the General Assembly has fallen short of its duty to enact legislation to provide for an efficient system of common schools throughout the state." The key term here is *efficient,* which was a stated expectation in Kentucky's constitution. The court went on to say, "Lest there be any doubt, the result of our decision is that Kentucky's entire system of common schools is unconstitutional." The court directed the legislature to develop a new system of public education for the state. The result was the Kentucky Education Reform Act (KERA) of 1991.

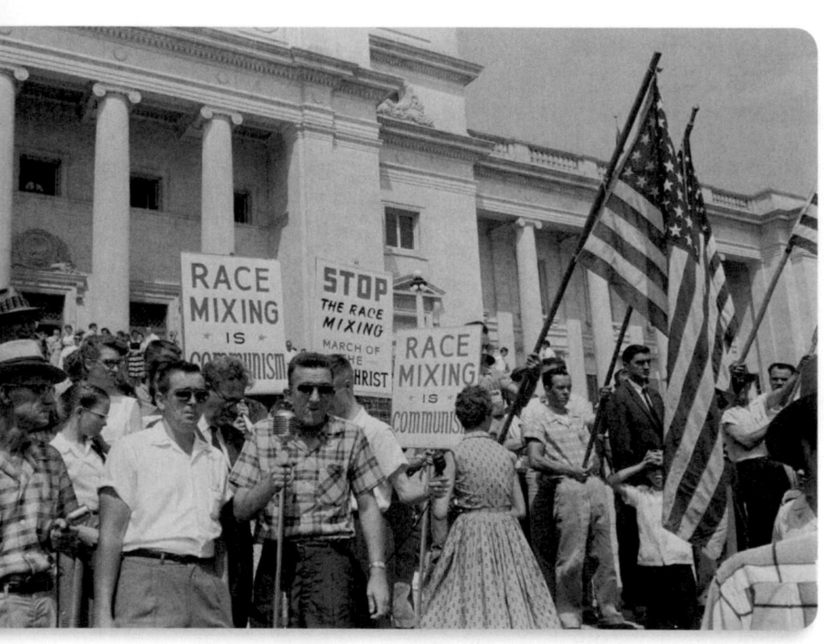

Achieving integration has been a long, and continuing, struggle.

Segregation, Desegregation, and the Risks of Resegregation

Another important dilemma that has a long history is achieving and sustaining nondiscriminatory practices in society in general and in schools in particular. Over the last 200 years, the courts have been on both sides of this dilemma. You need to keep in mind two important terms in considering this dilemma. **De facto** segregation refers to segregation that has developed through the "facts" of a situation, which are outside of the actions of government. **De jure** segregation refers to segregation that is brought about through laws *and* the actions of state and local officials.

Separate but Equal Was Constitutional

In 1896 in *Plessy v. Ferguson,* the Supreme Court ruled that public facilities and services for blacks could be "separate but equal." For the next 58 years de jure segregation led to dual school systems (one for whites and another for blacks). This included black teachers for segregated schools and white teachers for white students. Mainly, but not only, in Southern schools the state constitutions, statutes, and local school policies reinforced having dual school systems. This also was the time when Southern states adopted Jim Crow laws that required whites and blacks to use separate facilities, including drinking fountains, toilets, hotels, restaurants, and seats on public transportation.

Separate but Equal Becomes Unconstitutional

In 1954 the U.S. Supreme Court in *Brown v. Board of Education* reversed its ruling of 50-plus years before. "We conclude that in the field of public education the doctrine of 'separate but equal' has no place. Separate educational facilities are inherently unequal." In other words, de jure segregation is now unconstitutional. *Brown* only dealt with public schools; however, its consequences have evolved to affect all of American society.

Audio Link 10.1
Learn more about school segregation.

Implementation of *Brown* has continued to require court engagement. The overall strategy was to achieve **integration** whereby there would not be bias in the distribution of facilities, students, and school personnel. The first strategy of the courts was to direct dismantling of the dual systems of schooling. In many instances the courts' directive of implementing desegregation with "all deliberate speed" was not resulting in observable movements. So in cases such as *Alexander v. Holmes County Board of Education* (1969) the Court mandated that districts must immediately terminate dual school systems.

Release From Court Order

Over the intervening years there have continued to be suits related to progress in achieving integration in schools. Many school systems have been placed under court supervision, and their procedures as well as the assignment of students and personnel have been closely monitored. As the vestiges of the dual systems have been eliminated and the distribution of students and personnel has become equalized, in other words integration has been achieved, school systems have been released from supervision by the court. In many communities this has been a process that has taken many years.

Risk of Resegregation

Much has been achieved over the decades since the 1954 *Brown* decision. De jure segregation has been widely challenged and in most settings eliminated. However, now there is a new risk, **resegregation.** Now most of the segregation in schools and communities is de facto. For many reasons a large proportion of people of one race will be living in one neighborhood. One driving force for the current situation was the earlier "white flight." As the courts directed that schools integrate white and black students, many white families moved to other school districts. There also have been economic factors contributing to where people live. The end result can be de facto resegregation.

In Summary: Solving Dilemmas Takes Time

As the dilemmas of separation of church and state, financing of public schools, and desegregation well illustrate, many of today's challenges are not easily addressed. Most certainly they do not have simple solutions that will bring each to a final conclusion. Instead each of these dilemmas is enduring and likely to require concerted effort not only by the courts, but by government leaders, citizens, and especially teachers. As is readily seen within each of these dilemmas, the one institution that continues to be seen as a tool for solving them is education.

UNDERSTANDING AND USING EVIDENCE

Schoolwide Data About Student Learning

As a teacher, one of your opportunities to become involved schoolwide is to become a member of the School Improvement Team (SIT). The SIT will include teachers, the principal or vice principal, team leaders/department chairs, and perhaps an outside resource such as a district office person and possibly a university faculty member.

Each year the SIT reviews the test scores for all students and then develops the School Improvement Plan (SIP) that details the "action steps" the school will take the next year to improve student learning. Reviewing the data is where the SIT work begins. For this activity you are to assume that you a member of the SIT for a large (2,700 students) high school. The table presents two years of scores for a "proficiency" test. This is a test that students must pass in order to graduate from high school. It is typically taken the first time at the end of the sophomore year.

The Questions

Study the data in the table and answer these questions:

1. What patterns or trends do you see in the data?
2. Are there areas where students improved from one year to the next?
3. Are there areas where students did not improve?
4. Which groups of students would you want the SIP to address in planning for the next school year?
5. Given your developing knowledge of the law, what cautions would you keep in mind in developing the SIP action steps?

Answer the Questions

Answer the questions above for yourself before proceeding to the discussion below.

Reading	**Year One**			**Year Two**		
Population	**Number**	**% Proficient**	**% Nonproficient**	**Number**	**% Proficient**	**% Nonproficient**
Hispanic/Latino	230	54.5%	45.5%	274	63.4%	36.6%
Black/African American	89	60.5%	39.5%	85	62.0%	38.0%
White/Caucasian	85	73.9%	26.1%	78	76.5%	23.5%

STUDENTS' RIGHTS AND PROTECTIONS

Another area where beginning teachers can get in trouble is dealing with students with disabilities. For example, there is great controversy around the country now about what is called "restraint and seclusion" as ways of dealing with students who are out of control. Both school districts and individual employees have been sued in recent years either for confining a student with disabilities in a room until he or she

Reading	Year One			Year Two		
Population	Number	% Proficient	% Nonproficient	Number	% Proficient	% Nonproficient
IEP	14	20.9%	79.1%	14	19.4%	80.6%
LEP	144	50.3%	49.7%	209	61.8%	38.2%
FRPL	59	57.8%	42.2%	161	68.8%	31.2%

IEP – Individualized Education Plan LEP – Limited English Proficiency FRPL – Free or Reduced-Price Lunch

Discussion

There are several trends in these data. How many of these did you identify?

- Hispanic/Latino students had an increase in their pass rate.
- There is no change for Black/African American students.
- White students' scores might have increased a little.
- There was no change in the number or pass rate for students with IEPs.
- There was a significant increase in the pass rate for LEP and FRPL students.

Plans for Next Year

What did you recommend that the SIT address in planning for next year? For example, shouldn't something different be done to address Black/African American students? Whatever has been done to help Hispanic/Latino, LEP, and FRPL students probably should be continued. What are your thoughts about serving students with IEPs? Perhaps there should be more inclusion? If there isn't co-teaching (where the regular classroom teacher and the special education resource teacher work together), maybe it should be tried.

Legal Cautions

What did you identify about legal aspects of a School Improvement Plan? For example, you would want to be cautious about permanent classes or groups of any one of the student categories. This could be seen as discrimination. An important step would be to have more data. For example, ask that the test scores be disaggregated by standard. Then group students according to the standards where they need extra attention.

In summary, data-driven decision making always begins with looking at the data and disaggregating the data so that instruction can be customized. At the same time, keep in mind that there may be legal implications if some strategies are implemented without the data to support how student learning will be enhanced.

calms down (that's called seclusion) or for physically restraining a student, for example, by tying his hands to a chair to keep him from hitting himself or others.

Beginning teachers also need to know the ins and outs of how IDEA (the Individuals with Disabilities Education Act) works because every new teacher will likely have one or more students in each class with IEPs and BIPs (behavioral intervention plans). They will have to sit in on IEP meetings. They really need to have a grasp of what rights students have under IDEA and Section 504, and what their responsibilities are.
—Mr. Simpson

Although in many ways students have the rights of all citizens, in some ways their rights as students are more prescribed. In the distant past a commonly held view was that school officials were acting in place of the parents, in other words *in loco parentis*. This is no longer the case. Teachers and school administrators have to be careful to protect the rights of students and follow established procedures in all matters including discipline, searches, bullying, disseminating information from student records, and seeing that students are safe. Table 10.3 presents some of the findings of the courts. These and other cases are described here.

Statutes Related to Students With Disabilities

Students with disabilities and IDEA were described in Chapter Three, "Addressing Learners' Individual Needs." Here we begin by identifying legal aspects of students with disabilities. The remainder of the section describes other important aspects of student rights

The Least Restrictive Environment

Not all students have common capabilities for learning. Some students may need more time to learn a concept or skill that will lead to meeting academic standards. Some students may need special instruction or materials and resources to help them process instruction. Laws have been established to regulate and determine the placement of such students in schools. The Individuals with Disabilities Education Act (IDEA) is the federal law governing the education of children with disabilities. IDEA and its regulations define least restrictive environment (LRE) and require that all states demonstrate they have policies and procedures in place to guarantee they meet the federal LRE requirements.

Does a student with disabilities have an individualized education plan (IEP) that indicates what the extent of his or her least restrictive environment should be? Yes. The 1997 Amendments to IDEA require that in a situation where a child will not participate fully with peers without disabilities, the IEP must include an explanation of why and to what extent the child will not be included.

Inclusion

Is inclusion a right? No. People often assume that IDEA regulations require schools to practice inclusion. However, the term *inclusion* is not included in the IDEA statutes. The terms **mainstreaming** and **least restrictive environment** are included in the IDEA regulations, and these terms require school districts to educate students with disabilities in regular classrooms with their nondisabled classmates in the school they would attend to the maximum extent

Table 10.3 Student Rights

Question	Case	Decision
Do schools have a free hand in engaging in student searches?	*New Jersey v. T.L.O.* (1985)	No, there must be reasonable cause.
Can a student be suspended without a hearing?	*Goss v. Lopez* (1975)	Only in an emergency.
May states constitutionally authorize corporal punishment?	*Ingraham v. Wright* (1977)	Yes, and many states have.

appropriate. According to the definition of a least restrictive environment, a child with a disability may only be removed from the regular classroom when the nature or severity of the disability is such that the education in regular classes cannot be achieved satisfactorily, even with the use of supplementary aids and services. Students with disabilities may at times be removed from the regular classroom to work in a small group or in one-on-one situations designed to provide them with additional education in a specific academic area.

IDEA requires that students with disabilities be included in the regular classroom to the maximum extent that is appropriate.

Paying for Special Education

Do parents of students with disabilities have to pay for the special services provided by the school? No. Reauthorization of the IDEA in 1997 extended federal funding for special education services to assure that all children with disabilities were provided with a free appropriate public education (FAPE), and that the student's placement and the services he or she receives depend on the student's individual needs, not on administrative convenience.

Student and Teacher Qualifications Under IDEA

Is there a test to determine a student's eligibility for IDEA services? Yes. In a two-part test, a student's disability must fit within one of the categories of eligibility, and then it must be proven that the child needs special services because of this disability. Not all children with physical or mental impairments will satisfy IDEA's two-part eligibility test and so are not eligible for IDEA services.

Are there special requirements for classroom teachers who will teach students with disabilities in the least restrictive environment? Yes. All general and special education teachers responsible for providing services to students with disabilities must receive appropriate training, resources, and support necessary to help such students achieve academic goals. Specifications for a teaching certificate require that some college coursework related to the special needs of students with disabilities be included on a licensure applicant's transcript.

Student Rights

The rights of students as well as teacher and school responsibilities have been tested in the courts, and in most instances there now are established policies, rules, and procedures. Now is the time for you, as a future teacher, to begin to understand the rights of all students and your role in protecting those rights.

Deeper Look 10.2
Read more about FERPA.

Family Privacy Rights

Do families have rights to review student records? Yes. In 1974, Congress passed Public Law 93-380, the Family Educational Rights and Privacy Act (FERPA), to protect the confidentiality of student records. It allows parents the right to review their children's records and to file complaints. Non-English-speaking parents must be notified of these rights in their native language. The law requires the withdrawal of federal funds if a school (1) does not allow parents access to their children's records, or (2) releases information (with some exceptions) without the parent's permission. FERPA also applies to colleges and universities, but parental approval is not required for students over 18 years old. Approval must be granted by the college student.

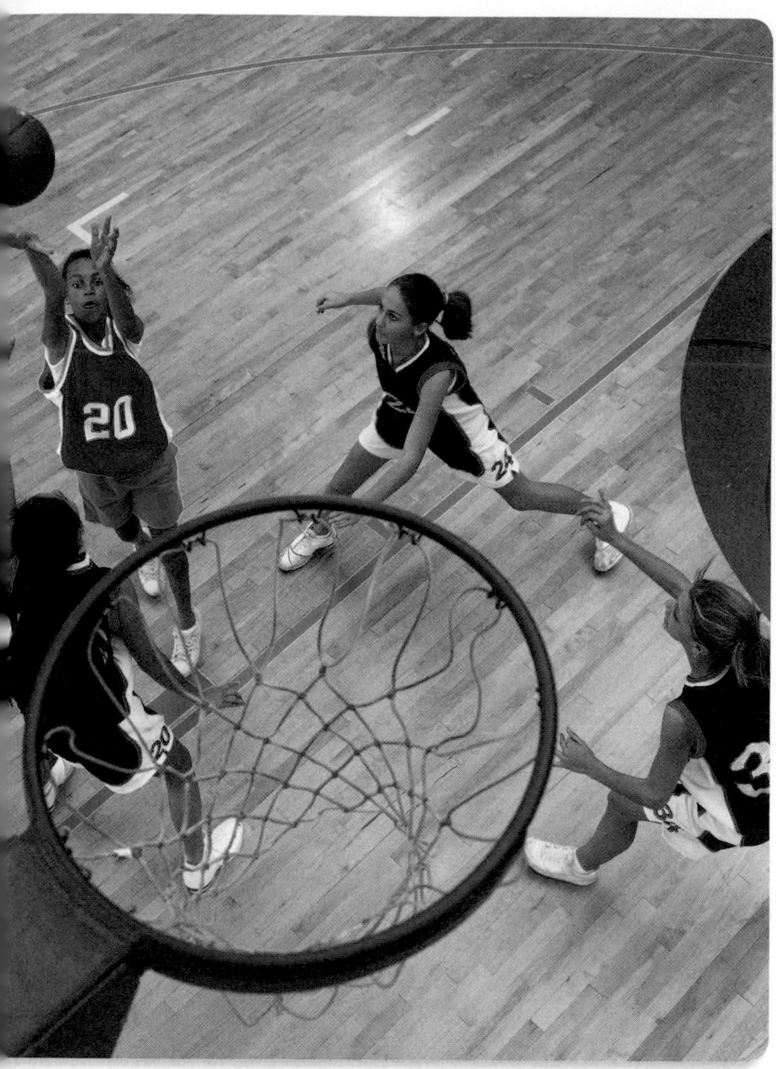

Under Title IX and other statutes, girls must have equal opportunities to participate in sports.

Recent court cases have clarified applicable violations under FERPA. For example, a college student filed for damages in *Gonzaga University v. Doe* because the university had released to the state department of education records indicating an unsubstantiated allegation of sexual misconduct, which led to the denial of a teaching license. The Supreme Court ruled in 2002 that individuals are not entitled to damages awards under FERPA. In 2002, the Supreme Court also ruled that peer grading practices did not violate FERPA in *Owasso Independent School District v. Falvo*.

Student records can sometimes be released without parental approval. For example, schools can release official student records to another school to which a student is transferring if the school has a clear policy that it routinely transfers such records. Student records are also made available for accreditation visits and audits and evaluations of federal programs.

State Interests Versus Individual Rights

Can compulsory attendance laws require all children to attend public schools? No. In 1922 the Oregon legislature passed the Compulsory Education Act, which required the parents and custodians of children between the ages of eight and 16 to send them "to a public school for the period of time a public school shall be held during the current year." This statute required attendance at *public schools only*. The Society of Sisters, which had been organized in 1880 to care for orphans, challenged the statute. In its ruling, *Pierce v. Society of Sisters* (1925), the Supreme Court declared that states may require compulsory attendance, but they may not require that all children attend public schools.

Public High Schools

Do states have the authority to establish public high schools? Yes. The answer to this question came in *Stuart v. School District No. 1 of Village of Kalamazoo* (1874). Kalamazoo College, a private academy, had been established in 1855. As demand for preparation for university increased, in 1858 the district superintendent created a union high school. The school was successful. The college was concerned because it pulled some students away and some taxpayers objected. In 1873 the college and a group of prominent citizens filed suit. The case was decided in support of public high schools by the Supreme Court of Michigan.

Sports for Girls

Can separate playing seasons be scheduled for girls' and boys' teams that are playing the same sport? No. This practice violates the equal protection clauses of federal and state constitutions. Some school districts argue that they do not have the facilities or coaches for both teams to practice and compete during the same season. The courts in Michigan and West Virginia ruled that if the two teams cannot play during the same season, the burden of playing during the off-season must be shared. For example, the boys' team would have to play during the off-season in alternating years.

Undocumented Students

Can the undocumented children of alien parents be denied a public school education? No. In 1975, the Texas legislature decided to withhold funds from local school districts for children who were not "legally admitted" into the United States. The act also empowered school districts to deny enrollment to undocumented children. In *Plyler v. Doe* (1982) the Supreme Court was asked to determine the constitutionality of the Texas statute. The equal protection clause of the Fourteenth Amendment, which says that "No State shall . . . deprive any person of life, liberty, or property, without due process of law; nor deny to any person within its jurisdiction the equal protection of the laws," does not limit protection to citizens.

The Court found that although public education is not a right granted by the Constitution, it is not merely a governmental "benefit" indistinguishable from other forms of social welfare. Education was found to be important in both maintaining our basic institutions and having a lasting impact on the life of the child; mark the distinction. In sum, education is seen as having a fundamental role in maintaining the fabric of our society. We cannot ignore the significant social costs borne by the nation when select groups are denied an education. Illiteracy is an enduring disability. Paradoxically, by depriving the children of any disfavored group an education, we foreclose the means by which that group might raise the level of esteem in which it is held by the majority.

Deeper Look 10.3
Read more about the legal rights of students.

Students' Freedom of Expression

Can students criticize governmental policies or practices in school? Yes. In 1965 three students in Des Moines, Iowa, were sent home for wearing black armbands to protest the United States' involvement in Vietnam. The Supreme Court in *Tinker v. Des Moines Independent Community School District* (1969) ruled that students (and teachers) do not "shed their constitutional rights to freedom of speech or expression at the schoolhouse gate." However, they must present their views in an orderly way and not be judged to be disruptive.

The First Amendment allows both students and adults the right to express themselves and the right to be silent. For example, students cannot be forced to salute the American flag or say the Pledge of Allegiance. However, some student expression is not covered by the First Amendment. School officials can take action against a student whose written or oral language is defamatory, shaming, or ridiculing others (remember the social media and bullying discussions at the beginning of this chapter?). The Supreme Court in 1986 ruled in *Bethel School District No. 403 v. Fraser* that school officials could censor lewd, vulgar, and indecent student behavior. Courts have also upheld a school's right to discipline students for inflammatory expression such as threatening other students or teachers.

Searches of students and their property at school are legal.

I will never forget the craziness of my "rookie" year. A parent came to my classroom totally unannounced. Board policy mandated visitors check in at the office and wait to be escorted to a classroom. Somehow the policy wasn't followed that day.

The parent barged in and began a tirade about how I was a horrible teacher. Her son was bored, he hated my class, and as a result, was requesting a transfer! I told her I was very sorry; I thought he loved my class, and liked how I acted like the characters in the stories we read or practiced writing sentences on the tennis courts with chalk. Her skin changed immediately from red to pink. Her jaw hung open as tears poured down her cheeks.

As I reached out to comfort her, she grasped my hand tightly and told me that she had made a huge mistake. She wanted to visit the seventh-grade geography teacher, not me. As it turned out, I was, in fact, his "favorite" teacher. She told me that he couldn't wait to get to my class or go home to tell what happened that day.

Once I assured her no harm was done, she left my classroom only to return the next day bringing large bags of freshly made popcorn and soft drinks to show her appreciation and to further state how bad she felt for her case of mistaken identity.

Although the principal enjoyed my story, he made sure at the next staff meeting that everyone was reminded of the importance of following board policy for the safety of not only the students, but the teachers as well.

Dr. Robert Allen Moody
Fort Hays State University
Hays, Kansas

Student Body Search

Is searching a student or student's personal belongings lawful? Yes. It is not uncommon for school administrators to be placed in the unfavorable position of having to search students or student lockers when there is a suspicion that a student or students may possess some illegal substance, a weapon, or property that is not rightly theirs. When such searches are deemed necessary by administrators or teachers it is possible that students will complain that their rights according to the Fourth Amendment of the U.S. Constitution have been violated. Courts must then come to a decision about an individual student's rights versus the responsibility of the school administration to maintain a safe and secure school environment for all students.

In 1985, in *New Jersey v. T.L.O.*, the courts concluded that a search of a student's belongings for evidence of cigarettes, which further turned up evidence of drug dealing, did not violate the Fourth Amendment. According to the courts the search was reasonable, but only because there was evidence that provided a substantial suspicion that the student was indeed in possession of an illegal substance.

Locker Search

Can a student's locker be searched without a warrant? Yes. Courts allow locker searches on the grounds that schools ultimately retain control over lockers as school property. Schools are also held responsible for protecting the educational function of the school and students' welfare. Lockers can be searched to prevent their illicit use.

TEACHERS' RESPONSIBILITIES, RIGHTS, AND LIABILITIES

One of the difficulties that beginning teachers need to understand is that when they are first hired they have very few employment rights unless the union has negotiated a section in the contract protecting probationary teachers. Currently, even many of the rights of veteran educators are being taken away by a number of state legislatures and governors: Arizona, Florida, Wisconsin, Ohio, and on and on. There are some ways that the union can assist because many states now require a close evaluation of beginning teachers, and if the teacher is found to be deficient in some way he or she must have an opportunity to improve under a plan of improvement.

It also is important to join a union because you get liability insurance. We live in such a litigious society that it is hard to imagine doing a job where you are uninsured, where you can be sued for tens of thousands of dollars and lose your house. NEA, and I am sure AFT as well, provides its members with a million dollar liability insurance policy. If you are sued for something you did on the job you will be defended, and the insurance will pay up to a million dollars.—Mr. Simpson

Signing a teacher's contract brings with it legal as well as professional responsibilities.

Mr. Simpson has touched on several aspects of the responsibilities and liabilities related to being a teacher. Now is the time for you to start developing an understanding of teacher-related legal topics including the rights of probationary teachers, employment contracts, liability, and due process. Some of the important cases are presented in Table 10.4. These and other cases are described briefly here.

Teacher Responsibilities as a School District Employee

Teachers are employees of a school district. As such, teachers must follow all of the policies, rules, and procedures that each district has established. For example, teachers do not have complete autonomy to decide what to teach. They must follow state standards and the curriculum as specified by the state and the district.

Determining the Content of the Curriculum

Do teachers determine the content to be taught? No. There is a never-ending debate about which topics should and should not be taught. One of the most famous cases, *State v. Scopes* (1927), more commonly referred to as the Scopes Monkey Trial, was held in Tennessee in the summer of 1925. This case clearly demonstrates the emotions that discussions of "what will be taught in schools" can evoke. Douglas Linder (2002) has written a fascinating narrative of the trial. He begins his description with the historical perspectives that added fuel to the debate:

> The early 1920s found social patterns in chaos. Traditionalists, the older Victorians, worried that everything valuable was ending. Younger modernists no longer asked whether society would approve of their behavior . . . Intellectual experimentation flourished. Americans danced to the sound of the Jazz Age, showed their contempt for . . . prohibition, debated abstract art and Freudian theories. In a response to the new social patterns set in motion by modernism, a wave of revivalism developed, becoming especially strong in the American South.
>
> Who would dominate American culture—the modernists or the traditionalists? Journalists were looking for a showdown, and they found one in a Dayton, Tennessee courtroom in the summer of 1925. There a jury was to decide the fate of John Scopes, a high school biology teacher charged with illegally teaching the theory of evolution. The guilt or innocence of John Scopes, and even the constitutionality of Tennessee's anti-evolution statute, mattered little. The meaning of the trial emerged through its interpretation as a conflict of social and intellectual values.

When Parents Disagree With Teachers

Will parents complain to the school board about what a teacher is teaching? Yes. You might be surprised at what some parents would consider inappropriate content for teachers to teach, as one of the authors of this text experienced when teaching third grade in Beaverton, Oregon.

> I read my students Baum's *The Wizard of Oz*. Parents of a child in my class took umbrage to the text because of the "communistic" overtones it contained. They asked the school district to remove the book from the school libraries and to forbid teachers to share it with their students. I was amazed. I thought the flying monkeys were the worst things in the book.

Audio Link 10.2
Listen to a clip about corporal punishment.

Corporal Punishment

Are there statutory provisions designed to protect teachers and administrators from suits resulting from their administration of corporal punishment? Yes. The use of corporal punishment in this country as a means of disciplining schoolchildren dates back to the colonial period. It has survived the transformation of primary and secondary education from the colonials' reliance on optional private arrangements to our present system of compulsory education and dependence on public schools. In many states **corporal punishment**, a teacher paddling or spanking a student, is legal and happens regularly.

In 1977, the U.S. Supreme Court upheld the practice of corporal punishment. The law was challenged in *Ingraham v. Wright* (1977), with Mr. Justice Powell delivering the opinion of the court. Two issues were raised during the court case: (1) Does the punishment represent cruel and unusual punishment in violation of the Eighth Amendment of the U.S. Constitution?, and (2) whether or not prior notice and the opportunity to be heard were required. According to the court, three categories of corporal punishment exist.

> Punishments that do not exceed the traditional common law standard of reasonableness are not actionable; punishments that exceed the common law standard without adequate state remedies violate procedural due process rights; and finally, punishments that are so grossly excessive as to be shocking to the conscience, violate substantive due process rights, without regard to the adequacy of state remedies. (p. 135)

More than half of the states do not allow the practice of corporal punishment. In some instances, local school boards, in states which allow corporal punishment, have banned or curtailed the practice. Teachers must be aware of any statutory provisions pertaining to corporal punishment in the state where they teach and whether practices within a school district are in conformance with state and local provisions.

Reporting Child Abuse

Can teachers be held liable for not reporting suspected child abuse? Yes. Teachers are among the professionals who are required to report signs of child abuse. Penalties for not reporting include fines and/or prison terms. School districts may also impose disciplinary action. For example, the Seventh Circuit upheld the suspension and demotion of a teacher-psychologist who did not promptly report suspected abuse in *Pesce v. J. Sterling Morton High School District 201, Cook County, Illinois* (1987). School districts usually have procedures for reporting suspected abuse, including to whom the abuse should be reported. In 1998, the Kentucky Supreme Court ruled that once the abuse is reported to a supervisor, the supervisor has responsibility for reporting it to the appropriate authority. However, teachers should check to ensure that the appropriate agency has been notified.

The Basis for Student Grouping

Can students be grouped by ability or achievement? Yes, unless it results in discrimination against a group of students. In the most publicized case, *Hobson v. Hansen* (1967), parents

Table 10.4 Teachers' Rights

Question	Case	Decision
May teachers criticize a school board and superintendent in a letter published by a local newspaper?	*Pickering v. Board of Education* (1968)	Teachers cannot be "compelled to relinquish their First Amendment rights."
Can school districts have a policy forcing all pregnant teachers to take mandatory maternity leave?	*Cleveland Board of Education v. LeFleur* (1974)	No.
Do untenured teachers have property rights when dismissed?	*Board of Regents of State Colleges v. Roth* (1972)	No.

in Washington, D.C., argued that their children were assigned to lower tracks with limited curriculum and little chance for moving to higher levels. The court found that the testing methods used by the school district discriminated against students of color. Testing instruments used to make decisions about placement must be reliable, valid, and unbiased. They cannot be racially biased or administered in discriminatory ways. They must be administered in the student's native language or with appropriate accommodations for students with disabilities.

Video Link 10.4
Watch a video about teacher accountability.

Teacher and School Accountability

Can teachers be held responsible for their students not meeting federal standards? Yes. Since the passage of NCLB in 2001 the goals and benchmarks states and school districts set must address the established national standards and federal mandates. It is probably pretty well understood that no school district wants to have any of its schools classified as "in need of improvement" or "failing." For sure, teachers will not see high status in working at a school that is on the "watch list." In all schools teachers are expected to assume responsibility for seeing that their students' achievement meets the standards. As the new **value added** teacher evaluation systems come into use, each teacher will be under even more pressure to "raise those test scores." In more and more states, legislatures are mandating that improvement in student test scores will count for as much as half of a teacher's evaluation.

Teachers need to continue to learn through participating in staff meetings and professional development opportunities.

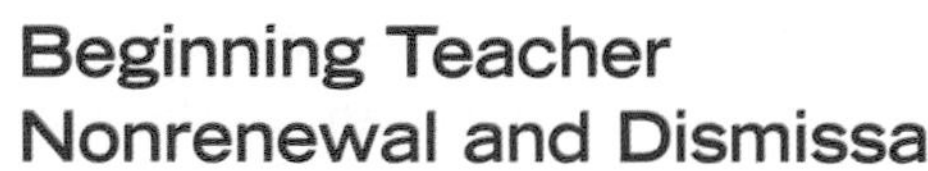

Beginning Teacher Nonrenewal and Dismissal

Do administrators have to provide reasons for dismissal of a nontenured teacher? No. School administrators have the responsibility for evaluating the fitness of teachers and determining whether their level of performance is satisfactory. They must follow the provisions outlined in state statutes; however, the U.S. Supreme Court in *Board of Regents of State Colleges v. Roth* (1972) decided that nontenured teachers need not be given reasons for nonrenewal. Note that this case addressed the dismissal of a college faculty member. As with many other cases, court decisions that have addressed questions related to higher education have been interpreted as applying to public school teachers as well. Each state has statutes that address the dismissal of tenured teachers, or ones under a continuing contract. These provisions lay out the due process requirements. Grounds for dismissal, such as insubordination, incompetency, failure to comply with reasonable orders, and conviction of crimes involving moral turpitude are addressed. These same grounds apply to probationary teachers, but in most states school officials are not required to provide any reasons for dismissal.

Due Process

Note that the idea of due process is referenced in several of the cases introduced here. It also was discussed in Chapter 9. The term *due process* gets mentioned frequently in social conversations. In the legal system there are two important meanings. **Procedural due process** addresses the actions that must be taken to ensure that teachers' and students' rights are protected. As stated in the Fourteenth Amendment, no "State shall deprive any person of life, liberty, or property, without due process of law." A teacher must have an opportunity to be heard, and the procedures must be stated and in place.

Substantive due process directs that the process must be fair. In other words, the actions cannot be arbitrary, unreasonable, or discriminatory. Both meanings of due process must be addressed in school administrative actions and will be considered by the courts. However, as you have read above for students and will read below about teachers, their due process rights are not fully the same as their rights as a citizen.

Individual Teacher Rights and Responsibilities

There are many areas where the actions of teachers have been examined by the legal system. Questions about how to dress, freedom of speech, and drug testing are some of the many topics that have been examined by the courts.

Teacher Freedom of Public Expression

Do teachers have freedom of public expression? Yes, but there are limits. Historically, teachers were seen as government employees and therefore had less freedom of public expression. This view was formalized at the federal level in the Hatch Act (1939). However, this view has been questioned in the last 50 years. In *Pickering v. Board of Education Township High School District 205* (1968), a teacher (Pickering) was dismissed for writing a letter to the newspaper that was critical of actions taken by his school board. He challenged in court his loss of First Amendment rights as a citizen. The Court stated in part, "The problem in any case is to arrive at a balance between the interests of the teacher, as a citizen, in commenting upon matters of public concerns and the interest of the state, as an employer, in promoting the efficiency of the public services it performs through its employees."

However, *Pickering* does not mean that teachers can say anything they want and not have it lead to employment consequences. For example, in *Mt. Healthy City School District Board of Education v. Doyle* (1977), a nontenured teacher, Doyle, had an altercation with a colleague, argued with cafeteria employees, swore at students, and called a radio station. He was dismissed. He then alleged that his not being rehired was in conflict with his First Amendment rights. The Court ruled that the school board would not have rehired him regardless of his "protected conduct."

Deeper Look 10.4
Read about the teacher dress code policy.

Teacher Dress

What about teacher dress? Can school districts impose dress standards? Yes. For example, a high school English teacher in East Hartford refused to wear a tie. In court he argued that requiring him to wear a tie would deprive him of his right to free speech. The courts in *East Hartford Education Association v. Board of Education of Town of East Hartford* (1977) had to balance the policy of the school board, which required teachers to dress more formally, with the teacher's individual rights. In these cases the courts have weighed heavily the community standards and values as reflected through the school board's policies and procedures. In this case, and others, the courts have supported the school boards' interest in requiring a degree of uniformity.

Drug Testing of Teachers

Can teachers be screened for use of drugs? Yes. As drug use has become widespread among students and adults, some school districts have implemented policies related to teacher use of drugs. When teachers have challenged these policies the courts have had to balance the interests of schools in having a drug-free environment with the Fourth Amendment privacy interests of the teacher. Considerations

Challenging Assumptions

Are there more negligence suits now than in the past?

Studies about questions of law generally use a different approach than is typical in regular education research. Instead of using questionnaires, surveys, and interviews, legal research typically involves reviewing what has been stated in statutes and examining previous court decisions. Law journals then report these reviews. In addition, legal scholars and attorneys will add to these analyses in court proceedings and some will write occasional papers. Law reviews most certainly can incorporate quantitative data, such as crime statistics, the frequency of certain incidents, and dollar costs.

The Questions

A general perception is that there are now more civil suits against teachers and schools than was true in the past. Another commonly held perception is that most of the time schools and teachers lose.

The Facts

A review by Zirkel and Clark (2008) examined 212 published decisions related to these two assumptions. The cases involved personal injuries to students and covered the 15-year period from 1990 to 2005. The authors examined the frequency of decisions within four-year intervals.

Is the frequency of negligence suits on the rise?

Number of negligence case decisions in 4-year intervals			
1990–1993	1994–1997	1998–2001	2002–2005
49	56	49	46

Several themes can be deduced from these frequencies and the related data. First of all, there is no clear pattern suggesting that the rate of negligence decisions is increasing. Within the data the authors found that during the 15-year period 40 of the 212 decisions were in New York State. Louisiana had more decisions that went against schools (9 out of 14 cases). This pattern suggests that there are state-by-state differences.

Who won the majority of cases?

In 63% of the cases the district won conclusively. In only 9% of the cases did the student win conclusively. A related finding was that there was a higher frequency of cases based in secondary schools. This makes sense, since secondary students are engaged in more risky activities including sports, which probably explains why coaches were most frequently named as being negligent. At the same time, elementary school decisions had a higher proportion (16% vs. 7%) in favor of the students as plaintiffs.

Regardless of whether you plan to be an elementary or secondary teacher you need to continually strive to protect students from injury. Your "duty to protect" includes providing adequate supervision and close supervision when students are engaged in more risky activities, especially on field trips. Also, be sure to monitor equipment for correct operation and maintenance.

Sources: Zirkel, P. A., & Clark, J. H. (2008). School negligence case law trends. *Southern Illinois University Law Journal, 32,* 345–363.

A related review with implications for school officials is Dragan, E. F. (2010). Understanding liability in school cases. Education Management Consulting LLC. Retrieved March 27, 2012, from http://www.edmgt.com/pdfs/publications/0067.pdf

include how extensive the drug problem is, how intrusive the search, and how significant the action that led to the search. In *Knox County Education Association v. Knox County Board of Education* (1999) the Sixth Circuit Court ruled that the Fourth Amendment was not violated. The school district had a two-part policy: (1) Suspicionless drug testing of all candidates for "safety sensitive" positions (e.g., teacher and principal), and (2) "reasonable suspicion" drug testing of individual employees.

Teachers are liable for what happens in their classroom, across the school campus, and during all other school-related activities.

Teacher Liability

Can teachers as individuals be sued? Yes. Teachers must constantly be aware of the potential of being personally liable for damages as a result of what they do, or don't do. They must always act in ways that are seen as reasonable and prudent. It is not likely that anything a teacher does will result in a lawsuit, but foolish behavior can possibly lead to unpleasantness in court. Recent cases include a teacher's use of duct tape to quiet a chatty 6-year-old, a student injured while jumping from a moving bus in order to avoid being disciplined, a principal pointing a toy gun at a student, and a coach's verbal abuse and comments about a student's weight.

Teachers being sued is another part of the law called **tort law.** This area of law deals with civil wrongs instead of criminal wrongs, although there may also be a criminal component. The plaintiff is seeking compensation for a loss or damages. Liability for alleged injury, death, malpractice, or depriving someone of his or her constitutional rights, while under the teacher's or school's supervision, can lead to legal action.

Negligence that leads to a student being injured within a classroom, on the school grounds, or on a field trip can lead to questions of teacher liability. Assault and battery is another area of torts. Threatening a child in anger, even without striking the child, can be interpreted as assault. Striking someone, even without harming them, can be interpreted as battery. Teachers can only use sufficient force for self-protection when attempting to restrain a student.

In addition to being aware of district, state, and national statutes regarding what is considered reasonable in managing student behavior, you should consider whether joining a professional association or purchasing liability insurance could be a wise investment. Typically coverage is included as part of membership in the NEA or AFT, and as part of membership in some professional organizations. To protect themselves from monetary loss, it is possible for teachers to obtain liability insurance.

Law and Ethics Are Not the Same

An all too common view of teachers and citizens at large is to think in some way about law and ethics being the same, or at least interconnected. Actually they are not the same and often teachers will find themselves in situations that are conflicted. Under the law one set of actions will be required, but from a value and belief point of view the teacher sees an alternative action being what is needed.

Deeper Look 10.5
Read a case study about a teacher who gets sued.

This tension between what the law expects from an employee and what an individual may see as "ethical" can lead to what a wonderful former colleague, Dr. Joan Curcio, called *crises of integrity.* It is likely that within your first several years as a teacher you will experience one of these moments. The law, rules, and procedures will be directing you to do one thing, but your moral beliefs will be telling you to do something different. Let's consider the two frames separately and then consider some ways to negotiate a constructive outcome.

The Perspective of the Law: Is It Legal?

As you have read in this chapter, through the legislative process various laws, policies, and procedures are developed. All of these apply to everyone in the affected group, whether it be teachers, public health workers, or all citizens. As a teacher you must understand what the law expects in terms of your actions and those of your students. Outlining the legal perspective has been the primary objective of this chapter.

The Ethical Perspective: What Is Right?

As you are becoming a teacher, one of your ongoing activities is developing your philosophy of education. An important reason for your reading Chapter 6 (about history) and Chapter 7 (about philosophies) was to provide you with information that you can use to refine your own philosophical framework. It is through this framework that you are judging what you think is right and good.

As a teacher you will not be alone in developing your philosophy. The different education associations have professional codes. You bring with you values related to the American ideals as well as moral codes and standards offered by religion, such as the Ten Commandments, and either implicitly or explicitly your parents will have brought you up to know the differences between right and wrong. All of these elements of morality and ethics become combined in what you will be as a teacher.

Audio Link 10.4
Learn more about ethical issues in schools.

Resolving Dilemmas: Legal and Ethical Processes

Earlier in this chapter the idea of a dilemma was introduced. As was illustrated with the dilemmas of school finance, desegregation, and separation of church and state, the legal processes to address each of these has been extensive and continuing. As each process has unfolded, specific problems have been addressed and solutions established. In each instance there has been processing by both perspectives: legal and ethical. As a simple example, if someone murders another the law will find them guilty and they will have violated a Commandment (Thou shall not kill another.). Both the legal and ethical perspectives have made it clear about what to do and what is right.

The problem comes when something new or different occurs. One or both perspectives will be challenged to rethink and determine what is the best course of action. To do this each frame has a process for review, deliberation, and developing a solution. However, there is a major difference between the two processes. The legal process results in a law that all are directed to follow, while the ethical process results in guidelines or a moral code that each individual may, or may not, follow.

As you have read, the legal system turns to the courts to resolve disputes and to the legislative process to develop new laws. The ethical process is less structured and formal. You as an individual can engage in considerations of right and wrong. Different groups such as church members and physicians can work together to consider what should be done in a critical situation. As another example, professional associations establish committees to develop and update ethical principles and codes of conduct.

As an individual teacher you have a more private process for review and reflection to determine what you will do in a certain situation. As you experience new problems and dilemmas you have to work out what you think is right (and wrong). Further, you have to decide to take action or delay doing anything.

Making the Final Decision

Ultimately, when confronted with a difficult problem, what you decide will be a product of your basic values and moral compass. The questions in Table 10.5 are suggested starting points for you to consider ahead of the time so that you will be better prepared when you are facing one of those crises of integrity. These questions will help you in considering what is the "right" thing to do.

At the same time you need to be aware that when legal and ethical questions reach the courts the judgments are increasingly taking the side of the school district. For example, in *Woodlock v. Orange Ulster B.O.C.S.* (2006/2008) a third-year probationary school counselor was not given tenure. She had repeatedly raised concerns to administration about lack of certified gym and art instructors and escalating safety incidents related to a special education student. She had left messages for administrators and continued to express her professional concerns. She received several disciplinary memoranda for "taking it upon yourself to go out of process." In her eyes she was guided by the ethical norms of advocacy for students. However, the court made its decision based more on *Garcetti v. Cegallos* (2006), which held that the First Amendment does not protect statements that public employees make as part of their official duties.

It is in this processing that you as a teacher will decide what you believe is good teaching and how best to help all of your students learn. The more you now think about what you see as important, good, and right for teachers, the clearer you will be about your personal moral code and your philosophy of education.

Table 10.5 Key Topic Areas and Beginning Questions to Consider in Developing an Ethical Framework About Good Teaching

Education	What do you see as the reason for having public schools? Why are they important to individuals and to society?
Student learning	What are your beliefs about how students learn? How much should learning be teacher directed? Should students have many opportunities to talk out their thinking? Should students work individually most of the time, or is group work important too?
Teachers as learners	How important is it for teachers to be continuing to learn about and try new instructional approaches? Do teachers learn best individually or is learning in groups and as a whole staff useful?
Teachers as members of a school staff	What should be the role of the teacher with other teachers? What types of beyond-the-classroom activities and efforts should teachers embrace?
Parents	To what extent and about what topics should teachers communicate with parents? Should parents be involved in your classroom? If so, in what ways?
Hills to die on	Are there any topics, problems, or directives where you would say, "No, I won't do that"?

A Final Thought

The many topics touched upon in this chapter may have you worried. Worry needs to be balanced with keeping the joy of teaching in mind. Mr. Simpson, our Educator in the Real School interviewee for this chapter, said the following when asked where he saw joy in teaching.

> The quote that I read at my mother's funeral, and I think you ought to put it in your book, is attributed to American scholar and teacher Forest Witcraft:
>
> A hundred years from now it will not matter what my bank account was, the type of house I lived in, or the kind of car I drove, but the world may be different because I was important in the life of a child.

CONNECTING TO THE CLASSROOM

From the legal perspective teachers have to continually be thinking about what they are doing and possible consequences for students and/or themselves.

1. Think twice about possible implications and consequences before placing anything on your social media sites. Once there, you cannot retrieve it.
2. Only communicate with your students about teaching and learning-related topics and only do this with school/district media.
3. Student records are confidential and not to be shared, except when parents request to see them.
4. Always consider possible safety risks in your classroom, at school, and especially on field trips. There may be liability risks.
5. Bullying includes more than punching and kicking. It includes verbal insults, face-to-face and via social media.
6. When grouping students, consider possible subtle indications of discrimination such as mainly having boys in one group and girls in another.
7. Students and teachers do not have complete freedom of expression.

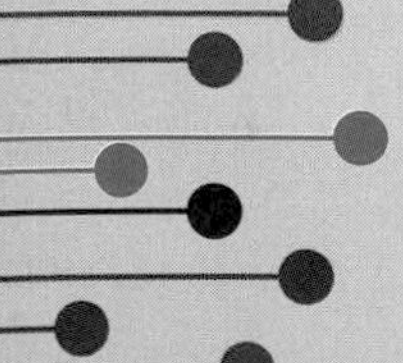

SUMMARY

Given the many tasks and areas of responsibilities that teachers have, it is important that you begin now to understand legal aspects of teaching. These major topics were introduced in this chapter:

- Student (and teacher) uses of social media can be a benefit to learning and at the same time the cause of serious problems.
- Teachers, as well as administrators, must continually keep in mind potential issues related to school safety and bullying.
- There are a number of dilemmas, such as separation of church and state, desegregation, and equitable school funding, that continue to be addressed through the courts.
- Students and teachers have limits to their rights as citizens.

CLASS DISCUSSION QUESTIONS

1. Under what conditions can teachers use social media such as Twitter and Facebook to communicate with their students?

2. With your classmates, list example topics and content that teachers are duty-bound to cover that might result in a conflict of values with parents and the community. Consider this content from varying social, economic, ethnic, political, and religious perspectives. If one of these topics were to become a court case, what do you think the courts would decide?

3. Which aspects of the rights and protections of students with disabilities are new to you?

4. What are your thoughts about the fact that in most states and school districts no explanation has to be provided when a probationary teacher is not rehired?

5. Have you seen situations where a teacher could have been held liable for something that occurred that placed students at risk?

KEY TERMS

Administrative law 285
Case law 285
Corporal punishment 304
De facto 294
De jure 294
Dilemma 290
Fair use 289
Integration 295
Least restrictive environment 298
Mainstreaming 298
Problem 290
Procedural due process 306
Resegregation 295
Sexting 287
Statute 285
Substantive due process 307
Tort law 309
Value added 306

SELF-ASSESSMENT

WHAT IS YOUR CURRENT LEVEL OF UNDERSTANDING AND THINKING ABOUT THE LAW AS IT RELATES TO TEACHING AND LEARNING?

One of the indicators of understanding is to examine how complex your thinking is when asked questions that require you to use the concepts and facts introduced in this chapter. After you answer the following questions as fully as you can, rate your knowledge on the Complexity of Thinking rubric to self-assess the degree to which you understand and can apply the law to you as a teacher and future school employee.

1. Name three key questions related to the dilemma of separation of church and state. What has been the legal reasoning underlying the related court decisions?

2. What do you see as implications for you as a teacher of the limits the courts have set in regard to free speech rights of students and teachers?

3. How would you respond to a colleague who claims that teachers can freely use copyrighted material as long as it is only for their class?

4. What are aspects of the conditions as set within IDEA you will need to consider in setting the least restrictive environment?

Assess your current level of understanding of how the legal system affects what you do as a teacher and the rights of your students.

Complexity of Thinking Rubric

	Parts & Pieces	Unidimensional	Organized	Integrated	Extensions
Indicators	Elements/concepts are talked about as isolated and independent entities.	One or a few concepts are addressed, while others are underdeveloped.	Deliberate and structured consideration of all key concepts/ elements.	All key concepts/ elements are included in a view that addresses interconnections.	Integration of all elements and dimensions, with extrapolation to new situations.
Understanding and applying the law	Names one or two court cases but is unclear about the issues or what was decided.	Describes the elements and decision in one court case, but is less knowledgeable about other cases.	Names and describes court decisions related to major dilemmas, along with the reasoning for each decision.	Describes the themes across court decisions and explains how these are related to teachers.	Presents an "integrated" description of court decisions, draws clear implications for teaching, and suggests possible directions that might emerge in the near future.

STUDENT STUDY SITE

Visit the Student Study Site at **www.sagepub.com/hall** to access links to the videos, audio clips, and Deeper Look reference materials noted in this chapter, as well as additional study tools including eFlashcards, web quizzes, and more.

Field Guide

for Learning More About the Law as It Relates to Teaching and Learning

• • • • •

In Chapter 1 you were introduced to the concept of a field guide for learning more about your surroundings. The artifacts and information you will collect for this part of your field guide will involve collecting information related to legal aspects of schooling. Remember to take field notes as you complete the activities suggested here. These notes should include your identifying topics and issues that could have legal implications. Your field notes should also include date, time of day, the grade or group you are observing, and your reflections and aha moments. As was said in an earlier chapter, this form of journaling will help you understand the steps you are taking to becoming a teacher. Remember, also, to collect pictures and samples. A picture can be worth a thousand words.

Ask a Teacher or Principal

Experienced teachers and most certainly principals will be knowledgeable about school problems they have experienced that have had a legal component. Ask them to describe the legal aspects. What legal resources and counsel do they turn to when a problem with potentially legal implications comes up?

Make Your Own Observations

Legal representation and counsel will be part of many venues. For example, attend a school board meeting and observe the role of the district's attorney and in what ways the law guides proceedings. You also could visit a court and observe the proceedings. The purpose of these observations is to see how the law provides the framework for the consideration of a question. The particular topic should not be the center of your attention.

Reflect Through Journaling

It is very likely that much of the content in this chapter has been new to you. Take some time to think about implications of the legal system for your future as a teacher. Which of the topics and cases did you find most relevant. Construct a table of legal topics. For example you could label one column "student rights," another "teacher rights," and another "schools and society." Within each column list what you now see as key "do's" and "don'ts."

Build Your Portfolio

Two useful resources to keep abreast of legal issues in education are *Education Week* and *Phi Delta Kappan*. Each issue of *Education Week* will have reports on current court cases and judicial decisions. Most issues of the *Kappan* will have a column called "Courtside," by Perry A. Zirkel. These columns are easy to read and summarize legal proceedings about a particular topic. Search through several issues of one or both of these publications and develop a set of notes about current issues about which you need to become knowledgeable.

Read a Book

Teachers and the Law (8th ed.), by David Schimmel, Leslie R. Stellman, and Louis Fischer (2011; Upper Saddle River, NJ: Pearson), is an easy-to-read text that addresses many of the critical legal topics. Each chapter expands on the topics that were introduced in the chapter you have just been reading. You can learn more about teacher and student rights, and other topics such as how collective bargaining works, and the meaning of due process.

Although *Responding to Cyber Bullying: An Action Tool for School Leaders*, by Jill J. Myers, Donna S. McCaw, and Leaunda S. Hemphill (2011; Thousand Oaks, CA: Corwin), has been written for school leaders, it still is a useful resource for teachers. In your teaching career you will most certainly be confronted with bullying in general and through social media in particular. This book reviews student rights and your responsibilities. There are suggestions for how to balance free expression with providing a safe environment. The authors even provide the "Top Ten Rules" for addressing cyberbullying.

Search the Web

As with any topic, the web is an important resource for finding information about legal matters. The organization of courts, past decisions, and current cases under consideration can be found. One useful website about U.S. Supreme Court decisions (http://www.streetlaw.org) has been developed specifically to help teachers find resources and activities that can be used in teaching about major Court decisions.

Oyez (**http://www.oyez.org/about**) has easy-to-follow summaries of major U.S. Supreme Court decisions. Each case is presented in a summary format that includes the Term, Facts About the Case, the Question, and the Decision.

You also can find a website for each state's court decisions. For example, the Kansas site—**http://www.kscourts.org/kansas-courts/supreme-court/**—describes the number of justices, cases under consideration, and how justices are selected. As an activity, take a look at your state's judicial branch website. Are there current cases related to schools and teaching? What education cases has your state dealt with in the past?

PART III

Teaching for Student Learning

Chapter 11 Standards, Curriculum, and Accountability

Chapter 12 Managing the Classroom and Student Behavior

Chapter 13 Teaching Strategies

Chapter 14 Using Technology to Improve Student Learning

Chapter 15 Assessing Student Learning and Results

TEACHER INTERVIEW

Lorraine (Reina) Floyd

Lorraine (Reina) Floyd teaches pre-algebra and honors algebra at Irmo Middle School, home of the Yellow Jackets, in District Five of Lexington and Richland counties in South Carolina. There are 65 teachers at Irmo, 81% of whom have advanced degrees. There are 400 white, 409 African American, 40 Hispanic, and 25 Asian Pacific Islander students at Irmo; 146 of these students have disabilities, and 23 have limited English proficiency. Sixty-seven percent of the seventh and eighth graders at Irmo are enrolled in high school credit courses. In 2011, Irmo Middle School exceeded standards for progress toward the 2020 South Carolina performance vision: *By 2020 all students will graduate with the knowledge and skills necessary to compete successfully in the global economy, participate in a democratic society, and contribute positively as members of families and communities.*

CHAPTER 11 Standards, Curriculum, and Accountability

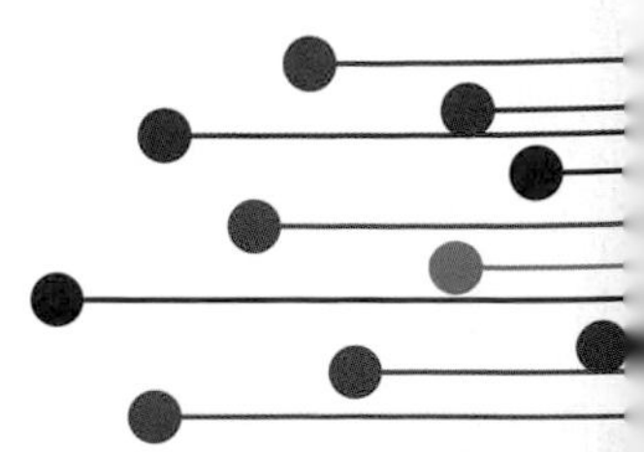

• Why did you decide to become a teacher?

My interest in teaching was first sparked when as a young child my father regularly played "school" with me. He let me "teach" him basic math concepts like addition and subtraction well before I formally learned them in school. Later, in the eighth grade, I had the distinct pleasure of having both my language arts and social studies classes taught by Mrs. Bowers. She approached classroom management and assessment in an engaging and inspirational manner. Ultimately, I went into teaching in hopes of sparking a love of learning in students like she did with me.

Where do you find joy in teaching?

I derive my joy from watching students become more comfortable with themselves and each other as mathematicians. They build their confidence in their math abilities by discussing and supporting their thinking process. I love hearing my students participate in mathematical discourse.

It's sad, but so many of my students start the school year with a defeatist attitude. Somewhere along the way someone sent them the message that they aren't capable of learning, and therefore it's not worth the time or effort. The degree to which these students gain confidence varies. At first, many of these students view my encouragement as bothering them, but the joy on their faces when they gain understanding is more than worth their initial discomfort. Unfortunately, not all of my students experience the level of success that I would like them to, but they all experience enough success in our classroom that I see an improvement in their effort and self-efficacy by the end of the year.

How would you describe excellence in teaching?

To me excellence in teaching is like perfection—it isn't something to be obtained, but to continuously strive for. I strive to engage my students, meet them where they are, and help them rise to where they need to be.

In what ways do you focus your instruction on student learning?

I guess it can be easy for teachers to get off track and focus more on sharing what they know about a topic rather than focusing on student learning. I have a few tools to keep me on track and help me remember that it's all about student learning. The first tool I use in my instruction is my knowledge of my students. I have them take inventories—learning and personal interests—at the beginning of the year and pretests before teaching each unit. The second tool I use is me—my personality, my understanding of the content, and my unabashed geeky devotion to all things math. Some of the day-to-day tools I use are cooperative learning, informal formative assessments throughout a lesson, and summative assessments that inform any remediation efforts that must be made.

Questions to Consider

1. Mrs. Floyd indicated that both her father and a former teacher helped her decide on teaching as a career. Do you believe family members might have a stronger influence on a person's decision to become a teacher than a former teacher? Why or why not?
2. Mrs. Floyd finds joy in teaching as her students become more comfortable with their abilities in mathematics. How might a teacher help the students to become "comfortable" in a content area?
3. Mrs. Floyd describes excellence in teaching as a something to "continuously strive for." Why might excellence in teaching be something that a teacher must always seek to achieve?
4. Consider how one of your teachers might have used the knowledge they had of you to help you learn. What did that teacher's knowledge of you feel like?
5. What are some ways mentors might help teachers survive their first year?

What are some tips you might have for college students considering teaching?

When interviewing with a district or school, be sure to ask about their mentorship program. If they do not have one, it is not the place for you. So many educators leave the profession because education courses do not prepare us for the daily grind of teaching. We all need guidance and support. Without it, getting overwhelmed is inevitable.

Learning Outcomes

After reading this chapter, you should be able to

1. Understand why there are standards for student learning.
2. Know how standards are established.
3. Recognize the ways standards and benchmarks can be used as a framework for lesson plans.
4. Understand ways the focus on standards and benchmarks can improve teaching practices and student learning.
5. Know ways that standards, curriculum, and accountability are interrelated.
6. Know ways teachers can use standards to increase their own professional growth.

INTRODUCTION

You are starting down the road to becoming a teacher at a time when all eyes—public, political, parental, and even those of your peers—are focused on student learning as something that can be viewed as a direct result of teacher performance. You are going to be in the spotlight. The long, hard look at what students and teachers know and know how to do has given rise to all manner of standards, benchmarks, and criteria for determining ways education—and especially teachers—are accountable. Standards have become an integral part of schooling: establishing them, using them to improve schools, using them to improve instruction, and using them as a means toward determining student progress.

There is an indisputable logic behind having a certain level of achievement in mind when undertaking any project. If a hostess is planning a dinner and decides to make a lemon meringue pie for dessert, she has a certain ideal in mind for what the pie should look like. There should be exactly the right amount and consistency of sunshine-yellow filling in a tan crust. Two inches of firmly swirled white meringue on top should have peaks toasted golden brown with at least a half dozen or more crystal pearls of moisture adding the final touch. The end result is beautiful to look at and delicious to eat. And anything below that standard just won't do. Students are not pies, but their fillings should meet equally high standards, and teachers who plan for and prepare their lessons to fill students' minds should be well aware of the role standards, curriculum, and accountability play in promoting student learning.

WHAT ARE STANDARDS AND BENCHMARKS?

When Mrs. Floyd was asked in what ways standards were implemented in her classroom, she replied, "Last year several teachers at the district level unpacked the standards and noted where there are areas that overlap or gap between the common core standards and those that we are currently teaching. This coming school year, we will start implementing the common core standards. By the school year 2013–2014, the common core standards will be fully implemented."

Deeper Look 11.1
Read more about standard
American education.

Standards are statements about overarching values in education that the majority of people agree upon. A standard is an acknowledged measure of comparison for quantitative or qualitative value, a criterion, a norm, or a degree or level of excellence that is achieved. Deciding what PreK–12 students and their teachers should know and be able to do is a major concern of educational policymakers as well as schools and departments of education. Their solution to this problem is the development of standards. What should be learned is also of concern to the teachers and students who grapple with standards on a daily basis. A teacher's job is to transform standards into enriched learning experiences that engage the intellect of students.

Standards are necessary in order to measure the learning that takes place in one school or place against other schools and other places. Setting such standards may seem like a simple task, but it was probably easier to standardize the size and width of railroad cars in the 19th century than to standardize anything having to do with education. Performance-based standards are designed to assure accountability and improve schools through exerting top-down control by holding students, teachers, schools, and districts accountable for the results of student achievement. Additionally, an underlying agenda of standards is also to see that public tax dollars are well spent. Setting standards in education has become a huge undertaking. It is complex, political, and fraught with challenges.

Standards are a general statement of a final goal; **benchmarks** are specific waypoints, turning points, or landmarks along the way to achieving the goal. Benchmarks denote the measurable stages along the journey to successfully achieving standards. For example, when a stagecoach left St. Louis for Custer, South Dakota, it began with a fast, fresh team of horses. During the trip, however, there were regular stops along the way to refresh the horses or hitch up a new team, and to give the travelers some time to check on their own condition. The stops where this change of horses or taking stock occurred were the benchmarks: measurable, familiar points along the way to reaching the final goal. Each time a new stagecoach left St. Louis, its forward journey was measured by reaching predetermined stage stops. Individual journeys might be filled with novel experiences but the stage stops, "benchmarks," along the way were familiar and well established.

There is always a degree of difference in the ways standards of performance are judged.

Characteristics of Standards

Standards are conceptually nothing new. Standards for student achievement have probably existed since the first student had to read from the Bible in the first Massachusetts school. The "Old Deluder Satan Act" of 1647 definitely set standards for what students of that era were expected to know since it was assumed that one chief aim of Satan was to keep man from knowledge of the Scriptures. Every township of 50 or more families was ordered to appoint someone within the town to provide all children with an elementary education so they could, of course, read the scriptures.

Benjamin Franklin's 1749 *Proposal Relating to the Education of Youth in Pensilvania* [*sic*] was intended to make English the standard of instruction rather than Latin and to establish a curriculum that was both scientific and practical. Thomas Jefferson's 1779 "Bill for the More General Diffusion of Knowledge" planned to establish cumulative and consecutive levels of education, from elementary schools, to secondary schools, and then possibly on to college. Jefferson's plan also called for states to control the schools rather than the church or the federal government. The curriculum of the Common School Movement of the 1800s outlined the skills needed for everyday life, for ethical behavior, and for responsible citizenship (Cremin, 1951, p. 62). President George W. Bush's No Child Left Behind Act of 2001 supported reading instruction to ensure that every child in public schools could read at or above grade level by third grade. The No Child Left Behind Act also strove to strengthen teacher quality for public schools by investing in training and retention of high-quality teachers. Each of these efforts, in addition to a multitude of other proposals, bills, and plans, to establish standards and improve American education have contributed to and continue to contribute to setting criteria for a cumulative and consecutive system of universal public education for all children who attend the nation's schools.

While the establishment of standards may appear to be the purview of lawmakers, politicians, and educators, parents also have major concerns about what schools will expect of their children. Parents want some measures of **accountability.** They want their children to succeed in school, and to have rewarding and enriching experiences there. Some standards are easy for parents to understand, for example, "all children will learn to read," while some standards are less clear, such as "children will be ready to learn." Readiness for elementary school is an implicit standard for beginning formal schooling in the United States. Although school attendance is not mandatory in most states until first grade, national surveys of parents of early elementary pupils show that a large majority of primary school children attended kindergarten before entering first grade. Such reports provide evidence that parents are concerned that their sons and daughters will begin school well prepared to meet the standards.

There are standards for content, for student achievement, for teachers, and for teacher education. In Chapter 1 you learned about the Interstate New Teacher Assessment Support Consortium (InTASC) Standards, stated as principles, and about national certification for teachers by the National Board for Professional Teaching Standards (NBPTS). You can learn more about the purposes of each of these organizations by visiting their websites, **http://www.ccsso.org/intascst.html** and **http://www.nbpts.org**, respectively. You will become very familiar with the InTASC Standards during your teacher education course work and with the NBPTS later in your career.

Common Core Standards

At the Common Core Standards website (**http://www.corestandards.org/the-standards**), the National Governors Association Center for Best Practices, Council of Chief State School Officers state that "standards do not tell teachers how to teach, but they do help teachers figure out the knowledge and skills their students should have so that teachers can build the best lessons and environments for their classrooms. Standards also help students and parents by setting clear and realistic goals for success. Standards are a first step; a key building block—in providing an accessible roadmap for our teachers, parents, and students" (2010).

Video Link 11.1
Watch a clip about the common core state initiative.

The U.S. Department of Education has declared that "all states and schools will have challenging and clear standards of achievement and accountability for all children, and effective strategies for reaching those standards." As a result, the Common Core State Standards initiative has been created. This initiative, while coordinated by the National Governors Association Center for Best Practices (NGA Center) and the Council of Chief State School Officers (CCSSO), is truly a state-led effort. Check the *Education World* website (http://educationworld.com/standards/) to view the process of establishing Common Core Standards in different states.

According to the CCSSO, the Common Core Standards are informed by the highest, most effective models from states across the country and countries around the world, and provide teachers and parents with a common understanding of what students are expected to learn. Consistent common core standards will provide appropriate benchmarks for all students, regardless of where they live. The Common Core Standards developed by each state define the knowledge and skills students should have within their K–12 education so they graduate from high school able to "succeed in entry-level, credit-bearing academic college courses and in workforce training programs." Directions for each state to develop Common Core Standards are clear, and states' standards must

- align with college and work expectations;
- be clear, understandable, and consistent;
- include rigorous content and application of knowledge through high-order skills;
- build upon strengths and lessons of current state standards;
- be informed by other top-performing countries, so that all students are prepared to succeed in our global economy and society; and
- be evidence based.

Common core standards are defined for each grade level and subject. For example, standards in grade 6 in English and language arts (ELA) are delineated into strands of (a) key ideas and details, (b) craft and structure, (c) integration of knowledge and ideas, and (d) range of reading and level of text complexity. Each strand is accompanied by a list of additional standards that should be articulated through curriculum and instruction.

The path from standard to curriculum to accountability is clearly marked so there should be little excuse of teachers losing their way. As common core standards are applied across the nation,

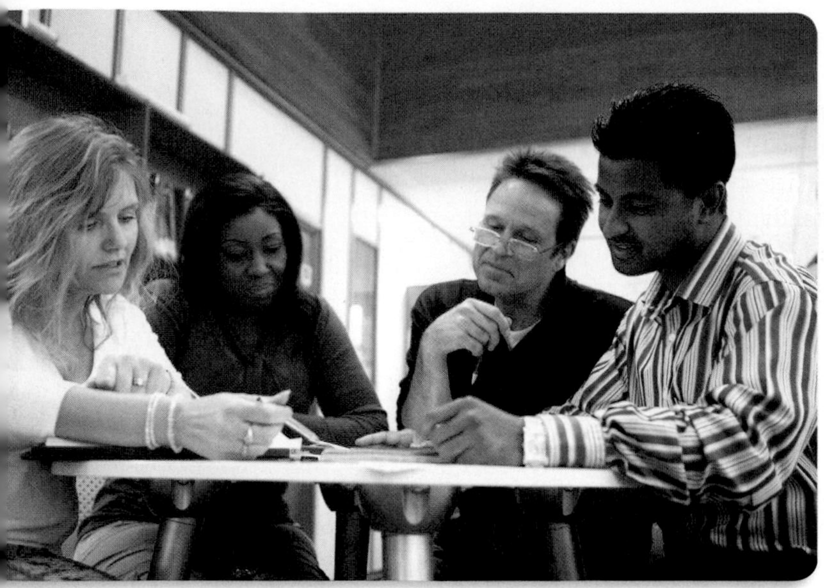

Teachers often reference standards documents when planning lessons to be sure necessary standards and benchmarks are included.

curriculum must be developed to help teachers design appropriate instruction that will match the goals of the standards. This can only be achieved through teachers' knowledge of the common core standards and their implementation.

STANDARDS FOR CONTENT

Mrs. Floyd believes that teachers have many excellent ideas that never reach the people who make decisions. Throwing money at educational reform is not going to result in the changes that are necessary to improve education. Teachers need to have their voices heard in schools in the districts and on the street. They need to be the voice for their students who have no voice in what or how they should learn. Teachers shouldn't rely too heavily on established organizations to be the only entity to determine standards.

In order to help you understand the scope and design of the standards movement, it seems wise to provide you with a brief history of the effort to standardize content goals and establish assessments that are intended to provide accurate data on student performance. The amount of time invested, the manpower needed to staff the numerous committees that were created, and the funding from tax dollars over a 15-year time period should make it crystal clear that the establishment of national standards in education was not a frivolous endeavor.

At the beginning of the 1990s, the National Council on Education Standards and Testing (NCEST) was created to make recommendations regarding voluntary national standards. This council in turn proposed an oversight board to establish guidelines for standards setting and assessment development. This board became the National Education Standards and Assessment Council (NESAC); its purpose was to review and evaluate content standards and assessments proposed by specialized professional associations. Of course, before all these councils and boards were created by the federal government, the National Council for Teachers of Mathematics (NCTM) published *Curriculum and Evaluation Standards for School Mathematics,* in 1989, blazing the trail for other content areas to follow (Marzano & Kendall, 1996).

Many content standards were drafted and finalized during the last decade of the 20th century. Part of the Goals 2000: Educate America Act, signed into law by President Bill Clinton, created the National Education Standards and Improvement Council (NESIC) to certify national and state content and performance standards. Federal funding was made available to support content area organizations in creating standards.

Creating standards for each content area in schools was often a controversial task garnering few rewards for the initial designers. For example, the National Endowment for the Humanities and the National Geographic Society worked together on a first draft of geography standards. When the standards for U.S. and World History, Civics and Government, and Geography were released, the history standards were denounced by the U.S. Senate as being unacceptable.

Other groups had more success. For example, the Committee for National Health Education Standards was funded by the American Cancer Society. The Consortium of National Arts Education Associations published the arts standards (dance, music, theater, and the visual arts). National standards for sport and physical education were published, standards for foreign language learning were published, national science education standards were published, and the National Council of Teachers of English and the International Reading Association also published standards.

Creating standards for student learning can result in controversy and conflict that will only be resolved through thoughtful discussion.

Developing the Content Standards

Standards for each content area have seen much revision since the first installments. They have undergone strict scrutiny from peers and from the general public for their cost, for their ability to truly reform education, for their content, and for their voluminous size. Through decades of lively discussion, the current standards and assessment criteria have survived and are rapidly becoming a permanent pillar of the education panorama.

For most taxpayers, it often seems the federal government only takes money away. However, in the case of creating national standards for education, the federal government established grants to support the process of designing standards and it also withdrew funding for certain organizations when controversy over the standards ran counter to national goals. In many ways the flow of funding from the federal government sometimes seemed like a rich uncle promoting a favorite nephew's desires and withdrawing those favors when the nephew did something the uncle didn't like.

A rich source for learning more about standards can be found on the *Education World* website (**http://www.educationworld.com/standards/national/**). Navigating the ocean of standards can sometimes seem like an impossible task for teachers and teacher education candidates, but the thread of content standards in education is strong and easy to follow. The manner in which national standards are articulated can help teachers understand the ways in which courses and subjects are defined. Standards help describe levels of student performance, and they also help determine how student performance is graded and reported. Table 11.1 offers a snapshot of how specific overarching concepts in six different disciplines are categorized by the standards movement.

Organizing the Standards

National standards are intended to serve as frameworks that will assist state departments of education and local districts in organizing knowledge and skills into curricula. National standards do not define a national curriculum per se. They do, however, specify broad areas of agreement on content that all students are expected to be exposed to. Some national standards are divided

Table 11.1 Examples of Standards as Lesson Plan Objectives

National Standards	Common Core Standards	Example of Standards as Lesson Plan Objectives
NCTM—Algebra Using mathematical models to represent and understand quantitative relationships	Student models problem situations with objects and uses representations such as graphs, tables, and equations to draw conclusions.	Grades 3: Students will determine how many packages each of 18 napkins, 10 plates, 5 cups, and 2 cupcakes they will need to purchase in order to serve a group of 33 guests.
National Standards for History—World History 5–12 Understanding the search for community, stability, and peace in an interdependent world	Student understands how population explosion and environmental change have altered conditions of life around the world.	Grade 11: Students will compare the negative population growth in Russia with the burgeoning population growth in Mexico and draw conclusions about the economic and social development in the two countries.
National Standards for Art Education—Visual Arts 5–8 Understanding and applying media techniques and processes	Student intentionally takes advantage of the qualities and characteristics of art media, techniques, and processes to enhance communication of his or her experiences and ideas.	Grade 5: Students will create original works of art by applying different media (salt, tissue, Saran Wrap) to water colors.
NCTE—K–12 Applying language skills	Student uses spoken, written, and visual language to accomplish his or her own purposes (e.g., for learning, enjoyment, persuasion, and the exchange of information).	Grade 4: Students will develop an infomercial on the causes and possible solutions for the dead zone at the mouth of the Mississippi River.
Science Content Standards—Physical Science 5–8 Developing an understanding of • properties and changes of properties in matter, • motions and forces, and • transfer of energy	Student observes and measures characteristic properties, such as boiling and melting points, solubility, and simple chemical changes of pure substances, and uses those properties to distinguish and separate one substance from another.	Grade 8: Students will describe the changes of states in relation to heat and temperature, and discover conditions for raising solubility of a solution.
U.S. National Geography Standards—K–12 Places and regions	Student recognizes places as human creations and understands the genesis, evolution, and meaning of places.	Grade 5: Students will produce a presentation or performance describing the unique features of their hometown to welcome visitors.
National Health Standards—Health information, products, and services	Student identifies characteristics of valid health information and health-promoting products and services.	Grade 3: Students will explain how media influences the selection of health information, products, and services.
National Educational Technology Standards—K–12 Technology problem-solving and decision-making tools	Student uses technology resources for solving problems and making informed decisions.	Grade 8: Students will use evaluation criteria to locate sites on the Internet that provide useful information and useless information on a predetermined topic.

into grade level bands (i.e., K–4, 5–8, 9–12) to further articulate content deemed especially relevant to particular grade levels. National Standards for Social Studies are divided into sets of standards for civics, economics, geography, U.S. history, and world history. Each professional association determines the range of its standards and the exact number of standards that will cover the structure of each discipline. Table 11.2 offers a glimpse of overarching concepts captured by the standards movement.

Table 11.2 National Standard Concepts

Physical Education	Health	Science	Mathematics	Language Arts
Movement forms	Health promotion and disease prevention	Science as inquiry	Number and operations	Reading for perspective
Movement concepts	Health information, products, and services	Physical science	Algebra	Reading for understanding
Physical activity	Reducing health risks	Life science	Geometry	Evaluation strategies
Physical fitness	Health influences	Earth and space science	Measurement	Communication skills
Responsible behavior	Using communication skills to promote health	Science and technology	Data analysis and probability	Communication strategies
Respect for others	Setting goals for good health	Science in personal and social perspectives	Problem-solving process	Applying knowledge
Understanding challenge	Health advocacy	History and nature of science	Reasoning and proof processes	Evaluating data
			Communication processes	Developing research skills
			Connections process	Multicultural understanding
			Representation	Applying non-English perspective
				Participating in society
				Applying language skills

National standards are intended to serve as frameworks that will assist state departments of education and local districts in organizing knowledge and skills into curricula. Each set of national standards provides details for developing student abilities and understandings as well as suggestions for curriculum planning. For example, there are seven broad content areas for science. Each area is separated into grade-level bands. In the 5–8 band for "science as inquiry," it is expected that all students should develop abilities necessary to do scientific inquiry and understandings about scientific inquiry. Examples are provided in the content standards documents illustrating how intermediate objectives might be achieved through lessons. State departments of education and district curriculum committees establish subsets of objectives, and classroom teachers deliver these objectives through instructional practices. The route from the overarching concepts embedded in national standards to a specific objective may be long, but it is clear, and at the end of the journey, it is the teachers who convey all of the standards to the students through curriculum. Since the content of education is of extreme importance to the future of our society, the absence of standards would leave society vulnerable to all manner of misfortune.

Video Link 11.2
Learn more using common core standards in the classroom.

Using the Standards

Beginning teachers use published standards as a guide for what they can and should do and as a caution against things they shouldn't do. New teachers also depend in some ways on the advice of others who are experienced with the actual ways standards are enforced and assessed. Teachers, both new and experienced, rely on established guidelines and standards to help them navigate the educational sea without going adrift. There are guidelines for professional behavior and for professional relationships between students and teachers. There are curriculum guides that set benchmarks for student achievement. There are standards for attendance, for grading, for discipline, and for dress. There are even standards for textbooks and protocols for the ways states and districts adopt one textbook over others.

Teachers create lesson plans that reflect district, state, and national goals for student learning. The process of planning is one of the crucial tasks teachers constantly perform.

Using Benchmarks

Since benchmarks denote stages on the path to achieving standards, it is logical and perhaps more doable that students' progress be assessed at benchmarks rather than at the end of the journey to achieving standards. At benchmarks, administrators and teachers can ascertain whether redirection or re-teaching is indicated, and determine what steps are necessary to rectify problems. Consider each benchmark as a point of curriculum accomplishment. How each benchmark might look in actual professional practice is clearly articulated on the Oregon Department of Education website (**http://www.ode.state.or.us/teachlearn/standards**). This website provides portals to understanding the Oregon Department of Education's Academic Standards and benchmarks at each grade level leading to the knowledge and skills expected of an Oregon high school graduate.

In 2011, the Oregon Social Sciences Standards were organized using the Common Core Standards structure to better articulate what graduates in Oregon need to know. The benchmarks' standards describe what students should know and be able to do at various grade levels. Benchmark requirements for students in Oregon are readily available to students, to their parents, and to their teachers. The Oregon Department of Education website (**http://www.ode.state.or.us**) allows visitors to select and view standards in all subject areas and at all grade levels. There is little excuse for being surprised by what students are expected to know and be able to do as they move through elementary, middle, and high school in Oregon.

Deeper Look 11.2
Read about teacher attitudes toward standard-based learning in a middle school.

Schools and classrooms have been likened to egg cartons, with each teacher and class in a separate environment having little or no contact with other ones. The advent of standards across all levels of school, student, and teacher performance has increased the opportunity for teachers to work together to develop strategies for achieving common short-term and long-term goals. Setting measurable goals and benchmarks is an integral part of any school reform planning process.

> Studies of high performing schools indicate that school quality is a people process. It requires that teachers collaboratively implement a focused curriculum and clear goals for students, and that teachers continually improve their instructional and assessment methods. Teachers design units and look at evidence of student learning together so that classrooms are deprivatized and teachers become learners in the sense of finding better ways to help all students be successful. (Robertson, 2004, p. 2)

While standards alone cannot bring about school improvement, they provide useful guidelines for states and local curriculum framework developers to define the knowledge and skills they want their students to have. Standards and benchmarks can help bring coherence to disjointed curricula. They can help planners determine what to teach, how to teach it, and how to assess it. Standards and benchmarks can help define a base for teacher content knowledge and for coordinating professional development for teachers. With such guidelines, the task of school improvement can become a well-organized project.

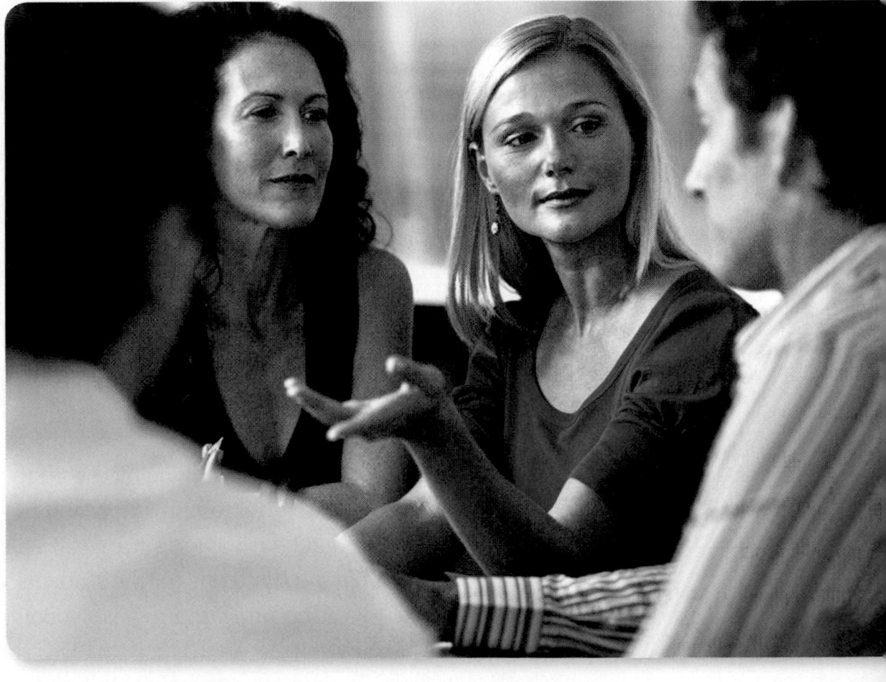

Students' achievement can be improved when teachers work together to promote effective instructional practices and establish goals for student learning.

Keeping Track of Benchmarks and Standards in Lesson Planning

Effective teachers know and think about standards every day when they plan lessons and write down what they expect from their students. Standards guide teachers in focusing instruction on the essential knowledge and skills their students should learn. Each teacher becomes responsible for teaching to a standard, measuring student mastery of the knowledge or skill, and re-teaching when mastery is not achieved. Teachers are held accountable through assessments by their supervisors and through the results of student learning.

Standards are translated through effective instruction. Benchmarks provide records of progress toward achieving the ultimate goal of a standard. Knowing the culminating standards students will be expected to meet helps teachers use benchmarks to check student progress toward these goals. "In a standards-based system, the end is held constant for all students; each one is expected to meet the standard" (Jamentz, 2002, p. 11). Additionally, in a standards-based system teachers are expected to articulate how the objectives and assessment of the lesson are tied to local, state, or national benchmarks or standards. School districts develop curriculum documents and standards that teachers must know and refer to in planning and instruction.

Video Case 11.1
Lesson Planning

1. What are some of the benefits to all students when teachers collaborate in planning lessons and curricular units of study?
2. Planning is one of the most important tasks that teachers must perform. When teachers plan lessons together with other teachers, what are the challenges? What are the rewards?

In Texas, the state standards for science in grade 4 are divided into three categories of (1) Knowledge and Skills, (2) Scientific Processes, and (3) Science Concepts. A series of benchmarks are listed for each category. One part of the scientific processes category states "the student knows how to use a variety of tools and methods to conduct science inquiry." The benchmarks for this standard list the tools students are expected to use in collecting and analyzing information (calculators, safety goggles, microscopes, cameras, sound recorders, computers, hand lenses, rulers, thermometers, meter sticks, timing devices, balances, and compasses). The benchmarks listed for this standard also expect students to be able to demonstrate that repeated investigations may increase the reliability of results.

Computerized lesson planning software applications can aid teachers in this effort. An example of a detailed application can be found on the TaskStream Learning Achievement Tools (LAT) website (**https://www.taskstream.com/pub/LAT.asp**). IBM also offers a product for lesson planning for use on iPhone, iPad, and Android-based devices. There are numerous Internet sites to help teachers plan lessons. These sites often illustrate ways standards can be expressed in lesson objectives. An excellent site to begin a search for help with standards, benchmarks, and lesson plans is Education World (**http://www.educationworld.com/**).

Web-based tools, among other things, enable educators to design lessons and units, map and track standards, and create rubrics. It is important for teachers to be able to explain what the students will be required to do at the end of the unit, and the use of rubrics helps students understand what criteria will be used to judge their performance. Effective planning helps teachers keep track of the benchmarks their students have passed and the ones that need to be revisited.

Knowing the Standards

You may begin to feel overwhelmed with the topic of standards, but if you can talk about standards during your job interview and how they can be integrated into instruction, you may be the top candidate for the job since most schools have adopted a **standards-based curriculum.** It is not only the standards for the students you will be teaching that affect your work. The teacher education program in which you are enrolled should be standards based. Your program should be preparing you to meet InTASC standards and professional standards for your field (for example, mathematics or early childhood education). You should become familiar with a range of standards.

Standards for Students

New teachers should know the student standards for the subject they will be teaching or the students with whom they will be working. All states have developed student standards that indicate what students at different grade levels should know and be able to do in a subject area. The tests that students are required to take annually in mathematics, reading, science, and social studies are based on the state standards. Many of the state standards have been adapted from the standards of national organizations such as the National Council of Teachers of Mathematics (NCTM), International Reading Association (IRA), National Council of Social Studies (NCSS), and American Association for the Advancement of Science (AAAS). These standards should provide the guide for what you should be teaching in those core curriculum areas. They can be used to develop your own **performance assessments** to determine what students are learning. The state tests also provide feedback, although limited, on what students have learned. State standards can be accessed on the website of your state department of education. Chapter 10 in this text explores the legal ramifications of student learning.

Standards for Teachers

Standards for teaching and for learning to become a teacher are not a new phenomenon. Teachers have always been held to some form of standards and accountability. Even before a degree and graduation from an accredited institution was mandatory, school boards or directors of schools demanded a level of respectability demonstrated by social status, family background, or gender. In 1867 *the American Educational Series, A Full Course of Practical and Progressive Text-Books; and ALMANAC* offered a list of 26 suggestions for what a teacher should do (Gutek, 1986, p. 99). Perhaps the male reference in this list implies that most of the teachers at that time were men. Even today, regardless of gender, what a teacher knows and knows how to do are fundamental to being employed. They are also keys to success in one's identity as a teacher and level of confidence in teaching. However, what a teacher does with this know-how is far more important to the achievement and success of students than simply having the knowledge.

When students are informed of the standards and objectives for a lesson, they have a better idea of what is expected of them.

As early as 1899, a report to the nation's normal schools (special, usually two-year colleges for preparing teachers in the 19th century) contained standards for almost all phases of teacher education. These standards were set in the areas of admission, clinical experiences, and administration. For admission to a "normal" school or school of education, applicants had to have completed a grammar school course, at least have graduated from elementary school, and be "reasonably proficient" in English grammar, geography, United States history, physiology and hygiene, drawing, civil government, music, grammar school algebra, nature study, reading, penmanship, spelling, and English literature. One wonders who determined what "reasonably proficient" was since entry exams such as SAT, ACT, and PRAXIS did not exist in 1899.

Teacher education candidates are required to pass standards-based examinations often before they are allowed in the K–12 classrooms. Results from such tests help state departments of education and colleges of education determine whether a student is qualified to be admitted to and matriculate through a teacher education program. Some state departments of education require the ETS PRAXIS series of tests for licensure, and some states require test results from the Pearson Evaluation Systems. The Florida Teacher Certification Examinations are administered by the Evaluation Systems group of Pearson. Once the state receives the test results, student scores are compiled in a Title II report that is sent to institutions. Visit the Florida Department of Education website (**http://www.fl.nesinc.com/**) for a summary of certification tests.

Teacher education programs across the nation either require candidates to pass the PRAXIS II or teacher certification test through the Evaluation Systems National Evaluation Series prior to graduation or recommend that it be taken soon after graduation. Test results can help determine whether candidates meet state criteria for licensing.

An example of how standards have become a standard fixture of the professional scene is the way in which the InTASC Standards (mentioned in Chapter 1) were conceived, constituted, and

Teachers are held to standards and are required to sit for exams that measure their knowledge of content as well as their knowledge of how to design instruction.

connected to every aspect of teacher preparation and performance. The standards were originally created to promote in-district professional development of beginning teachers, but these standards have evolved into a system for evaluating teaching performance at all levels. There is no question that standards and accountability will be in your teaching future.

Teacher education candidates should be aware that state departments of education can establish their own pedagogical standards for beginning teachers. Iowa State has identified eight standards for beginning teachers who have earned a two-year initial license. Visit **http://www.state.ia.us/boee/stndrds.html** to see these standards. To receive a standard Iowa State Teaching License, teachers must be approved by their building principal as passing the Iowa State Teaching Standards. In the future all Iowa teachers, not just beginning teachers, will be evaluated using the Iowa Teaching Standards. You need to become knowledgeable about how the state where you want to teach assesses beginning teachers.

National professional associations have also developed standards that describe what teachers should know and be able to do to teach a specific group of students (for example, English-language learners or students with disabilities) or a specific subject such as language arts or physical education. If teachers meet these standards, they should be able to help students meet the student standards.

Standards for Professional Education Areas

- American Alliance for Health, Physical Education, Recreation and Dance (AAHPERD)—**http://www.aahperd.org**
- American Association of Physics Teachers (AAPT)—**http://www.aapt.org**
- American Council on the Teaching of Foreign Languages (ACTFL)—**http://www.actfl.org**
- American Association for Health Education (AAHE)—**http://www.aahperd.org/aahe**
- Association for Childhood Education International (ACEI)—**http://www.acei.org**
- Association for Education in Journalism & Mass Communications (AEJMC)—**http://www.aejmc.org/**
- Association for Educational Communications and Technology (AECT)—**http://www.aect.org/newsite/**
- Council for Exceptional Children (CEC)—**http://www.cec.sped.org**
- International Reading Association (IRA)—**http://www.reading.org**
- International Technology and Engineering Educators Association (ITEEA)—**http://www.iteaconnect.org/**
- International Society for Technology Education (ISTE)—**http://www.iste.org/**
- Modern Language Association of America (MLA)—**http://www.mla.org**
- Music Teachers National Association (MTNA)—**http://www.mtna.org**
- National Art Education Association (NAEA)—**http://www.arteducators.org**

- National Association of Biology Teachers (NABT)—**http://www.nabt.org**
- National Association for Bilingual Education (NABE)—**http://www.nabe.org**
- National Association for the Education of Young Children (NAEYC)—**http://www.naeyc.org**
- National Association for Gifted Children (NAGC)—**http://www.nagc.org**
- National Association for Multicultural Education (NAME)—**http://nameorg.org/**
- National Association for Sports and Physical Education (NASPE)—**http://www.aahperd.org/naspe**
- National Business Education Association (NBEA)—**http://www.nbea.org**
- National Council for the Social Studies (NCSS)—**http://www.ncss.org**
- National Council of Teachers of English (NCTE)—**http://www.ncte.org**
- National Council of Teachers of Mathematics (NCTM)—**http://www.nctm.org**
- Association for Middle Level Education (AMLE)—**http://www.amle.org/**
- National Science Teachers Association (NSTA)—**http://www.nsta.org**
- Teachers of English to Speakers of Other Languages (TESOL)—**http://www.tesol.org**

Standards for Undergraduates

The **National K–12 Standards for Student Learning** developed by the Committee on Undergraduate Science Education, in collaboration with the Center for Science, Mathematics, and Engineering Education and the National Research Council (1999), addresses the teaching of science, mathematics, engineering, and technology at the college level in an attempt to provide potential teachers with the best undergraduate education possible. The primary goal of this committee is that "institutions of higher education provide diverse opportunities for all undergraduates to study science, mathematics, engineering, and technology as practiced by scientists and engineers, and as early in their academic careers as possible" (Center for Science, Mathematics, and Engineering Education & National Research Council, 1999, p. 1).

The committee recognizes that achievement of this goal relies in part on precollege experiences that include quality instruction in standards-based classrooms and a clear awareness that achievement in science, mathematics, and technology become prerequisites for admission to college. Standards are woven through the education process in an attempt to articulate the connections among all levels of learning.

Standards for Colleges of Education and Universities

There are also standards for school districts, universities, and colleges of education. Such institutions are also expected to meet standards. Through the consolidation of the National Council for Accreditation of Teacher Education (NCATE) and Teacher Education Accreditation Council (TEAC), the Council for the Accreditation of Educator Preparation (CAEP) was created to serve as a single accrediting agency for reform, innovation, and research in educator preparation. In addition to national accreditation agencies, regional agencies such as the Northwest Commission on Colleges and Universities (NWCCU) are recognized by state and federal departments of education as the regional authority on educational quality of higher education institutions in a specific area. These regional agencies establish criteria and evaluation procedures for reviewing institutions and qualify students enrolled in these institutions for access to federal funds to support student financial aid.

Deeper Look 11.3
Read about standards for colleges and universities.

Teacher education programs at accredited institutions have been approved by the Specialized Professional Associations and by state departments of education. Candidates at these institutions must pass standardized tests and maintain a required GPA. Most states with institutions that have received national accreditation have reciprocal agreements with other states for licensure. This means if you get your degree in New York and want to be licensed to teach in Indiana, the Indiana State Board of Education will consider whether you graduated from an accredited institution and if so, your chances of being granted a license to teach in Indiana will be better than if you graduated from an institution that has not achieved national, regional, or state accreditation. It is in your best interests to become aware of the standards underpinning your teacher education program and do your best to exceed these standards at every opportunity.

Standards for Professional Practice

When you begin your teaching career you will be evaluated on your performance as well as the achievement of your students. States may develop their own set of standards for evaluating teachers such as Iowa has. Some districts rely on published works of experts in the field of teacher practice evaluation. In *Enhancing Professional Practice: A Framework for Teaching* (1996), Charlotte Danielson describes the elements of a teacher's responsibilities that promote student learning. These elements are derived from the findings of research studies on the connection between teaching behavior and students' learning. Danielson's framework divides the complex act of teaching into four domains of teaching responsibility—(1) planning and preparation, (2) classroom environment, (3) instruction, and (4) professional responsibilities—and then describes the distinct features of each domain. Frameworks such as Danielson's provide teachers and supervisors benchmarks by which to document teacher progress toward a specific goal.

Standards for Teacher Professional Growth

Mrs. Floyd, introduced at the beginning of this chapter, is certified by the National Board for Professional Teaching Standards. She offers her reflections on this rigorous process.

> Although I already held a master's in education, I was looking to become a better, more effective teacher. I considered getting my PhD in education, but with my husband still in school, we couldn't afford the investment of time or money. In talking with National Board certified teammates of mine, I realized it was a great opportunity for professional development. I think that every teacher wants to improve in their craft but finding the time, and oftentimes money, holds many of us back from doing just that. Here was an avenue that would offer me great professional development at little to no financial cost.
>
> In South Carolina teachers are offered an incentive through the Center for Educator Recruitment, Retention, and Advancement (CERRA) to apply for and obtain National

> Board certification. The application fee is a quite sizable one, but CERRA offers a scholarship to cover that cost. Once a scoreable portfolio is submitted to the National Board for Professional Teaching Standards (NBPTS), half of that loan is forgiven. The other half is forgiven when National Board certification is obtained.
>
> What I learned about my teaching style, the great lesson plans I found and created to help differentiate that teaching style, and the ways I learned to collect and use data were worth the time and effort it took to become a National Board Certified teacher. My husband tells people it was hard not having me around much for the two weeks before the portfolio deadline, but that the supplemental pay made up for it. He's a pragmatist.

After you have taught for three or more years, you may decide to go through the yearlong process for National Board certification. The NBPTS expects accomplished teachers to

- be committed to students and their learning,
- know the subjects they teach and how to teach those subjects to students,
- be responsible for managing and monitoring student learning,
- think systematically about their practice and learn from experience, and
- be members of learning communities.

In addition to these general expectations, the NBPTS has standards for teaching each subject area for specific age levels such as early childhood, middle childhood, early adolescence, and young adulthood. Your teacher education program should be helping you develop the foundation to meet these standards later in your career. A number of colleges and universities have redesigned their master's degrees to reflect these standards and help teachers become nationally certified.

Knowing When Students Have Met the Standards

Audio Link 11.1
Hear how teachers are focusing on student needs.

Lately, it seems that every time students turn around they are being asked to take yet another test. It happens at all levels and in all schools. This increase in testing is part of the focus on accountability, though there is much current debate regarding whether standardized tests accurately reflect student learning. Not too long ago, tests were administered at distant intervals, when students were at a point of transition in developmental levels or at increased demand of content knowledge (fourth grade, seventh grade, or ninth grade). However, now that states and school districts must keep a closer eye on student progress in order to maintain accountability, tests are being administered with more intensity and more frequency. It is not uncommon to have all students, even primary students, taking districtwide competency tests at midpoints in each school quarter.

It would be unnatural if parents and teachers alike didn't question the validity of the increase in testing or ask "What's the point," or "When will I have time to teach?" Testing is part of what you must contend with as a teacher. Think of it as a challenge, not as an unsettling catastrophe. Tests can provide teachers useful data. They can be used for improvement, not just to condemn. As a new teacher, you will have to understand that testing is a large part of the education scene, reconcile yourself to that fact, and do what you can to make it most effective (Popham, 2009). Your response to the testing of your students is of extreme value to your students' success, to your peace of mind, and to the overall standing of your school.

UNDERSTANDING AND USING EVIDENCE

Are Standards for American Students Set Too Low?

The National Center for Education Statistics (NCES) collects and reports reliable data on student assessments in the United States and other nations in its ongoing examination of education systems around the world. One report, the Program for International Student Assessment (PISA), conducted in 2003, focused on 15-year-olds' capabilities in reading literacy, mathematics literacy, and science literacy. The data presented here represents the combined mathematical literacy scores for each country.

Finland	544
Korea	540
Netherlands	538
Japan	534
Canada	532
Belgium	529
Switzerland	527
New Zealand	526
Australia	524
Czech Republic	516
Iceland	515
Denmark	514
France	511
Sweden	509
Austria	506

Germany	503
Ireland	503
Slovak Republic	498
Norway	495
Luxembourg	493
Poland	490
Hungary	490
Spain	485
United States	483
Portugal	466
Italy	466
Greece	445
Turkey	423
Mexico	385

Using the list of combined mathematics literacy scores from the 29 member countries of the Organization for Economic Cooperation Development (OECD), discuss why you think U.S. standards for student achievement in mathematics literacy might need to be, or not need to be, revised. What does the data mean and how might you interpret it?

Taken at face value, the U.S. ranking of 24th in the 29 countries listed indicates that American 15-year-old students' capabilities in mathematics literacy are poor. The data point out a discouraging fact, and one could quickly jump to the conclusion that, yes, standards for American students are set too low.

Teachers are often presented with data that provide an overall picture of the state of the profession or the achievement of students. Sometimes such data can be encouraging, and sometimes it can leave one in a state of wondering how things could have gone so poorly. Data presented in a simple format like the one provided above requires teachers to take a critical look at what important information might be missing. Questions about the missing information should include these:

- What are the requirements for a teaching license in mathematics in each country listed?
- How does the elementary and secondary school curriculum in mathematics in each country compare with that in the United States?
- What is the diversity of the students tested in each country?
- What cultural and linguistic advantages might each country listed have over any of the others?

While the showing of U.S. 15-year-olds is nothing to be proud of, the idea of raising standards to improve these scores does not take into account other variables that might have as great an impact. Teacher excellence is undeniably one of the key components of student success. While standards provide a goal, excellent teaching is the path to that goal.

Teachers are programmed to recognize the individuality of students and to celebrate student achievements, whether or not a distant set of standards is followed. Sometimes, because of this orientation, and the accepting dispositions all teachers are expected to possess, teachers can lose sight of the importance of the nudge they are to exert on all students to achieve to their highest ability. There is a major difference between encouragement and acceptance. Understanding this difference and recognizing ways highly qualified teachers combine the two is a difficult lesson to grasp, but it is within your reach. It is human nature to respond to the raising of any bar as a challenge. We set our own bars and mentally raise them again and again each time we succeed in meeting the goals we have set for ourselves. Standards and benchmarks set the bar for students and teachers alike. Thank goodness teachers have the characteristic of perseverance, and that they continuously help their students over the bars they encounter. When administrators recognize the importance of the teacher's role in implementing standards and benchmarks, and when these administrators support the teachers' efforts, student achievement and school improvement are a likely result.

WHAT IS CURRICULUM?

When asked how she would describe the relationship between curriculum and assessment, Mrs. Floyd answered,

> Good assessment is based on the curriculum and shapes the implementation of that curriculum. I pretest my students to gauge their current level of understanding. This shapes my instruction.
>
> I always use investigation, direct instruction, and peer teaching within a given unit, but the pretest allows me to decide how much of each is appropriate for my students. The informal formative assessment that takes place within my direct instruction lets me know if my students are ready to move on or if we need to spend more time practicing. Sometimes it lets me know that I need to change my approach entirely, shifting my focus to more investigation or peer teaching than I had initially planned to use.
>
> When I was a student I thought that the chapter or unit test was the end of my learning on that topic. As a teacher, I see things completely differently. For me, summative assessment is one more opportunity for the students to learn. I allow my students to make corrections to missed problems, through an in-depth process I adapted from a "Teaching Mathematics" article I read in 2001. It helps build students' metacognitive skills by walking them through the missed problem—What did you do incorrectly? If you don't know what you did incorrectly, or you guessed, what about the problem confused you? I coach them through the correct problem-solving process. The last step is for them, in their own words, to explain how to work through the problem.

Curriculum is as old as any education institution. It is a dynamic field, complex and sometimes messy. Descriptions of curriculum range from "everything that happens in a school" to "a set of performance objectives" (Oliva, 2009, p. 3). Oliva also provides a list of 13 ways curriculum can be described, as well as a quote from Madeline R. Grumet, who labeled curriculum as a "field of utter confusion" (1988, p. 4). Perhaps the field of curriculum is a bit less chaotic today with the advent of easy to understand and follow national and state standards and benchmarks. Curriculum is essential to standards and benchmarks, for without curriculum standards lack

Perseverance, knowledge, effort, and skill can help teachers overcome any hurdles standards and benchmarks might pose.

movement. While standards and benchmarks create the goals for education, it is curriculum that provides the various paths, avenues, and highways to reaching these goals.

Curriculum is one of the key concerns of schooling in the United States. Excellent schools for the future cannot be created without an understanding of curriculum theory and practice. McNeil (2003) says that curriculum is the teacher's initiative. When teachers become active participants in determining the curriculum and the instructional practices that translate it into action, there is a greater chance that excellence will be achieved. Hilda Taba wrote, "All curricula, no matter what their particular design, are composed of certain elements. A curriculum usually contains a statement of aims and of specific objectives; it indicates some selection and organization of content; it either implies or manifests certain patterns of learning and teaching, whether because the objectives demand them or because the content organization requires them. Finally, it includes a program of evaluation of the outcomes" (Taba, 1962).

Even though schools look pretty much the same today as they did at the turn of the 19th century, the present never exactly mirrors the past. Curriculum has gone through some major changes since the first schools were established in the Plymouth Colony nearly 400 years ago. From schooling in Colonial America to the present day, concerns with teaching reading and equal access for all students to learn, as well as the intensity of debates among educators, politicians, and the population in general about what should be taught and how it should be taught has never faltered.

Students will always be expected to know the basics, which might include, in addition to reading, writing, and arithmetic, how to conduct a search on the Internet or create a media presentation. When Bob Dylan wrote that "the times they are a-changing," school curriculum was no doubt not in his thoughts; but he was right on the mark. Curriculum has been the conduit through which educational ideas and goals become evident in practice and programs. There has always been an ebb and flow to school curriculum as it reacts to the pull of American life. In the beginning, the waves of curriculum reform were gentle, while the undertow was hardly noticed. As American society and the American system of education grew in tandem, the pull of new ideas and novel educational practices became stronger and was, in turn, resisted with ever greater force. Curriculum always changes, but a useful and purposeful curriculum is never far removed from the students and society it serves.

Characteristics of Curriculum

To understand the nature of curriculum it helps to have a framework for thinking about curriculum. Oliva (2009) offers a view of curriculum through 10 different lenses he terms "axioms." These axioms provide guidelines for educators seeking ways to improve curriculum and solve curriculum problems. In the following, we have directed your thinking to something you may have experienced that reflects the intent of each axiom.

Challenging Assumptions

Does setting standards automatically result in increased student academic achievement?

● ● ● ● ●

The Assumption

The idea behind the No Child Left Behind (NCLB) initiative was that if there are specific standards for student achievement and if students' abilities to meet such standards are assessed over time in standardized and organized procedures then teachers and school districts will be held accountable and will make the necessary adjustments to practice and organization to assure that all students have equal opportunity to meet the national standards.

The Research

Not all school districts have the wherewithal to make the necessary changes to meet the mandates of NCLB. Some large school districts continue to struggle to fill each classroom with a teacher who meets the qualifications of the High Objective Uniform State Standard of Evaluation (HOUSSE) rules that each state must determine in order to show that teachers in all classrooms are highly qualified. Some school districts lack the funding to adjust class size and/or to provide each classroom with the materials and technology that are viewed as necessary support for students to meet mandated standards. Schools that are classified as "in need for improvement" often find themselves in an untenable position to demonstrate how they have improved to meet standards when they had not been able to meet them in the first place. However, increased funding for schools has not always provided a better learning environment for students. What is to be done?

In May 2006, the U.S. House of Representatives began a hearing related to NCLB to examine how the federal government can help states reach the goal to have all students proficient in reading and math by the year 2014. One way some public organizations are beginning to approach this problem is to demand that school districts allow students zoned for a school categorized as "in need for improvement" to go to another school which is not. A class action suit against the New Jersey schools is demanding that students in low-performing schools receive vouchers to attend a public or private school of their choice. Clint Bolick, the president and general counsel of the Alliance for School Choice, vows that such measures would provide educational relief for the 60,000 students attending the 97 New Jersey schools cited as failing. Approximately half of the students in New Jersey schools have failed to meet state standards in language arts and mathematics.

Implications

The school of choice movement has been around for some time now, and the voucher system has been in place for students; however, the mandates of NCLB placed a greater emphasis on the potential for parents to demand that their children have an equal opportunity for an education in a high-quality school with a highly qualified teacher. As a candidate in a teacher education program, you should know about the voucher programs in your state and the status of the schools in the area where you wish to teach.

Source: Hoff, D. J. (2006). Choice advocates seek vouchers as remedy for N.J. students in low-performing schools. *Education Week.* Retrieved from **http://www.edweek.org**

Axiom 1: Change is both inevitable and necessary, for it is through change that life forms grow and develop.

Though change is never easy, it is a fact of life. Some of the changes in American education occurred because of social issues, some because of philosophical debates, and some because of new inventions. Think for a moment of the problems a school you are familiar with has faced due to societal or technological influences. Consider any philosophical differences that have risen in the community you are familiar with. Then, ask yourself, in light of these changes, what curriculum changes might benefit the students in the school as well as the larger community?

Axiom 2: A school curriculum not only reflects but is a product of its time.

Something happens, then something else happens. Stuff happens. Events overlap. Societies change. People move. Scientific innovations, pandemics, war, and the media change the way we perceive the world. Consider the changes in technology, the environment, and population shifts that have occurred in your lifetime. Did any of these shifts cause a change in the school curriculum?

Axiom 3: Curriculum changes made at an earlier period of time can exist concurrently with newer curriculum changes at a later period of time.

You're probably familiar with educational reform being likened to a pendulum. School curriculum swings from one extreme to another, back and forth—from learning basic skills in math to "new math" concepts and back, from emphasis on direct instruction to classrooms that are student centered and back, from phonics to whole language and back. Ideas fall out of favor at some point in time and then later are embraced as exactly what is needed. Teachers who have been trained in one method of instruction often resist the newer methods being promoted. New teachers are often eager to try the latest innovation. No doubt you have been aware of some of the back and forth swing of curricular ideas in your own history of schooling. Ask your grandparents or parents what curriculum was important when they went to school. Is it similar to what you experienced? Dissimilar?

Axiom 4: Curriculum change results from changes in people.

Alice Miel, in *Changing the Curriculum: A Social Process* (1946), wrote: "To change the curriculum of the school is to change the factors interacting to shape that curriculum" (p. 10).

Teachers enact curriculum. They translate words on a page into meaningful lectures, demonstrations, or projects for students. Reading the curriculum for *Sesame Street* and seeing the curriculum come to life through Big Bird and the Muppets are two very different experiences. When educators want the curriculum to be changed they must also help the teachers who will translate the curriculum into changing their instructional practices. Sometimes it is even necessary for parents and the entire community to change their attitudes and beliefs about what should be taught and how it should be taught. Anyone involved in creating changes in curriculum must themselves change. Are you aware of any curriculum changes in your high school? If there were changes, how were they received by parents and the community?

Axiom 5: Curriculum change is effected as a result of cooperative endeavor on the part of groups. Teachers, professional planners, and curriculum developers must work together to effect positive curricular change. Significant curriculum improvement comes about through group activity.

Margaret Mead's famous quote, "Never doubt that a small group of thoughtful, committed citizens can change the world. Indeed, it is the only thing that ever has," can be applied to groups of people who come together to develop a curriculum that will meet the needs and expand the learning of students in any specific time or place. Hilda Taba's idea for a curriculum based on key concepts, organization, and facts was practiced and perfected by groups of educators who saw Taba's ideas as a way to teach critical-thinking skills in social studies to K–8 students. In 1969 this was a positive change in teaching the social studies curriculum, and it was made possible by a "cooperative endeavor on the part of groups" (Oliva, 2009, p. 33). Consider how groups of people may have made changes in the curriculum you experienced as a student.

Axiom 6: Curriculum development is basically a decision-making process.

Choices have to be made—what content should be included or excluded, what curriculum best serves the needs of the local society? Decisions about instructional methods need to be made. (How did you learn to read?) The types of programs that will exist in the school must be determined. How will classes and grade levels be organized? How will the teachers work to assure that all students have an equal opportunity to learn? "What knowledge is of most worth?" is a question Herbert Spencer asked in 1909, and that question has echoed through American education as policymakers, school administrators, and teachers wrestle with what students should know and be able to do.

Axiom 7: Curriculum development is a never-ending process.

Once you've got it the way you want it, it's time to go back to the drawing board. Curriculum planners must constantly monitor the curriculum they have developed to make sure it is fulfilling its original promise and is not creating unforeseen problems. As you read in Chapter 7, there have been good ideas in teaching and learning and ideas that were not so productive. Keeping track of what a curriculum poses to accomplish and the final results in student learning from that curriculum is of utmost importance in determining if the curriculum should be modified or not. Students constantly ask teachers, "Why do I need to know this?" When curriculum is well developed, the answer should be easy.

Axiom 8: Curriculum development is a comprehensive process.

Curriculum planning should not be piecemeal, patching, cutting, adding, plugging in, shortening, lengthening, or troubleshooting (Taba, 1962). If one aspect of the curriculum is out of whack, the whole curriculum can be a disaster. Every aspect of the curriculum must be taken into consideration—Oliva advises curriculum planners to be aware of the impact of curriculum development not only on the students, teachers, and parents directly concerned with a programmatic change but also on the innocent bystanders, those not directly involved in the curriculum planning but affected in some way by the results of planning (2009). Can you think of an experience in your education when a curriculum seemed confusing or irrational?

Axiom 9: Systematic curriculum development is more effective than trial and error.

Having a final goal in mind, just as state-established core standards aim for a final result, will direct curriculum development to a productive end. The whole picture should be apparent from the beginning. In the same way that a talented sculptor sees the form inside a block of stone, curriculum developers must be able to see through the existing curriculum to envision something more meaningful, effective, and purposeful, and then follow a specific set of procedures to achieve the desired goal. Results from curriculum changes do not happen overnight or at the rapid pace school administrators would like, so changes in curriculum may occur more often than would benefit any long-range systematic plan. How often did you see curriculum change in your own educational journey?

Axiom 10: The curriculum planner starts from where the curriculum is just as the teacher starts from where the students are.

What has come before should not necessarily be tossed aside. Preexisting ideas and modes of delivery may have some merit that will fit into new ideas for curriculum. Perhaps all that is needed is a reorganization of current practices and future goals. If a spiral curriculum for the development of math skills has been carefully developed, then it will not make sense to eliminate one section of the spiral and expect students to move forward through the curriculum with all the required skills and knowledge. Most drastic changes are caused by trauma. Young students and their teachers do not need to experience the stress that could result from a poorly conceived curriculum.

Viewing curriculum as one side of a coin and instruction as the other side can help you understand the close relationship between the two. One cannot exist without the other.

I was out of my driveway and down the block before realizing I should have turned right instead of left. I've never been very good at directions. My wife likes to call it being "directionally challenged." The lack of a strong, internal geographical compass would make life without maps and GPS exciting to say the least. Thankfully, when we're driving somewhere unfamiliar, I can rely on any number of direction-supportive devices.

The parallel in the debate related to curriculum development and accountability is clear and leads to several logical questions: What if, as an educational system, we had no compass or "road map"? How would we measure success? If each teacher sets an individual bar, how do we communicate excellence? Will that "relative" definition even make sense in a future marketplace? Without at least some general agreement related to the process and goals of what students should learn and be able to do, how might we measure whether or not we had successfully "arrived" at our intended destination?

Early in my career, I sat in a crowded conference hall listening to a keynote speaker address how much educators love their students and do not need accountability. She seemed to believe that somehow, once we don the role of professional educator, all selfishness, poor judgment, and personal drive are forever leeched from our souls. While most would accept that people who come into professional education do so for at least some noble reasons, we still come as fallible people. As such, we need some form of a map to guide the direction of our work.

Though finding the proper role and fit for accountability is complicated, failing to establish and maintain a reasonable system of checks and balances creates an environment with too much ambiguity to ensure we are effective. There are many fair criticisms of accountability systems in their current form; however, while perfection may be difficult to obtain, accountability in some form or another helps provide a more clear direction for the journey of teaching and learning.

Kevin Badgett
Assistant Professor of Educational Leadership,
University of Texas of the Permian Basin
Odessa, Texas

Teachers Making Curriculum Come Alive

A very talented teacher you met in Chapter 7, Diane McCarty, is especially able to weave different strands of curriculum through multiple forms of delivery and make learning fun for the students. She uses "Travel Bears" to help her students develop skill and knowledge in language arts, mathematics, social studies, art, and science as they track the travels of their chosen stuffed bears. Another integrated curriculum project she developed sent her students off on a virtual bike ride to learn the history, geography, political boundaries, and unique characteristics of their state. Both projects require the teacher to preplan extensively and garner a wealth of resources. The lessons are fun and memorable for the students, but more important, they set an example for the students of enjoyable ways to learn, to investigate, and to solve problems. It's likely that the students who participate in these projects learn to be aware of indicators of their own knowledge base and how it is acquired. Translating curriculum into action is similar to writing a lesson plan, though the perspective is not so much on objectives as it is on making ideas come to life, to be intriguing to students, and to motivate them to learn what is required.

In Chapter 13 you will read about some of the curriculum Jason Choi and his colleagues have created for the middle school and high school students in the Tarrytown School District in New York. Teachers who incorporate engaging curriculum projects and then share them with other

Deeper Look 11.4
Read about a problem-solving curriculum aligned with standards.

teachers are following Hilda Taba's plan for curriculum development. Teachers may be handed a curriculum guide when they begin their careers, but the lessons they create to help students meet standards and benchmarks can only be produced by spending time with learners, knowing their abilities and interests, and knowing the content. Diane McCarty and Jason Choi are teachers who share their own enjoyment of learning with their students by making curriculum come alive. Read more about Diane McCarty's curriculum projects in NCTM's *Teaching Children Mathematics* (February 1998) and, with coauthor Maribell Betterton, "Scientifically Speaking: Connection to the Past, Present and Future," in *Teaching K–8* (March 1999).

Accountability Measures Through Standards, Benchmarks, and Curriculum

Schools and, to a greater extent, teachers have always been held accountable in some manner of form for student learning. Accreditation agencies, local school districts, and state and national departments of education demand some sort of evidence of teacher effectiveness before initial licensure and tenure of teachers. In the past, evidence of teacher effectiveness was based mainly on supervisory reports conducted by administrators and standardized tests of teacher competencies. In the future, evidence of student learning based on accountability measures identified through standards and curriculum goals will also be used to determine teacher effectiveness.

Value-Added Assessment of Teacher Effectiveness

That teachers are accountable for student learning is a reasonable claim. However, crediting student learning to a specific teacher's actions over a specific period of time is difficult to pin down. The variables that determine student academic achievement comprise physical, mental, and emotional aspects that might be, at any given moment, unrelated to a teacher's actions. In value-added assessment of teacher effectiveness, statistics are used to determine an individual student's potential results on standardized tests. In any year that a student's results exceed his or her potential, the teacher is viewed as contributing to the student's academic growth (i.e., being effective). Such statistics can be used by school district administrators and departments of education to determine teacher retention and merit pay for teachers.

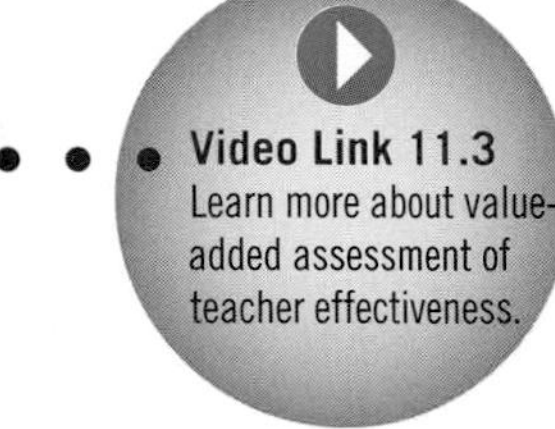
Video Link 11.3
Learn more about value-added assessment of teacher effectiveness.

The effort to determine the effect of teacher behavior on student academic achievement has been around since 1971. In 1996, Sanders and Rivers stated that effective teachers could be distinguished from ineffective teachers through rigorous research methods. In 2010, the Bill and Melinda Gates Foundation released initial results from a yearlong study indicating that value-added assessments could determine teacher effectiveness. Some school districts have adopted the practice of value-added assessment for teachers. Visit **http://www.cps.edu/SiteCollectionDocuments/REACHStudentsValueAdded.pdf** to learn about the Chicago Public Schools approach to value-added assessment for teachers.

Using statistical analyses and the results of student test scores has never had unanimous support. Teachers often respond to claims that test scores can be used to determine their effectiveness by countering that test scores can be influenced by time of day, noise level, hunger, and even the weather. It seems likely that the debate on ways teacher effectiveness can be determined will continue throughout your professional career. Whichever way the debate unfolds, it is in your best interest to recognize the professional standards by which your effectiveness might be judged.

School Accountability

Schools are evaluated on student achievement; when student achievement is low, and Adequate Yearly Progress (AYP) is not met, schools are sanctioned and may be forced to undergo some form of restructuring. The existing faculty at a school may be let go and new teachers hired in an attempt to "turn the school around." Visit the TurnAround Schools Institute website at **http://www.turnaroundschools.com** to become familiar with some of the strategies common to the turnaround school process.

When accountability is not met through standards and curriculum, policymakers must examine current practices and find some way to change or improve existing practices. In 1955, Rudolf Flesch published *Why Johnny Can't Read*. This publication forced curriculum developers to examine current instructional practices in reading. In 1983, Flesch published a second attack on instructional practices in reading, *Why Johnny Still Can't Read*. That same year President Ronald Reagan's National Commission on Excellence in Education published *A Nation at Risk: The Imperative for Educational Reform*. Such publications did much to heighten professional and public awareness that standards and accountability were necessary in order for the nation's educational programs to improve. As concern over problems in the education system increase so will efforts to hold teachers and schools accountable through establishment of standards and benchmarks.

Audio Link 11.2
Learn more about school accountability.

Accountability is not an evil construct with which to badger schools and teachers. If we are not held accountable for our actions and for the result of our actions, then what is the value of our efforts? Education is the great leveler in the field of life. Standards that can help students navigate this field successfully should be embraced. Standards that help teachers become more effective and a greater force in student learning should be met. Standards that can help schools be shining examples of American education should be integrated into every phase of the school curriculum. Accountability is nothing to worry about when standards, benchmarks, and curriculum are designed for student success and are followed with the creative flare only teachers can bring to translating them into instruction.

CONNECTING TO THE CLASSROOM

Students frequently ask, "Why do I have to learn this?"

Explaining that they have to learn something because it will be on the test or that they will use the information sometime in the future doesn't seem to carry much weight with students. When students ask why it is important to learn something, they want to know how it will be important *now*. Effective teachers—teachers who are successful in getting students to learn the standard-based curriculum—are masters at relating whatever content they are teaching to the students' here and now, creating ways to tie the content to students' lives, to make the standards relevant.

When you have the opportunity to observe a teacher responding to the question, "Why do I have to learn this?," make note of how the teacher responds.

1. Does the teacher's response engage the student's thinking?
2. Does the teacher ignore the question and continue on with the lesson?
3. What seems to be the most common teacher response?
4. Following the teacher's response, does the student appear more interested in the content? Why or why not?

SUMMARY

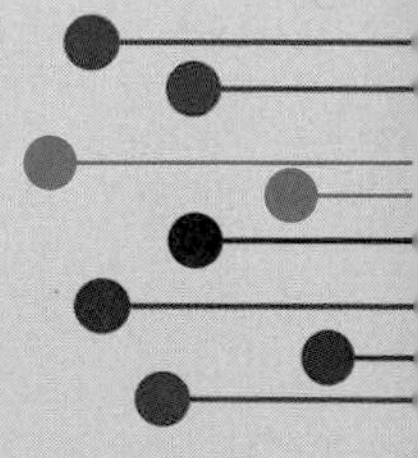

Four major topics have been addressed in this chapter:

- Standards: the statements that indicate what students should know and be able to do at specific points in their education
- Benchmarks: the intermediate goals that guide students toward achieving standards
- Curriculum: one of the key concerns in education, which provides the link between standards statements and instruction
- Accountability: the way schools, teachers, and students can show they have met standards, benchmarks, and curriculum goals

CLASS DISCUSSION QUESTIONS

1. Discuss some of the ways one of your teachers' focus on local, state, and national standards helped you learn specific concepts.

2. Effective teachers must also meet standards for teaching by reflecting on their practice and the behavior of their students in order to improve their instructional practices and student achievement. Name some of the ways focus on teacher standards can affect student learning.

3. Think back to your own experiences as a student. Describe one time when you knew you were "learning" something. Did you want to discuss your new knowledge with others (peers, parents, and teachers)?

4. How did your teachers reinforce your new learning? Were you ever aware as a student that the results of your learning were evidence that you were meeting standards and achieving specified benchmarks?

KEY TERMS

Accountability 322
Benchmarks 321
National K–12 Standards for Student Learning 333
Performance assessments 330
Standards-based curriculum 330

SELF-ASSESSMENT

WHAT IS YOUR CURRENT LEVEL OF UNDERSTANDING AND THINKING ABOUT STANDARDS, CURRICULUM, AND ACCOUNTABILITY?

One of the indicators of understanding is to examine how complex your thinking is when asked questions that require you to use the concepts and facts introduced in this chapter.

Answer the following questions as fully as you can. Then use the Complexity of Thinking rubric to self-assess the degree to which you understand and can use the ideas presented in this chapter.

1. How many types of standards can you explain?
2. What is the relationship of benchmarks to standards?
3. Why is it important for teachers to understand national, state, and local standards for student achievement?
4. What conditions influence the changing nature of the school curriculum?

What is your current level of understanding? Rate yourself using this rubric.

Complexity of Thinking Rubric

	Parts & Pieces	Unidimensional	Organized	Integrated	Extensions
Indicators	Elements/concepts are talked about as isolated and independent entities.	One or a few concepts are addressed, while others are underdeveloped.	Deliberate and structured consideration of all key concepts/elements.	All key concepts/elements are included in a view that addresses interconnections.	Integration of all elements and dimensions, with extrapolation to new situations.
Standards, benchmarks, and curriculum	Names some standards and benchmarks without explaining relationships.	Describes basic role of standards but not of benchmarks and curriculum.	Describes multiple roles of standards in curriculum design and implementation.	Describes standards and benchmarks are all levels and relates theses standards to present curriculum practices.	Describes ways standards can effect student learning and teaching practices.

STUDENT STUDY SITE

Visit the Student Study Site at **www.sagepub.com/hall** to access links to the videos, audio clips, and Deeper Look reference materials noted in this chapter, as well as additional study tools including eFlashcards, web quizzes, and more.

Field Guide

for Learning More About Standards, Curriculum, and Accountability

• • • • •

In Chapter 1 you were introduced to the concept of a field guide for learning more about your surroundings. The artifacts and information you will collect for this part of your field guide will involve the evidence of standards-based curriculum in the schools and classrooms that you visit during your teacher education program.

Ask a Teacher or Principal

Ask a teacher to talk about ways standards can facilitate the planning process. How do teachers incorporate the Common Core Standards into instruction?

Make Your Own Observations

Join a department meeting as the teachers plan a lesson or lessons for a specific content area. Note how often the teachers refer to standards as they plan these lessons. How often do they refer to particular students or groups of students and consider how they may have to differentiate the instruction to meet the learning needs of these students?

After you have observed the planning session, visit one of the teachers' classrooms to see how the standards and curriculum are expressed through instruction.

Reflect Through Journaling

One of the reasons people give for becoming teachers is the desire to enter a field where their creative talents can be expressed. Discussions of standards-based curriculum can often dampen the creative spirit teachers have. Write in your journal about ways you want to express your creative spirit in the classroom and how you might be able to do this even in an environment of standards.

Read a Book

Creating Standards-Based Integrated Curriculum, by Susan M. Drake (2007; Thousand Oaks, CA: Corwin), provides a wealth of information on accountability in standards-based curriculum and standards-based interdisciplinary curriculum, and offers a process model for designing curriculum.

Understanding Common Core State Standards, by J. Kendall (2011, Denver, CO: McREL/ Alexandria, VA: ASCD), offers educators an overview of the ways Common Core Standards can improve teaching and learning across the United States.

Search the Web

There is an interesting program at **http://www.wirelessgeneration.com/** under the Assessments link titled mCLASS Beacon. This program seems to put all of the standards at your fingertips while helping you assess student learning of the standards.

Common Core Standards Lesson Planning at **http://coreplanner.com/** will provide you with the tools to create a lesson plan around common core standards and allow you to track your lessons.

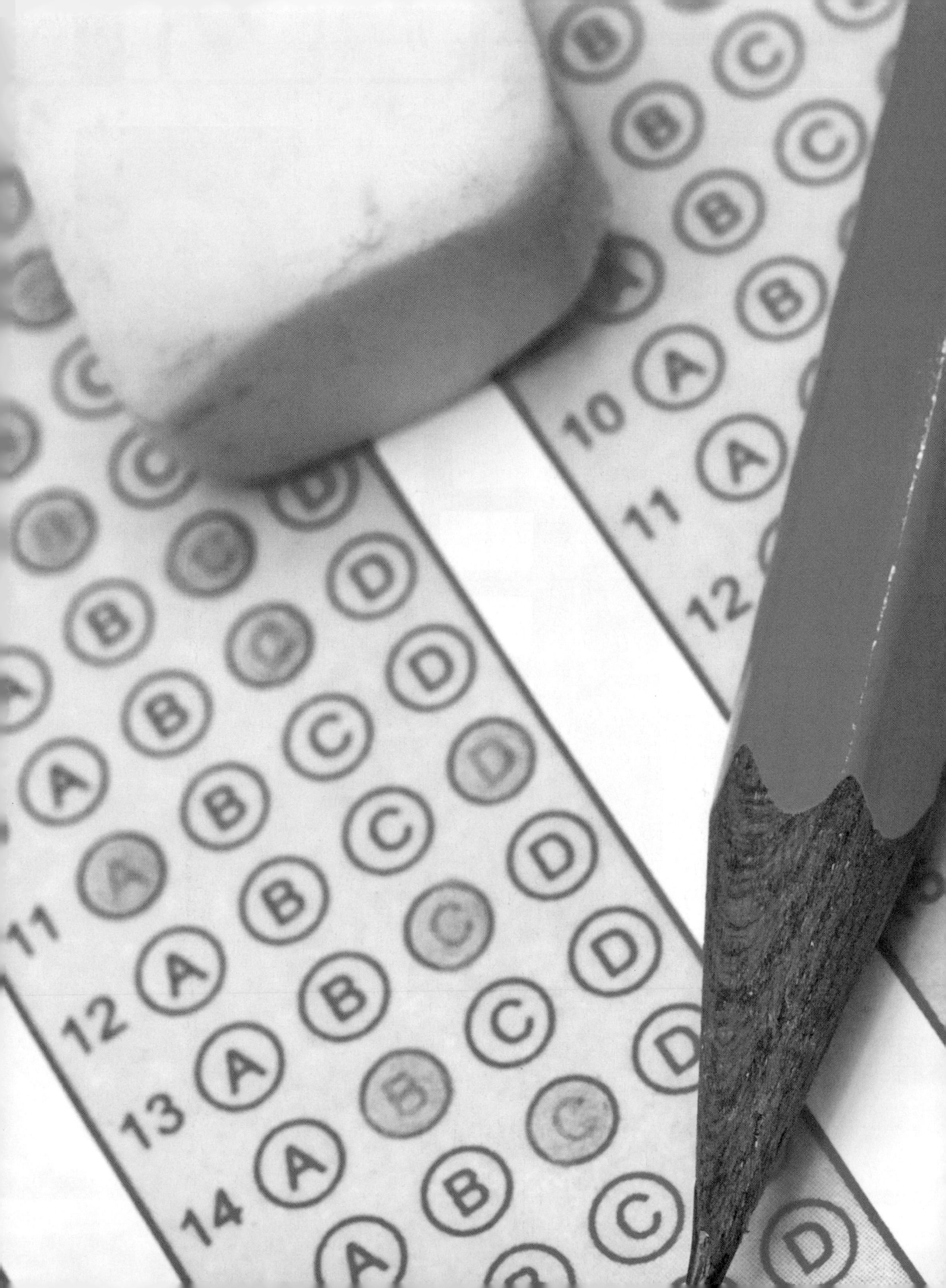

10 A B C
11 A
12
11 A B C D
12 A B C D
13 A B C D
14 A B C D

TEACHER INTERVIEW

Lena Mann

Lena Mann is a high school math teacher at Pinon High School, a public school located on the Navajo Reservation in northeastern Arizona. More than 425 students are enrolled in the high school. Ms. Mann says that after 42 years in the classroom she still enjoys coming to work every day. *I walk into the classroom and all of the problems that I had outside of the classroom disappear.*

Managing the Classroom and Student Behavior

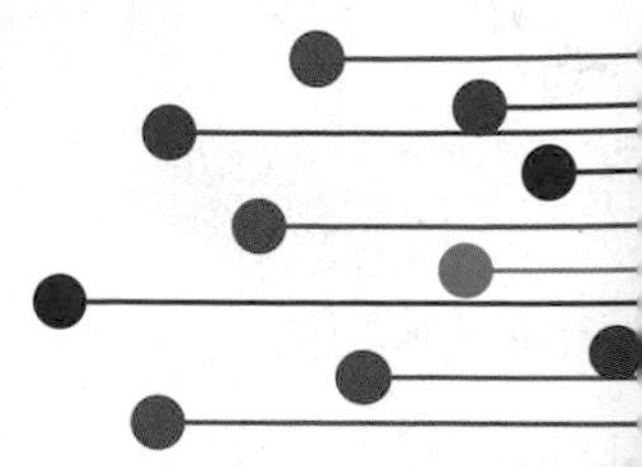

• *Why did you become a teacher?*

I actually went to school to be an architect. But then, I needed money and I started tutoring and discovered that I really liked teaching people about math and numbers and helping other people learn. I went back to college and got my teaching degree at Northern Arizona University. After two years of teaching I found out that students were having a lot of difficulties and couldn't read and couldn't understand the concepts they needed to know. Again, I went back to college and got my master's in special education so I could understand why some students had difficulty learning and why others learned the way they did. I wanted to be able to differentiate between the students and help them learn the ways they could learn.

How do you describe excellent teaching?

It's that place where there is rapport between the teacher and the students, where both teacher and students are comfortable and there is no friction. Excellence in teaching is when a teacher can make mistakes and the students can make mistakes but both the teacher and the students feel that the mistakes can be remedied. The classroom is a safe place where mistakes can happen and be corrected. I have seen a lot of teachers try hard to be excellent. Some go overboard being friendly with the students, while others focus on being disciplinarians instead of making students feel comfortable learning. There has to be a balance in teaching. To become an excellent teacher you do not need to be a disciplinarian. You need to help students learn how to take care of their own behavior. If you do this for the students, they will become empowered.

How do you know if students are learning?

The first thing I look for is that the students' eyes show they got it. Once I see the light in their eyes that they understood a concept or got the idea I am trying to teach them, I know they are with me. They are participating, and I don't have to push them because they have confidence in themselves. And then they can turn around and teach someone else. When I don't see the light in their eyes I go back to work with them once everyone else is settled. Sometimes students are surprised that I recognized that they didn't understand what I was trying to teach and they ask me how I knew they were lost. An excellent teacher can tell when a student has missed the point. When that happens, I will walk over to the student and ask, "Where did I lose you?" Probably most beginning teachers wouldn't have the skill to tell from a student's eyes whether they got the lesson or not; unless it was second nature to them, that they had a special talent for reading people. What I've always told young teachers to help them develop skill in teaching is to journal. Journaling is like having a diary. When you're a teacher, every day is a new day.

Questions to Consider

1. Think back to your days as an elementary, middle, or high school student. What was it about the classroom that was most appealing to you? Why?
2. What does the term *a friend to my students* mean to you?
3. How might asking a student, "When did I lose you?" contribute to effective classroom management?
4. What type of feedback would you most like to hear from your students?
5. What does Lena Mann mean when she says her "radius is very large now"? Is this something all teachers eventually experience?

It is important to make note of the things that you are learning about student learning. What you learn one day might work for you in the future. After each week, go back and read your notes and think about what went well or ways your teaching practice might be improved.

What brings you joy in teaching?

When I started teaching I thought that I would get immediate feedback from my students about what they were learning. But it took 10 years before I finally got the feedback I was hoping to get my first year of teaching. A student came back and told me she was finally doing something with the math she had learned in my classroom. She was working out of New York City and had helped design the iPad. Another student was a Navajo and he just sort of sat back and rolled his eyes during class. He made it to MIT and graduated from MIT. He came back and told me that I was the one who motivated him. That is the joy in teaching—to see that you have really made a difference. Young teachers really don't know the impact they are making on students until years later. Your connection with students and leaving your footprint on their lives is the true joy in teaching. Your family of students grows and expands to children of your students and grandchildren of your students. Teaching is like paying something forward. Your circle of influence grows and grows. My radius is very large now. It is a shame that some teachers don't stay in the profession long enough to recognize their influence on many lives. Persistence is so important in teaching.

Learning Outcomes

After reading this chapter, you should be able to

1. Understand how teachers begin to formulate a management approach (style) that is compatible with their individual personalities.
2. Recognize the ways classroom management facilitates teaching and learning.
3. Understand how the use of data on student behavior can help teachers determine the effectiveness of their classroom management plans.
4. Know the connection between effective classroom management behavior and national expectations for teacher knowledge.

INTRODUCTION

Winston Churchill once said, "We shape our dwellings, then our dwellings shape us" (1943). It is also likely that teachers shape their classrooms and then the classrooms they have created shape the learning that occurs there as well as the behavior of the learners. What every teacher wants is a classroom of students who want to learn, who feel good about being in school and about what they do when they are there. Expert classroom management can make that desire become a reality.

All schools, classrooms, students, and teachers are not the same. What works in one setting or for one group of learners may not work for another. School days begin and end on different notes, and the times in between are strung together by a variety of events that can perplex even the most experienced teachers. Each day in a classroom unfolds through actions and reactions influenced by environmental impacts, emotions, expectations, and sometimes frustration. Some people believe that what happens is inevitable and outside their control. Others may believe they have some degree of control over what happens. A teacher with a strong locus of control probably has a better chance of creating a well-managed classroom than a teacher who believes everything that happens in the classroom is outside of her control.

Teachers must develop plans for managing their classrooms that create a comfortable atmosphere for the teacher and students to work in, that allow for professional and personal choice, and that are acceptable within a given school culture. Any classroom management system must support teaching and learning, recognize individual needs and desires among students, and encourage growth of acceptable behaviors. Every teacher holds an ideal classroom in mind. The challenge is to make that classroom come to life through knowledge of oneself, through an awareness of the wide range of techniques and strategies available for building a management plan, and through communicating with students to inform them of that vision.

Learning about ways to manage a classroom and why certain teacher behaviors can be beneficial while others might be detrimental to teaching and learning will help you begin to articulate a plan for the way you want your classroom to look, feel, and function.

Developing a managing plan requires the same skills you use to plan a lesson. You have to have a goal in mind. You need to establish objectives and implement instruction that will help the students achieve the objectives. There needs to be an assessment of student success in meeting the objectives and reaching the desired goal so that you can evaluate whether the plan is actually working. This chapter will help you begin to envision a management plan.

WHAT IS CLASSROOM MANAGEMENT?

Deeper Look 12.1
Read an article about pro-social classrooms and student learning.

Lena Mann says classroom management is about teaching the students how to be responsible for their own behavior. According to Ms. Mann,

> the teacher organizes the environment and manages the environment. Students that come into that environment already know what their limitations on behavior should be. I set limitations on ethical behavior only such as bullying or cheating. The rest will evolve as the year begins. In the beginning of the year, the students and I look at the rules the district has established for the school and for the students. Then I ask students if they are comfortable with those rules. I have them write an essay about their comfort level with the district rules and as a class we discuss the concerns that are mentioned in the essays.
>
> There are days when you are challenged and on such days I always ask myself what did I do to make this happen. I am a person, my students are people so I always look to myself first when something doesn't seem to be going the way I want it to. Teachers should always look to themselves first. When things aren't going the way you think they should ask the students what might be the problem. Tell them how you feel and ask them if you should do something differently. Ask the students to help you to know what to do to help them learn.

Classroom management involves all of the tasks that teachers and students perform in any given day, covering a wide range of actions and attitudes associated with teaching and learning. Educators discuss classroom management from differing perspectives, but these different perspectives

There is a world of difference between a well-managed classroom and one that is chaotic. Teachers usually prefer the former.

all take into consideration the interaction among students, teachers, and the content to be taught in an effective learning environment. McEwan's (2000) view of classroom management encompasses a range of conditions from the interactions among and between students and the teacher, to the establishment and reinforcement of rules, to the room arrangement, to student access to materials and resources and to the frequency of teacher interactions with parents.

Weber (1994) defined classroom management as "that complex set of strategies that a teacher uses to establish and maintain the conditions that will enable students to learn" (1994, p. 234). Wong and Wong (1998) view classroom management as "all the things that a teacher does to organize students, space, time and materials so that instruction and student learning can take place" (p. 84). Iverson (2003) defines classroom management as "the act of supervising relationships, behaviors, and instructional settings and lessons for communities of learners" (p. 4), and views management as separate from discipline in that discipline refers to "teaching students how to behave appropriately." To Emmer, Evertson, and Worsham (2002), classroom management involves a series of decisions teachers make to create classroom communities where students are engaged in worthwhile activities that support their learning. Lemov (2010) views management as teaching students to do something right through building relationships that are "nontransactional."

If one considers the alternative to managing a classroom, which is *chaos,* effective classroom management can be viewed as central to all that is good and right about teaching. Since the responsibility for managing a classroom rests almost entirely on the teacher's shoulders, this is perhaps the main reason that managing a classroom is often cited as the number one concern of beginning teachers. Such concern is not just a recent phenomenon in education. Consider the following excerpt from D. H. Lawrence's (1915) novel, *Rainbow,* in which Ursula Brangwen begins her teaching career and is faced with the daunting task of managing the behavior of her students.

> The day passed incredibly slowly. She never knew what to do. There came horrible gaps, when she was merely exposed to the children. . . . Before this inhuman number of children she was always at bay. She could not get away from it. There it was. This class of fifty collective children, depending on her for command, for command it hated and resented. It made her feel she could not breathe: she must suffocate, it was so inhuman. They were so many, that they were not children. They were a squadron. She could not speak as she would to a child, because they were not individual children, they were a collective, inhuman thing. (pp. 355–356)

Ursula's experience may seem a bit extreme and out of the ordinary, but it is a rare teacher indeed who has never felt outnumbered or outmaneuvered by an unmanageable group of students. Teacher education candidates can take comfort in the fact that a modicum of knowledge about human behavior and skill in implementing management strategies can provide even a novice teacher some degree of self-confidence and competence in managing a classroom. It is a huge undertaking, but it does not have to be overwhelming.

Video Case 12.1
Classroom Management

1. What are some of the suggestions teachers in this video offer for managing student behavior and instruction? Which suggestions do you feel would work best for you?
2. Debbie Dogancay talks about starter exercises to get students' brains immediately focused on the lesson to be taught. What are some other ways teachers in the video focus student attention on learning?

Establishing and maintaining an effective learning environment through management of space, time, instruction, and behavior requires a teacher to have expert knowledge of the learners, the content, and the context. Teachers' ideas about classroom management often go through a series of transformations as they observe, learn, and reflect on the success of the management plans they have enacted. The way a particular teacher chooses to manage a classroom also derives from a specific system of values and priorities for attending to a range of educational functions. As you develop your personal professional philosophy of teaching introduced in Chapter 7, you will most likely include some of the ideas you have for managing a classroom.

Using What You Already Know About Classroom Management

In learning theory the technique of activation or the use of advance organizers helps bring the students' full attention to what they are about to study. For example, if a teacher wants to teach a science lesson about weather, he might ask the students to recall a time they had experienced stormy weather. He will talk about the sound of the wind moving objects around or the sound of rain and the smell of ozone or dust in the air. These are all things students would be familiar with, and recalling the memory of them will help students build a **cognitive framework** of weather to include additional information.

Likewise, we've all had some experience with management. If you've ever packed a suitcase, loaded a car, decorated a house or a room, planned a wedding or birthday party, or been shopping you probably already have a good idea about the importance of organization, time management, and access to resources. If you have spent any time at all working with young children, you no doubt know quite a bit about behavior management. You've also spent considerable time in classrooms observing how other teachers organize tasks and activities and manage the behavior of their students.

Frameworks for Learning About Classroom Management

Performance in managing a classroom does not rest entirely on rules, routines, rewards, and reprimands, but it is a far more complex combination of all that a teacher is, knows, and does. As an aspiring teacher education candidate, you need to recognize the relationships between teacher dispositions, teacher knowledge, pedagogical and management skills, and the level at which a teacher performs.

Three Areas of Classroom Management

Content management includes planning the physical environment, deciding on the procedures that will occur during the instructional day, and instruction (Iverson, 2003). Planning is the key. Teachers plan during the summer break for the coming school year. They plan on weekends. They plan before and after school, and during free periods. The planning that teachers do has a profound effect on instruction, student behavior, and the relationships that are formed with their

Table 12.1 Examples of Classroom Rules (Elementary, Middle, and High School)

Some rules of conduct are appropriate for all grade levels, for example, *Treat other students the way you would like to be treated.* Some variations are required to address the specific behaviors and attitudes of different age-groups.

Elementary Classroom Rules
Try hard
Speak softly
Ask before you act
Clean up after yourself
Middle School Classroom Rules
Respect other people's property
Keep a tidy workspace
Keep your hands to yourself
Act as if your grandmother is watching
High School Rules
Express yourself appropriately
Straighten up your area before you leave the room
Respect the rights of others
Turn off cell phones, beepers, and other communication devices

students. You will learn more about the planning cycle in Chapter 13.

Conduct management is maintained through the establishment of rules and guidelines of behavior. Three to five rules for appropriate behavior seem to be the ideal numbers. How these rules are established depends on grade level, the teacher's philosophy of classroom management, and what is considered acceptable behavior in the school. (See Table 12.1.) "Be nice" is a little vague for a rule. A fifth-grader might interpret "Be nice" as an invitation to chat with whoever is in earshot, while a high school senior might choose to be "nice" by doing a friend's homework. Rules and procedures must be taught so that students know how to succeed in the classroom.

Children in different grade levels react in different ways to rules, regulations, and procedures, so naturally what works in a kindergarten class to get students' attention may not work in a middle school class. Experienced teachers have found out that each developmental level has a set of typical behaviors that help determine which strategies teachers can use to best advantage. Third-graders tattle. Fourth-graders will do everything the teacher does. Middle school students will do whatever their friends do, and high school students usually make behavior choices based on a combination of the norms set by the school administration and the norms of their peers.

Covenant management is about managing relationships, having highly developed communication skills, and knowing ways the combined effects of content management and conduct management will influence interactions in the classroom. The relationships teachers are able to build with students, their parents, and the other teachers and staff in a school often provide a safety net when management problems arise. Any teacher who uses good listening skills, exhibits a willingness to understand another person's perspective, and treats students with "**unconditional positive regard**" (Rogers & Freiberg, 1994)—letting students know that it is their behavior meeting with disapproval, not them—will be viewed as caring and thoughtful. Teachers who make the effort to build personal relationships are usually given more leeway when they must make difficult management decisions that might clash with what the students desire or what parents consider just. A checklist for implementing covenant management, along with applications and examples, can be found on the University of Northern Iowa INTIME website (**http://www.intime.uni.edu/model/teacher/covenant.html**). A copy of the checklist is provided in Table 12.2.

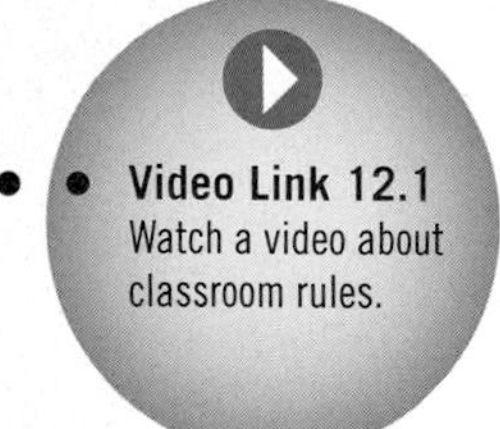
Video Link 12.1
Watch a video about classroom rules.

The Personal and Parental Affect in Classroom Management

From the first day of school, teachers should greet their students by name, make one personal comment to them each day, and note individual efforts and achievements in social, personal, and academic areas. Teachers who make an effort to communicate with parents will learn from the insights parents can provide about their children. Parents should be viewed as being in partnership with teachers in the education of children. Parents love their children and want them to be successful. Let parents know how much you appreciate the gift of their children that they entrust into your care each day.

The *Keeping Current* newsletter produced by the Teacher Institute (2003) offers five suggestions for helping teachers communicate with parents.

1. Encourage parents to spend time in your classroom.
2. Chat with parents when they pick up their child after school.
3. Invite active parents to bring along another parent when they visit your classroom.
4. Call a parent you don't know well and ask for help.
5. Give parents your phone number or e-mail address.

Table 12.2 Checklist for Implementing Covenant Management

For solutions to discipline problems, problem solve with the student.
☐ 1. Get involved with the student.
☐ 2. Deal with the student's present behavior.
☐ 3. Get the student to make a value judgment about the behavior.
☐ 4. Help the student develop a plan to change behavior.
☐ 5. Get a commitment from the student to stick to the plan.
☐ 6. Do not accept excuses for a failed plan.
☐ 7. Do not punish or criticize the student for broken plans.

Source: Adapted from Iverson, A. M. (2003). *Building competence in classroom management and discipline* (4th ed.). Columbus, OH: Merrill, Prentice Hall.

The Paradoxes of Classroom Management

In many ways the concept of classroom management can be seen as paradoxical. It is inconsistent to implement classroom management practices focused on rules, rewards, and punishments when the curriculum encourages problem solving and critical thinking. Students must be orderly but active, curious but follow the directions of the leader, self-motivated but follow established rules and guidelines. Management should be student centered and culture centered yet meet the norms of the local educational community, build interpersonal relationships yet get the job done. This list of conflicting ideas could be endless.

Effective teachers build personal relationships with their students. Teachers greet each student in the morning and make them feel welcomed.

Effective classroom management requires expert decision making by the teacher, and the multitude of decisions a teacher must make in any given day must be based on a clear understanding of a wide range of educational goals determined by the teacher as well as entities beyond the classroom. Here, then, is another paradox of classroom management: If management is a decision-making process, how can it be reduced to a set of recipes? And if it can't be reduced to some guidelines, what is a beginning teacher to do? It really is difficult to move someone else's experiences into your own instinctive behavior. To do this you have to work hard at understanding the behavior of others. It's so much easier to learn from your own experience, to learn firsthand with the support of a mentor or expert guide. Think about this: When you give a speech in your own words it's pretty easy. When you use someone else's words you have to memorize them.

HOW DO YOU BUILD A PERSONAL PHILOSOPHY OF CLASSROOM MANAGEMENT?

Deeper Look 12.2
Read about the principles of culturally responsive classroom management.

Lena Mann's classroom management techniques reflect who she is as a responsible, trusting, and quiet person. Ms. Mann says that teacher presence is something that you earn. *It is very hard to trust teenagers and in order to do that you have to get inside of their brains and be there mentally and physically to know what is going to work with them and what is not going to work. If you are afraid of them they will take advantage of you.*

Ms. Mann's advice to new teachers is to think about where they did their student teaching.

> I would tell them to begin the year by using what they learned in a student teaching situation and also by what they learned in classes. They should begin with what they know. New teachers should not try to be somebody they are not. Be true to yourself. Once new teachers have set their routines they should stick to them. Don't be uncertain. Look at the rules and find what you are comfortable with. Try to give yourself at least five years to learn what teaching is all about and what you need to do to be a fantastic teacher. Give yourself time to grow and analyze what is happening.

Establishing a personal philosophy of classroom management must naturally begin with knowledge of some of the common models and theories in the field. With an understanding of the basic tenets of numerous models, any teacher education candidate can begin to incorporate specific strategies and key elements from each model into a personalized perspective. Most of us try out new skills beginning with what feels comfortable for us or with what we think might work given past experiences and personal attributes. In that respect, learning how to manage a classroom is not much different from learning how to snowboard. There are certain things you should know before starting out, and there are many things you will learn along the way. Attempting to learn either can meet with resistance and create heat, but both should be fun. Here are some of the theories you should be familiar with when learning about classroom management.

Theorists, Theories, and Models

Teachers as well as teacher education candidates have access to a wide range of classroom management methods. While having many choices is nice, making the right ones in a highly charged classroom situation can present a challenge. The best-prepared teachers become familiar with many approaches and are ready to act effectively when called upon to do so. Each theory or model of classroom management discussed in this section can serve as an advance organizer for a set of strategies and teacher behaviors. You may be learning or have learned some of the philosophical and psychological underpinnings of the theories in course work associated with human learning and development and psychology.

As you read about these models, make notes on which strategies you would most like to incorporate into your own personalized classroom management style. As Madeline Hunter (1994) wrote in response to criticism of her *Instructional Theory Into Practice* model, "Models are judged on their ability to guide behavior, predict outcomes, and stimulate research, not on being the final answer to the establishment of any one method of classroom management" (p. 36).

Behavior Modification

Behavioral psychology tells us that behavior is learned and can be modified through positive reinforcement, punishment, extinction, and negative reinforcement. Burrhus Frederic Skinner, as discussed by Wattenberg (1967), is most often associated with the ideas of behavior modification in classrooms. The most common use of Skinner's theories, briefly mentioned in Chapter 7, is the idea of positive reinforcement—providing students with tangible rewards or praise for completing work or demonstrating acceptable behavior. The expected outcome is that when children are rewarded for acceptable behavior they will continue to exhibit that behavior and nonproductive behavior will be "extinguished." Positive reinforcement can be a powerful classroom management tool; however, there is disagreement in the professional community about the effect continued use of extrinsic rewards will have on self-motivation.

One of the most common mistakes in the use of behavior modification strategies by teachers is the practice of taking back a reward once it has been earned. For example, if a teacher distributes "behavior bucks" to students who are following directions and then demands that they are paid back to the teacher when directions aren't being followed, or if marbles are put in a jar when the whole class is doing a good job, working quietly, or staying on task and then marbles are taken out of the jar when the opposite occurs, a reward that has been earned is being taken away. This practice only serves to reinforce a negative attitude in students toward working for a goal. If the goal might be moved or removed entirely, the uncertainly of attaining it would negate even trying for it in the first place. Consider how many of us would run a race without a clear understanding of the finish line. Even a race car driver going around and around the track knows how many laps to the checkered flag.

Assertive Discipline

Lee and Marlene Canter (1992) established a system to manage behavior that relies, in part, on a set of hierarchical consequences. In their **Assertive Discipline** model, teachers must insist upon responsible behavior from students. The most easily recognized example of Assertive Discipline in elementary classrooms is the use of a set of colored cards for each student, usually kept in individually named pockets on a wall chart. When students display irresponsible behavior, they are directed to rearrange their individual cards from green, to yellow, or to red. Each colored card represents a corresponding consequence. Ask any student in any classroom in America and they have probably had some experience with the Canter model of behavior management. Visit **http://www.canter.net/** to learn more about Lee and Marlene Canter's model.

In middle schools and high schools, students are often directed to write their names on the board if misbehavior occurs and to place tally marks after the name if the misbehavior continues. This method makes it easier for middle and secondary teachers to keep track of student behavior over time given the frequent change in class venue. Keeping track of student behavior is a prerequisite to changing it. Tracking behavior and the effectiveness of interventions to improve behavior is a critical aspect of any kind of classroom management plan. And it is one of the most difficult things for teachers to stay on top of in light of their already taxing schedules.

Teachers often use an Assertive Discipline behavior chart to help students stay on track.

Social-Emotional and Group Dynamics Management Approaches

Classroom management methods based on the theories of group dynamics and social psychology, and **Judicious Discipline**, a philosophy that creates an environment respectful of the citizenship rights of students (Gathercoal, 1997), focus on the importance of membership in a group, the need for individuals to control their own behavior, and the need for teachers to provide guidance and create environments conducive to a candid exchange of ideas. William Glasser's (1997) **Choice Theory** model calls for teachers to help students satisfy their five psychological needs (the need for survival, the need to belong, the need for power, the need for freedom, and the need for fun), so that students can choose appropriate behavior individually and as a group. Glasser believes that performance is raised by doing what's real, responsible, and right.

Quay and Quaglia (2004) suggest providing opportunities for students to be leaders in the classroom and to take responsibility for their choices. For example, when students feel that they are an important part of the classroom, that their opinions matter, that they have the chance to lead, and that they are held accountable for their decisions, increased enthusiasm for learning can be the result.

Deeper Look 12.3
Read about culturally responsive classroom management.

The **democratic classroom** uses class meetings to engage students in shared decision making and in taking responsibility for building a democratic learning environment. Democratic classrooms depend on a teacher who recognizes the worth and dignity of every person, who can build a sense of community within the classroom, and who has the ability to build positive relationships with students, parents, and members of the professional community. Teachers employing democratic classroom strategies view students as social beings who want to be accepted into the group, and use encouragement rather than praise to direct student behavior. Robert Sylwester (2003) argues that a democratic classroom provides an excellent venue for brain maturation.

The Class Meeting

The students in Mr. T.'s second-grade classroom participate in a class meeting every Thursday morning. Students sit around the edges of a large square carpet to one side of the classroom. Since the last class meeting, students have written agenda items on pieces of paper and placed them in a jar on Mr. T.'s desk. These agenda items range from altercations between students, to complaints, to suggestions students have for changes in classroom procedures, or suggestions of topics they would like to study. Before the first topic is pulled from the jar and the meeting begins, Mr. T. reminds students of the procedures for class meetings:

1. The person who placed the topic in the jar will explain why it is important.
2. Three students who wish to react to the topic will be chosen by the class president.
3. These three students will express their comments within the 2-minute time limit.
4. At the end of the comments the topic initiator will be allowed to respond.
5. If a vote is deemed necessary, the class president will ask for a show of hands.
6. The decision of the class is final and must be abided by, except in the case of what to study. What to study is not up for grabs in a student vote.
7. The class meeting will last only 30 minutes.
8. Any issues not resolved at this meeting will be dealt with the following week.

As the meeting begins, Mr. T. moves outside the square of students and intervenes only if students request assistance in resolving an issue. Mr. T. admits that the class meetings take time away from instruction, but he firmly believes that the conflict resolution skills his students are

Classroom Rhythms

In classroom management, procedures and routines are vital. However, getting to know your students is also equally important. I remember in my fifth-grade classroom, I would often use music in order to manipulate the mood of my students. On those days when the sun was blazing overhead and my students were squirming in their chairs while trying to wait for recess, I would use a piano sonnet or instrumental saxophone CD in order to calm their mood. And, on those days when it seemed as if they were lacking the amount of energy I needed for a particular assignment or group work, I would use an upbeat, faster-paced music piece in order to pump up the mood. While using music often accomplished my goal, I had a particular student who still, regardless of the music manipulation, lacked any spirit in my class. She was very quiet and very sweet, but, to no avail, still no energy.

One morning, I used the old song, "Can't Get Enough of Your Love, Baby" by Barry White because of its awesome groove and rhythm. I looked up to see that same student who constantly lacked motivation, dancing in her seat. She was alive and had a great smile on her face that I had never seen. I was so excited! I took that "open door" to inquire about why that song made her dance. She stated that that song was her dad's favorite song, and they often danced to that song together before he passed away two years prior. On that day, regardless of our classroom procedures and routines, I had found a way to reach that one student. Mission accomplished!

Dr. TaLisha Givan
Henderson State University
Arkadelphia, Arkansas

developing along with respect for others is knowledge that all students should learn. Classroom meetings such as the ones in Mr. T.'s second-grade class are an example of the shift from a teacher-centered classroom to a classroom in which the teacher and students share leadership responsibility.

A class meeting is an effective management strategy to teach students to solve individual and group behavior problems.

Instruction and Communication Approaches to Classroom Management

Communication models of classroom management rely on the teacher's ability to provide effective instruction and to shape the classroom environment through effective communication that facilitates positive behavior and fosters harmony and cooperation. In such classrooms teachers talk to their students like the sensitive, intelligent individuals they are. Teachers refrain from threatening comments and sarcasm, they guide rather than criticize, and they learn to let some misbehavior slip by. When teachers learn to use Gordon's (1989) **I-messages**, which avoid any negative or neutral use of the word *you*, and to use the principles of **active listening**, by intentionally focusing on who they are listening to, they show respect for students' needs, interests, and abilities.

• • • UNDERSTANDING AND USING EVIDENCE • • •

Reviewing Data on Time Spent on Management Tasks and on Classroom Interruptions

Teachers have to plan and implement strategies for starting each day, and maintaining a purposeful pace throughout the day keeps students focused on learning and completing required tasks. The Stallings (1990) *Time Spent on Organizing and on Classroom Interruption* checklist provides teachers with a snapshot of the time that it actually takes to complete certain management tasks as well as tracking instructional time that is lost during interruptions. The checklist is easy to complete and summarize, and analysis of the data provides instant information about events which are, to some extent, out of the classroom teacher's control but which influence instructional activities.

Tracking the rate at which instructional time is diminished through poor classroom management can help a teacher gain a greater awareness of the value of efficient and effective routines. Actions or behaviors that infringe on the finite amount of time for teaching and learning in any given school day can have an accumulative effect of student opportunity to learn. An average school day begins at 8:55 and ends at 3:06. With time reserved for lunch and transition between specialists, the amount of time for classroom instruction is roughly five hours a day.

Your Task

Use the data on the *Time Spent on Organizing and on Classroom Interruptions* checklist below to analyze approximately how much time can be consumed by management in an average school day. What conclusions can you draw from the data? Is the teacher represented on this checklist an effective classroom manager?

TIME SPENT ON ORGANIZING AND ON CLASSROOM INTERRUPTIONS

School:	Teacher:	Observer:	Time Started	Time Stopped
Observation of Classroom Organizing				
Taking attendance			8:57	8:58
Collecting lunch money			8:57	9:00
Collecting homework or seatwork			8:57	8:58
Making assignments for seatwork			9:50	9:54
Making assignments for homework			2:55	3:05
Distributing books and materials			9:05	9:07
Explaining activities and procedures			9:00	9:05
Organizing groups			1:15	1:18
Shifting from one activity to another			10:20	10:22
Disciplining students			9:45	9:46

D. W. Johnson and Johnson (1999b) advocate cooperation as the key to promoting a well-managed classroom and propose the three Cs (cooperating, conflict resolution, and civic values) as the basis for effective learning environments. Visit the website of the Cooperative Learning Center at the University of Minnesota (**http://www.co-operation.org**) to learn more about the Three Cs of School & Classroom Management.

For Evertson and Emmer (2009) classroom management becomes routine once rules and expectations are made clear and instruction is well managed and related to the individual needs

School:	Teacher:	Observer:	Time Started	Time Stopped
Observation of Classroom Interruptions				
Students enter late			9:10	9:12
Students leave early			2:30	
Parents enter			2:27	2:30
Administrator enters			11:10	11:15
Other visitors enter		Observer	8:55	
Loudspeaker announcements			9:00	9:05
Special sales		5th-graders selling tickets to drama extravaganza	2:15	2:25
School events				
Outside noise				

Source: Adapted from Stallings, J. A. (1990). *Effective use of time program.* Houston, TX: University of Houston.

This teacher has spent approximately 30 minutes of the day managing class activities and getting ready for instruction. The short times spent for each management routine add up, and at the end of a week two and half hours of instructional time have been lost.

Your first question after considering the data could have been, why does it take the teacher a minute to take attendance? Good question. Establishing a routine that has students entering the room for the first time in the morning and moving a tag with their name or picture on it to a designated slot would make it possible for a teacher to take attendance in a glance. Homework should also be placed in a designated folder at the same time that each student marks his or her attendance.

A second question about the amount of time spent making assignments is certainly called for. Assignments for seatwork can be on the board or in folders located at centers around the room. And the same goes for homework assignments. Time at the end of the day should be spent summarizing what was learned during the day while homework assignments should be given immediately following the related instructional episode.

Too much time seems to be consumed when moving from one activity to another or getting students ready for group work, in this example. Time can be saved here by well-established routines and procedures. When students know what they are supposed to do when they enter the classroom, arriving late should not cause an interruption, and students who have been taught how to get ready for group work can certainly do so in less than three minutes. Teachers may have little control over the interruptions that come from outside the classroom, but there is no crime in placing a "Do Not Disturb" sign or a "Testing" sign outside the door when the teacher feels any interruption would be detrimental to student learning.

The teacher represented on this checklist is no doubt conscientious and aware of the benefits of a well-managed classroom. Collecting data that would indicate the time actually spent in organizing and in interruptions can only serve to help her improve her professional practice.

and talents of the students. In this well-managed classroom, it is vital that teachers recognize the relationship between their own behavior and that of their students and understand the support classroom management provides for instruction.

Kohn (1996) invites teachers to move beyond rules, to understand the needs of children and how these needs can be met. This seems a reasonable challenge given the diversity of culture and backgrounds represented by students in classrooms today. Visit Alfie Kohn's homepage at **http://www.alfiekohn.org/** for a better understanding of the ideas of *Beyond Discipline: From Compliance to Community*.

Challenging Assumptions

What matters most in classroom management?

• • • • •

The Assumption

Many beginning teachers worry most about their ability to manage the movement and behavior of their students. They have heard horror stories and observed unfortunate examples of teachers who have little or no effect on getting students ready for learning. Having no control over a classroom is a frequent concern of teacher education candidates. Cooperating teachers who work with practicum or student teachers may advise them to begin the year with a stern and strict attitude, and to reserve smiles for later in the year. Experienced teachers often advise new teachers not to become a friend too soon. So what really works in classroom management, and how is a new teacher to approach this aspect of teaching?

The Research

There are probably as many approaches to managing a classroom as there are teachers who implement one course of action or another. What approach works for each teacher really does depend on individual attitudes and capabilities. Certainly having a high level of self-efficacy is important. Teachers who view themselves as capable of managing a classroom are more likely to be successful doing so than a teacher who is unsure. One way researchers have approached the study of effective classroom management is to observe teacher behaviors and document those behaviors that result in positive student actions and attitudes.

The study cited here looked at two teachers who represented contrasting styles of classroom management. One teacher used an authoritarian style of classroom management and the other used a style that encouraged students to take responsibility for their own behavior. Three variables—student interactions (behaviors), teacher questioning, and quality of teaching—were used to analyze the effectiveness of the teacher's management styles. Both teachers used lower-level questioning skills and it was determined in the study that the overall quality of instruction was poor. The study found that neither of these two teachers' classroom management styles effected "consistent positive student interactions." The study concluded that the "quality of instruction is central to the interplay between student's interactions and teacher's classroom management practices."

Implications

While this study is very small in scope, and perhaps the teachers who participated in the study did not employ the most effective instructional strategies, it does provide a small piece of evidence regarding the connection between management style and instructional practices. When students are engaged in learning they are more likely to exhibit positive behaviors. The success of the approach a teacher uses for classroom management may be highly influenced by the instructional practices that are in place. Teachers who teach well usually have few problems with classroom management.

Source: Jeanpierre, B. J. (2005). Two urban elementary science classrooms: The interplay between student interactions and classroom management practices. *Education, 124*(4), 664–676.

No one shoe will fit all. We learned that from the story of *Cinderella.* The students you will meet in your future classrooms will possess skills society has only begun to imagine. Additionally, the technology that is shaping student thinking and behavior is creating changes the profession has yet to fully understand. As you meet these children and lead them to ever higher levels of understanding, consider ways that order in your classroom and increased student learning can be maintained by a range of positive approaches.

Principle No. 5 of InTASC Standards (see Chapter 1) states that the teacher uses an understanding of individual and group motivation and behavior to create a learning environment that encourages positive social interaction, active engagement in learning, and self-motivation. It is not too soon for you to being to acquire a more in-depth understanding of the many theories surrounding classroom management.

WHAT CONSTITUTES A WELL-MANAGED CLASSROOM?

Lena Mann believes that a well-managed classroom begins by helping students figure out the rules and the consequences for classroom behavior, and by teaching them how to have some control over managing themselves. According to Ms. Mann,

> Once you do that you really don't need to spend too much time on managing student behavior. I really don't think of teaching as work. Much of the way I manage the classroom is based on the way I was raised. I grew up in a family where mistakes were used to make us become wiser. I have tried different methods and have read a lot about behavior modification and right-brained/left-brained behavior. Kids are pretty much what they are going to be. I try to address all ways of learning. I take bits of information and journal about what I am learning. I am not much of a talker. I spend a lot of time watching the ways students interact and use some of that knowledge to keep me in tune with the students because I am two generations away from theirs. In this way I build trust with the students and they talk to me. The class becomes a family of sorts, and we help one another out. Building rapport with students is key, but I was never buddy-buddy with my students. I was always the professional adult in the classroom.

William Morris (1834–1896) might have said that décor is what makes a home a thing of beauty and a joy forever. While students spend almost as much time in school as they do at home, schools are built from a utilitarian viewpoint, with maintenance and durability the determining factors of what goes where. Nearly all classrooms are rectangular in shape. Most have windows, though it is cheaper to build schools without windows. The desks, bookcases, shelves, and tables in classrooms are institutional in style and by themselves don't offer much in the way of décor. Teachers are wonderfully creative people, however, and have the power to turn a somewhat bland environment into a scintillating palace of learning. Wise teachers let the students help build the environment that is the most comfortable for their needs and expressive of their individual and group personalities, while the teacher keeps in mind simply that room arrangement should promote learning in every nook and cranny.

Room Arrangement

The arrangement of a classroom can contribute to the responsibility students may feel toward a specific classroom. If it is a pleasant place to be, a place the teacher seems happy in, a place to be proud of, a place where significant things happen, then students are likely to perform in ways conducive to learning. The placement of furniture and materials in a classroom can also contribute significantly to instruction. Jones (2003) discusses the "interior loop" of a classroom and describes the ways in which room arrangement relates directly to time on task and fewer behavior issues.

In order for classroom arrangement to support learning, students need to have a clear view of the focal point for instruction. The teacher must be able to move easily around the classroom to monitor students' work, and materials and resources should be easily available to keep lessons moving. Teachers need to identify traffic routes and be ever on the lookout for obstacles that would impede movement or create a management problem.

Evertson and Emmert offer four key elements to good room arrangement (2009, p. 4):

- Keep high-traffic areas free of congestion.
- Be sure students can be easily seen by the teachers (and vice versa).
- Keep frequently used teaching materials and student supplies readily accessible.
- Be certain students can easily see instructional presentations and displays.

Classroom arrangements are dictated by the size of the classroom, the number of students, and the types of furniture in the room. The Teach-nology website (**http://www.teach-nology.com/ideas/**) provides a seating arrangement section as well as diagrams of different types of arrangements.

Helping Students Be Comfortable in the Room You Have Arranged

Students need to know what is expected of them, how to act in certain situations, and what instructional purposes are assigned to different spaces in the classroom. Everyone wants to know what is theirs. So, helping students find their own space and becoming comfortable in it might be one of the first orders of building a productive teacher–learner relationship. Students should be taught everything from how to enter the classroom, to where personal possessions should be kept, to how materials should be passed out and collected, to rules regarding the teacher's personal space. For students to feel comfortable in the space you have arranged, they need to know the procedures for success in the classroom. When students understand what they must do and why they must do a certain thing a certain way, they have a tendency to do what is expected.

Hardly anyone learns a thing perfectly the first time it is taught. Rules and regulations that are taught and learned on the first day of school or during the first week will no doubt have to be reviewed from time to time to reinforce students' comfort in your classroom. Re-teaching can take the form of gentle reminders or practice accompanied by a clarification of the goals and intended outcomes for the procedure. Certainly some things that were stressed at the beginning of the year may change, but once a teacher has established a process for learning a procedure, future changes to the procedure will be simplified.

Managing Paperwork

Have you ever stood in a post office and watched folks empty out their mailboxes? There is usually someone standing near a huge wastebasket throwing away what is commonly referred to as "junk" mail. Even the advent of the digital age and e-mail has not appeared to reduce the amount of paperwork that floods our lives. As a student, you have more than enough experience dealing with paperwork. Mostly you learn to organize paperwork in files, notebooks, or stacks. Dealing with paperwork can seem like a never-ending job. One of the benefits of technology is the way it can reduce paperwork, though losing a file on a computer can be as easy for the disorganized person as losing a piece of paper.

Developing a plan or system for handling the huge amount of documents and other paper forms associated with teaching is absolutely necessary in order for the management of paperwork not to interfere with effective instruction. The first step in dealing with documents, records, reports, and resources is to create one or more filing systems. Efficient filing systems provide ways of tracking individual student performance and progress, organizing forms and letters that are used on a regular basis, organizing lesson materials (plans, assessment criteria, teacher reflections on success or shortcomings of lessons, student evaluations of lessons, and resources), dating entries, and keeping track of schedules. Technology helps but teachers have to establish a mental picture of where every item is stored.

Students Managing Classroom Paperwork

In the classroom, teach students to manage their assignments. Even first-graders can keep a folder of the week's work in their desks. Teach them to arrange items chronologically. This can be done easily on a blog. Students can learn to check their e-mail or the class blog for assignments and return them to the drop box created for electronic documents. Students can be held responsible for making entries in an electronic homework log to assist the teacher in keeping track of individual student progress. Once you have established a routine for handling assignments in hard copy or electronically, you will have more time for instruction and the students will have more time for learning.

A Multidimensional Look at Classroom Management

Walter Doyle (1986) described five dimensions of classroom life that provide a framework for theorists, researchers, and practitioners to study the myriad events and interactions that can occur in any given time span in classrooms. Doyle's five dimensions—(1) multidimensionality, (2) simultaneity, (3) immediacy, (4) unpredictable and public climate, and (5) history—can serve as a guide for teachers to develop and organize a range of management strategies that will address the activities they must orchestrate in any given day.

Multidimensionality

Classrooms are complex, tightly populated social structures. Many events take place, and every single action can result in multiple effects. This variety of events with multiple effects that occur in a classroom can challenge a teacher's ability to keep student attention focused and to manage student behavior. For example, the domino effect of one student reaching down to get something out of a backpack may disturb another student, with the result of an exchange of words that causes a student across the room to stand up to see what is going on. Which action is the teacher to respond to, if at all? Or enthusiastic comments from students working on a group project may create a wave of excitement that draws other students to see what all the talk is about. How does a teacher manage such a situation and keep learning at a peak?

Simultaneity

Many actions occur at the same time in a classroom. A teacher is aware of many actions occurring in the classroom and processes information on student behavior or idleness to adjust lesson pace, input, and interest to keep the attention of all students. Students are also aware of the teacher's response to them. Students make their own adjustments to the events occurring around them, and these adjustments may give rise to additional actions. An effective classroom manager must be aware of what students are paying attention to and constantly be aware of the impact the simultaneousness of events will have on the learning environment.

In a well-managed classroom students can be engaged in a variety of learning activities while the teacher helps individuals.

Immediacy

Life in classrooms is fast paced and up close, and some events must be taken care of immediately. The movement in a classroom is perpetual; some students move at a faster pace than others, but no one really stands still. Immediacy in the classroom can come in the form of a call over the intercom asking someone to report to the office, or students leaving the classroom at odd times for special programs; something is misplaced, a necessary book can't be found, a pencil is broken, someone gets sick. Each day a teacher must respond to a hundred such interactions that often require immediate attention. Having routines and contingency plans in place can help both teacher and students adjust smoothly to some of the immediacy of the classroom.

Unpredictable and Public

Everything that happens in a classroom is public, and many of the events that occur are unexpected. An experienced teacher once explained to her practicum students that the first time she meets with parents she tells them that she won't believe anything the children tell her about what happens at home if the parents won't believe anything the children tell them about what happens in the classroom. She was joking, of course, but her humor did illustrate the fact that everything that goes on in a classroom is very public and can be unpredictable. A teacher in a sour mood can overreact to a minor problem, and every student within earshot can hear and be ready to spread the word. Even the way a teacher responds to different students is viewed by many pairs of eyes. The teacher may smile and listen to one student, but turn away from another student in midsentence. Teacher behavior is always public and can have lasting effects on students and their ability to learn.

History

History is a powerful force in any classroom and is constantly in the making. It takes a strong will and much determination to live down past mistakes or to change direction once a particular path has been chosen. Classroom histories are created as norms and common understandings develop in a single class over a single year. What happens in the very beginning when a class is formed can have long-lasting consequences. The history of each classroom is often being constructed even before the school year begins. Parents will have swapped details of the teachers their children had the previous year and the classrooms these teachers managed. Judgments are being formed that will be either confirmed or dismissed as the year gets under way. The manner in which each teacher begins the year, how well she has planned for the multitude of activities that will take place within the first week, how well-organized resources and materials are, and how the teacher deals with minor upsets or behavior malfunctions start a classroom's history.

Management of Movement on School Grounds and in Hallways

Movement in schools is almost constant. Students are moving between their own classrooms and other rooms in the school at regular and irregular intervals. Some schools do not allow students to move around the school alone or unsupervised while other schools may leave student movement outside of the classroom up to the discretion of individual teachers. The advent of school violence and dangerous weapons in the hands of elementary and secondary students has given rise to stricter rules governing student movement outside classrooms and to the utilization of metal detectors to assure that harmful instruments will not be available to students on school property.

While "lockdown" situations do not exist in most schools (such restrictions are usually reserved for detention centers or correctional centers), the freedom to move around in the school environment is carefully managed by administrators and teachers in the form of bells and hall passes. In high schools and middle schools, short periods of time are allocated for students to go from one class to another. Teachers or "hall guards" stand watch at strategic locations throughout the building during the break between classes. In elementary schools, teachers generally lead students to special classes such as music, art, or technology.

Teachers can learn about their students through play while observing them on the playground.

Teacher responsibilities include duties assigned by the administration to supervise large groups of students at recess or during lunch. As a teacher you will spend many hours on the playground watching students interact and play games. You may learn to play four-square and tetherball with students from your own classroom and from other classrooms. It is educational to observe the ways students behave outside of the classroom and to have conversations with students in a relaxed atmosphere. Playground, lunch, or hall duty should not be seen as drudgery or a responsibility to avoid, but it should be welcomed as an opportunity to learn more about your students.

Routines, Rules, and Schedules

Ms. Mann says that students don't like a lot of rules. She encourages the students to come up with the consequences for breaking the rules that do exist.

> When students set the consequences they become responsible for the behavior. One student told me he didn't want to do the work. I asked him to write to me why he didn't want to work. He sat there for 20 minutes and finally said he didn't know why he didn't want to work and that maybe he should just do the work. You can change the attitude of children just by talking to them.

Routines, rules, and schedules provide the framework in which our actions take place. When a routine is established, some of the uncertainty of life is laid to rest. Rules provide security. Rules and schedules relieve stress. They also encourage responsibility. Routines, rules, and schedules do not discourage spontaneity or creativity. The self-discipline that they encourage can give rise to disciplined expressions of creativity.

Deeper Look 12.4
Read about classroom management in different countries.

Rules provide guidance and clarity to routines. Who makes the rules should be determined for the most part by the person or people who are going to enforce them or monitor students' response to them. Keep in mind that any rule that is set forth may be scrutinized by students, parents, other teachers, and the school administration, and that the First and Fourteenth Amendments of the U.S. Constitution address students' and teachers' rights and responsibilities related to the establishment and enforcement of rules. Rules and procedures should be developed in conjunction with teaching strategies that help students meet their personal and academic needs. Table 12.3 lists specific requirements for classroom rules.

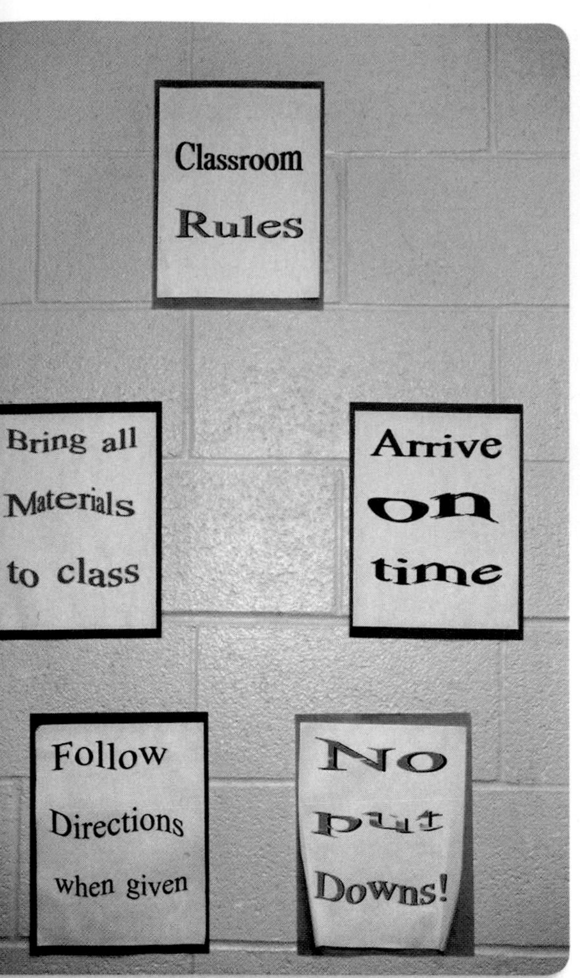
Classroom
Rules
Bring all
Materials
to class
Arrive
on
time
Follow
Directions
when given
No
put
Downs!

Rules should be brief, to the point, and posted where everyone in the classroom can see them.

Some rules are predetermined and everyone at school is expected to follow them. Some rules are determined by space and school structure. Smart teachers seek cooperation from the students, so in most classrooms rules are determined by the teacher with input from the students, and the smartest teachers allow the students to believe they are the ones who determine the rules. The possibilities for establishing and implementing classroom rules are endless and result from variables such as standards, student needs, and expectations.

Schedules form a framework for routines. Imagine getting through a day or a day at school without at least the semblance of a schedule. In fact, when schedules at school are interrupted, it doesn't take long for disorder to ensue. Getting from point A to point B in a timely manner depends mightily on a schedule. If a class of sixth-graders is to be at an assembly at 9:45 a.m., the teacher had better have them in the gym and quietly seated at the time the assembly is to begin or suffer the consequences of reprimands by the principal or other teachers.

Schedules are usually set by school administrators and to some extent determine ways routines will be enacted in individual classrooms. For example, in a high school with block scheduling, or an A/B class schedule, routines take on quite a different shape than if classes meet every day for 55 minutes. A block schedule also provides extended class time and opportunities to enhance instruction through project work and role-playing experiences, thereby dictating the need for routines governing such activities.

The Characteristics of a Well-Managed Classroom

The characteristics of a well-managed classroom are usually apparent even to the untrained eye. Students are involved in academic work, they know what is expected of them, time in the classroom is used wisely, all work in the classroom is being conducted in a purposeful manner, and students are not disrupting one another. While the elements of a well-managed classroom are easy to understand, translating these characteristics into purposeful actions is a major undertaking for teachers. Just as important as laying the groundwork for a great

Table 12.3 Key Components of Classroom Rules

1. The rule must be publicized to students. Whether it is issued orally or in writing, school authorities must take reasonable steps to bring the rule to the attention of students.
2. The rule must have a legitimate educational purpose.
3. The rule must have a rational relationship to the achievement of the stated educational purpose.
4. The meaning of the rule must be reasonably clear.
5. The rule must be sufficiently narrow in scope so as not to encompass constitutionally protected activities along with those which constitutionally may be proscribed in the school setting.
6. If the rule infringes on a fundamental constitutional right of students, a compelling interest of the school (state) in the enforcement of the rule must be shown. (Reutter, 1975, p. 6)

beginning to the year, teachers have to plan and implement strategies for starting each day and maintaining a purposeful pace that keeps students focused on learning and completing required tasks.

Maintaining on-task behavior when students are actively engaged in learning is one of the most important responsibilities of a teacher. The more time students have to learn, the more chances they have for success. Many events can interfere with students' time to learn, and it is a teacher's job to anticipate and eliminate distractions that interfere with learning time. In order to accomplish this responsibility, teachers must possess knowledge of classroom management strategies and be able to implement procedures in an efficient and timely manner.

Deeper Look 12.5
Read more about proactive ideas for classroom management.

Students are compelled by law to attend public school whether they want to be there or not, and while at school the U.S. Constitution's Fourteenth Amendment of due process and equal protection under the law protects students in the classroom and ensures their rights to a full range of opportunities. Given that all students must be provided equal and a full range of opportunities to learn, a well-managed classroom may be the first step in making this goal attainable.

WHAT IS THE CONNECTION BETWEEN DISCIPLINE AND MANAGEMENT?

Ms. Mann believes that discipline builds a chasm between a teacher and the students, and students can only cross that chasm if they do what you want. She says that when teachers establish their own territory, with strict rules, the students always have to do what the teacher says.

Audio Link 12.1
Listen to a clip about classroom management techniques.

> This doesn't allow the students to be open-minded and flexible. Under a rigid system of discipline, students won't venture out and want to learn more. Teachers put limitations on students when they set rigid discipline, and then, of course, teachers have to watch students closely to make certain that they don't break any of the rules. That's too much work. I want to focus on the students learning the content.

One view of discipline is gaining control by enforcing obedience or order. In this view, teachers are seen as enforcers or controllers. Another view of discipline sees teachers as the trainers or guides that help mold and develop student behavior. Discipline can also be viewed as a way to get students to change their misbehavior. When students misbehave, teachers must make decisions about how to manage the misbehavior. Managing furniture and classroom space is much easier than managing students' behavior. Students talk back. They disagree. They have their own ideas about what should be done and how it should be done. Managing behavior or disciplining students who have misbehaved requires communication and effective interpersonal skills.

Discipline problems do pop up in even well-managed classrooms, and when they do it is the knowledgeable teacher who has the best chance of coming up with fair and just solutions. The classroom discipline landscape changes constantly throughout a school year.

Four Stages of Classroom Life That Influence Behavior

Within the framework of content, conduct, and covenant management described earlier in this chapter, Iverson (2003) describes four stages that can influence management and discipline in a classroom. The stages are (1) Forming, (2) Storming, (3) Norming, and (4) Performing. There are a number of effects that can disrupt these clearly delineated stages of behavior. One effect results from the rapidly changing demographics in America's schools. Another disruption can be caused by the frequent movement of students from one school to another. Rapid changes in the growth of students can also disrupt the stages. Fourth-grade students who begin the year as gentle beings may soon begin to show signs of the exuberance and impatience of fifth-graders. Likewise seemingly "out-of-touch" sophomores can become mature, thoughtful seniors. Little ever stays the same in elementary or secondary classrooms, and the more prepared teachers are to respond to the changing environments they will experience, the more competent they will become at exhibiting best practices.

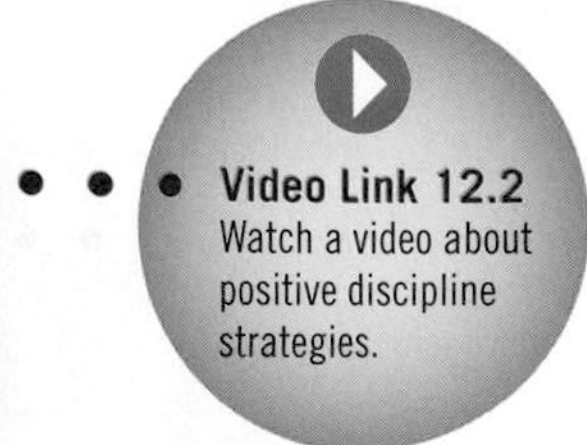

Video Link 12.2
Watch a video about positive discipline strategies.

Forming

The forming stage takes place at the beginning of the year, when students are learning information about their new surroundings as roles and procedures are established. In some instances, this first stage presents a sort of "honeymoon" period, when for the most part, everyone is trying to put their best foot forward. The more effective the teacher is in content management at the beginning of the year, the longer the honeymoon period can last.

Storming

As the year progresses, students may begin to test the limits that have been outlined and through peer pressure or for some other reason begin to distance themselves from established norms of behavior.

Norming

Somewhere around the middle of the year nearly all behavioral and management struggles have been reconciled and the content and conduct standards have been accepted. There are few reasons for behavior problems to interrupt opportunities for students to learn, and both teacher and students feel a sense of accomplishment.

Performing

During the performing stage, students exhibit self-reliance and self-discipline. They have formed close relationships with their classmates and with the teacher and can rely on support from them when needed. With expert teacher management, it is possible for behaviors associated with the performing stage to be evident throughout the school year. When teachers understand these stages, there is less opportunity to be caught off guard or frustrated by the changing climate of the classroom.

The Importance of Communication in Behavior Management

Most forms of management begin with talk. Teachers explain rules, they correct behavior, they give directions, and they issue orders. The manner in which teachers conduct their communication with students can have an enormous influence on the ways their students behave. Spock's trademark salutation of "Live long and prosper" conveys an emotional message full of kindness and hope. Teachers should emulate Spock in the ways they communicate their desires and expectations to students.

Large class sizes, the number of details to keep track of, and so little time all contribute to decreasing the amount of friendly and polite conversation a high school teacher can have with students. Because some high schools are as large as towns, once teachers leave their familiar section of the school they may seldom meet anyone they know. Knowing the names of the students they teach is a challenge in itself, and knowing the names and faces of the other 3,000 students in the school is close to impossible. A high school nurse indicated the number of traumas in any given day in her school far exceeded those cases that show up at a quick care medical facility in the neighborhood. Having the skills to communicate in positive and productive ways becomes exceedingly important in such environments.

All talk contains some type of emotional content. Imagine how boring communication would be if there was never any emotion in what people had to say. When teachers talk to students, when students talk to teachers, and when students talk to one another, the resultant messages are likely to contain emotional content that has the ability to shade the actual meaning of the words being expressed. Certainly a pouting child or teenager can be intimidated into saying what a parent wants to hear, but the emotional overtones in such a forced message can speak volumes in resentment and anger.

Every communication you have with your students is filtered through personal sieves woven together of hopes, fears, needs, and intellectual potential. When you talk to students, when you ask them to do something or to behave in a particular way, you must always be aware of the emotional impact your words will have. Learn ways to communicate that show you are aware of students' personal issues and that help the students also understand your concerns. Much of what we communicate to students comes through physical stance and tone of voice and contradicts the words we say.

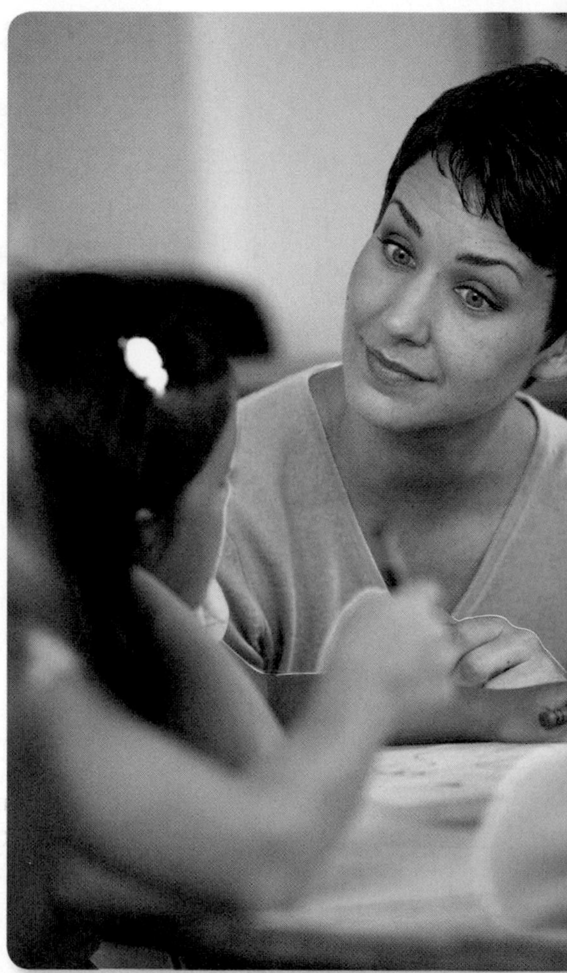

Teachers must practice the art of giving their full attention to students who are speaking.

Basic Rules of Engagement

Listen, listen, listen, and listen some more. Otherwise you might not hear what your students are saying. Two students come in from the playground or hallway, yelling and pushing one another, followed by a growing number of spectators. The great lesson you are ready to start will have to be postponed until tempers have cooled and you have defused the anger. What do you do? First, take charge. Give some orders in a low, clear voice. Send students from other classes back to their rooms. Tell your own students to go to their desks. If you are in an elementary grade, you might hold the hands of the two students who created the disturbance, keeping them near you. In high school you might ask the students to remain standing by the door until you are ready to LISTEN to them. State some rules. For example,

- Each of you will be able to tell me in your own words what happened.
- NO ONE will be allowed to interrupt.
- I will talk when you are finished.

Then you magically pull out the small circular disk you have in your pocket (one side heads, one tails), ask one of the students to choose heads or tails, and flip the disk. In a flash, what has happened on the playground or in the hallway becomes of lesser interest to most of the students than what is about to happen in the classroom. The key is that you have made decisions, the students know what to do, and you have not added to either student's frustration or humiliation. Now, do what your mother always told you to do: Take a deep breath, count to three, and listen.

When teachers listen actively to what the students have to say, they use a variety of response strategies. They make eye contact. They nod or make sounds indicating that they are taking in every word. They encourage students having difficulty expressing their thoughts to "Tell me more," or "Go on." Teachers who listen well don't interpret but try to identify with honest labeling the feelings and attitudes they are hearing. Teachers who are good listeners help students recognize how they feel and the ramifications of these feelings for themselves and for others.

Ms. Mann's advice when trying to modify the behavior of a student is to start with one small thing. She says,

> Don't try to change the whole behavior or make the student into something they are not. Some behaviors that are normal for new teachers also need to be modified to work with any specific group of students. Be calm and watch and listen to the students and soon they will be trying to please you. Try not to be pushy. Build trust.

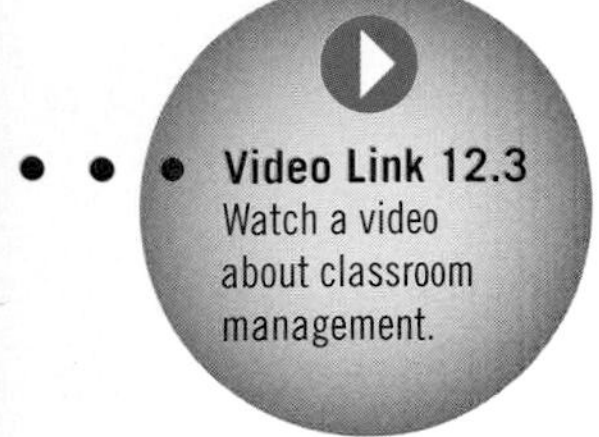

Video Link 12.3
Watch a video about classroom management.

HOW DO TEACHERS MANAGE THE STRESS OF MANAGING A CLASSROOM?

The stress of teaching can be relieved when teachers find out what each student can do and work from that point. Ms. Mann says teachers need to build on the students' successes.

> Failure is not a motivator, and student failure can cause teachers stress. Sometimes when you set your expectations too high the students are not willing to jump that high. Students don't know what they are going to be two years from now. They don't know how important what you are teaching them will be to their future lives. The learning comes from inside the kids, and they have to want to do the learning. They go to school to be cool, and you have to start from what is cool for the students.

Managing a classroom and student behavior often result in stressful interactions and situations. Teachers often talk about the stress of keeping up with demands of their profession such as learning new programs, taking university classes, balancing the instruction and assessment components of student learning, and taking on teacher leadership responsibilities at their schools. They have so much on their minds that they can't fall asleep at night and so they get up in the morning already stressed by their lack of sleep.

Many teachers are parents that have children they must help get ready for school as well as themselves. Some teachers live long distances from their work, and driving to school causes additional stress. Stress can have long-term effects on the heart, mental well-being, and overall health. Teachers have to be healthy. They have to go to school every day, and they have to arrive there with a sense of well-being and mental acuity. Teachers must learn to manage stress as they have learned to manage their classrooms. A little support can go a long way in helping teachers manage their personal stress levels. Once they have managed stress, teachers can manage almost anything else.

Stress comes to students as well as teachers, and management problems can result from a buildup of anxiety in the classroom for no apparent reason. When teachers provide a small amount of time each day for students to take stock of their personal sense of well-being, students can better understand and deal with some causes of stress. Reflection in the classroom can take different forms such as journal writing, class meetings, writing comments for a suggestions box, or experiencing a few minutes of silent reflection time each day. When students are able to manage the stressful situations they encounter, teachers may also experience less stress.

Three Dimensions of Psychological Support for Teachers

The degree of psychological support teachers need in order to be successful, to be able to manage the stress of their profession, and to recognize the joy and rewards that come from teaching are threefold. The three dimensions of this support are emotional-physical, psychosocial, and personal-intellectual. When teachers don't deal with daily stress it can gradually become overwhelming. Teachers need to be strong in mind and body.

Emotional-Physical Support

The emotional-physical dimension focuses on self-esteem, security, acceptance, self-confidence, and even the ability to resist illness. In psychology 101 we learned that the emotional stability of an individual can have a profound effect on the physical well-being of that person. A mild headache can lead to distraction and irritation at others, and a prolonged illness can render us incapable of coping with even the most routine events. Teachers' self-esteem is high when they know they are doing a good job and others acknowledge their successes. An administrator or fellow teacher who offers congratulations on a job well done is providing necessary emotional-physical support to keep the teachers happy and healthy.

Psychosocial Support

The psychosocial dimension focuses on an individual's need for belonging, for friendship, relationships, collegiality, and interactions with others. Teachers generally like people. They liked going to school as students and enjoyed the interactions they had with classmates and with their teachers. Becoming part of a school faculty and working with other professionals interested in helping children and youth learn can be a rewarding way to balance the stress that is a normal by-product of living.

Audio Link 12.2
Listen to a clip about the making of great teachers.

Personal-Intellectual Support

The personal-intellectual dimension relates to an individual's desire to grow mentally and professionally. When teachers are encouraged in the belief that they can make a difference in their profession they assume responsibilities with eagerness and confidence. When teachers have opportunities to learn new methods and strategies to become more effective they find self-expression in their work instead of stress. Teachers who are inspired by membership in a professional learning community see the horizon, not the trench.

Laughter in the Classroom

There is nothing wrong with having fun in the classroom. Moments of unexpected laughter and fun are the ones we remember. Laughter can ease the strain of following rules and sticking to schedules. It can turn a tense situation into a lighthearted learning experience. It can relieve stress. School should be more fun than playing hooky. It might be okay to smile before Christmas, maybe even laugh a little. It doesn't mean becoming a stand-up comic or running a steady stream of knock, knock or elephant jokes. The line between teacher and student must be maintained. But maybe if your students see you as a happy person, they will be happy to be in your classroom.

CONNECTING TO THE CLASSROOM

Try the visualization exercise (described below) from Stallings's *Effective Use of Time* program to create a personalized mental image of a classroom. When you have finished creating a mental image of your classroom, draw a picture of it. Then think about how your choices for placement of desks and other furniture match Evertson and Emmer's (2009) guidelines for effective use of classroom space described earlier in this chapter.

Visualize Your Classroom

1. With your eyes closed, visualize an empty classroom.
2. In your mind's eye, look carefully at the space you have to work with.
3. Imagine a space for the large group, a space for small-group learning, and a space for individual learning (a space where a student can be alone).
4. Decide on a place for your desk.
5. Think about sound: quiet places and noisy places.
6. Consider storage.
7. Think about what will be on the walls.
8. Think about putting some color in the room (red and orange for energy, blue and green for quiet, and purple for deep thought).

Remember that people space is more important than furniture space. Compare your room arrangement to the arrangement of a classroom you have recently visited. What are the differences? The similarities?

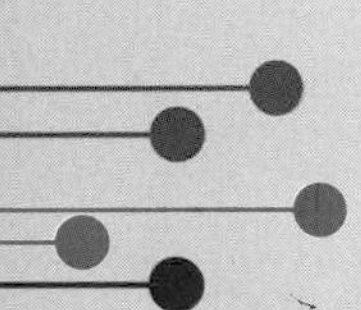

SUMMARY

This chapter on classroom management addresses a range of models and approaches to creating and maintaining an effective learning environment. An overarching theme of this chapter is that classroom management does not occur through happenstance. It requires teacher knowledge, skill, and a particular set of dispositions that recognize the individual worth of students and their right to an effective learning environment. Classroom management is also dependent on specific actions by teachers to communicate expectations to students and to enlist student acceptance of these expectations. Life in classrooms is complex and changeable. Developing the ability to manage such a dynamic environment is an essential function of learning to teach.

This chapter addressed five areas of classroom management:

- The multiple tasks associated with classroom management and ways of categorizing them
- Models of classroom management that require different teacher actions, and making decisions regarding which of the models will work within your personal belief system, a special group of learners, and the classroom environment
- The physical and emotional components of classroom management
- The relationship between management and discipline
- The ways that stress resulting from managing a classroom and student behavior can be lessened through positive approaches and interactions with other teachers

CLASS DISCUSSION QUESTIONS

1. We have all had the experience of managing something. We have organized our personal space and time and have arranged furniture to suit our tastes. Recall a time when you were required to manage something. How successful were you? What do you consider your strengths in making arrangements and in organization?

2. When you have had to include others in your plans, how did you convince them to go along with your ideas? What did you do to enlist their support? If someone disagreed with your plans, what did you do to change their minds? How did you make them comfortable with your expectations?

3. Teachers are required to manage the behavior of students so that everyone in the group has the greatest opportunity to learn. When teachers are faced with difficult behavior issues that infringe on the rights of other students in the class, they must often enforce consequences that might seem harsh and unreasonable to the unpracticed eye. Think about a time when you observed a child or youth being disciplined that made you uncomfortable. How might you have handled the situation differently? What about the situation might have been unknown to you?

4. What about your life is most stressful to you? What do you do to manage that stress? Would this method of managing stress be appropriate for use in a classroom?

KEY TERMS

Active listening 362
Assertive Discipline 359
Choice Theory 360
Cognitive framework 355
Conduct management 356
Content management 355
Covenant management 356
Democratic classroom 360
I-messages 362
Judicious Discipline 359
Unconditional positive regard 356

SELF-ASSESSMENT

WHAT IS YOUR CURRENT LEVEL OF UNDERSTANDING AND THINKING ABOUT MANAGING THE CLASSROOM AND STUDENT BEHAVIOR?

One of the indicators of understanding is to examine how complex your thinking is when asked questions that require you to use the concepts and facts introduced in this chapter. Answer the following questions as fully as you can. Then use the Complexity of Thinking rubric to self-assess the degree to which you understand and can use the ideas presented in the chapter.

1. Why is it important for teachers to develop a personalized approach to managing a classroom and student behavior?
2. How can building relationships with students and their parents help a teacher manage a classroom and student behavior?
3. What is one framework for thinking about classroom management that you believe matches your personal philosophy of teaching?
4. In what regard is communication a key component of managing student behavior?
5. Why is it important for teachers to learn ways to minimize stress in teaching?

What is your current level of understanding? Rate yourself using this rubric.

Complexity of Thinking Rubric

	Parts & Pieces	Unidimensional	Organized	Integrated	Extensions
Indicators	Elements/concepts are talked about as isolated and independent entities.	One or a few concepts are addressed, while others are underdeveloped.	Deliberate and structured consideration of all key concepts/ elements.	All key concepts/ elements are included in a view that addresses interconnections.	Integration of all elements and dimensions, with extrapolation to new situations.
Managing the classroom and student behavior	Discusses frameworks and theories in isolation from one another.	Describes basic approaches to managing a classroom only from a teacher's point of view.	Describes multiple ways classrooms and student behavior can be managed.	Describes multiple ways classrooms and student behavior can be managed for various purposes.	Describes ways the use of certain approaches to classroom management might influence and advance student achievement.

STUDENT STUDY SITE

Visit the Student Study Site at **www.sagepub.com/hall** to access links to the videos, audio clips, and Deeper Look reference materials noted in this chapter, as well as additional study tools including eFlashcards, web quizzes, and more.

Field Guide

for Learning More About Managing the Classroom and Student Behavior

• • • • •

To further increase your understanding about today's students, do one or more of the following activities.

Ask a Teacher or Principal

Chances are that teachers in most schools lean toward different strategies for handling similar problems. Ask six teachers for advice on how to cope with a specific management problem, and you'll more than likely receive six or seven different responses. This can be somewhat confusing for a beginning teacher or for someone who has not yet developed a personal classroom management game plan, system, or approach.

In the 1995 film *Dangerous Minds,* the protagonist, Lou Anne Johnson, is desperately seeking ways to connect with her inner-city students. One scene shows Lou Anne sitting in her apartment, taking notes from a classroom management book and then wadding up her notes and throwing them across the room. This scene could leave viewers with the impression that there was nothing in the book that was going to help Lou Ann succeed as a teacher. But, in finally gaining the attention and respect of her high school students, she employs techniques and strategies research has shown to be effective in managing student behavior.

- She made her lessons relevant to the students' lives,
- she piqued their interest so they became engaged in learning,
- she rewarded their efforts, and
- she showed them the respect she, herself, so desperately sought.

Ask the teacher you are observing (or practice teaching with) how she addresses the four strategies mentioned above in their daily management of the classroom and student behavior.

Make Your Own Observations

Use the grid below to document the ways that the teacher you are observing manages different events during the day. Some—but not all—management concerns are listed on the grid. You may need to add some others that you observe. Choose one of the management strategies the teacher exhibits and ask how he learned and decided to use it.

Events to Manage and How to Manage Them PKS

Event	Management Strategy
Students entering classroom	n/A
Beginning instruction/focusing attention	"attention scopes" "one voice" visual cues
Distributing materials/resources	centers
Monitoring students during guided practice	walking + observing
Responding to individual requests	n/A
Getting students ready to leave classroom	activity then line up
Providing individual attention	"attention-scopes" "one voice" "visual cues"

Reflect Through Journaling

Learn what experts or researchers have determined are important things to know and to know how to do in regard to classroom management. Include ideas, actual events, and observations in your journal. Write about how a particular teacher handled a particular event. Ask yourself if you would act in the same way. Consider how the students reacted. Mark down what happened, how the teacher handled it, and ways a particular student or many students reacted. There is no lack of information about classroom management strategies available. The teacher's task is to learn enough to know which of the multitude of strategies is worth testing or adapting, and which ones might work best for you.

Build Your Portfolio

What did the classrooms you most enjoyed as a student look like? What kinds of things happened during the day that made these classrooms comfortable places for you to be? Do you remember a teacher who seemed to take care of problems with little effort or without disrupting your learning? Did you have a teacher who made you laugh; made you look forward to each school day?

Reflect on your responses to these questions and then describe how your ideal classroom might be managed. How might your classroom be arranged? What type of learning activities might take place? How might you interact with each of your students? Give reasons from your personal experiences and from what you have read about classroom management to support your rationale for the classroom you have described.

Read a Book

Setting Limits in the Classroom: How to Move Beyond the Classroom Dance of Discipline, by Robert J. Mackenzie and Lisa Stanzione (2010; New York, NY: Random House), provides techniques on how to establish structure in your classroom.

Positive Discipline in the Classroom, Revised 3rd Edition: Developing Mutual Respect, Cooperation, and Responsibility in Your Classroom, by Jane Nelson, Lynn Lott, and H. Stephen Glenn (2000; Roseville, CA: Prima Publishing), provides strategies to help you restore order in your classroom and foster cooperation.

Search the Web

The Internet is loaded with sites for teachers seeking information on classroom management and discipline. Conduct a web search to locate at least two sites that have information on different aspects of classroom management that interest you. Briefly describe what information on the sites you think might be of value to you in the future. Include the descriptions of the two sites in your portfolio. For example, you could visit **http://www.teacher-institute.com** for newsletters on a variety of subjects, or you could visit **http://www.pecentral.org** to find out how to create a positive learning environment. Using the Internet as a resource should become one of your professional habits as a teacher.

Watch a Movie

If you haven't seen it already, you should watch *Dangerous Minds.* Just remember that it is a Hollywood perspective. Some events in the film must be taken with a grain of salt, though overall it does a good job showing some of the management problems teachers might face in inner-city high schools.

Simpson, D., Bruckheimer, J., Robins, S., & Foster, L. (Producers), & Smith, J. (Director). (1995). *Dangerous minds* [Motion picture]. U.S.: Hollywood Pictures, Via Rose Productions, Simpson-Bruckheimer Productions.

Workstations
should
night
WORDS
WORDS

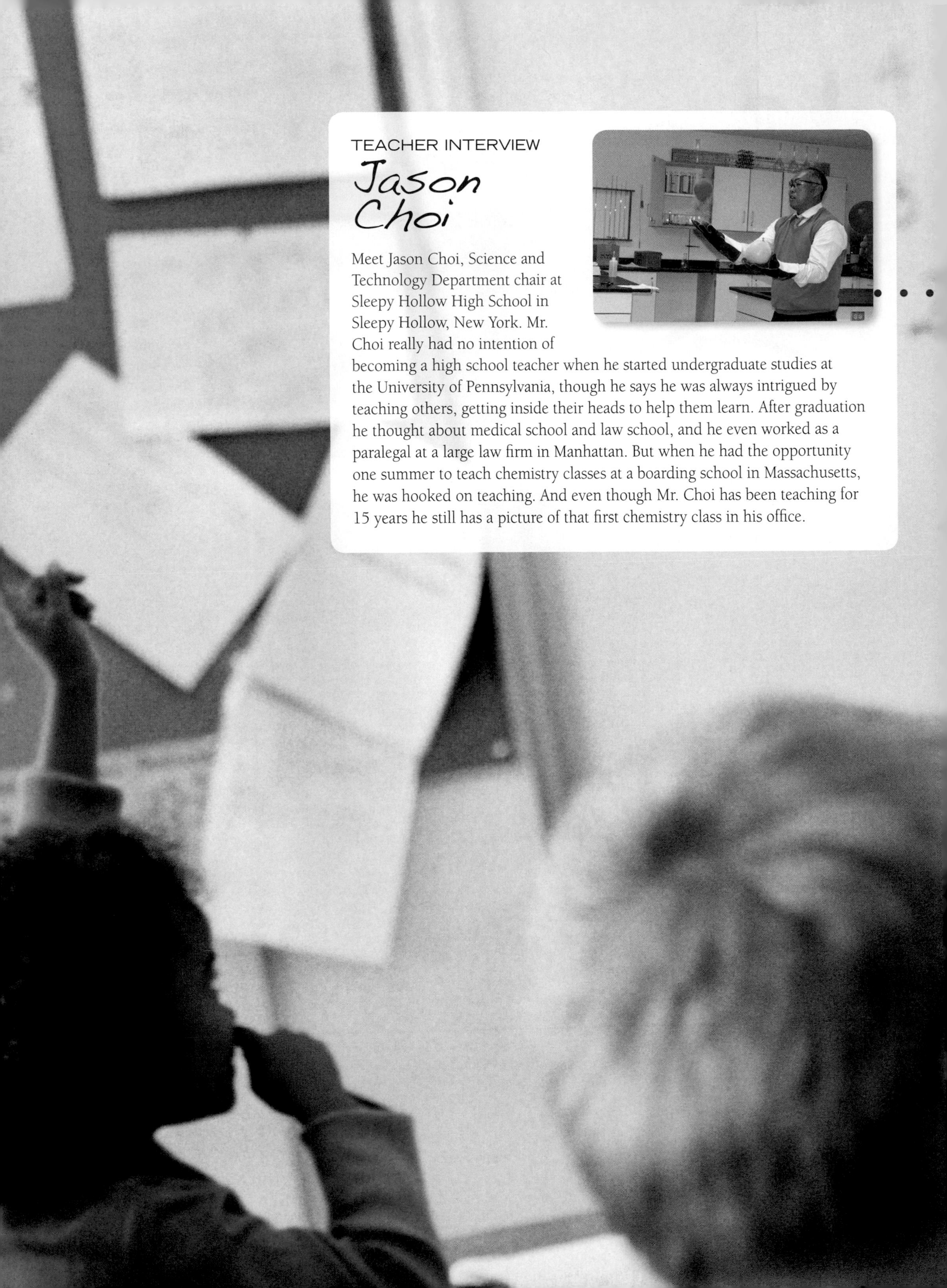

TEACHER INTERVIEW

Jason Choi

Meet Jason Choi, Science and Technology Department chair at Sleepy Hollow High School in Sleepy Hollow, New York. Mr. Choi really had no intention of becoming a high school teacher when he started undergraduate studies at the University of Pennsylvania, though he says he was always intrigued by teaching others, getting inside their heads to help them learn. After graduation he thought about medical school and law school, and he even worked as a paralegal at a large law firm in Manhattan. But when he had the opportunity one summer to teach chemistry classes at a boarding school in Massachusetts, he was hooked on teaching. And even though Mr. Choi has been teaching for 15 years he still has a picture of that first chemistry class in his office.

CHAPTER 13

Teaching Strategies

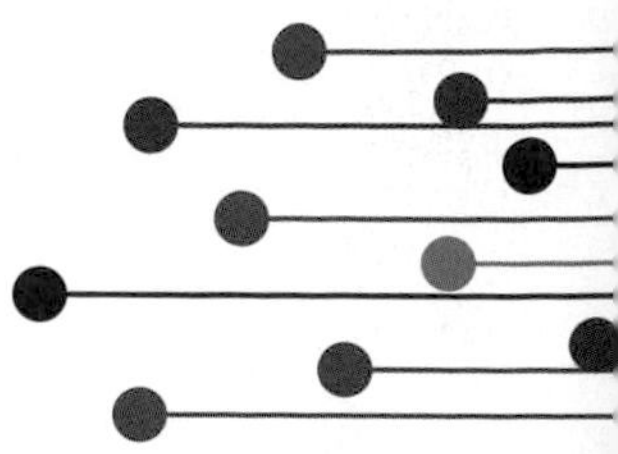

• In what ways do you focus on student learning?

Most chemistry lab manuals tend to be "cookbook" style with limited flexibility and creativity. In the same way I put my personal spin on recipes I cook at home, I try to provide some flexibility in the chemistry activities and labs I plan for the students. When I previously taught reaction rates and the factors that affect reaction rates, I would have the students perform an activity in which two clear solutions are mixed and then turn black after a certain amount of time. The students were provided a set of directions in which the solutions were diluted or the temperatures were changed. This year, I decided to show the reaction and then challenged the students to make the chemicals change color at the 25-second mark. By making it a competition, I was able to engage a few students who normally dislike lab activities. Each group was asked to make a list of questions that they needed to answer and were allowed time and resources to research online resources and experiment for a certain amount of time. The competition provided a great platform to introduce the factors that affect reaction rates; moreover, the students were more engaged.

How would you describe excellence in teaching?

Excellence in teaching goes well beyond the classroom and beyond the end of the year assessment. Excellence in teaching is about making a long-lasting connection, impression, or mark on my students. In return they make an impression on me. Although I teach chemistry, chemistry is not the most important thing I teach in my class—the more important things are thinking critically, articulating ideas, keeping an open mind, working well with others, meeting deadlines and juggling assignments, asking for help, persevering, understanding the value of hard work, and striving to be better. Having said this, I would not be doing my job well if my students did poorly on the standardized assessments. My belief is that if I teach the content and focus on the important things previously mentioned, my students will succeed on whatever test they take in the future.

Teachers need to make education a personal experience for each student. They need to engage students. How each student learns or how each teacher engages the students is different, but there are many similarities in good teaching. First, teachers need to show the relevance of what they are teaching to the students' lives. Teachers must encourage students to become active learners by incorporating activities that provide opportunities for students to observe, analyze, synthesize, and articulate. In science, demonstration and experiments are vital to achieve this purpose.

I have been lucky to be at Sleepy Hollow since 1997. I have had the opportunity to connect with thousands of students. Since my wife, Sarina,

Questions to Consider

1. What are some of the strategies the teachers at Sleepy Hollow use to engage students in learning?
2. What do excellent teachers do to help students learn?
3. Mr. Choi finds joy in teaching when his students ask him "What if?" questions. How might such questions indicate that students have truly understood the lesson?
4. What are some of the ways the teachers at Sleepy Hollow help one another create relevant lessons that require critical thinking? Would you enjoy being part of these lessons? Why?
5. Have you had a teacher who made learning a personal experience for you? Explain.

is an English teacher at the same high school, it makes it easier to attend student activities, for example, school plays, sporting events, fundraisers, and so forth. In fact, we've attended former students' college graduations, weddings, baby showers, and unfortunately, funerals. Last February we flew to Dublin and then rode a bus to Belfast to watch a former student play basketball in the Irish professional basketball league.

Where do you find joy in teaching?

As a science teacher, I enjoy seeing the "a-ha" moment in my students. I try to use a wide range of activities and demonstrations to teach chemistry. The purpose of these hands-on experiences is to help students connect the abstract, mathematical concepts with the physical world. It is the best when students ask questions that extend the demonstration or experiment. Rather than just asking to see a demonstration again, I particularly relish when students will ask "If we do A, would B happen?" It informs me that the students are engaged and have internalized the concepts that we are studying.

There is great joy when former students return to say hello and tell you that you've made a mark on their lives. I love the fact that Sleepy Hollow is a small school, which gives the faculty a chance to know each student. I also coach three sports—JV volleyball, JV basketball, and varsity golf. Coaching allows me to interact with the students in a different light. I get an opportunity to work with students of all abilities who would most likely not sign up for my honors chemistry or AP chemistry. Although coaching is physically taxing, it is rewarding to see your players grow as athletes and as individuals. The idea is to help students mature into well-rounded individuals who are ready to face the challenges that lie ahead.

You mention that members of your department believe that inquiry-based learning is the best way for students to learn; please explain.

The science department at Sleepy Hollow High School has been working collaboratively with Pace University through monthly meetings to discuss various aspects of the inquiry-based learning model. After the initial meetings the teachers wrote proposals to implement in their classes. This is the third year of this joint venture, and eight teachers participated (three last year and two the year before). The science teachers are joined by one English, two math, and three foreign language teachers. Each participant in the Inquiry-Based Learning Project is working collaboratively or independently on "tilting" some aspect of his or her course toward inquiry. Carlos is teaching acid-base chemistry through the lens of acid rain. Peter and Rachel are exploring hands-on application of electrochemistry by having students make their own "batteries" or copper plate leaves using electricity. Leana and Christine are developing engaging ways to incorporate the Hudson River into the AP Biology and AP Environmental Science curricula. David and Leila are helping students articulate their thoughts more clearly by holding a series of scientific debates. I am using a variety of activities (photo essay, demonstrations, reflections, and video clips) to connect science to the real world by having students explore the application of chemistry concepts. The teachers are working hard to balance the rigors of standardized testing with the excitement and enthusiasm that comes with discovery.

What else would you like to tell the preservice teachers who will be reading this text about using inquiry-based learning?

The best way to establish a good class atmosphere, reduce behavioral issues, and improve student performance is to deliver relevant and engaging lessons. Inquiry-based learning provides a method to do this by piquing students' natural curiosity and using it to introduce or teach concepts. Teachers should be prepared and the lessons should be well planned; however, teachers must recognize that each class and each student is unique and therefore, teachers need to be flexible and adaptable. Preservice teachers should realize that teaching is a work in progress. Teachers are continually reflecting on lessons and revising them. The teaching profession needs new teachers to come into teaching with enthusiasm and passion, as well as a strong work ethic. Veteran teachers and new teachers can and should learn from one another.

Learning Outcomes

After reading this chapter, you should be able to

1. Understand why some teaching strategies appear to work better with one content area than another.
2. Know why it is important for teachers to become skillful in using more than one teaching strategy.
3. Recognize the importance of detailed planning prior to teaching a lesson.
4. Learn some of the strategies teachers use to prepare students for learning.

INTRODUCTION

Teaching has been described as both an art and a science. Teaching as an art requires a level of intuition seldom demanded of other professionals. The intuition aspect of teaching develops through a process of **reflection** that is automatic and continuous, and that draws on all manner of visual and sensory awareness of the multitude of stimuli emanating from learner/teacher interactions in a specific context. As teachers practice their art, and reflect on the outcomes of that practice, they construct a framework for intuitive and spontaneous actions that promote student learning. Although it may seem that way, intuition and spontaneity in teaching are not random. Some beginning teachers walk into the classroom with a well-developed sense of intuition. They already possess some of the experiences necessary to the development of the intuitive aspect of teaching. However, for most teachers, their intuition grows through experience and develops over time.

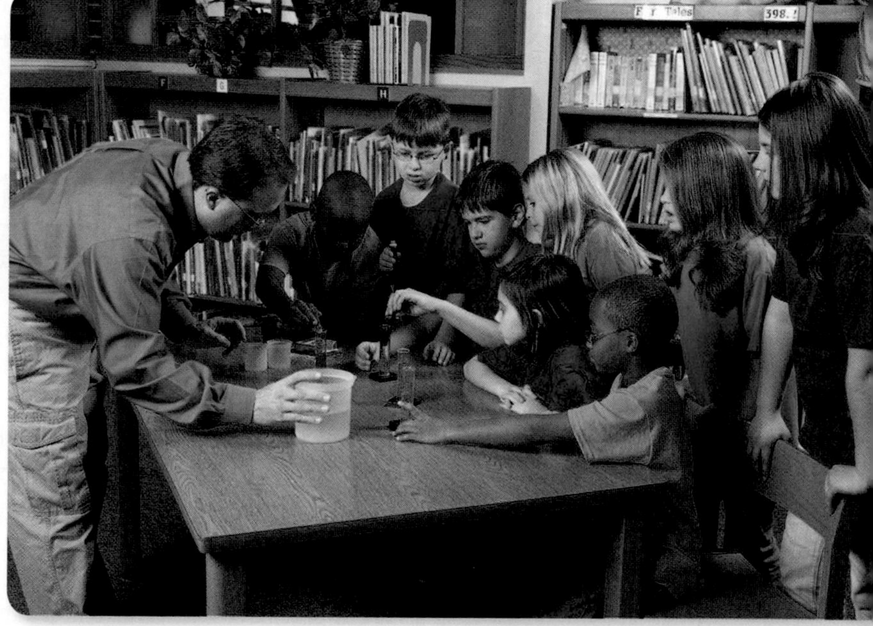

Students learn in different ways. A teacher who recognizes this can capture the attention of all students.

Teaching as a science is evident in the strategies that teachers learn to use to achieve desired results in student learning. Strategies are used to capture and hold student attention, to direct that attention to a specific detail of knowledge, or to develop a skill students will begin to incorporate into their own framework for learning. Other strategies help students practice and connect new bits of information to what they already know and to what they will be expected to know in the future. These and other strategies are all part of the science of teaching.

The science of teaching is concerned with keeping track of where students are in the **learning cycle** (Kolb & Fry, 1975), who has just fallen off the cart and who has already made a leap of learning to dimensions beyond the scope of the lesson. The science of teaching is in the planning, the tactical adjustments teachers make in action, and in documenting their own progress and performance and that of the students.

Audio Link 13.1
Learn more about the art and science of teaching.

When you ask your college instructor for a definitive answer about what particular strategy will work in a classroom and the instructor answers, "Well, it depends," your frustration at such an equivocal answer may not be entirely warranted. What your instructor knows is that intuition is developed through experience and since nearly every day in the classroom represents a different set of experiences, how a teacher might respond in any given situation depends often on an unpredictable set of conditions. Your instructor also knows that the science of teaching can be learned and what will work for you in a classroom will depend on how well you learn to use a range of teaching strategies and how well you monitor the effects of the applied science of your teaching.

You have probably heard the comment that teachers are born, not made. The truth is that some people are born to be teachers with all the natural talents necessary to produce excellent results in student achievement. However, most of us must learn and practice the science of teaching skills that comprise the characteristics of excellent teachers. We also learn through persistence, practice, and patience to develop the same art of teaching talent that others may be born with.

This chapter will introduce you to a variety of teaching strategies that work in classrooms and will help you understand a scientific approach to teaching. You will also learn ways specific strategies can be used to meet the learning needs of the range of student abilities and learning styles most commonly found in a single classroom. The art of teaching will emerge as you begin to practice these skills in classrooms.

WHAT ARE TEACHING STRATEGIES?

Mr. Choi provides some insights into teaching strategies and instruction.

> In education, it seems as if every year or two, a new theory or instructional model appears on the horizon. I think it is important to realize that there is no cure-all or panacea for struggling students. I am reminded of Leo Tolstoy's family line from Anna Karenina, "All happy families resemble one another, each unhappy family is unhappy in its own way." I believe that good instruction, whether it is in science, mathematics, English, or foreign language, all resemble one another. The students are engaged, challenged, and supported. However, poor instruction can have many roots—insufficient content knowledge, poor understanding of students and their lives, unsupportive colleagues or administration, or a lack of passion. The last cause—a lack of passion—is the most crucial aspect of teaching. Carlos, one of our chemistry teachers, often says that teaching is his calling; and many other teachers in our department cannot imagine themselves in any other profession. Some days and some years are more difficult than others, but they truly enjoy their jobs and the impact they have on their students.

Any teaching **strategy** certainly falls into the category of something that is carefully planned, a method, or a stratagem for reaching a desired goal. The word *stratagem* has a somewhat negative connotation, defined as being a cleverly contrived trick or scheme for gaining a desired end, but effective teachers know they have to invent all manner of activities to encourage their students to drink from the fountain of knowledge. Consider the admonition, "You can lead a horse to water, but you can't make it drink." Well it's a smart farmer who sprinkled alfalfa sprouts on the watering trough, or a Mary Poppins who figures out a clever way to get the "medicine to go down." Teaching strategies properly used make it possible for teachers to help students acquire useful and necessary information, sometimes contrary to the students' desire.

There are as many ways to teach as there are teachers. Since human societies first emerged, knowledge and skills have been handed down from one generation to another through the use of specific teaching strategies. The apprentice model worked for King Arthur and even today some aspiring potters spend weeks, months, or even years carrying the master teacher's clay from the source to the wheel to the kiln. In Iran students learn the Persian alphabet through repetition and spend hours each day at a table writing a single Arabic symbol over and over until it is so etched in the mind that only an act of Allah could erase it. Children in school in China or Japan must learn more than 8,000 symbols to properly communicate in an educated society, and they copy these symbols until every individual brush stroke becomes as natural as taking a breath.

Deeper Look 13.1
Read about teaching strategies.

Generic Teaching Strategies

In their "Framework of Universal Teaching Strategies," Freiberg and Driscoll (2004) describe generic instructional strategies along a continuum that ranges from a teacher focus or teacher-centered perspective to a student focus or student-centered perspective (see Figure 13.1). The strategies are truly universal as they cut across grade levels and content areas. The strategies described by Freiberg and Driscoll consider the context of teaching situations, the curriculum to be taught, and the diverse learners present in classrooms.

Some learning requires hours of practice. Learning to write *kanji* requires hours of painstaking repetition in making the proper strokes.

The lecture is the strategy used most often in classrooms and provides the teacher with the most immediate control over what content the students are exposed to, the expected behavior of the students, and the valuable commodity—time. When teachers are expected to cover a set amount of curriculum in a specified period of time, the lecture is often the favored strategy. David Ausubel, an educational psychologist that you read about in Chapter 7 of this text, argued that lectures provided the most efficient use of time when trying to impart large amounts of information to a group of students. Since teachers and students have the gift of language, Ausubel's (1963) contention was that teachers should use language to impart knowledge.

At the student-centered end of the strategies continuum described by Freiberg and Driscoll, students interact with books, audio and video tapes, computer programs, and the Internet. Students use these resources to investigate topics assigned by the teacher or topics that they are interested in and are highly motivated to learn. Use of resources as a teaching strategy requires a high level of teacher competence and knowledge of a range of subjects and of what resources are available. The teacher must be able to guide students to resources that will give them adequate, useful, and accurate information.

Figure 13.1 A Continuum of Teaching Strategies

Teacher Focus			Student Focus			
Lecture	Demonstration	Question/ discussion	Guided practice	Group work	Role play/ simulation	Reflective learning inquiry

There is a logical organization to the strategies on the continuum. Since students can't be expected to discuss what they know nothing about, inputting information is important, usually done most efficiently through lecture or presentation. Group work also requires that the students know how to ask questions of one another and discuss topics in a civilized manner. Role playing and drama require students to demonstrate their knowledge of a subject using higher-level thinking skills. Students who engage in inquiry need to know how to access information, what to do with it, and how to synthesize it. All learning has to begin with some level of knowledge. As you progress through your teacher education program, you will learn more details of a range of teaching strategies and the optimum application of each for specific content areas. The AEA 267 website (**http://www.aea267.k12.ia.us/cia/framework/strategies**) offers more than 30 teaching strategies and suggestions on how each might be implemented in kindergarten through high school classrooms.

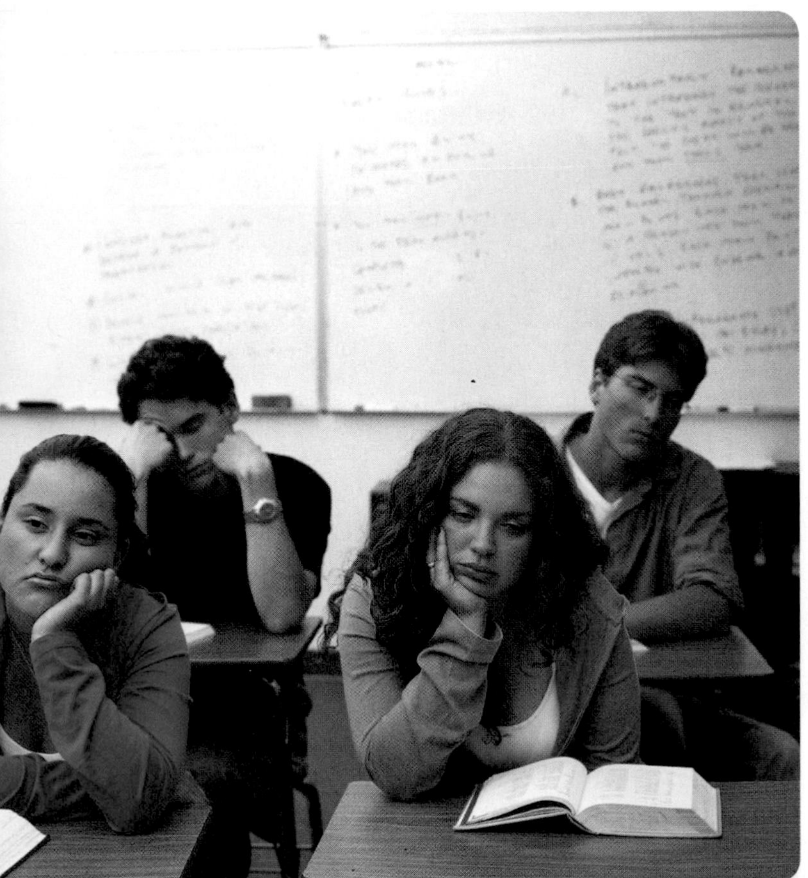

There are many ways to enhance student interest in a lecture by following the five elements of an effective lecture. The lecture teaching strategy does not need to bore students.

Lecture

We've all had the experience of being "talked to." Sometimes it was inspirational, sometimes it was not. There were probably even times when we had no idea what the lecturer was talking about. Fortunately or unfortunately, the lecture teaching strategy has survived for more than 2,000 years and is used in all content areas and at all grade levels. While the lecture may not always enjoy a favorable reputation, it can be effective in both elementary and secondary settings.

To gain information from a lecture, the listeners must attend to what the speaker is saying and, in the case of a presentation, be able to see what the lecturer is talking about. Al Capp, the creator of the Li'l Abner comic strip, once said in an interview that the length of time a person could attend to a lecture was equal to their age: one minute for every year. He then qualified his statement by adding that once a person reaches the age of 13 this rule does not apply and that most people despite their age can seldom listen for more than 20 minutes. Sometimes the main problem with lectures is that some people just never know when to stop talking.

Perhaps the unfavorable reputation the lecture might have as a teaching strategy could be, in part, a result of the failure of teachers to recognize and use the guidelines that help make this teaching strategy effective. The research on effective instruction provides guidelines for effective delivery of lectures and presentations (Rosenshine & Stevens, 1986). For the teacher education candidate or beginning teacher who is just becoming familiar with delivering a lecture or presentation, these guidelines can be reduced to five major elements essential for planning and delivering an effective lecture (see Table 13.1).

Table 13.1 Know Your Students

Audience	Know what is developmentally appropriate for them—be aware of their interests, their abilities, and what prerequisite skills and knowledge they need to have to understand what you are talking about.
Focus	Know your subject, be enthusiastic about it, and stick to it. We all can be seduced into talking about things we really don't know much about. Everyone wants to have an opinion, but an educative lecture should be a learning experience for the listener, not just an opportunity for the speaker to spout his or her opinion. Present ideas in small chunks, one idea at a time. Make sure your students are with you; keep their attention.
Organization	Know how to introduce the topic, to expand on it, and to summarize what has been talked about. Know when to change pace and when to stop.
Clarity	Know how to present an idea from the listeners' perspective. Provide examples that are relevant, make the subject come alive through explanations, and are colorful, unusual, or startling.
Pacing	Know when to shift gears, check for understanding, and bring an idea to its logical conclusion. Make students think about what you are saying by having them take notes, for example by writing down the names of important people or important dates. Provide students with an outline of your lecture before beginning so that they can make notations.

The following examples demonstrate how a teacher might use the five elements of an effective lecture.

Audience

A class of fifth-graders in St. Louis is learning about the Westward Migration during the 19th century in the United States. The students have already had lessons on the Westward Migration and have talked about why people in the 1800s chose to leave their homes and head westward. The teacher knows that her students will be able to listen for about 10 minutes at the most, so she has planned her lesson accordingly. Two objectives the teacher has for this lecture are for her students to be introduced to the major routes followed by the pioneers as they left Independence, Missouri, and headed westward, and to recognize and remember place names and why certain places along the routes became settlements.

Focus

To generate interest, the teacher relates how the pioneers prepared for their cross-country trek to how her urban students might prepare for a vacation or trip to some other part of the country. She relates details about the rigors of the pioneers' journey to what it might be like for her own students to walk across Missouri today, and lists some of the dangers and hardships both sets of travelers might face.

Organization

The teacher reminds the students of previous learning and gives each student a map with certain routes outlined with dots and lines for students to write place names and dates. As the teacher talks about the three major trails pioneers could take—The Oregon Trail, The Santa Fe Trail, and The California Trail—students mark the starting points for these trails on their individual maps and identify where the trails meet up or split, and the forts that were established along the way.

Clarity

There is a large map in the front of the room that the teacher refers to during the lecture. The teacher also writes the names of places on the board when the students are expected to mark them on their individual maps.

Pacing

The teacher ends the lecture by asking questions to help students recall the information and extend their thinking. The teacher tells the students that tomorrow they will be placed in small groups to gather detailed information about the experiences pioneers had on their journeys crossing the rivers, plains, and mountains. The teacher has provided a special selection of books on the Westward Migration for students to browse through at the end of the lesson. Students are also directed to the simulation "Oregon Trail," loaded on the classroom computers. While the students look at the books and run the simulation, the teacher plays music from the soundtrack *The Way West*, by Brian Keane (1995).

A variety of teaching resources can help teachers create images in students' minds to enhance their learning.

The lecture strategy can be a very effective teaching tool. Using a lecture makes it possible for teachers to present information in the least amount of time. All members of the class as well as the teacher hear the same information at the same time. And a lecture can be a perfect beginning to a unit or to introducing a new concept. However, when using the lecture strategy, it is difficult to address individual needs since the information is presented to all students in the same mode.

Questioning and Discussions

We all learn from the questions we ask and from the questions others ask us. We have questions we want answered, we have questions we are sometimes afraid to ask, and sometimes people ask us questions that we have no answers for. People ask questions to gain information, to increase understanding, and even to draw attention. Some of the questions people ask are silly, some are shocking, and some are just downright wrongheaded. Sometimes teachers are so concerned with answers that they miss the importance of questions, of asking the right questions, and of listening to and learning from the questions their students ask of them.

Teachers ask questions of their students for many reasons. Questions such as "Have you ever had an alligator nibble at your toes?" are asked to generate interest and gain student attention. Teachers ask questions to check for student understanding, to encourage student thinking, and to structure and redirect learning. Questioning is used by teachers as a diagnostic tool in determining the level of instruction at which students need to begin learning. Questions asked to manage student behavior or classroom organization are usually intended to help students remember rules, while some questions allow students to express their own feelings and opinions.

Questioning is a frequent activity in classrooms. Responses by students to teacher-posed questions can provide immediate feedback of student learning.

Questioning is the predominant method of checking for student understanding. Questions can be delivered in a rapid sequence for review of content or used as final evaluations of student learning. Learning the art of asking the right question at the right time and in the right way can be one of the most challenging aspects of teaching.

Guidelines have been created to help teachers with this task. Decades ago, John Dewey (1934) developed an "Art of Questioning Guide" that still holds true today.

- Questions should not elicit fact upon fact, but should be asked in such a way as to delve deeply into the subject, i.e., to develop an overall concept of the selection.
- Questions should emphasize personal interpretations rather than literal and direct responses.
- Questions should not be asked randomly so that each is an end in itself, but should be planned so that one leads into the next throughout a continuous discussion.
- Teachers should periodically review important points so that old, previously discussed material can be placed into perspective with that which is presently being studied.
- The end of the question asking sequence should leave the children with a sense of accomplishment and build a desire for that which is yet to come.

Other classification systems, **taxonomies**, have been created to aid teachers in developing questions for multiple purposes. There are multiple ways of organizing questions to encourage higher-order thinking skills, but you will most likely be introduced to Benjamin Bloom's (1956) taxonomy in your teacher education course work. You have also read about Bloom's taxonomy in Chapter 3 and will read more about Bloom in Chapter 15 of this text.

Six levels of questioning identified by Bloom are knowledge, comprehension, application, analysis, synthesis, and evaluation. Figure 13.2 shows the types of questions that elicit different responses from students and that require differing types of cognitive activity.

Figure 13.2 Bloom's Taxonomy of Question Types

Question Type	Student Performance	Examples
Knowledge	tell, list, describe, recall, which	How many queens have ruled Great Britain?
Comprehension	summarize, compare, contrast, explain, define, make comparisons	What happened in the experiment?
Application	demonstrate, use prescribed methods, restate, transfer	Using the population grid, which of the three cities has the largest population?
Analysis	list why, make inferences, generalize, categorize, break into parts	When did you know that Goldilocks was tired?
Synthesis	create, suppose, make predictions, write an essay	What is the best air route to take from Tokyo, Japan, to Disney World in Florida? Why?
Evaluation	judge, evaluate, rate, prove, give opinions about issues	Should world governments control population growth?

Wassermann (1992) identified both unproductive questions and less-than-productive questions that teachers ask. In her unproductive category she lists irrelevant questions, too complex questions, teacher-answered questions, trick questions, and questions that humiliate. An example in the irrelevant question category is this:: Student: I want to learn more about the aurora borealis. Teacher: Have you got a library card?

A too complex question is usually impossible to answer intelligently in a short answer. Teacher-answered questions need no explanation. Those of us who have seen the movie *Ferris Bueller's Day Off* watched with humor as the high school social studies teacher asked, "Anybody? Anybody?" and then either answered his own question or went on to the next question. Once a teacher starts answering his or her own questions, the students soon learn to wait the teacher out; and that's exactly why teachers have to learn to use **Wait-time** and **Wait-time II** during questioning and group discussions. Teachers who consistently use Wait-time II are helping their students learn the fine art of discussion. Wasserman's "less-than-productive questions" category includes questions that don't require students to examine their own responses. They often fall short because they deal with trivia or are too difficult for the students, or because their wording is ambiguous (p. 15).

One purpose of asking questions is to promote thought. When teachers ask questions that promote thoughtful responses, the students are encouraged to develop the habit of thinking. Grant Wiggins and Jay McTighe's (2004) text *Understanding by Design* introduces the concept of big ideas and that the questions essential to any unit of study need to be identified before instruction for the unit begins.

From Questions to Discussions

A lot of talk goes on in classrooms. Not all of this talk is productive. Productive talk is structured by the teacher and engaged in by the students. Teachers who understand the art of questioning teach their students how to answer and ask thoughtful questions in a courteous manner. This prepares students to engage in productive discussions. Discussing issues with one's peers can help students solve problems, attain goals, and develop concepts. Discussions can get students actively engaged in the content they must learn. Through discussion students can learn to think and value their own ideas as well as those of others. Effective teachers prepare their students for their role in discussions. Knowing how to participate in a productive discussion is a necessary step toward learning how to be a productive member of a cooperative learning group. Students may find it difficult to work productively in groups if they do not understand that discussions require active listening, respect for the ideas of others, and noninterference when others are speaking.

When introducing a group of students to new instructional strategies, a useful rule of thumb is never to teach a new strategy with new content. Teachers who want their students to engage in meaningful discussions let them practice the discussion skills. Teachers make certain all students understand the skills they have been practicing by asking the following questions.

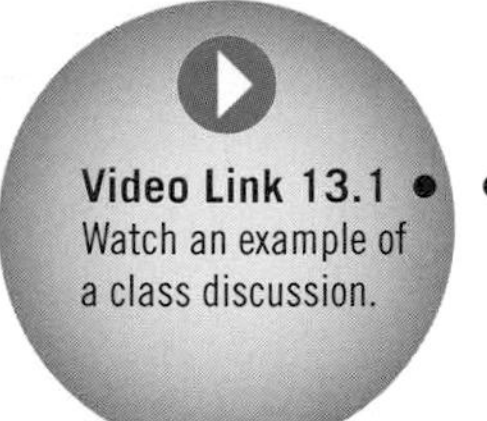

Video Link 13.1
Watch an example of a class discussion.

1. Were your comments relevant to the current discussion?
2. Were your comments supported by facts?
3. Did you consider the importance of your comment before you made it?
4. Did your comment broaden the discussion or clarify a point being discussed?
5. Were your comments complete and concise?

The School Improvement Network at **http://www.schoolimprovement.com** offers several resources that show teachers how to effectively implement differentiated instruction to assure that each student has the opportunity to learn and achieve.

Grouping

Humans are not born with the ability to collaborate, though learning to cooperate has been a major factor in the survival of our species. We have to learn how to get along with others even though it may take much energy and patience. Parents remind their children to share, to take turns, to let someone else be first. Teachers organize classroom activities and playtime so that students have opportunities to practice behaviors necessary for life in a community and in a democracy. Henry Ford developed a model of teamwork for mass production of cars. His motto was simple: "Coming together is a beginning; Keeping together is progress; Working together is success." Working together may not come naturally for everyone, but through every step of formal education, students are prompted to develop more and more skill at becoming productive members of a group. The seminal research of Johnson and Johnson (1990) emphasized that the skills needed to interact effectively with others need to be taught just as systematically as math or social studies.

Humans are not born with an innate ability to share. Students must be taught and then continuously reminded of the guidelines for working peacefully with others.

Formal group work has been a teaching strategy used in schools since the early 1800s. Grouping students for instruction usually involves grouping students by age to form grade-level classes and then within-class grouping by ability. (Remember the reading group you were in during elementary school!) Students can be grouped to study specific subjects, for tutoring purposes, and in **cooperative learning groups.**

When teachers think of grouping students it is usually to accomplish a specific goal and provide students increased opportunity to learn both academic content and group participation skills. Johnson and Johnson (1999a) define cooperative learning as the instructional use of

• • • UNDERSTANDING AND USING EVIDENCE • • •

Using Third-Grade Math Scores on a Unit Test to Create Cooperative Learning Groups

The following data provide the individual scores of third-grade students on an end-of-unit test. It has been determined by the teacher that a majority of the students could benefit from review work on regrouping when subtracting three-digit numbers. The teacher has decided to place the students in heterogeneous groups for cooperative group work. The purpose of the group work will be to provide students with the opportunity to ask questions of one another and to practice and develop skill in regrouping.

End-of-Unit Test Scores on Regrouping During Subtraction of Three-Digit Numbers

Student Name	Test Score (Highest Possible Score = 100)	Student Name	Test Score (Highest Possible Score = 100)
Carl Adams	96	Timette McKay	74
Garcia Bloom	60	Richard Power	72
Caitlin Broker	100	Jaylynn Price	88
Tiffany Brown	40	Patrick Quest	28
Carla Castenada	88	Stacy Romano	68
Nancy Dimmer	24	Kenneth Sharp	80
Neil Fox	76	Angelica Spooner	64
Pete Lowinsky	68	Marilyn Timon	52
Andrew Maxwell	84	Susan White	48

small groups so students work together to maximize their own and each other's learning. Slavin (1993) provided an organizational structure for managing cooperative learning in the classroom.

Deeper Look 13.2
Read more about cooperative learning.

Early socializing activities can begin by teachers handing out cards with numbers or symbols. Students find the classmates with the same number or symbol, form groups, and start to get to know one another. An "In the Bag" activity has small groups of students working together to blow a paper cup into bags taped at the edge of their desks or tables. In a strategy called "Number Heads Together," each student in the group has a number. The teacher asks a question and then

Your Task

Establish cooperative learning groups of three or four students.

Establish heterogeneous groups including high- and low-performing students and reflecting gender difference.

Teachers must constantly assess student learning through reflection on data and then organizing that data in useful ways. The teacher of this class has decided to put the students into cooperative learning groups so that the students can have more practice in using regrouping strategies. Teachers always know, or should know, more about their students than just raw data can show, and so they may make decisions based on personal experience rather than what the raw data indicate. This is a teacher's professional right and one that all effective teachers exercise from time to time.

The teacher has decided to put one high-performing student in each group. There were 25 items on the test and the teacher also considers the number of questions missed along with the raw score.

Caitlin missed no problems and works well with all other students in the class, even with Neil who can sometimes be a behavior problem, so the teacher has placed Caitlin, Neil, and Nancy in one group. The teacher wants Nancy to have as much practice as possible during the group work time and so has decided that a smaller group will be better suited to Nancy's needs. Also, a smaller group may give Neil less of an opportunity to act out.

Carl is also an excellent student, though sometimes he disregards others' feelings. The teacher is placing him with Timette, who has a calming personality, and with Patrick, who is Carl's friend, and with Susan. The teacher believes a larger group with numerous interactions will engage Carl's helper potential.

Carla and Kenneth scored close in their performance on the test and have often helped one another in the past. The teacher is placing Marilyn and Tiffany in this group because all of these students are hard workers and have demonstrated their ability to cooperate during group work in the past.

Jaylynn and Andrew performed very close on the test, and the teacher feels they will provide great assistance to Angelica and Garcia. Jaylynn also speaks Spanish and will be able to help with translation of any terms that may be unfamiliar to Garcia.

Pete, Stacy, and Richard will form a group. Richard scored in the middle range on the test, but he is very thoughtful and patient. The teacher feels that she will be able to spend some extra time with this group if her calculations about the other groups are correct.

says, "Put your heads together and make sure everyone knows the answer." Students discuss the answer; then the teacher calls a number and that student answers.

In high school classes students are often given the task of working together to solve problems or complete lab assignments. Group activities of this nature can provide a virtual experience for students' future roles as citizens in the larger community of their city or state or country. Such activities also make learning fun. When students learn the strategies and skills necessary to work together in productive groups, the end result can be enjoyable and intrinsically rewarding. Initial group activities should be short and simple and should concentrate on positive social interaction. Assessment of academic work in groups should not be addressed until students have learned to successfully interact with one.

The Learning Together Model of Johnson and Johnson contains five key steps:

Step One: Teacher presents students with a specific academic learning task.

Step Two: Students understand the social skills necessary to complete the task through group effort.

Step Three: Teacher checks for student understanding of both academic and social skills.

Step Four: Groups work together demonstrating a high level of verbal interaction and positive interdependence.

Step Five: Teacher assesses individual accountability for the academic task and initiates a class discussion of the group process.

Video Case 13.1
Group Work

1. Why did Seana Mekari use a "silent symposium" group work activity to facilitate student comments on a recent reading assignment?
2. Teachers must carefully plan every facet of group work. Which part of a group work lesson might be the most difficult for teachers to plan for?

The following scenario is an example of how a teacher designs, implements, and coordinates cooperative group learning. Clearly, preparing for effective cooperative learning groups in the classroom is no small undertaking.

One evening during a unit on anatomy, Ms. Lynn drives across town with two large, well-iced cool cans in her pickup truck. She collects sterilized pigs' hearts from the local meat processing plant through an arrangement she has made with the school administration, the PTA, the parents and students in her seventh-grade science classes, and the managers of the processing plant. The next day her students, already aware of their task for the day, get into their appointed groups around the tables in the science lab, don medical gloves, and assume their posts.

Ms. Lynn states the plan for the day, placing special emphasis on the timing of the lesson since there will be no opportunity for students to complete their work at a later date. She questions the students to make certain they understand their assignment and the role each will assume in the group. As the hearts are dissected and parts identified, one member of each group is using a scalpel, one is making notes, and another is drawing pictures, while another is offering suggestions from a sheet handed out by Ms. Lynn, asking questions, and keeping an eye on the clock. Ms. Lynn circulates among the lab tables, stops to praise a group for their progress, prompts them to look at specific areas, and moves on to the next group. She allows the students to work at their task for most of the period, reminding them that they will debrief the lesson the next day.

Cleanup is handled efficiently, all pig's heart parts are placed back in the cool cans, and Ms. Lynn tells the class she is checking for fingers and toes before she closes the lids. Just before the bell rings she asks the students to place their index and middle fingers on the wrist of one of the other members of their group, making a circle of heartbeats. She thanks them for their contribution to today's lesson. As the students leave the lab there is much chatter and excited energy and even some anticipation of the lesson on the brain and the sheeps' heads they will be expected to investigate.

Table 13.2 Common Characteristics of Cooperative Learning

Heterogeneous groups	Group members represent a mixture of gender, ethnicity, and ability.
Positive interdependence	Everyone in the group has a meaningful task to complete
Verbal face-to-face interaction	Students engage in purposeful discussion.
Individual accountability	Each member must complete an assessment appropriate to the group goal.
Social and academic goals identified	Guidelines for group work have been explained and practiced.
Group processing conducted	During group work, the instructor monitors student involvement; at the close of group work, the level of success of the group is assessed.

Before groups of students can work together successfully they must learn the skills of cooperative work, communication, and division of labor. Before teachers can implement cooperative learning strategies effectively they must know how to organize materials, equipment, and workspace. Teachers must carefully plan and schedule group work. For your benefit, at **http://math.sfsu.edu/hsu/talks/asilo-groupthoughts.html**, Eric Hsu, a math teacher, asks and answers questions on teaching with group work. Marzano, Pickering, and Pollack (2001) say that cooperative learning activities instill in learners important behaviors that prepare them to reason and perform in an adult world. Teachers are expected to pose problems for students to solve. When students can work together to find solutions to problems that may emerge through other sources, they are using critical-thinking skills in interactions with others.

Role Play, Simulation, and Drama

Teaching strategies that involve students in acting a part or responding to a specific set of circumstances are perhaps the most emotionally charged of all teaching strategies. Role playing, simulations, and drama allow students to experience tough, real-life problems in a controlled environment. Students in a first-aid class learn to resuscitate drowning victims and administer CPR with the assistance of lifelike dummies whose touch and response is similar to that of a living person. Second-graders learn to "drop and roll" to extinguish flames and to crawl along the floor of an escape route to exit a burning building.

Through role play, we learn how to act in places we have never been and how to negotiate unknown territory. Simulations can help students learn empathy, to understand the predicaments life creates for others. In simulations students are faced with dilemmas. They must make choices, take action, and then experience the consequences of their actions. Training for medical triage groups and rescue teams relies heavily on simulation and role playing. Role play, simulation, and drama can help students learn by doing, thinking, feeling, or responding and develop their own knowledge, skills, and dispositions. They allow students to have vicarious experiences that can substitute for firsthand experiences that may be impossible to achieve. Teacher education candidates often cite field experience as the most informative and influential part of teacher education course work. Perhaps that's because fieldwork puts them in the "role" of teacher.

The Powerful Effect of Role Play and Simulation

An infamous simulation exercise, "Blue-eyed/Brown-eyed," had its birth in 1968, in Jane Elliott's fourth-grade classroom in Riceville, Iowa. Following the assassination of Martin Luther King, Jr., when one of her students asked why this had happened, Elliott decided to provide her students with firsthand knowledge of racial discrimination. Since Elliott's students lived and attended school in an all-white community, she had to create a hypothetical situation that would demonstrate to her students what racial discrimination looked and felt like and the demoralizing effects it could have on individuals. Blue-eyed and brown-eyed students in her classroom were assigned to two groups; one group was not allowed to enjoy the benefits enjoyed by others in the classroom, and one group enjoyed all of the benefits plus special considerations. After a time of being in one group, students switched roles.

Elliott's Blue-eyed/Brown-eyed simulation exercise is a classic in teaching about racial discrimination and is a perfect example of the impact a well-planned teaching strategy can have on students. Elliott's simulation was such a powerful piece of teaching that her students still remember it today. Read more about Elliott's lesson at **http://www.horizonmag.com/4/jane-elliott.asp** or check out copies of Elliott's videos, *The Angry Eye, The Eye of the Storm,* and *The Stolen Eye.*

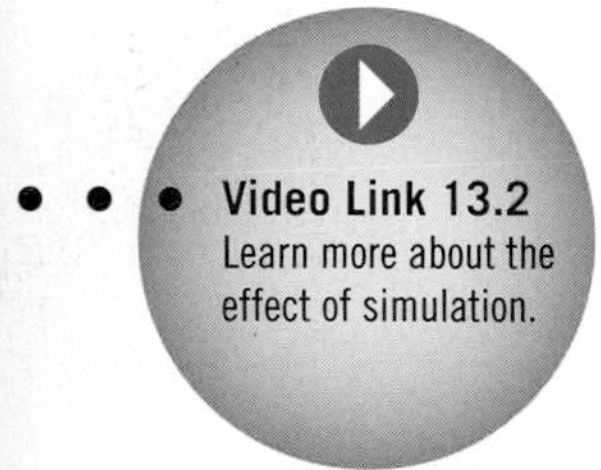

Video Link 13.2
Learn more about the effect of simulation.

The website **http://www.simulations.com** offers educators and students a wide range of well-planned simulations to explore. The website **http://www.sciencesimulations.com** offers simulations in chemistry, biology, and physics that combined create a complete classical lab for experimentation.

Reflective Learning/Inquiry

Discovering something for yourself is intrinsically rewarding because you are actively involved in exploring and manipulating your environment. Most people love a well-planned scavenger hunt and movies that have the hero fight nature, the forces of evil, and doubting Thomases to finally discover some wondrous prize. It's the reason scientists of all kinds spend long hours laboring over test tubes, ancient texts, or computer programs to finally solve a puzzling piece of nature, history, or engineering, to say "I did it."

Reflective learning strategies deal with a problem or problems the students must solve. In reflective learning students are often asked to contend with circumstances that lie outside the range of what is commonplace and normal to them. Students involved in reflective learning must discover facts and concepts and knowledge that are new to them. They also have to compile evidence to support or refute a solution. Students must develop hypotheses.

One well-known reflective learning teaching strategy is the Social Inquiry Model, described by Joyce and Weil (2008). This model, specifically developed for the social studies curriculum, has six phases that help students develop cooperation and collaboration skills in addition to the cognitive benefits of the inquiry process. The six phases are

1. Orientation: presentation and clarification of a puzzling situation
2. Hypothesis: development of a hypotheses to structure an exploration or solution to the problem
3. Definition: process of defining, clarifying, and understanding the hypothesis

4. Exploration: looking for the assumptions, implications, and logical validity of the hypothesis
5. Evidence: assembling relevant facts and evidence to support or refute each hypothesis
6. Generalizations: arriving at an acceptable solution based on evidence

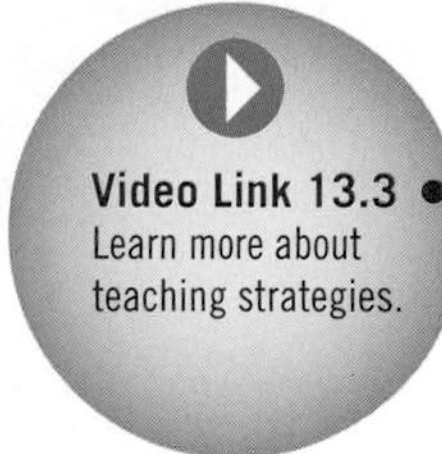

Video Link 13.3
Learn more about teaching strategies.

Viewing Teaching Strategies as Direct or Indirect Instruction

Teaching strategies can also be grouped into two overarching categories of **direct** or **indirect instruction** sometimes referred to as **explicit** and **implicit instruction.** Explicit instruction can be viewed as instruction that helps students increase and broaden their existing knowledge or skills. Teaching strategies that are explicit or direct are successful in helping students acquire information that is highly structured. Implicit teaching strategies are intended to assist students in thinking about their own thinking, also called **metacognition,** deciding on a specific choice or solution, and acting on their decisions. Each area of instruction requires different behaviors from teachers and responses from students.

Direct instruction represents a teacher-centered approach with the teacher providing the instructional input. The teacher's role in direct instruction is to pass facts, rules, or action sequences on to students in the most direct way possible (Borich, 2011). Direct instruction has been shown to correlate highest with student achievement as measured by standardized tests emphasizing facts, rules, and sequences. Direct instruction strategies make it possible for teachers to serve up information in chunks palatable to students, to make dry, boring information interesting, and to help students master content.

Indirect instructional strategies help students work together to solve existing problems.

Rosenshine and Stevens (1986) wrote a seminal essay on the power of direct instruction that has provided a framework for understanding the components of direct instruction. Additionally, Carnine, Silbert, Kame'enui, Tarver, and Archer (2012) provide many examples of the use of direct instruction strategies. Remember the lecture on the Westward Migration referred to earlier in this chapter, and the way the teacher provided stimuli to pique student interest and attention.

Indirect teaching strategies encourage students to think beyond the facts given, to draw conclusions or make generalizations. Teachers who use direct instruction focus learner attention on a problem and then provide students with background information (Woolfolk, 2004). This approach activates the cognitive processes required to form concepts and to recognize patterns and abstractions. Borich and Tombari (2003) suggest that indirect teaching functions are most useful in providing behaviors that students will use in their adult lives. Reaction to the world outside the classroom requires students to be able to analyze situations, make decisions, organize information, and adapt. These skills are not learned through memorization of rules and facts, but must be constructed through experiences demanding higher-level thinking. They are using information to draw conclusions and they are thinking. When students think well while learning, they learn well.

Deeper Look 13.3
Read more about metacognition and student learning.

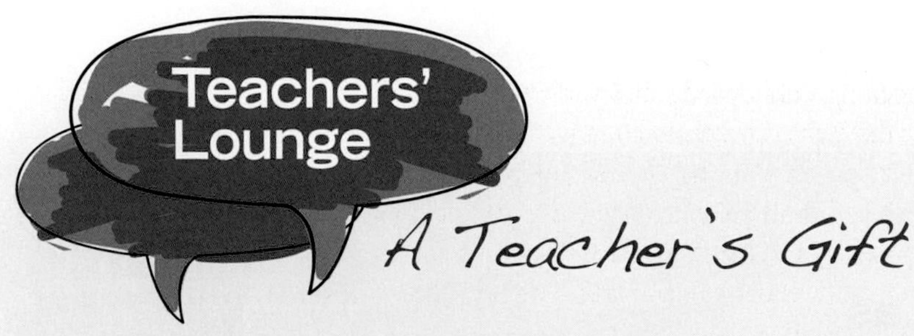

One of the most difficult, but most rewarding classes I taught came the year I was assigned a LA/SS block of 15 of the lowest-achieving, least-motivated eighth-graders in our middle school. I worked hard to reach these students, and sometimes wondered if I had. On the day before Winter Break, I saw two of my students in the corner of the classroom working hard on something that was not an activity I had prepared for them. I put on my best "teacher face" and walked over. As I approached, they turned around and offered up a small, plastic bell that they had physically cracked; with grins, they exclaimed "Merry Christmas! Do you know what this is?" I choked up as I identified the Liberty Bell from our social studies lessons. It was only later that I learned they had stolen the bell from the tree at the entrance of the school! This bell is still one of my prized holiday decorations.

Lorae Roukema, EdD
Campbell University
Buies Creek, North Carolina

A Constructivist Approach to Teaching

As you learned in Chapter 7 of this text, a constructivist approach to teaching is built on the idea that each student actively creates, interprets, and reorganizes information in ways that are unique. Present knowledge is used to achieve predetermined educational goals. Students engage in **problem-based learning,** inquiry activities, and dialogues with others to connect elements in the learning environment. They come together in communities of learners with an opportunity to think critically by challenging and explaining their thinking to one another. Students experience the ideas, phenomena, and artifacts of the discipline before having formal explanations of them.

In a constructivist environment teachers do not prescribe, but instead are more likely to respond to the needs of learners, the content, and the context. The teacher's role is that of a facilitator of learning, one who responds to the students' needs in a flexible manner. By allowing students to construct knowledge as learners, teachers help them to think critically about concepts (Gabler & Schroeder, 2002; Martin-Dunlop & Fraser, 2008) and design and sequence lessons that encourage learners to use their own experiences to actively construct meaning (Richardson, 1997).

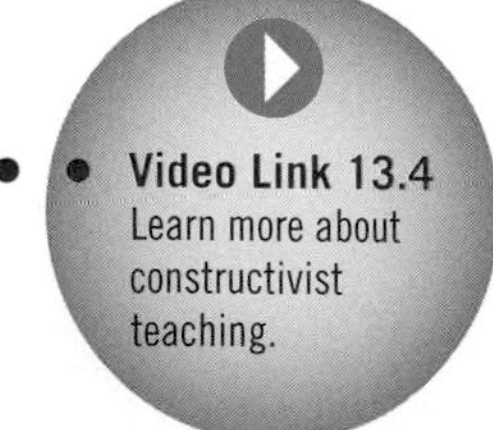

Video Link 13.4
Learn more about constructivist teaching.

There are many constructivist strategies that a teacher might employ when teaching a particular content area. **Scaffolding** allows the learner to make sense of a complex task. **Modeling** requires teachers to think aloud about the process they have gone through to solve a problem. Teachers probe students' thinking through coaching, guiding, and advising. To create a constructivist learning environment, teachers must clearly understand how the theory of constructivism translates into practice (Windschitl, 1999).

Activity Learning

Simply put, the **activity approach** to teaching is exactly what it implies. Students develop understanding of the link between the conscious and the objective world by engaging in activities.

Through the manipulation of objects and tools, students can gain knowledge in a variety of domains. Piaget (1985) proposed that individuals gain knowledge through active exploration in which they form schemes, cognitive structures that help them organize patterns, or thoughts to interpret their experiences. A teacher might allow a student to choose either a pictorial or a, concrete representation to solve a math problem (e.g., 2 × 3). The student then can either make two groups with three cubes in each group or draw two circles with three boxes in each, thus concluding the answer is six. The objective of the activity is achieved through a physical or mental product.

When teachers plan an activity for their students, they consider the curriculum objectives for that activity, what resources should be available, and what prerequisite knowledge the students must have to complete the activity. Teachers take into account the context in which the activity will take place.

Teachers know that as students become actively engaged things will happen that may change the intended outcome, and that sometimes students will come up with solutions or answers that the teacher may not have considered. Teachers using constructivist and activity teaching strategies must be both well prepared and flexible. That is not a contradiction. It is just one of the phenomena of teaching from a constructivist perspective.

Deeper Look 13.4
Read about five strategies to improve student learning.

Never Just One

It would be nearly impossible to use only one teaching strategy in a single lesson. Even lectures usually include some questions. Discussions are loaded with questions. When students work together in groups, they share information with one another, ask questions, and carry on discussions. Inquiry, whether done individually or in groups, depends on questioning and working through hypotheses and sometimes acting out a problem. Role playing, simulations, and drama draw on any number of teaching strategies to achieve desired results. When students are using resources, audiovisual equipment, computers, and the Internet they are receiving lectures of sorts from books and videos, asking and answering questions, and sharing their information through discussions and presentations with their classmates.

Teachers who use a variety of strategies are likely to have a high degree of instructional success since students learn in so many different ways. Selecting the best teaching strategy to match students with subject matter is a teaching skill not easily mastered. But it can be accomplished when a teacher keeps in mind the needs and abilities of the learners, the content goals to be achieved, and the time and resources allowed by the context. Teachers must make hundreds of decisions a day regarding what they are going to teach and how they are going to teach it. Teacher knowledge of the best uses for a particular teaching strategy, how to most effectively implement the strategy, and the learner response to a particular approach are the key ingredients in any instruction.

WHAT MAKES TEACHING STRATEGIES WORK?

As Mr. Choi describes, it is the teachers that continually strive to improve lessons that make teaching strategies work.

> As a department chair, I have the opportunity to visit and sit in on numerous classrooms. Watching a wide range of teaching styles is a great learning experience. I encourage all my teachers to visit other classrooms; and this year, I gave the teachers a list of periods that I would cover so that they could visit other teachers. Unless the culture of the school

> encourages and supports peer visitations and observations, it is difficult to implement. Peer visitations are a requirement of the inquiry program. Each class presents a unique challenge and a unique experience. Teachers should continually try to improve lessons and revise the curriculum. I try to implement technology into my classes when it proves useful. Technology can help engage students, allow for differentiated structure, and provide multiple opportunities. Last year I started using WebAssign with my AP and Honors Chemistry classes. This website allows teachers to assign problems that vary from student to student and provide immediate feedback. This year, we have used iPads to help differentiate instruction so when we studied chemical formulae, the students were able to work at their own pace and at their level of proficiency. We are fortunate to have Smart Boards in our classroom. Technology is no panacea; however, if used properly, it can make instruction more efficient and effective.

Teacher knowledge, skill, dedication, disposition, enthusiasm for helping students learn, and ability to assess student learning are the catalysts that can bring any teaching strategy to its full potential. Teachers such as Jason Choi, featured at the beginning of this chapter, who can motivate students to learn by making the content engaging and meaningful, who can use the context in which the students must learn to best advantage, and who understand the needs of the students, use a variety of teaching strategies.

Knowing a variety of instructional strategies and having the flexibility to change them both within and among lessons are two of the greatest assets a teacher can have (Emmer, Evertson, & Worsham, 2003). Without variety and flexibility to capture the interest and attention of students, it is unlikely that any other key behavior, however well executed, will have the desired effect (Borich, 2011).

Mr. Choi provides an example of ways teaching strategies can be combined to increase student participation in lessons.

> The AP chemistry course is quite expansive and rigorous. I use direct instruction to present certain materials or explain certain phenomena. I often model problem analysis and problem solving in this manner. However, I usually follow up with some cooperative learning activity and provide opportunities for students to find out for themselves what they know and what they don't know. Cooperative learning encourages metacognition skills since students have to articulate and justify their ideas.

During your first attempts at teaching a small group of students or an entire class, it may be that you will feel more confident and competent with only one teaching strategy. The fear of losing control, that the students won't pay attention to you, or that they won't learn what you need to teach them may keep you locked within the parameters of this one teaching strategy. That's natural. We begin learning in small chunks, and we feel very comfortable when we know how to do something, so we practice it and get better at it and feel even more confident as we continue to practice that particular skill. However, the research base in education tells us that teachers who use a range of teaching strategies have a greater chance of meeting the learning needs of their students and of helping students develop academically. It becomes every teacher's responsibility to develop skill in using a variety of strategies to help students connect with the content. Over time, effective teachers learn to make any teaching strategy work for them.

The Importance of Planning

Planning is of the utmost importance in making a variety of teaching strategies work for you and the students. Some types of plans work better with some types of teaching strategies. You will

Challenging Assumptions

Is cooperative group work beneficial to high-performing students?

• • • • •

The Assumption

High-performing students do not benefit from working cooperatively on group projects with students who are achieving at lower levels. Students, and occasionally their parents, may complain that by being placed in groups with lower-achieving students they simply end up doing the work for others and are not challenged to learn at the high levels that they are capable of.

The Research

The benefits of cooperative learning have been extolled through extensive research. It has been claimed that cooperative learning is one of the best researched of all teaching strategies. The research indicates that cooperative learning consistently improves achievement and that students who learn cooperatively have greater retention of the information learned. Working in cooperative learning groups has been shown to encourage positive relationships among all students, improved relations among different ethnic groups, and improved relationships between mainstreaming students with learning disabilities and others. Cooperative learning groups also promote positive feelings about learning and about one's own abilities. Higher-level thinking is promoted through cooperative group learning.

Implications

While the reasons to use cooperative learning groups in a classroom are clear, the potential for individual student success of any cooperative learning group often rests directly on a teacher's ability to plan tasks that require input from each student and address individual needs. In addition to planning appropriate tasks, a teacher must also make certain that all students have the opportunity to stretch their learning and reach ever-increasing levels of achievement.

Sources:

Johnson, D. W., & Johnson, R. (1999). *Learning together and alone: Cooperation, competition, and individualization* (5th ed.). Boston, MA: Allyn & Bacon.

King, A. (2002). Structuring peer interactions to promote high-level cognitive processing. *Theory Into Practice, 41,* 31–39.

hear and read about the importance of planning in nearly all of your teacher education course work. In your personal life you have no doubt had much opportunity to plan, but as a student you have been mainly concerned with enacting the plans of others. Your teachers have told you what they expect you to do, and in best-case scenarios have provided you with examples, directions, and a time line for achieving the objective. In becoming a teacher, it is necessary to make the shift from enacting the plans of others to creating plans for others to follow.

Plans need to be detailed, thorough, and doable. Plans must be based on accurate content information, a comprehensive understanding of the context, and both theoretical and practical knowledge of learner capabilities and potential. Plans must include objectives that will meet established curricular goals. In other words, they must make sense across many dimensions. There are many lesson plan formats for teacher education candidates to follow. The website at **http://www.lessonplans4teachers.com/templates.php** offers a variety of lesson plan templates for you to follow. Often individual teacher education programs and specific content area instructors will provide a "homegrown" lesson plan format that they expect all of the candidates to use. The concept of what should be included in a lesson plan has a theoretical base, while variations on the concept are widespread among educators.

Instructional Theory Into Practice

Madeline Hunter's (1994) seven basic elements of an effective lesson—(1) anticipatory set, (2) instructional objective, (3) instructional input, (4) example of intended learning outcome, (5) check for understanding, (6) guided practice, and (7) independent practice—help form the foundation for any plan involving any teaching strategy. These elements might not be arranged in the same order, and some of the elements might not be shared with the students to encourage discovery or inquiry learning. Whether or not all elements of Hunter's seven basic elements of an effective lesson are shared with the student, they should be part of the instructional plan in one form or another.

Jarolimek, Foster, and Kellough (2005) define a lesson plan as a step-by-step plan of action, or a trip map through the lesson that can be followed easily while the lesson is being taught. Beginning teachers and teachers in training need to keep their plans close by for easy reference. How many of us have had the experience of driving to a new destination, map on the car seat next to us if we have no GPS navigator, checking reference points, and trying to read street signs. Cell phones can be used as homing devices when we're on the road, but most school administrators would frown on teachers calling out to get advice on exactly how to proceed with a lesson in progress. Plans help teachers reach benchmarks and goals and bring the students along. It is not an easy task to write a lesson plan. It is complex and time-consuming. One reason for developing the skill of writing effective lesson plans early in your career is so that once you do write a plan, use it, and judge it as top-notch, you won't have to write the whole plan over again and again, though you may have to modify it for different groups of students. The Internet is a rich resource of lesson plans to provide examples and get you started on planning your own lessons.

Figure 13.3 A Lesson Planning Cycle

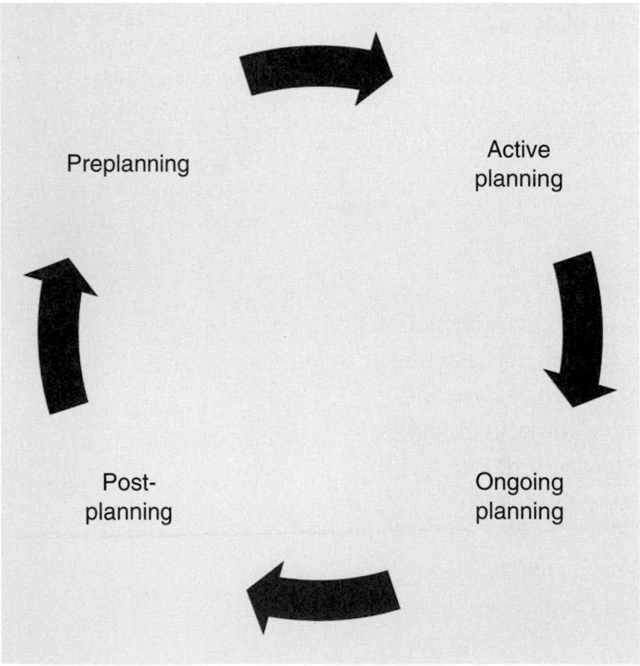

Source: Adapted from Freiberg, J. H., & Driscoll, A. (2004). *Universal teaching strategies.* Boston, MA: Allyn & Bacon.

The Planning Cycle

Effective teachers are always planning. They think through the design and implementation of lessons long before it is time to actually teach them. They collect artifacts, talk to other teachers and friends about what they want to do, and maybe even try out a plan for a lesson on an unsuspecting family member. Freiberg and Driscoll (2004) explain teacher planning through four phases of a planning cycle (see Figure 13.3).

The first phase may find a teacher sitting quietly in a backyard swing looking at a sky full of clouds and listening to the sound of the wind in the trees. Ways to teach a unit on climate and weather to next year's third-graders come to mind. What do 8-year-olds need to know about weather? What would they find most interesting about weather? How would it be possible for them to experience weather conditions in other parts of the world? How many children's books does the school library have on weather? Questions come together in ideas, and ideas spur teachers on to action. Resources are collected and organized. Before you know it, it is fall, the school year has begun, and it is time to teach a lesson on weather.

Effective teachers access a variety of resources when planning lessons. Maintaining a file of lesson examples provides a starting point for lesson planning.

The active planning phase of Freiberg's cycle is when teachers actually write the lesson plans they intend to teach. The teacher opens the mental box of weather lessons that has been created in the brain, or the filing cabinet, or the computer program where all the ideas collected during the preplanning stage have been stored, and begins to write the actual plan.

Ongoing planning takes place while the teacher is actually teaching the lesson. A student's question may prompt the teacher to include a bit of information that wasn't in the original plan, or a super book recommended by the school librarian may be read, or an unbelievable weather pattern develops outside that the children simply must see. The world is full of reasons teachers need to be ready to include ongoing planning in their teaching strategies repertoire.

Postplanning is what teachers do when the lesson is over, the school is quiet, and most everyone has gone home for the day except the custodian and the principal. In postplanning the teacher asks if the goals of the lesson were achieved, if necessary standards were covered, if student learning met expectations, and if there are changes that should be made next time the lesson is taught. In postplanning the teacher is engaging in reflection on practice. After this period of reflection the planning cycle begins again as the teacher considers how this lesson might be taught in the future.

Experienced teachers will suggest that it's a good idea to plan more than you actually expect to teach. Teachers should also let the students know the plan. No one likes to be kept in the dark. In explaining or discussing the plan with the students, the teacher may become aware of an approach or idea that the students or a particular student may be interested in that the teacher had not included. Through interactions with students about plans, an opportunity to uncover the curriculum may present itself.

Getting Students Ready to Learn

One of the most critical parts of any teaching strategy is how it is applied in the beginning of the lesson. How do your university instructors begin their lectures? With stories? With anecdotes? By directing your attention to a picture or a chart? Did math classes you attended begin with a "stumper" problem on the board for you to try to solve in the first few minutes of class? When you entered your psychology class was there a sealed envelope on each desk with instructions not to open it until an exact moment in time? Such simple devices can capture our attention. They are often mysterious, and frequently so compelling that we don't need to be reminded to pay attention. Our own internal monitoring devices are turned on, and learning has us in its grasp.

Attention-getting activities may include a quick demonstration with an unexpected outcome or asking students to close their eyes and visualize an unlikely event. Riner (2000) says that gaining attention need not be elaborate, but the event should cause all students to be involved.

Bracketing or: Let's See, Where Was I?

Did you ever walk into a room in your own house and wonder why you were there? Have you ever forgotten something you went to the store to buy? Have you ever left your house and worried that maybe you forgot to turn off the stove? Of course you have. Some students come to school and can't remember what you talked about the day before. So much has happened to them in the interim that they may have misplaced the last bit of information they received at school before heading home, or to their part-time job, or to soccer practice. There's a lot going on in teachers' and students' lives. Part of a teacher's job is to help the students remember where they are in the process of learning in school.

"First, you have to get their attention."

Bracketing is a strategy that teachers can use at the beginning of a lesson or at the end of the lesson. Teachers talk the students though the process of bracketing what happened between yesterday's lesson and today's lesson and setting it aside so that the ideas from content studied previously can be easily associated with the ones they are about to learn. For example, a teacher reminds students of the class discussion on magnets held the previous day. She acknowledges that after class the students were engaged in activities unrelated to the discussion and that particles of information from other experiences may have gotten mixed in with the information the students were carrying around about magnets. Then she tells the students it is time to organize the information and ideas surging around in their thinking. Find all the information about magnets, focus on it, and attempt to set aside unrelated information to access at a later time. Bracketing used often becomes a habit of mind and can aid considerably in focusing attention on instruction.

Sponges

Another simple yet effective technique used by teachers to gain student attention at the beginning of a lesson, or to keep student attention during the lesson, is the sponge. This term describes review or extension activities that help to keep learning on track. Sponges can also be used effectively to summarize a lesson through an enjoyable activity. For example, at the end of a lesson on parts of speech or sentence construction, have students in the classroom call out four letters as you write them on the board or overhead projector. Then ask the students to come up with a four-word sentence where each word in the sentence begins with the letters written on the board. It may take a few seconds for the first sentence to be formed, but once you have written two or three sentences on the board the students' ideas will come at you like wildfire. Such an activity could be used to introduce a lesson or as a wrap-up. Visit **http://www.atozteacherstuff.com/Tips/Sponge_and_Transition_Activities/** for additional ideas on sponge activities.

Evaluating Learning

The purpose of assessment is to measure student learning. Since different teaching strategies tend to stimulate different types of learning, it is important for teachers to learn about and be able to use a wide variety of assessment strategies. It would be illogical to evaluate student learning following a role play situation with a multiple-choice test. And a test on the facts and rules of one content area would not work for a classroom of students who were researching different subjects. Assessment should become a part of every teacher's repertoire of teaching strategies so that knowledge of assessment is applied in planning, in decision making, and in communicating with students.

Knowledge about learners is gained through interactions with and observations of the students. Teachers need to observe students, to record their observations, and to seek information about students from outside the classroom. Teachers also need to be clear about the methods of assessment they are using and to what end they are using them. You will learn more about assessing student learning in Chapter 15 of this text, and as you do, keep in mind the connection between the content, the context, the learner, and assessment and teaching strategies.

Teacher Work Sample or Analysis of Student Work

Teachers can also document student work and their own effectiveness as teachers by a process of work samples. Perhaps you have already been introduced to Teacher Work Samples (TWS) or Analysis of Student Work (ASW) in your teacher education program. The process of developing a TWS or ASW offers evidence of your ability to design and implement standards-based instruction, assess student learning, and reflect on the teaching and learning process. These products also provide credible evidence of your ability to facilitate learning of all students. A TWS and ASW are sources of evidence your instructors and supervisors use along with classroom observations and other measures to assess your performance as a teacher relative to national and state teaching standards.

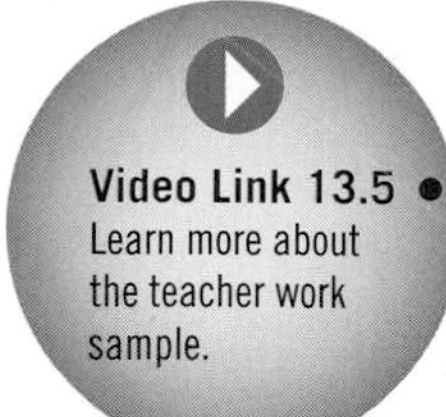

Video Link 13.5
Learn more about the teacher work sample.

Understanding the Connection Between Teaching Strategies and Curriculum

At the beginning of this chapter, Mr. Choi creates lessons that reflect practical applications of the required content. In Chapter 11 of this text you were introduced to the role curriculum plays in instruction and learning. You read the ways a teacher used exceptional instructional strategies to deliver the curriculum in engaging and long-lasting applications that can be disseminated to other teachers.

What we discover in learning about teaching strategies is that they share a symbiosis with curriculum. Teaching strategies cannot really exist without curriculum and vice versa. They rely on one another for successful delivery. Of what use would a teaching strategy be if there was no purpose for using it? Curriculum supplies the purpose. Curriculum is what we teach. Instruction is how we teach the curriculum.

In many ways the teacher is in control of the curriculum, though sometimes it may seem otherwise, given the heft of district curriculum guides and state and federal curriculum policies. Curriculum materials can be used in different ways. Teachers use curriculum materials according to their own personal practical knowledge. They consider how curriculum can be applied in the context and best meet the needs of the students. Teachers use different approaches to teaching to make the relevance and significance of curriculum apparent to the students. Teachers have to be able to visualize what written curriculum looks like in action. The talent it takes to make the transition from text to action is much greater than the talent it takes to recognize it once it occurs, but a teacher must possess both talents.

HOW ARE DIFFERENT STRATEGIES USED FOR DIFFERENT PURPOSES?

When Mr. Choi was asked if he thought all students would respond to an inquiry-based teaching strategy, he answered both yes and no.

I believe that all human beings are curious by nature. Inquiry-based learning taps into one's natural curiosity and desire to explore and discover. Unfortunately, this curiosity has been stamped out of some students and they want to be told what to do and what to think. Surprisingly, sometimes these are the top students with the highest grades. Initially, some students do not respond favorably to inquiry-based learning; however, if the teacher can gradually lead the students toward discovery and independent thinking, all students eventually respond favorably to the model.

We have a thriving science research program that provides students the opportunity to choose a particular topic and research an original hypothesis. I participated in a science research for teachers program at Columbia University for two summers. I was lucky enough to study carbon nanotubes with a great group of professors and graduate students. This program gave me insight into science research and allowed me to see, firsthand, the role of creativity in science. Ultimately, we want our students to have both the sound foundation and the innovative spirit to succeed in science.

We all remember clearly the teachers we had who were able to help us "see" and understand concepts that were new to us or difficult for us to grasp—teachers who used all manner of paraphernalia to help us connect what we already knew about the world in general to what we had to learn specifically. These were the teachers who carried schoolbags full of objects they had collected that we could hold and manipulate, while they talked us through ideas, lessons, and experiments.

Doing math is different from teaching math. Teaching math, as well as other subjects, is as much an art as it is a science. Teachers must train themselves to think like artists at times. They must constantly draw on creativity in their approach to teaching. If you approach teaching strictly from an empirical perspective, you're painting by the numbers. Art is a creative way of organizing reality. The logic of teaching is the logic of the well-organized artist whose palette is arranged methodically so that his or her creativity can have full reign.

Culturally Relevant Teaching Strategies

Culturally relevant teaching strategies refers to the ways generic strategies are modified or implemented to address the fact that students' orientations to learning may be influenced by their cultural backgrounds. The ways in which students interact with one another and with the teacher also may be influenced by their cultural background (Irvine & York, 2001). Students who live in an Italian or Jewish neighborhood in New York City, students from a fishing town in Florida, students who attend an inner-city school in Chicago or Los Angeles, and students from a small mining town in a remote area of Northern Nevada will bring different backgrounds to school and have different orientations to learning. Teaching strategies that accommodate learning styles influenced by culture have a greater chance of matching students' varying orientations to learning.

Some students require less structure and want to solve problems on their own with a minimum of teacher help. Planning lessons that provide opportunities for students to learn within differently structured contexts is part of what makes teaching such an interesting and engaging profession. Visit the website at **http://www.lab.brown.edu/tdl/tl-strategies/crt-research.shtml** to learn more about culturally responsive teaching through reviews related to learning styles, culture, and research on effective teaching strategies.

Multiple Intelligences

Learners view the world from different perspectives and react to it with differing abilities. You read about Howard Gardner's (1999) belief that children develop abilities, "intelligences," by their own spontaneous interaction with the world in which they live. According to Gardner, curriculum and teaching strategies should respond to the individual differences in intellectual potential related to the eight intelligences he identified: (a) linguistic, (b) musical, (c) logical-mathematical, (d) spatial, (e) bodily-kinesthetic, (f) interpersonal understanding, (g) intrapersonal understanding, and (h) naturalistic intelligence. People generally possess all eight intelligences, and these intelligences interact with one another. Yet individuals are likely to be more highly developed in some of the intelligences than others. Some students perform well on standardized tests, and some don't. Students who have not yet mastered computation skills but perform well on story problems may be using their ability to understand the meaning and order of words to solve problems rather than mathematical skills.

Inclusion Strategies: Least Restrictive Environment (LRE)

As a teacher, you will be expected to create a classroom environment that provides all students equal access to learning. An intended goal of federal and state special education requirements has been to afford opportunities for students with disabilities, to the maximum extent possible, to interact with their nondisabled peers. The Individuals with Disabilities Education Act (IDEA) presumes that all children with disabilities are, to some extent, educated in regular classes. Special education and related services provided to special needs students are to be in addition to and affected by the general education curriculum, not separate from it.

Response to Intervention (RTI)

Response to Intervention (RTI) is an instructional program that guides teachers in making instructional decisions for students who may not be able to access information at the same rate as other students in the classroom. The program involves data-based problem solving, monitoring of student progress, and universal screening. When specific students are identified as benefitting from RTI, the intensity and duration of additional instruction is determined. The implementation of RTI has provided evidence that through additional high levels of instruction the learning abilities of struggling students can be improved.

Strategies for English-Language Learners (ELL)

Audio Link 13.2
Listen to a clip about teaching English Language Learners.

Many students in your future classrooms will have limited or no English-language capacity. You will be responsible for helping these students learn the content. Since the role of language has a strong influence on student learning and may place students who do not speak, read, or understand English at a disadvantage, you will be expected to implement strategies that diminish this disadvantage. Some schools may use a "pullout" approach, allowing limited English proficient (LEP) students to spend part of the day in a special bilingual class. However, chances are that all teachers will need to possess some skill in using strategies to help LEP students learn. The first step in teaching LEP students should always be to show respect for students' cultural backgrounds. It doesn't take much energy for a teacher to learn how to pronounce a student's name correctly, but the effort will make a world of difference in the student's attitude toward the teacher and consequently toward learning.

Homework as a Teaching Strategy

One of the best pieces of advice I received from an experienced teacher when I began my professional career was to never have students do homework that they had not started in class

Deeper Look 13.5
Read more about the effect of homework on student achievement.

or that they weren't sure how to complete. No teacher wants a student to go home and report, "I don't know why I'm doing this, and I don't understand it at all."

Homework is a form of interactive practice in which the learner is interacting with the content, but when the teacher is not present to mediate this interaction, the student had better be absolutely clear about what needs to be done and why. Homework is an extension of classroom learning and when planned carefully can assist student achievement; but like every other strategy a teacher uses, homework should fit the content, the context, and the learner. If practice makes perfect then it becomes a teacher's responsibility to somehow monitor the practice that occurs during homework so that it will not become imperfect practice. One educator suggests that no homework should be assigned until the teacher has completed the same work. Ten common reasons why teachers assign homework were identified by Joyce Epstein and Frances Van Voorhis (2001). Epstein called these the 10 Ps, for purposes of homework: Practice, Preparation, Participation, Personal development, Peer interactions, Parent–child relations, Parent–teacher communication, Public relations, Policy, and Punishment.

CONNECTING TO THE CLASSROOM

This chapter introduced you to some of the teaching strategies that teachers employ in the classroom. There are many reasons teachers use a variety of teaching strategies to help students access information. As you visit classrooms for observation and practice, be alert to the rationale a teacher might have for using one strategy over another. Here are some ideas to help focus your observations.

1. Not all students learn in the same manner.
2. Learning skills and facts are more easily facilitated by some strategies.
3. Space and time have a major influence on the strategies teachers can use.
4. Materials and resources may influence the strategies teachers use.
5. Most effective lessons utilize more than one teaching strategy.
6. A teaching strategy should always match the method by which students will be assessed.

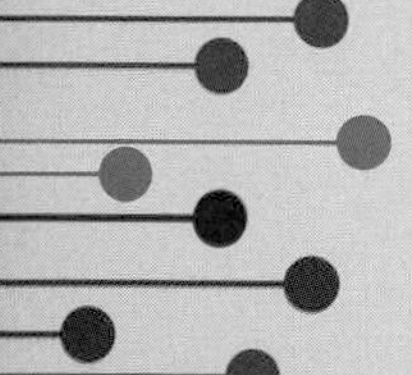

SUMMARY

Understanding that instruction is the systematic delivery of content to a unique set of individuals in a specified context is part of the specialized knowledge of a professional teacher.

- What are teaching strategies? A teaching strategy is the yeast in the lesson that makes it rise to meet students' interests and abilities. Teaching strategies provide the pedagogical framework for the professional teacher to deliver the content and to build instruction and activities around standards and the required curriculum.
- What makes teaching strategies work? Part of making teaching strategies work is being able to assess their impact on student learning, so teachers have to collect data and use that data to guide future practice. Teaching strategies used correctly have the power to transform a ripple on a pond to wave length and frequency in a student's mind.

- How are different strategies used for different purposes? We're not the same as people or as learners. Each of us sees the world from a single perspective born of a million different influences and affects. Not all students discover the same bit of information simultaneously, if at all. Teachers must always look though the eyes of their students to see where learning connects for each of them.

CLASS DISCUSSION QUESTIONS

1. It would be unreasonable to expect a novice practitioner to enter the classroom highly knowledgeable of and skilled in the use of multiple approaches to teaching. Which teaching strategy would you like to learn first? What advice is of most worth in this process? How might you practice a teaching strategy even before you have a classroom of your own?

2. Resources are like advice; they fall into categories of useful and not so useful. What types of resources are most likely to help teacher education candidates increase their knowledge of teaching strategies? What are some ways to store and organize resources so they will be readily available when needed?

3. The diversity of student characteristics in a classroom can make some teachers lack confidence in their ability to meet the learning needs of all students. What examples have you seen when the strategy clearly matched the students' backgrounds?

4. Helping students identify and build on their strengths is an often underemphasized tenet of teaching. Recognizing one's own strengths can lead to confidence. Feeling confident when teaching a group of students leads to competence. Consider your strengths. How will these help you in teaching? Which strategies do you believe will benefit most from the strengths you possess?

KEY TERMS

Activity approach 399
Cooperative learning groups 393
Direct or explicit instruction 397
Indirect or implicit instruction 397
Learning cycle 386
Metacognition 397
Modeling 399
Problem-based learning 398
Reflection 385
Scaffolding 399
Strategy 387
Taxonomies 391
Wait-time 392
Wait-time II 392

SELF-ASSESSMENT

WHAT IS YOUR CURRENT LEVEL OF UNDERSTANDING AND THINKING ABOUT TEACHING STRATEGIES?

One of the indicators of understanding is to examine how complex your thinking is when asked questions that require you to use the concepts and facts introduced in this chapter. After you answer the following questions as fully as you can, rate your knowledge on the Complexity of Thinking rubric to self-assess the degree to which you understand and can apply a variety of instructional strategies.

1. What ways would a teacher have to plan differently for a lecture and organizing cooperative group work?

2. What is the planning cycle that teachers use in lesson implementation?

3. What activities might teachers use to get their students ready for learning?

4. Why should teachers be aware of Howard Gardner's multiple intelligences when planning lessons?

Assess your current level of understanding of how the teaching strategies can improve student learning.

Complexity of Thinking Rubric

	Parts & Pieces	Unidimensional	Organized	Integrated	Extensions
Indicators	Elements/concepts are talked about as isolated and independent entities.	One or a few concepts are addressed, while others are underdeveloped.	Deliberate and structured consideration of all key concepts/ elements.	All key concepts/ elements are included in a view that addresses interconnections.	Integration of all elements and dimensions, with extrapolation to new situations.
Using teaching strategies to improve student learning	Able to name one or two phases of the planning cycle.	Can describe the planning necessary for use of one strategy but does not compare this process to another strategy.	Describes ways teachers' knowledge of strategies can promote student learning.	Combines knowledge of strategies and students' learning styles.	Adjusts planning and teaching strategies to students' learning styles to prepare students for learning.

STUDENT STUDY SITE

Visit the Student Study Site at **www.sagepub.com/hall** to access links to the videos, audio clips, and Deeper Look reference materials noted in this chapter, as well as additional study tools including eFlashcards, web quizzes, and more.

Field Guide

for Learning More About Teaching Strategies

• • • • •

Go back and read the introduction to the Field Guide in Chapter 1. Think about what you are learning about teaching and what you might include in your field guide related to the topics in this chapter.

Ask a Teacher or Principal

Ask a teacher what her favorite teaching strategy is and why she prefers it over others. Have her tell you how she learned it and developed skill in using it. Also, ask the teacher if the strategy is most effective with any particular content area.

Make Your Own Observations

Plan a short lecture on a subject you feel will be of interest to students at a specific grade level. Be sure to follow the five guidelines discussed in the chapter (audience, focus, organization, clarity, and pacing). Make an outline of your lecture. Visit a classroom when the teacher is delivering a lecture. Compare your lecture structure to the one the teacher used. If the teacher used a lecture structure different from the one you outlined, ask why.

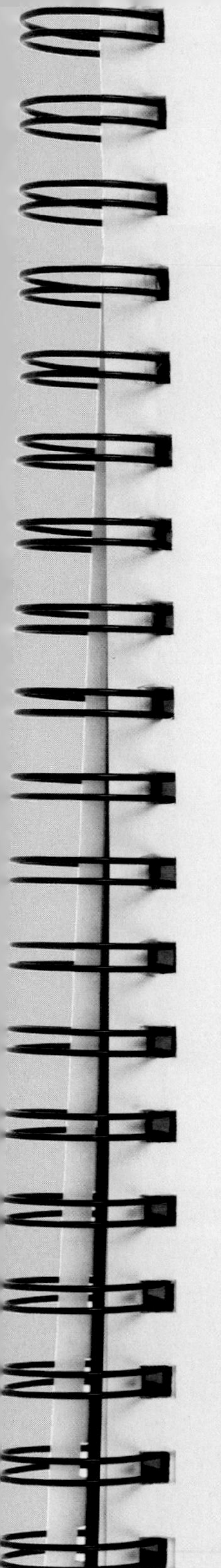

Reflect Through Journaling

Think of something you learned and who taught it to you. For example, how did you learn to tie your shoes, scramble an egg, play a musical instrument, dance, or wash a load of clothes so all the clothes didn't come out some shade of pink or dusty brown? Describe the process. How did the person who helped you learn teach you? What strategies did he or she use? Did the teacher use repetition, written instructions, or a demonstration? Did you have to practice on your own or did the teacher work through the process with you? Write a brief description of the learning process you went through. What teaching strategies work best for you?

Build Your Portfolio

Teachers who continue to grow and learn access the resources available to them, work with other professionals, and collect data representing their teaching performance and the performance of their students. You have no doubt already begun a professional development portfolio..This is a perfect place to keep a record of your growth in understanding and using an array of teaching strategies. Make a list of the key components of one teaching strategy you have observed and understand. Describe how you might have used it in one of your practicum experiences.

Select a content area (e.g., reading, math, science, social studies, art, music) that you are interested in teaching. Write six questions you could ask the students that would be designed to elicit differing levels of student thinking. Make certain the questions you write will help the students achieve the objective of a particular lesson. Write one question for each of the levels in Bloom's taxonomy.

Read a Book

Everyone who teaches should read *Enhancing Teaching,* by Madeline Hunter (1994; New York, NY: Macmillan). It is easy to read, addresses many aspects of designing instruction to help students achieve success in school, and is written from the personal perspective of an educator who understands the teacher's role.

The Teacher's Guide to Success: Teaching Effectively in Today's Classrooms, by Ellen L. Kronowitz (2008; Boston, MA: Pearson), provides a wealth of suggestions for making every classroom the perfect environment for learning.

Search the Web

Visit the In Time website (**http://www.uni.edu**) to see examples of the ways teachers incorporate standards into lesson plans. Download two lesson plans using different teaching strategies and compare the elements and style of the two lessons. Focus on teacher behaviors and expected student behaviors as you consider the content, the context, and the learners.

Visit **https://www.teachingchannel.org/videos?** to see some of the great strategies teachers use in their classrooms to engage students in learning.

TEACHER INTERVIEW

Nira Dale

Nira Dale teaches English and journalism at the Florence Freshman Center in Florence, Alabama. Ms. Dale teaches in a collaborative setting with four other English teachers who encourage and motivate one another and their college-bound students. Ms. Dale has seven periods for teaching, one for planning, and a 20-minute lunch period, which she often spends tutoring students. When asked why she became a teacher, Ms. Dale replied, “Why would I not be a teacher? I always wanted to be a teacher.”

Using Technology to Improve Student Learning

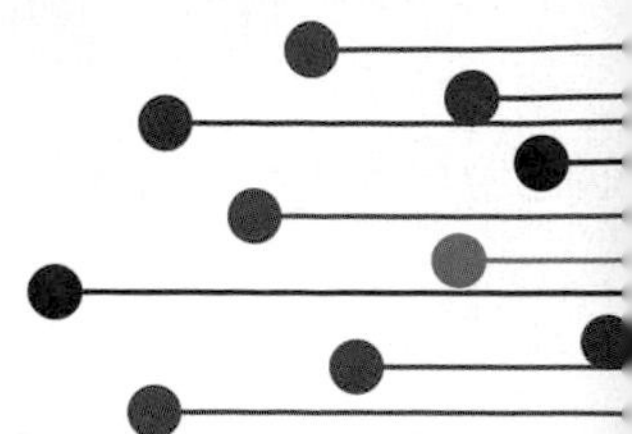

What does excellence in teaching look like to you?

Excellent teaching requires three main things: (1) Setting high standards, (2) making sure the students believe they can achieve the high standards because attitude about learning exceeds aptitude, and (3) creating a climate that allows the students to have some sort of peer interaction and opportunities to explore and investigate what they have learned through group work. I want every student to leave each lesson knowing more than they did when it started.

How do you know when your students are learning?

Students are learning not simply when they can give a correct answer, but when they can explain *why* an answer is correct. I stress the "big ideas" in what we are learning and make certain that each student understands them. Effective teachers create opportunities for the students to show what they learn. Teachers should assess learning in ways that make the student enjoy learning.

I believe that using clickers [student remote response systems] provides an accurate example of what students know. Clickers have proven to be a great technological aid to me in knowing quickly what the students know about the subject I am teaching.

What brings you joy in teaching?

I just get excited about everything in the classroom—the kids learning, the subject we are studying, and the chances I have to work with my colleagues. I find joy when I see the kids realize that they can do something, when they are proud of themselves, when they can make connections between what they are learning and how the content relates to their lives, and when I hear them say how much they appreciate what I do.

How would you describe the use of technology in the classroom?

Technology is a fantastic resource. It's like having a personal assistant. Using the whiteboard, the class blog, my website, clickers, the mobi [mobile interactive whiteboards], the iPad, and different applications, helps any teacher make an extra connection with the students. My website [http://www.dalesdigitalclassroom2.weebly.com] was created so that parents could follow what their children were doing in my classes, but it really helps the students, too.

What are some problems you see with the Internet?

It is a problem if students can access inappropriate sites. There are a lot of filters at my school, so I don't worry about that. We have iGoogle days that are focused on searching a topic that sometimes the filters block the students

Questions to Consider

1. How does Ms. Dale's knowledge of technology and the Internet help her create engaging lessons for her students?
2. Can Ms. Dale's ninth-graders be passive learners in her classroom? Why, or why not?
3. How can technology help Ms. Dale's students show her what they have learned?
4. In what ways does Ms. Dale use technology to inform parents of the expectations she has for the students?
5. How might technology assist Ms. Dale in evaluating student learning?

from. I do my best to set the stage for what the students are studying and get them to investigate something that may have happened around the time of the play or story they are studying (Globe Theatre, Black Plague). I ask the students to find at least three or four different sites that give details about a chosen topic. Most of the time in general instruction the students won't stay engaged for more than 10 to 12 minutes, but when they do Google searches they work hard at research for 20 minutes. They also spend time during the Google search teaching one another. I love it when the students are teaching one another.

Why do you think that it is necessary for teachers to use technology?

Teachers have so much to compete with for students' attention. If we don't use technology we are making it that much harder to engage the students. It is necessary to use technology in some way, shape, or form to give the students something that lets them share something on their turf. Students have been told that they are the technology generation, and they have developed skills in using technology that are often beyond the skills of their teachers. They love to be able to show you what they know.

Learning Outcomes

After reading this chapter, you should be able to

1. Understand the knowledge and skills teacher education candidates should accumulate in order to integrate technology in their future classrooms.
2. Recognize the differences between how technology might be used for personal communication and how it can be appropriately used for teaching and learning.
3. Understand the importance of integrating technology into teaching and learning.
4. Recognize ways technology can assist a teacher in managing a classroom.
5. Know the ways technology can be used to promote your own professional growth.

INTRODUCTION

Human beings love to communicate. Since the first verbal grunts, hand signals, and stacked rocks along pathways, humans have wanted to let others know where they have been and what they were doing. Cro-Magnon cave paintings, Mayan and Aztec symbols, and Aboriginal drawings were early attempts on the part of primitive humans to leave pictorial records of events viewed as important in the lives of their tribes. Much later, spoken language became the popular means of communication, with bards and performers carrying news throughout the domains. Tribal storytellers were revered as celebrities for their talent in keeping fireside audiences enthralled with tales from the past. Everyone could talk, but not everyone could remember the story line of an epic poem.

Written forms of language and the later advent of the printing press in the 15th century created a whirl of communication and a healthy rise out of the morass of illiteracy. Of course there were elements of society that saw evil in education and deemed darkness better than light. But humans love to communicate and there was no way to keep the flood of information and print material from having a huge impact on the path humanity was destined to take. As Columbus and Magellan sought out new horizons and Newton and Galileo challenged long-standing beliefs, folks learned to read, went to plays, and listened to symphonies by Mozart and Beethoven. Of course this all took time, but the 15th, 16th, and 17th centuries truly changed the ways humans went about the business of sharing their news and ideas.

Video Case 14.1

Technology

1. Technology is part of 21st century life. How do teachers in this video describe ways technology can benefit and should be part of teaching and learning?
2. In what ways can technology assist teachers in providing immediate feedback on student learning?

Fast forward three centuries; there were still wars with ever more powerful and frightening weapons. Humans were beginning to look to the stars for new horizons, and at Iowa State University, Professor John Atanasoff and a graduate student, Clifford Berry, were building the first electronic computer. It wasn't a handheld device, but it was a beginning. Visit http://inventors.about.com/library/blcoindex.htm for a great timeline of the invention and development of computers. Now, handheld computers are commonplace and folks let everyone know where they've been and what they've been doing by texting or posting their personal information through applications designed to link us all.

This chapter will help you consider today's array of technology from a teacher's perspective. Since you are likely a member of the generation of "technology natives," using technology for personal endeavors is nothing new. However, using technology to help improve student learning may present challenges that you have yet to explore. Communicating with students in professional and engaging ways is one of the most important roles that teachers perform whether with or without technology.

WHAT ROLE DOES TECHNOLOGY PLAY IN THE LIVES OF TEACHERS AND LEARNERS?

Ms. Dale says her classroom instruction consists of three to five online digital assignments (digital flashcards for vocabulary, posts in blogs, online quizzes in Edmondo [**http://www.edmodo.com/**], etc.). These assignments that must be submitted by the end of the week not only help students develop digital literacy skills; they also develop the ninth-grade reading objectives of "following directions."

The types of technology available to teachers for instructional purposes have changed remarkably.

Technology has always provided tools for teaching and has been part of education in America since the first student in Massachusetts etched a numeral or letter on a slate. From stones for etching softer rocks, to styluses for making marks in soft clay, to shaved brushes for painting icons, teachers have used tools to enhance their practice. Chalk and blackboards made it possible for teachers to invent their own text in classrooms. Imagine where Albert Einstein would have been without a chalkboard. The science of photographic reproduction in the 19th century made it possible for teachers to show students photographs of famous art objects and historical sites in faraway places. The first Kodak slide projector, produced in 1937, offered another piece of technology for teachers to enhance instruction. Teachers also learned to use 8 millimeter and 16 millimeter movie projectors to show select films to their students, and nearly anyone graduating from a teacher education program in the 1950s had to take a course on audiovisual aids.

When television was introduced in schools, there was a consensus among educators that the small screens installed in many classrooms would revolutionize teaching and learning. Televisions did not revolutionize teaching and learning. Unfortunately, typical television programming puts the viewer in passive mode, except maybe for programs like "Dora the Explorer." Three-year-olds are known to stand up during one of Dora's silences and yell "backpack." Technology is not something new, but the technologies available to teachers today are certainly fantastically improved.

Much of what happens when you begin teaching is a mystery. In many ways, what happens from day to day in any classroom can be surprising. You might be prepared for the worst and find the best. You might discover something wonderful that you weren't quite prepared for that stretches your knowledge and skills in ways that are new and occasionally frightening. Teaching with the technology tools available to teachers today adds a dimension of magic to the art and science of teaching. It poses challenges that can leave your head spinning and surprises that make you and your students go, "Wow!"

GPS devices provide students new avenues for discovery.

Teachers today must consider technology as a tool for student learning that can foster critical thinking, and must learn to use the virtual interactive tools that their students use in their personal lives (McGrail, Sachs, Many, Myrick, & Sackor, 2011).

Imagine this:

As students enter the classroom they approach the classroom computer console and click on the square after their name to mark their attendance in class. The time and date are registered automatically in the teacher's electronic grade book and in the central office of the school. When the students take their seats, homework assignments are scanned and evaluated on their individual desk consoles by programs designed to recognize correct responses. Within minutes of the first bell the teacher receives a printout showing who has done what and how well. From a technology station at the front of the room, the teacher can post grades and send private messages to students who might need clarification of the grade. The teacher can also schedule times to visit privately with individual students about their work and attendance. While these messages are being sent, the teacher has directed the students to a National Geographic website where they are to read about the Alashan Plateau section of the Gobi Desert as an introduction to the unit on natural deserts. Questions for discussion are listed on the board. Little time is wasted. The students are engaged in learning and soon a lively, thoughtful, and informed discussion is taking place about barren landscapes, fragile soils, and scarce water sources.

The Evolving Face of Technology

Deeper Look 14.1
Read more about technology in education.

In the late 1960s, the mothers' club at Lakeside Middle School in Seattle, where Bill Gates was a student, used the proceeds from a rummage sale to install a computer terminal and buy computer time for the students at Lakeside. Students spent lunchtime and other free time playing games and experimenting with the computer. It was novel, it was fun, and the students had the freedom to "mess around with the computer, speeding things up or making the games on the computer more difficult" (Gates, 1995). School environments have changed enormously since then.

There is no technological parallel in history to the speed at which the digital/electronic revolution has changed the way we communicate. People started accumulating a digital life during the 1990s. The first digital camera was invented in 1975, but it didn't become available on the consumer market until the mid-1990s. You could take pictures on your digital camera, download the ones you wanted to keep to your computer, and delete the rest. Cameras with film became obsolete and so have most of the companies tied to that technology.

Digital video disc (DVD) players had limited availability in the late 1990s, and now nearly every personal computer comes with a DVD player. And a DVD is now called a digital versatile disc because it has greater capacity than video. Voice recorder applications are available on most cell phones, and cell phones no longer come in suitcases. Cell phone companies vie for customers on the basis of speed of connectivity and range of applications with the goal of ever faster, ever further, and ever more fashionable in mind.

The government is puzzling over ways of legislating usage of technology and particularly the Internet, but the industry has held them at bay so far. People are so attached to the digital side of their lives that any restriction of the personal freedom technology creates results in a public outcry.

The Cloud

Keeping all the technology devices available to you in sync prompted Apple to create a digital hub in the sky. The iCloud provides access to all information uploaded to the iCloud from any one of your Apple digital devices. Businesses often buy applications to create a private cloud. For example, Amazon has both a private and a public hybrid cloud. Go to *Amazon S3* to check out the exponential growth of one cloud and see where such technologies might take us in the future. Public clouds make it possible for entrepreneurs to try out their new ideas. Hooking into a cloud is inexpensive, and it doesn't take much development time to advertise your ideas. Schools use cloud technologies to set up school websites, where assignments can be posted and where what was taught in class can be reinforced through a homework assignment link within the cloud. Even the federal government has adopted cloud computing.

Technology for Communication

Technology makes it easier and easier to stay in touch, and as technology evolves so do the ways we communicate. Michael Ian Borer, associate professor of sociology at the University of Nevada, Las Vegas, says that "technology has advanced so quickly that social etiquette and rules and norms haven't caught up" (Bornfeld, 2011, p. 3). When eating out with friends or colleagues, is it okay to text or answer your cell phone? This probably depends on the norms of behavior for whatever group you are with.

Social Networking

Kevin Bacon's six degrees of separation, SixDegrees.org, an attempt to establish a charitable social network among actors and actresses, blossomed in 1994 and quickly became a game for everyone. Mark Zuckerberg started Facebook in 2004. If you've seen the movie *Social Network,* you know all about the intrigue connected with the start of the Facebook.com phenomenon. Since the beginning, Facebook has undergone improvements and invented ever more intricate ways to communicate with friends and enemies.

Audio Link 14.1
Listen to a clip about teachers and social media.

When teachers use a social network tool to connect with friends and family, they must be careful not to post pictures or comments that will be seen by someone other than the people they are intended for. As has been demonstrated, pictures or comments that have been posted during a lapse of common sense have ended up in the media, causing retribution from parents and employers. Given the current technology and the applications that are available to everyone, hardly anything remains secret. Julie Spira, founder of RulesofNetiquette.com, says that every time you tweet or post something online you create a *permanent* digital footprint. The idea of creating a public, permanent photo or comment should make you think twice before hitting the Enter button.

Blogs

You probably already have one. If not, it is easy enough to establish one. Blogs are an integral part of the Internet and there are beautiful, customizable templates just ready and waiting for your personalized input. Blogs are online journals arranged in chronological order, and some people believe blogs were the death of the evening news. Ms. Dale, the teacher at the beginning of this chapter, uses a blog to keep her students up-to-date on assignments and to let the students know exactly what is happening at school. In Chapter 12 of this text you learned about the importance of history in influencing students' behavior in the classroom. Keeping a class blog is a perfect way for teachers and students to track class history. Visit http://EzineArticles.com/3084842 to learn more about blogs from Patricia Fioriello.

YouTube

Like Apple, YouTube started out in a garage. It quickly became a hugely popular site. YouTube makes it possible for individuals to share videos—mostly hilarious, but it also can provide informational lectures and experiments for use by teachers and learners. Blogs also can be found on YouTube. Next time you visit YouTube, consider how what you chose to view might be used for instructional purposes. Think about the grade level you hope to teach, what might appeal to that age-group, what the curriculum is at that grade, and how you might use YouTube to help the students learn. Inviting someone into your classroom to provide a change of venue for learning is easily accomplished through YouTube technology. And students love using the technology during class time that they already know how to use outside the classroom. You might even learn something that will help you improve your instruction the next time you teach a particular lesson.

Twitter

Twitter is another online social networking service. Think of it as a mini blog, though Twitter is a real-time communication device. If you can keep your information to 140 characters, imagine the speed with which you can let someone know not just where you are and what you are doing, but also what you are thinking. Twitter is free, and it is an excellent learning device for posting and receiving information. Even pictures can be sent through Twitter as TwitPics. Facebook used to be the social network site of choice for many teens, but once their parents and grandparents also became members of Facebook teens turned to Twitter—creating another "proprietary" space for teens to communicate (Irvine, 2012).

Can teachers use Twitter in the classroom? Sure! Twitter streamlines dissemination of information. Teachers can send news to students and tell them to remind their friends who don't have access. In class, teachers can have the recorder in a cooperative learning group send the groups' results through a tweet to the large computer-connected Smart Board at the front of the room, and then have the other groups tweet back. Technology is amazing in the classroom, but only when the teachers know how to use it for student learning.

Technology Changing the Teacher–Learner Relationship

When you become a teacher, you create a personal teaching identity. You establish a philosophy toward teaching and learning that guides your actions as a teacher. If technology is introduced into your world after your ideas of teaching and learning are well established, you are faced with the question of how using technology will change who you are as a teacher. Change can be disturbing. Being asked to integrate technology into your teaching when you are not comfortable using technology in the first place can be a little like learning to ride a horse in the Kentucky Derby. You're probably not going to win the race even if you can stay in the saddle.

The Internet provides a wealth of educational and entertaining learning opportunities for students.

Introducing technology into your teaching can place a considerable strain on your most deep-rooted perceptions of a teacher's role. The abundance of ready information on the Internet and the World Wide Web (WWW) has the potential to alter or undermine the relationship between the teacher and the students. Teachers set goals and objectives, follow plans, and assess results. Students follow, the teacher leads. But 24/7 access to information can set this well-established pattern on its ear. This change in the teacher–learner relationship can create tension among teachers, even those who may embrace classroom technology.

Consider the following example of the way technology can challenge a teacher's perception of the traditional teacher–student relationship.

The teacher tells the students that tomorrow the class is going to learn about arachnids. Later that day, ever precocious Irelynn accesses the Internet through her iPad, enters *arachnids* on Google, discovers amazing facts and myths about arachnids that the teacher hadn't included in the well-planned lesson, sends texts to her friends about arachnids, and comes to school the next day loaded with information to share. So what does the teacher do?

The teacher is no longer the premier source of information on arachnids. Once again, the teacher has to make a decision. Certainly the teacher doesn't want to stifle Irelynn's incentive to learn, and also wants to set an example for the rest of the students that "finding stuff out" is what good learners do. So the teacher makes a deal with Irelynn, telling her that since she is the teacher, she will introduce the unit on arachnids and then Irelynn can share the information she has located and where she located it.

The teacher put Irelynn in charge of making a digital presentation of pictures and myths from the website with a brief description of each myth that she discovered. It's an easy adjustment if the teacher is flexible and knows the topic. This example shows how a teacher can make the transition from the "sage on the stage" to the "guide on the side."

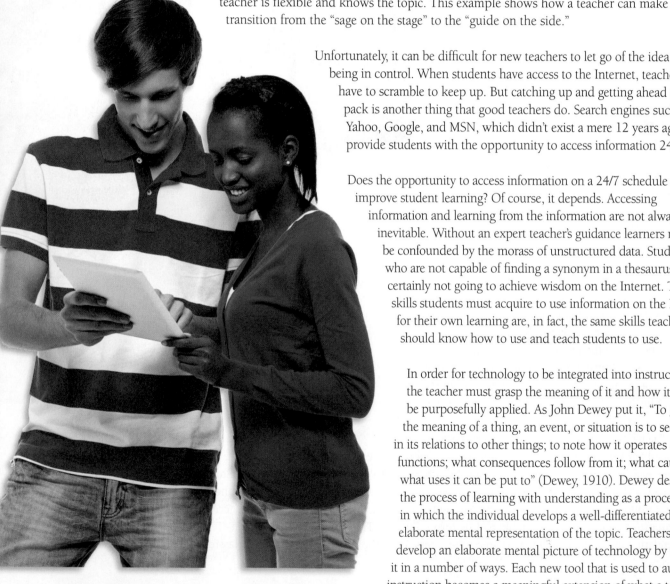

Presentations can be enhanced through the use of technology.

Unfortunately, it can be difficult for new teachers to let go of the idea of being in control. When students have access to the Internet, teachers may have to scramble to keep up. But catching up and getting ahead of the pack is another thing that good teachers do. Search engines such as Yahoo, Google, and MSN, which didn't exist a mere 12 years ago, now provide students with the opportunity to access information 24/7.

Does the opportunity to access information on a 24/7 schedule improve student learning? Of course, it depends. Accessing information and learning from the information are not always inevitable. Without an expert teacher's guidance learners may be confounded by the morass of unstructured data. Students who are not capable of finding a synonym in a thesaurus are certainly not going to achieve wisdom on the Internet. The skills students must acquire to use information on the Internet for their own learning are, in fact, the same skills teachers should know how to use and teach students to use.

In order for technology to be integrated into instruction the teacher must grasp the meaning of it and how it can be purposefully applied. As John Dewey put it, "To grasp the meaning of a thing, an event, or situation is to see it in its relations to other things; to note how it operates or functions; what consequences follow from it; what causes it, what uses it can be put to" (Dewey, 1910). Dewey described the process of learning with understanding as a process in which the individual develops a well-differentiated, elaborate mental representation of the topic. Teachers develop an elaborate mental picture of technology by using it in a number of ways. Each new tool that is used to augment instruction becomes a meaningful extension of what a teacher knows and does. Without the tool, the teacher is unable to discover the meaningful uses it can be put to.

Teachers must prepare students to learn on their own, both during school years and after graduation. Since individuals engaged in lifelong learning will be best positioned to survive cultural, technological, and thought transitions, and to actively and intelligently interact in a global arena, teachers must become facilitators and guides in technology's learner-centered classrooms. They must use technology to show students what can be learned from the past, to understand current information, and to adapt presently acquired knowledge to tomorrow's ideas. Teachers need to help their students understand the BEAR fundamentals of self-directed learning:

Base intelligent decisions on accurate and comprehensive information.
Evaluate information critically.
Access reliable information.
Recognize inaccurate and misleading information.

Teachers and learners can work together to use strategies for locating reliable information sources and then share the information they access.

One way to close the technology gap between teacher and learner is to talk about the first time either of you saw a computer, a remote control, a calculator, a cell phone, or better yet, a cell phone with a camera, a digital camera, an MP3 player, a handheld computer, a video game system, or computerized navigation systems. Compare your students' initiation into the world of technology with yours. Then consider what type of technology both you and your students will see for the first time. Talking with your students about technology can be a helpful step in closing whatever gap may exist between your understandings and uses of technology and theirs.

Audio Link 14.2
Learn about using technology in the classroom.

WHY INTEGRATE TECHNOLOGY IN TEACHING?

Ms. Dale talks about how writing a grant made it possible for her to purchase a 55-inch high-definition TV for her classroom.

> I use it daily to illustrate some point I am trying to make in instruction, to let the students see performances, or hear actors talk about the motivation of the character they are portraying. Teachers have to use anything they can to keep the students engaged, but they should never waste instructional time showing movies. Before I even show a clip from a film the students will have already discussed and understood every aspect of the story.
>
> When I was teaching for the U.S. Department of Defense Dependents Schools (DoDDS) in Avellino, Italy, I had the wonderful experience of taking the students on a field trip to Pompeii. It was, to say the least, extraordinary. I wished at the time that any student in any school could have such a close-up perspective on the ruins of ancient civilizations. Never in my wildest dreams did I imagine my wish would become reality.

Today, students have access to archeological museums around the world and can take virtual tours of many of them. For example, go to the IBM website (**http://www.eternalegypt.org**) and explore the culture of Egypt through virtual visits to famous sites and museums. It is only one of many sites available to help teachers and students increase their knowledge and understanding of the world, its past, and its peoples.

The WWW resides within the Internet as your mind resides in your brain. One is really not much good without the other. The WWW and the Internet together provide a wealth of information for teachers to create unusual learning opportunities for students, to manage student work, to develop presentations for introducing and investigating topics, to plan virtual field trips, to find games students can play with other students across the nation to improve skills, or even to get help in creating their own games. Using technology to improve student learning is not a difficult task, but it is up to the teacher to make it happen.

Interesting ways for teachers to incorporate technology in the classroom range from helping students create a talking avatar (**http://www.Voki.com**) to teachers themselves creating lessons in a movie format (**http://www.Xtranormal.com**). The resources that are available to teachers on the Internet seem never ending, and every day there is something new to explore.

In addition to the decisions teachers make about students, curriculum, and instructional strategies, they have to now make decisions about the purposes of technology in their teaching, quality software, and equal access for students. Visit a classroom at any grade level and look around the room to see what technology tools are available for teacher use and for student use. It is likely that you'll see a desktop PC, some laptops, a Smart Board, Student Response System (SRS; aka "clickers"), an Elmo document projector, an LCD projector, a DVD or VCR player, and perhaps some view pads. Nearly every class has some technology available. The difference technology can make in student learning resides in how it is used. Andy Carvin's EdWeb site at **http://www.edwebproject.org/resource.cntnts.html** also provides a wealth of information for educators wishing to know more about the technology in education.

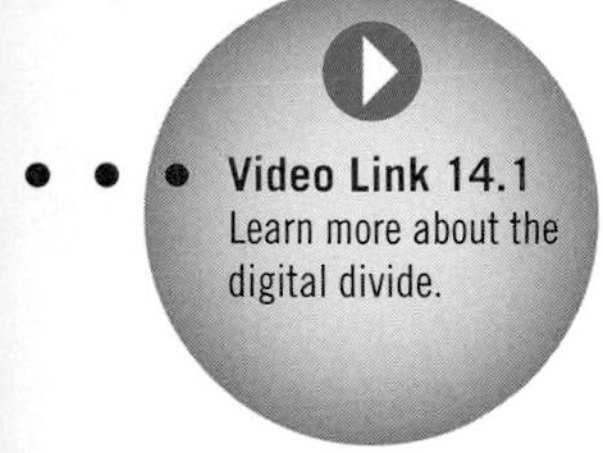

Video Link 14.1
Learn more about the digital divide.

Not all educators are enthusiastic about the use of technology in teaching and learning. Some refer to the "digital divide" that separates those who have access to the Internet from those who do not. Disparities also exist in terms of socioeconomic status, geography, and race. A study by Day, Janus, and Davis (2005) demonstrates these disparities and suggests that the issue of the digital divide will become increasingly troublesome as there is ever more dependency upon digital technologies. Teachers must be aware of the disparities in the use of technology among their students and find creative ways to overcome them.

Here is an example of ways technology can influence teaching:

The Explore Knowledge Academy (EKA) in Clark County is Nevada's first iSchool. A recent article by Paul Takahashi (2012) in the *Las Vegas Sun* portion of the *Las Vegas Review-Journal* describes the school as a charter school that uses project-based learning methods to allow students to demonstrate their learning through "presentations, plays, dances and dioramas" (p. 9). Each of the 720 students and 54 staff members at EKA receives an iPad. According to the article, "Students use iPads to access educational websites and applications as well as electronic textbooks. They use iPads to take notes and the tablet's camera to photograph whiteboards filled with teachers' lessons. Some students even record lectures using the iPad's digital voice recorder or video-camera. Starting in second grade, students are assigned EKA e-mail addresses to send assignments to teachers, and student accounts are monitored for cyberbullying and inappropriate content. The hope is that iSchool students will have an advantage in becoming self-directed learners through their engagement with technology."

Technology for Teaching

Teachers have a wealth of entertaining resources at their fingertips through websites. Some are free. Some are not. Once you start to visit different sites you will become a regular, looking for new interactive content and resources. You have probably been directed to conduct a WebQuest in one of your college classes. If you haven't been on a WebQuest before, now is a good time to get started. First explore a topic that interests you and then one that might interest students from a range of grade levels. Refer to Table 14.1 for a list of websites and topics to explore.

Table 14.1 Starting Your Own WebQuest

Duke University Library	http://library.duke.edu/	Tour exhibit of early newspaper comic strips (1899–1916)
Kidsmart Guide to Early Learning and Technology	http://www.kidsmartearlylearning.org	Find out how to make computers a regular part of any childhood program
Froguts	http://www.froguts.com	A virtual dissection service—science with no smell
National Library of Virtual Manipulatives	http://nlvm.usu.edu/en/nav/vlibrary.html	K–12 emphasis in mathematics instruction
Try Science	http://www.tryscience.org	Contemporary science and technology through on- and offline interactivity with science and technology centers worldwide
National Geographic	http://www.nationalgeographic.com/education/	Find ways to help students learn more about geography

You likely use a variety of technology tools for personal needs. Technology is all around us, and we use it for our personal pleasure and business without giving a moment's thought to how or why it works. In fact, the only time we really think about it is when it doesn't do what we want it to. Digital media in our homes comes at us constantly through music, voice, data, and video. The digital generation of kids and young adults have no problem watching TV, listening to music, e-mailing friends, or surfing the Internet to see what's happening—all at the same time. Multitasking is a new vocabulary word and for many has become habitual. It is not always safe, and it sometimes causes important pieces of information to be missed, but it is a part of our culture.

Switching perspectives from using technology for personal need or pleasure to using it in a classroom to augment student learning requires a focus of attention on what the technology does and what it can be used for. A beginning teacher who is digitally oriented may need to change her mind-set toward technology tools. Integrating technology into teaching requires knowledge and skill. Perhaps more important, though, it requires that teachers who wish to integrate technology into teaching possess a curiosity about new ways of doing things and a willingness to learn how to do something they haven't done before. Teachers who grow with the changes in their profession will find joy in the amazing technology tools that become available to them. Following are some examples of ways teachers can use common technology tools and applications in instruction and managing a classroom.

Smart Boards, MP3 Players, and Tablets

Regardless of their product name, Smart Board, Promethean Interactive Whiteboard, or just Whiteboard, the technology behind the product provides an interactive display connected to a computer and projector. Users are able to control the display using a pen, a finger, or a stylus. Since, in this case, a video is better than words, go to **http://www.YouTube.com** and type in

"Smart Boards." Why are they so easy to use? You will see teachers use interactive whiteboards for a variety of purposes.

From numerous cell phones and stereo systems, MP3 players can be found just about anywhere. MP4 players will play files that are either audio or video or a combination. iPads are MP4 players. They can deliver highly compressed digital files such as movies, games, books, and a wealth of applications. Tablets provide easy access and freedom of use through their connectivity and light and robust casings. Teachers can keep track of student assignments, check the library for availability of specific texts, plan next month's field trip, develop a data chart for collection of artifacts during the field trip, and download a topographical map of the designated field trip site.

Digital Cameras

Will Weber, a professor in the College of Education at University of Houston, would tell his college classroom management students to "catch students being good." He said that positive reinforcement is the most powerful management tool in a teacher's possession. Take pictures of your students being wonderful and load the pictures on a computer that everyone can see or the Smart Board. When things get a little out of hand in the classroom, run the photos as a slide show. Soon all students will get the picture and order will be restored without you having to say a word. A picture really is worth a thousand words.

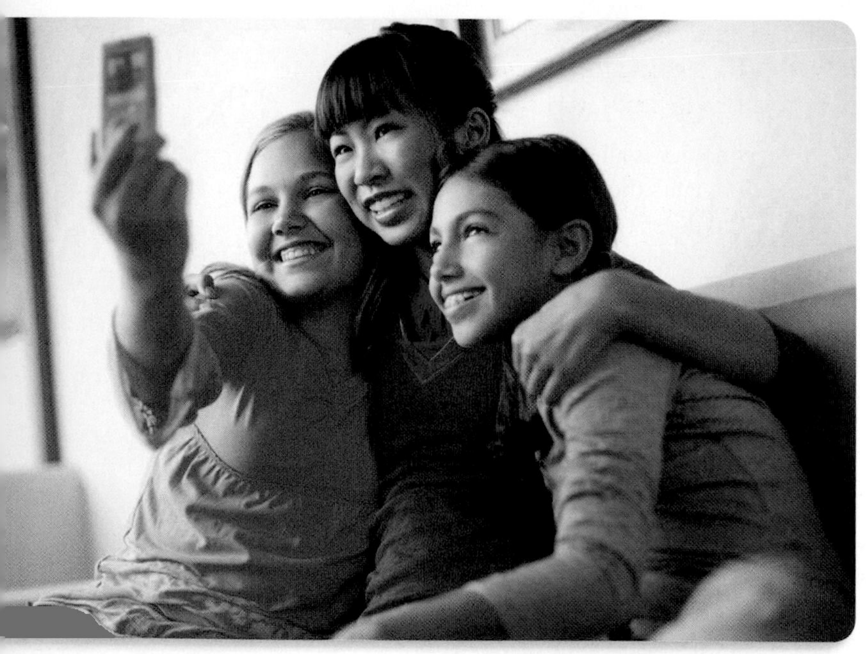

A picture can be worth a thousand words, and pictures allow us to see things as they are and not as we imagine them to be.

An opposite approach would be to take a series of pictures of a classroom out of control, put them on a computer monitor, and ask the students to explain what's happening, and what can be done so it does not happen again. Students sometimes think they are invisible to the all-seeing eyes of a teacher. They're wrong, of course, but the difference between having a teacher tell students what they see and showing the students what is seen can be a mighty behavior management tool.

Digital pictures can be used to show student progress and what it looks like when students are learning and growing. Teachers take pictures of class accomplishments and create slide shows. With current technology it is easy to share these slide shows with parents and other teachers. Each student can have a photo journal of his or her personal record of achievement.

Pictures can provide background for a story or lesson. If you are teaching a story set in Yosemite National Park, you can download pictures of Yosemite from the Internet and create a slide show so the students have visual images of the park during the reading of the story and afterward during questions about the story. Maybe no one in the class has actually been to Yosemite, but the addition of pictures provides a virtual trip for all students and adds an engaging dimension to the story.

Video Recording

In addition to the video recording capacity of most digital cameras, nearly all cell phones have camera and video recording applications. Gone are the days of having to "tape" an event with a

In the early days of technology integration, I was helping a teacher prepare for a class lesson using a computer and projection device. I was standing beside her as she operated her desktop computer, guiding her through the steps to access a program. She was a little unsure in using the mouse to click and open the program. After a few missed tries, I leaned over and pointed on her screen directing her to move the mouse and click "there." She calmly picked up the mouse and put it on the computer screen exactly where I had pointed—and clicked.

Karen Grove
Associate Professor in the Department of Teaching and Learning, University of Nevada, Las Vegas

cumbersome tape recorder. At any school performance parents have their cell phones and small video recorders ready to capture images of their children. Teachers can also record students' performances in the classroom. Sometimes it is difficult to record students and teach them at the same time, but more than likely even elementary students will have no difficulty assuming the role of photographer to assist the teacher.

Teachers can also help one another record lessons. Want to know how you're doing in the classroom? Have one of your colleagues capture you teaching on video (more about that under using technology for professional development). Watching an event over and over or at a later time provides viewers (learners) ample time to react to the information delivered as well as the meaning behind the scenes. TIVO and cable digital video recording (DVR) make it possible to set your own time frame for watching what you want when you want to watch it.

Filming lessons can make learning entertaining. Imagine the titles "Kate Learns to Add," "Shannon and Sean Build an Ant Farm," "Room 68 Crosses the Potomac," and "Terry Totally Rocks at Soccer." The possibilities are endless, and the learning potential through technology is exceptional.

Filming a lesson also can be a powerful learning experience for preservice teachers. I once had a student who on first watching her teaching segment said it looked like her hands were attached to her hips. Her family watched it with her, hooted with laughter, and mocked her stance. Luckily she had a sense of humor.

Another student who had been teaching for five years said that she had never watched the videotape she made during student teaching. She had kept it but was too "chicken" to watch it. After she filmed another segment of her teaching as a graduate course requirement, watched it, and made comments on her teaching ability, she finally got up the courage to watch the video she had made five years earlier. I didn't get to see that one, but she said it wasn't as bad as she had anticipated, and that comparing the two videos showed that her teaching had improved over five years of practice.

Teachers who go for National Board certification have to include a video of their teaching with the application. All teachers, whether or not they apply for National Board certification, should record one of their lessons and then watch it. Watching yourself teach can be a powerful learning experience.

Learning Games

Deeper Look 14.2
Read about ways to include technology into early learning.

When something is fun we want to do it again and again. Children learning a new game that they enjoy are very persistent. Persistence is one of the prerequisites to learning. According to Jenn Shreve, who writes about technology, "A good game can motivate students to understand things they couldn't or wouldn't learn before" (Shreve, 2005, 30). As a student, did you ever encounter the video game "Oregon Trail" (1974) or "Where in the World Is Carmen Sandiego?" (1985)? Game machines blend a range of digital media into one hub, making possible things that traditional teaching cannot.

Sid Meier's "Civilization III" computer game has motivated failing middle and high school students to high levels of involvement and achievement. Go to **http://www.civ3.com/** to learn more about Meier and his games. Students who design their own games have additional opportunities to connect content to other skills and ideas. Games and simulations are also used to train teachers. A Vermont-based SimSchool, PT3 Project, has developed a game that gives preservice teachers "a chance to try out their lesson plans before subjecting an entire classroom to them" (Shreve, 2005, 30). The world of technology is making possible amazing opportunities for teachers and learners.

Computer-generated activities provide students time to learn and practice skills at a personal pace they determine.

Audio Recordings

Audio recordings can be used to augment single pictures. Today's technology makes it easy to do voiceovers for video. Audio recordings are great for feedback on progress in learning to read or explaining how to compute a math problem. Students read stories into a recorder, read the story again as they listen to their own words, and begin to make self-corrections all the while learning to monitor their own learning. Students who record their thinking processes are often able to recognize where they may have gone astray without having someone else point out their mistakes.

Go to "What did you do in the war, Grandma?" at **http://www.stg.brown.edu/projects/WWII_Women/** for an example of an oral history project. Students in the honors English program at South Kingstown High School interviewed 26 Rhode Island women to create photos, audiotapes, and essays about women and World War II.

Teachers Using Technology Effectively

Think about the fact that computers don't teach people. People teach people. People design programs and tell the programs how to run. Lousy instruction, whether it is backed up with technology or not, is still lousy instruction. The teacher's task is to determine the purpose and effect of the benefit of technology in any given situation. Teachers need to focus on what they want the students to learn and then consider how the use of technology can help them achieve their goals. They have to modify all of the technology tools available to them to fit their needs as teachers, the needs of the learners, and how effectively the curriculum can be augmented through the use of any specific technology tool.

Technology can provide the individual focus that some students need to learn.

Using Technology With Diverse Learners

Many schools already have the technology resources to accommodate individual differences in learners. Teachers at the EKA iSchool mentioned earlier claim that using iPads is especially helpful for the special needs students because curriculum can be tailored to individual students and iPads provide a visual, tactile, and creative outlet. Software available for individualized approaches to learning provides students with a range of venues to learn content, examine ideas, and demonstrate understanding (Tomlinson, 2001). A report from Wahl and Duffield (2005) explains that technology-related tools, such as talking text, web resources, graphic organizers, and features of the word processor are readily available in most classrooms and can be leveraged to meet the needs of diverse learner groups. Use of technology allows flexible adaptations or alternative ways in which students can interact with the curriculum (p. 3). Related professional-development materials on how to use technology with diverse student groups are now available on a PDF called Technology Tips for Diversified Instruction (http://daretodifferentiate.wikispaces.com/file/view/NewTThandout.pdf). Technology makes it possible to match instruction to students' individual learning styles, allowing students to interact with content at differentiated levels of difficulty while taking individually appropriate amounts of time to work through learning tasks.

Software to Enhance Teaching and Learning

It seems that almost daily new software is developed to support learning through technology. Teachers can access a range of tools that will support their teaching and student learning. For example, **http://www.ultralingua.net** provides vocabulary support for students who may have difficulty reading online texts through an immediate computer-assisted tool. Immediate feedback on word meaning may provide the necessary encouragement for such students to continue to use their language skills. The Supportive Inquiry-Based Learning Environment (SIBLE) is developing a software tool to help students acquire the skills of reflective inquiry through computer-based investigation environments (**http://www.letus.org/sible/**). Online tutorials for developing skills in Internet searches and gathering research information are available from Monash University (**http://www.lib.monash.edu.au**). Teachers can download a software tool called the Progress Portfolio (**http://www.progressportfolio.northwestern.edu**). Technology will help you quickly find many ways to enhance student achievement. The HP New Education Center, a mobile classroom by HP, is a computer-assisted education system that connects a teacher and up to 20 students to the Internet, a projector, and a laser printer. Imagine the possibilities.

Deeper Look 14.3
Read about using technology to teach students with disabilities.

Challenging Assumptions

Does access to technology necessarily translate into increased student achievement?

• • • • •

The Assumption

Much attention has been directed toward preparing schools and teachers for the technological age of the 21st century. Elementary and secondary schools have rapidly become "wired" to the Internet. In 2004, virtually all public schools in the United States had Internet access (Lazarus, Wainer, & Lipper, 2005). Teachers and teacher education candidates have received training through support from the Department of Education's Preparing Tomorrow's Teachers to Use Technology (PT3) program. Over 400 PT3 grants have been funded in the belief that projects directed at faculty development, course restructuring, and new and better uses of electronic formats will transform teaching and learning. Private companies such as IBM Corporation and Microsoft have provided funding to school districts and individual schools in the belief that the presence of technology and technological expertise will support and encourage student learning. There is a very strong assumption in education today that in order for each student to have an equal opportunity to learn they must have access to technology.

The Research

Researchers that seek to accurately identify the effect of the use of technology in student achievement will have to design studies that take into account both the technology in use and teacher expertise in understanding and using the technology to help students learn. The study cited here examined the relationship between computer use and fourth- and eighth-grade students' mathematics achievement. The findings indicate that higher mathematics scores were related to adequate access to computer technology and access to a teacher who knew how to apply the technology to help the students learn higher-order concepts. It was also pointed out in the study that the most pronounced inequities in computer use and teacher training were across socioeconomic status, race, and geographic locae. It appears that technology does help students learn, but a knowledgeable teacher is still key to the process.

Implications

This study provides one example of the interaction necessary between teacher expertise and available resources to increase the potential for student learning. Sometimes a knowledgeable and effective teacher can be all the enticement a student needs to excel in any given subject. However, the availability of up-to-date equipment coupled with teacher expertise in specialized uses of the technology can sometimes increase student performance. According to the study, computer use was associated with increased performance when the following conditions were met:

- Students had adequate access to up-to-date computer technology.
- Computers were used specifically to help students learn higher-order concepts.
- Teachers were well trained and capable of assisting students in using the technology for specific purposes.

Source: Wenglinsky, H. (1998). *Does it compute? The relationship between educational technology and student achievement in mathematics.* Princeton, NJ: Educational Testing Services (ETS).

Difficulties in Teaching With Technology

When introducing a new technology tool in instruction, you might find that students are more interested in the technology than the content you are trying to teach them. Before this occurs, provide time for students to spend a little time playing around with the technology (i.e., How does a clicker work? What can it do? What is it used for?), and then show the students how it can help them learn. Effective teachers know that when a new strategy or new materials are introduced to students they may need a little time to play with or practice with the technology outside of a formal assignment.

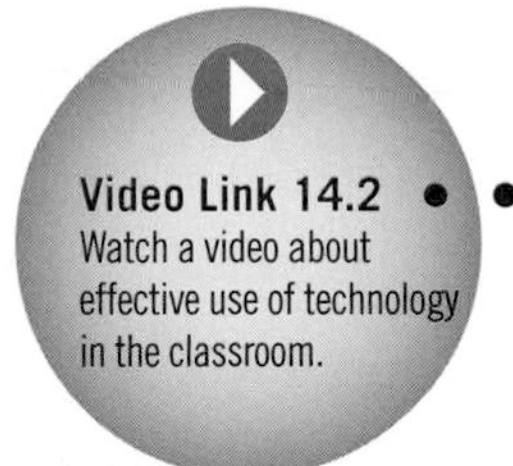

Additionally, the use of technology can be confounded by having equipment that is not in excellent working order or might be missing. Using technology in the classroom requires considerable preplanning. Teachers who are new to how necessary equipment can be accessed and are unfamiliar with the use of the equipment must engage in considerable fieldwork and practice prior to integrating technology into lessons. Nothing can make students lose interest faster than technology that isn't working.

Students Using Technology for Learning

Technology transforms learning in the way it transcends classroom walls and brings information to the learner. Whether the school of the future is just around the corner or not depends on teachers who integrate technology in teaching and use technology to enhance learning and student achievement. The North Central Regional Educational Laboratory (NCREL) Blue Ribbon Panel of 2004 came to the conclusion that a continued integration of technology will transform education. However, it is unlikely that this hoped-for integration of technology will occur unless teachers make the effort to truly bring technology to the classroom. To this end, the use of technology in educational settings is now focused on how to use technology for instructional purposes and to improve student learning (Salpeter, 2003). Teachers must anticipate and be able to deal with a two-way flow of information in the classroom.

Using technology in the classroom is a team sport. No member of the class should be only a spectator. It is likely that the students will be more capable of coping with the technology in the classroom than the teacher. In the same ways that a smart teacher shares power with the students through designating student helpers and leaders, students can be given responsibility for the use and care of classroom technology tools. Students can prove extremely resourceful in straightening out glitches in computer use. I use technology in my teaching, but whenever there is a problem, it is a student in my class who knows exactly where to click or why a screen isn't popping up the way I want it to. Your future students will truly be technology natives. It is always important for teachers to listen to their students, and no less so regarding the uses of technology.

Presentations and Research

Even very young students can prepare digital presentations to share with their classmates. Developing presentation skills helps students to focus on the critical details of a topic, to present a solid argument, and to summarize information in concise forms. Students should be constantly involved in collecting and organizing information, accessing and compiling lists of resources, or inserting video clips to illustrate details of their chosen topics. Sometimes the best way to learn a thing is to teach it.

Evaluation of student work should also emphasize these details; otherwise, the student research presentation can become a cut-and-paste exercise. In order for students to think about technology as a learning tool and not just one to use for personal pleasure, they will have to use the technology to learn, not just watch the teacher use it to teach.

Student Work Samples

How did you keep track of your progress through your teacher education course work? Formerly, cumbersome, paper portfolios were required as summative evidence of a teacher education candidate's achievement. Most likely you are now expected to keep an electronic record of meeting each standard and goal set forth by your college and state licensing agency. There are a variety of ePortfolio programs available for organizing, assessing, and presenting work. Chalk and Wire's ePortfolio at **http://www.chalkandwire.com** allows students to create, maintain, and showcase their work. Folio by ePortaro at **http://www.eportaro.com** is advertised as a cradle-to-career portfolio tool.

Maybe at the time you compiled your ePortfolio you considered the activity of keeping a record of your progress just one more hurdle before graduation, with the thought that once you'd done it you could put it behind you. Not so. Your skill in establishing a personal electronic record will be put to use in helping your own students set up electronic portfolios of their assignments and assessments over time. Visit **http://www.lasw.org/resources_stuwork.html** for many examples of student work websites. When students know their work will be published in a public venue, they are inclined to take greater pains in making certain it is correct.

Learning My Way on My Time

Technology is making it possible for students at all levels to be able to go to school without ever leaving home. No more waiting for the bus. No traffic jams to blame for tardiness. No more stress over bad hair or what to wear. For some online students it's roll out of bed and turn on the computer. For example, American education is experiencing a fast-growing trend in high school online education. Suggestions for making a virtual high school successful for administrators, teachers, and students include leaving the heavy technology task of maintaining servers to another company, carrying out continuous evaluations of programs and progress, offering interactive courses that are easy for both instructors and students to negotiate, and setting the bar high and keeping it there. It takes a dedicated student to be successful in online courses. Such students have to assume responsibility for their own learning and to engage with their instructors, the other students in the course, and the content. Possibly the best candidates for a virtual education are ones who enjoy learning, who like to solve problems, and who enjoy reading and learning independently.

The virtual high school distance education program in the Clark County School District of Nevada provides interactive online courses, televised instruction, and DVDs/videotapes. Courses can be taken from any location, providing the student has access to the required technology. All classes are curriculum based and meet or exceed the standards established by the Nevada Department of Education. Students can enroll full time and earn a high school diploma from home.

Distance education can also expose students to ideas and content they cannot access in their local community. For example, in Center, Colorado, physics is offered to students with no local physics teacher, and in Amman, Jordan, and Alaska students take a geometry course previously unavailable to them. The University of Maine supports online learning for high school students who live in remote areas and who otherwise would have little opportunity to take calculus and statistics classes that prepare them for attendance at major universities. The possibilities for online learning are infinite.

Table 14.2 Technology and Some of Its Functions in Teaching and Learning

Technology	Function
E-mail	Connectivity among teachers, students, and parents
Web log (blogs)	A place to record ideas, experiences, and challenges; also a communications tool
Podcasts Odeo.com	Build communities of teachers with common interests
Search engines and encyclopedias	Assist teachers in finding accurate, relevant, and useful information
WebQuests	Provide access to teacher-guided research and inquiry-based instruction
Rubistar at Rubistar.4teachers.org	Rubric-building tool for assessing student work
Delicious at del.icio.us	Social bookmarking tool to tag sites appropriate for assignments
Skype Skype.com	Worldwide voice and visual communication through an Internet-connected computer

HOW CAN TEACHERS MANAGE THE USE OF TECHNOLOGY AND USE TECHNOLOGY TO MANAGE THE CLASSROOM?

According to Ms. Dale, teachers should monitor technology to make it work for everyone involved. Stay close to your students so you can see at a glance what they are doing. Having them work in pairs on computers encourages cooperative learning, and it also makes it easier to see and hear how the students are using the technology.

Teachers' work has always been complex and complicated. Teachers must discern the personalities and abilities of a new group of students each year. They must evaluate the academic growth each student achieves. They must make decisions regarding student achievement and then weigh these decisions against future demands and possibilities. They must keep parents abreast of their children's progress and school expectations for student achievement and behavior. They must learn new teaching methods and programs that are touted to improve student learning. If they are lucky, training is offered to help them learn how to use the new programs effectively. When no training accompanies new programs, teachers rely on one another to help make the curriculum the students must learn meaningful and educative. It is, after all, the teacher who makes learning possible. Technology can help teachers spend more time on instruction and less time on management. Table 14.2 provides a sample of websites that can help teachers become more effective.

Managing the Use of Technology

Some schools and classrooms are technologically rich. Other schools and classrooms may not contain the technology you have become accustomed to using. Some school systems have excellent connectivity for "Skype-ing" around the globe and accessing the Internet, while other schools may have a minimum of connectivity, if any. Regardless of what is available in individual classrooms, teachers have a responsibility to see that the equipment is maintained in good working order and always ready for use. Just as a pilot completes a check of equipment and operations before taking off with a plane full of passengers, teachers should complete a check of any technology they plan to use for instruction before the actual lesson.

Regardless of the age of the available technology or what it can do, there are guidelines for using technology for instructional purposes that every teacher should follow. The checklist below will help any teacher make integrating technology in instruction a plus rather than a frustrating, time-wasting experience.

- Is the equipment ready to be used? (Have you tried it yourself to make certain it is in good working order and that it will not stop in the middle of the lesson?)
- Are directions for student use of the equipment available? (Are they posted near the equipment? Have you gone over them with the students?)
- Does the program to be run fit within the time limit you have set for the lesson? (Have you previewed the program from start to finish?)
- Will students be able to run the program without assistance? (If not, who will assist them?)
- If you are planning to access the Internet, do you know the content of the webpage?
- Are you sure all of the links you plan to use are available?
- Do all the students who need it have visual or physical access to the technology?
- Are follow-up activities to the lesson communicated to the students?

Taking care of the technology that makes learning more engaging should not take time away from instruction. In Chapter 12 you learned about the benefit of teaching the students classroom rules and routines. Students can just as easily learn their role in caring for the technology in the classroom. Remember that even a six-year-old can manipulate applications on a cell phone or program a DVR.

Technology for Managing the Classroom

Audio Link 14.3
Learn more about using technology in the classroom.

Technology can make managing the classroom a breeze. Paperwork is kept to a minimum, and information is processed and stored without the teacher having to worry about losing data that is supposed to make its way to the central office. Any teacher can develop an electronic format for keeping track of student information. Spreadsheets can be filled out by students at the beginning of the day and entered into a database by an aide, a parent helper, or even a student helper. Teachers and students can keep in touch during the day through Twitter or e-mail. Don't laugh. Twitter or e-mail communication may cut down on interruptions from students when the teacher is working with a small group or with a single student. Teachers often require that students with burning questions ask them of other students in the classroom before they ask the teacher. Putting the question on e-mail would be one additional step in thinking through the question and perhaps coming up with an answer before requiring the teacher's assistance.

Teachers have to keep track of books, supplies, borrowed resources, and schedules. Amazingly, teachers have the capacity to keep all of that information stored in a special part of the brain teachers have for miscellaneous information. Even though teachers can come up with all the right answers at the right times, it would be comforting to know that the information was stored somewhere else and that it could be accessed by other people without the teacher having to stop what he was doing or thinking about to find a specific piece of information within a well-developed teacher cognitive framework. Computer programs provide great storage places for documents and information. And, when they are connected to a printer, a clean copy of any document can be produced even if the first one had someone's lunch spilled on it.

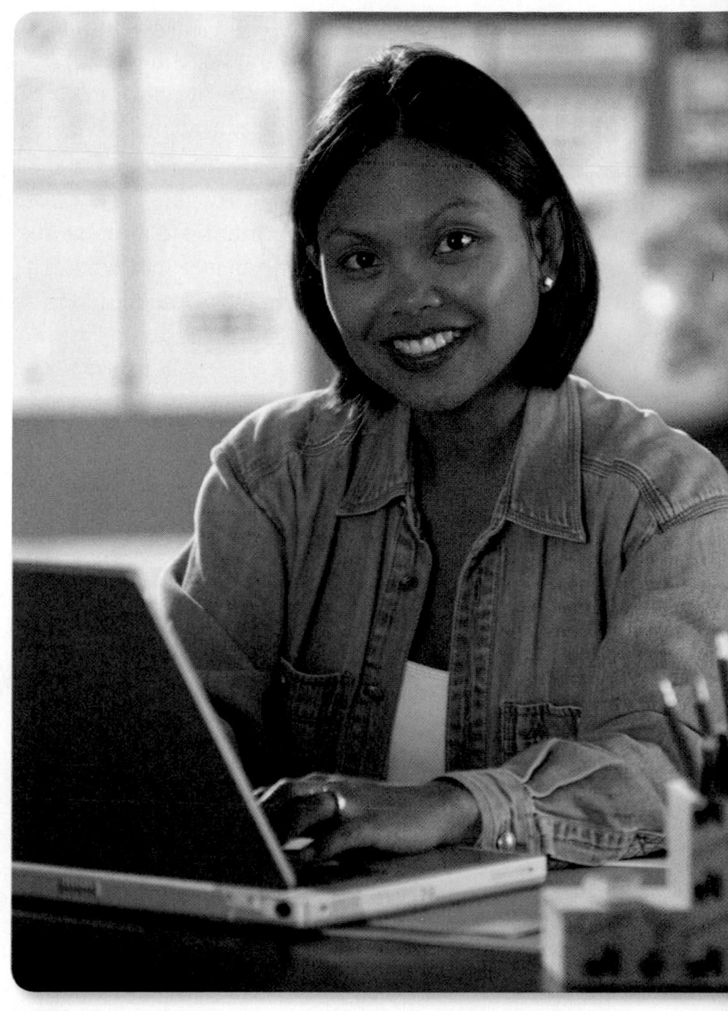

Teachers preparing for National Board certification can access the Internet to help them create records of their professional growth.

Creating a Technology-Rich Learning Environment

Most teachers give a great deal of thought to how their classrooms will be arranged. Creating a technology-rich learning environment should be part of that planning. Creating spaces that are rich in sound and visual experiences is no problem with technology. If a fish tank or pets are not allowed in classrooms, screen savers can provide scenes that are visually calming. A required text for your grade level can be saved electronically on individual tablets and notebooks. Students can read the text aloud to one another or quietly to themselves. No more, "I can't find my book!" when students own their personal copies of study material.

Music can be anywhere the teacher wants it to be. MP3 player docking stations can add a dimension of soothing baroque strains to calm the wiggliest students. A teacher might keep a digital camera available for students to take pictures of meaningful moments, within guidelines of course. There should be areas in each classroom for play, for meetings, and for contemplation. With a little imagination and help from technology, even the smallest classroom can provide productive learning space for all of the students.

HOW CAN TEACHERS INTEGRATE TECHNOLOGY INTO THEIR OWN PROFESSIONAL DEVELOPMENT?

It is not uncommon for first-year teachers to spend most of their efforts managing the day-to-day duties of teaching. Ideas for professional development or keeping a record of professional accomplishments take a backseat to learning curriculum standards and helping students raise their achievement to meet district and state criteria. If you are in the process of constructing a professional portfolio, you already have a start toward using technology for your own professional development. Your next steps should be directed toward meeting specific criteria for teacher performance. The website for the National Board for Professional Teaching Standards has a Twitter feed and a Facebook link to help you keep abreast of ways teachers are using technology to create a record of their professional growth.

Audio Link 14.4
Listen to a clip about technology in the classroom.

Educational Technology Standards for Teachers

The International Society for Technology in Education (ISTE) has developed a set of standards for effectively integrating technology into the classroom. These standards, the National Educational

Technology Standards for Teachers (NETS-T), focus on preservice teacher education and define the fundamental concepts, knowledge, skills, and attitudes for applying technology in educational settings. All candidates seeking certification or endorsements in teacher preparation should meet these educational technology standards.

The instructors at your institution are responsible for making sure that you have had the opportunity to meet the six NETS-T Standards. Table 14.3 lists NETS-T's six standards areas with performance indicators. The standards are specific enough to define the broad goals of using technology in educational settings, yet general enough to allow for a comfortable fit with local circumstances.

Visit the National Educational Technology Standards for Teachers website at **http://www.iste.org/standards.aspx** to learn more about the performance indicators for teachers. These performance indicators will give you a better understanding of what will be expected of you once you begin teaching.

Table 14.3 Educational Technology Standards and Performance Indicators for All Teachers

I. Technology Operations and Concepts
Teachers understand technology operations
• Teachers possess the knowledge and skills necessary to use technology
• Teachers increase their knowledge and skill in using technology to stay abreast of changes in technologies
2. Planning and Designing Learning Environments and Experiences
Teacher use technologies in instruction
• Teachers use technology enhanced lessons to meet the needs of all students
• Teachers use current research on technology in instruction when planning lessons
• Teachers evaluate the accuracy and suitability of technology resources
• Teachers develop plans for managing the technology and for managing student use of technology
3. Teaching, Learning, and the Curriculum
Teachers maximize student learning by using technology methods and strategies
• Teachers address content standards and student technology standards in their instruction
• Teachers use technology to address the needs of all students
• Teachers encourage problem solving and creativity through the use of technology
• Teachers use technology to manage student learning

4. Assessment and Evaluation
Teachers use technology to assess and evaluate student learning
• Teachers use technology in a variety of assessment techniques
• Teachers use technology to analyze data from student learning and to use such data to improve practice and student learning
• Teachers evaluate student's use of technology
5. Productivity and Professional Practice
Teachers use technology for their own professional development
• Teachers use technology for life-long learning
• Teachers use technology to improve their practice and to increase their knowledge of ways technology can support student learning
• Teachers use technology to become more productive
• Teachers use technology to communicate for the improvement of student learning
6. Social, Ethical, Legal, and Human Issues
Teachers understand the many issues involved in using technology in PreK 12 schools.
• Teachers model and teach the legal and ethical use of technology
• Teachers use technology resources to help all students learn
• Teachers use technology resources to affirm the diversity of all students
• Teachers use technology resources in a safe and healthy manner
• Teachers make sure that all students have equitable access to technology resources

Source: Adapted from the NETS for Teachers website, http://www.iste.org/standards/nets-for-teachers.

Using the Internet for Professional Development

You know that everyone learns at a different pace and through different stimuli. Your development as a teacher will also take its own path and move forward at a pace that you choose and are comfortable with. The online learning opportunities for professional development will allow you to choose when and what you learn. When you do chose an online learning environment, Levin, Waddoups, Levin, and Buell (2001) suggest you look for (1) relevant and challenging assignments, (2) coordinated learning environments, (3) adequate and timely feedback from instructors, (4) rich environments for student-to-student interaction, and (5) flexibility in teaching and learning. It's no surprise that these are the same characteristics you should strive for in any lesson you plan to teach.

UNDERSTANDING AND USING EVIDENCE

Impact of Increased Computer Use in Classrooms

The December 2005/January 2006 issue of *Educational Leadership* (2005/2006) was devoted to an examination of learning in the digital age. Numerous statistic sources cited in this issue provide evidence of the increase of student access to and use of computers in classrooms. The National Center for Education Statistics (http://nces.ed.gov/) provided the following percentages of U.S. students who used computers in school in 2003:

- 97% of high school students,
- 95% of middle school students,
- 91% of students in grades 1–5,
- 80% of kindergarten students, and
- 67% of nursery school students.

In this same issue of *Educational Leadership,* the South Central Regional Technology in Education Consortium reported frequency of classroom technology use by percentage.

Electronic presentation:	81%	Web editors:	36%
Word processing:	68%	Spreadsheets:	6%
Internet:	50%	Databases:	<1%
Publishing:	40%	E-mail:	<1%

The data are based on observations and teacher self-reports in 10 low-income middle and high schools (Burns, 2005/2006).

Your Task

So what's happening here? Are today's schools well equipped to educate students for success in the digital age? Do you see any problems that might be lurking in the data? Is the focus on computer use in schools the direction in which educators should be headed as they prepare students for the future?

Educators are inundated with megabytes of information regarding the state of teaching and learning. Most of these bytes are designed to alert and amaze the reader and often to prompt some sort of action that will respond

Most education websites contain professional development links. The professional development link on the *Education World* website at **http://www.education-world.com/** is a rich source of opportunities to manage your own professional development. Many school districts also offer online professional development sites to aid teachers in learning new skills and improving the ones they already possess. One example of an online professional development site is the "lifelong learning" website of Jefferson County Public Schools. As you get closer to the end of your teacher education course work, check out the websites of the school districts you intend to apply to and see what offerings are available for professional development.

to the information. The evidence that can be gleaned from the data presented in in this chapter could lead a person to presume that all is quite well and good with the use of technology in today's classrooms. There are, however, some questions that you should consider from a review of the two sets of data.

1. U.S. students who used computers in school in 2003.
   - 97% of high school students,
   - 95% of middle school students,
   - 91% of students in grades 1–5,
   - 80% of kindergarten students, and
   - 67% of nursery school students.
2. Frequency of classroom technology use by percentage.

Electronic presentation:	81%	Web editors:	36%
Word processing:	68%	Spreadsheets:	6%
Internet:	50%	Databases:	<1%
Publishing:	40%	E-mail:	<1%

3. Average expenditure of $103 per pupil for educational technology.

Is it more important for high school students to use technology than elementary school students?

Should the use of word processing in classrooms be higher than 68%?

Why is use of the Internet at a low 50%? Is it possible that teachers do not include the resources on the WWW in lessons?

What benefit do students receive from the $103 spent on educational technology?

What other technology tools besides computers and the accompanying software should schools be investing in for student learning? Marc Prensky (2005) says that "one of the most important tools for 21st century students is not the computer that we educators are trying so hard to integrate, but the cell phone that so many of our schools currently ban." Students already know this.

Data provide us with starting points to think about teaching and learning. Data should never be taken as the final word.

Source: Prensky, M. (2005). Listen to the natives. *Educational Leadership, 63*(4), 12.

Using Technology for Self-Improvement

Everyone has a blind spot. Even teachers! There is something they don't see about themselves, something in their manner of teaching that they are not aware of, content that they do not properly or adequately present, comments that they make that are unnecessarily harsh. Who will point out your flaws? Your mother is certainly not going to sit in the classroom every day and watch you teach, and even if she did, she might not be aware of the nuances of teaching or the content. Someone not afraid to tell you the truth might be hard to find. Technology is your answer. The hard truth of a videotape viewed in solitude can help you see the changes you need to make, the habits you need to break, and the outstanding acts you need to repeat. Watching yourself teach a lesson can be a startling and educative experience. You won't be able to do it without the use of technology.

CONNECTING TO THE CLASSROOM

Using technology in teaching is not necessarily a new idea. What is novel to many teachers though is making a transition from telling, explaining, and demonstrating to helping students find information on their own from a worldwide resource pool, and then assisting the students in explaining and demonstrating what they have learned. This requires a huge shift in defining a teacher's purpose in a classroom of the 21st century. For some it is a slow, often painful process. Here are three major points to think about when establishing your own personal–professional philosophy of becoming an effective teacher in the information age.

1. Learn to ask divergent questions that will encourage students to consider possibilities rather than pat answers.
2. Listen to the questions that students ask and extend those questions rather than provide answers.
3. Teach as though tomorrow is a mystery and the students are as much a part of solving the mystery as you are. Be like Watson and Sherlock Holmes. Search for clues and rely on one another.

SUMMARY

Four major topics have been addressed in this chapter:

- The role that technology plays in our lives and the impact it can have on teachers and learners is discussed through the ever-present need for humans to communicate.
- There are many ways that technology can be integrated into teaching.
- Technology can help diminish the challenge of keeping ahead of student work, record keeping, and reports that are all part of the profession, providing the teacher more time to focus on instruction.
- Keeping track of one's accomplishments as a professional can be facilitated through technology.

CLASS DISCUSSION QUESTIONS

1. Is it possible that anyone beginning a teaching career in the 21st century would not have some skills in using technology? Why would this be possible? Why not?
2. In what ways might a beginning teacher help create technology-rich learning environments in a school setting where there is little use of technology?

3. How might teachers support one another in the integration of technology in instruction? How might students support their teachers?
4. Why should all teachers commit to using technology for their own professional development from their first day as a new teacher?

SELF-ASSESSMENT

WHAT IS YOUR CURRENT LEVEL OF UNDERSTANDING AND THINKING ABOUT USING TECHNOLOGY TO IMPROVE STUDENT LEARNING?

One of the indicators of understanding is to examine how complex your thinking is when asked questions that require you to use the concepts and facts introduced in this chapter.

Answer the following questions as fully as you can. Then use the Complexity of Thinking rubric to self-assess the degree to which you understand and can use the ideas presented in the chapter.

1. Why should teachers develop skill in using a wide range of technologies?
2. How can using technology in teaching help students have learning experiences beyond the classroom walls?
3. What issues might the integration of technology in instruction create among teachers and learners?
4. How might teachers use technology to advance their professional growth?

What is your current level of understanding? Rate yourself using this rubric.

Complexity of Thinking Rubric

	Parts & Pieces	Unidimensional	Organized	Integrated	Extensions
Indicators	Elements/concepts are talked about as isolated and independent entities.	One or a few concepts are addressed, while others are underdeveloped.	Deliberate and structured consideration of all key concepts/ elements.	All key concepts/ elements are included in a view that addresses interconnections.	Integration of all elements and dimensions, with extrapolation to new situations.
Using technology to improve student learning	Names some programs and reasons for using technology in teaching.	Describes basic uses of technology but not in relationship to learning.	Describes multiple ways technology can be integrated in teaching.	Describes ways technology can be integrated in teaching for various purposes.	Describes ways uses of certain technologies can influence student achievement.

STUDENT STUDY SITE

Visit the Student Study Site at **www.sagepub.com/hall** to access links to the videos, audio clips, and Deeper Look reference materials noted in this chapter, as well as additional study tools including eFlashcards, web quizzes, and more.

Field Guide

for Learning More About Using Technology to Improve Student Learning

• • • • •

In Chapter 1 you were introduced to the concept of a field guide for learning more about your surroundings. The artifacts and information you will collect for this part of your field guide will involve the evidence of technology in the schools and classrooms that you visit during your teacher education program. Remember, also, to collect pictures and samples. A picture can be worth a thousand words.

Ask a Teacher or Principal

Teachers have different learning styles and preferences just as their students do. Ask a teacher what technology she uses on a regular basis and why. Ask her when she was introduced to the technology and to explain how she learned it. Do teachers at the school where she teaches share their expertise in the use of technology?

Make Your Own Observations

Join a department meeting as the teachers plan lessons for the following weeks. Note how often the teachers refer to the use of technology as they plan these lessons. Do they use technology to plan the lessons? After the planning session, visit one of the teachers' classrooms to see how technology is used in instruction.

Classrooms usually contain a variety of technology for teacher use. Make a list of the technology tools in two classrooms. Remember to include all types of technology (e.g., listening station, tape recorder, TV, metronome, overhead projector, computer, record player). Indicate whether the technology is being used by the teacher, the students, or no one. After comparing your two lists, make an inference about each teacher's comfort level with technology. What conditions that you observed in the classrooms might either facilitate or inhibit the use of technology?

Reflect Through Journaling

One of the reasons people give for becoming teachers is the desire to enter a field where their creative talents can be expressed. Write in your journal about ways you want to express your creative spirit in the classroom and how you might be able to do this through the integration of technology. Include how viewing the ways other teachers integrate technology into their teaching might give you ideas for integrating technology into your own future lessons.

Build Your Portfolio

Take three pictures of a child or young person engaged in some activity. This could be your own child or the child of a friend. Remember to get the child's permission and explain what your intentions are. Show the pictures to the individual and ask him or her to tell you what he or she is doing or thinking. Develop a PowerPoint presentation of the pictures with excerpts from the person's comments. Summarize the PowerPoint by reflecting on what the pictures may have helped the person notice about his or her actions and thoughts, and what you learned about the person through the process. Comment on the ways this reflection provides evidence of your understanding of the

Interstate New Teachers Assessment and Support Consortium (InTASC) Principles 3 and 4 introduced in Chapter 1 of this text.

Read a Book

The Future of Ideas: The Fate of the Commons in a Connected World, by Lawrence Lessig (2001; New York, NY: Random House), proves a provocative look at the impact connectivity through the Internet will have on society, learning, and creativity. This interesting book covers a range of topics related to control of intellectual property.

Technology Integration for Meaningful Classroom Use: A Standards-Based Approach, by Katherine Cennamo, John Ross, and Peggy Ertmer (2009; Mason, OH: Cengage Learning, Inc.), is organized around the ISTE standards and can help future teachers integrate technology into instruction. It also helps teachers and learners navigate the constantly changing environment of technology.

Search the Web

The website **http://www.netc.org/classrooms@work**, maintained by the Northwest Educational Technology Consortium, provides four examples of ways teachers have successfully integrated technology into teaching. The examples range from applications in first grade to a ninth-grade research and analysis project. Visit this website, review the ways these four teachers have integrated technology into their teaching, and then write a short journal entry on how viewing the work of these teachers might give you ideas for integrating technology into your own future lessons.

For a detailed description of the transition from "sage on the stage" to "guide on the side," go to **http://proc.isecon.org/2008/3114/ISECON.2008.Saulnier.pdf**. Also, visit **https://flippedlearning.eduvision.tv/default.aspx** for a fast-paced look at a learner-centered classroom, to the tune of the "Flight of the Bumblebee."

Additional Web Resources for Support and Information

Digital Kids—**http://www.apple.com/education/digitalkids/**

Technology and Special Needs—**http://coe.nevada.edu/nstrudler/29332s.pdf**

ABCs of Web Site Evaluation—**http://Kathyschrock.net/abceval/ABC.PDF**

Net Wise Teens—**http://www.techlearning.com/db_aera/archives/TL/2002/08/netwise.html**

One Computer Classroom—**http://coe.nevada.edu/nstrudler/31142w.pdf**

ISTE Nets—**http://cnets.iste.org/teachers/**

Here are two links to Ms. Dale using the iPad applications for instruction:

http://www.showme.com/sh/?h=ruuBDxQ

http://www.screenchomp.com/t/3Yy3Bsrxwu

TEACHER INTERVIEW

Dr. Elliott Asp

Meet Dr. Elliott Asp, an assistant superintendent in the Cherry Creek (Denver, Colorado) School District. Dr. Asp has an unusual title: assistant superintendent for performance improvement. Usually assistant superintendents will be responsible for administration, curriculum and instruction, facilities, or finance. Dr. Asp's title reflects the high priority that his school district is placing on student learning. In fact, in his school district there are two assistant superintendents for performance improvement! He is in charge of curriculum, assessment, staff development, and instructional technology. The other assistant superintendent is in charge of supervision and evaluation of principals and teachers.

> I was hired here to change the system. The mission here is continuous improvement. No matter how good you are you can get better. Our job is to push the district in the direction of positive change.

Dr. Asp also is a nationally recognized expert in assessment of student learning. He has published many papers and is regularly sought after to assist school districts engaged in improving the assessment of student performance.

CHAPTER 15 Assessing Student Learning and Results

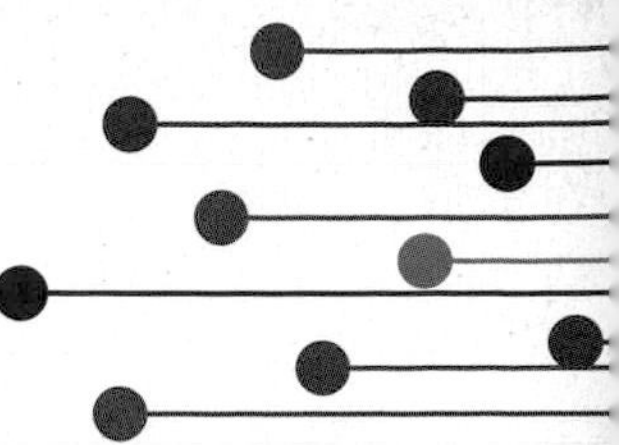

- ***What do you see as being important for teachers to know about assessment?***

The first thing teachers need is to have a firm understanding of the difference between formative and summative assessment. They need to understand how formative assessments can be used as a process to inform instruction and really improve student achievement. In the past teachers would be more focused on testing and "how do I give grades?" rather than on "how do I give meaningful feedback?" In particular, they need to see assessment as being broader than just a test or quiz.

What do you see as being the key differences between testing and assessing?

Testing is usually viewed as an event. For example, some sort of summative event that says we are going to see how you are at this point in time. I see formative assessment as much more of a process. The teacher is trying to get a handle on where kids are and where to go next with instruction. The teacher is seeing how much progress they have made over time in terms of achieving a goal. Testing is more of an event: "I do something and I am done, rather than charting progress and growth, and using the information to determine where I go next."

Do you see that secondary teachers can apply these ideas?

They are learning more about assessment too. In addition, they have to reeducate their students so that they understand and use formative assessments. Secondary students tend to come in thinking that all that is important is the grade, not what I learned. These students ask, "How come you are not grading this piece, just giving me feedback?" Secondary teachers not only have to learn the techniques (of formative assessment); they have to change the mind-set of the kids.

We use a book called *Mindset: The New Psychology of Success*, by Carol Dweck (2006). It deals with changing the mind-set of kids to a growth mind-set. It is not that you are either smart or dumb. The reason you do well is because you work hard.

What do you expect a first-year teacher to know and be able to do in relation to assessing student learning?

More than anything, I really want them to have at least some knowledge and skill in the area of a variety of ways of assessing, particularly in formative assessments. There are a variety of techniques, but they come down to two things: feedback and questioning. Feedback can take the form of teachers

Questions to Consider

1. If you were being interviewed for a teaching position by Dr. Asp, what questions would you expect him to ask?
2. What do you think he means when he says he expects teachers to "understand how formative assessments can be used as a process to inform instruction and really improve student achievement"?
3. Dr. Asp keeps talking about the differences between formative and summative; do you know what he is talking about?
4. What are your current ideas about how to give "meaningful feedback" to students? Is there more to it than providing test scores and grades?

giving feedback to students and thinking about how to do that in an effective and efficient way. Thinking about what effective feedback looks like and how do I manage that in a classroom. Second is the ability to ask questions that get at what kids are thinking and gets at it in a way that sets high expectations for all students. This is tricky since the way you ask questions and give feedback conveys high expectations.

How do you see joy in teaching?

That is a great question! You can see joy in teaching in several ways. First is in the relationships with kids and families. If you don't find joy in kids and developing relationships with their families, you probably are not going to be very happy in teaching. Another is in watching students grow both academically and personally. Also seeing teachers grow professionally. Seeing their skills improve and get better at handling various situations, whether they are academic growth of kids or how to motivate and get kids involved in more meaningful ways in classrooms. Also, teachers having support of colleagues and being part of professional learning communities, and where there is excitement about improving their practice.

We interviewed you for the last edition of this book; what have you learned since?

I have been giving a lot of thinking to how much time districts and the state spend on the annual testing. The tests are administered in the spring and the schools get the results back about time for the beginning of the new school year. If they spend more than September on the results it is a waste of time. In the end, they don't tell you a whole lot. Another point is how important formative assessment is in defining high-quality instruction.

Learning Outcomes

After reading this chapter, you should be able to

1. Understand the purposes and characteristics of formative and summative evaluations.
2. Identify the different ways to check on student learning.
3. Explain the difference between norm-referenced tests (NRTs) and criterion-referenced tests (CRTs).
4. Recognize what is entailed in using formative assessments to adjust instruction.
5. Know what RTI is and what role it has in improving student learning.

INTRODUCTION

Today's teachers cannot escape hearing, talking, and reading about testing and assessing. Teachers are told that assessing is a key component of all lesson plans. Curriculum and instruction experts constantly talk about assessing student learning. Teacher educators, as well as school district administrators like Dr. Asp, are constantly pointing out that good instruction involves high-quality teachers continually assessing their students and making adjustments in instruction. At the same time, school districts, state policymakers, and the federal government have mandated annual testing of students, and licensing tests for teachers. Policymakers and the media focus intently on test results and use the scores to rank schools, school districts, and states. Now there is increasing interest in using test scores to evaluate teachers.

So, what's all the fuss about? Teachers continually observe their students, evaluate their homework, give tests, and assign grades. Why do some people talk about *testing* and others seem to prefer the term *assessing*? The answer to these questions is found inside of three other questions. The first two important questions for aspiring teachers are, "What are different methods for assessing student work?" and "How do I determine grades and prepare report cards?" As important as each of these questions is, a third question is even more to the point: "How do I use the information about students' current level of understanding to adjust my instruction?" Each of these questions is addressed in this chapter. Highly effective teachers have the knowledge, skills, and understanding to address all three of these questions in their teaching.

WHY IS ASSESSING SO IMPORTANT?

> *We find a lot of confusion when teachers are giving benchmark tests two or three times a year, which tends to be more summative. This is different than having an ongoing process. Yes, the benchmarks can be used in a formative way, but they tend to be only used to make final judgments.*—Dr. Asp

Most school years begin with district and school-based staff meetings. One of the major topics will be how the district and each school did on the previous year's state mandated testing. The talk will include terms like *CRTs, NRTs,* and *cut scores.* Principals and teachers will ask: "Will we be using the same CRTs as last year?" "What about the NRTs that the district had us doing in January?" "You know, that is the real problem, the CRTs are performance based, while the NRTs are multiple choice. No wonder our test scores are not improving." NRTs? CRTs? Performance based? Many beginning teachers will have no idea what they are talking about!

Audio Link 15.1
Learn more about testing and assessment.

Teachers, administrators, policymakers, and parents talk a lot about testing and assessing. But it is not always clear that they are talking about the same things. There are very important differences to keep in mind. **Tests** are structured opportunities to measure how much the test taker knows and can do at a particular point in time. The test conditions should be consistent for all test takers, and there is an expectation that each individual will make a maximum effort. **Assessing** is the process that entails interpreting test results and developing a plan for what will be done next.

The Whys and Hows for Assessing

Teachers need to keep in mind why they are testing and/or assessing. Just because it is Friday does not necessarily mean that it is time for a test. There should be a clear understanding about the purpose of all assessment efforts. There are a number of reasons for assessing that will be of help to the teacher. Often forgotten is that there are a number of purposes for assessing that are of direct benefit to the students. Teachers need to think carefully about why they are assessing, and they need to pay particular attention to how the assessment activity will contribute to increasing further student learning.

A metaphor to illustrate these two important concepts is how property tax rates are determined. Every few years, the value of your home is reexamined. The potential sale price is estimated by comparing its value to like properties that had been sold recently. That price is similar to a student's score on a test. The tax assessor examines the property and its likely sale price, if it was for sale, and sets the amount of tax to be paid accordingly. Determining the final tax amount requires some interpretation and judgment. The tax bill is not a simple calculation; rather, the assessor takes into consideration a number of factors such as condition, trends in the neighborhood, and the amount of taxes paid for like properties.

A parallel process takes place in assessing student learning. The test score has little meaning until the assessor interprets it, compares the results to those obtained by students in similar and different situations, and takes into consideration the special needs of each student. The assessor then develops recommendations and plans for next steps for instruction.

Deeper Look 15.1
Read more about formative assessment.

Formative Versus Summative Assessments

An expert assessor also keeps in mind how the test results will be used. If the purpose is purely to provide feedback on student progress and to guide preparation of tomorrow's lessons, which is called **formative evaluation,** then there will be less concern about the rigor of the testing. When test results are used to make conclusions about how much a student has learned or to decide whether a student is ready to move to the next grade level, which is called **summative evaluation,** then the assessor must be much more careful in considering the quality of the test and the consequences of the final decision.

Teachers make formative decisions about student learning continually within each lesson and throughout the day. They also make summative decisions when they assign report card grades and at the end of the school year recommending promotion, or not. In most states, the results of mandated testing are used to make summative judgments about high school graduation, the ranking of schools, and teacher licensure.

Good teachers are always checking for student understanding through observation and listening to student discourse.

Purposes for Assessing

Within these two general ways of thinking about testing and assessing there are a number of different purposes. For each purpose the design of the assessment is different, but each must have an acceptable level of quality, given understanding of how the results will be used. Also, the type of learning being assessed is associated with certain kinds of assessments being more appropriate. An additional very important consideration is taking into account the characteristics of the students being assessed. For example, there is an obvious mismatch when English-language learners are given a mathematics word-problem test in English and their scores are treated the same as for those students whose native language is English.

Table 15.1 is a summary of purposes for assessing, along with examples. In reviewing this table you will see that there is a flow from top to bottom. The purpose of assessments at the top is formative, while for those at the bottom it is summative. At all times the primary aim for teachers is to determine the extent of student learning and to figure out next steps in instruction.

Table 15.1 Different Purposes for Testing and Assessing

	Type	Purpose	Examples
FORMATIVE ↓	Diagnosing readiness for learning	Finding out what they already know, and don't know, and whether they have the prerequisite knowledge and skills for an upcoming lesson; finding out if students have certain learning difficulties or skill deficiencies	A diagnosis indicating that students are not writing introductory sentences for paragraphs, or that when given a table of numbers most students cannot construct bar graphs correctly
	Checking for understanding within lessons	Continually checking for understanding during lessons	The Teacher-Question-Student-Answer strategy during a lesson, having students do a sample problem, having one or more students solve an example in front of the class, having students explain to each other how they solved a problem
	Checking for progress learning across lessons	Seeing what has been learned, retained, understood, and misunderstood from lesson to lesson	Reviews, "pop quizzes," homework assignments, online discussions, and submission of drafts
	Adjusting instruction	Monitoring to see the effects of adjustments in instruction within each lesson and across each day	Obtaining information about the current understanding of students, engaging in self-reflection, and thinking about what can be done next to improve student learning
	Assessing gains in student learning	Determining the amount of growth in student learning at the end of lessons, units, and terms	Teacher-made tests, grading of student reports, and major products
	Reporting progress	Providing grades to students and parents	Report cards, parent conferences
SUMMATIVE	Gatekeeping	Decisions about pass/fail, promotion/retention	End-of-term grades, scores on district and state standardized tests

Considering the Quality of Assessments

Careful and thorough assessment work is absolutely necessary when it is time to report progress or to make gatekeeping decisions. Even though talking about it makes us feel uncomfortable, a reality today is that much of the testing that is being done by school districts, states, schools, and teachers is for the purpose of sorting students. Students are not being allowed to advance to the next level of schooling (e.g., middle school to high school) unless they pass a test. **No Pass No Play** policies prohibit students from participating in sports and band unless they maintain a certain grade point average (GPA). And teacher education candidates cannot become licensed to teach unless they pass a state-mandated licensure exam. When tests are used to gatekeep there is likely to be little room for interpretation or accommodation of special situations or unique individual differences. Instead there is **high-stakes testing**, where the score on the test is the determinant for passage to the next level.

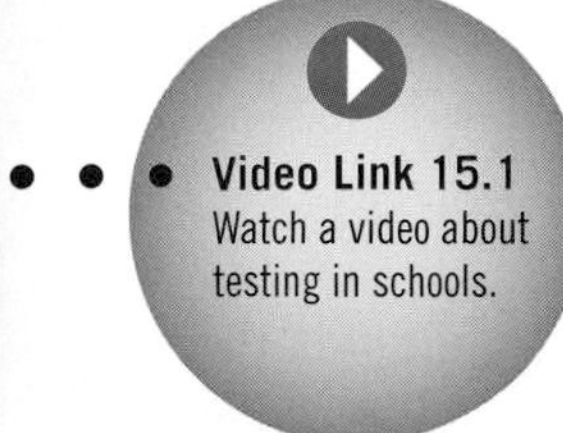

Video Link 15.1
Watch a video about testing in schools.

One way to view the tensions between the purpose of the assessment and the quality of the test is presented in Figure 15.1. The left-hand side of the continuum signifies major teacher responsibility for the design of tests and the interpretation of the results. As your eyes move across the continuum from left to right the role of the teacher as test maker decreases, while expectations for test quality increase. A teacher-made test should not be used to make a high-stakes grade promotion or graduation decision. Note also that there should be multiple assessments employed for all purposes, especially in making gatekeeping decisions. This is one of the hotly debated issues in today's state and federal education policy environment, where frequently the score on a single test is used to make a high-stakes decision.

Teachers need to think through how the amount of rigor in their assessments compares with the weight of the decision being made. Assessing learning at the end of a unit requires more rigor than daily checking for understanding. Assessing learning for a semester or a year is an even larger responsibility requiring much more careful construction of the measure(s) and extensive consideration of how to interpret and report the results.

Teachers also need to make sure that the tests that they construct are closely based in the curriculum standards and benchmarks. Students doing well on a teacher-made test that has little correlation with the district and state standards will not be as helpful to the students or the teacher as will the measure that has a clear relationship to the standards and benchmarks.

Figure 15.1 Comparing Purposes and Quality of Assessments

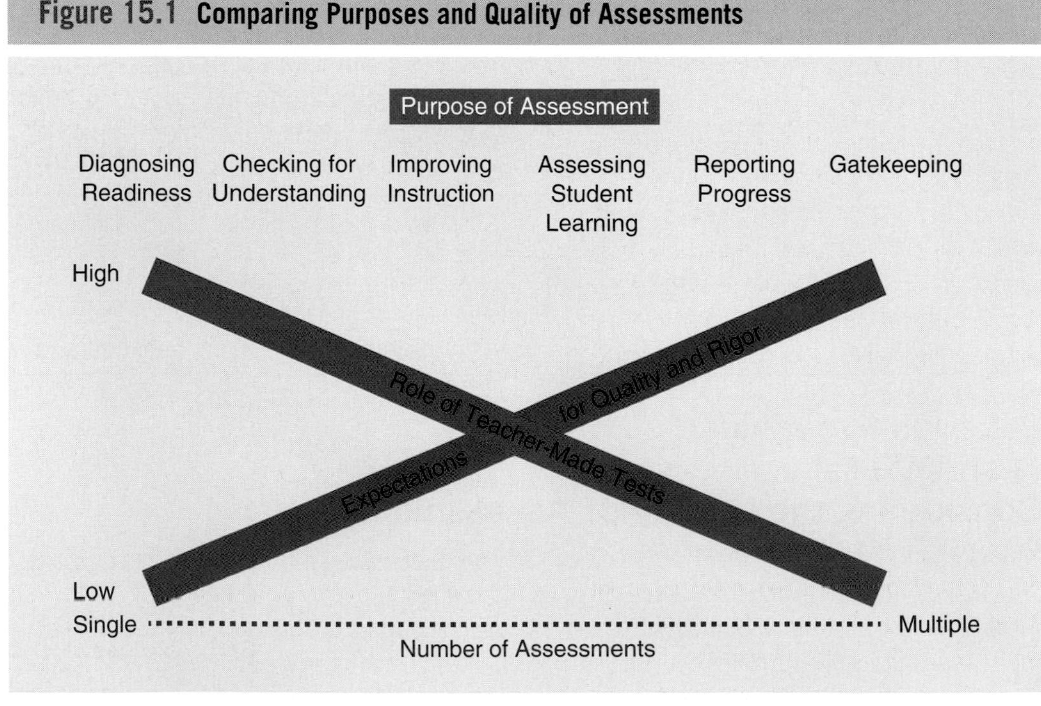

One important caution for teachers to keep in mind is that all of their assessments can face close scrutiny if someone initiates legal action. The legal action could come from a number of fronts. For example, a suit could be filed on behalf of a student where there is an indication of discrimination, or where there is parent disagreement about promotion. Another possibility for legal action arises when there is a belief that a particular test was not scored correctly or that the test used was not an appropriate estimate of the amount of student learning. In summary, it is very important for teachers to think carefully about each assessment activity and its purpose, and to keep careful documentation of all assessments.

Two Very Different Kinds of Tests

Whenever testing is done, one of the most critical decisions relates to how the resulting test scores will be compared. A test score by itself has no meaning. A student could have a test score of 33, or 5, or 357. The score does not make any sense until it is compared with something. One of the interesting and important parts of testing is determining which comparison to make. In today's schools two very different ways of comparing test scores are being used. One way to interpret the test score is to compare it with how other students did on the same test. The other way is to compare the score with a certain level of performance. Teachers need to understand these two very different ways of interpreting test results. Unfortunately, there is a great deal of confusion and misunderstanding about the two ways of thinking and their consequences.

Deeper Look 15.2
Read more about norm-referenced testing.

Norm-Referenced Tests (NRTs)

The most widely used and well-understood approach to comparing test scores is when the test score of one student is compared with the scores of other students. This is called a **norm-referenced test (NRT).** The comparison group for teacher-made tests is typically the other students in the class. For standardized tests and high-stakes tests the comparison group of test takers will be a large sample of similar students. The sample could be all other third-graders in the state, or a national sample of like students.

When all of these students take a well-designed test, the distribution of their scores will form a "normal" curve. If a perfect test score was 100, then the scores for all students would be distributed across the total possible range of test scores as is illustrated in Figure 15.2. Very few students would have extremely low or extremely high scores, and the one test score received by the highest number of students would be 50. The average, or "mean" test score for all students would be 50. Regardless of how the comparison group is assembled, in norm-referenced testing one student's test score is compared with the scores of other students.

Figure 15.2 The Normal Curve: A Statistical Description of the Chance Distribution of Test Scores for a Theoretical Population

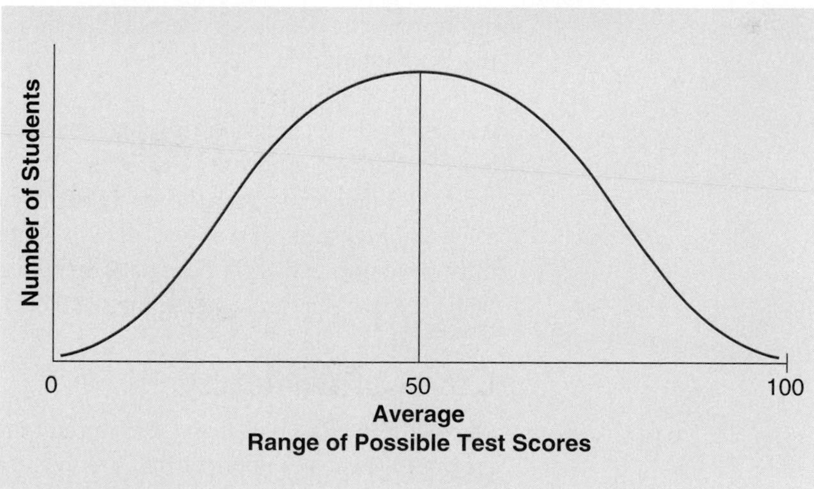

Criterion-Referenced Tests (CRTs)

An important alternative way to compare test scores is to identify a level of performance, a *criterion,* and then check to see if a particular student's score is above or below that level. As the name implies, with **criterion-referenced tests (CRTs),** each student's test score is

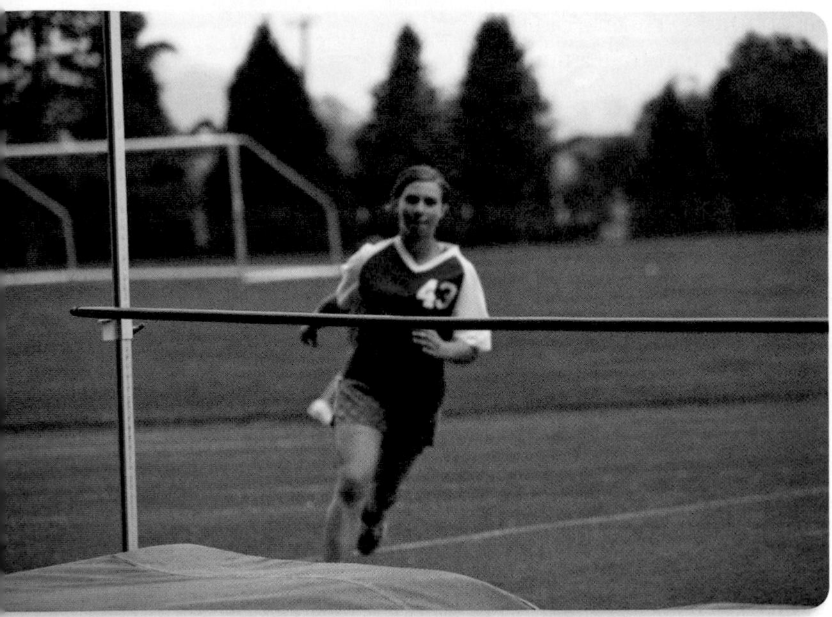

Criterion-referenced tests (CRTs) compare each student's level of performance with a particular level of accomplishment. Clearing the bar is what counts, not how other students do.

compared with a defined level of performance, rather than with how other students have done. This approach is particularly useful when student learning is being defined in terms of standards and benchmarks.

With CRTs the evaluation asks: Has the student attained the desired standard or benchmark? Rather than comparing the student's level of learning with how well a comparison group of students has done, the test result is compared with the level of learning stated in the benchmark or standard.

Comparing NRT and CRT Test Scores

Teachers, school leaders, and policymakers often confuse the two ways of thinking about test results. Some simple examples can be helpful in clarifying the differences between NRTs and CRTs. In high school track meets, one of the standard events is the high jump. Athletes run up to a horizontal bar and attempt to roll their body over the bar without knocking it off its brackets. In a norm-referenced view, the height that one athlete is able to clear would be compared with the heights reached by a sample of other students. If the average 10th-grade girl can clear 48 inches and Malinda cleared 60 inches, her performance is far above average. In the criterion-referenced view, a certain height would be set as the "benchmark," and if the student cleared that height that would be seen as success. Ralph cleared five feet, which was the minimum level of performance set for his age-group. This example is not used here to identify the "winner"; instead, this is a visual example to illustrate the different comparisons that are made in norm-referenced and criterion-referenced testing.

Characteristics of Effective Assessments

Test and assessment experts have identified several criteria that teachers should use when considering the selection and uses of assessments developed by others and in making their own. For example, one important question is, how hard should the assessment be? If the test is too easy then it will not discriminate between those students who know a lot and those that have limited understanding. However, a test that is too difficult will lead to student frustration and the teacher having little information about how much students have learned. Another important characteristic of good assessments is that they are related clearly to the desired learning outcomes, that is, the standards.

Addressing these characteristics of good tests is why a driving license test has a written part and a **performance** part (driving a car with an observer/evaluator). Knowing the meaning of rules of the road is important. So is the ability to drive the car on the right side of the road and to drive safely in heavy traffic. Having only a written test would not be credible. Aspiring license holders must demonstrate that they can perform by driving. (This is a good example of an **authentic task.** The task directly relates to the standard.)

Level of Difficulty

One of the biggest challenges for expert test makers and teachers is developing test items that are not too easy, and not too hard. A test can be too difficult for many reasons. If the assessment includes words that the students don't know, or if an activity or diagram is not clear, then students will do poorly. They may know the information, but they do not understand how to show it. Of course, there also are the tests that ask students about information that was not covered in class, projects, readings, or other assignments. Many beginning teachers are concerned that all of the students might get high grades on a test and therefore *As*. To prevent this from happening they may make test items too complicated or difficult. In these situations the teacher has not thought about the reason for the assessment. Is it to check for understanding (i.e., formative)? Or is it to determine the amount of learning, or to determine a final grade (i.e., summative)?

"Yes, I'm counting off for misspelling. We're having a spelling test."

Validity

Another important characteristic of tests is that they measure what is intended, in other words **validity.** The first way to judge validity is to look at the items/tasks that students must do. Do these look like they are related to the standards, benchmarks, and learning objectives? For example, if the learning outcome has to do with reading comprehension and the test does not ask students to read, there is a clear need to question the validity of the test. A test of students' ability to multiply and divide probably should not be done with a handheld calculator. Having students in marching band play the music without looking at the sheet would be a direct and valid test if the criterion was that the music be memorized. In constructing test items take time to look them over and ask, is what I am asking the student to do in this test clearly representative of the learning objective?

Reliability

Another important characteristic of tests has to do with whether or not the test scores for students who seem to be similar in their learning are similar, in other words **reliability.** Test reliability is important for teachers to consider when they plan to use the same test with different classes. The high school history teacher may want to use the same test item with different classes. Or the elementary teacher may use last year's test with this year's students. Or two teachers may use the same test. A highly reliable test should provide similar results from similar students. There is a problem when two groups of students score dramatically different on the same test! The question then confronting the teacher(s) is, was the same material covered with each set of students, or is there something wrong with the test, that is, a question of test reliability?

Deeper Look 15.3
Learn more about validity and reliability.

Performance Tasks

Another characteristic of good assessments is asking for student performance, in other words doing an activity rather than only a mental exercise. When the assessment is based in students applying their learning through accomplishing an activity there is greater certainty that they really have learned the benchmark and standard. This emphasis on performance is built into the descriptions of most standards and benchmarks. Actually, these descriptions can be very helpful to teachers who are constructing their own assessments. Visualizing the actions that students can do when they have learned the material can lead to assessment tasks that require them to demonstrate through action what they have learned.

Authentic

Assessment tasks that are clearly related to the benchmarks and standards, as well as to real-world applications, are called *authentic*. It is much easier for students to demonstrate what they have learned when the tasks are related to the student's background and world experiences. There are many disturbing examples of assessments that were not authentic such as asking low-income students in the desert southwest to write about a white Christmas. Teachers, as well as commercial test makers, must be extremely careful in constructing assessment tasks to make sure that they are not assuming background and context that has not been a part of the knowledge and experience of the students being assessed.

Assessing for Different Types of Learning

Authentic performance tasks are based in the standards and benchmarks and also in real-world applications.

Up to this point our discussion of testing and assessing has addressed the different purposes, two ways of thinking (formative/summative), differences between NRTs and CRTs, and some of the characteristics of good assessments including asking for performance and using authentic tasks. What hasn't been addressed is the type of learning being assessed. There are a number of useful models that teachers can use for organizing and sorting the level and extent of student learning. One of the most widely used is *Bloom's Taxonomy of Educational Objectives Handbook I: Cognitive Domain* (Bloom, 1956). This taxonomy was developed as a way to describe different levels of learning, or **depths of knowledge (DOK).**

Bloom's taxonomy (see Table 15.2) provides a very useful set of categories for gauging the type of learning that is expected in assessment tasks. The taxonomy is equally useful for teachers and other test makers, as they think about the type of learning they want students to demonstrate when tests are being constructed. Asking students to provide facts and figures (Level I, Knowledge) is very different from asking students to use their knowledge of certain facts to solve a problem (Level III, Application). An even higher level of learning is required to provide reasoned judgment about the strengths and weaknesses associated with certain phenomena (Level VI, Evaluation). Of course Bloom's taxonomy has to be adjusted for the grade level and subject area being assessed. What would represent Analysis at seventh grade would not be the same for high school seniors or second-graders. Still, within each class all levels of Bloom's taxonomy can be applied in the construction of assessments and in making clear the expectations in objectives.

Accommodating Different Types of Learners

The final assessment topic to be introduced has to do with accommodating different types of learners and special needs students. An assessment that is perfect for middle-class suburban students may not be appropriate for urban poor students. The reverse may also be true; an

Table 15.2 The Six Levels of Bloom's Taxonomy of the Cognitive Domain

Level VI: Evaluation	Making judgments about the quality of a solution or solution to an issue or problem.
Level V: Synthesis	Using original thinking to develop a communication, make predictions, and solve problems for which there is not a single right answer.
Level IV: Analysis	Identify causes, reasons, or motives; analyze information to reach a generalization or conclusion; find evidence to support a specific opinion, event, or situation.
Level III: Application	Applying previously learned information to answer a problem. Using a rule, a definition, a classification system, or directions to solve a specific problem which has a correct answer.
Level II: Comprehension	Going beyond simple recall and demonstrating the ability to arrange and organize information mentally. Putting previously learned information into one's own words.
Level I: Knowledge	Using memory or senses to recall or reorganize information.

assessment that worked well with an urban high school English class may not make sense with a rural high school English class. And exceptional learners (see Chapter 3) must be considered in all assessment work. Two particularly important student learner populations that all teachers must consider are English-language learners (ELL) and special needs students.

Accommodating Special Needs Students

A particularly challenging problem for teachers as well as professional test makers is developing assessments that are appropriate for special needs students. Each student will have unique needs and is likely to have a tendency to do better with certain types of test situations. However, there is a legal distinction for students that have been formerly identified as having special needs. Students with *recognized* learning disabilities, physical handicaps, and other special needs will have an assigned school district team, including the parents, and an **individualized education plan (IEP).**

Video Link 15.2
Learn more about Bloom's Taxonomy.

A key component of each student's IEP will be information related to any **accommodations** that must be made in assessments. Accommodations are those adjustments that are made in order to ensure that a student with special needs is not placed in an unfair or disadvantageous situation for instruction or testing. In developing tests and with other assessments, the classroom teacher has a responsibility to be knowledgeable about any and all accommodations that have been specified in student IEPs.

In addition to whatever accommodation information is provided in a student's IEP, another readily accessible resource is each state's department of education website. A federal requirement is that each state will provide a list of acceptable accommodations. As an example, some of Pennsylvania's accommodations are presented as Table 15.3.

Always keep in mind that teacher initiative is a very important element in student success. Teacher initiative is important to student success in testing too. For example, one high school teacher had a student who did well with all assignments, but failed every test. The teacher reflected on

Table 15.3 Examples of Appropriate Testing Accommodations for Special Needs and English-Language Learner Students

Test Preparation
• Read directions to the student (reread as necessary).
• Use sign language or the student's native language to give directions or to simplify the directions. This may include American Sign Language or spoken English with sign support.
• Provide audiotape directions verbatim.
Test Administration
• Prompt the student to remain on task.
• Read test items (for Mathematics or Writing items only). (Do not read Reading test items.)
• Check periodically to make sure student is marking in correct spaces.
• Provide materials to students to mask portions of test to direct student's attention to specific areas.
• Provide materials to student to use colored stickers or highlighters for visual cues.
Test Response
• Allow student to answer questions orally (Mathematics and Reading only).
• Use enlarged answer sheets.
• Allow student to point to response.
• Allow student to answer on a typewriter or computer. (Turn off Spelling, Grammar Checker, and Thesaurus.)
Timing/Scheduling
• Increase or decrease opportunity for movement.
• Permit additional breaks or extended rest breaks for student during testing session.
• Increase test time.
Setting
• Allow student to use adaptive or special furniture, such as a study carrel.
• Test in a separate room or in a small group to reduce distractions.
• Test in a special education or bilingual classroom, if appropriate.
• Reduce stimuli (e.g., limit number of items on desk).
• Provide for reduced acoustical distraction.
Assistive Devices
• Allow augmentative communication systems or strategies, including letter boards, picture communication systems, and voice output systems. (No voice output for Writing.)
• Provide magnifier, large print, or Braille materials.
• Provide pencil grips.
Other Options
• Provide sign language interpreter, if necessary. (Mathematics and Reading only—no sign language output for Writing.)

Source: Testing Accommodations for the Pennsylvania System of School Assessment 2002–2003.

this discrepancy between consistent indications of achievement during instruction and the string of Fs on tests. The teacher called a parent to help in understanding what was happening. It seems that the student would freeze and not be able to read the test questions during formal test taking situations. The teacher then adjusted the test setting by presenting the test questions on audiotape and allowing the student extra time. From then on the student passed the tests.

Formal testing of student learning, especially for high-stakes decisions, must be done in secure and closely monitored settings.

Accommodating ELL Students

The accommodations examples presented in Table 15.3 also can be appropriate for ELL students. With their continually increasing number there is additional pressure on schools and school districts to do all that they can to assure a fair opportunity for ELL students to demonstrate what they have learned. Under No Child Left Behind (NCLB) 95% of all students, including ELL and those with special needs, must take the annual state tests. Much of the reasoning that states use in setting accommodations for ELL students is applicable in the classroom as well. For example, the New Mexico State Department of Education has identified a useful list of guidelines for making accommodations as long as they

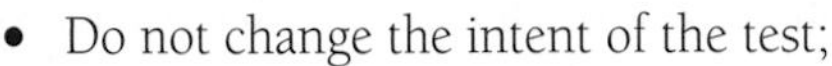

- Do not change the intent of the test;
- Do not change the purpose of the test;
- Do not change the content of the test;
- Do not provide the student with an unfair advantage;
- Continue to allow the testing contractor to be able to score the test;
- Do not violate test security; and
- Do not change the focus of what is being assessed.

Each of these points is important for teachers to keep in mind as they develop their own assessments. Teachers have the responsibility of providing all students with the opportunity to fairly demonstrate what they have learned.

WHAT ARE SOME WAYS TO TEST STUDENT LEARNING?

I want to be looking at samples of student work and seeing how those are changing over time. I would look at whether students can apply what they are learning in different settings, including new and novel settings. I would be looking at how kids rate their own work and provide feedback to others about their work. How sophisticated their feedback is about writing or a project they are working on. These are indicators of the goals of the class and whether or not students' knowledge and understanding of these goals is increasing in meaningful ways.—Dr. Asp

Video Case 15.1
Checking for Understanding

1. Compare and contrast the different techniques used by two of the teachers to assess student understanding.
2. What is Ms. Dogancay's first priority in checking her students for understanding? What are the different types of learning that she is checking in the lab reports?

Testing has become a very important component of the work of teachers and students. Teachers must continually assess developing student understanding, and each year school districts and the state are testing students' learning in several subjects. An important message for beginning teachers is that from the very first day in the classroom they must have expertise in developing different types of tests. From the first day onward each of the purposes for assessing must be addressed. Within each lesson and across the school day teachers need to be engaged in informal assessing of each student. Across the weeks and semesters teachers must develop summative tests and report student grades. All of these activities are done in order to make adjustments in instruction and increase student learning. They also are done within the context of anticipation of the testing that the school district and state will require toward the end of the school year.

Checking for Understanding Within Lessons

When the term *testing* is used, don't think only of paper-and-pencil exams. That is why in this chapter we have used the term *assessments*. There are a variety ways to probe and examine student's understanding and the extent of their learning. Expert teachers continually assess by using informal ways before, during, and in follow-up to each lesson. For example, when teachers employ the all too familiar "Q&A" tactic during a lesson their intent is to use short questions that require lower-level (Bloom's taxonomy Levels I and II) student responses as a way to spot-check understanding across a number of students.

Some of the ways to check for understanding within a lesson are summarized in Table 15.4. Most certainly as a student you have experienced all of these at one time or another. The reason for summarizing them here is to refresh your memory about the variety of ways that teachers can easily appraise how student learning is progressing. None are particularly difficult to use; however, using a variety is important since some students will naturally do better with some strategies than with others.

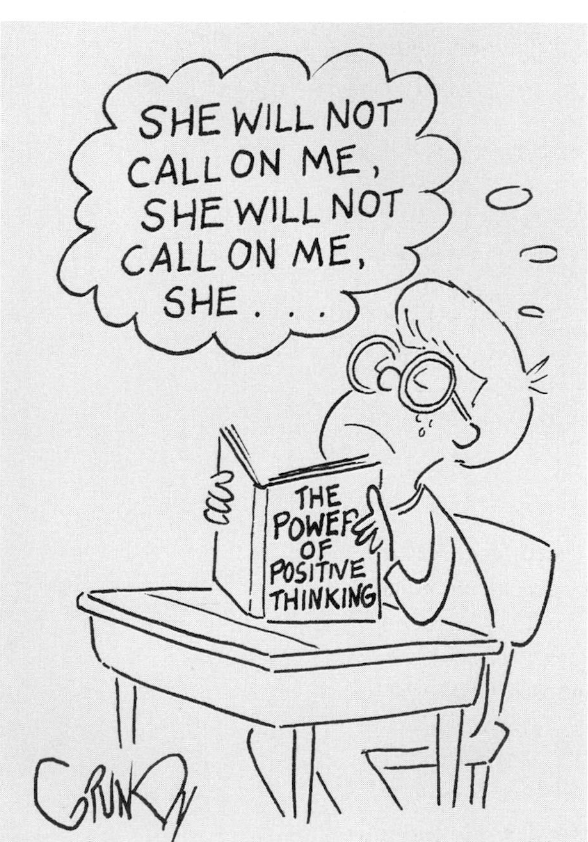

Teacher Observation

Quite naturally one of the most prevalent concerns for beginning teachers is classroom management. When teachers have these concerns their observations of students focus on whether all students are attentive, they are not misbehaving, and they are not creating distractions. Observing student behavior in order to assess classroom management is a necessary first step. When observing for classroom management, keep in mind that one significant reason for student misbehavior is they are not understanding what they are supposed to be doing.

A critical difference between novice teachers and expert teachers is found in the extent to which the purpose for a teacher's observations of students extends beyond a focus on classroom management. Expert teachers go further by continually observing students in order to pick up clues about their extent of understanding and engagement with learning the material. For example, by looking around the classroom teachers can immediately see if students are reading or writing or calculating. During group work expert teachers are monitoring to see that all students are participating. In lab work teachers check to see if each student has set up the equipment properly and it is working

Table 15.4 Checking for Understanding Within Lessons

Strategy	Teacher Actions	What to Look For
Teacher observation for classroom management	Looking around, listening for procedural questions/confusions; asking if they understand what they are to be doing	Proportion of students that are engaged, not misbehaving or creating distractions
Teacher observation for student understanding	Walking around, listening for student use of academic language, looking for student focus on tasks	Students using academic language, doing assigned activities, contributing to the assigned topic
Teacher questioning	Closed questions for short answers; open-ended questions to encourage higher levels of thinking	Short facts and yes/no answers; extended answers from several students
Pop quizzes	At any point inserting one or a few questions that all students must respond to	Percentage of correct answers
Homework	Assignments that can be accomplished outside of class time	Proportion of correct submissions; points of confusion and misunderstandings
Drafts of assignments	Review of early outlines and drafts of major products	Gaps in understandings and areas of omission
Student self-reflection	Student talk, student journals	Students can describe what they know/don't know and what they need to learn next

safely. By walking around the classroom teachers can look over shoulders at student work and listen in on student-to-student talk.

Some teachers walk around the classroom primarily to monitor for misbehavior. Expert teachers have a higher-level purpose; they are checking for student learning and understanding. [It is disappointing to be able to report that in some classrooms teachers do not walk around the classroom and monitor closely what students are doing. They just sit at the teacher's desk, doing some other task, only occasionally looking up to see what students are doing. *Do not become this type of teacher.*

Teacher Questioning

Of course teacher questioning is a very useful way to check on student understanding. Teachers are always asking **closed questions,** those that ask for a yes/no reply or seek specific information about procedures and facts. With closed questions student answers are brief so many students can be spot-checked in a few minutes. Another type of teacher questioning uses **open-ended questions,** which require students to provide an explanation, interpretation, or elaboration. Open-ended questions will require higher-level student thinking (Bloom's taxonomy Levels IV, Analysis; V, Synthesis; and VI, Evaluation).

Open-ended questions also require more time for the teacher to ask and for students to construct their responses. One way to save time and take advantage of open-ended questions is to pose a

Challenging Assumptions

Most students, especially those in elementary school, cannot self-assess and set their own learning goals.

• • • • •

The Assumption

A major theme in this chapter is that not only teachers but their students should be assessing what they know now and what they need to learn next. The standards and related benchmarks provide the target. Students should be able to "unwrap" the standards and be able to describe what they are learning. Through this process students can be more purposeful in how they approach learning, and through the use of evaluation tools such as rubrics they can map their progress and celebrate their accomplishments. Additionally students need to be understanding of which learning strategies work best for them.

Most parents and too many teachers either do not understand or accept this assumption. The following is a frequently heard comment: "Well, that might work with some students in high school, but it won't work in elementary schools."

The Research

In two randomized controlled trials researchers found positive effects when students were given assessment data and provided with feedback about strategies that they could use. In one study (Phillips, Hamlett, Fuchs, & Fuchs, 1993) the teachers provided the feedback. In the other study (May & Robinson, 2007) the students had access to an interactive website that gave them their test scores and provided advice for improving their scores. The findings from these and related studies have been summarized by Hamilton et al. (2009). These study findings are consistent with Popham's (2008) emphasis on teachers and students engaging in formative assessing. The findings also are supportive of instructional strategies that lead to students understanding the learning targets of each lesson and the related standards and indicators of learning success. Although not directly addressed in the research, students engaging in formative assessment is an accepted expectation in many schools and school districts, as was described in this chapter's interview with Dr. Asp.

Implications for Teaching and Learning

The IES document cited below provides a set of recommendations for improving student learning based in research. The document offers a direct recommendation in relation to the assumption challenged here: **Teach students to examine their own data and set learning goals** (p. 19). Teachers should (1) explain expectations and assessment criteria; (2) provide feedback to students that is timely, specific, well formatted, and constructive; (3) provide tools that help students learn from feedback; and (4) use students' data analyses to guide instructional changes.

The report also identified potential roadblocks, including the possibility that students will view feedback as a reflection on themselves rather than seeing it as a focus for improvement, and that teachers may be concerned about taking the time to explain rubrics and to help students analyze feedback. Actually, if all teachers were to facilitate the development of self-assessment skills in their students, each of these roadblocks would go away.

Sources:

Hamilton, L., Halverson, R., Jackson, S. S., Mandinach, E., Supovitz, J., & Wayman, J. D. (2009, September). *Using student achievement data to support instructional decision making.* Washington, DC: U.S. Education Department, IES, National Center for Education Evaluation and Regional Assistance.

May, H., & Robinson, M. A. (2007). *A randomized evaluation of Ohio's Personalized Assessment Reporting System (PARS).* Philadelphia, PA: Consortium for Policy Research in Education.

Phillips, N. B., Hamlett, C. L., Fuchs, L. S., & Fuchs, D. (1993). Combining classwide curriculum-based measurement and peer tutoring to help general educators provide adaptive education. *Learning Disabilities Research & Practice, 8*(3), 148–156.

Popham, W. J. (2008). *Transformative assessment.* Alexandria, VA: Association for Supervision and Curriculum Development.

single well thought out open-ended question and then allow several students to present their responses. The teacher may ask closed questions for clarification purposes as each student responds. This way more students are able to construct a thoughtful response. With both types of questions the teacher is listening for the extent and depth of student understanding and learning.

In standards-based education it is important that students understand how their current work compares with key benchmarks. A student is explaining to the teacher in what ways he can improve his writing.

Student Self-Reflection

Teacher questioning is used continually to check on student understanding and learning. In fact it is overused in most classrooms. There are some other ways to check on student progress during lessons. One tactic that is underused is student self-reflection. Instead of the teacher assuming all of the responsibility for determining where students are, place some of the responsibility on the students. After all, it is the students who have to do the learning. Asking students to talk or write about what they know or don't know is an important activity. This type of self-reflection should be tied to the learning objectives for the lesson, which should be based in the curriculum standards and benchmarks. In today's environment of high accountability, it is especially important for students to be assessing themselves in terms of the extent of their current understanding and learning in relation to how they will be tested. So ask them to describe their current level of understanding in relation to a specific benchmark and its standard.

Objective Tests

The more formal tests that teachers develop frequently use test items that are called objective. **Objective tests** get their name from the characteristic that the answers are either right or wrong. There is no gray area in scoring well-constructed objective test items. Everyone who scores the test items will agree on which of the possible student responses is correct. One advantage of using objective test items is that scoring the student responses can be done quite quickly. Another advantage is that a wide range of student knowledge can be assessed relatively quickly since answering objective test items takes less time than items that require students to construct an original response. A disadvantage is that constructing good objective test items is not as easy as it seems and takes considerable time.

There are different types of objective test items ranging from true–false to fill-in-the-blank, to multiple choice. Each format is particularly good at testing a certain type of learning, and each has certain keys to construction that teachers need to keep in mind. Regardless of the item format it is important to be sure that there is a clear relationship to the learning objective(s), benchmark(s), and standard(s). Several of the typical objective test item formats are presented in Table 15.5. This table also offers a few tips for constructing good objective test items.

Watch Out for Bias in Test Items

No matter the test item format, an important responsibility for teachers is to make sure that each item does not unwittingly include some form of bias. It is all too easy to accidentally write a test

Table 15.5 Test Item Formats and Tips for Writing

Objective Test Item Formats	Tips for Writing Good Items
True–False	• Write items that are clearly true or false. • Avoid using absolute terms such as *always, never,* and *only.* • Avoid double negatives. • Don't include two ideas/parts in a single item.
Matching Items	• Provide a title for the list of items. • Place the longest list on the left. • Consider having one or two extra response options.
Fill-in-the-Blank	• It is best to require one-word responses. • Include the label for an amount of something. • Write clear statements.
Subjective Test Item Formats	
Short Answer	• Set a limit (number of pages) to the size of the response. • Specify the number of elements. • Delimit the range to specific areas that the students should have learned.
Essay	• Be careful to circumscribe the topic without being too prescriptive. • Decide in advance which items will be scored. • Decide if spelling and grammar will count.
Open-Ended	• Determine whether there will be group or only individual responses. • Establish in advance the criteria for evaluating group work. • Plan to monitor student work during the response construction process. • Consider ways for students to share/publish their works.

item that includes a sexual, racial, or cultural bias. There also is risk of including a socioeconomic status (SES) bias. SES refers to the level of wealth, education, social class, and range of experiences that a teacher and students bring to the classroom. Check all test items for the following:

1. Overuse of *he* or *she,* or stereotyping of boys and girls.
2. The use of terms that may be offensive to certain ethnic and cultural groups.
3. Using examples from a middle-class experience that poor children may not have had (e.g., travel to Disneyland).
4. Selecting content and examples that will have different meanings to students from different parts of the country (e.g., a *blizzard* for students from New England will likely mean a heavy snowstorm, while for students in Arizona it is a special type of milk shake from Dairy Queen).
5. Built-in implicit expectations that *some* (boys, girls, ELL, special needs, the "brightest") will do betteror or worse on the test item than others.

Subjective Tests

Objective test items take time to write, provide students with a limited number of response options, and can be scored quickly. An alternative test item format is called **subjective.** Subjective test items pose a problem or task and students must construct an original response, which must be scored individually. Subjective test items are easier to write, more challenging for students to answer, and require judgment and interpretation by the teacher in scoring each response. A very important strength of subjective test items is that each student's response is the student's own work and usually requires higher-order thinking. The following are examples of different types of subjective test items along with a few tips for constructing effective ones. Table 15.5 includes summary points to keep in mind when developing subjective test items.

Short-Answer Items

DIRECTIONS:

If you were writing objective test items for seventh-grade students in an inner-city school, what are three elements of good test items that you would want to be sure to attend to? Be sure to explain your reasoning.

____

____

____

Short-answer test items are an effective way to test for students' use of vocabulary, their ability to think using key concepts, and their success at constructing a brief narrative response. Another advantage of short-answer items is that several of them can be presented within a typical class period. A challenge is that each student's response will be unique and open to interpretation. Variations in interpretation come when some students interpret the test item in different ways. There also can be variation in how the teacher interprets what students have written. This challenge of interpretation is a component of all subjective test items, thus the name.

There are a number of techniques that can be used to reduce the subjectivity, while still requiring originality in the student response. For example, in the test item presented above the number of elements is specified (i.e., three). This removes any debate about a whether a response that only provides one or two elements is sufficient. Without adding the request for the response to include the reasons there could be debate about the need to provide more in the response than the number of elements. The challenge in writing subjective test items is to reduce the unnecessary ambiguity in what is expected while at the same time delimiting what the students are to demonstrate based on what they have learned. The following are two other types of open-ended test items.

Essay Test Items

DIRECTIONS:

A very important skill for teachers to develop is writing good test items. In this chapter you have been reading about different test item formats. Each format is particularly useful for testing certain levels of learning and understanding, and each has particular technical elements that must be addressed. Teachers must understand when to use each test item format. For a subject area that you will be teaching, describe the types of test items that you would use in writing an end-of-unit, one-class-period test. Use at least three test item formats and include an example test item for each. Be sure to describe your reasoning. Use five to eight pages to write your answer. Organization, composition, and spelling will count.

Do I Have To?

Antonio is a fifth-grader attending a Title I school in a predominantly Hispanic section of a large southwestern city. He and his classmates realize he is one of the top three math students in the class of nearly 30 students. However, this knowledge has not diminished his willingness to help others understand their assignments. It is common to observe Antonio helping those who ask him for assistance.

Antonio's teacher has taught third grade and been the school's science specialist. Due to budget cuts that eliminated her position, she returned to a regular classroom assignment. She earned her teaching credentials through an alternative licensure program and has stayed in contact with her elementary mathematics methods instructor since the instructor had been involved in grant activities at the school for several years.

When she was assigned to a fifth-grade class, she asked me, as her former math methods instructor, to visit the class during math time a couple of days a week and assist in any way possible. Sometimes I work with small groups. I often participate in large group instruction by asking probing questions the classroom teacher might not think to ask.

The mathematics program used at Antonio's school is *Investigations in Number, Data, and Space*. This program is designed to help elementary students develop conceptual as well as procedural knowledge and skills. A common assessment procedure is to require students to explain how they solved a problem.

During a recent unit on volume, the students had been doing activities that help them understand the difference between area and volume, as well as "discovering" for themselves that volume can be found by multiplying length, width, and height. In order to determine how many of the students had developed the formula $(1 \times w \times h)$, the teacher presented the following assessment item:

> How many one-inch cubes will fit in a box that's 20 inches long, 12 inches wide, and 10 inches high? Explain how you solved the problem so you could convince your classmates your answer is right.

As soon as the teacher finished reading the item, Antonio turned to me and said, "I know the answer." The professor responded, "I'm sure you do, but we're really interested in how you'd convince your classmates."

Antonio's gaze passed over his classmates, he rolled his eyes, looked up me and asked, "Do I have to convince *all* of them or can I just convince *most* of them?"

Dr. Virginia Usnick
Professor of Mathematics Education
University of Nevada, Las Vegas

One of the most useful ways to test higher-order student thinking is the essay. Essay writing requires students to organize complex ideas and to use what they have learned in new ways. Essay test items present a situation or problem and each student must construct his or her own response. Essay test responses are expected to be long and well organized, and to include detail as well as analysis, synthesis, and evaluation. The challenge in writing essay test items is to circumscribe the topic without making the item so prescriptive that students do not have to think long and hard in composing their essay. We all have experienced essay test items that were so open and vague that we had no clear idea of what a good response would include.

The major challenge for the teacher comes when it is time to score an essay test. First of all, the ease with which an essay test item can be constructed is out of balance with the time it takes to read each student's multipage response. It takes extended time to read each paper and to decipher student penmanship. Another challenge is deciding which components will be scored. How much weight will be given to the quantity of facts and terms that are used? Will there be a clear distinction between lower-level and higher-level thinking? Will grammar and spelling be counted? Will there be one composite score or will each of these questions result in a separate score? An additional challenge with older students is judging whether a particular response really reflects understanding or is bluffing.

Open-Ended Formats

DIRECTIONS:

By the end of this semester you should have in place the foundations for what will become your professional portfolio. This foundation should include (a) a summary of your education and work experience, (b) a description of your academic record, (c) documentation that you have passed all entry tests and requirements, (d) artifacts that indicate the type of product you produce, and (e) the first draft of your education philosophy statement.

There are a number of other formats that teachers can use to assess the extent of student learning and especially their higher-order thinking. These various formats are **open-ended.** They require students to organize and construct their response in creative and unique ways. Open-ended formats include portfolios, exhibits, group projects, investigations, creative works and performances, technology-based productions and presentations, panels, and juries. Student work in response to an open-ended format task will take extended time and should be based in a number of weeks of cumulative class work. Don't forget that open-ended format items can be structured for students working in groups or as teams.

Group projects add a challenge for the teacher when it comes to evaluating the contributions of each student individually. One way to accommodate this challenge is to assign each student an individual grade and each student a grade for the group. Another approach is to have each student grade the other members of the group in terms of the effort and/or the extent of their contributions to the group's product.

Teacher supervision during the time period when students are constructing their open-ended response can be tricky. Beyond monitoring student engagement and the effort of each student there is the need to not provide too many suggestions and hints while at the same time facilitating having all students succeed with producing a final product.

Audio Link 15.2
Learn more about the future of assessment.

Open-ended formats require extended time for students to produce the final product. One way to maximize student learning is to build in time for students to report, share, present, or exhibit their product. This can become a major celebration and a highly visible way for students and teachers from across the school to see what has been going on in your classroom. In one elementary school as part of the writing program all students made a book. Examples of their writing were displayed all around the school, and there was a book fair held so that everyone could see and read the works of other students.

Which Format Is Best?

Deciding on which test item format to use, as with so much of teaching, comes back to consideration of the expected learner outcomes. What are the most important facts, concepts, and understanding that students should be acquiring? These are the elements that should be tested.

Some of the test item formats can be fun for students to do, especially the open-ended ones. But teachers must always keep in mind that testing in the classroom must be grounded in state and district standards and benchmarks. Also continue to think about the level of thinking, learning, and understanding that is expected. Bloom's taxonomy (Table 15.2) has been used in this chapter because it is such a useful way to think about the level of learning and depth of understanding that is being tested. Fill-in-the-blank test items work well for recall of vocabulary, but they are not useful for testing application of what has been learned. Table 15.5 also provides a number of tips for writing open-ended test items. For every test item that teachers develop, one final check should be made for any sort of bias or discrimination. It is surprisingly easy to accidentally build into a test item favoritism for certain students or an unfair disadvantage for certain students. Teachers must be very careful in constructing test items to ensure that all students have an equal opportunity to show what they have learned.

Table 15.6 Rubric for Assessing High School Student Writing Proficiency.

Domain	Score "One"	Score "Two"	Score "Three"	Score "Four"
Development of Ideas	Simply repeats the topic with no development of the idea.	Some focus, with little development of a theme/idea.	Main idea is clear and in general the idea is developed toward a theme or conclusion.	Main idea is fully developed with additional ideas introduced while not losing track of the overall theme.
Strength of Persuasion	Fails to take a position.	Position is vague/unclear.	States a position and defends/persuades with support and use of relevant evidence.	Presents a position clearly, presents evidence in support of the position, and frames the issues.
Writing Style	Shows almost no structure, organization, or coherence.	Has minimal organization; digresses, rambles.	Uses a variety of sentence structures and word choices.	Demonstrates involvement with the text; speaks purposefully to the audience.
Grammar/ Mechanics	Many and serious violations of standard grammar and mechanics.	Limited sentence structure and word choices; consistent errors in grammar.	Uses a variety of sentence structures and word choices; a few errors in grammar and mechanics.	Uses multiple sentence structures and word choices; few, if any, errors in grammar and mechanics.
Use of Sources	No, or only a single source is cited; citations are partial or incorrect.	A few sources are cited, but not clearly tied to theme of paper; citations are partial or incorrect.	At least five appropriate sources are cited; citations are correct.	At least five sources are cited; several additional well-selected sources are cited; citations are correct.

Rubrics Are an Important and Informative Assessment Tool

Very useful tools for assessing student work are **rubrics.** Rubrics are multiple-point continua that describe different levels or degrees of quality, or completeness, of a student's work or a product. Within a rubric there will be brief descriptors or indicators of the different levels of accomplishment. An example of a rubric for assessing four-year high school student writing of research papers in the Edmond (OK) public schools is presented in Table 15.6. With rubrics of this type a large part of the mystery is taken out of subjective evaluation. Each of the points in the rubric describes a level of performance that can be observed and that is distinguishable from the other levels.

The beginning point for developing a rubric is writing down observable descriptions of different levels of quality or completeness. For example, teachers (and their students) could note example elements for each letter grade and use these as the beginning steps for developing rubrics. Rubrics can be **holistic** for evaluating the total effort. Rubrics also can be used to evaluate subparts or components of the effort. For example, one rubric could be used to assess the overall level of thinking (Bloom's taxonomy again) that was used in a student report, while another rubric could be used to evaluate the correctness of grammar and spelling. Some useful tips to keep in mind when developing rubrics are presented in Table 15.7.

Audio Link 15.3
Listen to a clip about student assessment.

HOW DO TEACHERS USE FORMATIVE ASSESSMENTS TO ADJUST INSTRUCTION AND IMPROVE STUDENT LEARNING?

Even with a summative test or a grade at the end, I would want to look at the progress the student has made, specific ways their work has improved, and look at how much better they are at understanding their own strengths and weaknesses. Those kinds of features would tell me a lot more about what a student knows.—Dr. Asp

Table 15.7 Tips to Keep in Mind When Developing Rubrics

1. Both cognitive and performance rubrics can be developed.
2. Have the different levels cover a broad range of possible student performance.
3. Have students brainstorm examples and indicators for each level of performance.
4. Rubrics may have any number of levels, but typically three to five.
5. Describe each level of performance so that it can be easily observed and distinguished clearly from other levels.
6. The levels of performance may be associated with letter grades: A = "Exceeds Expectations"; B = Meets Expectations"; C = "Almost Meets Expectations"; D/F = "Does Not Meet Expectations."
Have students use rubrics to evaluate their own and peer work.

Developing tests and evaluating student assignments are important tasks. More important are the related tasks of analyzing each student's work and determining how instruction needs to be adjusted in order to improve student learning. In addition, at the end of the marking period teachers must compile the various scores and determine a final report of each student's progress. Rather than focusing on making summative decisions, such as preparing report cards, in this section we will take a formative assessment approach.

Four Levels of Formative Assessment

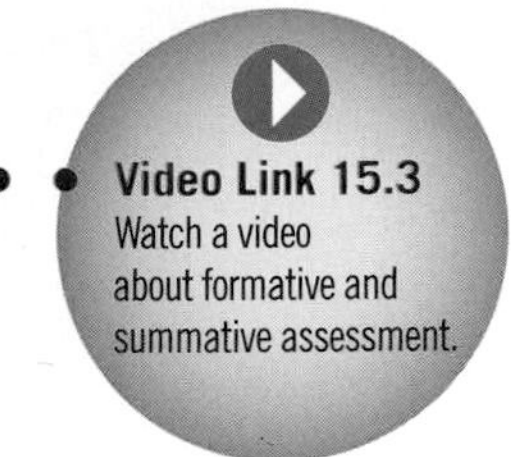

Video Link 15.3
Watch a video about formative and summative assessment.

One of the most influential scholars in regard to formative assessing is W. James Popham, a UCLA Emeritus Professor. Dr. Popham's career-long academic work has centered on ways to think about and apply evaluation methodologies in teaching. He has proposed four levels of formative assessments (Popham, 2008), which are introduced in Table 15.8. Review of this figure may lead to one or more ah-ha moments for you, especially if you have been thinking of teaching in the traditional summative way.

Teachers' Instructional Adjustments

Keep in mind that instruction and assessment are not the same thing. Instruction is what the teacher does to help students learn the curriculum and especially the standards. Formative assessment is a process that helps a teacher, and students, to improve learning. The teacher's task naturally begins with review of the desired learning outcomes. Then appropriate instructional activities are planned. Another task is to plan for formal pre- and post-assessments. What do students know already, and following the lesson how has their understanding changed? Don't forget to include within the lesson spot-checks on understanding: At key points what questions will the teacher ask? What should be observed about student talk that will be indicators of increasing understanding? In a

Table 15.8 Popham's Four Levels of Formative Assessment

Level 1: Teachers' Instructional Adjustments
Teachers collect evidence by which they decide whether to adjust their current or immediately-upcoming instruction in order to improve the effectiveness of that instruction.
Level 2: Student's Learning Tactic Adjustments
Students use evidence of their current skills-and-knowledge status to decide whether to adjust the procedures they're using in an effort to learn something.
Level 3: Classroom Climate Shift
Teachers consistently apply formative assessment to the degree that its use transforms a traditional, comparison-dominated classroom, where the main purpose of assessment is to assign grades, into an atypical learning-dominated classroom, where the main purpose of assessment is to improve the quality of teaching and learning.
Level 4: Schoolwide Implementation
An entire school (or district) adopts one or more levels of formative assessment, chiefly through the use of professional development and teacher learning communities.

Source: Popham, W. J. (2008). *Transformative assessment* (p. 49). Alexandria, VA: Association for Supervision & Curriculum Development.

UNDERSTANDING AND USING EVIDENCE

Looking for an Achievement Gap

The Problem

A very important task for teachers is to be able to use data to understand and illustrate achievement gaps. Unfortunately, achievement gaps are all too common in today's schools.

Examine the table of data for fifth-grade student achievement in mathematics in one school. What can you say based on these test score means? Is there any indication of an achievement gap? What are the trends across the school years? How else could these data be displayed in order to better "see" any patterns?

Achievement in Mathematics by Racial/Ethnic Categories
Fifth-Grade Means (One Elementary School)

	1999–2000	2000–2001	2001–2002	2002–2003	2003–2004	2004–2005	Across Years
Caucasian & Asian	53.67	51.43	54.44	55.41	53.05	53.57	53.58
Nonwhite	32.56	31.06	33.22	35.08	36.29	39.71	36.87
Whole Group	47.32	44.30	47.18	45.24	44.67	46.64	45.89

Interpreting the Data

Rarely will trend data be a perfect straight line from low to high, or high to low. The data presented for the Caucasian and Asian fifth-grade mathematics scores is quite typical. From year to year the means vary but there is no clear direction other than each year being about the same. However, there is a clear pattern for the test score means with nonwhite fifth-graders. The average test score increases each year after the 2000–2001 school year. But this trend by itself does not tell us if the achievement gap is shrinking. A comparison has to be made of the differences in means with the Caucasian and Asian test takers.

One interesting way to illustrate the size of the achievement gap is to determine its size each year by subtracting the nonwhite mean from the Caucasian and Asian mean. When a bar graph is constructed using these differences, the decreasing achievement gap is readily seen. Note that the significant drop took place in the most recent two years. Why do you suppose this pattern occurred?

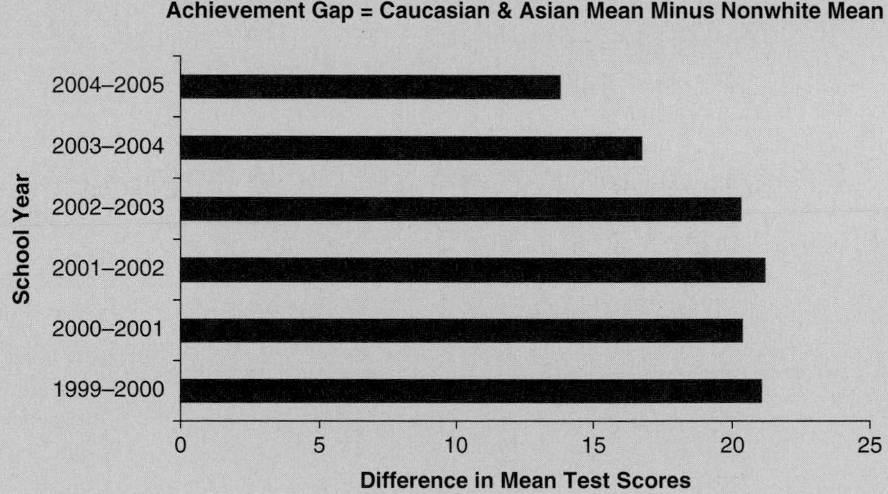

formative assessing approach, all of these sources of information are considered, and adjustments in instruction are made *within* the lesson as well as in *planning* the next lesson. Key subtasks are to consider each student's progress as well as progress of the whole class.

Students' Learning Tactic Adjustments

This level of formative assessment may be a new idea for some teacher candidates. Even up to this point in this chapter we have pretty much been describing the teacher's role in assessment. It also is important to keep in mind the student's role. Students should be engaging their own formative assessment processes to aid in improving their learning. They need to be self-assessing too. How well do they see themselves doing? What are they doing to make adjustments in their learning strategies? As Popham points out, "Level 2 formative assessment consists of *student-determined* adjustments in learning tactics, not *teacher-dictated* adjustments the students are then supposed to make" (p. 72).

More than likely, most students will not automatically know how to do this; they will need instruction in how to consider the types of tactics that will help them learn. With the teacher's help students need to come to understand the learning expectations for each lesson. They need to know what's coming next. They need to know how their learning progress will be judged. This latter point means that they also need to know the steps they need to take to progress in their learning.

Classroom Climate Shift From Traditional to Formative Assessment

As important as are the teacher's and the students' approaches to formative assessment, in the end the feel of the whole classroom has to change. The climate or culture of a classroom is different when formative assessment is foundational. Popham identifies three key dimensions of the classroom: *learning expectations, responsibility for learning,* and *the perceived role of classroom assessment* (p. 94). He talks about a shift from *traditional classroom climate* to *assessment-informed classroom climate* (p. 94). For example, there is a shift from an expectation that the most motivated students will progress to a view that "substantial" learning will occur for all students. Responsibility for learning shifts from the teacher as primarily responsible for learning to students assuming major responsibility for their own learning *and* that of their classmates. Instead of tests being seen as data for comparing students and assigning grades, assessments are used to inform adjustments in instruction *and* students adjusting their approaches to learning. Development of this type of classroom culture requires teacher leadership, trust, and social construction by the teacher and the students. By the way, this type of learning-centered classroom culture can be constructed in the primary grades and kindergarten. It is not something that can only exist with older students.

Schoolwide Implementation of a Formative Assessment–Centered Culture

As you will have read in the excerpts from the interview with Assistant Superintendent Elliott Asp, it is possible not just for a few classrooms, or one or two schools, but for an entire school district to make the shift to formative assessments as the shared way of teaching and learning. One key to a school or a district making this major change in thinking and action is leadership. Without the understanding, vision, and active support of the principals and district office leaders, teachers and students will be hard-pressed to make the change. Another important resource is access to related professional development that goes beyond teacher workshops. Modeling and coaching supports are other required strategies. When all of these elements come together it is possible for teachers, administrators, and students to construct a professional learning community.

As Dr. Asp stated in his interview when asked about when he sees joy in teaching,

Deeper Look 15.4
Read more about RTIs.

> Seeing teachers grow professionally. Seeing their skills improve and get better at handling various situations whether they are academic growth of kids or how to motivate and have kids involved in more meaningful ways in classrooms. Also teachers having support of colleagues and being part of professional learning communities to where there is excitement about improving their practice and there is a working environment that is supportive.

Response to Intervention (RTI)

Our description of formative assessment began with what a teacher and his or her students can do in a classroom. We, as well as Drs. Asp and Popham, then suggested that a whole school or district could approach teaching and learning using the principles of formative assessment. A related approach that is receiving increasing attention is called **Response to Intervention (RTI)**, or **Response to Instruction (RTI).** RTI is a multilevel approach for addressing the needs of all students by differentiating between those who are keeping up and those who are struggling or seriously falling behind. The approach combines screening, progress monitoring, and a multilevel prevention strategy into a process for data-based decision making for all students (National Center on Response to Intervention (n.d.).

Figure 15.3 Response to Intervention (RTI): Different Levels of Schoolwide Support and Instructional Interventions to Address Increasingly At-Risk Students

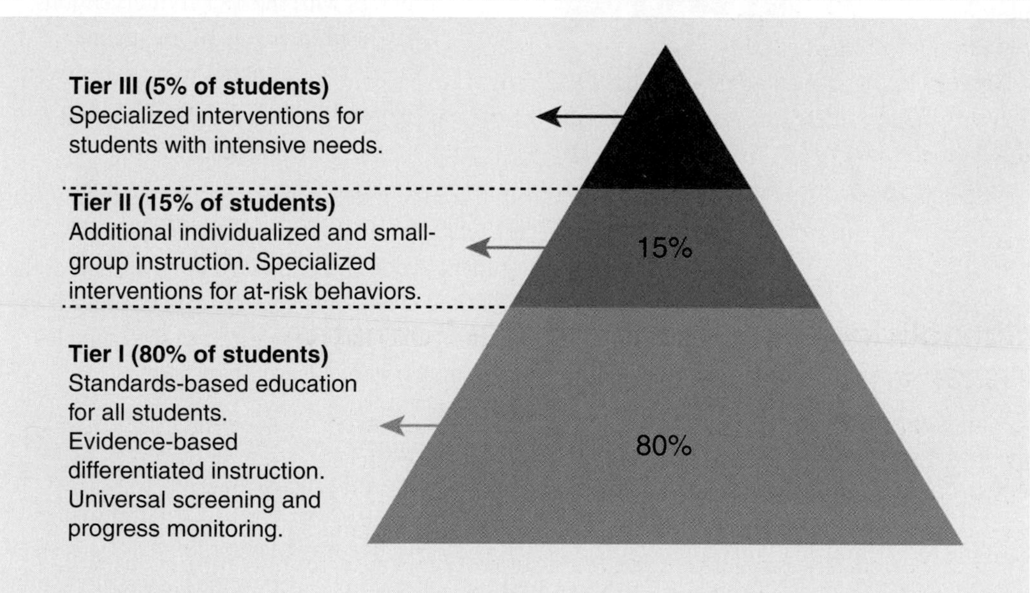
Tier III (5% of students)
Specialized interventions for students with intensive needs.
Tier II (15% of students)
Additional individualized and small-group instruction. Specialized interventions for at-risk behaviors.
15%
Tier I (80% of students)
Standards-based education for all students.
Evidence-based differentiated instruction.
Universal screening and progress monitoring.
80%

Student Improvement Team (SIT) and RTI

Implementing RTI involves all of a school's staff, teachers (regular and special education), administrators, and instructional strategy specialists. One frequently observed mechanism for sustaining RTI is to establish a special committee with a name such as **Student Improvement Team (SIT)**. The SIT will have representatives for all grade levels/subjects, a school administrator, reading and mathematics specialists, one or more special education teachers, and at least one member who is skilled at organizing and displaying student data.

Typically, the SIT will meet once a week for 30 to 60 minutes. At each meeting the performance of individual students is reviewed. The heaviest attention will be given to those students who are struggling. Assessment information will be displayed. The SIT will discuss alternative "instructional and/or behavioral interventions" that might help. An agreement is reached about the exact steps that will be taken and how student progress will be monitored. The students' teacher(s) will then proceed to implement the interventions, assess student progress, and bring a report back to a subsequent SIT meeting.

An important organizing framework within RTI is "the triangle" (Figure 15.3). Within the triangle are different levels of "intervention." Three levels, or tiers, have been defined:

- Tier I. For all students, RTI begins at the bottom of the triangle by monitoring their learning progress. Tier I entails the use of evidence-based instructional strategies and differentiated instruction for all students.
- Tier II focuses on students who are identified through assessments and teacher observations as being at risk of having lower learning outcomes. They are falling behind the others in their class. Through the SIT there is discussion and development of a plan for these students to receive targeted supplemental instruction that usually takes place within the regular education classroom.
- Tier III is for those students who did not progress with the Tier II interventions. They need intensive supplemental instruction that needs to be delivered in small groups or individually.

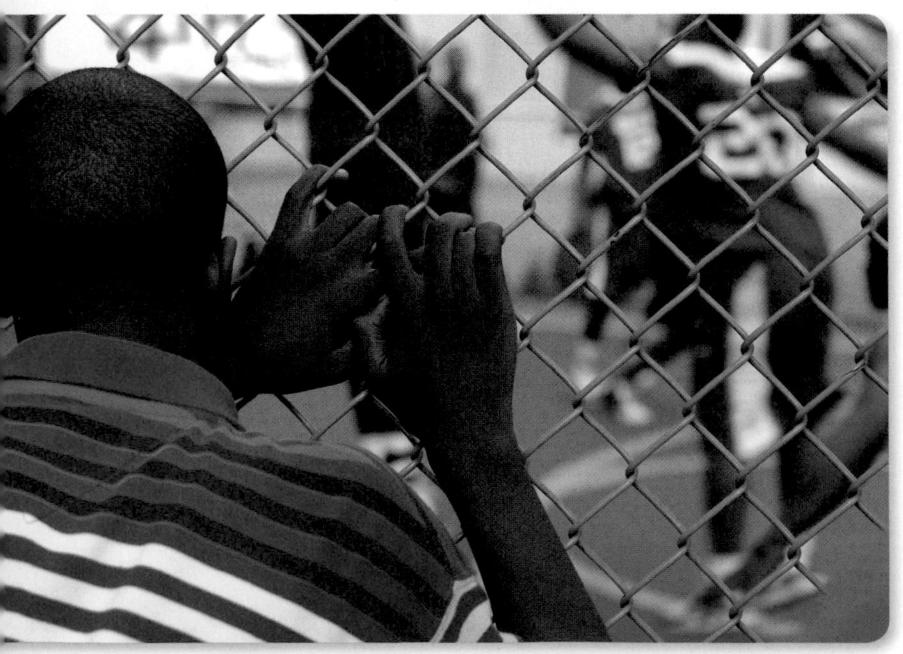

In the RTI model there is continuous monitoring of progress and regular review of how each student is doing. Following efforts at each of the RTI tiers, if students are not making progress in learning they may be referred to screening for determination of a learning disability.

Reducing the achievement gap requires that all students have the opportunity to learn.

The RTI framework along with the use of a school-based committee, such as a SIT, provides one very constructive approach to improving learning for all students. This approach represents a very effective way to incorporate all aspects of the formative assessment model. It provides a systematic approach to continuous assessment, time for careful reflection, use of evidence-based interventions, and review of the outcomes of making adjustments in instruction—all of which is designed to address the goal of learning for all students.

Don't Forget the Achievement Gap

Whether we are talking about NRTs versus CRTs, or testing versus assessing, or summative versus formative, or RTI, it is imperative that as a teacher you continually be thinking about all of your students having opportunities to learn. Monitor your assessment notes, the results of tests, and your reports of summative grading to see if any categories of your students are not making satisfactory progress. Often teachers are not aware that they are treating girls or boys, or ELL or some other category of students differently. Disaggregating your assessment information by category of student will tell you a lot about how well you are matching instruction with the needs of all your students.

CONNECTING TO THE CLASSROOM

This chapter first introduced seven purposes for assessment. Then different approaches to testing, including CRTs and NRTs, and the construction of different types of test items were described. The remainder of the chapter focuses on formative assessment. The importance of continuously checking for understanding and being ready to adjust instruction cannot be overemphasized. Also, the importance of students doing self-formative assessing at all grade levels and for all content areas cannot be overemphasized. The following summary points should be kept in mind as you engage with assessing student learning.

1. The primary purpose for assessment should be to help students learn, which means that teachers must be continually using a variety of methods to assess the extent to which each student's understanding is increasing.
2. Don't forget that students have a responsibility to self-assess and to use the results of tests and other assessments to reflect and identify steps they can take to improve their learning.
3. Norm-referenced tests (NRTs) compare one student's achievement with how other students have done.
4. Criterion-referenced tests (CRTs) compare one student's achievement with a particular level of proficiency or performance.
5. Bloom's taxonomy is a very useful tool for classifying test items and teacher questions. Low-level questions seek recall of facts and procedures. High-level questions ask students to analyze, synthesize, and evaluate using what they know and understand.
6. Objective test items take more time to write and are quick to score. Subjective test items may take less time to construct, but require extended time to score.

SUMMARY

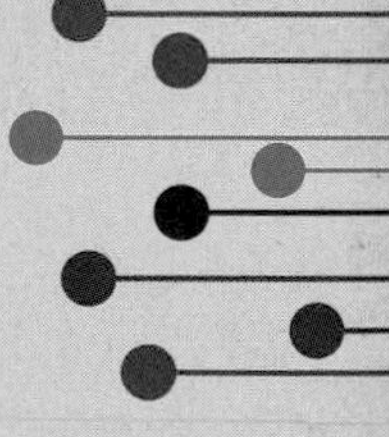

In this chapter we have introduced basic concepts and procedures for assessing student learning. We also have focused on the importance of thinking about teaching and learning in terms of formative assessing. These were the key topics:

- Norm-referenced tests (NRTs) compare the performance of one student with the performance of a comparison group of students.
- Criterion-referenced tests (CRTs) compare the performance of each student with a particular level of accomplishment.
- Teachers need to develop knowledge and skill in constructing different types of objective and subjective test items.
- Formative assessment is now the foundational perspective for planning, delivering, and adjusting instruction in order to continuously improve learning.
- Response to Intervention (RTI) is an organized school- or districtwide three-tier approach to data-based decision making that entails assessing learning, making adjustments in instruction, and monitoring progress for all students.

CLASS DISCUSSION QUESTIONS

1. A major emphasis in this chapter has been on having you think less about summative assessments for the purpose of grading, and to think much more about the uses of assessments to improve student learning. The idea is to have teachers shift their thinking from preoccupation with "what I am teaching" to continuously thinking about "what evidence do I have that each of my students is learning?" What do you see as being the biggest challenges to making this transformational change in thinking?
2. One of the purposes for assessment that was introduced in this chapter is for students' self-reflection about their learning. What can teachers do to help students use assessments for self-reflection and to adjust their learning tactics? At what grade level are students ready to self-assess? In other words, do you think that it would be useful for primary grade teachers to work with their students on self-assessment? Or in elementary school is this really only the teacher's job? What about changing the mind-set of high school students who are only interested in their grade?

KEY TERMS

Accommodations 455
Assessing 447
Authentic task 452
Closed questions 459
Criterion-referenced tests (CRTs) 451
Depths of knowledge (DOK) 454
Formative evaluation 448
High-stakes testing 450
Holistic 467
Individualized education plan (IEP) 455
No Pass No Play 450
Norm-referenced tests (NRTs) 451
Objective tests 461
Open-ended questions 459
Performance 452
Reliability 453
Response to Intervention (RTI) or Response to Instruction (RTI) 471
Rubrics 467
Student Improvement Team (SIT) 472
Subjective 463
Summative evaluation 448
Tests 447
Validity 453

SELF-ASSESSMENT

WHAT IS YOUR CURRENT LEVEL OF UNDERSTANDING AND THINKING ABOUT ASSESSING STUDENT LEARNING AND RESULTS?

Answer the following questions and then score your responses using the Complexity of Thinking rubric.

1. What types of assessments are you most comfortable in using at this time?
2. In your teaching, how will you engage students in assessing their own learning?
3. There are major differences between CRTs and NRTs; when and in what ways should teachers use each of these test designs?
4. As a teacher, what balance between the use of subjective and objective assessing will you strive for?

What is your current level of understanding? Rate yourself using this rubric.

Complexity of Thinking Rubric

	Parts & Pieces	Unidimensional	Organized	Integrated	Extensions
Indicators	Elements/concepts are talked about as isolated and independent entities.	One or a few concepts are addressed, while others are underdeveloped.	Deliberate and structured consideration of all key concepts/elements.	All key concepts/elements are included in a view that addresses interconnections.	Integration of all elements and dimensions, with extrapolation to new situations.

	Parts & Pieces	Unidimensional	Organized	Integrated	Extensions
Assessing student learning and results	Names one or two concepts, such as the types of test items, without placing them into a formative or summative context; or can only name one or two of the RTI tiers.	Only describes one model, such as summative evaluation and assigning grades; describes one tier of RTI in detail, but provides little information about other tiers.	Describes and compares NRTs and CRTs with implications; or describes formative assessment and the components of RTI.	Describes the concepts of NRT, CRT, formative and summative assessments, and the role of the teacher in RTI.	Presents an integrated view of formative assessment (or RTI) and identifies areas where she or he plans to develop more in-depth understanding.

5. You will likely teach in a school that has some model of RTI. What do you see as being implications of RTI for you and your students?

STUDENT STUDY SITE

Visit the Student Study Site at **www.sagepub.com/hall** to access links to the videos, audio clips, and Deeper Look reference materials noted in this chapter, as well as additional study tools including eFlashcards, web quizzes, and more.

Field Guide

for Learning More About Assessing Student Learning and Results

To further increase your understanding about testing, formative assessment, and RTI, do one or more of the following activities.

Ask a Teacher or Principal

Ask a teacher or principal to describe for you how he or she does RTI. Listen for how much his or her approach is formative versus summative.

Look over the various assessments that a teacher has used across a term to evaluate student work. Ask the teacher to explain the reasoning for the different forms of assessment that have been used. To what extent does she or he focus on thinking in terms of summative versus formative assessment? Are his or her students expected to engage in formative assessment?

Make Your Own Observations

Attend a meeting of the SIT or other committee in a school that is organized to review student progress. This committee may be organized around RTI, or it may be a screening committee, to determine whether or not a student should be referred for screening for a possible disability. What data does this committee use? Have there been different adjustments to instruction for certain students? Does it appear that the committee is thinking more in terms of summative or formative assessment?

Find a rubric for some component of student learning for a subject that you plan to teach. When you next visit a classroom where that subject is being taught, use the rubric to score examples of student work. Compare your scoring with that of the teacher. Did the teacher use a rubric or some other scoring system? If possible, check with some of the students about how they have assessed their learning. Do they use rubrics as well? Do the students benchmark their learning to the standards?

Reflect Through Journaling

One of the biggest concerns for all teachers, not just beginning teachers, is wading through all of the paperwork. For example, every time teachers give an assignment there is likely to be a student product that has to be reviewed and graded. Take a few minutes to think about the whole business of testing and assessing. Write down some of your current ideas for how the assessing you will do can be made most efficient. Which forms of formative assessments will be most useful for you as a teacher, and which will be most useful for your students? Be sure to record your notes from observations of expert teachers managing this work efficiently. How do they do it?

Build Your Portfolio

It is never too soon to start drafting ideas about the strategies you will use to check for understanding. For a subject that you plan to teach, select a unit, chapter, or week's worth of lessons and construct a set of questions you could use. Be sure to keep in mind a combination of objective and subjective probes. Use Bloom's taxonomy (Table 15.2) as a guide for developing checks that will assess different levels of DOK (depths of knowledge). One easy way to test your ideas can be done the next time you visit a classroom. Ask the students about what they are doing. How do they assess how much they know? Can they describe what they need to learn next?

Read a Book

In his interview, Dr. Elliott Asp talked about the challenges involved in helping students (and teachers) make a change in their thinking about the purposes of assessment. He has his teachers read a book about mind-sets: *Mindset: The New Psychology of Success,* by Carol Dweck (2006; New York, NY: Random House/Ballantine Books). You will find this to be an interesting read.

Assessing learning progress with special needs students can be a challenge for teacher education candidates and beginning teachers. *Assessing Students With Special Needs,* by John J. Benn (2004; Upper Saddle River, NJ: Pearson Merrill Prentice Hall), addresses the issues and makes clear what teachers can do to assess general performance and academic achievement. Each chapter offers many concrete ways for teachers and their students to be successful. For example, Chapter 3 includes description of a dozen approaches to alternative grading including contracts, level, and IEP grading.

Understanding by Design, by Grant Wiggins and Jay McTighe (2005; Alexandria, VA: Association for Supervision & Curriculum Development), is one of the classic references for developing an understanding of the relationships between learning outcomes, assessment, and the design of curriculum. The authors walk the reader through each topic and then draw implications for the design of instruction, including examination of how the way teachers teach is linked to how and what students learn.

Each of the nine chapters of *Grading and Reporting Student Progress in an Age of Standards,* edited by Elise Trumbull and Farr Beverly (2000; Norwood, MA: Christopher-Gordon), is written by an expert who has carefully thought through the challenges and approaches to grading in a standards-based environment. Topics covered include different grading methods, avoiding bias, special populations, and reporting to parents. Examples of report cards and strategies for addressing standards are presented throughout each chapter.

Search the Web

RTI is an important framework for you to know about. In most states some form of RTI will be required. The U.S. Department of Education, Office of Special Education website (**http://www.osepideasthatwork.org**) is one important source. Another important source of RTI information and tools is the National Center on Response to Intervention (**http://www.rti4success.org**). For a content area or topic that you will be teaching, use one or more of these websites to guide you in identifying questions you can ask your students about their level of understanding. Design these questions with consideration of the three tiers of RTI in mind.

Go to the website for a school or school district where you would like to become a teacher. Search within the site for information about the types of assessments and tools that are provided to teachers. Does the information provided on this website suggest that there is more interest in summative or formative assessment? Does the site provide any information about how they are doing RTI? Develop a list of questions you will want to ask in order to learn more details about what they are doing.

The web represents a powerful resource for obtaining information about any of the public schools in the country. However, there always has to be caution in assuming that all of the information is accurate. Exploring and comparing information about student performance in different schools and school districts can be informative. For example, go to **http://www.greatschools.net** and search for high schools in the Cherry Creek, Colorado, school district. This is the district where Dr. Asp, the interviewee for this chapter, is an assistant superintendent. You will be able to see and compare information about each school in terms of academic performance rating, the ratio of full-time equivalent (FTE), and other factors. Then search for where you went to high school. Develop a table that compares high schools in the two districts. What inferences would you make?

Becoming Tomorrow's Highly Effective Teacher

Chapter 16 Succeeding in Your Teacher Education Program, and Beyond

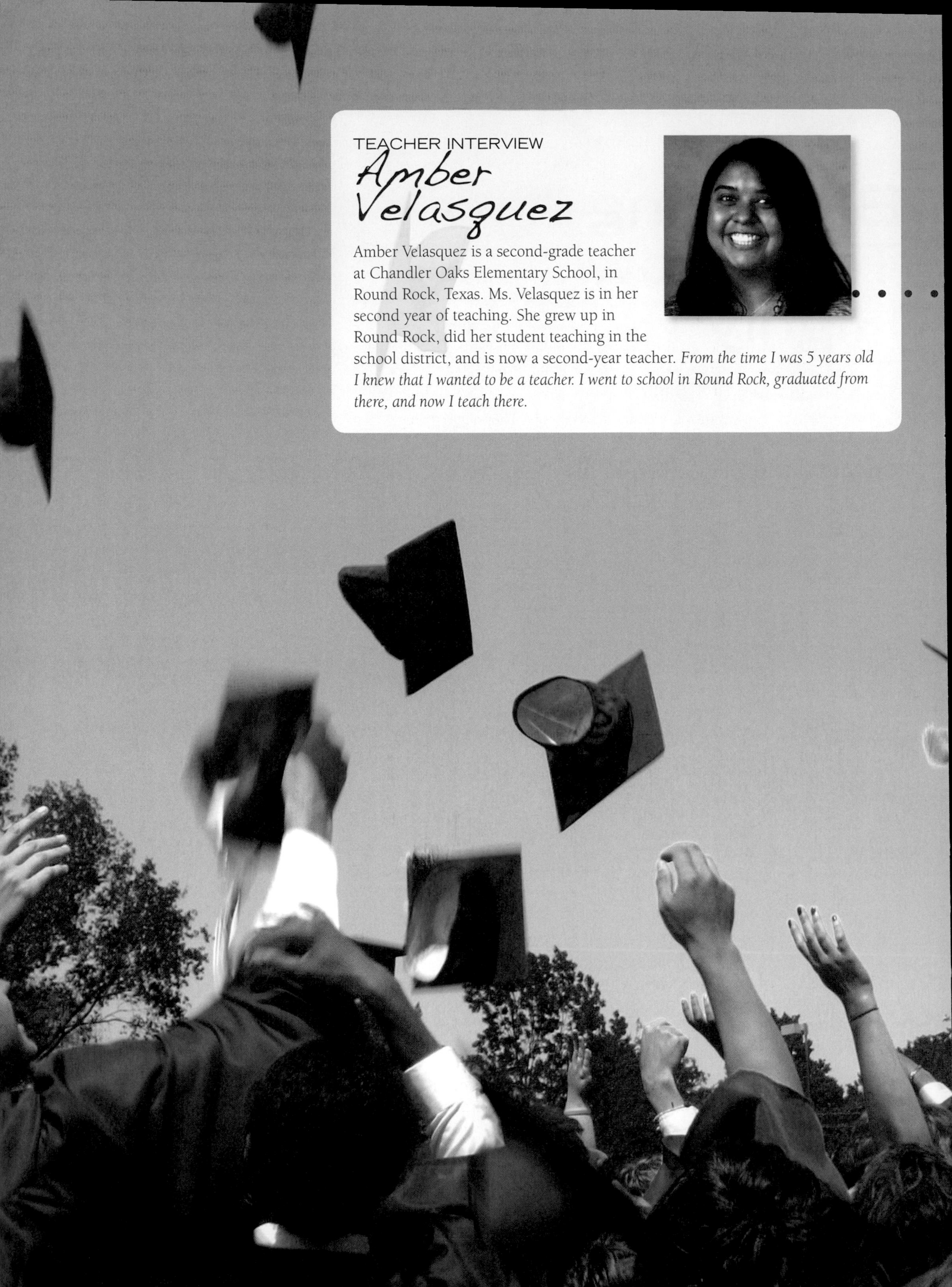

TEACHER INTERVIEW

Amber Velasquez

Amber Velasquez is a second-grade teacher at Chandler Oaks Elementary School, in Round Rock, Texas. Ms. Velasquez is in her second year of teaching. She grew up in Round Rock, did her student teaching in the school district, and is now a second-year teacher. *From the time I was 5 years old I knew that I wanted to be a teacher. I went to school in Round Rock, graduated from there, and now I teach there.*

Succeeding in Your Teacher Education Program, and Beyond

• • *What is your school like?*

The school has grades K–5 and is in its second year with 600-plus students. Our families are middle and upper class, depending on where they live. The two-story building is brand new, with lots of technology. Our district has a contract with Dell, a big company in Austin, so we have lots of technology.

We have windows on the outside of each classroom. They are fairly big. We also have windows looking into the hallway. The school expectation is that your blinds are always up for the windows looking outside and the ones facing inside. In many ways you are teaching in a fish bowl!

All six of the second-grade classroom doors face a big central area called the "Village." This area is an extension of our classrooms. The Village houses technology including a big document camera and Smart Board that we can use for grade-level presentations and lessons. Each classroom has a bathroom, so there are no big bathroom breaks. Also, there is a back walkway joining each classroom.

What advice do you have for teacher education candidates?

Let me fast forward to something I wish I had known: I just want to share that this profession is a changing profession. There are going to be lots of trends that happen. There is going to be a lot of curriculum that you will learn is the "right way," and the only way during your teacher preparation classes. Then you will learn that in the real world it will be taught in a different way.

Best practice is a growing practice. It is OK to feel passionate about the way a curriculum is taught, but you still need to be knowledgeable about other ways to deliver the same curriculum. Set high expectations for yourself as a personal learner. As you move closer to securing a teaching position and even after you have obtained one, seek out professional development opportunities, conferences, seminars, and books. The pressure of learning best practice increases once you earn your license. Hold yourself accountable for meeting your learning expectations.

To what extent are parents involved in your school?

Our parents are very involved. They are on campus all the time. If teachers have something they need done, such as a bulletin board, copies, or something cut out, a parent will volunteer to do that for you. There is a room called the Pro Center. Parents can work on projects there. What is wonderful about utilizing parent volunteers is that a teacher can spend her time working on things that are more academic, rather than spending time putting up bulletin boards. They really help out!

Questions to Consider

1. How would you feel about having so many windows in your classroom and teaching in a "fish bowl"?
2. In Ms. Velasquez's school, parents are in the school all day, every day. In what ways will you expect to involve parents?
3. Ms. Velasquez talks a lot about how important it is to continue learning once you are a teacher. Is this a new expectation for you?

Our parents support the school beyond taking on bulletin boards and copying; they organize events and fundraisers that directly benefit the campus and the students as well. We had a "Cheetah Walk"—that was an amazing fundraiser held at the school in the fall. Lots of hard work was poured into the event to make it a successful fundraiser by the parents and the teachers. The parents routinely organize monthly Spirit Nights at surrounding local restaurants also. The local restaurants donate a percentage of their earnings back to the school between the set hours. Parents also lend their hand outside of the school; several volunteers join teachers on field trips to help chaperone small groups of children. The parents work hard to make sure all needs of the teachers and students are met daily!

What brings you joy in teaching?

Knowing I am giving back to my community. That's a huge part of it. I get a chance to teach in my own community. Seeing the children grow. You can see a child grow in reading. You can see a child grow in writing. And you also can see them grow socially through their interactions every day.

Also, you become a person of many strengths. You start the day as a teacher and as the day progresses you adapt into several different side roles to accommodate the needs of your students: mother, nurse, confidant. The job is not one-dimensional. It's fast paced; the next day will never be the same as the one before, and each day will try you. That's pretty rewarding.

Learning Outcomes

After reading this chapter, you should be able to

1. Name and have plans for what you will want to accomplish during your teacher education program in order for you to become a high-quality beginning teacher.
2. Have notes about the key steps you will need to take to get your first teaching position.
3. Describe ways teacher education candidates and beginning teachers can be leaders.
4. Identify questions and topics related to what you can learn from talking with a highly successful teacher.

INTRODUCTION

Teaching is one of the most important professions. Now, more than at any other time in history, students, parents, communities, and the nation need outstanding teachers. As has been described in Chapters 1 through 15, because the need is so great and teaching is so complex, the preparation to become a teacher is more rigorous than ever before. The expectations for beginning teachers are higher too. For all of these reasons it is very important for you to take advantage of every opportunity presented throughout your teacher preparation program. Now is the time to begin anticipating what you will need to know, be able to do, and have on record as you seek and obtain your first full-time teaching position. Failure to be thinking ahead could result in not obtaining your most preferred beginning teaching position.

This chapter begins with recommendations for succeeding in your teacher education program. The remainder of the chapter describes themes, offers recommendations, and identifies issues related to being a successful and influential beginning teacher. Again, it is not too early for you to begin thinking about, preparing for, and anticipating what you will need to have and be able to do to be a successful beginning teacher. How will you apply for a teaching position? What kinds of documentation will you need to have, and how can you prepare for the position interview? If you start anticipating and planning now you will see how much of what you do in the remainder of your preparation program will be useful to you in seeking, applying for, and obtaining the perfect teaching position.

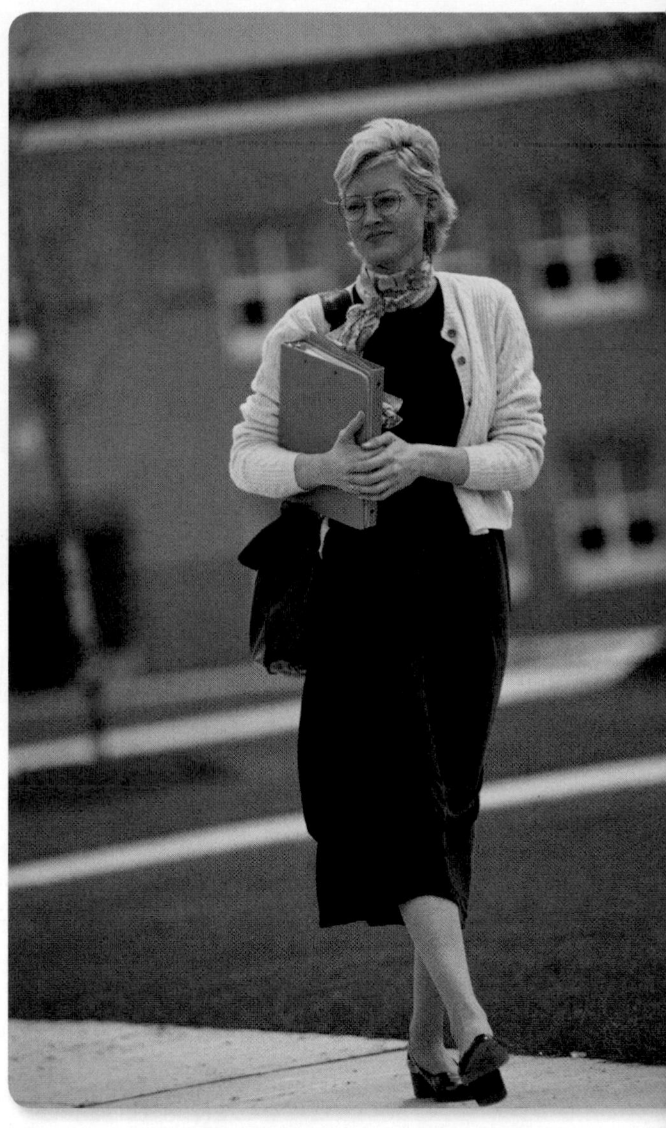

Walking into the school as a teacher for the first time is exciting and a little scary.

WHAT ARE KEYS TO SUCCEEDING IN YOUR TEACHER EDUCATION PROGRAM?

Something that is very important is reflection. I kept a journal my first year of student teaching and my first year as a teacher. I would write down things as they happened. Then I would look back at how I handled different situations. Sometimes I would tweak it and write what I would do the next time that happened. I still have that journal. I would recommend reflection, because you can learn so much.—Ms. Velasquez

There are three very important components to reflection. The first is to appreciate how important the process of reflecting can be to your learning and continually improving in your teaching. Second, keeping a journal provides a record of your efforts, what worked well, and what you will want to do differently next time. The third important aspect is that reflection is a personal experience. Your journaling and thinking about what you have done, what you are doing, and what you will do is all about your becoming an exceptional teacher. These same notes and insights also become important examples for you to draw from when you are applying for your first teaching position.

To help you in refining your reflection efforts, we offer two sets of conceptual tools. Each of these is a generic framework that you can use in reflecting upon your teaching and thinking about how well your students are learning. The first provides a research-based method to reflect about your developing perceptions and feelings about becoming a teacher. The second framework introduces two very useful ways to think about learning-centered instruction.

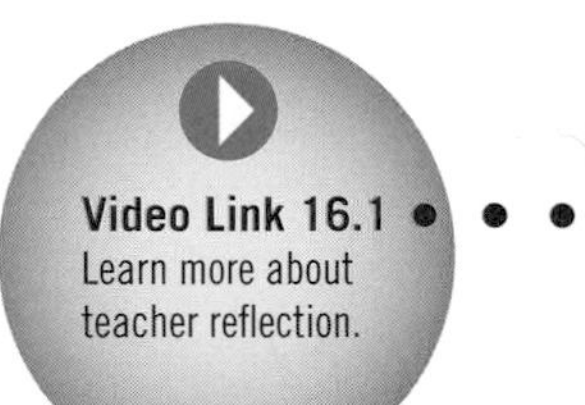

Video Link 16.1
Learn more about teacher reflection.

As you continue with your preparations to become a teacher, you will take a number of professional education courses and have a variety of clinical and field experiences. As you will have heard already from your fellow candidates, some courses and experiences are perceived as being "better" than others. What you will discover is that regardless of the perceived quality of the course or experience, the really good candidates use them to advantage. They use every assignment and activity as an opportunity to learn more about teaching, student learning, and what classrooms and schools are like. Regardless of the situation, the high-quality candidates

Teachers need to share their concerns about individual students as well as how the whole school is doing.

learn and contribute to the learning of others. They are able to do this because they understand themselves, what teaching is about, and the importance of using every experience and opportunity to learn more. They also collect evidence to document their efforts and what they have learned, and artifacts that indicate the differences they make. They do all of this in spite of their feelings of not knowing it all and being very busy. The following frameworks can help you understand and use every situation as a learning experience.

Understanding Your Concerns

In order to understand their students, teachers must first understand themselves. This does not require a complex psychological analysis; however, each of us will have certain feelings and perceptions about every situation. In addition, each of us may perceive the same situation differently. Depending upon our own perceptions, we construct our personal interpretations of what each situation means. Teachers do this all the time when talking with students and colleagues, and when thinking about what they and others are doing.

What Are Your Concerns Right Now?

Teacher education candidates worry about getting good grades and wondering what it will feel like to be in front of a whole class of students. Understanding that all of us filter and ascribe personal meaning to events and actions is very important, especially for teachers. This is the personal side of teaching: understanding our **concerns.** At any time you will have a mixture of feelings, perceptions, worries, and preoccupations about teaching. To illustrate this idea, take a minute to respond to the following task.

Open-Ended Concerns Statement

As you think about your becoming a teacher, what are your concerns? Don't say what others are concerned about; instead, what are *your* concerns at this time? (Write/type a description of your concerns using complete sentences.)

Don't read any further until you have written your response.

• • • • • • •

The activity of writing your concerns is easy. Developing an understanding of what you have written is guided by more than 40 years of research. Researchers have documented that the concerns of teacher education candidates can be placed in categories and used by candidates and the program faculty to improve learning. In the end teachers who understand their own concerns are better able to understand the concerns of their students and colleagues.

It turns out that our concerns can be sorted into a set of easy-to-understand categories. The original research on teacher concerns was pioneered by Frances Fuller (1969), a professor at the University of Texas at Austin. Since then the analysis of concerns has expanded beyond teachers and now includes understanding the concerns of people involved in change (Hall & Hord, 2011).

Table 16.1 Stages of Concern

Stages of Concern About the Innovation

IMPACT	6	REFOCUSING	The focus is on the exploration of more universal benefits from the innovation, including the possibility of major changes or replacement with a more powerful alternative. Individual has definite ideas about alternatives to the proposed or existing form of the innovation.
	5	COLLABORATION	The focus is on coordination and cooperation with others regarding use of the innovation.
	4	CONSEQUENCE	Attention focuses on impact of the innovation on students in his/her immediate sphere of influence.
TASK	3	MANAGEMENT	Attention is focused on the processes and tasks of using the innovation and the best use of information and resources. Issues related to efficiency, organizing, managing, scheduling, and time demands are of utmost importance.
SELF	2	PERSONAL	Individual is uncertain about the demands of the innovation, his/her inadequacy to meet those demands, and his/her role with the innovation. This includes analysis of his/her role in relation to the reward structure of the organization, decision making, and consideration of potential conflicts with existing structures or personal commitment. Financial or status implications of the program for self and colleagues may also be reflected.
	1	INFORMATIONAL	A general awareness of the innovation and interest in learning more detail about it is indicated. The person seems to be unworried about himself/herself in relation to the innovation. She/he is interested in substantive aspects of the innovation in a selfless manner such as general characteristics, effects, and requirements for use.
	0	UNCONCERNED	Little concern about or involvement with the innovation is indicated.

Source: For more information, see Hall, G. E., & Hord, S. M. (2011). *Implementing change: Patterns, principles and potholes* (3rd ed.). Upper Saddle River, NJ: Pearson.

Describing Teacher Concerns

Teacher education candidates, teachers, and others will typically have concerns in one of four areas: *Unconcerned, Self, Task,* and *Impact.* Researchers have divided these major areas of concern into a set of **Stages of Concern** that people may move through as they experience any type of change. Since becoming a teacher represents a major change process, the Concerns Model certainly applies. A typical question that a teacher would ask when she or he has concerns in each of these areas and stages is presented in Table 16.1. The following are general descriptions of each of these areas of concern:

Unconcerned There is little or no concern about teaching. Instead the concerns are about other topics such as work, a family problem, getting along with a roommate, or an upcoming event such as getting tickets for a concert.

Self Concerns Having enough information and wanting to know more are of concern, as well as concerns about one's adequacy and ability to be a successful teacher. Doubt might be about knowing enough content, controlling the class, knowing how to teach a particular lesson, or being uncomfortable when standing in front of the class. These concerns can pop up each time you enter a new classroom or are getting ready to teach a lesson for the first time.

Audio Link 16.1
Listen to a clip about teacher concerns.

Task Concerns Finding the time to fit everything in, getting all the materials organized, preparing lesson plans, and grading papers are likely topics of concern. Learning the how-to-do-its of teaching and coordinating schedules are other indicators of Task concerns. Teachers have a lot to do, so being concerned about getting it all done should make sense to you.

Impact Concerns Having ideas about what could be done to further improve your effectiveness as a teacher and especially concerns about student learning are indicators of Impact concern. Thinking about ways to increase all students' learning, improving one's effectiveness as a teacher, and getting the last two students to understand are clear indicators of Impact concern. Another concern could be about working with one or more fellow teachers so that *together* you can have a greater effect on student learning.

There Is a Developmental Pattern to Teacher Concerns

It is very important to keep in mind that there are no "bad" areas of concern. All areas of concern are possible. In fact, there are some general patterns to how teacher concerns evolve. Teacher education candidates will have more Self and Task concerns, while experienced teachers have more Impact concerns. If you think about it, this difference in the distribution of concerns makes sense. Beginners are more likely to have doubts about their ability to do something (Self concerns) and to be more preoccupied with logistics and getting everything done (Task concerns). These areas of concern are also characteristic of first-year teachers.

Impact concerns are more likely to be present with those who are comfortable and confident with what they are doing. This is the time when teacher concerns can truly focus on improving student learning. Most teachers won't have a majority of their concerns being about Impact until after they have taught for several years.

Assessing Your Concerns

Assessing one's concerns is easy to do. Once there is an understanding of the four areas of concern and the more specific Stages of Concern, as outlined in Table 16.1, a person's concerns can be analyzed. Whether written or spoken, most concerns can be sorted into one of the four areas and then the specific stage can be identified using the descriptions in Table 16.1.

As a first example of how to assess an open-ended concerns statement, read what you wrote in response to the open-ended concerns statement that was presented above. Do the following:

1. Which area of concern (Unconcerned, Self, Task, or Impact) is most present? Were your concerns mainly related to teaching, or more about other things? Were your concerns centered mainly on your ability to succeed in your college courses? Did they relate to how you will manage teaching? Did any part of your statement relate to student learning? As you read what you wrote, what is the overall view—Unconcerned, Self, Task, or Impact?

2. Which Stage(s) of Concern was most present? Use the definitions presented in Table 16.1 as the guide for determining which Stages of Concern are most often reflected in your statement. Sometimes what you have written will not be as easy to figure out, but with a little practice sorting concern statements becomes easier.
3. Keep this analysis of your concerns in mind as you read below.

Implications of the Concerns Model for Teacher Education Candidates

Once a teacher's concerns have been analyzed, the very important follow-up question should be this: What needs to be done to address the concerns and to facilitate the teacher continuing to improve? This question is what makes the Concerns Model so important for teacher education candidates and inservice teachers. When you understand your concerns, you can do something about them. Effective teacher education programs are designed with candidate concerns in mind. For example, most candidates have concerns about managing the classroom (Task concerns), so many preparation programs include a course on classroom management. Another important component of effective teacher education programs is how to assess student learning (Task and Impact concerns).

Candidates that understand their concerns can do many things on their own to address them. For example, candidates with Self concerns will be more hesitant to ask questions of others. "What if they think my question is stupid?" Understanding this tendency can help you to assert yourself more. This insight should also help you to be more understanding when your students have Self concerns.

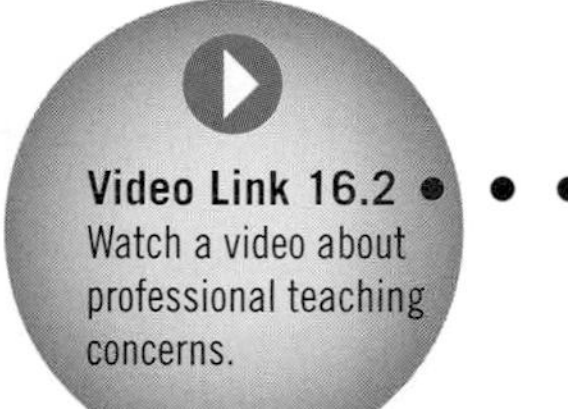

Video Link 16.2
Watch a video about professional teaching concerns.

Monitoring Your Concerns About Teaching

As you continue in your teacher education program and as you become a first-year teacher it will be important for you to document the evolution of your concerns. At regular intervals, respond again to the open-ended concerns statement. You will likely see a progression in your concerns. Ideally, by the end of student teaching you will have fewer Self and Task concerns and more Impact concerns. However, as you become a first-year teacher, what do think will happen to your concerns?

Most first-year teachers will return to having more Self and Task concerns. They have a lot to learn, many lessons to prepare, and meetings to attend, and they also have to get to know their colleagues and the principal. It makes sense that first-year teachers will have more Self and Task concerns. This is OK. It is what happens to any of us when we are experiencing something new (Hall & Hord, 2011).

Implications for You

We have introduced the idea of concerns with the hope that understanding your concerns will help you in being reflective. This understanding will help you to take steps to resolve many of them. As we stated above, the more you understand about yourself, the more quickly you can become an exceptional teacher.

The Concerns Model can help you in another way too. What about your classmates? What do you hear about their concerns? Do you hear more Unconcerned, Self, Task, or Impact concerns? The concerns idea also applies to your students. What concerns are they reflecting when they say, "I don't know if I can do this"; "Ah, homework tonight; I already have two hours of it for two of

• • • UNDERSTANDING AND USING EVIDENCE • • •

Analyzing Teachers' Concerns About Teaching

In most of the chapters in this text, the Understanding and Using Evidence box has required you to work with quantitative data. The task required working with numbers or graphic representations and developing an interpretation. In addition, each of these activities was based in data about students or schools. The task for this chapter is different in two ways. First of all, the subject is teachers and aspiring teachers like you. Second, the data are qualitative instead of quantitative.

Open-Ended Concerns Statements From Three Student Teachers

The following paragraphs were written by student teachers.

JoAnne

Yesterday, right in the middle of my lesson, one of my students raised his hand and asked me who I went out with Saturday night! I said that we were in the midst of the lesson now. I just went on with the lesson. It really shook me. I don't really mind saying whatever I was doing, because they really did see me Saturday night. Should I have had him stay after school for asking? I felt like ignoring it—it was the only thing I could do. But I'm not sure if I was losing control. Will they disrespect me for it? I don't know how to react to it.

Greg

Now, I am less concerned about their learning the facts and more interested in their seeing the general patterns and understanding the concepts. If there is a word or concept they don't understand, we stop and go over it. I realize more clearly now how little they know and how lacking their background is. When I can help them make the connections, they really get it.

Sue

My father wants me to get a teaching certificate. Right now I am most concerned about getting married. We have booked the hotel and have the photographer too. But there is so much to do in the next two months!

Your Task

Analyzing concerns statements: Use the descriptions of the four areas of concern presented in Table 16.1 to assess each of the concerns statements. What areas and Stages of Concern are represented in each statement? First reread

my other classes!"; or "I have compared my writing to the rubric on the wall. I need to work on topic sentences."

What About Ms. Velasquez's Concerns?

Reread the opening interview with Ms. Velasquez. Which areas of concern and which specific Stages of Concern did she talk about? Clearly her overall perspective is based in Impact concerns. She not only expressed concerns about her students learning (Stage 4, Consequence); she also offered suggestions for your learning as a teacher education candidate (Stage 4, Consequence). Ms. Velasquez also expressed Impact concerns about the importance of working with colleagues (Stage 5, Collaboration). Given that at the time of the interview she was nearing the end of her each concerns statement and determine its overall flavor. Does it sound most like Unconcerned, Self, Task, or Impact? Then read each sentence and assign a specific Stage of Concern to it. How could you summarize your analysis?

Analyzing and Summarizing Teacher Concerns Statements

The three open-ended concerns statements reflect very different Stages of Concern. One way to summarize each teacher's concerns would be to construct a table.

Student Teacher	Overall Area of Concern	Stage(s) of Concern
JoAnne	Self	Stage 2 Personal
Greg	Impact	Stage 4 Consequence
Sue	Unconcerned (about teaching)	Stage 0 Unconcerned

Addressing Their Concerns

Given how different each student teacher's concerns are, probably each person should be supported individually.

JoAnne's concerns could be addressed through a talk with her cooperating teacher or student teacher supervisor. There will definitely be times when students ask inappropriate questions or ask them at the wrong time. JoAnne's not letting the question disrupt the flow of the lesson certainly made sense. In this particular case, JoAnne might also consider not going to the certain places on the weekend where her students will see her.

Greg clearly has Impact concerns at Stage 4, Consequence. He is focused on how well his students are learning. He also is discovering how important it is to be knowledgeable about the learning background and experiences each student brings to his classes. Now his challenge is in helping students build a bridge/scaffold from where they are to understanding the concepts that Greg is teaching. He might want to read more about informal ways to assess student understanding, and learn more about his students' background of out-of-school experiences that could be used to help them understand in-class content.

Sue doesn't seem to have teaching-related concerns. Although each of us will have personal things going on in our lives, when it comes to being a successful teacher the nonteaching concerns need to be set aside. Someone needs to help Sue focus on her responsibilities as a teacher. She also should seriously consider this question: Do you *really* want to be a teacher?

second year of teaching, in terms of the Concerns Model she clearly already is a high-quality teacher.

Strive for Quality in Your Teaching

In everything that you do in your teacher preparation program, *strive for quality.* If an instructor makes an assignment that is confusing, ask for clarification. If you are not fully satisfied with a field placement, think through what you can do to still learn from the experience. Use every assignment and experience as an opportunity to learn more about teaching. In every situation there is the potential to find an idea that can help you become a better teacher. Finding these

Teachers need to spend time thinking/reflecting and considering what to do next based on what their students are doing now.

ideas is your responsibility. Here are three particularly useful strategies:

1. Have in mind a generic teaching model that can be used to examine any teaching situation.
2. Take advantage of every field experience to learn something.
3. Whenever possible, collect samples of teacher and student work.

Elliott's General Model of Effective Instruction

Throughout this text the authors have emphasized the importance of teachers focusing on student learning (back to Impact concerns). We have described a broad array of contextual factors (e.g., student diversity, special needs, and ELL) and introduced several instructional strategies (e.g., different ways of grouping students). The importance of assessing student learning and methods for doing so (e.g., rubrics) has been emphasized. Given the large number of methods, strategies, and factors that have been introduced, it now should be helpful to offer a general model that can serve as an overall organizer, reminder, and guide. Such a model can help you keep in mind all that teachers need to do to have high-quality teaching that results in all students learning.

One such model has been proposed by Emerson Elliott (2005) (see Table 16.2), who is a national expert on accreditation of teacher education and assessing high-quality teaching. His model "defines expectations for evidence that PreK–12 student learning has occurred, constructed around a core of activities in which the candidate takes responsibility for a significant unit of instruction" (p. 1). This model is generic; it can be applied to all levels of schooling, different kinds of students, and all subject areas. Each of the core activities is basic to effective and high-quality teaching. The elements outlined in Table 16.2 have been introduced and emphasized throughout this textbook.

One of your major responsibilities as you complete your preparation program is to become knowledgeable and skilled at doing each of the elements outlined in this model. They may be given different names. Whatever they are called, these are the essential components of high-quality instruction. By the end of your program you will need to have artifacts in your portfolio that document your capabilities to do each of the components of this model. Be sure to collect specific examples and artifacts related to each component of the model.

One useful approach that addresses each of the activities of this generic model is the Teacher Work Sample (TWS) methodology that was described in Chapter 13.

The Importance of Each and Every Field Experience

Striving for quality in field experiences is very important for aspiring teachers. Candidates consistently report that the most important part of their preparation program was student teaching. This is the capstone experience where everything that has been introduced, studied, and dissected throughout your professional education courses is brought together in the "real"

Table 16.2 Core Activities for a Significant Unit of Instruction That Leads to PreK–12 Student Learning

Setting appropriate expectations for evidence that PreK–12 student learning has occurred, constructed around a core of activities in which the candidate **takes responsibility for a significant unit of instruction,** and	
JUDGES PRIOR LEARNING	Undertakes a systematic assessment (based in standards and benchmarks) to understand the prior PreK–12 student learning in the area he or she will teach;
PLANS INSTRUCTION	Plans an appropriate sequence of instruction to advance PreK–12 student learning, based on the prior assessment;
TEACHES	Teaches PreK–12 students to acquire and use content knowledge in meaningful ways, engaging those who bring differing background knowledge and learning needs, and providing students opportunities to demonstrate the use of critical and creative thinking skills;
ASSESSES	Conducts a concluding objective test or alternative assessment(s);
ANALYSES	Analyzes the results of the concluding assessment(s), documenting the student learning that occurred at individual and group levels, including explanations of results from students who learned more or less than expected, and results from each subgroup of students; and
REFLECTS	Reflects on change in teaching that could improve results.

Source: Elliott, E. (2005). *Student learning in NCATE accreditation.* Washington, DC: National Council for the Accreditation of Teacher Education.

world. This is the time when you get to teach. Naturally your first concerns will be about preparing each lesson (Task concerns). However, do not lose sight of why you are there and presenting the lesson: It is to help each and every student learn. Be sure to incorporate formative assessment questions and tasks, and obtain evidence of the extent to which your students are learning.

As important and significant as student teaching is, do not underestimate the important learning opportunities that come with every other clinical activity and field experience. Whether it is observing a lesson, or monitoring student behavior on the playground or in the cafeteria, there are opportunities to learn. Your learning will not always be about teaching; it might be about characteristics of students, or classroom or school procedures. The Impact-concerned candidate always takes advantage of every activity as an opportunity to learn something new. One way to do this is to set a personal objective: *In every experience I will seek to learn at least one new thing.* When you engage each experience with the expressed intention of learning something new, you will!

Be sure to express your appreciation to the teacher(s) who permitted you to be there. They did not have to open the door. Teachers are under tremendous pressure to make every minute count. Many are self-conscious (Self concerns?) about letting anyone observe them. Without their openness you would have to learn the basics of teaching OJT (on the job). So be sure to say "thank you."

Challenging Assumptions

Should student teaching be done in the most difficult and hard-to-staff settings?

• • • • •

Many suggest that student teaching assignments should be in the most challenging schools—schools with more low-performing students and more teacher turnover—the rationale being that these schools are the most likely settings for the first assignments of beginning teachers and that more can be learned from having intensive experiences in these settings. The counterrational is that student teachers can learn more in schools that are easier to staff and offer desirable teaching conditions.

Most studies of learning outcomes focus on what the school students learn. In the study reported by Matthew Ronfeldt (2012), the focus was on examining the outcomes of the school placements of student teachers. Two of the study questions were (1) Were teachers who had student taught in a difficult-to-staff school more or less likely to leave teaching in the first 5 years? and (2) Did teachers who had student taught in a difficult-to-staff school have higher or lower student gains when compared with teachers who had student taught in easier-to-staff schools?

Study Design and Method

Administrative and survey data from nearly 3,000 New York City teachers, their students, and their schools were analyzed. The teachers in the study sample were, on average, 30 years old, 65% white, and three-fourths female. Forty-seven percent of the sample came through an early entry teacher education program, either Teach for America or Teaching Fellows.

Study Findings

The study found that: (1) teachers who student taught in easier-to-staff schools had higher retention rates, (2) teachers who student taught in easier-to-staff schools were more effective at raising test scores, and (3) teachers who did their student teaching in easier-to-staff schools had better retention and achievement gains even if they had their full-time teaching assignments in the hardest-to-staff schools with the most underserved student populations.

Implications

The findings from this study suggest that future teachers learn more about teaching when their student placement is in schools that are functioning more effectively. In these settings they can experience more effective instruction, be mentored by more effective functioning teachers, and experience what it is like to be in a school that overall is doing well. The findings from the Ronfeldt study suggest that what is learned in these settings is carried into their succeeding years as full-time teachers.

As your time for student teaching nears, you will want to think about the alternative beliefs about where to be placed for student teaching and to consider carefully the findings from this study.

Source: Ronfeldt, M. (2012, March). Where should student teachers learn to teach? Effects of field placement school characteristics on teacher retention and effectiveness. *Educational Evaluation and Policy Analysis, 34*(1), 3–26.

WHAT ARE THE KEYS TO BEING HIRED AS A BEGINNING TEACHER?

I am Round Rock bred and have made the full circle. I went to school here, graduated from here, I did my student teaching here, and now I teach here. Also, I always have been a mentor to children, even in high school. It is something I enjoy doing. I feel so strongly about doing something in my own community. I want to help the upcoming generation. This is my way of staying in tune with what I like to do.—Ms. Velasquez

Video Link 16.3
Learn more about teacher training.

Back in Chapter 1 we introduced you to the big picture of what is entailed in becoming a teacher. In each of the succeeding chapters another major aspect of teaching was introduced. It is not too early for you to now begin thinking about what will be needed and what it will be like to seek and get your first teaching position. There will be a number of applicants competing for most positions. This is especially true for low-need areas such as elementary, social studies, and physical education. As was introduced in Chapter 1, there are a number of steps and requirements that must be completed to become a fully qualified teacher. Now is the time to begin anticipating and preparing what you will need to have accomplished and be able to demonstrate so that you are the one that will be hired for the teaching position you would most like to have.

Requirements for Obtaining a Teacher License

The licensing requirements for public school teachers are set by each state. In addition, federal legislation, such as what happened under NCLB, can mandate that each state has to establish certain requirements for teachers that are "highly qualified." For example, over the last several years each state has had to develop a teacher evaluation model that is at least in part based in student test scores.

Deeper Look 16.1
Read about teacher certification requirements.

The following are typical basic requirements for obtaining a teaching license:

- Successful completion of a state-approved preparation program. Programs may be offered by a higher education institution, a school district, or another agency.
- **Criminal background check**, including fingerprinting. No one with a criminal record may teach.
- Passing state-required tests, typically of content and pedagogical knowledge. In some states examples of teaching performance, such as a portfolio or teacher work sample, may be required.
- Having a major and perhaps advanced study in the subject(s) you plan to teach.

In addition to state requirements, each school district may have additional requirements. If you have not done so, check both your state and your preferred school district websites for the specific requirements you must meet in order to be eligible to apply for a teaching position.

In a job interview it is likely that teacher applicants will be asked to provide evidence of how they have affected student learning.

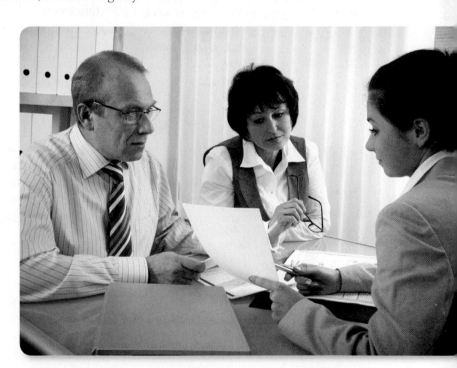

Getting Your First Teaching Position

All of the effort that you are putting into becoming a teacher will be for naught if you are not successful in obtaining a teaching position. Until recently there was a demand for teachers in all areas, especially the Southwest. Now with budget cuts there is heavy competition for each and every opening. The following are a few suggestions for being successful in the search.

Where to Look for Teaching Positions

All public school openings will be published and open to all qualified applicants. The place to begin, if there is a particular school district where you would like to teach, is by checking its website. The district home page will include a link to the human resources department or may directly link to positions that are currently open. Even if you will not be teaching for several years, now would be a good time to check a district's website and study the position requirements. Take careful notes about what is entailed in making an application.

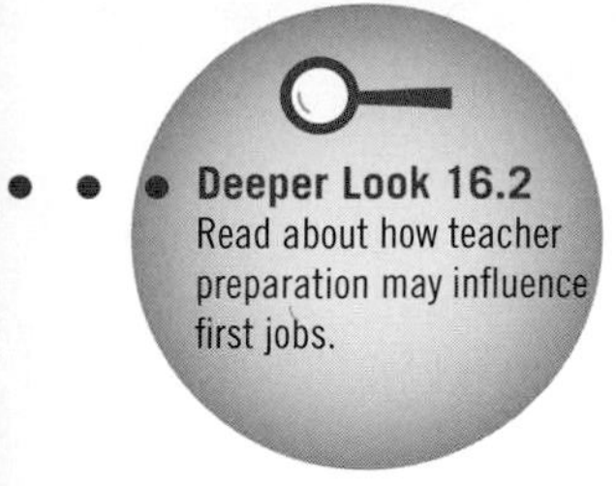

Deeper Look 16.2
Read about how teacher preparation may influence first jobs.

Another useful resource for finding out about openings is *Education Week*. This is the national newspaper for the K–12 education profession. It is published weekly during the school year and reports on national, state, and local education topics. At the back will be many pages of classified advertisements, where school districts publish their position openings.

Don't forget to check out state education department websites, many of which list job openings. If you are interested in teaching overseas, it is possible:

Department of Defense Education Activity (DoDEA)

To serve the families of U.S. military personnel stationed overseas, the Department of Defense (**http://www.dodea.edu**) operates schools and districts in many locations in Europe, Japan, Korea, and the Middle East. DoDEA also operates schools on some military bases in the United States.

Overseas Schools

The U.S. Department of State (**http://www.state.gov**) and many other government agencies have personnel working in other countries. Many of these families support the operation of independent local schools. These schools are not funded directly by the U.S. government, but they are supported by them through teacher professional development and website links. Although each school does its own hiring, school administrators and teacher recruiters regularly visit association meetings in the United States.

Private Schools

There are many private schools in other countries that employ American teachers. For example, children of oil company employees based in the Middle East can attend company-supported schools, which use American curriculum and teachers (e.g., Aramco in Saudi Arabia, http://jobs.saudiaramco.com). Various church groups support schools in other countries too. Probably the best approach to finding out about openings for teachers is to make direct contact with a particular school's office.

Teaching English Abroad

Another strategy for gaining a teaching position overseas is to teach English to students of the host country. A number of countries such as Japan, South Korea, and China are very active in recruiting teachers of English. A potential downside to this strategy is that many of the positions provide little if any salary. Many of the opportunities are in very rural areas, which means one needs to be more adventuresome and ready to live, and teach, with fewer of the accustomed amenities.

Ideas for Your Professional Resume

An important document, that you can begin preparing now, is a professional resume (see Table 16.3). This is a one- (or no more than two-) page summary of your qualifications and related experiences. Although most of the categories seem obvious, preparing a strong resume will take

Figure 16.1 Professional Resume: Suggestions for Topics and Elements

NAME

ADDRESS

PHONE NUMBER

E-MAIL (DON'T USE A SILLY E-MAIL ADDRESS.)

Philosophy/Bio Paragraph: In one paragraph, describe who you are and why you want to be a teacher. What do you believe about teaching and students? Why are schools important?

QUALIFICATIONS

Education: List college degrees and any specialized certificates. Don't forget to name the institution(s), and probably the dates for each. You might want to include GPA or other indicators of strength and quality.

Licensure: Name the license and areas of certification.

Special Certifications: Name any endorsements, such as special education or ELL.

Recognitions: List honors, awards, and other forms of recognition.

Special Skills: Do you have areas of expertise or special skills, such as speaking a second language? Have you lived in different places, or abroad? Have you had leadership experiences in work, your community, or your church?

Examples of Your Teaching: Have available artifacts of the work and evidence of the learning that has taken place when you have been teaching. Be able to provide photos of students and their work (don't forget to have parent permissions) and/or videos of your teaching.

Work Experience: List past work experiences. These may include nonschool work. List those that demonstrate that you are reliable, that you can hold a job over time, and that you will bring a range of experiences to the classroom.

Community Service: Describe ways that you have been, or are, involved in giving back through volunteer activities, or in other ways providing service to one or more parts of your community.

Outside Interests: Perhaps you will want to list hobbies or other activities that are an important part of your life. These can be especially useful for high school teachers who are expected to work with co-curricular activities.

Select, organize, and present these in a format that matches you to the position requirements.

some time and thought. Your portfolio tasks and artifacts will be a useful resource. Keep in mind that employers are looking not only for teachers who have good grades, but also for ones who can document that they can make a major difference in student learning. They also will be looking for teachers who will be a resource to the school and contribute to the community. (What did Ms. Velasquez have to say about this?) They will be interested in your past work experiences, even if they were not in education. Your resume provides the opportunity to document not only that you meet the basic requirements for the position but also that you bring additional related expertise and valuable experience.

Teacher Dispositions Are Very Important

Deeper Look 16.3
Read about the importance of teacher dispositions.

As necessary as meeting the official licensure requirements and completing program requirements are, an unstated, but very important criterion for becoming a teacher is **dispositions.** The attitudes, beliefs, and values that teachers hold about students, the subjects they teach, their colleagues, parents, and the school are critical. Teachers who are not excited about the subjects they teach cannot develop enthusiasm for the subject in their students. Teachers who do not believe that certain students (boys/girls, poor, brown, special needs, or ELL) can learn cannot help those students learn. Teachers who do not see value in their colleagues, parents, and the school cannot help the school be successful. Reflect back on the interview quotes from Ms. Velasquez. There is nothing negative or undercutting about anything that she says. She is enthusiastic, and she reflects a belief that all students can learn and that she can be a positive influence on students, colleagues, and her community. Everything that she said had to do with opportunities and possibilities, not barriers. High-quality teachers always think, teach, and lead with a view that the glass is half full, not half empty.

IN WHAT WAYS CAN CANDIDATES AND TEACHERS BE LEADERS?

I have colleagues, specialists, the principal, and many parents coming into my classroom. Also, I am on the District Advisory Council. A teacher from every school is on this council. We meet with the superintendent once a month to discuss issues going on within the district. He bounces ideas off the teachers to see which way he wants to go. I will continue to work on my teaching craft during the summer months, teaching enrichment courses to students for the district and by attending professional development trainings focused on my personal learning goals.

As a leader, I go back to the idea that it is business, not personal. If anything needs to be addressed it is because it is going to affect the overall wellness of my kids. So, I just lay out expectations. If I have a problem with a parent, I address it with them.

As a leader you are responsible for maintaining professionalism at all times. Problems that threaten your goal of the academic achievement of your students need to be addressed immediately. Laying out expectations and norms with the colleagues you work with not only promotes collaboration, but guarantees respect for all professionals. Concerns with parents need to be handled confidentially and immediately. Establish a positive rapport with parents at the start of the year. Concerns can easily be resolved if you are both aware that each is working toward the academic achievement of their child!—Ms. Velasquez

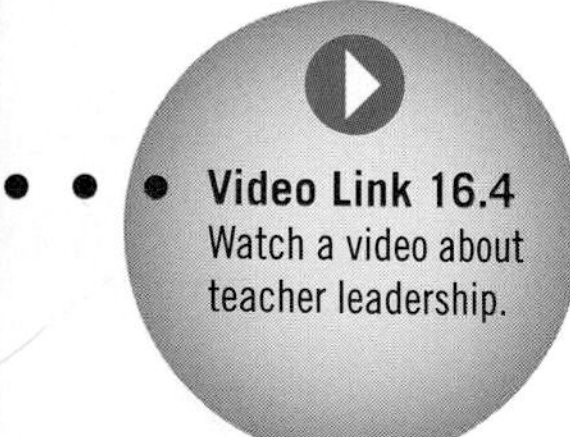
Video Link 16.4
Watch a video about teacher leadership.

Contrary to what you may have thought, leadership is not reserved to the principal or the superintendent. All members of an organization have leadership responsibilities. This is true for schools, businesses, church groups, and families. Unfortunately, too many teacher education candidates and teachers assume that they have no leadership responsibilities. In fact, the opposite is true—every member of the school staff, including those who refuse to participate, affects potential progress and success. Leadership skills and functions can be learned, and participating in different ways can be informative, influential, interesting, and even fun. There are many unofficial and informal ways to contribute to leadership, and there are formal leader positions and career paths for those who are motivated to make a difference in what the whole school or district accomplishes.

Different Ways Teachers Can Lead

Teachers tend to first think about leadership as something that administrators do. In this way of thinking the only people who are leaders are those who have official titles and responsibilities such as the principal, department chair, vice principal, and superintendent. However, scholars make a careful distinction between **leaders** and **leadership.** Leaders are those with formal, and informal, roles and responsibilities related to a group or the whole school accomplishing its objectives. Leadership encompasses the actions of leading. All members of the school staff have a leadership responsibility. You cannot escape this responsibility; you either help or hinder the attainment of the desired ends. Teacher leadership is accomplished through a number of ways.

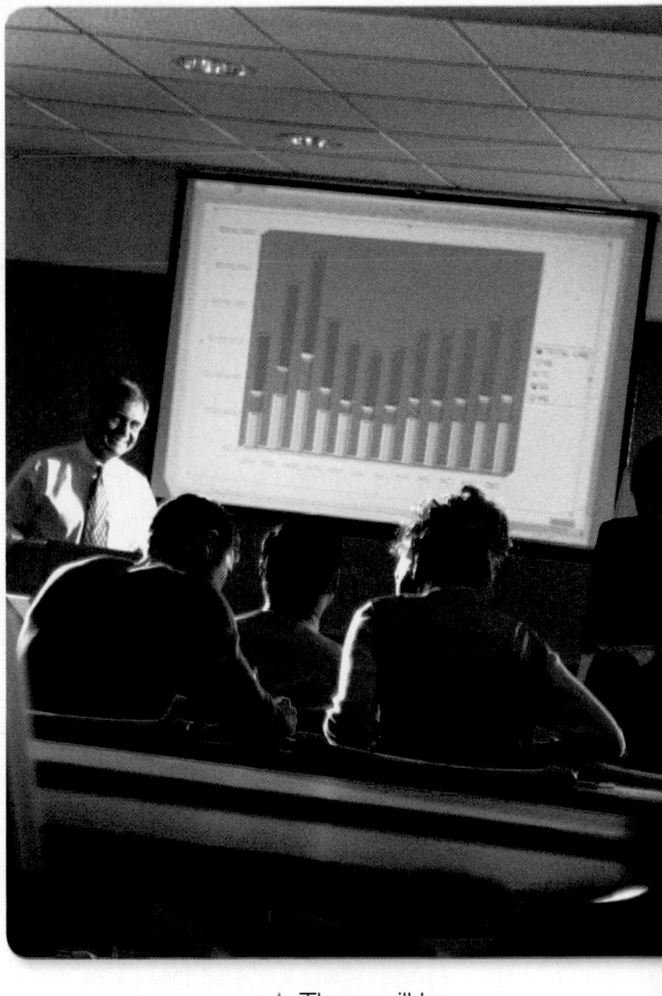

There will be opportunities throughout the school year for beginning teachers to share and learn from colleagues.

Formal Teacher Leadership

There are many opportunities for teacher education candidates and beginning teachers to have formal leader responsibilities. For example, Ms. Velasquez is providing leadership within her second-grade team of six teachers. "Our campus is very big on collaborative planning. We write our lessons together. Then there is the expectation that we will tweak them to meet our students." Other ways that a beginning teacher can lead include chairing school committees, serving as grade-level team leader, and being the coordinator of a co-curriculum such as pep squad or yearbook, or by being an assistant coach.

During the remainder of your teacher education program there will be a number of opportunities to be a formal leader. These include serving as the representative to organize candidates for an accreditation visit, chairing the student education association or honor society, and serving on the student advisory board. During student teaching there may be opportunities to assume some responsibility within the school. The basic message here is that rather than avoiding leader assignments, take them on. This is the best way to learn more about being a leader—by doing it!

Working With Parents

There is a big difference between **engaging** parents and **involving parents**. It is relatively simple to engage parents by having occasional notes for students to take home. A much higher level of investment is needed to fully involve parents in the school and teachers' classrooms (see Figure 16.2). Involving parents means making them a necessary part of what goes on. Involving parents in the school is very important for many reasons. The more parents understand about what is going on the more supportive they can be. The students of involved parents are likely to have better attendance and better grades. They also are more likely to complete homework assignments. An additional outcome in most schools is additional funding for the school. In some schools parents

Figure 16.2 Suggestions for Increasing Parent Involvement

1.	Give your students "talking points" to tell parents about what they are learning.
2.	Help parents develop a home environment that supports their children learning (e.g., "No TV nights").
3.	Provide parents with a way to guide and check on their child's homework (e.g., a rubric, or a description of the learning objective, or an assignment that parents can do with their child).
4.	Establish a way to have two-way communication: Teacher to parents *and* parents to teacher, *in their language.*
5.	Encourage parents to volunteer in your classroom (e.g., putting up bulletin boards and/or guiding small-group work).
6.	Attend events and activities in the community.
7.	Survey parents about what their children like about your classroom and about any concerns they might have.
8.	Place your lesson plans and assignments online. (This is a state mandate in Alabama.)
9.	Keep in mind that parents are likely to have Self concerns about meeting you, so be calm, supportive, and informed.
10.	Keep your school administrators informed about the ways you are planning to involve parents in your classroom.

will be a direct support to teachers. For example, in Ms. Velasquez's school there is a designated room for parents. There are three to six parents there every day!

> Our parents are very involved. They will be on campus every day. If teachers have something they need done, such as a bulletin board, copies, something cut out, a parent will volunteer to do that. There is a room called the Pro Center. That is where the parents are and they take on jobs that a teacher might not have time for. They are there all the time. Also, they organize events and fundraisers.

At a minimum, teachers must communicate with the parents of the students in their classroom. This is another form of leadership. In some schools parents will be available to help in the classroom. In those situations, teachers must develop skill organizing and guiding what parents do. In Ms. Velasquez's school there is more:

• Audio Link 16.2
Learn more about parent and school partnerships.

> In my case lots of the parents have college degrees. Two of my parents are former second-grade teachers. So they conduct small reading groups. We also have a program called "Watch D.O.G.S." (Dads of Great Students; http://fathers.com). It is pretty much a dads' organization. The dads take off from work and come to our school for the whole day. They come to their child's classroom and go to other classrooms, or they help the teacher with whatever she needs.

Informal Teacher Leadership

As important as formal leader roles can be, the informal roles are important also. One of the least understood is that of **followership.** As good as the formal leader may be, he or she will accomplish little unless the members of the group/team/committee/staff do their parts. Being a constructive member of the group, offering to help, contributing positively to the discussions, and being sure to complete assigned tasks, with quality and on time, are important skills for all followers. Each of us has experienced the colleague who sits in meetings with folded arms, and the one who grades papers rather than contributing to the discussion. We also have experienced the team member who promises to do a task and then doesn't deliver. Effective followership entails participating and volunteering help. Ms. Velasquez offers these thoughts:

> Outside of school I volunteer for the Neighborhood Conference Committee (NCC), which addresses truancy within the Round Rock School District. It deals with first-time truancy offenders. Once they have been visited by a truancy officer, their last step before they are referred to the courts is to come before NCC. They make a positive action plan to help this kiddo see the light, so to speak.

Deeper Look 16.4
Read about how teachers can and should be leaders.

A related concept is that of **distributed leadership.** The primary assumption in this model of leadership is that rather than leadership being the sole responsibility of the formal leader at the top of the organization, aka the principal, leadership should be distributed to many people and be seen as a shared responsibility. Distributed leadership is particularly useful in schools where teachers are seen as professionals whose work is not to be closely supervised. As professionals, teachers are expected to assume and share responsibilities for leadership.

Leading Adults Is a Big Challenge for Beginning Teachers

As good as being a teacher leader may sound, there will be challenges—especially for first-year teachers. Based on her experience, Ms. Velasquez offered the following insights:

> I do find it challenging. Last year I found it more challenging, because not only did I have the first-year teacher stigma, I had my age. What parent wants to be talked to about any problem with their child from a 22-year-old? It was difficult. I found that I not only had to have inner confidence, but that I also had to have outer confidence. The more confidence that I showed the better I was received.
>
> As much of a cliché as it sounds, dressing professional helped a lot. Through my actions, showing them that I know what I am talking about. Their coming into my classroom, seeing how I run my classroom, how my classroom management skills are, and how I interact with their child really calmed down my parents who knew I was a first-year teacher. At the beginning of the year, I had a really lot of parent involvement. Then around December it all went away. So it was kind of like they were testing me out, then once I built a relationship with them, and they knew what I was about, all my parents kind of eased up.

Career Path Options for Teachers

Although at this point you are thinking mostly about completing your initial teacher education program, becoming licensed to teach, and obtaining your first full-time teaching position, it is not too early to learn about the various career options that are open to teachers. In the past most teachers stayed in the classroom as teachers for 20 or 30 years. (One of your authors once interviewed a teacher who had taught kindergarten in the same school and in the same classroom for 26 years!) Today, the career options for teachers are many including changing grade levels and schools within the same district.

Terror! That was the only way I can describe my reaction when my mentor for student-teaching told me he was being moved from the middle school back to the high school, where he had taught thirteen years ago. "So," he said, " instead of teaching Introductory French to seventh and eighth-grade students, you will be teaching ninth-grade French Honors, and tenth- and eleventh-grade French Regents." Honors! How was I going to be smart enough to do that? Eleventh grade? I was nineteen years old, 5′ 2″ tall and 105 pounds soaking wet! Why would they listen to me? He sensed my concern. "Look, as teachers we use whatever we've got to reach the students. I'm 6′ 4″ with a booming voice. You have a warm, exuberant smile and tremendous energy. That's what you'll use."

Believe me, I practiced my French (and my smile) nonstop during the summer leading up to student-teaching. To my amazement, my mentor teacher was right. I was able to build rapport quickly and easily and make my behavior expectations clear. I never needed a big voice, not then nor in any phase of my teaching.

As a new teacher, I wanted to learn as much as I possibly could. I embraced every professional development opportunity I could find. I was such a regular participant in workshops that, after ten years of teaching children, I was hired to teach workshops to teachers.

Terror again! I was thirty years old and going to tell veteran teachers how to do their jobs better? What was I thinking? I discussed this with my boss. His reply?

"We have a phrase around here that might help you—Fake it until you make it!" I thought that sounded like good advice until I looked at the list of teachers who would attend my workshop the next week. My fifth-grade teacher (who I had adored) was attending! I knew I couldn't fake it. It was then that I remembered my student teaching mentor's advice. "Use what you've got" became my mantra and, still teaching workshops twenty-four years later, the smile and energy seem to be working!

Lauri Pepe Bousquet
Le Moyne College

Becoming a School Administrator

The most obvious career step is to "move up" the administration ladder. Becoming a department chair, an assistant principal, and then principal is the career path chosen by some teachers. Nearly all school and district administrators will have been teachers earlier in their careers; this includes the superintendent. There also are many staff assignments open to teachers. Within schools there are a number of specialist positions such as for literacy or technology, as well as community liaisons and special education resource teachers. Many other staff positions are available in the district office, including curriculum coordinators, staff developers, technology directors, and the professionals that work with federal funds such as Title I, bilingual, compensatory education, and special education. In brief, there are many career options within schools and the district office for teachers who wish to expand their horizons and move into leadership positions.

Graduate Studies

Pursuing one or more graduate degrees is another way to keep learning and to advance your career. In most school districts obtaining a certain number of hours of advance study or a graduate degree will be reflected in increases in salary. There are many possibilities in terms of degree options and areas of concentration. The first step for most teachers is to take graduate course work and obtain a master's degree. This degree could be in curriculum and instruction, educational technology, or a subject area such as literacy, history, mathematics, or science education. Other teachers will want to receive advance preparation in special education, learning, or assessment. Master's degrees in special education or educational psychology will address these areas.

Another direction for graduate study is educational leadership. Most of these programs will include meeting the state qualifications for an administrator license. Some focus less on license preparation and more on leadership development per se. Most master's degrees will entail around 35 semester hours of course work.

Once a master's degree has been completed, there is the possibility of pursuing the doctoral degree. Depending on the institution of higher education, one of two doctoral degrees will be available. The EdD is a doctoral degree specifically designed for educators. In most institutions this will be a practitioner-oriented course of study. The PhD may be practitioner oriented but more often is more research focused. In either case, the program will include further course work and the penultimate component will be the dissertation study. This will be an original research study addressing some aspect of teaching, learning, curriculum, or leadership, or some other aspect of schooling. Most doctoral programs will include 30 to 40 hours of course work "beyond the master's," and approximately 12 hours of credit for the dissertation.

Teachers who wish to become faculty members in colleges or universities will need a doctoral degree. Although this possibility for you is a number of years away, beginning to understand now what the steps and qualifications are for career advancement introduces some of the many possibilities and provides background information for use in future planning.

HOW DOES A MASTER TEACHER THINK ABOUT THE JOY OF TEACHING?

One of the major themes embedded within each chapter of this text is *the joy of teaching.* The authors see this theme being critical, since having joy in what you do as a teacher is so important to you and to the students and adults you work with. Joy is about emotions. It is seeing success in each student, taking delight in their learning and how the class is growing. Joy includes the great pleasure that comes from making a difference in each and every student. It comes in the satisfaction of having a lesson go well. It also comes in grappling with the major challenges in teaching and schooling, and knowing that being a teacher is important.

Video Case 16.1
Keys to Succeeding

1. What are these teachers saying are the most important reasons for becoming a teacher?
2. How well do your expectations align with the views of these teachers?

When asked about joy Ms. Velasquez observed,

> Knowing I am giving back to my community. That's a huge part of it. I get a chance to teach in my own community. Seeing the children grow. There is very quantitative

data. You can see a child grow in reading. You can see a child grow in writing. And you also can see them grow socially through their interactions every day.

People in business gain a great deal of their satisfaction from the amount of money they make and through their efforts to grow a business. Teachers most certainly are not joyful when they see the size of their paychecks. For teachers the joy comes from the difference they make in the lives of their students. There is joy in seeing the lightbulb come on for a student who has been struggling to understand a concept. There is joy in seeing the whole class work together to share strategies for solving a puzzling problem. Teachers have enormous responsibilities. Almost completely by themselves, elementary teachers are responsible for the care and learning of 30 students for an entire school year. Secondary teachers will be responsible for 150 students each day! There is satisfaction and purpose in this level of responsibility and in making a positive difference.

Joy and Satisfaction in Teaching Can Be Career Long

Teaching is a very significant and special profession that most people do not get the opportunity to do. Most adults never have the opportunity to teach. Yet, nearly every adult can readily name one, two, or even three teachers that made all the difference to them and what they have become. This is another of the many ways that teachers experience joy in teaching. When one of their former students returns and describes the difference the teacher made in their lives and how successful they are now, their teacher will be delighted.

Deeper Look 16.5
Read about beginning special education teachers.

Your authors can readily point out elements of this theme within each chapter. However, some of the elements of this theme are more subtle. The inclusion of less obvious elements of joy has been intentional. Seeing the joy in teaching is in large part the responsibility of the observer. Some teachers can list everything that is wrong with teaching and have to think hard to remember the good parts. Other teachers only see the joy in their students, themselves, and their school. This difference in teachers is not simply a matter of how old they are, or how long they have been teaching. It is a part of one's spirit. There are really old teachers who are still enthusiastic and looking for opportunities to learn new things. Some teacher education candidates already are grumps, while others are laughing at themselves and overflowing with excitement about learning to teach. In many ways, experiencing the joy in teaching is your responsibility.

To illustrate the joy of teaching and how master teachers never lose this perspective, we end this text with an interview with Mrs. Joyce Schneider. She retired after 42—yes, 42—years of teaching! Parents would press the principal to have their children assigned to Mrs. Schneider's classroom. She was known across the entire school district as being a phenomenal teacher. As a result of her status as a master teacher she was asked to serve on district and state committees, to lead teacher workshops, and to teach teacher education courses. She worked with the local university's student teaching supervisors to develop their student teaching handbook. She is known by all as a master teacher who always sees the joy in teaching.

We asked her about where she found joy in teaching. As you will see in the interview excerpts, she continues to have high enthusiasm about teaching and continues to be involved. As a result, our interview wandered over many topics and experiences, and concluded with one of those unplanned happenings that so clearly illustrates the joy of teaching.

"First of All, I Love Kids"

I love kids. That's the key. When I walked into the classroom, I wanted everyone to feel valued. They have to feel that they are a very important part of the family that I was working with as my classroom. I never looked at my class as a class. I looked at them as individuals that came together.

Every year I got to know them as completely as I could and then say, how can I help that person be the best he or she can be? It was fun! I would do a lot of activities to get them to empower themselves.

For example, at the start of every year I would watch them. I would greet them at the door, welcome them to my room, and say, "I am so happy you are here." We would exchange smiles and positive things. If they were working on something I would make sure that I asked, "How did you do on your writing last night?" "Did you finish that chapter in the book that you were enjoying?" There was that positive connection, and it was individual. I was never a phony; kids pick up on that real quick.

I did the same thing when they left: "OK now, I know that you are going to work on your 5s in multiplication tonight. Which ones are you still struggling with, and which ones are you good at?" I would be specific and always focus on the positives. "I see you improving in your sentence structure and here's why." Those kids would skip out of the room. Do you think they wanted to come back on Monday? Absolutely!

Retired teacher Mrs. Joyce Schneider continues giving and learning.

I am a positive person. I taught the whole class to focus on the positives. As they saw me do it, they would begin to see the same things I saw. They would see that this kid improved on his writing, or reading, or became a much better thinker.

"I Saw That I Was Making a Difference"

I stayed in teaching because I saw that I was making a difference. I love talking with kids. I love building and empowering people. I was not always a strong person. I was very quiet. I had to build positiveness in me first, and then I could build it in others. Not only did it work in the classroom; parents would come to me and say, "Whatever you are doing is making a huge difference in our family." It's the same in business and elsewhere; if you value that human being, the results are magnificent and the joy is there.

How adults think and how kids think is so different. They are so literal. One time we were selling something for PTA. It was chocolate or something. There also was a coupon that the buyer could exchange for something. I pointed out to the kids that it didn't cost them that much for the chocolate because they would get the price back through the free coupon. The kids went out to sell and one came back and said, "This didn't work. We didn't get it for free." He had thought that it was really free, instead of having to buy the chocolate. They think in very literal ways and have to develop high-level thinking.

I know that people keep saying that "kids are different today," but I didn't see that difference. I always taught the child. When you teach the child and address their

There is much joy to be found in teaching and learning—for students and their teachers.

needs, it isn't a whole lot different. You look at the person and say, "He needs organizational skills." This other person needs . . . I think a lot of people use those statements as cop-outs. I never felt that way. I always taught individual kids. I taught kids to love to learn.

My [students'] parents would say to me, "I can't put my finger on it, but what you do with kids is phenomenal. You bring in current events. You bring in human interest stories and you talk about them. You get them to look at the whole world in a different way. Then they come home and teach us the same things."

"I Loved Sharing With Others"

If something worked for me, I loved sharing it with others. I loved starting something that worked, sharing it, and making it even better. Or, if somebody would say, "Boy, am I having a struggle with this," I loved sharing ideas with them. They would go back, and then I would say to them, "How did that work?" And, if it didn't work we would spend some more time figuring out what to try next.

I got a lot of joy out of student teachers too. I had at least 25 student teachers. We would evaluate lessons, how they thought it went, what they liked about it, and what they didn't. For the things they didn't like, I would say, "OK, what can we do differently?"

However, some teachers didn't want to share. You just learn not to share if they didn't want to. You just stay being a positive teacher.

Principals can make or break you in the classroom. I loved it when principals would say specific things they saw. Not that you were a good teacher. But when they would say, "When I walked into your classroom, I could not tell which of the students were struggling." That was one of the highest compliments I would get, because I would always involve my kids in discussions and teach them how to think. When the principal would come and she would say, "I cannot tell. All of them are involved. They have their hands up and all of them are coming up with great ideas." That was one of the highest compliments I could get.

I was very fortunate to seek out those kinds of principals. It always was the same thing. They saw my love for teaching, they saw the success I had, and the results I got. When they were assigned to a new school they would always take me with them.

I only had one principal that was not that way. He was insecure. I always tell my student teachers, "It doesn't make any difference whether you work for a man or woman, you look for that secure person and then you will have a wonderful time."

"I Was Always Bringing Human Interest Stories to Share With the Kids"

Mrs. Schneider continually kept informed about the world at large, not just what was required to teach. "I listened to the *Today Show.* I listened to all news." She also read books and would read them to her classes. For example, at the time of our interview she had just completed reading Thomas Freidman's book *The World Is Flat: A Brief History of the Twenty-First Century.*

> In front of my classroom is "Yes I can." You see, the only thing that ever stops us from doing something is ourselves. I think we can do anything in life if we believe we can. I would constantly reinforce this through human interest stories that were appropriate to their level. For example, I read them Michael Jordan's book, *I Can't Accept Not Trying: Michael Jordan on the Pursuit of Excellence.* When he was in high school he tried out for basketball and did not make it. He said he never wanted to feel that way again. So he practiced and practiced. So we talked about that and how important it is to practice. I would always bring books like that and read them to kids. My classrooms were always literature rich.

You Need to Have a Notion of What You Want Your Classroom to Be Like Before You Get There

Our last interview question for Mrs. Schneider was, "What advice do you have for teacher education candidates?"

> First of all, they need to have a notion of what they want their classroom to be like before they ever step in it. I would always say, what is it that I would want my child to experience in my classroom? You have to have a working knowledge in your head of what you want your classroom to be like. Here is mine: They had to get ready for life. It made a huge difference when I decided that, because all of the things I taught were then related to this goal.
>
> Once you decide, you need to have consistent routines. I was consistent in my expectations. I greeted them at the door every morning. My one rule was respect for yourself, respect for the earth, and respect for each other. Why would you not put your hands on the wall? Because you would just make more work for the custodian. I always focused on their actions and made sure that they didn't think that I was not supporting them as a person.
>
> Today, I think we are overtesting. When I was in the classroom, I never let it bother me. But I know that it is huge on teachers' minds. I would just test, get it over with, and get back to teaching. I never worried about testing because my kids always did well. I just taught the curriculum, and they always did well.
>
> The most important thing on entering the classroom is that you have a positive outlook on life. I never allowed things to not be a joy.

Serendipity Occurs as We Are Concluding the Interview With Mrs. Schneider

Our interview with Mrs. Schneider took place in a neighborhood coffee shop. Just as we were concluding the interview, a middle-aged woman came up. Mrs. Schneider stood up; they greeted each other with smiles and a hug. It turns out that the woman's son had been in Mrs. Schneider's classroom. He now was a senior in college. The mother proudly reported on how he was doing and acknowledged the important contributions Mrs. Schneider had made. Mrs. Schneider smiled and showed great interest in her former student's successes. What a wonderful anecdote to illustrate the joy of teaching.

An Epilogue

We can report that Mrs. Schneider can't stay away from teaching. One year she called up a principal and volunteered to serve as the mentor for all the new teachers in that school. For the last seven years she has been the vice chairperson of the Discovery Children's Museum, which opened its doors in 2012. "Having worked with the whole child in my classroom for many years has helped me to communicate with the fabricators and designers for our exhibits and to emphasize how important it is to build exhibits that inspire the love for lifelong learning." She also has served on and been chair of the Development Committee for the UNLV College of Education. What more can be said about Mrs. Schneider's lifelong engagement with teaching and learning? Perhaps her final quote during our interview says it best:

> My grandchildren inspire me to stay involved and feed that growing mind with the best practices we know.

• • • • • • • • • •

Becoming a teacher is an exciting, intense, and time-consuming process. Teachers are dedicated professionals who have to learn a lot in order to help all of their students learn a lot. There are going to be many new experiences, challenges, and, yes, concerns along the way. As busy as you will be, be sure to still take time to reflect and to enjoy the many opportunities as each unfolds.

Halfway through her second year, second-grade teacher Ms. Velasquez summed up her first year of teaching this way:

> I am very family oriented. In my first year of teaching I also worked on my master's degree. It was very, very hard, but I am so glad I did it. I would find myself crying lots of time when I couldn't go see my family because I had to complete an assignment, or I had to finish lesson plans. So my life was balanced out between graduate school and being at this school. Then in December, as my life transitioned from college to being a young professional, I began to have more balance. I started to force myself to leave at 4:30 and only to come in 30 minutes ahead of time. But it was a very hard thing to do, because if you are so committed to something it bothers you if it is not perfect.

CONNECTING TO THE CLASSROOM

Key themes in this chapter have been related to your being successful in your teacher education program and being successful in your first year of teaching. Two important additional themes addressed the importance of teacher leadership and looking for the joy in teaching. The following suggestions will help you apply these themes as you advance through your teacher education program and anticipate your first year as a teacher.

1. Understanding your concerns is as important as understanding the concerns of your students. No one has Impact concerns all of the time. For example, teacher education candidates have many Self and Task concerns, which is understandable given all that they have to learn and be able to do.
2. Eisner's Generic Teaching Model outlines the basic tasks and steps that should be a part of planning, presenting, and evaluating each lesson. Keep these components in mind when observing other teachers, and in reflecting on your teaching. The model also can be a guide for reflecting on a whole day or week of instruction.

3. As you move through your teacher preparation program check carefully and make sure that each course you take will count in two ways: (1) toward program completion, and (2) toward obtaining a teaching license from the state. All too often candidates get to what they think is the end of their program and then discover that a course did not count or they have not taken one that is required.
4. Approach every field and clinical experience as an opportunity to learn. Make it a personal challenge to identify one learning about teaching from every assignment.
5. Make a personal commitment not just to participate but to lead some type of activity or effort each term.
6. Schedule a 15-minute period each week where you stop doing and reflect on this question: What was joyful about the things I did this week?

SUMMARY

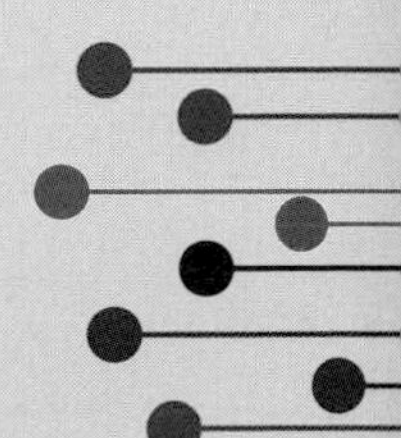

This chapter addressed achieving success in your teacher education program and in your first year of teaching. These key topics were discussed:

- Take advantage of every experience to be successful in your teacher education program.
- Understanding your concerns and the concerns of others is a useful guide for your own professional learning.
- A general teaching model can be a guide for all grade levels and subject areas.
- Obtaining your first real teaching position requires advance preparation.
- Continue developing your leadership experiences and skills.
- Much can be learned from master teachers.

CLASS DISCUSSION QUESTIONS

1. How do you think the different areas of concern (Unrelated, Self, Task, and Impact) relate to whether a teacher experiences joy in teaching? Do you have to have Impact concerns to see the joy?
2. A major theme in this chapter is teacher leadership. How realistic do you think this theme is? What opportunities do you have now to practice leadership? Followership?
3. What did you learn from the interview with Mrs. Schneider? Do you think you will be teaching for 42 years? If you did, how many students would you have taught?
4. What tips have you picked up about steps you should take in the remainder of your teacher education program that will help you obtain your desired teaching job?

KEY TERMS

Concerns 484
Criminal background check 493
Dispositions 496
Distributed leadership 499
Engaging parents 497
Followership 498
Involving parents 497
Leaders 497
Leadership 497
Stages of Concern 485

SELF-ASSESSMENT

WHAT IS YOUR CURRENT LEVEL OF UNDERSTANDING AND THINKING ABOUT SUCCEEDING IN YOUR TEACHER EDUCATION PROGRAM, AND BEYOND?

One of the indicators of understanding is to examine how complex your thinking is when asked questions that require you to use the concepts and facts introduced in this chapter. After you answer the following questions as fully as you can, rate your knowledge on the Complexity of Thinking rubric to self-assess the degree to which you understand and can apply the law to you as a teacher and future school employee.

1. Where do you see yourself at this time in terms of the different areas of teacher concerns? What do you plan to do next to address these concerns?
2. What are the different elements of Elliott's teaching model? Which of these elements can you now do well? What will you do to learn more about those elements where you feel less proficient?
3. What items are important to include in a resume? For the items you have already, what does each represent about your potential to be a high-quality teacher?
4. What aspects of leadership/followership do you need to work on? When and where will you be engaging these?
5. What areas of knowledge and skill do you need to target in order to be well qualified for your first teaching position? Explain why you see these as being so important.

One of the indicators of understanding is to examine how complex your thinking is when asked questions that require you to use the concepts and facts introduced in this chapter.

Answer the following questions as fully as you can. Then use the Complexity of Thinking rubric to self-assess the degree to which you understand and can use the organization ideas presented in this chapter.

What is your current level of understanding? Rate yourself using this rubric.

Complexity of Thinking Rubric

	Parts & Pieces	Unidimensional	Organized	Integrated	Extensions
Indicators	Elements/concepts are talked about as isolated and independent entities.	One or a few concepts are addressed, while others are underdeveloped	Deliberate and structured consideration of all key concepts/ elements.	All key concepts/ elements are included in a view that addresses interconnections.	Integration of all elements and dimensions, with extrapolation to new situations.
Succeeding in your teacher education program & beyond	Offers only general or vague items to be learned about; does not name different areas of concern, or elements of a generic model of instruction.	Identifies only one area for growth, such as classroom management; provides no elaboration of why this is important.	Names major categories such as parts of a resume, areas within the Concerns Model, and/or aspects of leadership and describes why these are priority areas for growth.	Goes beyond naming major areas and identifies specific knowledge and skill areas, and explains how each will help increase teaching expertise.	Describes major areas for growth, identifies knowledge/ skills that need to be developed, and charts actions to be taken short term and longer term to learn more.

STUDENT STUDY SITE

Visit the Student Study Site at **www.sagepub.com/hall** to access links to the videos, audio clips, and Deeper Look reference materials noted in this chapter, as well as additional study tools including eFlashcards, web quizzes, and more.

Field Guide

for Learning More About Succeeding in Your Teacher Education Program, and Beyond

• • • • •

In Chapter 1 you were introduced to the concept of a field guide for learning more about your surroundings. The artifacts and information you have collected for each of the earlier chapters provides a rich array for you to consider as you move with your teacher preparation program. For this chapter the field guide tasks and activities need to be viewed as a combination that is a summary of the whole and a foundation for charting your professional growth from here. Remember to keep taking field notes as you complete the activities suggested here. These notes should include facts and descriptions of your observations. Your field notes should also include date, time of day, the grade or group you are observing, and your reflections and ah-ha moments. As Ms. Velasquez pointed out in her interview, noting your reflection is important too. You will be able to look back at these notes at various times in the future to see how your concerns have changed, and to review how particular teaching situations were handled. All of this is a form of journaling that will help you understand the steps you are taking to becoming a teacher. Remember, also, to collect pictures and samples. A picture can be worth a thousand words.

Ask a Teacher or Principal

Ask a first- or second-year teacher what knowledge or skill he or she wished he or she had learned more about during his or her preparation program.

Ask a principal what she or he looks for in hiring a beginning teacher. Compare what the principal says with what you now have on your resume.

Make Your Own Observations

There are many indicators of joy in teaching. Walk around your college classrooms and building, or a school's classrooms and building. Take field notes on the activities and indicators of joy. Which students and which teachers seem to be enjoying what they are doing? Which seem not to be joyful? What explains the differences?

Use the topics presented in the interview with Mrs. Schneider to interview one or two very experienced teachers. Develop a chart to compare their views with those of Mrs. Schneider. Use Table 16.1 to assess their concerns about teaching. Which seem to be their biggest areas of concern? In which areas do they seem to have little or no concern?

Reflect Through Journaling

The Concerns Model provides a useful framework for you to chart your continuing development as a teacher. Review your journal notes for each of the preceding chapters. How have your concerns changed? What new areas have popped up? Do you see any type of pattern in terms of how the amount of concerns at each level (Unconcerned, Self, Task, Impact) has evolved? How do you think your concerns will change over the next year?

In this chapter there have been excerpts from interviews with a second-year teacher and a retired teacher. As you read these quotes and now as you think about yourself as a future teacher, what are your thoughts, feelings, and concerns? What are your priority topics and areas where you know you must learn more? In what areas have you already experienced joy? Jot down your current thoughts and reflections about how you are developing as a teacher and what your learning priorities are for the next parts of your teacher education program.

Build Your Portfolio

Start a folder for storing each of the open-ended concerns statements that you write. By the end of your program you should have six to ten of these. Develop a table or graph to illustrate how your concerns have changed over time in your teacher education program. As part of your reflections, write a short analysis of how your concerns have evolved.

Review the list of suggested items for a professional resume outlined in Table 16.1. Start now collecting documents, artifacts, and the records that you will need to have to prepare your resume. When the time comes to apply for your first full-time teaching position, you will find it very helpful to have collected materials and examples along the way. Also, be sure to note those item areas where you currently have very little or nothing.

At various times as you have been reading this text you have probably thought about one or more of your teachers who made a significant difference in your life, and perhaps in your decision to become a teacher. Now is the time to write a letter to that teacher. Tell him or her what you are doing now and describe the way(s) that teacher impacted you. The following is what one aspiring teacher wrote to one of her teachers. In your teaching career hopefully some of your students will take the time to write similar letters to you.

Read a Book

As the title of Alan M. Blankstein's book *Failure Is Not an Option: 6 Principles for Making Student Success the Only Option* (2010; Thousand Oaks, CA: Sage) makes clear, the mission of every teacher and school needs to be having all students learning. This award-winning book provides a positive and proactive stance about what to do and what not to do. Leadership by teachers is essential to a school having trust, a shared vision, a focus on student success, and engaged parents.

Building and sustaining partnerships between schools, parents, and communities requires ongoing involvement of teachers. *Educational Partnerships: Connecting Schools, Families, and the Community,* by Amy Cox-Peterson (2011; Thousand Oaks, CA: Sage) goes beyond presenting the need and provides steps for developing and sustaining connections with families and the broader community.

Ann Lieberman and Lynne Miller, the authors of *Teacher Leadership* (2004; San Francisco, CA: Jossey-Bass), are nationally recognized professional development experts and have championed teachers being leaders for many years. In this book they describe why teacher leadership is important, summarize the research, and present case studies of teacher leaders who have made a difference.

Search the Web

Surf the web using the term "teacher leadership." You may be surprised at the number of resources and efforts to support teacher leaders, their professional development, and ways to network. For example, the Center for Teacher Quality (**http://www.teacherleaders.org**) has organized the Teacher Leaders Network. They offer a free newsletter, provide information about teacher leaders, and facilitate conversations through listserv

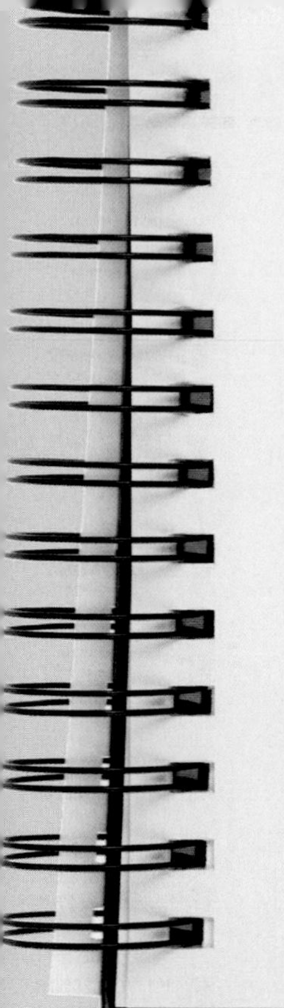

discussions. Virginia Commonwealth University has a Center for Teacher Leadership (**http://www.ctl.vcu.edu**) that has been established "to promote and support teacher leadership in order to improve teaching and learning."

Explore several of these websites and contact one or two to learn more about the ways that teacher education candidates and beginning teachers can learn about and serve in leadership roles.

As another activity, carefully think about the characteristics of teacher leaders that are being identified. Develop a checklist of different knowledge and skills that teachers should possess. Add a column to assess your current level of leadership expertise. Add another column where you can name activities you have done and plan to do to further develop your leadership skills.

Check out the website for the school district where you want to teach. Go to the Human Resources section and review the teacher position description. Make notes about what you will need to have in order to qualify for a position. Also, what can you do between now and then to make you extra well qualified to be hired to teach in that district?

E-mail From a First-Year Teacher (to One of Her Teacher Education Faculty)

In my previous life as an Air Force airman, we were taught three core values: (1) Integrity First, (2) Service Before Self, and (3) Excellence in All We Do. It usually takes a few years of working as part of a team to truly internalize how those values translate into consistent mission accomplishment. But since the moment I got it, I've found that those three guidelines can apply to almost any endeavor in life.

As a first-year teacher, I've felt all the normal pressures. Pressure every week to produce an organized lesson plan. Pressure every hour to keep the students' attention. Pressure every minute to avoid making mistakes that the kids can use against me later. Pressure to stay consistent with the rest of the department. And, of course, pressure to prepare my students for the proficiency exams. After a while, I realized that I wanted to spend more time actually teaching and less time analyzing all the various pressures of the job.

I learned that, in the crucible of the classroom, the only thing I really cared about were the kids. The other worries only came later. They were like irritating, but meaningful, afterthoughts. It eventually got on my nerves that I was even spending time thinking about it. And slowly, as I became a better teacher, I started to understand why I was becoming more irritated and less worried: I realized my heart was in the right place, and I was doing my best.

I believe we should all stop worrying about the "tensions" of teaching and simply use the Air Force core values to guide us.

Integrity: Have a philosophy about what you want *your* students to learn in *your* class. Make sure it includes overarching themes and specific learning goals. Stick to your philosophy—always.

Service Before Self: When you sign up to teach America's youth, you are in the service of our collective future. Yeah, that's a little soap-boxy, but it's true. Understand that educating is reason No. 1 why you go to work, above your paycheck, your benefits, or your summer vacation.

Excellence in All We Do: The word is *excellence,* not *perfection.* Do your best, and don't let mistakes get in the way of your performance. Keep your eyes open. Don't just learn from your own mistakes and successes; learn from others', too. Be involved enough with other teachers that you can accrue second- and third-degree experience, which will make you as excellent as possible.

I believe teachers who can adopt those three concepts will be happier and more effective. And they'll realize that the other "tension" is just noise that can get in the way of the mission.

Elissa Richmond

Glossary

Accommodations. Purposeful additional supports or adjustments in instruction that give students with disabilities access to the content being taught and ensure that a student with special needs is not placed in an unfair or disadvantageous situation for instruction or testing.

Accountability. Process that demonstrates that students are learning, teachers are improving student learning, and public resources for education are being effectively and efficiently used.

Accreditation. Recognition by members of a profession that an educational institution meets standards.

Achievement gap. The difference between performance on assessments, especially standardized tests, among groups of students.

Active listening. Intentionally focusing on the speaker and showing respect for students' needs, interests, and abilities.

Activity. Interactions with the environment that become more dynamic and change thinking as children grow.

Activity approach. Strategy that helps students develop an understanding of the link between the conscious and the objective world by engaging in activities.

Adequacy. The degree to which there are sufficient funds to accomplish the objectives.

Adequate Yearly Progress (AYP). A requirement of No Child Left Behind that students in a school be improving their achievement on standardized tests in mathematics and reading/language arts on an annual basis.

Administrative law. The regulations, rules, and procedures, based on legislation, that specify what states, schools, teachers, and others must do.

Affirmations. Positive comments and supports.

Afrocentric curriculum. A curriculum that is centered in African history, culture, and experiences.

Agnostic. A person who is not sure of the existence of a god and does not commit to believing whether God exists or not.

Annual measurable objective (AMO). State-established performance targets that assess the progress of student subgroups, schools, school systems, and the state annually.

Assertive Discipline. A model in which teachers insist upon responsible behavior from students.

Assessing. Process that entails interpreting test results and developing a plan for what will be done next.

Assimilation. Process by which groups adopt or change the dominant culture.

Atheist. A person who does not believe in the existence of a god.

At risk. Students who may fall behind in learning and may drop out of school.

Authentic task. Assessment tasks that are clearly related to the benchmarks and standards, as well as to real-world applications.

Authoritarian. Leadership that requires submission to the rule of teacher or another person.

Authorize. Legislative action that establishes authority for a certain activity to take place.

Axiology. The branch of philosophy that deals with questions concerning the nature of values.

Beliefs. The fundamental tenets that a person or a group holds to be true.

Benchmarks. A description of performances required to meet a standard at an expected level (for example, unacceptable, acceptable, and target).

Bilingual education. The use of English and the native language of students in instruction to ensure that students are able to understand the concepts being taught.

Board of trustees: Governing body that has responsibility for developing the official policies and guidelines for the educational system.

Born-again. Individuals who have had a religious experience that led them to recommit themselves to God and Jesus Christ as an evangelic.

Brain architecture. How the brain is "wired" through genetics and interactions with the environment and personal experiences.

Budget. Formal legislation that sets the amount of money available for an authorized activity.

Bullying. An act that occurs when a student or group of students intimidate or harass another student.

Canon. The books, values, and principles that guide education and society.

Case law. Law that is established as result of judicial decisions.

Catechism. Series of questions and answers, usually on religious doctrine.

Ceremonies. Activities based on rituals or customs that in schools range from the topics that are, and are not, announced on the PA system each day to the many activities that unfold around a football game or graduation.

Chain of command. Frequently used phrase to refer to the up/down line relationships in an organization chart that determine who reports to whom.

Charity schools. Schools established for poor children in urban areas prior to the common school.

Chief state school officer. State superintendent of public instruction or commissioner of education who may be elected or appointed by the state board of education or governor.

Choice Theory. William Glasser's (1997) model that calls for teachers to help students satisfy their five psychological needs (the need for survival, the need to belong, the need for power, the need for freedom, and the need for fun), so that students can choose appropriate behavior individually and as a group.

Civil rights. The rights of personal liberty guaranteed by the Thirteenth and Fourteenth Amendments to the U.S. Constitution and by acts of Congress.

Closed questions: Questions that require one word, facts or short answers

Coalition. Multiple interests groups that have joined forces to influence how a school board votes.

Cognitive framework. A set of intellectual abilities expressed through thought and action.

Color blindness. All students are treated the same without regard to their race and ethnicity.

Common Core State Standards. Set of learning standards developed by the Council for Chief State School Officers and other national groups for adoption by states that are guiding the development of new state tests.

Common schools. Eighteenth-century schools that mixed students from different socioeconomic levels in the same classes and taught the same curriculum to all students.

Compulsory attendance. Required attendance at school until an age (now 16 or older) set by state legislatures.

Concerns. Thoughts, preoccupations, and worries in relation to becoming a teacher and/or teaching.

Conduct management. Maintaining conduct through the establishment of rules and guidelines of behavior.

Confidence interval. A statistical tool to ensure accurate, reliable, and fair accountability decisions.

Consensus oriented. Decision making through open dialogue, rather than resorting to ultimatums and refusals to negotiate.

Content management. Planning the physical environment, deciding on the procedures that will occur during the instructional day, and instruction.

Cooperative learning groups. A heterogeneous group of students working together to solve problems or help one another learn content.

Corporal punishment. A teacher paddling or spanking a student.

Corporate income tax. Taxes paid by corporations to federal and state governments.

Covenant management. Managing relationships, having highly developed communication skills, and knowing ways the combined effects of content management and conduct management will influence interactions in the classroom.

Criminal background check. School district's process for determining whether teachers have a criminal record, which would prevent them from teaching. This process usually requires teachers to be fingerprinted.

CRISS (CReating Independence through Student-owned Strategies. A set of teaching strategies based in brain research and cognitive psychology that are designed "to produce thoughtful and independent learners."

Criterion-referenced tests (CRTs). Assessments in which each student's test score is compared with a defined level of performance, rather than with how other students have done.

Cultural borders. A social construct based on cultural membership that is political and involves differences in power.

Cultural capital. Endowments such as academic competence, language competence, and wealth that provide an advantage to an individual, family, or group.

Culturally responsive teaching. An educational strategy that affirms the cultures of students, views the cultures and experiences of students as strengths, and reflects the students' cultures in the curriculum.

Cultural match. Students and teachers with the same or related experiences, which are used by teachers as representations to help students learn the concept being taught.

Cultural relativism. Judging other cultural groups through the lens of members of that culture rather than applying the standards of one's own culture.

Cultural safety. An environment that allows students to feel safe in terms of their unique background and experiences with shared respect and equitable interactions.

Culture. Socially transmitted ways of thinking, believing, feeling, and acting within a group. These patterns are transmitted from one generation to the next.

Current expenditures. Funds spent during a specific school year.

Cut score. The score determined by the state that must be achieved to pass a test such as the teacher licensure test.

Deculturalizing. The educational process that destroys a student's culture and replaces it with a new culture. Deculturalization was the goal of boarding schools that removed American Indian students from their homes at early ages with the goal of assimilating them into Christianity and the Anglo Saxon culture.

De facto. Action that has developed through the "facts" of a situation which are outside of the actions of government.

De facto segregation. The voluntary separation or isolation of racial, ethnic, or socioeconomic groups in a community, leading to neighborhood schools attended by students from one group.

Deficit ideology. Viewing individuals or groups as inferior to your own group.

De jure. Action that is brought about through laws *and* the actions of state and local officials.

Democratic classroom. Engagement of students in shared decision making and in taking responsibility for building a democratic learning environment.

Depths of knowledge (DOK). A taxonomy for describing different levels of learning.

Developmental. A model of how children grow and how they learn in which there are predictable phases and stages to child development.

Differentiate. To adjust instruction so that it matches the learning needs of each student.

Differentiated system of accountability. Expectation that school assessment systems will include multiple assessments and that accommodations will be made for some students, such as ELLs and those in special education.

Dilemma. A complex problem with two or more solutions.

Direct or explicit instruction. Instruction that helps students increase and broaden their existing knowledge or skills.

Disability. A long-standing physical, mental, or emotional condition that can make it difficult for a person to do activities such as walking, climbing stairs, dressing, bathing, learning, or remembering.

Dispositions. The attitudes, beliefs, and values that teachers hold about students, the subjects they teach, their colleagues, parents, and the school.

Distributed leadership. Distribution of leadership across teachers and administrators as a shared responsibility.

Effectiveness and efficiency. Time and resources used purposefully and well.

Elementary and Secondary Education Act (ESEA). Federal legislation, first passed in 1965, that establishes a number of national priorities for improving schools and education.

Empowering. Policies or guidelines that identify the target or vision and leave open the means for achieving the desired end.

Enculturation. The process of learning your culture's expectations for behavior, communications, and ways of knowing.

Engaging parents. Providing general information to parents without seeking their active participation.

English as a Second Language (ESL). An education program for teaching English to speakers of other languages without the use of the native language for instruction.

English for Speakers of Other Languages (ESOL). A program teaching English to children and adults who do not speak English.

Epistemology. Examines questions about how and what we know, and how knowing takes place.

Equity. The state of fairness and justice across individuals and groups; it does not mean the same educational strategies are used across groups, but all groups have equivalent opportunity.

Essentialism. School of philosophy based on the belief that there is a fundamental core of knowledge that any functioning member of society must possess.

Ethnicity. Membership based on one's national origin or the national origin of one's ancestors when they immigrated to the United States.

Ethnic studies. A curriculum or courses that focus on the history, contributions, and conditions of a specific ethnic group (for example, Asian American studies or American Indian studies).

Ethnocentric curriculum. A curriculum that is centered on the ethnic roots of the dominant culture, which is northern and western European. Such a curriculum neglects the contributions of other cultural groups, often denigrating them and implying that they are inferior to the dominant culture.

Evangelical. Identification with Christian groups who believe the bible is the actual word of God.

Existentialism. School of philosophy that sees a world in which individuals determine for themselves what is true or false.

Extra-curriculum. An activity in which students participate before or after school such as yearbook, pep squad, theater, or a music program.

Extrinsic rewards. Those rewards that are given to students by others; such rewards are external to a student's self-motivation.

Fair use: The conditions under which a teacher may use certain materials without the permission of the copyright holder.

The conditions under which a teacher may use certain materials without the permission of the copyright holder.

Federalism. Involvement of the federal government in making decisions about education for the whole nation.

Field-based supervisors. The teachers or other professional school personnel who provide support for teacher candidates when they observe and work in schools.

Followership. Being a constructive member of the group, offering to help, contributing positively to the discussions, and being sure to complete assigned tasks, with quality, and on time; entails participating and volunteering help.

Formative evaluation. Assessments of student work that provide feedback on student progress and guide preparation of future lessons.

Fourteenth Amendment. The amendment ratified during the Reconstruction era on July 9, 1868, to provide citizenship to all persons born or naturalized in the United States other than American Indians and Asians. It also reaffirmed and extended the civil rights act passed in 1866 and served as the foundation for *Brown v. Board of Education of Topeka* and other civil rights cases in the twentieth and twenty-first centuries.

Free and universal education. Public education for all children and youth.

Gender. The behavioral, cultural, or psychological traits typically associated with one sex.

General intelligence. A single ability that entails information processing and is used with all types of cognitive tasks. It is measured by standardized tests.

Governance. The processes of making decisions and implementing actions.

Growth scores. Comparison of test scores for each student from year to year with the expectation that students will show growth in each subject from year to year.

Heterosexism. An irrational fear or hatred of people whose sexual orientation is different than heterosexual that can lead to prejudice, discrimination, and violence against LGBTQ persons.

Hidden curriculum. The norms and values that define expectations for student behavior and attitudes and that undergird the curriculum and operations of schools.

Highly Qualified Teacher (HQT). Specifications in the federal No Child Left Behind legislation to assure that all classrooms are staffed by teachers who have met a set of minimum criteria, including minimum requirements for a teacher license.

High-stakes testing. Tests that are used for gatekeeping, such as passing to the next grade or being qualified for a job.

Holistic. Rubrics that evaluate the total effort such as overall level of thinking.

Horizontal communication. Communications *across* the various levels in the organization chart.

Human resources (HR). The department with responsibility for hiring employees and ensuring that they are paid and have health and retirement programs (benefits).

I-messages. Messages in communication that avoid placing blame and allow speakers to express their feelings directly and specifically.

Inclusion. The integration of students with disabilities into the regular classroom.

Indigenous. Population that is native to a country or region. In the United States, Native Americans, Hawaiians, and Alaska Natives are considered indigenous populations.

Individualized education plan (IEP). A plan that indicates the accommodations and special services that must be provided to a student with disabilities, which was developed by parents, teachers, special educators, and other specialists such as a school psychologist or occupational therapist.

Integration. (1) Students from different ethnic, racial, and socio-economic groups attending school together; (2) distribution of facilities, students, and school personnel without bias.

Intelligence quotient (IQ). A measure of intelligence by comparing a student's score on the Stanford–Binet Intelligence Scales to that of their age-group multiplied by 100.

Interest groups. A formal or informal group who advocate for a common interest.

Intermediate. Grades 4 through 5/6.

Intrinsic rewards. Importance due to internal satisfaction such as helping a child learn rather than external incentives such as salary or prestige.

Involving parents. Making parents a necessary part of what goes on at school.

Jim Crow laws. Laws and practices that segregated whites from blacks in the use of facilities such as water fountains, restrooms, hotels, buses, restaurants, and movie theaters.

Journals. Documents in which teacher candidates record their thoughts about a topic or their reflections on the teaching of a lesson, student behavior, and other classroom events.

Judicious Discipline. A philosophy that creates an environment respectful of the citizenship rights of students.

Kagan strategies. A set of evidence-based structures and activities produced by Kagan Publishing and Professional Development that teachers at all grade levels can use to increase academic achievement.

Knowledge. Knowing information, facts, and ideas about someone or a topic that has been learned through education or lived experience.

Leaders. Those with formal and sometimes informal responsibility for accomplishing a task or activity.

Leadership. A responsibility of all to help a group or whole school accomplish its objectives.

Learning centered. Focus in the classroom on students that is characterized by a shared belief in the importance of having all students learn.

Learning cycle. Kolb & Fry's (1975) "cycle of learning" is expressed as a four-stage cycle of learning, in which "immediate or concrete experiences" provide a basis for "observations and reflections." These "observations and reflections" are assimilated and distilled into "abstract concepts" producing new implications for action which can be "actively tested," in turn creating new experiences.

Least restrictive environment. Education of students with disabilities in regular classrooms with their nondisabled classmates to the maximum extent appropriate.

Lesson plans. A teacher's detailed guide for classroom instruction.

LGBTQ. A popular term used to identify lesbian, gay, bisexual, transgender, and queer or questioning individuals.

Line relationships. One position has direct supervisory authority over another.

Local control. Authority for decision making regarding schools is in the hands of those nearest the site, whether it is the district or a school.

Local education agencies (LEAs). School districts that include a cluster of schools in the same geographic area.

Looping. An educational practice in which teachers remain with the same students for two or more grades.

Mainstreaming. Education of students with disabilities in regular classrooms with their nondisabled classmates.

Manifest destiny. Future event that is believed to be inevitable or cannot be avoided.

Maturation. The genetically programmed way that thinking changes as a child grows older.

McKinney–Vento Homeless Assistance Act. The federal legislation that outlined the education rights and protections for homeless children and youth.

Mentors. Experienced teachers who coach and guide new teachers through their first years of practice.

Meritocracy. A system in which individuals who are the most talented and ambitious deserve to achieve at the highest social and economic levels.

Metacognition. Thinking about one's own thinking, which includes deciding on a specific choice or solution and acting on one's decisions.

Metaphysics. School of philosophy that is concerned with questions about the nature of reality and humans' attempts to find coherence in the realm of thought and experience.

Micromanaging. The tendency to become overly involved in the day-to-day operations of the district.

Modeling. Through modeling the teacher describes his or her thought process and provides an example for students to follow.

Model minority. A stereotype about a group that characterizes all members of the group as academically and economically successful because of the group's cultural norms that promote hard work and education.

Morals. Generally accepted notions of right and wrong or good and bad behavior.

Multicultural curriculum. A curriculum that incorporates the history, culture, contributions, and experiences of multiple ethnic, socioeconomic, language, and religious groups as well as females, males, and students with exceptionalities. A multicultural curriculum also addresses issues of power, discrimination, and inequality.

Multiple Intelligences (MI). Howard Gardner's theory that classifies intelligence into seven abilities. Gardner holds that everyone has strengths with some abilities and weaknesses with others.

Multiple perspectives. Views from people or groups of people whose histories and experiences provide different ways of looking at a current or past event, policies, research, and practices in the world.

National Assessment of Educational Progress (NAEP). Federal program that regularly assesses student learning within each state.

National Board for Professional Teaching Standards (NBPTS). The organization that has developed standards for accomplished teachers and a process for determining whether teachers meet the standards.

National K–12 Standards for Student Learning. Standards for the teaching of science, mathematics, engineering and technology at the college level that were developed by the Committee on Undergraduate Science Education in collaboration with the Center for Science, Mathematics, and Engineering Education and the National Research Council (1999).

Nihilism. A philosophical position that argues the world, and especially human existence, is without objective meaning, purpose, comprehensible truth, or essential value.

No Pass No Play. Policies that prohibit students from participating in sports and band unless they maintain a certain grade point average.

Norm-referenced test (NRT). The test score of one student is compared with the scores of other students.

Norms. The shared guidelines that define which actions and products are acceptable for a particular group.

Objective tests. Test items that can be scored as clearly being either right or wrong.

On-site staff developer. Master teachers who serve as mentor, model teacher, peer coach, and teacher trainer within a school.

Open-ended questions: Questions that require elaboration, higher level thinking and responses that will be longer.

Organization chart. A graphic representation of line and staff relationships and levels of authority.

Out-of-field teachers. Educators assigned to teach a subject in which they did not major in college and which they have not been licensed to teach.

Outsourcing/privatizing. Contracting with outside companies to provide services such as cleaning buildings or driving school buses.

Pan-ethnic. Ethnic membership based on national origin from a large geographic region that includes numerous countries; examples are African or Asian American.

Parent–teacher organizations (PTOs). Groups of teachers and parents that have organized to support student learning in a school.

Participation. Involvement of men and women in school governance with the freedom to express their views.

Perennialism. School of philosophy that offers a conservative and traditional view of human nature. In this school of thought, humans do not change much, but they are capable of analytical thinking, reason, and imagination, and should be encouraged along these lines.

Performance. An assessment that is based on students applying their learning through accomplishing an activity, which shows that they really have learned the benchmark and standard.

Performance assessments. Evaluations of teachers' or students' ability to meet standards as demonstrated in their accomplishments in a real situation such as teaching or a project.

Per-pupil expenditure. Total number of dollars spent divided by the number of students. It is used as an indicator of a community's commitment to and support of public education.

Personal income tax. Taxes paid by individuals to federal and state governments based on their level of income.

Pessimism. A general belief that things are bad and tend to become worse.

Physical safety. Elimination of the potential for students (and you as a teacher) to be injured.

Policies. The official stated overarching parameters for what can, and cannot, be done within an organization.

Portfolio. A compilation of works, records, and accomplishments that a student prepares for a specific purpose in order to demonstrate his or her learnings, performances, and contributions.

Pragmatism. School of philosophy that is concerned about practice and the practical, which is viewed as dynamic and evolving.

Prescriptive. Policies or guidelines that set limits and specify the procedures that are to be used.

Primary. Grades K/1 through 3.

Problem. A matter that needs fixing for which one or more solutions can be devised to fix it.

Problem-based learning. When instruction is focused on a relevant problem and data is provided to students to help them reach solutions.

Procedural due process. Procedure to ensure that a person has been treated fairly and that proper procedures have been followed.

Profession. A career that requires specialized knowledge and advanced college preparation often beyond the baccalaureate.

Professional Learning Communities (PLCs). An approach to organizing the adults in a school to meet regularly or a school-wide effort focused on developing a collaborative culture around student *and* adult learning.

Proficiencies. Knowledge, skills, or dispositions that students are expected to acquire to meet a set of standards.

Progressive. Income tax that is graduated with those having a higher level of income paying a larger amount.

Progressivism. School of philosophy marked by progress, reform, or a continuing improvement. The tenets of progressivism demonstrate respect for individuality, a high regard for science, and receptivity to change.

Prohibitions. Rebukes and telling a child not to do something.

Proselytize. Recruiting new members to one's own faith.

PT3 Project. U.S. Department of Education's Preparing Tomorrow's Teachers to Use Technology (PT3) grant was designed to address the growing challenge of using technology in teaching.

Race. A social category that groups people by the skin color of their ancestors.

Racism. The belief that one race is inherently superior to all others and thereby has the right to dominance.

Reduction in force (RIF). Eliminating jobs due to budget cuts.

Reflections. Thinking about one's actions and the result of such actions.

Refugees. Persons recognized by the U.S. government as being persecuted or legitimately bearing persecution in their home country because of race, religion, nationality, or membership in a specific social or political group.

Regressive. A form of taxation that has those with less ability to pay proportionately paying more.

Reliability. A characteristic of tests that indicates how similar the results are for students who seem to be similar in their learning.

Resegregation. The de facto segregation of students as a result of the return to neighborhood schools after de jure segregation has been dismantled for the most part.

Response to Intervention (RTI) or **Response to Instruction (RTI).** A multilevel approach for addressing the needs of all students by differentiating between those who are keeping up and those who are struggling or seriously falling behind.

Responsiveness. Establishment of time frames that are reasonable and at the same time sufficiently long so that all necessary information is available.

Rubrics. Criteria for judging a person's performance against standards that include descriptions of performance at levels such as inadequate, proficient, and beyond expectations.

Rule of law. Expectations and requirements that are enforced equally for all.

Scaffolding. Scaffolding denotes starting instruction with small tasks the learner already knows and building on that knowledge.

School board. The school district governing body that has responsibility for developing the official policies and guidelines for the educational system.

School board of trustees. The school district governing body that has responsibility for developing the official policies and guidelines for the educational system.

Schools in Need of Improvement (SINOI). Schools that fail to make Adequate Yearly Progress (AYP) in any one disaggregated category, leading to the school being placed on a list of Schools in Need of Improvement.

Schools of philosophy. Different perspectives on answering the broad philosophical questions posed through metaphysics, epistemology, and axiology from differing perspectives. The schools of philosophy most often mentioned in terms of the implications they have for education are idealism, realism, perennialism, pragmatism, progressivism, essentialism, and existentialism.

School-to-prison pipeline. The process in which factors such as student absenteeism, failing a grade, suspension, and expulsion become predecessors to being arrested and spending time in prison.

Secondary. Grades 9 through 12.

Secular. Not religious in nature; sometimes identified as based on science rather than religion.

Secular humanism. A dogma stressing the ethical consequences of human decisions that is based on science and philosophy rather than religion and faith.

Self-contained classroom. One teacher stays in a classroom and is assigned responsibility for teaching one set of students all subjects.

Self-fulfilling prophecy. A phenomenon in which a teacher's expectations for a student's achievement are established early in the school year and match the student's achievement at the end of the school year.

Sexting. The act of using a cell phone or other technology to send or receive sexually explicit pictures, video, and/or text.

Sexual orientation. One's sexual attraction to persons of the same or opposite sex or both.

Sin taxes. Taxes on products and services the value of which has been questioned on religious grounds.

Socialization. Process of learning the social norms and expectations of the culture.

Social justice. Caring for and supporting people who are less advantaged than you.

Socioeconomic status (SES). Composite of the economic status of families or persons on the basis of occupation, educational attainment, and income.

Socratic Method. A questioning strategy that guides students toward independent thinking.

Specific abilities. Particular tasks such as language development, memory, and auditory perception.

Staff relationships. One position does not have direct authority over another, but there is an expectation that the two positions will communicate, coordinate, and work together.

Stages of Concern. Levels that people may move through as they experience any type of change.

Standards-based curriculum. A course of study designed to help students meet the proficiencies identified in standards adopted by a school or state.

State education agency (SEA). The state agency responsible for public education in the state.

Statute. A law by a legislative body that sets the general boundaries and some of the limits, but not the specific details of the legislation, which is the administrative law.

STEM. Science, technology, engineering, and mathematics education.

Stereotypes. Generalizations about the behavior, attitudes, perspectives, and other characteristics of a group of people that could be positive, but are often negative, and against which persons from the group are judged.

Stereotype threat. A phenomenon in which the common stereotypes about our group influence how we perceive ourselves.

Strategy. A method or technique teachers use to deliver instruction.

Student Improvement Team (SIT). A special committee that reviews the performance of individual students. The team includes representatives from all grade levels/subjects, a school administrator, reading and mathematics specialists, one or more special education teachers, and at least one member who is skilled at organizing and displaying student data.

Subjective. A type of test item that poses a problem or task for which students must construct an original response, which must be scored individually.

Substantive due process. Protection against the loss of the rights granted in the Constitution, such as freedom of expression.

Summative evaluation. The use of test results to make conclusions about how much a student has learned or to decide whether a student is ready to move to the next grade level.

Superintendent. The chief executive officer (CEO) of a school district.

Symbols. The icons that reflect core beliefs and values through the meaning that is ascribed to them.

Taxonomies. Classification systems of the learning hierarchy that progress from simple to complex.

Team teaching. A staffing plan in which two or more teachers work together to plan and teach a common group of students.

Test-based accountability. Annual state testing that drives the evaluation of schools as well as teachers and administrators.

Tests. Structured opportunities to measure how much a test taker knows and can do at a particular point in time.

Tort law. Wrongs related to failure to act properly or acting improperly.

Toxic stresses. Past negative experiences such as extreme poverty or abuse that affect development.

Tracking. The practice of separating students based on their academic abilities to receive instruction that is supposed to be most appropriate for their abilities.

Transitions. The move from one level of schooling to another such as elementary school to junior high/middle school.

Transparency. A decision-making process in which the reasoning and output are open to the public and freely available.

Unconditional positive regard. Expressing basic acceptance and support of a person regardless of what the person says or does. This term is attributed to Carl Rogers.

Unfunded mandate. Legislation that requires certain activities to be done without provision of sufficient budget.

Unpaid furlough days. Requirement that employees, especially teachers and other public employees, take one or two days a month off without pay.

Validity. A characteristic of a test that indicates that the test measures what it is intended to assess.

Value added. Assessment that provides evidence of a teacher's performance in improving student achievement as measured by standardized tests.

Values. The elements of behaviors and principles that reflect what is viewed as important.

Vertical communication. Communication that moves down, and up, the organization chart of personnel in schools.

Vocabulary gap. The difference in the number of words children know at different stages of their development based on factors such as poverty and the education of their parents.

Wait-time. The time a teacher waits after asking a question that gives students the opportunity to think about a response.

Wait-time II. The time teachers should wait after a student has responded to a question, providing other students the opportunity to add an additional response or ask for clarification.

Zero tolerance. School policies that call for punishing any infraction of a rule.

References

AACTE. (2010). *The clinical preparation of teachers: A policy brief.* The American Association of Colleges for Teacher Education.

Akiba, M., LeTendre, G. K., & Scribner, J. P. (2007, October). Teacher quality, opportunity gap, and national achievement in 46 countries. *Educational Researcher, 36*(7), 369–387.

Alexander, K., & Alexander, M. D. (2001). *American public school law* (5th ed.). Belmont, CA: Wadsworth/ Thomas Learning.

Alexander v. Holmes County Board of Education, 396 U.S. 19 (1969).

American Library Association. (2012). Number of challenges by year, reason, initiator & institution (1990–2010). Chicago, IL: Author. Retrieved February 12, 2012, from http://www.ala.org/advocacy/banned/frequentlychallenged/challengesbytype

American Psychological Association. (2008). Answers to your questions: For a better understanding of sexual orientation and homosexuality. Washington, DC: Author. Retrieved March 28, 2011, from http://www.apa.org/topics/sorientation.pdf

Anderson, J. (1988). *The education of blacks in the South, 1860–1935.* Chapel Hill: The University of North Carolina Press.

The Annie E. Casey Foundation. (2011). *2011 kids count data book: America's children, America's challenge: Promoting opportunity for the next generation.* Baltimore, MD: Author.

ASCD. (2012). School culture and climate. Alexandria, VA: Author. Retrieved February 12, 2012, from http://ascd.org/research-a-topic/school-culture-and-climate-resources.aspx

Aud, S., Hussar, W., Johnson, F., Kena, G., Roth, E., Manning, E., Wang, X., and Zhang, J. (2012). *The condition of education 2012* (NCES 2012-045). Washington, DC: U.S. Department of Education, National Center for Education Statistics.

Aud, S., Hussar, W., Kena, G., Bianco, K., Frohlich, L., Kemp, J., & Tahan, K. (2011). *The condition of education 2011* (NCES 2011-033). Washington, DC: U.S. Department of Education, National Center for Education Statistics.

Ausubel, D. (1963). *The psychology of meaningful verbal learning.* New York, NY: Grune & Stratton.

Ausubel, D. (1967). *Learning theory and classroom practice.* Toronto, Canada: The Ontario Institute for Studies in Education.

Bailey, M. (2003). Learning, technology and educational transformation: From philosophy to pedagogy. Berglund Center Summer Institute. Retrieved from http://education.edu.pacificu.edu/bcis/workshop/philosophy.html

Bainbridge, D. (2009). *Teenagers: A natural history.* Berkeley, CA: Greystone.

Beane, J. A. (2001). Introduction: Reform and reinvention. In T. S. Dickinson (Ed.), *Reinventing the middle school.* New York, NY: RoutledgeFalmer.

Benjamin, R. M. (2011, April 19). Childhood obesity: Beginning the dialogue on reversing the epidemic (Surgeon General's Statement to the Committee on Health, Education, Labor, and Pensions of the United States Senate). Retrieved January 31, 2012, from http://www.hhs.gov/asl/testify/2010/03/t20100304i.html

Berg, E. L. (2003). Kindergarten. In P. S. Fass (Ed.), *Encyclopedia of children and childhood: In history and society.* Farmington Hills, MI: Gale. Retrieved March 1, 2012, from http://www.faqs.org/childhood/Ke-Me/Kindergarten.html

Berry, B. (2011). *Past as prologue: A historical overview of teaching in America.* Carrboro, NC: Center for Teaching Quality.

Bethel School District No. 403 v. Fraser, 478 U.S. 675 (1986).

Bill and Melinda Gates Foundation. (2010). *Learning about teaching: Initial findings from the Measuring Effective Teaching Program* (December). Seattle, WA: Author.

Bloom, B. S. (Ed.). (1956). *Taxonomy of educational objectives handbook I: Cognitive domain.* New York, NY: David McKay Co.

Blue Mountain School District and Layshock v. Hermitage School District, (2010) 593 F.3d 249 (2010).

Board of Education, Island Trees Union Free School District No. 26 v. Pico, 457 U.S. 853, 102 S.Ct. 2799, 73 L.Ed.2d 435 (1982).

Board of Education of Oklahoma City Public Schools v. Dowell, 498 U.S. 237 (1991).

Board of Education of the Westside Community Schools v. Mergens, 496 U.S. 226 (1990).

Board of Regents of State Colleges v. Roth, 408 U.S. 564 (1972).

Boeree, C. G. (2006). B. F. Skinner. Retrieved from http://webspace.ship.edu/cgboer/skinner.html

Boger, J. C., & Orfield, G. (Eds.). (2005). *School resegregation: Must the South turn back?* Chapel Hill: University of North Carolina Press.

Bolling v. Sharpe, 347 U.S. 497 (1954).

Borich, G. D. (2011). *Effective teaching methods* (5th ed.). Upper Saddle River, NJ: Pearson/Prentice Hall.

Borich, G. D., & Tombari, M. L. (2003). *Educational assessment for the elementary and middle school classroom* (2nd ed.). Upper Saddle River, NJ: Merrill/Prentice Hall.

Bornfeld, S. (2011, October 23). i-Manners. *Las Vegas Review-Journal,* 3.

Boykin, A. W., & Noguera, P. (2011). *Creating the opportunity to learn: Moving from research to practice to close the achievement gap.* Alexandria, VA: ASCD.

Bridgeland, J. M., DiIulio, J. J., Streeter, R. T., & Mason, J. R. (2008, October). *One dream, two realities: Perspectives of parents on America's high schools.* Washington, DC: Civic Enterprises.

Brown v. Board of Education of Topeka, 347 U.S. 483 (1954).

Bruner, J. (1966). *Studies in cognitive growth.* San Francisco, CA: John Wiley & Sons.

Burant, T., Christensen, L., Salas, K. D., & Walters, S. (2010). Creating classrooms for equity and social justice. In T. Burant, L. Christensen, K. D. Salas, & S. Walters (Eds.), *The new teacher book* (pp. 157–162). Milwaukee, WI: Rethinking Schools.

Burns, M. (2005/2006). Tools for the mind. *Educational Leadership, 63*(4), 50.

Bushaw, W. J., & Lopez, S. J. (2011, September). Betting on teachers: The 43rd annual Phi Delta Kappa/Gallup poll of the public's attitudes toward the public schools. *Phi Delta Kappan, 93*(1), 8–26.

Bushaw, W. J., & Lopez, S. J. (2012, September). Public education in the

United States: A nation divided. *Phi Delta Kappan, 94*(1), 9–25.

Bureau of Indian Affairs. (2011). What we do: Services overview. Retrieved October 11, 2011, from http://www.bia.gov/index.htm

Burris, C. C., Wiley, E., Welner, K., & Murphy, J. (2008, March). Accountability, rigor, and detracking: Achievement effects of embracing a challenging curriculum as a universal good for all students. *Teachers College Record, 110*(3), 571–608.

Cambron-McCabe, N. H., McCarthy, M. M., & Thomas, S. B. (2004). *Public school law: Teachers' and students' rights* (5th ed.). Boston, MA: Pearson.

Canter, L., & Canter, M. (1992). *Assertive discipline: Positive behavior management for today's classrooms.* Santa Monica, CA: Lee Canter & Associates.

Carnine, D. W., Silbert, J., Kame'enui, E. J., Tarver, S. G., & Archer, A. L. (2012). *Direct instruction reading.* Upper Saddle River, NJ: Prentice Hall.

Center for Science, Mathematics, and Engineering Education & National Research Council. (1999). *Transforming undergraduate, education in science, mathematics, engineering, and technology.* Executive Summary. Retrieved from http://www.nap.edu/html/transund/es.html

Centers for Disease Control and Prevention. (2010a, Summer). Suicide: Facts at a glance. Atlanta, GA: Author. Retrieved January 31, 2012, from http://www.cdc.gov/ViolencePrevention/pdf/Suicide_DataSheet-a.pdf

Centers for Disease Control and Prevention. (2010b, June 4). Youth risk behavior surveillance—United States, 2009. *Morbidity and Mortality Weekly Report, 59*(SS-5).

Centers for Disease Control and Prevention. (2011a, April 8). Vital signs: Teen pregnancy—United States, 1991–2009. *Morbidity and Mortality Weekly Report, 60*(13), 414–420. Retrieved January 31, 2012, from http://www.cdc.gov/mmwr/preview/mmwrhtml/mm6013a5.htm?s_cid=mm6013a5_w

Centers for Disease Control and Prevention. (2011b). Trends in birth rates, fertility rates and selected characteristics (VitalStats). Washington, DC: National Center for Health Statistics. Retrieved February 6, 2012, from http://www.cdc.gov/nchs/vitalstats.htm

Children's Defense Fund. (2011). *Portrait of inequality 2011: Black children in America.* Washington, DC: Author.

Churchill, W. S., 28 October 1943 to the House of Commons (meeting in the House of Lords). Retrieved August 2006 from http://www.winstonchurchill.org

Clark, C. M., & Peterson, P. L. (1986). Teachers' thought processes. In M. C. Wittrock (Ed.), *Handbook of research on teaching* (pp. 255–314). New York, NY: Macmillan.

Cleveland Board of Education v. LeFleur, 414 U.S. 632 (1974).

Coalition of Essential Schools. (2012). About the Coalition of Essential Schools. Providence, RI: Author. Retrieved February 29, 2012, from http://www.essentialschools.org/items

Cochran-Smith, M. (2004). *Walking the road: Race, diversity, and social justice in teacher education.* New York, NY: Teachers College Press.

Coles, R. (1989). *The call of stories: Teaching and the moral imagination.* Boston, MA: Houghton Mifflin Co.

College participation rates for students from lower income families by state: FY1993 to FY2009. (2010, October). *Postsecondary Education Opportunity,* #150.

Collins, E., & Scott, P. (1978). Everyone who makes it has a mentor. *Harvard Business Review, 56*(4), 89–101.

Cremin, L. A. (1951). *The American common school: An historical conception.* New York, NY: Teachers College Press, Columbia University.

Cuban, L. (2004). Why has frequent high school reform since World War II produced disappointing results again, and again, and again? In *Using rigorous evidence to improve policy and practice: Colloquium report.* New York, NY: MCRC. Retrieved March 1, 2012, from https://www.mdrc.org/publications/391/conf_agenda.html

Danielson, C. (1996). *Enhancing professional practice: A framework for teaching.* Alexandria, VA: ASCD.

Darling-Hammond, L. (1999). *Teacher quality and student achievement: A review of state policy evidence.* Seattle, WA: Center for the Study of Teaching and Policy, University of Washington.

Darling-Hammond, L. (2000). *Solving the dilemmas of teacher supply, demand, and standards: How we can ensure a competent, caring, and qualified teacher for every child.* Washington, DC: National Commission on Teaching & America's Future.

Darling-Hammond, L. (2010). *The flat world and education: How America's commitment to equity will determine our future.* New York, NY: Teachers College Press.

Darling-Hammond, L., Hammerness, K., Grossman, P., Rust, F., & Shulman, L. (2005). The design of teacher education programs. In L. Darling-Hammond & J. Bransford (Eds.), *Preparing teachers for a changing world: What teachers should learn and be able to do.* San Francisco, CA: Jossey-Bass.

Day, J. C., Janus, A., & Davis, J. (2005). *Computer and Internet use in the United States: 2003.* Washington, DC: U.S. Census Bureau.

DeCarlo, M., Johnson, N., & Cochran, P. (2008). *Survey and analysis of teacher salary trends, 2007.* Washington, DC: American Federation of Teachers.

Dewey, J. (1910). *How we think.* Lexington, KY: D. C. Heath.

Dewey, J. (1934). *Art as experience.* New York, NY: Minton, Balch & Co.

Dewey, J. (1943). *The school and society.* Chicago, IL: University of Chicago Press.

Dewey, J. (1963). *Experience in education.* New York, NY: Collier Books.

Dewey, J. (1974). *The child and the curriculum: And the school and society.* Chicago, IL: University of Chicago Press.

Dewey, J. (1997). *Democracy and education.* Detroit, MI: Free Press.

Downey, L. W. (1988). *Policy analysis in education.* Alberta, Calgary: Detselig Enterprises.

Doyle, W. (1986). Classroom organization and management. In M. Wittrock (Ed.), *Handbook of research on teaching* (3rd ed., pp. 392–431). New York, NY: Macmillan.

Dragan, E. F. (2010). Understanding liability in school cases. Education Management Consulting LLC. Retrieved March 27, 2012, from http://www.edmgt.com/pdfs/publications/0067.pdf

Duckworth, E. (1996). *The having of wonderful ideas and other essays on teaching and learning* (2nd ed.). New York, NY: Teachers College Press.

Dweck, C. (2006). *Mindset: The new psychology of success.* New York, NY: Random House/Ballantine Books.

East Hartford Education Association v. Board of Education of Town of East Hartford, 562 F.2d 838 (1977).

Educational Leadership. (2005/2006). Learning in the digital age [Special issue]. *Educational Leadership, 63*(4).

Education Week. (2011, July 7). Achievement gap. Retrieved January 2, 2012, from http://www.edweek.org/ew/issues/achievement-gap/

Egley, A., Jr., & Howell, J. C. (2011, June). *Highlights of the 2009 national youth gang survey* (OJJDP Juvenile Fact Sheet). Washington, DC: U.S. Department of Justice, Office of Juvenile Justice and Delinquency Prevention.

Eliot, L. (2009). *Pink brain, blue brain: How small differences grow into troublesome gaps—and what we can do about it*. Boston, MA: Mariner, Houghton Mifflin Harcourt.

Elliott, E. (2003). *Assessing education candidate performance: A look at changing practices*. Washington, DC: National Council for Accreditation of Teacher Education.

Elliott, E. (2005). *Student learning in NCATE accreditation*. Washington, DC: National Council for the Accreditation of Teacher Education.

Emmer, E., Evertson, C., & Worsham, M. (2003). *Classroom management for secondary teachers*. New York, NY: Longman.

Epstein, J., & Van Voorhis, R. (2001). More than minutes: Teachers' roles in designing homework. *Educational Psychologist, 36*, 181–194.

Everson v. Board of Education, 330 U.S. 1 (1947).

Evertson, C., & Emmer, E. T. (2009). *Classroom management for elementary teachers* (8th ed.). Upper Saddle River, NJ: Pearson.

Farkas, S., Johnson, J., & Duffett, A. (1999). *Playing their parts: Parents and teachers talk about parental involvement in public schools*. New York, NY: Public Agenda.

Farkas, S., Johnson, J., & Foleno, T. (2000). *A sense of calling: Who teaches and why*. New York, NY: Public Agenda.

Federal Interagency Forum on Child and Family Statistics. (2011). *America's children: Key national indicators of well-being, 2011*. Washington, DC: Author.

Ferlazzo, L. (2009, August 5). Going home. *Education Week's Teacher Magazine*. Retrieved January 15, 2012, from http://www.edweek.org/tm/articles/2009/08/05/tln_ferlazzo.html?r=720561725

Finkelhor, D., Turner, H., Ormrod, R., & Hamby, S. L. (2010, March). Trends in childhood violence and abuse exposure: Evidence from 2 national surveys. *Pediatrics and Adolescence Medicine, 163*(3), 242.

Flesch, R. (1955). *Why Johnny can't read*. New York, NY: Harper & Row.

Flesch, R. (1983). *Why Johnny still can't read*. New York, NY: Harper & Row.

Florey v. Sioux Falls School District, 619 F.2d 1311 (1980).

Foster, P. (2004). *Edmond Public Schools English IV research paper*. Edmond, OK: Author.

Frankenberg, E., Lee, C., & Orfield, G. (2003). *A multiracial society with segregated schools: Are we losing the dream?* Cambridge, MA: The Civil Rights Project, Harvard University.

Freiberg, H. J. (Ed.). (1999). *School climate: Measuring, improving and sustaining healthy learning environments*. London, England/Philadelphia, PA: Falmer Press.

Freiberg, J. H., & Driscoll, A. (2004). *Universal teaching strategies*. Boston, MA: Allyn & Bacon.

Fuller, F. (1969). Concerns of teachers: A developmental conceptualization. *American Educational Research Journal, 6*(2), 207–226.

Furstenberg, F. F., Jr. (1999). Family change and family diversity. In N. J. Smelser and J. C. Alexander (Eds.), *Diversity and its discontents: Cultural conflict and common ground in contemporary American society* (pp. 147–165). Princeton, NJ: Princeton University Press.

Gabler, C. I., & Schroeder, M. (2002). *Constructivist methods for the secondary classroom: Engaged minds*. Boston, MA: Allyn & Bacon.

Gallup, Inc. (2011). Religion. Princeton, NJ: Author. Retrieved October 15, 2011, from http://www.gallup.com/poll/1690/Religion.aspx

Garcetti v. Ceballos, 547 U.S. 410 (2006).

Gardner, H. (1999). *Intelligence reframed: Multiple intelligences for the 21st century*. New York, NY: Basic Books.

Gardner, H. (2005). *The development and education of the mind: The collected works of Howard Gardner*. London, England: Taylor and Francis.

Gardner, H. (2011). *Frames of mind: The theory of multiple intelligences*. New York, NY: Basic Books.

Gates, B. (1995). *The road ahead*. New York, NY: Viking Penguin.

Gathercoal, F. (1997). *Judicious discipline* (4th ed.). San Francisco, CA: Caddo Gap Press.

Gay, G. (2010). *Culturally responsive teaching: Theory, research, and practice* (2nd ed.). New York, NY: Teachers College Press.

Giroux, H. A. (2010, October 17). Lessons from Paulo Freire. *Chronicle of Higher Education*. Available at http://chronicle.com/article/Lessons-From-Paulo-Freire/124910/

Gitomer, D. H. (2007). *Teacher quality in a changing policy landscape: Improvements in the teacher pool*. Princeton, NJ: Educational Testing Service.

Glasser, W. (1997). A new look at school failure and school success. *Phi Delta Kappan, 78*(8), 597–602.

Glenn, C. L. (2011). *American Indian/First Nations schooling*. New York, NY: Palgrave Macmillan.

Goldberg, P. E., & Proctor, K. M. (2000). *Teacher voices: A survey on teacher recruitment and retention*. Scholastic, Inc., & the Council of Chief State School Officers. Retrieved from http://www.scholastic.com/content/collateral_resources/pdf/v/voices_part_1.pdf

Goldhaber, D. D., & Anthony, E. (2004). *Can teacher quality be effectively assessed?* Seattle, WA: Center on Reinventing Public Policy, University of Washington.

Gollnick, D. M., & Chinn, P. C. (2013). *Multicultural education in a pluralistic society* (9th ed.). Upper Saddle River, NJ: Pearson.

Gonzaga University v. Doe, 536 U.S. 273 (2002).

Gordon, T. (1989). *Teaching children self-discipline: Promoting self-discipline in children*. New York, NY: Penguin.

Gorski, P. (2011). Unlearning deficit ideology and the scornful gaze: Thoughts on authenticating the class discourse in education. In R. Ahlquist, P. Gorski, & T. Montaño (Eds.), *Assault on kids: How hyper-accountability, corporatization, deficit ideologies, and Ruby Payne are destroying our schools* (pp. 177–198). New York, NY: Peter Lang.

Goss v. Lopez, 419 U.S. 565 (1975).

Greene, M. (1988). *The dialectic of freedom*. New York, NY: Teachers College Press.

Gregory, A., Skiba, R., & Noguera, P. (2010). The achievement gap and the discipline gap: Two sides of the same coin? *Educational Researcher, 39*(1), 59–68.

Grumet, M. R. (1988). *Bitter milk: Women and teaching*. Amherst, MA: The University of Massachusetts Press.

Guerino, P., Harrison, P. M., & Sabol, W. J. (2011, December). *Prisoners in 2010*. Washington, DC: U.S. Department of Justice, Bureau of Justice Statistics.

Gurian, M., & Stevens, K. (2005). *The minds of boys: Saving our sons from falling behind in school and life*. San Francisco, CA: Jossey-Bass.

Gutek, G. (1986). *Education in the United States: An historical perspective*. Englewood Cliffs, NJ: Prentice-Hall.

Gutek, G. L. (2012). Friedrich Froebel (1782–1852)—Biography, Froebel's kindergarten philosophy, the kindergarten curriculum, diffusion of the kindergarten. Retrieved March 1, 2012, from http://education .stateuniversity.com/pages/1999/ Froebel-Friedrich-1782–1852.html

Guttmacher Institute. (2011a, December). Facts on American teens' sexual and reproductive health. New York, NY: Author. Retrieved January 31, 2012, from http://www.guttmacher. org/pubs/FB-ATSRH.html

Guttmacher Institute. (2011b, December). Facts on American teens' sources of information about sex. New York, NY: Author. Retrieved January 31, 2012, from http://www.guttmacher .org/pubs/FB-Teen-Sex-Ed.html

Hall, G. E., & Hord, S. M. (2011). *Implementing change: Patterns, principles and potholes* (3rd ed.). Upper Saddle River, NJ: Pearson.

Hamilton, L., Halverson, R., Jackson, S. S., Mandinach, E., Supovitz, J., & Wayman, J. D. (2009, September). *Using student achievement data to support instructional decision making.* Washington, DC: U.S. Education Department, IES, National Center for Education Evaluation and Regional Assistance.

Harris Interactive, Inc. (2009a, August 4). Firefighters, scientists, and doctors seen as most prestigious occupations. Retrieved February 5, 2012, from http://www.americanbar.org/content/ dam/aba/migrated/marketresearch/ PublicDocuments/harris_poll .authcheckdam.pdf

Harris Interactive, Inc. (2009b, May). A generation of change in American public education. *Trends & Tides,* 8(2), 1–5.

Hart, B., & Risley, R. T. (1995). *Meaningful differences in the everyday experience of young American children.* Baltimore, MD: Paul H. Brookes.

Hart Research Associates, Brossard Research, and the Insights Marketing Group. (2011). *Communities of color and public school reform: Findings from qualitative and quantitative research.* Retrieved February 5, 2012, from http://publiceducation.org/pdf/2011_ National_Conference/Communities_ of_Color_Slides.pdf

Hendrie, C. (2000). In black and white. In *Education Week, Lessons of a century: A nation's schools come of age.* Bethesda, MD: Editorial Projects in Education.

Hernandez, D. J. (2011). *Double jeopardy: How third-grade reading skills and poverty influence high school graduation.* Baltimore, MD: The Annie E. Casey Foundation.

Hill, C., & Kearl, H. (2011). *Crossing the line: Sexual harassment at school.* Washington, DC: American Association of University Women.

Hobson v. Hansen (1967) 269 F. Supp. 401 (1967).

Hollins, E. R. (2011). The meaning of culture in learning to teach: The power of socialization and identity formation. In A. F. Ball & C. A. Tyson (Eds.), *Studying diversity in teacher education* (pp. 105–130). Washington, DC: American Educational Research Association.

Hong, S. (2011). *A cord of three strands: A new approach to parent engagement in schools.* Cambridge, MA: Harvard Education Press.

Hord, S. M. (2004). Professional learning communities: An overview. In S. M. Hord (Ed.), *Learning together, leading together: Changing schools through professional learning communities.* New York, NY: Teachers College Press.

Horse, P. G. (2001). *Reflections on American Indian identity.* In C. L. Wijeyesinghe & B. W. Jackson III (Eds.), *New perspectives on racial identity development: A theoretical and practical anthology* (pp. 91–107). New York: New York University Press.

Howard, T. C. (2010). *Why race and culture matter in schools: Closing the achievement gap in America's classrooms.* New York, NY: Teachers College Press.

Howey, K. R., & Post, L. M. (2002). History of elementary education. In *Encyclopedia of education.* Gale-Macmillan Reference. Retrieved March 1, 2012, from http://www .answers.com/topic/history-of-elementary-education

Hunter, M. (1994). *Enhancing teaching.* New York, NY: Macmillan College Publishing.

Hussar, W., & Bailey, T. (2007). *Projections of education statistics to 2016.* Washington, DC: National Center for Education Statistics, Institute of Education Sciences, U.S. Department of Education. Retrieved from http:// purl.access.gpo.gov/GPO/LPS74331

Hussar, W. J., & Bailey, T. M. (2011). *Projections of education statistics to 2020* (NCES 2011-026). Washington, DC: U.S. Department of Education, National Center for Education Statistics.

Ingersoll, R. M. (2003). *Is there really a teacher shortage?* Seattle, WA: Center for the Study of Teaching and Policy, University of Washington.

Irvine, J., & York, D. (2001). Learning styles and culturally diverse students: A literature review. In J. Banks & C. Banks (Eds.), *Handbook of research on multicultural education* (pp. 484–497). San Francisco, CA: Jossey-Bass.

Ingraham v. Wright, 430 U.S. 651 (1977).

Irvine, M. (2012). Teens atwitter about Twitter: Micro-blogging service increasingly favored by youths. The Associated Press (March).

Iverson, A. M. (2003). *Building competence in classroom management and discipline* (4th ed.). Columbus, OH: Merrill, Prentice Hall.

Jamentz, K. (2002). *Isolation is the enemy of improvement: Instructional leadership to support standards-based practice* (p. 11). San Francisco, CA: WestEd.

James, W. (1975). *Pragmatism.* Cambridge, MA: Harvard University Press.

Jarolimek, J., Foster, C. D., Sr., & Kellough, R. D. (2005). *Teaching and learning in the elementary school* (8th ed.). Upper Saddle River, NJ: Pearson.

Johnson, D. W., & Johnson, R. T. (1990). Social skills for successful group work. *Educational Leadership,* 47(4), 30–32.

Johnson, D. W., & Johnson, R. T. (1999a). *Learning together and alone: Cooperative, competitive and individualistic learning* (5th ed.). Boston, MA: Allyn & Bacon.

Johnson, D. W., & Johnson, R. T. (1999b). The three Cs of school and classroom management. In H. J. Freiberg & J. E Brophy (Eds.), *Beyond behaviorism: Changing the classroom management paradigm* (pp. 119–144). Boston, MA: Allyn & Bacon.

Johnson, J., Duffett, A., Farkas, S., & Wilson, L. (2002). *When it's your own child: A report on special education from the families who use it.* New York, NY: Public Agenda.

Johnson, J. A., Dupuis, V. L., Musial, D., Hall, G. E., & Gollnick, D. M. (2005). *Foundations of American education* (13th ed.). Boston, MA: Allyn & Bacon.

Jones, F. (2003). More time on task, less goofing off. Fredjones.com, Discipline, Instruction, Motivation. Tools-for-Teaching.

Jones, J. M. (2011, May 20). *For first time, majority of Americans favor legal gay marriage.* Princeton, NJ: Gallup. Retrieved on June 1, 2011, from http://www.gallup.com/poll/147662/ First-Time-Majority-Americans-Favor-Legal-Gay-Marriage.aspx,

Joyce, B. R., & Weil, M. (2000). *Models of teaching* (6th ed.). Boston, MA: Allyn & Bacon.

Joyce, B., & Weil, M. (2008). *Models of teaching* (8th ed.). Englewood Cliffs, NJ: Prentice-Hall.

J.S. v. Blue Mountain School District, 593 F.3d 286 (2010).

Kaestle, C. F. (1983). *Pillars of the republic: Common schools and American society, 1780–1860*. New York, NY: Hill & Wang.

Kaestle, C. F., & Radway, J. A. (2009). *A history of the book in America: Print in motion: The expansion of publishing and reading in the United States, 1880–1940*. Chapel Hill: University of North Carolina Press.

Kagan, J. (1998). *Three seductive ideas*. Cambridge, MA: Harvard University Press.

Kauchak, D., & Eggen, P. (2005). *Introduction to teaching: Becoming a professional* (2nd ed.). Upper Saddle River, NJ: Merrill Prentice Hall.

Keane, B. (1995). *The way west* [Audio CD]. Shanachie Entertainment.

Keen, L. (2011, April 8). LGBTs comprise 3.5 percent of U.S. adult population. *Keen News Service*. Retrieved April 10, 2011, from http://www.keennewsservice.com/2011/04/08/lgbts-comprise-3-5-percent-of-u-s-adult-population/

Kimmel, M. (2008). *Guyland: The perilous world where boys become men*. New York, NY: Harper.

King, A. (2002). Structuring peer interactions to promote high-level cognitive processing. *Theory Into Practice, 41*, 31–39.

The Kinsey Institute. (2011). Data from Alfred Kinsey's studies. Bloomington, IN: Author. Retrieved March 24, 2011, from http://www.kinseyinstitute.org/research/ak-data.html#homosexuality

Kliebard, H. M. (2004). *The struggle for the American curriculum: 1893–1958* (3rd ed.). New York, NY: RoutledgeFalmer.

Knox County Education Association v. Knox County Board of Education, 158 F.3d 361 (1998).

Kohn, A. (1996). *Beyond discipline: From compliance to community*. Alexandria, VA: Association of Supervision and Curriculum.

Kolb, D. A., & Fry, R. (1975). Toward an applied theory of experiential learning. In C. Cooper (Ed.), *Theories of group process*. London, England: John Wiley.

Kosciw, J. G., Greytak, E. A., Diaz, E. M., & Bartkiewicz, M. J. (2010). *The 2009 national school climate survey: The experiences of lesbian, gay, bisexual and transgender youth in our nation's schools*. New York, NY: Gay, Lesbian and Straight Education Network.

Kottler, J. A., Zehm, S. J., & Kottler, E. (2005). *On being a teacher* (3rd ed.). Newbury Park, CA: Sage.

Kozol, J. (2007, September). Letters to a young teacher. *Phi Delta Kappan: The Journal for Education*, 8–20.

Kubota, R., & Lin, A. (2009). Race, culture, and identities in second language education: Introduction to research and practice. In R. Kubota & A. Lin (Eds.), *Race, culture, and identities in second language education: Exploring critically engaged practice* (pp. 1–23). New York, NY: Routledge.

Lareau, A., & Horvat, E. M. (2004). Moments of social inclusion and exclusion: Race, class, and cultural capital in family-school relationships. In J. H. Ballantine & J. Z. Spade (Eds.), *Schools and society: A sociological approach to education* (2nd ed.). Belmont, CA: Wadsworth/Thomson.

Lau v. Nichols, 414 U.S., 563–572 (Jan. 21, 1974).

Lawrence, D. H. (1915). *The rainbow* (pp. 355–356). New York, NY: Random House.

Layshock ex rel. Layshock v. Hermitage School District, 593 F.3d 249 (2010).

Lazarus, W., Wainer, A., & Lipper, L. (2005). *Measuring digital opportunity for America's children: Where we stand and where we go from here*. Santa Monica, CA & Washington, DC: A Publication of The Children's Partnership.

Lemon v. Kurtzman, 403 U.S. 602 (1971).

Lemov, D. (2010). *Teach like a champion*. San Francisco, CA: Jossey-Bass.

Let's Move! (n.d.). 5 simple steps to success. Washington, DC: U.S. Department of Health and Human Services. Retrieved January 31, 2012, from http://www.letsmove.gov/schools

Levin, S. R., Waddoups, G. L., Levin, J., & Buell, J. (2001, January). Highly interactive and effective online learning environments for teacher professional development. *International Journal of Educational Technology*.

Lewix, S., Simon, C., Uzzell, R. Horwitz, A., & Casserly, M. (2010). *A call for change: The social and educational factors contributing to the outcomes of black males in urban school*. Washington, DC: The Council of Great City Schools.

Lieberman, A., & Miller, L. (1984). *Teachers, their world, and their work: Implication for school improvement*. Alexandria, VA: Association for Supervision and Curriculum Development.

Linder, D. (2002). *The Scopes Trial: An introduction*, University of Missouri-Kansas City School of Law.

Lipsky, D. K., & Gartner, A. (1996, Winter). Inclusion, school restructuring, and the remaking of American society. *Harvard Educational Review, 66*(4), 762–796.

Loewen v. Turnipseed, 488 F. Supp. 1138 (N.D. Miss. 1980).

Lopez, M. H., & Velasco, G. (2011). *The toll of the great recession: Childhood poverty among Hispanics sets record, leads nation*. Washington, DC: Pew Hispanic Center.

Lortie, D. C. (1975). *Schoolteacher: A sociological study*. Chicago, IL: University of Chicago Press.

Lortie, D. C. (1977). *Schoolteacher: A sociological study* (2nd ed.). Chicago, IL: University of Chicago Press.

Losen, D. J. (2011). *Discipline policies, successful schools, and racial justice*. Boulder, CO: National Education Policy Center, University of Colorado–Boulder.

Lucas, J. L., Blazek, M. A., Raley, A. B., & Washington, C. (2005). The lack of representation of educational psychology and school psychology in introductory psychology textbooks. *Educational Psychology, 25*, 347–351.

Males, M. A. (2010). *Teenage sex and pregnancy: Modern myths, unsexy realities*. Santa Barbara, CA: Praeger.

Martin, J. (2002). *The education of John Dewey: A biography*. New York, NY: Columbia University Press.

Martin-Dunlop, C., & Fraser, B. J. (2008). Learning environment and attitudes associated with an innovative course designed for prospective elementary teachers. *International Journal of Science and Mathematics Education, 6*, 163–190.

Marzano, R. J., & Kendall, J. S. (1996). *A comprehensive guide to designing standards-based districts, schools, and classrooms*. Alexandria, VA: ASCD.

Marzano, R., Pickering, J., & Pollack, J. (2001). *Classroom instruction that works: Research-based strategies for increasing student achievement*. Alexandria, VA: Association for Supervision and Curriculum Development.

May, H., & Robinson, M. A. (2007). *A randomized evaluation of Ohio's Personalized Assessment Reporting System (PARS)*. Philadelphia, PA: Consortium for Policy Research in Education.

McCarty, D. (1993, April). Travelmates: Geography for kids (and stuffed pets). *Teaching Pre K-8,* 32–35.

McCarty, D. (1994, November/ December). Kids writing for kids. *Teaching Pre K–8,* 67–69.

McCarty, D. (1998, February). Books + manipulatives + families = A mathematics lending library. *Teaching Children Mathematics,* 368–375.

McCarty, D. (2003). Travelmates . . . One more time. *Teaching PreK-8, 34* Nov/ Dec (3) pp 60–61.

McCarty, D. (2004). A literacy luncheon. Essential Learning Products. Retrieved from http://www .essentiallearningproducts.com/ literacy-luncheon-diane-mccarty

McCarty, D., & Betterton, M. (1999, March). Scientifically speaking: Connecting to the past, present and future. *Teaching K–8,* 56–58.

McEwan, B. (2000). *The art of classroom management: Effective practices for building equitable learning communities.* Columbus, OH: Merrill/Prentice Hall.

McEwin, C. K., Dickinson, T. S., & Jenkins, D. M. (2003). *America's middle schools in the new century: Status and progress.* Westerville, OH: National Middle School Association.

McEwin, C. K., & Greene, M. W. (2011). The status of programs and practices in America's middle schools: Results from two national studies. Westerville, OH: Association for Middle Level Education.

McGrail, E., Sachs, G. T., Many, J., Myrick, C., & Sackor, S. (2011). Technology use in middle-grades teacher preparation programs. *The Journal of the Association of Teacher Educators, 33*(1), 63–80.

McNeil, J. D. (2003). *Curriculum: The teacher's initiative* (3rd ed.). Upper Saddle River, NJ: Pearson Education.

Meiners, E. R. (2007). *Right to be hostile: Schools, prisons, and the making of public enemies.* New York, NY: Routledge.

Mendez et al. v. Westminster School District et al., 64 F. Supp. 544 (C.D. Cal. 1946), aff'd, 161 F.2d 774 (9th Cir. 1947).

MetLife. (2008). *The MetLife survey of the American teacher: Past, present and future.* New York, NY: Author.

MetLife. (2009). *25th annual MetLife teacher survey looks back on more than two decades of education reform.* New York, NY: Author. Retrieved February 5, 2012, from http://www. metlife.com/about/press-room/index .html?compID=12296

MetLife. (2010). *The MetLife survey of the American teacher: Collaborating for student success.* New York, NY: Author.

Meyer, P. (2011, Winter). The middle school mess. *Education Next, 11*(1). Retrieved March 1, 2012, from http://educationnext.org/the-middle-school-mess/

Miel, A. (1946). *Changing the curriculum: A social process.* New York, NY: D. Appleton-Century.

Miller v. Mitchell, 598 F.3d 139 (2010).

Miller v. Skumanick, 605 F.Supp.2d 634 (2009).

Milner, H. R. (2010). *Start where you are, but don't stay there: Understanding diversity, opportunity gaps, and teaching in today's classrooms.* Cambridge, MA: Harvard University Press.

Mitchell, D. E., & Mitchell, R. E. (2003). The political economy of education policy: The case of class size reduction. *Peabody Journal of Education, 78*(4), 120–152.

Mt. Healthy City School District Board of Education v. Doyle, 429 U.S. 274 (1977).

National Assessment of Educational Progress. (2011). *2011 reading assessment and 2011 mathematics assessment.* Washington, DC: National Center for Education Statistics, Institute of Education Sciences, U.S. Department of Education. Retrieved January 29, 2011, from http://nces.ed.gov/ nationsreportcard/naepdata/

National Association for Gifted Children. (n.d.). *Advanced students in today's classrooms: What do we know?* Washington, DC: Author.

National Association for the Education of Homeless Children and Youth. (2011). Facts about homeless education. Retrieved October 13, 2011, from http://naehcy.org/facts. html#howmany

National Center for Education Statistics (NCES). (2005). Washington, DC: U.S. Department of Education. Retrieved from http://nces.ed.gov/

National Center for Education Statistics (NCES). (2010, July). Status and trends in the education of racial and ethnic minorities (Table 8.1b). Washington, DC: U.S. Department of Education. Retrieved June 11, 2012, from http:// nces.ed.gov/pubs2010/2010015/tables/ table_8_1b.asp

National Center on Response to Intervention. (n.d.). What is RTI? Retrieved from http://www .rti4success.org

National Clearinghouse for English Language Acquisition (NCELA). (n.d.). Types of language instruction educational programs (LIEPs). Washington, DC: Author. Retrieved April 29, 2012, from http://www .ncela.gwu.edu/files/uploads/5/ Language_Instruction_Educational_ Programs.pdf

National Commission on Excellence in Education. (1983). *A nation at risk: The imperative for educational reform.* Washington, DC: The Department of Education.

National Commission on Teaching and America's Future. (2003). *No dream denied: A pledge to America's children.* Washington, DC: Author.

National Education Association (NEA). (2003). *Status of the American public school teacher 2000–2001.* Washington, DC: Author.

National Governors Association Center for Best Practices, Council of Chief State School Officers. (2010). Common Core State Standards. Washington, DC: Authors. Retrieved from http://www.corestandards.org/ the-standards

National Scientific Council on the Developing Child. (2007, December). *The timing and quality of early experiences combine to shape brain architecture* (Working Paper No. 5). Cambridge, MA: Center on the Developing Child, Harvard University.

Neild, R. C., & Balfanz, R. (2006). *Unfulfilled promise: The dimensions and characteristics of Philadelphia's dropout crisis, 2000–05.* Baltimore, MD: Johns Hopkins University. Available at http://www.csos,jhu.edu/ new/Neild_Balfanz_06.pdf

Nelson, C. A., Lin, J., Carver, L. J., Monk, C. S., Thomas, K. M., & Truwit, C. L. (2000). Functional neuroanatomy of spatial working memory in children. *Developmental Psychology, 36,* 109–116.

Netterville, C. (2002). Sample portfolio contents. *2002 AAEE job search handbook.* Columbus, OH: American Association for Employment in Education, Inc.

New Jersey v. T.L.O., 469 U.S. 325 (1985).

Newport, F. (2011, May 20). For first time, majority of Americans favor legal gay marriage. Princeton, NJ: Gallup. Retrieved June 1, 2011, from http://www.gallup.com/poll/147662/ First-Time-Majority-Americans-Favor-Legal-Gay-Marriage.aspx

Newport, F. (2012, May 8). Half of Americans support legal gay marriage. Princeton, NJ: Gallup. Retrieved May 13, 2012, from http://www.gallup.com/poll/154529/Half-Americans-Support-Legal-Gay-Marriage.aspx

Nieto, S. (2008). Nice is not enough: Defining caring for students of color. In M. Pollock (Ed.), *Everyday antiracism: Getting real about race in school* (pp. 28–31). New York, NY: New Press.

Nieto, S. (2010). *Language, culture, and teaching: Critical perspectives.* New York, NY: Routledge.

North Central Regional Educational Laboratory. (2004). Learning Point Associates (2004). Blue Ribbon Panel Meeting, November 17–18.

Oakes, J. (1985). *Keeping track: How schools structure inequality*. New Haven, CT: Yale University Press.

Office of Justice Programs. (2011, October). OJP fact sheet: Bullying. Washington, DC: U.S. Department of Justice. Retrieved January 31, 2012, from http://www.ojp.usdoj.gov/newsroom/factsheets/ojpfs_bullying.html

Oliva, P. F. (2005). *Developing the curriculum* (7th ed.). Boston, MA: Pearson/Allyn & Bacon.

Oliva, P. F. (2009). *Developing the curriculum* (8th ed.). Boston, MA: Pearson Education.

Olson, L. (2000). The common good. In *Education Week, Lessons of a century: A nation's schools come of age.* Bethesda, MD: Editorial Projects in Education.

Orfield, G. (2004). *Dropouts in America: Confronting the graduation crisis.* Cambridge, MA: Harvard Education Press.

Owasso Independent School District v. Falvo, 534 U.S. 426 (2002).

Passel, J. S., & Cohn, D. (2011, February 1). *Unauthorized immigrant population: National and state trends, 2010.* Washington, DC: Pew Hispanic Center.

Passel, J. S., Cohn, D., & Lopez, M. H. (2011, March 24). *Hispanics account for more than half of nation's growth in past decade.* Washington, DC: Pew Hispanic Center.

Pavlov, J. (2011). Pavlov's dog. Nobelprize.org. Retrieved September 14, 2011, from http://www.nobelprize.org/educational/medicine/pavlov/readmore.html

Pergamit, M. R. (2010, April). *On the lifetime prevalence of running away from home.* Washington, DC: Urban Institute.

Pesce v. J. Sterling Morton High School District 201, Cook County, Illinois, 830 F.2d 789 (1987).

Phillips, N. B., Hamlett, C. L., Fuchs, L. S., & Fuchs, D. (1993). Combining classwide curriculum-based measurement and peer tutoring to help general educators provide adaptive education. *Learning Disabilities Research & Practice, 8*(3), 148–156.

Piaget, J. (1951). *The psychology of intelligence.* London, England: Routledge and Kegan Paul.

Piaget, J. (1985). *The equilibrium of cognitive structures: The central problem of intellectual development* (T. Brown & K. L. Thampy, Trans.). Chicago, IL: University of Chicago Press.

Pickering v. Board of Education Township High School District 205, 391 U.S. 563 (1968).

Plessy v. Ferguson, 163 U.S. 537 (1896).

Plyler v. Doe, 457 U.S. 202 (1982).

Popham, W. J. (2008). *Transformative assessment.* Alexandria, VA: Association for Supervision and Curriculum Development.

Popham, J. (2009). *Instruction that measures up: Successful teaching in the age of accountability.* Washington, DC: Association for Supervision & Curriculum Development.

Prensky, M. (2005). Listen to the natives. *Educational Leadership, 63*(4), 12.

profession. *Merriam-Webster Online.* Retrieved March 21, 2004, at http://www.m-w.com/home.htm

PTA. (2009). *PTA national standards for family-school partnerships: An implementation guide.* Alexandria, VA: Author.

PTA. (2012). History. Alexandria, VA: Author. Retrieved February 14, 2012, from http://pta.org/1164.asp

PTA. (n.d.). Making parent-teacher conferences work for your child. Alexandria, VA: Author. Retrieved February 14, 2012, from http://www.pta.org/2532.htm

Public Policy Research Institute. (2005). *Study of minority overrepresentation in the Texas juvenile justice system (final report).* College Station: Texas A&M University.

Quay, S. E., & Quaglia, R. J. (2004). Creating a classroom culture that inspires student learning. *The Teaching Professor, 18*(2), 1.

Ranck, E., & NAEYC's History & Archives Panel. (2001). Timeline of early care and education. In National Association for the Education of Young Children, *NAEYC at 75 (1926–2001): Reflections on the past, challenges for the future.* Washington, DC: Author.

Ratcliffe, C., & McKernan, S. (2010). *Childhood poverty persistence: Facts and consequences.* Washington, DC: Urban Institute. Retrieved January 29, 2012, from http://www.urban.org/UploadedPDF/412126-child-poverty-persistence.pdf

Redeaux, M. (2011). A framework for maintaining white privilege: A critique of Ruby Payne. In R. Ahlquist, P. Gorski, & T. Montaño (Eds.), *Assault on kids: How hyper-accountability, corporatization, deficit ideologies, and Ruby Payne are destroying our schools* (pp. 177–198). New York, NY: Peter Lang.

Reichert, M., & Hawley, R. (2010). *Reaching boys, teaching boys: Strategies that work—and why.* San Francisco, CA: Jossey-Bass, Wiley.

Renzulli, J. S., & Park, S. (2002). *Giftedness and high school dropouts: Personal, family, and school-related factors* (RM02168). Storrs, CT: The National Center on the Gifted and Talented, University of Connecticut.

Rethinking Schools. (2011–2012, Winter). Stop the school-to-prison pipeline. *Rethinking Schools, 26*(2), 4–7.

Reutter, E. Edmund, Jr. (1975) *The courts and student conduct*. The National Organization on Legal Problems of Education.

Richardson, V. (1997). Constructivist teaching and teacher education: Theory and practice. In V. Richardson (Ed.), *Constructivist teacher education: Building new understanding* (pp. 3–14). Washington, DC: Falmer Press.

Riner, P. S. (2000). *Successful teaching in the elementary classroom.* Upper Saddle River, NJ: Merrill/Prentice-Hall.

Rivkin, S. G., Hanushek, E. A., & Kain, J. F. (1998). *Teachers, schools and academic achievement.* (Working Paper No. 6691). Washington, DC: National Bureau of Economic Research.

Robelen, E. W. (2010, June 9). Some lawmakers seeking to rein in Texas board. *Education Week, 29*(33), 1, 20.

Robers, S., Zhang, J., & Truman, J. (2010). *Indicators of school crime and safety: 2010* (NCES 2011-002/NCJ 230812). Washington, DC: U.S. Department of Education, National Center for Education Statistics, and U.S. Department of Justice, Bureau of Justice Statistics, Office of Justice Programs.

Robertson, C. (2004). *Understanding comprehensive reform: Component four: Measurable goals and benchmarks.* SERVE: The University of North Carolina, Greensboro, (p. 2). Retrieved from http://www.serve.org/UCR/UCRCompFour.html

Robinson, S. (2011, February 16). Education master's programs: Add value or shut down. *Education Week*, February 16. Retrieved from http://www.edweek.org/ew/articles/2011/02/16/21robinson.h30.html

Rogers, C. (1969). *The freedom to learn.* Columbus, OH: Merrill.

Rogers, C., & Freiberg, H. J. (1994). *Freedom to learn.* Upper Saddle River, NJ: Prentice-Hall.

Ronfeldt, M. (2012, March). Where should student teachers learn to teach? Effects of field placement school characteristics on teacher retention and effectiveness. *Educational Evaluation and Policy Analysis, 34*(1), 3–26.

Rose v. Council for Better Education, 790 S.W.2d 186 (1989).

Rosenshine, B., & Stevens, R. (1986). Teaching functions. In M. C. Wittrock (Ed.), *Handbook of research on teaching* (3rd ed., pp. 376–391). Upper Saddle River, NJ: Merrill/Prentice Hall.

Rothstein, R. (2008). Whose problem is poverty? *Educational Leadership, 65*(7), 8–13.

Rumberger, R. W. (2011). *Dropping out: Why students drop out of high school and what can be done about it.* Cambridge, MA: Harvard University Press.

Rumberger, R. W., & Lim, S. A. (2008). *Why students drop out of school: A review of 25 years of research.* Santa Barbara, CA: California Dropout Research Project. Retrieved January 29, 2012, from http://cdrp.ucsb.edu/dropouts/pubs_reports.htm#15

Sadaker, M. P., & Sadaker, D. M. (2000). *Teachers, schools, and society.* New York, NY: McGraw Hill.

Sadovnik, A. R. (2004). Theories in the sociology of education. In J. H. Ballantine & J. Z. Spade (Eds.), *Schools and society: A sociological approach to education* (2nd ed., pp. 7–26). Belmont, CA: Wadsworth/Thomson.

Salpeter, J. (2003). Professional development: 21st century models. *Technology and Learning*, 24. Retrieved from http://www.techlearning.com/story/showArticle.jhtml?articleID=13000492

San Antonio (Texas) Independent School District v. Rodriquez (1973).

Sanders, W. L., & Rivers, J. C. (1996). *Cumulative and residual effects of teachers on future student academic achievement.* Knoxville: University of Tennessee, Value-Added Research and Assessment Center.

Santa Fe Independent School District v. Doe, 530 U.S. 290 (2000).

Savage, T. A., & Harley, D. A. (2009, Summer). A place at the blackboard: Including lesbian, gay, bisexual, transgender, intersex, and queer/questioning issues in the education process. *Multicultural Education, 16*(4), 2–9.

Schug, M. C., Tarver, S. G., & Western, R. D. (2001). Direct instruction and the teaching of early reading: Wisconsin's teacher-led insurgency. *Wisconsin Policy Research Institute Report, 14*(2). Retrieved from http://www.wpri.org/Reports/Volume14/v0114n02.pdf

Senate Committee on Labor and Public Welfare. (1969). *Indian education: A national tragedy—A national challenge,* 91st Cong., 1st sess. Washington, DC: U.S. Government Printing Office.

Shields, C. M. (2002, Spring). A comparison study of student attitudes and perceptions in homogeneous and heterogeneous classrooms. *Roeper Review, 24*(3), 115–120.

Short, D. J., & Boyson, B. A. (2012). *Helping newcomer students succeed in secondary schools and beyond.* Washington, DC: Center for Applied Linguistics.

Shreve, J. (2005). Let the games begin. *Edutopia, 1*(4), 29–31.

Simpson, D., Bruckheimer, J., Robins, S., & Foster, L. (Producers), & Smith, J. (Director). (1995). *Dangerous minds* [Motion picture]. U.S.: Hollywood Pictures, Via Rose Productions, Simpson-Bruckheimer Productions.

Slavin, R. E. (1987). Ability grouping and student achievement in elementary schools: A best-evidence synthesis. *Review of Educational Research, 57,* 347–370.

Slavin, R. (1993). *Student team learning: An overview and practical guide.* Washington, DC: National Education Association.

Smith, M. K. (1997). Johnann Heinrich Pestalozzi. Retrieved from http://www.infed.org/thinkers/et-pest.htm

Snyder, T. D., & Dillow, S. A. (2011). *Digest of education statistics 2010* (NCES 2011-015). Washington, DC: National Center for Education Statistics, Institute of Education Sciences, U.S. Department of Education.

Southern Poverty Law Center. (2004, Spring). 50 years later: Brown v. Board of Education [Special issue]. *Teaching Tolerance, 25.*

Spanierman v. Hughes, Druzolowski, & Hylwa, 576 F. Supp.2d 292 (D. Conn. 2008).

Sparks, S. D. (2011). Statistics shed light on costs and benefits of career paths. *Education Week Diplomas Count, 30*(34), 18–19.

Spring, J. (2001). *The American school: 1642–2004* (6th ed.). Boston, MA: McGraw Hill.

Spring, J. (2011). *The American school: A global context from the Puritans to the Obama era* (8th ed.). New York, NY: McGraw Hill.

Staessens, K. (1993). Identification and description of professional culture in innovating schools. *Qualitative Studies in Education, 6*(2), 111–128.

Stallings, J. A. (1990). *Effective use of time program.* Houston, TX: University of Houston.

State v. Scopes, Tenn. 105,289 SW 363 (1927).

Steele, C. M. (2010). *Whistling Vivaldi and other clues to how stereotypes affect us.* New York, NY: W. W. Norton.

Stuart v. School District No. 1 of Village of Kalamazoo, 30 Mich. 69 (1874).

Substance Abuse and Mental Health Services Administration. (2011). *Results from the 2010 national survey on drug use and health: Summary of national findings,* NSDUH Series H-41, HHS Publication No. (SMA) 11-4658. Rockville, MD: Author.

Swann v. Charlotte-Mecklenburg Board of Education, 402 U.S. 1 (1971).

Swanson, C. B. (2011). Nation turns a corner: Strong signs of improvement on graduation. *Education Week Diplomas Count, 30*(34), 23–25.

Sylwester, R. (2003). *A biological brain in a cultural classroom: Applying biological research to classroom management.* Thousand Oaks, CA: Corwin.

Szasz, M. (1974). *Education and the American Indian: The road to self-determination, 1928–1973.* Albuquerque: University of New Mexico Press.

Taba, H. (1962). *Curriculum development: Theory and practice.* New York, NY: Harcourt Brace Jovannovich.

Taba, H. (1965). *Teaching strategies and cognitive functioning in elementary school children.* (Washington, DC, H.E.W., U.S. Office of Education, Cooperative Research Project No. 2404, 1965).

Takahashi, P. (2012, February 26). A model of future classrooms? *Las Vegas Review Journal,* 9.

The Teacher Institute. (2003). Increasing parent involvement. Research-based ideas for teachers from the editors of Better Teaching. *Keeping Current.* Fairfax Station VA: Author.

Thomas, W. P., & Collier, V. P. (1997). *School effectiveness for language minority students.* Washington, DC: National Clearinghouse for Bilingual Education.

Thomas, W. P., & Collier, V. P. (2001). *A national study of school effectiveness for language minority students' long-term academic achievement.* Santa Cruz, CA: Center for Research on Education, Diversity & Excellence.

Thorndike-Law of Effect. (n.d.). Retrieved from http://www.youtube.com/watch?v=Vk6H7Ukp6To

Thurlow, M. L., & Johnson, D. R. (2011, September). *The high school dropout dilemma and special education students.* Santa Barbara, CA: California Dropout Research Project. Retrieved January 29, 2012, from http://cdrp.ucsb.edu/dropouts/pubs_reports.htm#15

Tillery, G. (2011, June 22). Teaching secrets: Communicating with parents. *Education Week Teacher.* Retrieved February 13, 2012, from http://www.edweek.org/tm/articles/2011/06/21/tillery.html?tkn=QXQFt3Cw2U8vql%2F5pl5gyKQf5AyB49x9RMM9&cmp=ENL-TU-NEWS1

Tinker v. Des Moines Independent Community School District, 393 U.S. 503 (1969).

Tomlinson, C. (2001). *How to differentiate instruction in mixed-ability classrooms.* Alexandria, VA: ASCD.

Torff, B. (2006). Expert teachers' beliefs about critical-thinking activities. *Teacher Education Quarterly, 33,* 37–52.

Torff, B. (2011, November). Teacher beliefs shape learning for all students. *Phi Delta Kappan, 93*(3), 21–23.

Tyler, R. W. (1949). *Basic principles of curriculum and instruction.* Chicago, IL: University of Chicago Press.

Urban, W. J., & Wagoner, J. L., Jr. (2009). *American education: A history.* New York, NY: Routledge.

U.S. Census Bureau. (2011). *Statistical abstract of the United States: 2012* (131st ed.). Washington, DC: Author.

U.S. Conference of Mayors. (2010, December). *Hunger and homelessness survey: A status report on hunger and homelessness in America's cities, a 27-city survey.* Washington, DC: Author.

United States Department of Education. (2011). *Digest of education statistics, 2010* (NCES 2011-015), Table 3. Retrieved from http://nces.ed.gov/programs/digest/d10/tables/dt10_003.asp

U.S. Copyright Law {Title 17 U.S.C. Section 101 et seq., Title 18 U.S.C. Section 2319)

U.S. Department of Education, National Center for Education Statistics, Common Core of Data (CCD). (n.d.). National public education financial survey, 2007–08. Retrieved from http://nces.ed.gov/

U.S. Department of Education, Office of Special Education Programs, Individuals with Disabilities Education Act (IDEA) database. (n.d.). Retrieved June 10, 2012, from https://www.ideadata.org/DACAnalyticTool/Intro_2.0sp

U.S. Department of Health and Human Services. (2011a). HIV and other STD prevention and United States students. Washington: DC: Author. Retrieved January 31, 2012, from http://www.cdc.gov/healthyyouth/yrbs/pdf/us_hiv_combo.pdf

U.S. Department of Health and Human Services. (2011b). The obesity epidemic and United States students. Washington, DC: Author. Retrieved January 31, 2012, from http://www.cdc.gov/healthyyouth/yrbs/pdf/us_obesity_combo.pdf

U.S. Department of Homeland Security. (2011, August). *Yearbook of immigration statistics: 2010.* Washington, DC: U.S. Department of Homeland Security, Office of Immigration Statistics.

Vavrus, F., & Cole, K. M. (2002). "I didn't do nothing": The discursive construction of school suspension. *Urban Review, 34,* 87–111.

Vygotsky, L. (1978). *Mind in society: The development of higher psychological processes.* Cambridge, MA: Harvard University Press.

Wahl, L., & Duffield, J. (2005). Using flexible technology to meet the needs of diverse learners: What teachers can do. *WestEd Knowledge Brief.*

Wallace v. Jaffree, 472 U.S. 38 (1985).

Wassermann, S. (1992). *Asking the right question.* Bloomington, IN: Phi Delta Kappa.

Wattenberg, W. (1967). *All men are created equal.* Detroit, MI: Wayne State University Press.

Wayne, A. J., & Youngs, P. (2003, Spring). Teacher characteristics and student achievement gains: A review. *Review of Educational Research, 73*(1), 89–122.

Weber, W. A. (1994). Classroom management. In J. M. Cooper (Ed.), *Classroom teaching skills* (5th ed., pp. 234–279). Lexington, KY: D. C. Heath.

Wenglinsky, H. (1998). *Does it compute? The relationship between educational technology and student achievement in mathematics.* Princeton, NJ: Educational Testing Services (ETS).

Wiggins, G., & McTighe, J. (2004). *Understanding by design.* Washington, DC: ASCD.

Wiggins, G., & McTighe, J. (2005). *Understanding by design: Expanded 2nd edition.* Alexandria, VA: ASCD.

Windschitl, M. (1999). The challenges of sustaining a constructivist classroom culture. *Phi Delta Kappan, 80,* 751–755.

Wong, H. K., & Wong, R. T. (1998). *The first day of school: How to be an effective teacher.* Mountain View, CA: Harry K. Wong Publications.

Woodlock v. Orange Ulster B.O.C.S., 281 Fed. Appx. 66-2008.

Woodward, C. V. (1971). *Origins of the New South, 1877–1913* (pp. 416–417). Baton Rouge: Louisiana State University Press.

Woolfolk, A. (2004). *Educational psychology* (9th ed.). Needham Heights, MA: Allyn & Bacon.

Wright, E. (1999). *Why I teach: Inspirational true stories from teachers who make a difference.* Rocklin, CA: Pima Publishing.

Youth Risk Behavior Survey. (2011). Selected health risk behaviors and health outcomes by sex: National YRBS: 2009. Washington, DC: U.S. Department of Health and Human Services. Retrieved January 31, 2012, from http://www.cdc.gov/healthyyouth/yrbs/pdf/us_disparityrace_yrbs.pdf

Zirkel, P. A., & Clark, J. H. (2008). School negligence case law trends. *Southern Illinois University Law Journal, 32,* 345–363.

Zohar, A., & Dori, J. (2003). Higher-order thinking and low-achieving students: Are they mutually exclusive? *The Journal of the Learning Sciences, 12,* 145–182.

Zusman, M., Knox, D., & Gardner, T. (2009). *The social context view of sociology.* Durham, NC: Carolina Academic Press.

Photo Credits

Front Matter

Photo, page xxxiii. © Gene E. Hall, professor, husband, father, grandfather, and road racer.

Photo, page xxxiii. © Linda F. Quinn, professor, wife, mother, grandmother, and traveler.

Photo, page xxxiii. © Donna Gollnick, administrator, mother, scholar, and golfer.

Chapter 1

Photo, chapter opener, page 2. © Siri Stafford/ Lifesize/Thinkstock.

Photo, page 2. © Katie Johnston.

Photo, page 5. © iStockphoto.com/kali9.

Photo, page 6. © iStockphoto.com/Steven Debenport.

Photo, page 8. © iStockphoto.com/kate_sept2004.

Photo, page 15. © iStockphoto.com/Terraxplorer.

Image, page 18. © Pearson.

Photo, page 22. © Istockphoto/Catherine Yeulet.

Photo, page 23. © Lloyd Goldberg.

Photo, page 30. © iStockphoto.com/Silvrshootr.

Chapter 2

Photo, chapter opener, page 36. © istockphoto.com/Rich Legg.

Photo, page 36. © Michele Clarke.

Photo, page 39. Wikimedia Commons – From Yale University Art Gallery. Author: Lewis W. Hine.

Cartoon, page 40. © Harley Schwardon.

Photo, page 44. Wikimedia Commons – author Moliverg.

Photo, page 47. © iStockphoto.com/Justin Horrocks.

Photo, page 53. © iStockphoto.com/iofoto.

Photo, page 54. © iStockphoto.com/Sarah Salmela.

Photo, page 56. © Peter Eley.

Photo, page 59. © iStockphoto.com/ Juanmonino.

Chapter 3

Photo, chapter opener, page 66. © Ryan McVay/Photodisc/Thinkstock.

Photo, page 66. © Brandy Donald.

Photo, page 69. © iStockphoto.com/Erna Vader.

Photo, page 73. © Pixland/Pixland/Thinkstock.

Photo, page 74. © Thinkstock Images/ Comstock/Thinkstock.

Photo, page 81. © iStockphoto.com/Melhi.

Photo, page 82, top. http://commons .wikimedia.org/wiki/File:Trailerpark.jpg.

Photo, page 82, bottom. © Ablestock.com /Ablestock.com/Thinkstock.

Photo, page 84. ©Thinkstock Images/ Comstock/Thinkstock.

Photo, page 86. © Jupiter Images/Brand X Pictures/Thinkstock.

Photo, page 88. © iStockphoto.com/Aldo Murillo.

Cartoon, page 89. © Martha Campbell.

Photo, page 90. © Thinkstock/Comstock/ Thinkstock.

Photo, page 92. © Susan Rakow.

Chapter 4

Photo, chapter opener, page 98. © iStockphoto.com/mbbirdy.

Photo, page 98. © Ava Evbuoma.

Photo, page 101. © iStockphoto.com/ Christopher Futcher.

Photo, page 103. © AP Photo/Daily Chronicle/ Kyle Bursaw.

Photo, page 107. © Bob Daemmrich/Alamy.

Photo, page 111. © iStockphoto.com/bonnie jacobs.

Photo, page 113. © Jupiterimages/Creatas/ Thinkstock.

Photo, page 115. © Jupiterimages/Comstock/ Thinkstock.

Cartoon, page 116. © Norman Jung.

Photo, page 118. © iStockphoto.com/quavondo.

Photo, page 120. © Amanda Glaze.

Chapter 5

Photo, chapter opener, page 128. © Ryan McVay/Digital Vision/Thinkstock.

Photo, page 128. © Arlene Costello.

Photo, page 134. © iStockphoto.com/Willie B. Thomas.

Photo, page 136. © iStockphoto.com/Mark Bowden.

Photo, page 138. © Jupiterimages/liquidlibrary/ Thinkstock.

Photo, page 141. © Peter Marshall/Demotix/Corbis.

Cartoon, page 144. © George Abbott.

Photo, page 147. © © iStockphoto.com/kali9.

Photo, page 148. © Michael Evans.

Photo, page 151. © AP Photo/The Advocate-Meesenger, Clay Jackson.

Chapter 6

Photo, chapter opener, page 158. © Thinkstock/Comstock/Thinkstock.

Photo, page 158. © Marvin Kuhn.

Cartoon, page 163. © Aaron Bacall; 2010, May. *Phi Delta Kappan, 91*(8):73.

Photo, page 163. U.S. National Archives and Records Administration via Wikimedia Commons.

Photo, page 165. © Getty Images.

Photo, page 170. © Bettmann/Corbis.

Photo, page 172. © iStockphoto.com/Chris Schmidt.

Photo, page 175. © Getty Images.

Photo, page 179. Library of Congress.

Photo, page 182. © Douglas Sturgeon.

Photo, page 183. © Getty Images.

Chapter 7

Photo, chapter opener, page 190. © iStock.

Photo, page 190. © Heather Cyra.

Photo, page 196, part A. © iStockphoto.com/ BulentGrp.

Photo, page 196, part B. © Comstock Images/ Comstock/Thinkstock.

Photo, page 197. © Thinkstock Images/ Comstock/Thinkstock.

Photo, page 199. © Crimsononmaroon.

Photo, page 202. © iStockphoto.com/Simon Ingate.

Photo, page 203. © Creatas Images/Creatas/ Thinkstock.

Photo, page 206. © Sky View/Digital Vision/ Thinkstock.

Photo, page 208. © Wikimedia Commons.

Photo, page 210. © Mary Bauer.

Photo, page 211. © Miguel A. Monjas.

Photo, page 212. © iStockphoto.com/clu.

Chapter 8

Photo, chapter opener, page 222. © Ryan McVay/ Digital Vision/Thinkstock.

Photo, page 222. © Dr. Kim Friel.

Photo, page 226. © iStockphoto.com/Alina Solovyova-Vincent.

Photo, page 227. © iStockphoto.com/Annedde.

Cartoon, page 229. © Cartoonstock.

Photo, page 232. © John Foxx/Stockbyte/ Thinkstock.

Photo, page 237. © David Eitan Arom.

Photo, page 238. © Dr. Kim Friel.

Photo, page 241. © U.S. Government—House of Representatives.

Photo, page 242. © U.S. Government—Architect of the Capitol.

Cartoon, page 244. © Dave Carpenter.

Chapter 9

Photo, chapter opener, page 250. © iStockphoto.com/Michael Hoerichs.

Photo, page 250. © Italia Negroni.

Photo, page 253. © U.S. Federal Government.

Photo, page 255. © iStockphoto.com/Trista Weibell.

Photo, page 256. © US Federal Government.

Photo, page 258. © Ralf Roletschek – Creative Commons.

Photo, page 260. Jeff Kubina.

Cartoon, page 261. © Martha F. Campbell.

Photo, page 262. © Jennifer Holloway.

Photo, page 263. © iStockphoto.com/Scott Dunlap.

Photo, page 268. © Sage Ross.

Cartoon, page 269. © Aaron Bacall.

Photo, page 269. © iStockphoto.com/Steve Weinik.

Photo, page 270. © Erich Schlegel/Corbis.

Photo, page 274. © iStockphoto.com/Daniel Padavona.

Chapter 10

Photo, chapter opener, page 282. © Photodisc/ Photodisc/Thinkstock.

Photo, page 282. © Michael Simpson.

Photo, page 285. © U.S. Government.

Photo, page 286. © iStockphoto.com/Sean Locke.

Photo, page 288. © Stockbyte/Stockbyte/ Thinkstock.

Photo, page 290, top. © iStockphoto.com/ Jennifer Byron.

Photo, page 290, bottom. © Comstock/ Comstock/Thinkstock.

Photo, page 293. U.S. Government.

Photo, page 294. U.S. Government.

Photo, page 299. © iStockphoto.com/Kim Gunkel.

Photo, page 300. © Brand X Pictures/Brand X Pictures/Thinkstock.

Photo, page 301. © AP Photo/Kingman Daily Miner, JC Amberlyn.

Photo, page 302. © Robert Moody.

Photo, page 303. © iStockphoto.com/Nathan Maxfield.

Photo, page 306. © iStockphoto.com/vm.

Photo, page 309. © iStockphoto.com/ constantgardener.

Chapter 11

Photo, chapter opener, page 318. © iStock.

Photo, page 318. © Lorraine (Reina) Floyd.

Photo, page 321. © iStockphoto.com/ AlbanyPictures.

Photo, page 324. © iStockphoto.com/Chris Schmidt.

Photo, page 325. © iStockphoto.com/ PaulaConnelly.

Photo, page 328. © SAGE.

Photo, page 329. © Stockbyte/Stockbyte/ Thinkstock.

Photo, page 331. © iStockphoto.com/Aldo Murillo.

Photo, page 332. © Jack Hollingsworth/ Photodisc/Thinkstock.

Cartoon, page 333. © Calvin and Hobbes ©1993 Watterson. Dist. By Universal Uclick. Reprinted with permission. All rights reserved.

Photo, page 338. © iStockphoto.com/Bill Grove.

Cartoon, page 342. © Non Sequitur ©1996 Wiley Ink, Inc. Dist. By Universal Uclick. Reprinted with permission. All rights reserved.

Photo, page 343. © Kevin Badgett.

Chapter 12

Photo, chapter opener, page 350. © iStock

Photo, page 350. © Lena Mann.

Photo, page 354 top. © iStockphoto.com/Terry J Alcorn.

Photo, page 354, bottom. © iStockphoto.com/ Terry J Alcorn.

Photo, page 357. © Jupiterimages/Comstock/ Thinkstock.

Photo, page 359. © Anna Baik, Kindergarten Teacher, Berkley, IL.

Photo, page 361. © Talisha Givan.

Photo, page 361. © iStockphoto.com/Alina Solovyova-Vincent.

Photo, page 368. © iStockphoto.com/zorani.

Photo, page 369. © Jupiterimages/Comstock/ Thinkstock.

Photo, page 370. © Thinkstock/Comstock/ Thinkstock.

Photo, page 373. © Jupiterimages/Photos .com/Thinkstock.

Chapter 13

Photo, chapter opener photo, page 382. © Bananastock/ Thinkstock.

Photo, page 382. © Jason Choi.

Photo, page 385. © iStockphoto.com/Jani Bryson.

Photo, page 387. © iStockphoto.

Photo, page 388. © Brand X Pictures/Brand X Pictures/Thinkstock.

Photo, page 390. © iStockphoto.com/Troels Graugaard.

Photo, page 390 (inset). © Comstock/Thinkstock.

Photo, page 391. © iStockphoto.com/SteveStone.

Photo, page 393. © iStockphoto.

Photo, page 399. © iStockphoto.com/ Christopher Futcher.

Photo, page 400. © Lorae Roukema.

Photo, page 405. © Comstock/Comstock/ Thinkstock.

Cartoon, page 406. © Martha Campbell.

Chapter 14

Photo, chapter opener photo, page 414. © Ciaran Griffin/ Stockbyte/ Thinkstock.

Photo, page 414. © Ms. Nira Dale.

Photo, page 417. © iStockphoto.com/Fred Fox.

Photo, page 418. © Thinkstock Images/ Comstock/Thinkstock.

Photo, page 421. © iStockphoto.com/Daniel Laflor.

Photo, page 422. © iStockphoto.com/Luis Alvarez.

Photo, page 426. © Jupiterimages/Brand X Pictures/Thinkstock.

Photo, page 427. © Karen Grove.

Photo, page 428. © Digital Vision/Photodisc/ Thinkstock.

Photo, page 429. © Ableimages/Lifesize/ Thinkstock.

Photo, page 435. © Brand X Pictures/ Thinkstock.

Chapter 15

Photo, chapter opener photo, page 444. © Jack Hollingsworth/Photodisc/Thinkstock.

Photo, page 444 © Dr. Elliott Asp.

Photo, page 448. © iStockphoto.com/ omgimages.

Photo, page 452. © iStockphoto.com/Colleen Butler.

Cartoon, page 453. © George Abbott.

Photo, page 454. © Jupiterimages/liquidlibrary/ Thinkstock.

Photo, page 457. © iStockphoto.com/Leontura.

Cartoon, page © Original Artist.

Photo, page 461. © Author.

Photo, page 472. © iStockphoto.com/ PeskyMonkey.

Chapter 16

Photo, chapter opener photo, page 480. © ©iStockphoto.com/ Heather Nemec.

Photo, page 480. © Amber Velasquez.

Photo, page 483. © Comstock/Comstock/ Thinkstock.

Photo, page 484. © Jupiterimages/Photos.com/ Thinkstock.

Photo, page 490. © iStockphoto.com/Svetlana Braun.

Photo, page 493. © iStockphoto.com/ Alexander Raths.

Photo, page 497. © Creatas/Creatas/ Thinkstock.

Photo, page 500. © Lauri Bosquet.

Photo, page 503. © Joyce Schneider.

Photo, page 504. © Digital Vision/Digital Vision/Thinkstock.

Cartoon, page 505. © David Quintanar.

Index

AAAS. *See* American Association for the Advancement of Science
AACTE. *See* American Association of Colleges for Teacher Education
Absolute truths, 211
Abuse, child, 118–119, 305
Academic ability
  intelligence, 73–74
  learning implications of, 75
  teaching implications of, 75
Academic achievement. *See also* Student achievement
  reforms to improve, 43
  setting standards and, 339
Academic performance
  federal mandates to improve, 101
  social context effects on, 100–101
  teacher's role in, 101
Academic success, 132–133
Academies, 166
Accommodations, 456–457
Accountability
  description of, 254
  differentiated system of, 264
  of school finance, 274
  of schools, 344–345
  standards and, 322
  of teachers, 306, 329, 344
Accreditation, 9–10, 335
Achievement gap
  description of, 42–44, 101–102
  discipline and, relationship between, 107
  reasons for, test scores used to identify, 102, 469, 473
  after school desegregation, 179
  teacher's effects on, 101
Active listening, 361
Activity learning, 400–401
Adequacy suits, 275
Adequate yearly progress, 43, 101, 261, 344
ADHD. *See* Attention deficit hyperactivity disorder
Administrative law, 259, 285
Administrator, 500
Advanced students, 89–90
African American(s)
  culture of, 39
  in early 20th century, 177–178
  education of, history of, 176–179
  imprisonment rate for, 118
  school desegregation for, 178–179
  in Southern states, 177
African American families
  academic success, 132
  educational concerns of, 132
  educational involvement by, 144
  structure of, 133
  working with, 149
African American students
  expulsion of, 107
  population forecasts for, 41
  suspension of, 107
Afrocentric curriculum, 45
AFT. *See* American Federation of Teachers
Agnostics, 59
AIDS, 117
Alaska Natives, 39
Alcohol, 122
Alexander v. Holmes County Board of Education, 295
Alvord, John W., 177
American Association for the Advancement of Science, 28, 330
American Association of Colleges for Teacher Education, 12
American Federation of Teachers, 182
American Indian Movement, 176
American Indian students, 41
American Indians
  boarding schools for, 175–176
  colonists' conversion of, 173
  deculturalizing of, 173
  description of, 39
  education of, history of, 173–176
  poverty rates for, 46
Amish, 59
Analysis of student work, 407
Analysis question, 392
Annual measurable objective, 43
Application question, 392
Aquinas, Thomas, 211
Aristotle, 198, 208, 211–212
Arkansas, 239
Armstrong, Samuel Chapman, 169, 177
Artifacts, in portfolio, 29
Asian American(s)
  education of, history of, 181
  poverty rates for, 46
Asian American students
  as model minority, 104
  population forecasts for, 41
  stereotypes for, 104
Asp, Elliott, 444, 446–447, 457, 460, 467, 470–471, 476–477
Assault and battery, 309
Assertive Discipline, 359
Assessing, 477
Assessment(s). *See also* Test(s)
  analysis of student work used in, 407
  authentic tasks, 452, 454
  characteristics of, 452–454
  criteria used in selection and use of, 452–454
  curriculum and, 338
  English-language learners, 456–457
  formative. *See* Formative assessments
  importance of, 447–457
  instruction versus, 468
  instructional adjustments after, 468, 470
  knowledge, 19
  learners and, 454–457
  learning types and, 454
  level of difficulty of, 452–453
  methods of, 447–448
  performance tasks included in, 453
  purposes for, 448–450
  quality of, 449–451
  reasons for, 447–448
  rigor of, 450
  rubrics used in, 466–467
  scrutiny of, 451
  special needs students, 455–457
  student learning, 20–21, 406–407
  students' learning tactic adjustments after, 470
  students with disabilities, 455–457
  summative, 445, 448
  testing versus, 445
  writing proficiency, 466
Assimilation, 57
Assistant principal, 226
Atanasoff, John, 417
Atheists, 59
At-risk students, 90–91
Attention deficit hyperactivity disorder, 71
Attention-getting activities, 405
Audio recordings, 428
Ausubel, David P., 203, 387
Authentic tasks, 452, 454
Authoritarian, 170
Authorize, 259
Autism, 71–72
Axiology, 208

Bachelor's degree, 8–9
Bacon, Francis, 165
Bacon, Kevin, 420
Bad governance, 254–255
Bagley, William Chandler, 169, 171
Bailey, Mark, 193

Basic Principles of Curriculum and Instruction, 200
Basic skills testing, 18
Beginning teachers. *See also* Teacher education candidates
- challenges for, 499
- content tests for, 19
- dismissal of, 306
- employment rights of, 303
- expectations for, 482
- hiring of, 223, 492–496
- leadership by, 497
- nonrenewal of, 306
- state-created pedagogical standards for, 332
- student learning assessments by, 445–446

Behavior management, 372–373
Behavior modification, 358–359
Beliefs
- cultural, 84
- personal, 196

Benchmarks. *See also* Standards
- definition of, 321
- lessons plans used to track, 329–330
- progress tracking using, 28
- use of, 328–329

Bethel School District No. 403 v. Fraser, 301
Bethune, Mary McLeod, 169
Bias, in objective tests, 461–462
Biculturalism, 137
Bilingual education, 16, 52–53, 141
Bilingualism, 50, 142
Bill of Rights, 256–257
Birney, Alice McLellan, 150
Blogs, 420, 433
Bloom, Benjamin, 205, 391–392, 454–455, 466
Board certification, 10
Board of Education of Oklahoma v. Dowell, 179
Board of Education of the Westside Community Schools v. Mergens, 292
Board of Education v. Pico, 139
Board of Reagents of State Colleges v. Roth, 305–306
Board of trustees, 237
Boarding schools, 175–176
Bodily-kinesthetic intelligence, 75–77, 201
Body search, 302
Bolling v. Sharpe, 178
Books
- readers, 165
- religious beliefs and, 139–140

Borders, cultural, 137
Borer, Michael Ian, 419
Born-again, 59
Boston Latin School, 159
Bourdieu, Pierre, 103
Boys
- equitable education for, 52–54
- girls versus, 53–54
- society's view of, 54
- suicide rates in, 121

Bracketing, 406
Brain
- development of, 79–81
- impoverishment effects on, 80
- plasticity of, 80–81

Brain architecture, 79
Brown v. Board of Education of Topeka, 178–179, 256, 292, 295
Bruner, Jerome S., 203
Budget
- balancing of, 273–274
- description of, 272
- examples of, 277
- revenue distribution, 272–273
- size of, 235

Bullying, 87, 119–120
Bureau of Indian Affairs, 176
Bush, George H.W., 104
Bush, George W., 260

CAEP. *See* Council for the Accreditation of Educator Preparation
California, 17, 239, 268
Candidate teachers. *See* Teacher education candidates
Canon, 109–110
Canter, Lee, 359
Canter, Marlene, 359
Cardinal Principles of Secondary Education, 167
Career path, 499–501
Career-themed academies, 107
Carlisle Indian School, 175
Carnegie, Andrew, 204
Carnivals, 270
Case law, 285
Catechism, 160
Catholicism, 59
Censoring of books, 139
Centralization, 276
Certification, national board, 10
Chain of command, 228
Change, 340
Charity schools, 163
Chicago Federation of Teachers, 182
Chicago Laboratory School, 199
Chief state school officer, 241
Child abuse, 118–119, 305
Chinese immigrants, 181
Chinese-Americans, 39
Choctaws, 173
Choi, Jason, 343, 382–384, 386, 401–402, 407
Choice Theory model, 360
Christianity, 173
Christians, 59, 139–140
Churchill, Winston, 352
Civil rights, 60
Civil Rights Act of 1964, 178
Civilization Act, 173
Clarke, Michele, 36–37, 45, 49, 54–55, 58
Class meeting, 360–361
Class size, 242, 244
Classroom
- changing focus in, 217
- computer use in, 438
- cultural safety in, 87–88
- culture in, 86, 88
- democratic, 360
- displays in, 86
- educational philosophies in, 213–214, 217
- environment of, 86–87
- ethics in, 209
- immediacy in, 368
- Lancastarian, 165
- organizing of, 362
- overview of, 352–353
- parent volunteers in, 148
- Popham's dimensions of, 470
- public nature of, 368
- race in, 44
- room arrangement in, 214–215, 217, 365–366
- rules for, 356, 369–370
- safe and caring environment in, 86–87, 245
- self-contained, 232
- simultaneity in, 367
- stages of, 371–372
- student-focused, 217
- teacher-focused, 213–214, 216
- unpredictable elements of, 368
- in urban schools, 165
- values in, 209
- well-managed, 370–371

Classroom history, 368
Classroom interruptions, 362–363
Classroom management
- areas of, 355–356
- Assertive Discipline, 359
- behavior management, 372–373
- behavior modification, 358–359
- class meeting, 360–361
- communication approaches to, 361–365
- conduct management, 356
- content management, 355
- covenant management, 356–357
- decision making involved in, 357
- definition of, 353–354
- description of, 353
- discipline and, 371–374
- group dynamics approach to, 359–360

instruction approaches to, 361–365
Judicious Discipline, 359–360
listening, 373–374
movement in hallways and on school grounds, 368–369
multidimensional view of, 367–368
paperwork, 366–367
paradoxes of, 357
personal and parental affect in, 356–357
personal philosophy of, 358–365
planning, 355–356
room arrangement, 365–366
routines, 369
schedules, 369–370
socio-emotional approaches to, 359–360
stress caused by, 374–375
studies of, 362–364
teacher's existing knowledge about, 355
technology used in, 433–434
Cleveland Board of Education v. LeFleur, 305
Clinical experience, in teacher education programs, 12
Closed questions, 459
Coalition, 255
Coalition of Essential Schools, 171
Code of ethics, 11
Cognitive development, 77–79
Cognitive domain taxonomy, 455
Cognitive framework, 355
Colleagues, sharing with, 26
Colleges of education standards, 335
Colonies, 160–161
Color blindness, 42
Committee for National Health Education Standards, The, 325
Committee of Ten on Secondary School Studies, 166–167
Common Core State Standards, 264, 271, 276, 323
Common schools, 161, 163, 322
Commonsense media, 289
Communication
behavior management through, 372–373
classroom management through, 361–365
history of, 416–417
horizontal, 228–230
with parents, 147–149, 357, 498
school structure and, 228–229
technology for, 419–421
vertical, 228
Community
school and, partnerships between, 151–152
school staff collaboration with, 146
social context of, 99
Comprehension question, 392
Compulsory attendance, 166, 300
Compulsory Education Act, 300
Computers, 438
Concerns, of teacher education candidates, 484–487
Concerns Model, 485–487
Concrete operational stage, of cognitive development, 78
Conditioning, 206
Conduct management, 356
Confidence interval, 43
Confucianism, 210–211
Confucius, 210
Congress, 259
Connecticut, 17
Consensus oriented, 254
Consortium of National Arts Education Associations, The, 325
Constitution
U.S., 256–257, 291, 294
Constructivist approach, 400
Content management, 355
Content standards
benefits of, 329
development of, 324–326
examples of, 326–327
as lesson plan objectives, 326–327
organizations involved in creating, 324–325
organizing of, 325–328
use of, 328
Content tests, 19
Cooperating teacher, 27
Cooperative groups, 233, 403
Cooperative learning groups, 393–397
Copyright
accessing material with, on the web, 288–289
fair use exceptions, 290
federal law protection for, 289
finding out about, 290
guidelines for, 289–290
infringement of, 289
Corporal punishment, 304–305
Corporate income tax, 267
Costello, Arlene M., 128, 134–135, 142, 150
Council for the Accreditation of Educator Preparation, 9, 335
Courts, 241
Covenant management, 356–357
Criminal background check, 493
Crises of integrity, 310
Criterion-referenced tests, 451–452
Critical pedagogy, 201
Critical thinking, 271
Cultural beliefs, 84
Cultural borders, 137
Cultural capital, 48, 103
Cultural conflicts, 138–139
Cultural identity, 135
Cultural Literacy, 211
Cultural match, 88
Cultural norms, 84
Cultural relativism, 136–137
Cultural safety, 87–88
Cultural symbols, 85–86
Cultural values, 84
Culturally diverse teachers
shortage of, 16
statistics regarding, 42
Culturally relevant teaching strategies, 407
Culturally responsive teaching, 111–113
Culture
adaptations by, 136
characteristics of, 136
in classroom, 86, 88
description of, 60, 81
elements of, 84–85
eye contact and, 87
family influenced by, 135–138
indicators of, 85
learning affected by, 87–88
religious beliefs, 139–140
student exceptionality and, 84
teaching affected by, 87–88
Culture of poverty, 103
Curcio, Joan, 310
Current expenditures, 272
Curriculum
Afrocentric, 45
assessment and, 337
axioms of, 340–342
changes in, 340–341
characteristics of, 338–342
common school, 163
comprehensive approach to, 341–342
content of, teacher's role in determining, 303–304
decision making involvement in creation of, 341
description of, 338–339
development of, 341–342
elementary school, 163
hidden, 138
history of, 170–172
Industrial Revolution effects on, 171
influences on, 170–172
multicultural, 111
multiple perspectives on, 109, 111
national, 276
progressivism effects on, 171–172
religion and, 110
Sputnik I effects on, 172
standards-based, 330
student-centered, 171

teacher's role in, 342–343
teaching strategies and, connection between, 407
Curriculum planner, 342
Custodians, 227
Cut score, for licensure tests, 18, 26
Cyberbullying, 119–120, 286–287
Cyra, Heather, 190, 192, 197, 205, 207

Dale, Nira, 414, 417, 420, 423, 433, 443
Danielson, Charlotte, 335
Darling-Hammond, Linda, 101
De facto segregation, 179, 294
De jure segregation, 294–295
Dean, 226
Deculturalizing, 173
Deficit ideology, 103–104
Defining moments, 195–196
Delicious, 433
Democratic classroom, 360
Department chairs, 226–227
Department of Defense Education Activity, 494
Department of Health and Human Services, 116
Departmentalization, 229
Depths of knowledge, 454
Desegregation of schools, 178–179, 292, 294
Development
cognitive, 77–79
human brain, 79–80
vocabulary, 83–84
Dewey, John, 113, 169, 171, 198–199, 205–206, 212, 391, 422
"Dick and Jane" readers, 165
Differentiated system of accountability, 264
Digital cameras, 419, 426
Digital presentations, 431–432
Dilemma, 290, 310
Direct instruction, 399
Disability
categories of, 70–72
definition of, 69
description of, 38
students with. *See* Students with disabilities
Discipline
achievement gap and, relationship between, 107
classroom management and, 371–374
Discovery method, 203
Discussions, as teaching strategy, 390–393
Dispositions
of students, 8
of teachers, 496
Distance education, 432
Distributed leadership, 499
Diverse families, 149
Doctoral degree, 501
DoDEA. *See* Department of Defense Education Activity
Donald, Brandy, 66–69, 73–74, 76, 81, 89
Doyle, Walter, 367
Drama, 397–398
Dress, 307
Dropouts, 92–93
Dropping out
contributing factors, 105
cost of, 106–107
description of, 92–93
incarceration rates and, 107
reasons for, 105–106
risk factors for, 105
sociocultural factors, 105
Drug testing, of teachers, 307, 309
Drugs, 122
Du Bois, W.E.B., 169, 178
Dual-language programs, 52
Duckworth, Eleanor, 201
Due process, 257–258, 306–307
DVD players, 419
Dyads, 233

Early childhood education, 168, 170
East Hartford Education Association v. Board of Education of Town of East Hartford, 307
Eating disorders, 115
Economic diversity, 45–48
ECS. See Equal cost sharing
EdD, 501
Education
bilingual, 16, 52–53, 141
early childhood, 168, 170
equality in, 173–175
multicultural. *See* Multicultural education
special, 299
Education, student
bilingual, 16, 52–53, 141
educator's view of, 130–133
family involvement in, 145
history of, 161–162
income levels and, correlation between, 106
public's view of, 130–133
Education, teacher
bachelor's degree, 8–9
five-year teaching degree, 13–14
master's degree, 10, 501
programs. *See* Teacher education programs
requirements, 8–9
Education as the Practice of Freedom, 200
Education for All Handicapped Children, 69
Education Week, 494
Education World, 438
Educational leadership, 501
Educational philosophies, in classrooms, 213–214, 217
Educational psychology
student learning understood through, 205
theorists of, 206–208
Educational Testing Services, 18
Effectiveness and efficiency, 254
Eggen, Paul, 213
Electronic Frontier Foundation, 289
Elementary and Secondary Education Act
description of, 176
goals of, 260
history of, 258
reauthorization of, 260, 264–265. *See also* No Child Left Behind Act
rewarding school success, 264
Elementary schools
classroom rules in, 356
curriculum of, 163
departmentalization in, 229
history of, 164–165
per-pupil expenditures for, 273, 277
state revenues for, 266
Elementary teachers
intermediate, 226
primary, 226
secondary, 226
ELL. *See* English-language learners
Elliott, Jane, 398
Elliott's general model of effective instruction, 490–491
E-mail, 433
Emergency action plan, 245
Emotionally disturbed students, 71
Emotional-physical support, 375
Empowering policies, 238
Enculturation, 136
Engaging parents, 497
English as a Second Language
description of, 52, 141
purpose of, 142
teacher education in, 53
teacher shortages in, 13, 16
English Classical School, 166
English for Speakers of Other Languages, 128, 141–142, 150
English High School, 166
English language
development programs for, 52
learning of, 141–142
English-language learners
assessment of, 456–457
bilingual education for, 52–53,141–143
deficit ideology view of, 103
languages spoken by, 50
population statistics for, 50
Supreme Court ruling, 140
teaching of, 50–53
teaching strategies for, 409
testing accommodations for, 456–457

Environment
classroom, 86–87
technology-rich, 435
Epistemology, 197–198, 208–209
ePortfolio programs, 432
Epstein, Joyce, 410
Equal cost sharing, 265
Equity school finance, 275
Escalante, Jaime, 88
ESEA. *See* Elementary and Secondary Education Act
ESL, English as a Second Language
ESOL. *See* English for Speakers of Other Languages
Essay test, 462–464
Essentialism, 211–212, 214, 216
Establishment clause, 257, 291
Ethics
in classroom, 209
code of, 11
law and, differences between, 309–310
Ethics Resource Center, 209
Ethnic studies, 44–45
Ethnicity
alcohol use based on, 122
ethnocentric curriculum for, 45
poverty rates based on, 46
reading test performance based on, 43
in schools, 41–43
Ethnocentric curriculum, 45
ETS PRAXIS, 331
Evaluation pay, 264–265
Evaluation question, 392
Evangelicals, 59
Evbuoma, Ava, 98–99, 106–107, 113, 120
Everson v. Board of Education, 291–292
Exercise, 116–117
Existentialism, 212–214
Explicit instruction, 399
Explore Knowledge Academy, 424
Expulsions, 107
Extra-curriculum, 226
Extrinsic rewards, 6
Eye contact, 87

Facebook, 420
Fair use, 290
Family. *See also* Parent(s)
cultural influences on, 135–138
diverse, 149
diversity of, 133–134
low-income, 45–46
middle-class, 47–48, 149
privacy rights of, 299–300
religion's importance for, 60
school involvement by, 145
single-parent, 134
size of, 134
structure of, 133
teacher involvement with, 144–146
Family Educational Rights and Privacy Act, 299–300
Family income
high school graduation and, correlation between, 105
low-income. *See* Low-income families
Fast food, 116
Federal government
branches of, 258–259
educational role of, 256–265
executive branch of, 259
First Amendment, 257, 301
Fourteenth Amendment, 257–258
judicial branch of, 259
legislative branch of, 260
public education role of, 242, 251
school funding sources from, 267–268
structure of, 256
Tenth Amendment, 257
Federal mandates, 101
Federalism, 276
Feedback, 445–446
Females, 53–54. *See also* Girls
Feminine identity, 56
Field events, 270
Field experiences
benefits of, 26
importance of, 491–492
learning opportunities during, 492
portfolio inclusion of, 29
professional development schools for, 22
Field trips, 152
Field-based supervisors, 18
Field-based teacher education programs, 12
Fill-in-the-blank tests, 462, 466
First Amendment, 257, 301
Fitness, 115–117
Five-year teaching degree, 13–14
Fixed groupings, 233
Flesch, Rudolf, 344
Flexible-group structure, 233
Florey v. Sioux Falls School District, 292–293
Florida Teacher Certification Examinations, 331
Floyd, Lorraine (Reina), 318, 321, 324, 334, 337
Followership, 498
Foraker Act, 180
Foreign countries, 494
Foreign-born population
description of, 40
education levels of, 50
Formal operational stage, of cognitive development, 78
Formative assessments
classroom climate shift to, 470
definition of, 445, 448
instructional adjustments by teacher, 468, 470
levels of, 468, 470–471
Popham's four levels of, 468, 470–471
schoolwide implementation of culture focused on, 470–471
students' learning tactic adjustments, 470
Formative evaluation, 448
Founding Fathers, 257
Fourteenth Amendment, 178, 257–258, 306, 371
Fourth Amendment, 302, 307
Franklin, Benjamin, 322
Free and universal education, 160, 177
Free appropriate public education, 299
Free or reduced-price lunch programs, 46
Freedmen's Bureau, 177
Freedom of expression, 301
Freedom of public expression, 307
Freedom of religion, 257
Freedom of speech, 257
Freire, Paulo, 200–201
Friel, Kim, 222, 225–227, 229–230, 233, 235, 238
Froebel, Friedrich, 169–170
Full inclusion, of students with disabilities, 72
Fuller, Frances, 484
Fundamentalists, 59
Funding. *See* School funding

Gambling, 269
Gangs, 121
Garcetti v. Cegallos, 311
Gardner's multiple intelligences theory, 74–75, 201, 408–409
GATE students. *See* Gifted and talented education students
Gay, 57
Gender. *See also* Boys; Girls
brain-based differences, 53–54
description of, 53–54
differences based on, 53–54
school reinforcement of society's view of, 54
sex versus, 54
Geography standards, 324–325
Gifted and talented education students, 89–91, 234
Girls
boys versus, 53
bullying of, 120
equitable education for, 54–56
society's view of, 54
sports for, 300–301
suicide rates in, 121
teen pregnancy among, 117–118
Glasser, William, 360
Goals 2000: Educate America Act, 324
Goggin, Catherine, 169, 182
Gonzaga University v. Doe, 300

Good governance, 253–254
Governance
bad, 254–255
definition of, 253
description of, 252–253
good, 253–254
overview of, 251
politics and, 255–256
Government
federal. *See* Federal government
levels of, 275–276
state. *See* State government
Governors, 240
Grade level-based licensing, 10
Graduate licensure, 14
Graduate studies, 501
Grandparents, 152
Great Recession of 2008, 242
Greene, Maxine, 212
Grouping
of students, 305–306
as teaching strategy, 393–397
Growth scores, 263–264

Haley, Margaret, 169, 182
Hall, G. Stanley, 167, 169–170
Hall, Reverend Samuel, 169, 183
Hall guards, 369
Hampston Institute, 177
Harassment, 119
Head Start, 147
Health, 115–117, 327
Hearst, Phoebe Apperson, 150
Hegel, Joseph, 211
Heritage language programs, 53
Heterogeneous structure, 233
Hidden curriculum, 138
High school(s)
academies as early model of, 166
classroom rules in, 356
in colonial period, 165
history of, 165–167
purpose of, 166
state authority to establish, 300
virtual education programs in, 432
writing proficiency assessments, 466
High school graduation
National Education Goals for, 104
rates of, 105, 264
socioeconomic status and, 105
High-ability courses, 49
Highly qualified teacher, 260–261
High-poverty schools, 99–100
High-stakes testing, 263, 450
Hirsch, E.D., 211
Hispanics. *See* Latino(s)
HIV, 117
Hobson v. Hansen, 305
Holidays, religious, 59
Holistic, 467
Homeless students, 47
Homework
lesson understanding assessed by reviewing of, 459
parental involvement in, 146
as teaching strategy, 409–410
Homogeneous structure, 233
Hord, Shirley, 231
Horizontal communication, 228–230
HQT. *See* Highly qualified teacher
Human resources department, 235
Hunter, Madeleine, 358, 404
Hutterites, 59

iCloud, 419
IDEA. *See* Individuals with Disabilities Education Act
Idealism, 211
IEP. *See* Individualized education plan
Illicit drugs, 122
Illiteracy, 301
I-messages, 361
Immediacy, 368
Immersion classrooms, 52, 101
Immigration Act, 181
Immigration/immigrants
educational experiences of, 50–51
native language preservation by, 52
population affected by, 40–41
Impact concerns, 486
Implicit instruction, 399
In loco parentis, 298
Incarceration, 107
Incentive pay, 264–265
Inclusion, 72, 298–299
Income
family. *See* Family income
low-income. *See* Low-income families
postsecondary education and, correlation between, 106
salary ranges, 16–17
supplemental sources of, 17
Income tax, 266–267
Indian Peace Commission, 175
Indian Removal Act, 173
Indigenous language programs, 53
Indigenous population, 39
Indirect instruction, 399
Individualized education plan, 69, 72, 298, 455
Individuals with Disabilities Education Act, 69, 298–299, 409
Industrial Revolution, 171, 244
Industrialization, 171
Informal leadership, 498–499
Infractions, 107
Ingraham v. Wright, 304
Inquiry, 398–399
Institute for Global Ethics, 209
Instruction
assessment versus, 468
direct, 399
Elliott's general model of, 490–491
explicit, 399
implicit, 399
indirect, 399
Instructional support function, 235
Instructional Theory Into Practice, 358
Intangible property, 267
Integration, 295
Intelligence
as basic ability, 73–74
multiple, 74–77, 201, 408–409
Intelligence quotient test, 73–74
Interest groups, 255
Intermediate teachers, 226
International Reading Association (IRA), 28
International Society for Technology in Education, 435–436
Internet
copying documents and other material from, 288
lesson plans obtained from, 404
problems with, 415
professional development using, 437–438
public domain issues, 289
World Wide Web and, 423–424
Interpersonal intelligence, 75–77, 201
Interstate New Teacher Assessment and Support Consortium (InTASC), 10–11, 19, 28, 322, 330–331, 365
Intrapersonal intelligence, 75–77, 201
Intrinsic rewards, 6
Involving parents, 497–498
Iowa, 332
IQ test. *See* Intelligence quotient test
Islam, 59
ISTE. *See* International Society for Technology in Education

James, William, 169, 171, 204
Jefferson, Thomas, 204, 291
Jim Crow laws, 179, 295
Job(s)
in foreign countries, 494
outlook for, 14–15
resources used to find, 494
search for, 493–495
success in, 27
Job interview, 493
Johnson, D.W., 362
Johnson, Lyndon B., 258
Johnson–Reed Act, 40
Johnston, Katie, 2, 5–6
Journals
description of, 30
field guide as, 34–36
J.S. v. Blue Mountain School District, 287
Judicial branch, of federal government, 259
Judicious Discipline, 359–360
Junior high school, 168

Kagan, Jerome, 204
Kauchak, Donald, 213
Kennedy, John F., 176
Kentucky Education Reform Act, 241, 294
Kilpatrick, William Heard, 169, 171
Kindergarten, 170
Knowledge
  assessment of, 19
  creation of, 110
  definition of, 109
  social construction of, 109–110
  specialized, 10–11
Knowledge question, 392
Knox County Education Association v. Know County Board of Education, 309
Kohn, Alfie, 363
Kozol, Jonathan, 6
Kuhn, Marvin, 158, 162, 165, 170, 181

Lancastarian classroom, 165, 171
Lancaster, Joseph, 165
Land Ordinance of 1785, 161
Language arts standards, 327
Latino(s)
  countries of origin, 39
  education of, history of, 179–181
  imprisonment rate for, 118
  middle class status of, 48
  poverty rates for, 46
  Puerto Ricans, 180–181
  students, population forecasts for, 41
Latino families
  academic success, 133
  educational concerns of, 132
  educational involvement by, 144
  working with, 149
Lau v. Nichols, 140, 181
Laughs, 6–7
Laughter, 375
Law. *See also* Legal issues
  administrative, 259, 285
  case, 285
  ethics and, differences between, 309–310
Law of Effect principle, 207
Lawrence, D.H., 354
Layshock ex rel. Layshock v. Hermitage School District, 287
Leaders, 497
Leadership
  distributed, 499
  educational, 501
  opportunities for, 496–501
Leading causes of death, 121
League of United Latin American Citizens, 180
Learning. *See also* Student learning
  academic ability effects on, 75
  activity, 400–401
  classroom culture centered on, 88
  conflicting perspectives in, 202–204
  cultural effects on, 87–88
  culturally responsive teaching effects on, 112
  developmental models effect on, 81
  expulsions effect on, 107
  online, 432, 437
  organizing students for, 232
  philosophical perspectives influence on, 210–213
  problem-based, 400
  research on, 205–206
  school culture effects on, 137
  self-directed, 423
  social class effects on, 87–88
  social context effects on, 108
  software used to enhance, 429
  student categorization effects on, 93
  student resistance against, 6
  suspensions effect on, 107
  technology effects on, 431–432
  vocabulary development effects on, 83–84
Learning cycle, 386
Learning disabilities, 70
Learning games, 428
Learning team, 25
Learning Together model, 396
LEAs. *See* Local education agencies
Least restrictive environment, 298–299, 409
Lecture, 387–390
Legal issues. *See also* Law
  copying documents and other material from the Internet, 288
  copyrighted material accessed on the web, 288–290
  cyberbullying, 119–120, 286–288
  desegregation, 292, 294
  MySpace, 286–288
  overview of, 285–286
  private-school teacher salaries paid with public funds, 291–293
  public funds used to pay for transportation to private schools, 291–292
  religious activities in schools, 293
  religious holidays, 292–293
  resolving of, 310
  school funding, 294
  school prayer, 139, 293
  segregation, 294–295
  separate but equal, 292–295
  separation of church and state, 291
  sexting, 287–288
  social media, 286–288
Legislature
  federal, 259
  state, 240
"Lemon Test," 291
Lemon v. Kurtzman, 291–292
Lesson plans
  benchmarks tracked using, 329–330
  bracketing, 406
  computerized software applications for, 330
  content standards as objectives for, 326–327
  cycle of, 404
  definition of, 29
  elements of, 404
  Internet as source of, 404
  standards tracked using, 329–330
  student understanding of, methods for assessing, 458–467
LGBTQ students, 57–58, 120, 134
Liability, of teacher, 309
Library of Congress, 290
Licensure
  alternative plans, 14
  description of, 10
  graduate, 14
  pathways to, 12–14
  requirements for, 493
  tests for, 18, 26–27
  withdrawal of, 9
Limited English proficiency, 89, 409
Linder, Douglas, 304
Line relationships, 227
Linguistic intelligence, 75–77, 201
Linguistically diverse teachers, 16
Listening, 373–374
Local control, 239, 276
Local education agencies, 235, 241
Lockdowns, 369
Locke, John, 205, 211
Locker searches, 302
Logical-mathematical intelligence, 75–77, 201
Looping, 229
Low-ability courses, 49
Low-income families, students from
  at-risk status of, 91
  description of, 45–46
  disciplining of, 107
  drop out risks, 105
  physical activity inadequacies, 117
  words heard and, relationship between, 82–83
Lunch duty, 369
Lunches, 116

Mainstreaming, 298
Making a difference, 7–8
MALDEF. *See* Mexican American Legal Defense and Education Fund
Males, 53–55. *See also* Boys
Manifest destiny, 173
Mann, Horace, 163, 169, 183–184
Mann, Lena, 350, 353, 358, 365, 369, 371, 374
Marshall, Thurgood, 169, 178

Masculine identity, 56
Maslow, Abraham, 206
Massachusetts Bay Colony, 160
Master of Arts in Teaching (MAT) program, 13
Master of Education (MEd), 14
Master teacher, 501–506
Master's degree, 10, 501
Matching items test, 462
Mathematics
core standards for, 172
national standards for, 327
McCarty, Diane, 202, 343
McGuffey, William Holmes, 165, 169
McGuffey Readers, 165
McKenney, Thomas L., 173
McKinney–Vento Homeless Assistance Act, 47
McTighe, Jay, 392
Mead, Margaret, 341
Media
social, 283, 286–288
youth as portrayed by, 114–115
Meier, Sid, 428
Mendez v. Westminster School District, 180
Mental retardation, 71
Mentors, 12, 27
Meritocracy, 103
Metacognition, 399
Metaphysics, 207
Mexican American Legal Defense and Education Fund, 180, 294
Mexican American students, 179–181
Micromanaging, 239
Middle level education, 167–168
Middle school classroom rules, 356
Middle-class families
classroom volunteering by, 149
students from, 47–48
Miel, Alice, 340
Miller v. Mitchell, 287
Miller v. Skumanick, 287
Model minority, 104
Modeling, 400, 470
Morals, 161, 184
Morris, William, 365
Mosques, 59
Movement, 368–369
MP3 players, 425–426
Mt. Healthy City School District Board of Education v. Doyle, 307
Multicultural education
characteristics of, 111–112
culturally responsive teaching, 111–113
curriculum to support, 111
social justice education, 111, 113–114
Multiculturalism, 137
Multiple intelligences, 74–77, 201, 408–409
Multiple perspectives, on curriculum, 109, 111
Musial, Diann, 208
Musical intelligence, 75–77, 201
MySpace, 286–288

NAACP. *See* National Association for the Advancement of Colored People
NAEP. *See* National Assessment of Educational Progress
Nation at Risk: The Imperative for Educational Reform, A, 345
National Assessment of Educational Progress, 258
National Association for Gifted Children, 90
National Association for the Advancement of Colored People, 178
National board certification, 10
National Board for Professional Teaching Standards, 10, 29, 323, 336
National Character Education, 209
National Commission on Excellence in Education, 345
National Council for Accreditation of Teacher Education, 9, 335
National Council of Social Studies, 28, 330
National Council of Teachers of English, 9
National Council of Teachers of Mathematics, 9, 324, 330
National Council on Education Standards and Testing, 324
National curriculum, 276
National Defense Education Act, 172
National Education Association, 5, 166, 182
National Education Goals, 104
National Educational Technology Standards for Teachers, 436
National K-12 Standards for Student Learning, 333
National Science Foundation, 172, 196
National standards, 325–328
National Standards for Social Sciences, 327
Native languages
learning and, 141
maintaining of, 142
use of, 140–141
NBPTS. *See* National Board for Professional Teaching Standards
NCATE. *See* National Council for Accreditation of Teacher Education
NCEST. *See* National Council on Education Standards and Testing
NCLB. *See* No Child Left Behind Act
NCSS. *See* National Council of Social Studies
NCTE. *See* National Council of Teachers of English
NCTM. *See* National Council of Teachers of Mathematics
NDEA. *See* National Defense Education Act
Neglect, 119
Negligence, 308–309
Negroni, Italia, 250, 252–254, 256, 265, 274
NETS-T. *See* National Educational Technology Standards for Teachers
Neural circuits, 79
New England Primer, 160
New Jersey v. T.L.O., 302
New mathematics, 172
New York, 17
Nietzsche, Friedrich, 212
Nihilism, 212
No Child Left Behind Act
adequate yearly progress, 43, 101, 262, 344
criticisms of, 264
description of, 43, 90, 101, 212, 276, 322
elements of, 260–263
English-language learner assessments, 457
goals of, 263–264
growth scores, 264
highly qualified teacher, 260
history of, 258
purpose of, 339
realities of, 263
Schools in Need of Improvement, 261–262
special needs children assessments, 457
teacher accountability under, 306
test scores, 264
waivers, 263
No pass no play, 255, 450
Normal curve, 451
Normal schools, 183, 331
Norm-referenced tests, 451
Norms, 84
Northwest Ordinance, 161
NRT. *See* Norm-referenced tests
NSF. *See* National Science Foundation
Nutrition, 115–116

Obama administration, 258
Obesity, 115
Objective tests, 461–462
Old Deluder Satan Law, 160, 322
Online learning, 432, 437
On-site staff developer, 230–231
Open-ended concerns statement, 484, 488
Open-ended questions, 459
Open-ended tests, 462, 465–466
Operant conditioning, 207
Oregon Social Sciences Standards, 328–329
Organization(s)
communication in, 228–229
line relationships in, 227

schools as, 224
staff relationships in, 227
Organization charts
description of, 227–230
school district, 235–236
Organizing students
for learning, 232
for work, 232–233
Out-of-field teachers, 16
Outsourcing, 273
Overseas schools, 494
Owasso Independent School District v. Falvo, 300
Owens, Robert, 169

Pacing, of lecture, 390
Padin Reform, 181
Pan-ethnic groups, 39
Paperwork, 366–367
Parent(s). *See also* Family
communication with, 147–149, 357, 498
disagreement with teacher, 304
engaging of, 497
importance of education, 144
involved, 497–498. *See also* Parental involvement
organizations for, 150–151
student learning affected by, 144
students with disabilities, 72–73
teacher involvement with, 143–145, 357
teacher quality and, 131
volunteering in classroom, 148
working with, 497–498
Parent Teacher Home Visit Project, 147
Parental involvement
description of, 497–498
in homework, 146
in school, 481–482
statistics regarding, 144
suggestions for increasing, 498
Parent–teacher conferences, 148
Parent–teacher organizations, 150, 270
Participation, 254
Partnership(s)
school–business, 270
school–community, 151–152
Partnership for Assessment of Readiness for College and Careers (PARCC), 276
Partnership schools, 23
Passive learning, 203
Pavlov, Ivan, 206–207
Pearson National Education Series, 18
Pedagogical tests, 22
Pedagogy, 198
Pedagogy of the Oppressed, 200
Peers
collaboration with, 30–31
dropping out and, 106
Peirce, Charles, 212
Perennialism, 211–212, 214, 216
Performance assessments, 18. *See also* Assessment(s)
Performance tasks, 453
Performance-based standards, 321
Per-pupil expenditures, 273, 276
Personal income taxes, 267
Personal philosophy
of classroom management, 358–365
of teaching, 191–197
Personal-intellectual support, 375
Pesce v. J. Sterling Morton High School District 201, Cook County Illinois, 305
Pessimism, 212
Pestalozzi, Johann, 171, 205–206
PhD, 501
Phi Delta Kappa/Gallup poll, 131–132
Philosophical perspectives
in classrooms, 213–214, 217
Confucianism, 210–211
essentialism, 211–212, 214, 216
existentialism, 212–214
idealism, 211
learning influenced by, 210–213
metaphysics, 207
overview of, 207–208
perennialism, 211–212, 214, 216
pragmatism, 212, 217
problem solving using, 217
progressivism, 159, 171–172, 203, 212, 214, 217
realism, 211
student learning and, 207–217
teaching influenced by, 210–213
Physical activity, 116–117
Physical education, 117, 327
Physical safety, 86, 88
Piaget, Jean, 78, 205–206, 209, 401
Pickering v. Board of Education Township High School District 205, 305, 307
Pierce v. Society of Sisters, 300
Planning
classroom management affected by, 355–356
teaching strategies affected by, 402–404
Plasticity, of brain, 80–81
Plato, 197–198, 211
Playground duty, 369
PLCs. *See* Professional learning communities
Plessy, Homer, 178
Plessy v. Ferguson, 178–179, 292, 294
Plyler v. Doe, 301
Podcasts, 433
Police officers, 107, 245
Policies
definition of, 238
school board's role in setting of, 238–239
state's role in creating, 239–240
Politics, 255–256
Pop quizzes, 459
Population
bilingualism in, 50
ethnicity of, 39–40
foreign-born, 40
immigration effects on, 40–41
indigenous, 39
race of, 39–40
Pornography, 287
Portfolio
artifacts in, 29
creating of, 29–30
definition of, 29
description of, 9, 18
ePortfolio, 432
Positive reinforcement, 359
Post-baccalaureate courses, 13
Postplanning, 405
Postsecondary education
income and, correlation between, 106
Obama Administration's goals for, 106
Poverty
drop out risks, 105
ethnicity-based rates of, 46
free or reduced-price lunch program qualifications, 46
homelessness and, 47
race-based rates of, 46
in single-parent family, 134
Pragmatism, 212, 217
Praxis III, 19
Prayer in school, 139, 293
Preoperational stage, of cognitive development, 78
Prescriptive policies, 238
Presentations, 431–432
Primary teachers, 226
Principal, 225
Prisons
race-based population statistics, 118
school-to-prison pipeline, 107, 118
Privacy rights, 299–300
Private school(s)
overseas, 494
public funds used to pay for transportation to, legal issues regarding, 291–292
Private school teachers
public funds used to pay for, legal issues regarding, 291–293
turnover rates, 15
Privatizing, 273
Problem, 290
Problem solving, 199, 203, 217
Problem-based learning, 400
Procedural due process, 258, 306
Profession
definition of, 8
standards and codes associated with, 9
teaching as, 8–10

Professional development
Internet used for, 437–438
technology for, 435–440
Professional development school, 212
Professional education areas, 332–333
Professional growth, 335–336
Professional knowledge tests, 22
Professional learning communities, 231
Professional resume, 494–495
Professionals, 9
Professors, collaboration with, 30–31
Proficiencies, 19–20
Program for International Student Assessment, 337
Progress Portfolio, 429
Progressive tax, 267
Progressivism, 159, 171–172, 203, 212, 214, 217
Project KNOTtT, 13
Project method, 171
Prop 13, 268
Property tax, 267, 292
Proselytize, 140
Protestants, 59
Psychological needs, 360
Psychosocial support, 375
PTA, 145, 148, 150
PTO. *See* Parent–teacher organization
Puberty, 53
Public
education as viewed by, 130–133
school problems according to, 132
Public domain, 289
Public education
description of, 161–162
federal government involvement in, 242
state government involvement in, 239–241
Public schools. *See also* School(s)
history of, 160–162
in nineteenth century, 164
public attitudes toward, 8
revenue sources for, 268
Puerto Rican Teachers Association, 180
Puerto Ricans, 180–181
"Pullout" approach, 409
Punishment, corporal, 304–305
Puritans, 160

Quality, in teaching, 489–491
Queer, 57
Questioning
closed questions, 459
lesson understanding assessed through, 459, 461
open-ended questions, 459
as teaching strategy, 390–393
Quincy School, 164

Race. *See also* specific race
alcohol use based on, 122
poverty rates based on, 46
reading test performance based on, 43
in schools, 41–43
Racial discrimination, 398
Racism, 44
Ramadan, 59
Reading
male underperformance in, 56
teaching methods for, 216
Reading tests, 43
Realism, 211
Reception-receptive method, 203
Recitation, 163
Recording Industry Association of America, 289
Recruiting New Teachers (RNT), 16
Reduction in force, 274
Reflection, 30, 385, 483
Reflective learning, 398–399
Refugees, 40
Reliability, 453
Religion, 110
Religious activities, 293
Religious beliefs, 58–60, 139–140
Religious holidays, 292–293
Research
on learning, 205–206
perspective based on, 204–205
on teaching, 205–206
technology used in, 431–432
Resegregation, 295
Response to Intervention, 409, 471–475
Responsiveness, 254
Resume, 494–495
Revenue distribution, 272–273
Revolutionary War, 176–177
Rewards, 5–6
Rice Boarding School, 175
RIF. *See* Reduction in force
Rights
of students. *See* Student rights and protections
of teachers, 307–311
Rigor, 271
Risk-taking behaviors, 114
Robinson, Sharon, 13
Rogers, Carl, 205, 213
Role play, 397–398
Room arrangement, 214–215, 217, 365–366
Rose v. Council for Better Education, 292
Rosh Hashanah, 59, 152
Rousseau, Jean Jacques, 171
Routines, 369
RTI. *See* Response to Intervention
Rubistar, 433
Rubrics, 10, 466–467
Rule of law, 254

Rules, classroom, 356, 369–370
Runaways, 119
Rural schools
history of, 163
job openings in, 16

Safety
in classroom environment, 86–87
description of, 245
Salaries, 16–17
Sales tax, 267
San Antonio (Texas) Independent School District v. Rodriguez, 292, 294
Santa Fe Independent School District v. Doe, 292–293
Sartre, Jean-Paul, 212
SBAC. See SMARTER Balanced Assessment Consortium
Scaffolding, 400
Schedules, 369–370
Schneider, Joy, 501–506
School(s). See also Public schools; Secondary schools
accountability of, 344–345
books read in, 139–140
current expenditures by, 272
deficit ideology influences on, 103
desegregation of, 178–179, 292, 294
equity in, 48–49
ethnicity in, 41–43
family involvement in, 145
learning to be comfortable in, 22
meritocracy ideology influences on, 103
movement in, 368–369
as organizations, 224
physical education in, 117
prayer in, 139, 293
professional development, 212
quality of, 131
race in, 41–43
religious beliefs in, 140
school districts and, relationship between, 233–235
school district/university partnership schools, 23
social context of. *See* Social context
sociopolitical context of, 101–104
School and Society, The, 199
School attendance
compulsory, 166, 300
historical laws regarding, 161
School boards
characteristics of, 253
composition of, 237
definition of, 237
meetings of, 252
policy setting by, 238–239
responsibilities of, 239
role of, 244–245, 251

School carnivals, 270
School culture
description of, 137
hidden curriculum, 138
histories, 138
traditions, 137–138
School districts
achievement gap closure by, 44
funding of, 235
licensing requirements based on, 493
organization of, 235–236, 244
partnership schools with universities, 23
schools and, relationship between, 233–235
size of, 235
sociopolitical context of, 102–103
superintendents, 236–237
support staff of, 237
teacher as employee of, 303
School finance
adequacy suits, 275
challenges for, 274
equity, 275
examples of, 277
questions about, 274–275
School funding
additional sources of, 268–269
citizen initiatives against, 268
creative sources of, 269–272
federal government sources of, 267–268
field events for, 270
gambling as source of, 269
income tax for, 267
inequality in, 274
legal issues, 291, 294
lotteries for, 269
property tax, 267, 292
revenue distribution, 272–273
sales tax, 267
school carnivals as source of, 270
school–business partnerships for, 270
sin taxes for, 270, 272
sources of, 265–268
special education, 299
U.S. Constitution coverage of, 294
School libraries, 139
School lunches, 116
School structure
class size, 242
communication and, 228–229
description of, 224
School–business partnerships, 270
School–community partnerships, 151–152
Schools in Need of Improvement, 261–262
School-to-prison pipeline, 107, 118
Science, 327
SEA. *See* State education agency
Secondary schools
out-of-field teachers in, 16
per-pupil expenditures for, 273, 277
school district responsibility for, 235
state revenues for, 266
Secondary teachers, 226
Secretaries, 227
Secular, 139
Secular humanism, 139
Segregation, 294–295
Self concerns, 486
Self-assessments, 460
Self-contained classroom, 232
Self-directed learning, 423
Self-esteem, 115, 375
Self-fulfilling prophecy, 48–49
Self-improvement, 439–440
Self-reflection, 30, 459–461
Senate, 259
Sensitive periods, in student development, 79
Sensorimotor stage, of cognitive development, 78
Separate but equal, 292–295
Separation of church and state, 291
SES. *See* Socioeconomic status
Sex education, 118
Sex versus gender, 53
Sexting, 287–288
Sexual behavior, 117
Sexual harassment, 119
Sexual identity, 57–58
Sexual orientation, 56–58
Sexuality, 117
Sexually transmitted diseases, 118
Shadowing, 25
Short-answer tests, 462–463
Shreve, Jenn, 428
SIBLE. *See* Supportive Inquiry-Based Learning Environment
Simpson, Michael, 282, 285, 297, 303, 312
Simulation, 397–398
Simultaneity, in classroom, 367
Sin taxes, 270, 272
Single-parent family, 134
SINOI. *See* Schools in Need of Improvement
SIT. *See* Student improvement team
Six degrees of separation, 420
Sizer, Theodore, 169, 171
Skinner, Burrhus Frederick, 206–207, 358–359
Skype, 433
Small-group structure, 233
Smart Boards, 425–426
SMARTER Balanced Assessment Consortium, 276
Smoking, 122
Social class
description of, 81
student expectations not affected by, 82
words heard and, relationship between, 82–83
Social context
academic performance affected by, 100–101
bullying, 87, 119–120
fitness, 115–117
gangs, 121
health, 115–117
knowledge construction affected by, 109–110
learning affected by, 108–109
nutrition, 115–116
overview of, 99–100
sexuality, 117
students affected by, 114–122
substance abuse, 121–122
suicide, 121
teen pregnancy, 117–118
violence, 118–121
Social development theory, 205, 207
Social Inquiry Model, 398
Social justice, 111, 113–114
Social media, 283, 286–288
Social networking, 420–421
Social norms, 136
Socialization, 54, 58, 136
Socioeconomic status
description of, 45
high school graduation rates affected by, 105
student expectations not affected by, 82
test bias, 462
tracking and, 49
words heard at home and, relationship between, 82–83
Socrates, 198
Socratic method, 198
Software, 429
South, 177
South Dakota, 17
Spanierman, Jeffrey, 286
Spanish language, 40, 179–180
Spatial intelligence, 75–77, 201
Special education funding, 299
Special education teachers
qualifications of, 299
shortage of, 16
Specialized knowledge, 10–11
Speech impairment, 70–71
Spira, Julie, 420
Sponges, 406
Sports for girls, 300–301
Spreadsheets, 434
Sputnik I, 172, 195–196
Staessens, Katrine, 231

Staff
assistant principal, 226
department chairs, 226–227
differences in, 243
principal, 225
roles of, 225–227
teacher leaders, 226–227
Staff relationships, 227
Stages of Concern, 485–486
Stand and Deliver, 88
Standards
academic achievement and, 339
benchmarks versus, 321
benefits of, 329
characteristics of, 322–323
colleges of education, 335
Common Core State Standards, 264, 271, 276, 323
content-based. *See* Content standards
definition of, 321
educational technology, 435–437
global comparison of, 337
Interstate New Teacher Assessment and Support Consortium, 10–11
knowledge of, 28–29
lessons plans used to track, 329–330
mathematics, 172
meeting of, 336–337
national, 325–328
National Board for Professional Teaching Standards, 10
national profession associations, 332
performance-based, 321
professional education areas, 332–333
professional growth, 335–336
professional practice, 335
public views on, 132–133
reasons for, 321
setting of, 9
state, 330
students, 28, 330–331, 336–337
teacher, 28–29
teachers, 331–332, 335–336
technology, 435–436
undergraduates, 333
universities, 335
upholding of, 9
Standards-based curriculum, 330
Stanford–Binet Intelligence Scales, 74
State boards of education, 241
State courts, 241
State education agency, 235, 241
State government
description of, 240, 251
educational responsibility of, 256–257
State governors, 240
State legislatures, 240
State license, 10, 13
State standards, 330
State v. Scopes, 303–304
STDs. *See* Sexually transmitted diseases
Steele, Claude, 104
STEM education, 262
Stereotype threat, 104
Stereotypes, 42
Stereotyping, 104
Stimulus-response concepts, 171
Stories, 194
Stress, 374–375
Structured English immersion programs, 53
Struggling students, 90
Student(s)
achievement gaps in, 42–44, 101–102, 469, 473
at-risk, 90–91
categorizing of, 89–93
copyright guidelines for, 289–290
deficit perspective of, 103
drop outs, 92–93
economic diversity of, 45–48
gifted and talented education, 89–91, 234
greeting of, 356
grouping of, 305–306
homeless, 47
learning about, 196–197
LGBTQ, 57–58, 120, 134
listening to, 373–374
from low-income families, 45–46
from middle-class families, 47–48
in poverty, 43
religious beliefs of, 58–60
resistance toward learning, 6
self-assessments by, 460
self-reflection by, 459–461
shadowing of, 25
standards for, 28, 330–331, 336–338
statistics regarding, 14
struggling, 90
teacher expectations for, 48–49
technology use by, 431–432
tracking of, 49
undocumented, 301
Student achievement. *See also* Academic achievement
gap in, 42–44, 101–102, 469, 473
reforms to improve, 43
teacher's influence on, 8, 338
technology effects on, 430
types of, 8
Student development
brain development, 79–80
cognitive development, 77–79
models of, 81
overview of, 76–77
sensitive periods in, 79
vocabulary, 83
Student diversity
achievement gaps secondary to, 42–44
economic, 45–48
ethnic studies for, 44–45
regional differences in, 51
religion, 59
statistics regarding, 41–42
teaching considerations, 42
Student fees, 274
Student improvement team, 472
Student learning. *See also* Learning
assessments of, 20–21, 406–407, 457–467
characteristics of, 89–93
data about, 296
Dewey's ideas about, 198–199
Duckworth's ideas about, 201
educational psychology used to understand, 205
Freire's ideas about, 200–201
ideas about, 197–202
improving, methods for, 100–101
McCarty's ideas about, 202
National K–12 Standards for Student Learning, 333
parental support effects on, 144
philosophical perspectives used to understand, 207–217
process of, 197–198
standardized tests for measuring, 8, 43
Taba's ideas about, 199–200
technology effects on, 421–423
testing of, 457–467
Tyler's ideas about, 200
Wiggins's ideas about, 202
Student records, 299
Student rights and protections
body search, 302
case law for, 298
family privacy, 299–300
freedom of expression, 301
overview of, 296–298
public high schools, 300
sports for girls, 300–301
state interests versus, 300
students with disabilities, 298–299
undocumented students, 301
Student teaching
benefits of, 26
description of, 12
in hard-to-staff settings, 492
student learning assessments, 20–21
Student-focused classroom, 217
Students of color
deficit ideology view of, 103
high school graduation rates for, 104–105
in high-poverty schools, 43
normalization of inequitable educational outcomes for, 44
stereotyping of, 104

Students with disabilities
assessment of, 455–457
attention deficit hyperactivity disorder, 71
autism, 71–72
characteristics of, 69–72
definition of, 69
disproportionate placement of, 73
emotional disturbance, 71
full inclusion of, 72
inclusion of, 72, 298–299
individualized education plan for, 69, 72
Individuals with Disabilities Education Act protections for, 69, 298–299, 409
learning disabilities, 70
least restrictive environment for, 298–299
mainstreaming of, 298
mental retardation, 71
parental involvement, 72–73
rights of, 298–299
school experiences for, 72–73
special education funding for, 299
speech impairment, 70–71
statutes for, 298–299
teachers of, 299
testing accommodations for, 455–457
Subjective tests, 463–466
Substance abuse, 121–122
Substantive due process, 307
Suicide, 121
Summative assessment, 445, 448
Summative evaluation, 448
Superintendents, 236–237
Supplemental income, 17
Support group, 26
Supportive Inquiry-Based Learning Environment, 429
Supreme Court, 259, 285
Suspensions, 106–107
Swann v. Charlotte-Mecklenburg, 179
Sylwester, Robert, 360
Symbols, cultural, 85–86
Synthesis question, 392

Taba, Hilda, 199–200, 338, 341, 343
Tablets, 425–426
Talking text, 429
Tangible property, 267
Tape, Mamie, 181
Tax, 267
Tax Payer Bill of Rights (TABOR), 268
Taxonomies, 391, 454, 466
TEAC. *See* Teacher Education Accreditation Council
Teach for America (TFA), 14
Teacher. *See also* Beginning teachers
academic performance affected by, 101
accountability of, 306, 329, 344
accreditation of, 9–10
behavior by, 183–184
beliefs of, 196
career path options for, 499–501
challenges for, 132
child abuse reporting by, 305
code of ethics for, 11
communication by, 372–373
concerns of, 485–486, 488–489
copyright guidelines for, 289–290
corporal punishment by, 304–305
creative thinking by, 204
culturally diverse, 16, 42
curriculum content determined by, 303–304
deficit ideology by, 103
demographics of, 15
disposition of, 496
dress by, 307
drug testing of, 307, 309
due process for, 306–307
education requirements for, 8–9
effectiveness of, 24
as employee of school district, 303
evaluation pay for, 264–265
expectations for students, 48–49, 82
freedom of public expression, 307
growth as, 28–31
high-need areas for, 16
high-quality, 101
incentive pay for, 265
leadership by, 496–501
liability of, 309
licensure of, 10
national board certification of, 10
obligation to practice in acceptable ways, 11
observation by, 458–459
out-of-field, 16
parent disagreement with, 304
parental involvement with, 143–145, 357
personal philosophy of teaching, 191–197
as professional, 9
professional growth of, 335–336
psychological support of, 375
public views on quality of, 131
questioning by, 459, 461
reasons for becoming, 5–8
reflection by, 30
responsibilities of, 229, 303–311
retirement of, 14, 16
rights of, 307–311
roles of, 226, 229
shadowing of, 25
specialized knowledge requirements, 10–11
standards for, 28–29, 331–332
stress management by, 374–375
student achievement affected by, 8, 338
turnover rate for, 15
value-added assessment of effectiveness of, 344
women as, 182–183
Teacher contracts, 17
Teacher Education Accreditation Council, 9
Teacher education candidates
advice for, 251–252, 481
basic skills testing of, 18
concerns of, 484–487
content tests for, 19, 331
as co-teachers, 26
disposition of, 496
leadership by, 496–501
learning to be comfortable in schools, 22
licensure tests for, 18, 26–27
pedagogical tests for, 22
performance assessments, 18
personal philosophy of teaching development by, 193–194
professional knowledge tests for, 22
shadowing a student or teacher by, 25
standards-based examinations of, 331
striving for quality by, 489–491
support group for, 26
tips for, 283
volunteering as teacher's aide or tutor, 25
Teacher education programs
acceptance into, 11–12
accreditation of, 9, 335
clinical experience with, 12
entry requirements for, 331
field-based, 12
five-year teaching degree, 13–14
getting started, 17
history of, 183
information sources about, 12
keys to success in, 483–491
Master of Arts in Teaching, 13
organization of, 12
post-baccalaureate courses, 13
striving for quality, 489–491
student learning assessment methods learned through, 20–21
succeeding in, 483–491
types of, 12–13
Teacher group, 25
Teacher leaders, 226–227
Teacher licensure. *See* Licensure
Teacher unions, 9, 255, 283
Teacher work samples, 407
Teacher-focused classroom, 213–214, 216

Teacher's aide, 25
Teachers of the Year, 6
Teaching. *See also* Student teaching
academic ability effects on, 75
activity approach to, 400–401
conflicting perspectives in, 202–204
constructivist approach to, 400
cultural effects on, 87–88
culturally responsive, 111–113
description of, 385–386
developmental models effect on, 81
evolution of, 181–185
excellence in, 223
goals of, 100
introduction to, 4–5
joys of, 3, 5–6, 99, 159, 191, 223, 251, 284, 319, 352, 415, 446, 482, 501–506
making a difference through, 7–8
personal philosophy of, 191–197
philosophical perspectives influence on, 210–213
as profession, 8–10
quality in, 489–491
reasons for leaving, 14–15
research on, 205–206
rewards of, 5–6
science of, 386
as semiprofession, 8
social class effects on, 87–88
Socratic method of, 198
software used to enhance, 429
standards for, 335
student categorization effects on, 93
teacher-focused approach to, 214, 216
team, 230
vocabulary development effects on, 83–84
women's role in, 182
Teaching fields, 15–16
Teaching locations
description of, 16–17
school diversity effects on selection of, 51
Teaching strategies
activity approach, 400–401
applications of, 407–410
constructivist approach, 400
continuum of, 388
culturally relevant, 407
curriculum and, connection between, 407
description of, 386–387
direct instruction, 399
discussions, 390–393
drama, 397–398
English-language learners, 409
generic, 387–401
for getting students ready to learn, 405–406
grouping, 393–397
homework as, 409–410
implementation of, 401–407
indirect instruction, 399
inquiry, 398–399
learning styles and, 407
least restrictive environment, 409
lecture, 387–390
limited English proficient students, 409
planning effects on, 402–404
questioning, 390–393
reflective learning, 398–399
Response to Intervention, 409, 471
role play, 397–398
simulation, 397–398
Team teaching, 230
Technology
audio recordings, 428
blogs, 420, 433
classroom management use of, 433–434
communication uses of, 419–421
difficulties in teaching with, 431
digital cameras, 426
digital presentations created using, 431–432
diverse learners' use of, 429
educational technology standards, 435–437
effective use of, 428–431
evolving nature of, 419
iCloud, 419
integration of, into teaching, 423–432
learning environment with, 435
learning games, 428
management of, 433–434
MP3 players, 425–426
overview of, 417–418
professional development uses of, 435–440
research completed using, 431–432
self-improvement uses of, 439–440
Smart Boards, 425–426
social networking, 420–421
software, 429
student achievement and, 430
student's use of, 431–432
tablets, 425–426
teacher–learner relationship affected by, 421–423
teacher's use of, 428–431
Twitter, 420–421
types of, 433
video recording, 426–428
YouTube, 420
Teen pregnancy, 117–118
Television, 418
Tenth Amendment, 161, 257
Test(s). *See also* Assessment(s)
basic skills, 18
content, 19
criteria used in selection and use of, 452–454
criterion-referenced, 451–452
essay, 462–464
level of difficulty of, 452–453
licensure, 18, 26–27
norm-referenced, 451
objective, 461–462
open-ended, 462, 465–466
pedagogical, 22
professional knowledge, 22
reliability of, 453
short-answer, 462–463
standardized, 8
student learning, 8, 43
subjective, 463–466
teacher education, 18
validity of, 453
Test concerns, 486
Test scores
achievement gap causes identified using, 102, 469
on criterion-referenced tests, 451–452
No Child Left Behind Act, 264
on norm-referenced tests, 451
Testing
accommodations for special needs students and English-language learners, 455–457
assessments versus, 445
purposes for, 449
student learning, 457–467
student self-reflection as method of, 460–461
teacher observation as method of, 458–459
Texas, 330
Texas Board of Education, 110
Thorndike, Edward, 169, 171, 206–207
Three Seductive Ideas, 204
Tillery, Gail, 147
Tinker v. Des Moines Independent Community School District, 301
Title IX, 55
Tort law, 309
Toxic stresses, 81
Tracking, 49, 234
Traditions, 137–138
Trail of Tears, 173
Transgendered persons, 57
Transitions, 91
Transparency, 254
Trends in International Mathematics and Science Study, 101
Tribally Controlled Schools Act, 176

Troops to Teachers, 14
Troy Female Seminary, 183
True–false tests, 462
Tutor, 25
Twitter, 420–421
Two-way bilingual programs, 52
Two-way immersion programs, 52, 142
Tyler, Ralph, 200

Unauthorized immigrants
children of, 41
countries of origin, 40
Unconditional positive regard, 356
Undocumented students, 301
Unfunded mandate, 260
Universal education, 160, 177
Universal truths, 211
Universities, standards for, 335
University of Southern California Rossier School of Education, 13
Unpaid furlough days, 273–274
Urban Institute, 47
Urban schools
classrooms in, 165
job openings in, 16
teacher turnover rates in, 15
U.S. Congress, 259
U.S. Constitution, 256–257, 291, 294
U.S. Department of Education, 259
U.S. Supreme Court, 259, 285

Validity, 453
Value added, 306
Value-added assessments of teacher effectiveness, 344
Values
in classroom, 209
cultural, 84
generational changes in, 215
Van Vorrhis, Frances, 410
Velasquez, Ambert, 480, 483, 493, 495–499, 501, 506, 509
Vermont, 239–240
Vertical communication, 228
Vice principal, 226
Video recording, 426–428
Violence, 118–121
Virtual education, 432
Vocabulary development, 83–84
Volunteerism, 148
Vygotsky, Lev, 205, 207

Wait-time, 392
Wait-time II, 392
Wallace v. Jaffree, 293
Washington, Booker T., 169
Weber, Will, 426
WebQuests, 425, 433
Websites, 425, 438
Webster, Noah, 163, 169
Weight lifting, 115
"White flight," 295
Whites, 46
Whole class structure, 233
Why Johnny Can't Read, 344
Why Johnny Still Can't Read, 345
Wiggins, Grant, 202, 392
Willard, Emma, 169, 183
William and Mary College, 173
Women teachers, 182–183
Woodlock v. Organe Ulster B.O.C.S., 311
World Wide Web
copyrighted material accessed on the web, 288–289
description of, 423–424
information from, 421
lesson plan design using, 330
Wright, Ester, 194
Writing proficiency assessments, 466

Yarmulkes, 59
Yom Kippur, 59, 152
YouTube, 420

Zero-tolerance policies, 107
Zuckerberg, Mark, 420

About the Authors

Gene E. Hall currently is a Professor of Urban Leadership at the University of Nevada, Las Vegas. He has had a career-long involvement with the development of programs and national accreditation of teacher education. He began his career as the science methods instructor and faculty team member for the experimental Personalized Teacher Education Program (PTEP) at the national R&D Center for Teacher Education, the University of Texas at Austin. Subsequently he was a faculty member at the University of Florida and the University of Northern Colorado. He has twice been the dean of a college of education. He also has had career-long involvement with studies of the change process and development of tools and applications of the Concerns Based Adoption Model (CBAM). He is coauthor of *Implementing Change: Patterns, Principles and Potholes* (3rd edition), and *The Foundations of Education* (16th edition).

Linda F. Quinn is a Professor in the Department of Teaching and Learning in the College of Education at the University of Nevada, Las Vegas (UNLV). She was a member of the UNLV faculty from 1991 to 1995, and rejoined the faculty in 1999 after four years as a visiting professor and associate dean at the University of Northern Iowa. Before coming to UNLV, she had a rich and varied career in public and private schools in the United States, and in Iran and Japan. She currently teachers upper division courses in curriculum development, classroom management, and instructional strategies. Her research interests focus on all aspects of teacher professional development, distance education, and global education. She is an annual contributor to national meetings of the Association of Teacher Educators and the Northern Rocky Mountain Educational Research Association. Reports of her research have been published in journals and as book chapters. She currently lives in Henderson, Nevada, with her poet husband and three loveable labs.

Donna M. Gollnick is a consultant for the National Council for Accreditation of Teacher Education (NCATE) where she is engaged in the transition to a new accrediting agency, the Council for the Accreditation of Educator Preparation (CAEP). She is co-author with Philip Chinn of *Multicultural Education in a Pluralistic Society,* which is in its 9th edition. She is also co-author of the textbook *Introduction to the Foundations of American Education,* in its 16th edition, and *Introduction to Teaching: Making a Difference in Student Learning.* Dr. Gollnick is also a past president of the National Association for Multicultural Education (NAME). The School of Family and Consumer Sciences at Purdue University has presented her a Distinguished Alumni Award as has the Rossier School of Education at the University of Southern California. AACTE honored her as an "Advocate for Justice" in 1998 and NAME has honored her for her years of work with the association with a number of awards, including a fellowship for research in multicultural education, which is named after her.